Warfare in History

THE WARS OF EDWARD III

SOURCES AND INTERPRETATIONS

Warfare in History

General Editor: Matthew Bennett
ISSN 1358–779X

Already published

THE WARS OF EDWARD III

SOURCES AND INTERPRETATIONS

EDITED AND INTRODUCED BY

Clifford J. Rogers

THE BOYDELL PRESS

First published 1999
The Boydell Press, Woodbridge

ISBN 0 85115 646 0

The Boydell Press is an imprint of Boydell and Brewer Ltd
PO Box 9, Woodbridge, Suffolk IP12 3DF, UK
and of Boydell and Brewer Inc.
PO Box 41026, Rochester, NY 14604–4126, USA
website: http://www.boydell.co.uk

A catalogue record for this book is available
from the British Library

Library of Congress Cataloging-in-Publication Data
The wars of Edward III : sources and interpretations / edited and
introduced by Clifford J. Rogers.
    p.   cm. – (Warfare in history, ISSN 1358–779X)
    Includes bibliographical references and index.
    ISBN 0–85115–646–0 (acid-free paper)
    1. Great Britain – History – Edward III, 1327–1377.
    2. Military art and science – History – Medieval, 500–1500.
    3. Great Britain – History, Military – 1066–1485.
    4. Edward III, King of England, 1312–1377.   5. Hundred
Years' War, 1339–1453.   I. Rogers, Clifford J.   II. Series.
DA233.W287   1999
944'.0254 – dc21   99–37411

This publication is printed on acid-free paper

Printed in Great Britain by
St Edmundsbury Press Ltd, Bury St Edmunds, Suffolk

CONTENTS

For Shelley

MAPS, FIGURES AND PLATES

Maps

War and Fourteenth-Century France

Figures

Plates

GENERAL EDITOR'S PREFACE

It is perhaps surprising that there is no modern military history of such an energetic war-wager as Edward III (1327–77). Biographies and general studies of the king and his reign abound and these cannot but discuss Edward's wars, yet it is over a century since any volume was dedicated to the subject. W.J. Ashley's *Edward III and his Wars 1327–60* (Oxford, 1887) consisted of translated fourteenth-century narratives and documents, heavily dependent upon Froissart in particular. It is a mark of how scholarship has developed since then that this collection can call upon a much greater variety of sources and a range of interpretations provided both by the editor and the authors of reprinted articles. It is also fair to say that Clifford J. Rogers has dedicated much of his academic career so far to the study of the military aspects of Edward's reign. He is therefore especially suitable to take on the role of editor for this book.

Modern readers are often suspicious of descriptions of medieval warfare, in the sense that it appears insufficiently chivalrous to their eyes. Modern commentators are therefore too ready to criticise medieval military practitioners for not living up to unrealistic standards of behaviour. As this collection shows, the experience of war in the fourteenth century combined most of the same elements of activity today. For example, mud is not an exclusively twentieth-century phenomenon, restricted to the Somme and Passchendaele. Just read Jean le Bel's plaintive account of the Scottish campaign of 1327, when the Scots avoided battle and watched as the English forces almost literally disintegrated before their eyes. Constant rain rotted the equipment and made both the under-fed men and horses sick [1]. Or there is the way that the civilian population was targeted by armies on campaign. The description of the destruction of the Cambrésis (in north-eastern France) is as chilling today as the papal commissioners intended it to be in 1340 [46]. Great swathes of property were burnt and destroyed and families reduced to penury. All this in order that Edward could demonstrate his superiority over Philip VI of France as a wrathful lord and potential protector of Philip's subjects. Part of this strategy was to encourage Philip to engage in battle with Edward's expeditionary force, put together with Continental allies at literally ruinous expense. Philip's refusal to offer battle defeated Edward more surely than the chivalrous charge of knights of which medieval warfare is still popularly believed to be entirely composed.

Of course, this did happen at Crécy in 1346. It was a great victory for Edward III, celebrated as a feat of arms by that chronicler of chivalry Jean Froissart, amongst others [77–78]. It did indeed help to deliver Calais into Edward's hands to form a bridgehead and bulwark for English ambitions in France for two hundred years. Yet it was unusual. Most encounters were on a much smaller scale. Sieges were by far the most common form of military operation. Calais only fell after a bitter siege of eleven months. Campaigning by *chevauchée*, a ride through enemy territory such as the Cambrésis campaign represented, was also far more frequent than open battle; sometimes they were. So much depended upon the immediate military circumstances as to what was possible for an English expeditionary force to achieve. In 1356, near Poitiers, Edward, Prince of Wales, was forced to fight a battle against much larger forces led by a vengeful King John [101–102]. By a mixture of luck and judgement (or rather French misjudgement) John's army was routed and he ended up a prisoner. This certainly played an important part in assuring Edward the most favourable treaty won by a king of England in France up to that point (Brétigny, 1360) [112–113].

Such an outcome was far from certain in 1340, however, with the English Crown bankrupt. Edward's small campaigns in 1342 and 1343 were almost proxy wars; interventions in a succession dispute for the duchy of Brittany, yet they yielded better results than his grandiose schemes in Flanders [65–67]. Similarly, the ambitious nature of his three-pronged attack in 1345 was superseded by the more limited objectives of his 1346 operations. The results of campaigns were frequently very uncertain and much could turn upon small accidents. Chroniclers revelled in personal detail. Here a raid, there a challenge to combat; here an ambush, there a night attack. So Avesbury's stories of Henry of Lancaster's 1356 *chevauchée* featured marvellous triumphs against the (often unlikely) odds [103]. Although written in chronicler's Latin they differ little from the chivalric fantasies of vernacular French accounts composed after the fashion of the Romances.

Yet, once again, the realities of war intrude upon tales of derring-do. The details of the administration of the invasion of 1346 show how deeply the war impacted upon all the areas of life in England [72–73]. For France, the situation was far worse. Not only did its population have to bear the burden of the cost of the war, but also the pain of the devastation it brought [109]. Fields went unploughed, crops unreaped; the human and animal populations were killed or driven into forests and caves; churches, town-houses and farms were burnt or torn down; the countryside was left at the mercy of roaming bands of mercenaries – the Free Companies – who also settled themselves in castles and towns. Not surprisingly there were revolts in town and country alike against lords who were perceived as failing in their role as protectors against the realm's enemies. Indeed, often they were seen as worse than the invaders against whom they supposed to fight. A game for some; misery for most – this collection of sources and interpretations lays bare the truth about the wars of Edward's reign. In the end he died having seen most of his gains lost to Charles V (1364–80); his strategies countered, his alliances undermined. Dr. Rogers has provided a valuable service to scholars, students and general readers alike in bringing together this fascinating collection.

Matthew Bennett
Royal Military Academy, Sandhurst
July 1999

ACKNOWLEDGMENTS

My thanks to Matthew Bennett for a number of suggestions which improved the translations section of this book. Research grants from the Faculty Development and Research Fund of the United States Military Academy made possible the inclusion of the texts from BN Ms. Fr. 693 and Ms. 78 of Corpus Christi College, Oxford. The assistance of the staff of the USMA Library, particularly Ms. Faith Coslett of the Interlibrary Loan department, has been invaluable. I am grateful to Uassar College for guest borrowers' privileges at the library. Col. Jim Johnson of the USMA history department has encouraged me to reflect on teaching methods and philosophy in ways which have contributed, I hope, to improving the value of this book as a teaching tool.

The editor and the publishers are grateful to the following authors, journals and institutions for permission to reprint the materials for which they hold copyright. Every effort has been made to trace the copyright holders; we apologise for any remission in this regard, and will be pleased to add any necessary acknowledgements in subsequent editions.

Ayton, Andrew. "English Armies in the Fourteenth Century," in Anne Curry and Michael Hughes, eds., *Arms, Armies and Fortifications in the Hundred Years War*, Woodbridge, Suffolk: Boydell Press, 1994.

Campbell, J. "England, Scotland and the Hundred Years War in the Fourteenth Century," in *Europe in the Middle Ages*, ed. J.R. Hale et al. London, 1965.

Harriss, G.L. "War and the Emergence of the English Parliament, 1297–1360," *Journal of Medieval History* 2 (1976).

Hewitt, H.J. "The Organisation of War," in Kenneth Fowler (ed.) *The Hundred Years War*, London: Macmillan, 1971.

Jones, Michael [C]. "War and Fourteenth-Century France," in Anne Curry and Michael Hughes, eds, *Arms, Armies and Fortifications in the Hundred Years War*, Woodbridge, Suffolk: Boydell Press, 1994.

Le Patourel, J. "Edward III and the Kingdom of France," *History* 43 (1958).

Rogers, Clifford J. "An Unknown News Bulletin from the Siege of Tournai in 1340," *War in History* 5, no. 3 (1998).

Rogers, Clifford J. "Edward III and the Dialetics of Strategy, 1327–60," *Transactions of the Royal Historical Society* 6th ser. 4 (1994).

Templeman, G. "Edward III and the beginnings of the Hundred Years War," *TRHS*, 5th ser. 2 (1952).

INTRODUCTION

Few monarchs have engaged in as much military activity as Edward III, and fewer still have, through their wars, had such an impact on British or European history. During his reign (1327–1377), Scotland won its first War of Independence, then nearly lost its second. Eight lowland counties were ceded to the English crown in 1334, and by 1336 – when Edward III and a small army under his command rode all the way to Moray Firth and burned Elgin without meeting any resistance – it seemed almost inevitable that the remainder of Scotland would be subjugated to the will of the Plantagenet monarch and his vassal-king, Edward Balliol. Scottish independence was rescued, not by the daring resistance of Andrew Murray and William Douglas, but by the outbreak of war between the English and Scotland's firm ally, Valois France, in 1337.

Aside from his desire to preserve a valuable thorn in England's side, Philip VI of France was also concerned to solidify his claims to sovereignty over English Gascony, just as Edward III was trying to enforce Plantagenet claims to suzerainty over Scotland. These were grounds enough for a major conflict, but the seriousness of the situation was ratcheted up to a new plane in 1340 when Edward (who had been the nearest male relative of Philip VI's predecessor, Charles IV, at the time of that king's death) claimed the French throne as his own rightful inheritance, and assumed the title and arms of King of France. Surprisingly, given the disparity of size, wealth, population and reputation between the two realms, Edward did very well in his war against the Valois. His great victories at Sluys and Crécy, and the even more significant triumph of his eldest son at Poitiers, shocked all of Europe and earned for him a reputation, even in France, as "the most valiant man in Christendom,"[1] and "the wisest and shrewdest warrior in the world".[2] The English battlefield victories, along with the harsh and destructive warfare which characterized their great *chevauchées* (war-rides) and the raids of the *routiers* who pillaged France in Edward's name, pushed France's reputation and economy into a precipitous decline from which they did not fully recover until the time of Louis XIV. By 1360 France was such a wreck that the captive King Jean II, the regent Charles of Normandy, and the Estates-General were alike willing to make unprecedented concessions to secure peace. Edward was to receive 3,000,000 *écus* ransom for the French King (an amount nearly ten times the English Crown's annual revenues at the beginning of Edward's reign) and, more importantly, was to gain a huge Greater Aquitaine –

---

[1] J. Viard and A. Vallée, *Registre du trésor des chartes* (Paris: Archives Nationales, 1979–84), no. 6707.
[2] *Chronique des quatre premiers Valois (1327–1393)*, ed. Siméon Luce (Paris: Société de l'histoire de France, 1862), 114.

comprising a full third of the realm of France – as his own independent principality, sovereign and free of any obligation to the French monarchy. It is difficult even to begin to imagine the consequences which this settlement would have had on European history had it endured much longer than its actual nine-year life.

When the war broke out again in 1369, Edward was already fifty-six years old, and no longer the vigorous campaigner he once was. Furthermore, his new opponents, Charles the Wise and Constable du Guesclin, developed a successful counter to the English *chevauchée* strategy, relying on sieges and political maneuverings while studiously avoiding open battle. By 1377, when Edward III died a few months after his eldest son, English holdings on the Continent had dwindled to a slimmed-down Gascony and the Calais Pale. Of the English dominions in Scotland, almost nothing beyond the walls of Berwick remained. Not until the reign of the other great soldier-king of the Hundred Years War, Henry V, would England's military renown (or conquests) rise again to the level to which Edward III had carried them by 1360.

Though it did not end in glory, Edward's career in arms was truly a dramatic one. His *chevauchée* to Lochindorb in 1336, his eager pursuit of the French fleet in 1340 despite the overwhelming odds against him, the splendid feasts and tourneys, his brash challenge to King Jean's army in Picardy in 1355, and of course Crécy and Poitiers: all these scenes (set out in the primary source readings below) seemed better matched to the *chansons de geste* of Roland and the romance of Lancelot than to the history of a real-life king. No wonder people said of him that he was "a second King Arthur."[3] The continuing popularity of Froissart's classic chronicles owes much to the inherent power of the material he had to work with, following this charismatic protagonist from the humiliating defeat of his first campaign, through his triumphs, and to the collapse of his conquests. The narrative of Edward's wars is, quite simply, a good story.

Sources

In the first section of this book, that story is told primarily in the words of Edward's own contemporaries. Indeed, a portion of it is related in the King's own words, taken from the campaign dispatches he regularly sent back to family and councilors in England. Henry of Lancaster, Edward the Black Prince, and other key figures also wrote similar letters, providing us with narratives of events which are as immediate and personal as they are well informed. Other portions of the story come from the pens of men who were personally involved in the campaigns they describe, though not in command positions: Jean le Bel details the 1327 campaign against the Scots, one of Sir John Wingfield's dispatches illustrates the Black Prince's *grande chevauchée* of 1355, and so on.

---

[3] Jean le Bel, *Chronique de Jean le Bel*, ed. Jules Viard and Eugène Déprez (Paris: Société de l'histoire de France, 1904), 1:118.

Most of the remainder come from chroniclers who were able to discuss the battles, sieges, and court dramas of the day with eye-witnesses. These accounts are sometimes awkward, sometimes mistaken, sometimes biased, but they bring the reader directly into contact with the people and events of the late Middle Ages in a way that no modern historian can fully replicate. They depict events and small details which later writers have tended to pass over as insignificant, yet which illuminate the military methods and the mind-set of the day.

The biggest problem with the work of the various chroniclers whose writings are included in this collection is their erratic quality. They do a good job of describing things of which they have personal knowledge, or for which they have a good source, but no one of them covers the whole range of Edward's wars effectively. Jean le Bel, for instance, provides by far the best narrative of the 1327 campaign in northern England, and gives an excellent account of Edward III's *chevauchée* in Picardy in 1355, but is almost valueless when it comes to the Scottish war after that first campaign. Giovanni Villani's Florentine chronicle misses the mark on many points, but it provides the only account of the Flemings' remonstrances with King Edward prior to the battle of Sluys. The Tournai Chronicles, unsurprisingly enough, provide the most details of the siege of Tournai in 1340, but little else of use here. So, to gain the advantages of primary source narratives without suffering from the limitations which come from relying on any single writer, I have drawn material for this book from the work of no fewer than twenty-four chroniclers, not counting the authors of the dozen-odd narrative letters which are also reproduced here. Thus, for each episode covered I was able to pick a source which is both informative and reasonably reliable.[4] In some cases, two or more different contemporary accounts have been included to illustrate the impact which different perspectives can have on narratives of the same events.

Freshness – along with accuracy, detail, inherent interest, and length – was one of the factors which affected my selection of source materials. Thus, I have made only limited use of Froissart's well-known chronicles (though I have included a number of selections from his main source for the period up to 1356, Jean le Bel) especially of the sections of his work available in the Penguin paperback translation,[5] and have tried to minimize the overlap between this collection and Richard Barber's excellent book of materials on *The Life and Campaigns of the Black Prince* (though not to the point of impeding this volume's ability to stand on its own). Teachers should find that the combination of that book, this one, and an edition of Froissart will give students the basis for research papers in which they can work with a good variety of primary sources.

In addition to the various types of narrative sources dealt with above, I have

4 Of course, the accuracy of any given source's description of any given event is likely to be subject to dispute. Readers wishing to understand my justifications for choosing particular texts should see my forthcoming monograph, *War Cruel and Sharp: English Strategy under Edward III, 1327–60* (Woodbridge: Boydell, forthcoming).

5 Jean Froissart, *Chronicles*, sel., tr. and ed. Geoffrey Brereton (New York: Penguin, 1978).

included a substantial leavening of "record" documents, originally created as elements of the practice of government, rather than histories for posterity: letters from Edward III demanding reinforcements or money, documents setting out the terms of alliances or surrenders, financial accounts, and so on. Records of this sort can be of value for many reasons. They provide the most reliable information about dates and quantities; like the narrative campaign dispatches, they show what people were saying to each other at the time, rather than retrospectively; and they cast a great deal of light on the details of medieval administration, logistics, and even social assumptions which do not find their ways into chroniclers' accounts.

Editorial notes (in italics) introduce the authors of the narrative texts and sometimes highlight particular issues or points arising from the documents.[6] These notes also serve to concisely fill in gaps in the primary-source narratives so as to maintain the continuity of the story. The majority of the entries in the sources section have never before been translated into modern English, though they have appeared in print in French, Latin, Middle English, Italian, or Occitan. Some, however, are published here for the first time in any language.

Interpretations

In the spring of 1357, three kings resided in London: Edward III, Jean II of France, and David II of Scotland. The latter two were prisoners; their presence left little room for doubt that the first was, by the standards of his day, the most successful king in Christendom. This state of affairs was symbolic of what contemporaries saw as the most dramatic results of King Edward's wars: England, formerly considered "inferior to the wretched Scot," (as Petrarch put it) had now humbled her two greatest enemies and emerged as perhaps the strongest military power in Europe. Yet, as we know with hindsight, these accomplishments (like Edward's great territorial conquests) proved transitory. From the perspective of the twentieth century, the most significant consequences of Edward's wars lie in other areas entirely.

Historians have long realized that the reign of Edward III holds a special place in England's constitutional history. During his half-century on the throne, parliament, which before his reign still seemed a little tentative, a little unfinished, solidified into a powerful and established institution. The division between the Houses of Lords and Commons appeared, and parliament's power of the purse expanded to include indirect as well as direct taxation. Redress of common grievances became an acknowledged purpose of the calling of parliament, and the practice of making grants of taxation contingent on the granting

---

6   See Antonia Gransden, *Historical Writing in England, II: c. 1307 to the Early Sixteenth Century* (Ithaca: Cornell University Press, 1982) and Robert Bossuat et al., *Dictionnaire des lettres Françaises: Le Moyen Age*, revised edition (Paris: Fayard, 1992), for more information (and bibliographical citations) concerning the chroniclers.

of political petitions was introduced. No longer could parliament be seen as merely a tool of the Crown. What has not always been realized is the degree to which these developments resulted from Edward's wars. The first separate meeting of the Commons was at a parliament in 1332 called to advise the King on how to respond to the success of English soldiers in defeating the Scottish royal host at Dupplin Moor. The ruinously expensive alliance strategy which Edward pursued in the first three years of the war with France, and the extraordinarily high tax revenues required to support it, led in 1340 to the first instance of parliament requiring major political concessions before agreeing to a subsidy.[7]

Equally laden with consequence for the history of the West was another change which Edward's wars greatly advanced, though it was neither created nor completed by them: the development of national sentiment in France, Scotland and England. For Frenchmen and Scots, the devastation wrought by English troops on *chevauchée* and the presence of unmistakably foreign garrisons on their soil, whether troops in Edward's pay or *routiers* fighting in his name, provided a clear, irritating "other" against whom patriotic sentiment could develop, as a pearl forms around a grain of sand. This process was strengthened by the vigorous use of propaganda by the Plantagenet and Valois monarchies. Each king worked to rouse the enthusiasm (or at least the cooperation) of his subjects by stressing the foreignness and perfidy of the enemy *nation* – not just the enemy monarch. From pulpits across the land English churchgoers were warned that the French were planning a great invasion of England, not just to defeat Edward in battle and put an end to his claims on France, but to eliminate *the English language* from the Earth. French polemicists harped on the inconstancy and tendency to regicide of the English people. Slowly but surely, the struggle between the two kings assumed more and more of the trappings of a war between two nations.[8] Similarly, the trials of the partial English occupation greatly strengthened the feeling of national unity among the Scots, so that by the end of his reign David II was in control of a Scotland more coherent, and an apparatus of state far more developed, than his illustrious father had ever known. Of course, the growth of royal power under David II arose in large part because of the improved fiscal strength of the monarchy which itself resulted, ironically enough, from the need to pay David's ransom to Edward III. The necessity to provide the huge payments required for King Jean's ransom similarly laid a foundation for a whole new system of taxation in France, one which largely bypassed the Estates and led to their decline at the very time parliament was rising to full prominence in England.[9]

---

[7] See G.L. Harris' article, below, for an introduction to these issues. His *King, Parliament, and Public Finance in Medieval England to 1369* (Oxford: Clarendon Press, 1975) provides a fuller treatment.

[8] See John Barnie, *War in Medieval English Society: Social Values in the Hundred Years War 1337–99* (Ithaca: Cornell University Press, 1974).

[9] For Scotland, see James Campbell's article in the "Interpretations" section of this book,

For all these reasons, a study of Edward III's wars proves very rewarding to the student of history, and indeed this period has attracted the attention of some of the finest historians working today. Although some of the themes mentioned above are illustrated by materials included in the "Sources" section of this book, the essentials of these complex interactions between military events and the development of British society as a whole are not well served by contemporary narrations. They require a breadth of perspective which comes only with hindsight, and a range of sources, especially archival documents, and methods to analyze them, not available to any medieval chronicler, or even any combination of chroniclers. These are stories, in short, that can only be told by a modern historian.

The articles in the "Interpretations" section are intended to make the results of a representative sample of the historical research on the wars of Edward III conveniently accessible to the general reader, or for the teacher wishing to include a section on the Hundred Years War in a college-level course. They deal with some of the issues indicated above, and also round out the narrative accounts by providing insights into *why* the events described by the chroniclers took place. They also serve to illuminate the "behind the scenes" action which was necessary to make possible the more dramatic battles, sieges, and *chevauchées* of the Plantagenet's wars. Because of the scope of the topic of this volume, I have selected studies which give broad coverage of some of the most important aspects of Edward's wars, rather than seeking to provide deep, multifaceted coverage of the more controversial issues. There is, however, enough disagreement among them to provoke some reflection and debate.

Like Edward's wars, these articles begin with Scotland. James Campbell's sweeping survey provides the context necessary for a deeper understanding of Edward's efforts to conquer Scotland, and shows how the Plantagenet's war there interacted over time with his war in France. Particularly useful is Campbell's analysis of King Edward's relations with his brother-in-law David Bruce after the latter's capture at Neville's Cross in 1346. Another interesting point in this article is the emphasis on Scottish affairs as the "immediate cause" of the Hundred Years War. Some more recent writers have echoed this view, but others – while acknowledging divergent Scottish policies as one of the factors which led to the outbreak of the great war between England and France – have instead seen conflicts over Gascony as the real root of the war.[10] Geoffrey Templeman's judicious study of this complex issue argues that, while Scotland may

---

and also R.A. Nicholson's *Scotland: The Later Middle Ages* (Edinburgh: Oliver & Boyd, 1974). On France, see J.B. Henneman, *Royal Taxation in Fourteenth Century France: The captivity and ransom of John II* (Philadelphia: American Philosophical Society, 1976).

[10] Among those who emphasize Scotland are Jonathan Sumption, in *The Hundred Years War, vol. 1: Trial by Battle* (London: Faber and Faber, 1990), and myself, in *War Cruel and Sharp*. The best and most elaborate case for the opposite view is made by M.G.A. Vale, in *The Angevin Legacy and the Hundred Years War, 1250–1340*, 2nd ed. (Oxford: Clarendon, 1994).

have provided the spark that led to the explosion, much of the force of the blast came from longstanding Anglo-French tensions over the status of Guienne.

It is natural to assume that the causes of war and the war aims of the combatants will be closely linked. If the war was caused by the French monarchy's meddling in Gascony, then we would expect to see sovereignty over Aquitaine as the primary objective of Edward III; if Scotland was the primary cause, then we might expect the war with France to continue until the issue of English suzerainty over the northern realm had been settled one way or the other. John le Patourel, in his essay "Edward III and the Kingdom of France," warns us that this presumption is not necessarily valid, for war aims can and indeed usually do vary with the vagaries of the course of the fighting. Still, the negotiations for peace must at the least be taken carefully into account as we study the origins of the war, particularly if we want to understand why the crisis of 1337 led not merely to a war, but to a Hundred Years War. Le Patourel's judgments concerning the evolution of Edward's strategic objectives are certainly subject to dispute, but his questions and his ideas must be given due consideration by anyone striving to understand the wars of Edward III.

The bridge between the causes and the ends of the war is the actual conduct of campaigns, and the strategy guiding that conduct. Here, too, Le Patourel's ideas – focusing on the concept of a "provincial" strategy aimed at building block by block the support Edward needed to secure the French crown – must be taken into account, and here, too, his conclusions may be questioned. A rather different view is presented in my own "Edward III and the Dialectics of Strategy, 1327–1360," which argues that the English, throughout the period, consistently sought to pull their enemies into battle, since a decisive victory in the field offered the best chance for Edward to reach his strategic objectives (regardless of whether he did in fact aim to secure the French throne, as Le Patourel argues, or rather sought a compromise peace which would give him a free hand in Scotland and Aquitaine). As the article points out, and as the reader can see in the "Sources" section of this book, Edward III was fairly clear on the matter in his own letters; the question is whether or not he should be believed, whether or not his actions (as reported in French as well as English sources) match his words.

If the foundation of strategy is the matching of ends to means, then before we can finally resolve our questions on that dispute, we must comprehend the means at King Edward's disposal. The next two articles in this collection serve to illuminate that topic. First, H.J. Hewitt gives us an informative overview of how fourteenth-century English armies were raised, equipped, transported, and even how they were employed on campaign (which provides us with yet another perspective on English strategy).[11] Second, Andrew Ayton provides a masterful summary of the composition and structure of the armies themselves.

One of the points highlighted by Ayton is the fact that in the first half of the

---

[11] The ideas and information outlined in this article are developed in much greater depth in two of Hewitt's books, *The Organization of War under Edward III* (Manchester: Manchester

fourteenth century, for the first time, England fielded armies whose members were all paid the King's wage. This helps explain the very high cost of Edward III's wars, for the government (and therefore the taxpayers) at least; for the individual soldier, the prospect of ransoms and plunder weighed in the balance against the risks and expenses of serving as a soldier.

How those burdens balanced out with those profits, for the nation as a whole, is a question which has elicited a great deal of consideration from historians, and some readers will be surprised that I have not chosen to include in the Interpretations section of this volume an article dealing with the debate on the subject between M.M. Postan and K.B. McFarlane.[12] There are several reasons for that choice. First, the debate on the cost of the war invariably addresses the Hundred Years War as a whole, rather than focusing on the phase of the struggle directed by Edward III, and so a substantial part of it falls outside the scope of this work. Second, the dispute centers around questions of economic history which the documents in the "Sources" section of this book cannot even begin to address (unlike the problems of the origin of the war, Edward III's war aims and strategy, or even the organization of the military effort). In any case, it has always seemed to me that the scale and importance of England's net loss or gain from the war were unquestionably much less than the war's impact on the *distribution* of wealth within English society, for most of the costs of the conduct of the war came from the farms and flocks of the country, and were paid out to English soldiers in the form of wages – came, in other words, from the community as a whole, and went to the fighting section of the population, which came disproportionately from the gentry and the nobility.

Parliament, and especially the House of Commons, which developed to maturity in Edward III's reign, was the primary engine for this redistribution. It was parliament which authorized the extraction of wealth from the community of the realm, knowing (indeed insisting) that the proceeds were to be directed to military activity. It was Edward's wars which made parliament so important to him, and which therefore gave the leaders of parliament the ability to enhance the assembly's role and power, primarily through the medium of petitions for redress of grievances, and particularly by means of grants of taxation made conditional on political concessions by the Crown. The political and social consequences of the conflicts with Scotland and France were profound in many ways, but it is difficult to imagine any elements of greater long-run import than the development of a more powerful and more institutionalized parliament which

U.P., 1966), and *The Black Prince's Expedition of 1355–1357* (Manchester: Manchester U.P., 1958).

12   K.B. McFarlane, "War, the Economy and Social Change. England and the Hundred Years War," *Past & Present* 22 (1962); M.M. Postan, "The Costs of the Hundred Years War," *Past and Present* 27 (1964); A.R. Bridbury, "The Hundred Years War: Costs and Profits," in *Trade, Government and Economy in Pre-Industrial England*, ed. D.C. Coleman and A.H. John (London: Weidenfeld and Nicolson, 1976); W.M. Ormrod, "The Domestic Response to the Hundred Years War," in Anne Curry and Michael Hughes, eds., *Arms, Armies and Fortifications in the Hundred Years War* (Woodbridge: Boydell, 1994).

G.L. Harriss discusses in his article, "War and the Emergence of the English Parliament, 1297–1360."

However great the expenditures of the English government on the war were, the costs to France were infinitely greater. Michael C. Jones provides us with a concise study which illustrates the consequences of Edward III's wars for France, in a way which may also, indirectly, help us understand why the Plantagenet's campaigns compelled the French to accept the Treaty of Brétigny, and therefore, perhaps, to understand Edward III's strategy.

Even with all of these, it is impossible for this book to provide more than a taste of what is being done by historians of the war. Propaganda; the role of the Church in supporting the war, or in seeking to resolve it; the use of spies; battle-field tactics; chivalry's impact on war and vice-versa; military technology (including the efficacy of the famous longbow); the effect of the war on literature, art, and architecture; naval developments; all these fascinating topics and many more are barely touched on in the articles chosen for inclusion here.[13] The sources section does provide some insight into most of these topics, but again only enough to whet a serious student's appetite. That, however, seems a reasonable aspiration for a single volume.

Clifford J. Rogers
West Point
August 1999

---

[13] See the bibliography for works covering these topics.

A note on money

In England, the basic monetary units were the silver penny (abbreviated "d.," from the Latin *denarius*), the shilling (abbreviated "s.," and worth 12d.), and the pound (£), worth 20s., or 240 pence. A mark was worth 2/3 of a pound (i.e. 13s. 4d.). An idea of purchasing power can be gained by considering that the daily wage for a farm laborer in the 1330s was under 2d.

French money of account was based on *livres* worth 20 *sous*, each worth 12 *deniers*. The value of the *livre* varied greatly depending on its origin and the current level of devaluation of the coinage, but the normal exchange in the fourteenth century was 5–6 *livres tournois* per pound sterling.

The florin was a gold coin of varying weight and value depending on its place and time of minting; the florin of Florence (the original) was worth 36d. sterling in 1338. The *écu* was a similar French coin, worth 40d. sterling in 1360.

A note on the translations

In translating the texts below, I have tried to maintain a balance between clarity and faithfulness to the original. Sometimes, in order to make what I believe to be the meaning of the original clear, I have had to translate rather freely, and (as is the case with any translation, but particularly any translation from medieval vernacular texts) I have often had to select a more definite English word to use for a more imprecisely defined term in the original language. It is very probable that in doing so I have sometimes gotten it wrong and distorted the intended meaning of the text. It seemed better, however, to give the reader the benefit of my best judgment even at the risk of introducing some error, rather than to use a more literal but also less informative translation.

The orthography of place and personal names can be extremely difficult, and even impossible, to decipher. Where I was able to identify (or at least able to make an educated guess as to the identity of) a place or person mentioned in the text, I have given the modern form. Text number 95 offers the reader an example of the difficulty of the problem. When I was entirely unable to identify the place or person, I left the source's spelling intact.

The majority of the texts are given in in new translations, but for a substantial number (e.g. most of the passages from the *Scalacronica*) I have employed extant English versions. In these cases I have often taken the liberty of making small changes to enhance the clarity of the translation, to correct small errors, to match spellings to the standard forms used elsewhere in this section, etc.

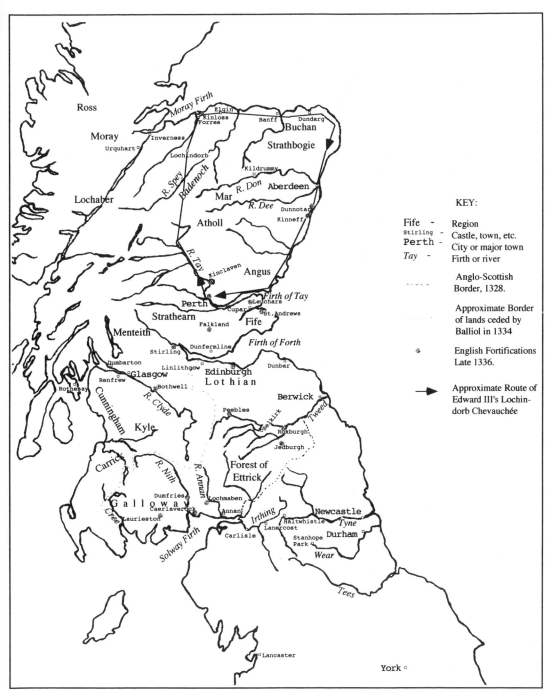

I. Map of Scotland and Northern England (showing the 1336 Campaign).

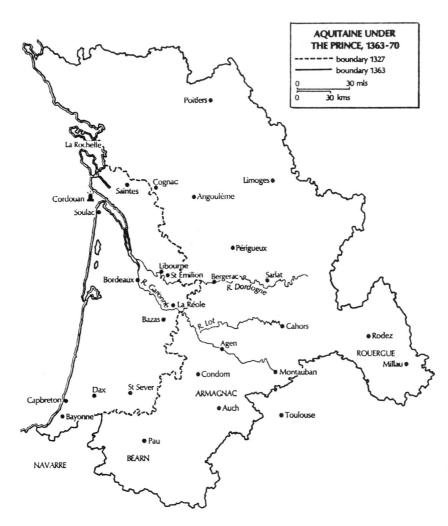

II. Aquitaine, 1327 and 1363.

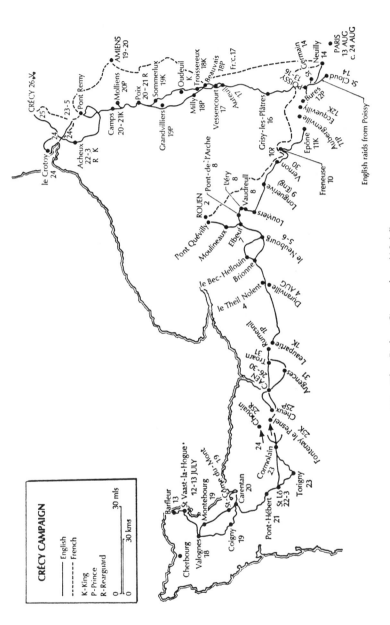

III. The Crécy Campaign (1346).

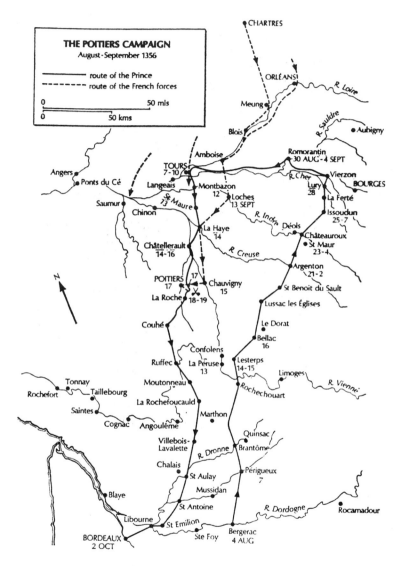

IV. The Poitiers Campaign (1356).

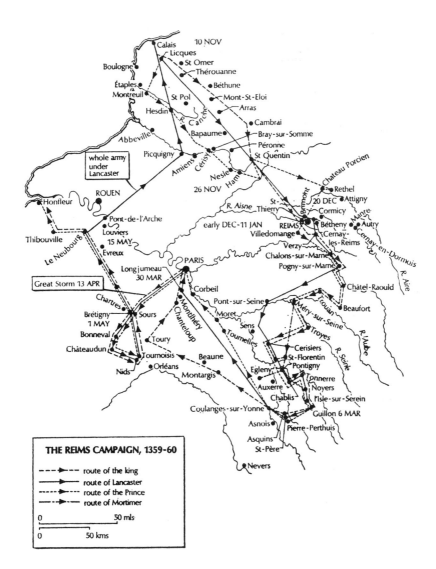

V. The Rheims campaign (1359–60).

PART I
SOURCES

LIST OF SOURCES

Starting in 1285, after the death of the Scottish King Alexander III, Edward I of England mounted a major diplomatic and military effort seeking to secure the Scots' acknowledgment of Plantagenet suzerainty over their kingdom. Edward first backed one claimant to the vacant throne, John Balliol, but then drove him out after Balliol proved unwilling to subordinate his realm to domineering English overlordship. From then through the 1320s, Edward and his son, Edward II, engaged in frequent warfare against the Scots, who from 1306 were led by Robert Bruce, in that year crowned as King of Scots.

Edward II, described by one chronicler as "always lily-livered and luckless in war," proved unequal to the challenge posed by the war in the North. In 1314 his army was crushed by Bruce at the battle of Bannockburn, and from then until 1323 the Scots harried the lands north of the Trent and the Humber almost without hindrance.

In that latter year, England was drawn into a war in Gascony, which began when Charles IV of France declared the duchy confiscate in response to Plantagenet officers' involvement in the burning of one of his towns. In 1324, King Charles' cousin Charles of Valois led an army into English territory, overran the Agenais, and forced Edward to sue for peace. The next year Queen Isabella (King Charles' sister) and her young son, Edward of Woodstock, were sent to France, the former to work towards a treaty and the latter to do homage to the Capetian King for the fiefs of Gascony and Ponthieu, thus enabling Edward II to avoid doing so himself.

Once she and her son were out of England, however, Queen Isabella joined Sir Roger Mortimer and other English exiles in plotting to overthrow King Edward, whose military failures, excessive generosity towards certain favorites, and personal peculiarities had left him in a terribly weak political position. Isabella got no help from her brother, who was troubled by her open liaison with Mortimer, but, by promising to marry Prince Edward to one of Count William's daughters, she was able to raise an army in the Imperial county of Hainault. This force of about 700 men-at-arms, led by Sir Jean de Hainault (brother of William, Count of Hainault) escorted the Queen and her entourage of exiles back to England in 1326. The country rallied to the Queen's side, and in short order Edward II found himself driven from power. Early in the next year, the elder Edward was formally deposed in parliament, and on the twenty-fifth of January his fourteen-year-old son was crowned as Edward III.

Although a thirteen-year truce between England and Scotland had begun in 1323, Robert Bruce was unable to resist the temptation to take advantage of the disorder in England. Shortly after the coronation of the new monarch, the Scots again began to raid the north of England, seeking thereby to extort an acknowledgement of their country's independence. In response, Mortimer and Isabella raised a substantial army of English knights, esquires, archers and "hobelars" (light cavalry or dragoons), reinforced by the men-at-arms who had come from Hainault to serve the Queen. The young Edward III was placed in nominal command of this force, which soon set out to meet and destroy the invading Scots. Among the soldiers from Hainault who served in this campaign was the

*young Jean le Bel, whose extraordinary narrative of the expedition (included in
the chronicle he initially composed in 1352 at the request of his friend Jean de
Hainault) is one of the best and most detailed eye-witness accounts of a medieval campaign ever written.*

1. Edward III's First Campaign. [Source: Le Bel, 42–77]

After [the arrival of reinforcements from Hainault,] the young King, so that he
might better fête these lords and all the people of their company, held a great
court on the day of the Trinity [7 June] in the house of the Minorite Friars [at
York]. He and milady his mother were lodged there, and held their courts separately; that is to say: the King for his knights, and the Queen for her ladies, of
whom she had a great number. At this court the King had a good 600 knights
sitting within the cloisters, and new knights were dubbed that day; and milady
the Queen held her court in the dormitory, and she had fully 60 ladies, whom she
had sent for in order to provide a better feast for Sir Jean and the other lords,
sitting at the table.

There could one see great nobility well served with a great plenty of dishes
and sweets – such strange ones that I wouldn't know how to name or describe
them. There one could see ladies richly adorned and nobly ornamented, if one
had had leisure to do so. But, soon after dinner, a great brawl began between the
servants of the Hainaulters and the archers of England, who were encamped
among them, which arose over a game of dice. Great evil came of it, as you shall
hear, for as these servants fought with some of the English, all the other archers
of the town and the others who were encamped among the Hainaulters gathered
up all their bows, [crying] *hahay hahay* like pigs, and wounded many of the servants and forced them to retire to their hostels. Most of the knights and of their
masters were then at court, and knew nothing of all this; and as soon as they
heard news of this struggle, each immediately went to his own quarters, if he
could get in; and if not, he had to remain outside, for these archers, of whom
there were a good two thousand, had the devil in their bodies and shot, with
amazing skill, to kill everyone, both lords and varlets, and to rob everyone. And
I myself, who was there, along with my companions, could not enter into my
hostel in order to arm myself, as I found such a great number of English in front
of our door trying to break in and steal everything; and we saw so many arrows
being shot at us, that we for our part were constrained to draw back to a different
place and, along with the others, await the outcome.

When those who were able to enter into their hostels had armed themselves,
they didn't dare issue out of them in front because of the arrows; so they sallied
out from the rear, through the gardens, broke the enclosures, and awaited each
other in a certain place, until there were 100 who were armed, aside from us and
many others who had been unable to get their arms. When these armed men
were assembled, they hastened to rescue the others of the company who were
defending their hostels on the main street, as well as they could. The armed men

passed through the hostel of lord d'Enghien, which had large doors in the rear and the front on the main street, and charged directly into the midst of the archers. Some of our men were wounded to the death with their arrows. In the end, the archers were defeated, and fully 316 of them were killed there, on the spot and in the fields, all of whom were the Bishop of Lincoln's men. So I believe that God never sent better fortune to anyone, than he did then to Lord Jean de Hainault and his company, for those men intended nothing other than to murder us and rob us, even though we had come there on their business. But know that we were not off the hook with that: for never did men remain in such great distress or in such great peril of death, without any hope of returning to our own land, as we were in every day and every night, for as long as we remained in that country, until we returned to Wissant. For because of that deed, in defending our persons, we fell into the hatred of the entire country, except for the great barons; indeed, they hated us rather more than they hated the Scots who burned their country. Every day someone came to say to our lords, on behalf of some knights who did not hate us, and on behalf of the King's Council as well, that we should be on our guard, for they knew of 6,000 English assembled in a town who were coming to kill us all and murder us by night or by day; and our men would not find anyone who would dare to aid or succor them on behalf of the King or his Council.

When we heard this news, we were of course very troubled at heart, as we did not know what to think, or see what we could do with this news. We had no hope of returning, and we did not dare separate ourselves from the King and his high barons; so if we could not expect any support from them, to aid us and guard us, then there was nothing left for us but to defend our bodies, and to sell our lives dearly, and to aid one another like good brothers. So our lords and their councilors made many good, prudent regulations, so that we might better protect and defend ourselves. According to them, we had to lie all night with our armor on, and by day keep inside our hostels and have armor ready to hand; and we were required always, by day and by night, to have Constables who watched the fields and roads around the towns, and to send some scouts out for half a league[1] out of the town to discover if anyone was coming – as was announced to us every day by men worthy of belief, knights and esquires, who thought they knew what they were talking about. These scouts, if they heard people moving towards the town, were supposed to draw back towards those who were keeping watch in the fields in order to guard us. Thus we could be mounted and assembled very quickly, and each would come to his place under his banner, where he had been assigned to go.

In such fear, in such distress, we remained in these suburbs for three weeks, and every day we had such news definitely reported to us, and many times even

---

[1] In his description of the 1327 campaign, it seems that Le Bel sometimes uses "lieue" to mean a league (three miles), and sometimes to mean a mile. I have translated the word either as league or as mile as seemed to make the most sense (or as was most accurate when that can be determined) in each instance.

worse, and several times we saw pretty good signs that it was true. This made us very downcast, because we did not then dare venture away from our quarters or our armor, nor to enter into the city, except for the lords, who sometimes went to see the King and the Queen in order to participate in feasts and to learn something of their counsel – how long we would be held in such distress without being put to the task which he had sent for us to perform. But if we had not been in such great difficulty and fear, we would have had a pleasant enough sojourn, for the city and the countryside around where we were was so plentiful, that during the more than six weeks that the King and all the princes and barons of the country and all their men-at-arms stayed there, there was no increase in the prices of commodities or victuals. And, although in all of England there is not (nor was there then) a single grape vine, yet in the said town there was so much Gascon and Rhenish wine (and more arriving) that, despite the lords who stayed there, and all the armies of England which passed through or nearby there, the price of four gallons only increased by a single silver penny; nor did the price of poultry increase so much that one could not have a large capon for three pennies, or four for the best ones; or two large pullets for three pennies, or a dozen fresh herrings for one penny. And every day, fodder, litter, and oats were brought to us for sale at such low prices that it was as if we were out in the countryside, not staying in the city. So we didn't have to trouble ourselves to go foraging for as long as we stayed there. And we never ceased to marvel how such a great abundance could come there; and it was a very good thing for us, for with standing watch and sleeping fully armed, we had plenty of trouble, care, and fear. But this much of goodness and of peace we did have: that we were all readily paid each week in good silver pennies, and everything was provided so that we could spend our pay without any great danger.

How the King and all his army departed from the city of York in order to go against the Scots

When we had thus sojourned for the space of three weeks, we were informed on behalf of the King and his Council that, within the next week, each person should provide himself with carts and with everything needed to camp in the fields, and with all cooking utensils, and everything else necessary to go against the Scots, for the King no longer wished to wait or to stay where he was. Then each person began to provide for himself according to his responsibilities and his status, and bought tents and carts, and small horses to pull them (in the local fashion); and there were plenty of them for sale, and at reasonable prices, as well as pots, kettles, and cauldrons and other such necessaries which are required in the army.

When everything was ready, the King and all the barons went out and took up lodgings a good six leagues' distance out of the town, and milord Jean de Hainault, and the other lords, and all the members of the company, were always lodged the closest to the King, because of the hate and suspicion of the English, and in order to do the greatest honor to these lords. And they stayed there two days to await the stragglers, and to advise each person if there was anything he [still] needed. On the third day, the entire army decamped and went forward, by day and by night, until reaching the city of Durham – a long day's travel – at the edge of a land called Northumberland, which is a wild country, full of waste-lands and large mountains and extremely poor, except in livestock. Through it runs a large river full of pebbles and large stones, which is named the Tyne. On this river,[2] higher up, is the castle and town which is called Carlisle in Wales, which once belonged to King Arthur; and lower down on the river sits another, called the New Castle on Tyne. The Marshal of England was there with a very large number of men-at-arms to protect the country from the Scots, who were camping in the fields in order to enter into England. And at Carlisle, too, a great plenty of Welshmen were stationed, in order to defend the passage of the river, for the Scots could not cross into the realm of England without passing this river, which is fully as large as the river Ourthe. Up until the King of England and his whole army came to the edge of this country, they could not learn any news of the Scots; but then they could easily see the smoke of the hamlets and villages which the Scots had burned in this area. They had crossed the river so quietly that neither those of Carlisle, nor those of Newcastle, knew anything of it, so they said; for it is a good fourteen English leagues between Carlisle and Newcastle. But, for a better understanding of the ways of the Scots, I will draw away from the English a little, and describe the ways of the Scots, and how they know well how to make war.

The ways of the Scots, and how they know well how to make war

The Scots are extremely bold and tough, and well endure the rigors of war. At that time they had very little fear of the English; I don't know whether that is still so now. And when they want to enter the realm of England, they lead their army forward 20 or 32 miles,[3] by day and by night, which amazes those who do not know their customs.

It is certain that when they want to pass into England, they are all mounted, except for the camp followers who are on foot; the knights and esquires are mounted on good, large rouncies, and all the other Scots on little hackneys. They bring no carts with them because of the mountainous terrain, nor do they carry any supplies of bread or wine; for such is their usual practice in war, and their frugality is so great that they can make do well enough, for a long time, on half-cooked meat, without bread, and good river-water, uncut with wine. They do without pots and kettles, since they cook their meat inside the hides of the animals which they have skinned, and they well know that they will find a great

---

2 Le Bel has conflated two rivers, the Eden (on which Carlisle sits) and the Tyne.

3 Or possibly "they spread their army out over 20 or 32 miles." The French ("ilz mainnent bien leur ost XX ou XXXII liewes loing") is obscure. Also, 32 (XXXII) could be a scribal error for 24 (XXIIII), as it is given in Froissart. Furthermore, it is possible that by "liewes" le Bel means leagues rather than miles; his usage elsewhere in the chronicle is inconsistent.

abundance of cattle in the country where they mean to go. So they carry no other supplies, except that each one carries a large flat stone between the saddle and the saddle-pad, and ties behind him a sack filled with oatmeal. When they have eaten so much of this badly-cooked meat that their stomachs feel weak and unhale, they throw this stone in the fire, and mix a bit of their oatmeal with water. When the stone is hot, they make a sort of round biscuit on it, which they eat to restore their stomachs. So it is no marvel that they make longer marches than other people, when all are mounted, except the camp followers, and they don't bring along carts or other equipment, as you have heard. In such a way they enter into England, and burn and devastate the country; and they find so many cattle that they don't know what to do with them all. They have a good 3,000 men-at-arms with iron armor, knights and esquires, mounted on good large rouncies and coursers, and fully 20,000 men armed in the local way, crafty and bold, mounted on their little hackneys. These are neither tethered nor curried, so that once their riders have dismounted they immediately send them to graze in the fields or the heath.

And know that they had two excellent captains, for King Robert of Scotland was then, it was said, ill with the great sickness, and was old, so he had given them as their captains a very noble and knightly prince, worthy in arms – namely, the Earl of Moray, who bore arms *argent*, three cushions *gules* – and Lord William Douglas,* who was held to be the boldest and most enterprising man of either country; and he bore arms *azur*, a head *argent*, and three small stars *gules* within the *argent*. And these two lords were the highest barons of the entire realm of Scotland.

How the King of England pursued the Scots, who burned and devastated his country

Well, I will return to my subject. When the King of England and his whole army saw the smoke of [the fires set by] the Scots, they realized instantly that it was the Scots who had entered into the country; so they immediately had the call to arms proclaimed, and also that each person should decamp and follow the banners. Thus it was done, so that three great divisions on foot were immediately organized, each of which had two wings of 500 men-at-arms each, who were supposed to remain on horseback. And it was said that there were 7,000 men-at-arms – knights and esquires – and 30,000 armed men, half of whom were mounted on little hackneys, the other half of whom were foot-sergeants selected and sent by the good towns, and at their wages, each town according to its assessment, and also there were a good 24,000 foot archers, not counting the camp followers. As soon as the divisions were arranged thus, everyone rode forward, all in formation, after the Scots, towards where the flames could be seen, until early evening. Then the army encamped in a woods on a little river to rest and to await the baggage and the supplies. All this time the Scots had been carrying the torch within five leagues of our army, yet we could not catch up with them. The next day, at dawn, everyone was armed, the banners were carried

---

*   It was actually James Douglas, not William, who was one of the Scottich leaders in 1327.

into the fields, and each person went to his division and his banner, as had been ordained. Thus the divisions rode forward in array, without disorder, over four mountains and through four valleys; but we could never come to grips with the Scots (who were continually lighting fires in front of us) because there were so many woods, marshes, uncultivated wastes, and rough mountains and valleys, so that there was not one person who dared, on pain of his head, to pass beyond or ride in front of the banners, except the marshals.

When it came to afternoon, towards evening, the men, horses and baggage train, and especially the footmen, were so wearied that they could go no further, and the lords perceived that they were tiring themselves out in this way for nothing, considering that if the Scots did want to wait for them, they [the Scots] would post themselves advantageously on a mountain or in a pass in such a way that they could not be attacked without the result being a complete disaster. So it was ordered that camp be made there, each one where he was, until, on the morrow, each would be informed of what was going to be done. Thus all the army lodged that night in a woods along a little river, and the King was quartered in the poor court of an abbey which was there. The men-at-arms, horses, baggage train, one and all, even the cattle which followed the army, were exhausted, as you'd expect.

When each had taken a piece of ground to camp on, the lords all took counsel together concerning how the Scots could be brought to battle, considering the country where they were. It seemed to them that the Scots were making their way back towards their country, burning everything; and that it would be impossible to fight with the Scots among these mountains, except to our own great harm; and that they could not overtake them anyway; but that the Scots would have to cross the river Tyne, and so if one were to rise before midnight, and hasten a bit on the morrow, one could block the passage over the river against them. Then the Scots would be compelled to fight at a disadvantage, or all remain in England, caught in a trap.

With this intention, which I have told you, it was ordained and agreed that each should go to his lodgings to dine on whatever could be had, and each explained to the members of his company that each man should saddle up and ready his horses as soon as the sound of the trumpets was heard; on hearing the trumpets the second time, he should arm himself; and, the third time, he should mount without delay and draw to his banner. Also, each person should take only a single loaf of bread, and tie it behind in the manner of a poacher; and all military equipment and baggage and other supplies should be left there, since on the next day they would be fighting, to whatever outcome, so that all would be won or lost. Just as it was ordered, so was it done; and everyone was arrayed and mounted directly at midnight; there were few who slept, despite the extremely hard labor of the day. As soon as the divisions were arrayed and assembled properly, the daylight began to appear.

Then the banners began to ride in terrible haste, through heaths, over mountains and through difficult valleys without any flat land at all. And below the mountains and in the lowlands of the valleys there were difficult defiles and marshes, and such treacherous passages that it is a wonder that no one was left behind, for everyone rode forward ceaselessly without waiting for lord or companion. And whoever took a tumble had great difficulty finding anyone to help him. And so a great number of drovers remained behind, in many places, with all their horses and a great profusion of packhorses and horses, the like of which has never since been seen. Very often that day the alarm was cried, and it was said that the people in front were fighting with the enemy, so that everyone who believed that to be true rushed as fast as he could through marshes, over stones and pebbles, over mountains and through valleys, with helm on head and shield [strapped around] the neck, lance or sword in fist, without waiting for father or brother or companion. And when one had thus rushed forward a half-league or more, and come to the place where the cry had begun, one discovered that one had been deceived, for it had been only a stag or hinds or other wild beasts, of which there was a great plenty in these woods and moors, who took off and fled before these banners and these horsemen, who rode thus.

How the English sought the Scots, and did not know where they were

Thus the young King rode that day with all his army through these mountains and wastelands – without holding to a road, not coming across any towns, walled or otherwise, without a path or a trail, except as could be determined by the sun – all day until early evening, when we came to the river Tyne, which the Scots had crossed, and which they would have to re-cross, as the Englishmen said. When we had arrived there, as exhausted and severely tormented as one can imagine, we crossed over this river at a ford, with great difficulty because of the large stones in it; and when we had crossed, each went to set up camp along this river, as he could find a spot of ground. But as soon as we had taken a piece of ground to encamp upon, the sun began to hide away. And also there were few people who had a hatchet or an ax, or any other tool for making camp or for cutting wood. Also, there were those who had lost a large portion of their company and didn't know what had become of them. So if they were uncomfortable, it's no wonder. And in particular the infantry had remained behind; and if one didn't know where or whom to ask, that was no wonder, for those who knew the country said that we had ridden a good 28 English miles that day, rushing, as you have heard, without stopping except to piss, or to re-girth a horse.

Worn out in such a way, men and horses, we all had to lie that night fully armed along the river, each holding his horse's reins in his hands, since no one knew where to tie them, for lack of daylight and of our baggage, which we had not been able to bring with us through such countryside, as you have heard. And so they had no hay or oats or forage to eat that night. We ourselves had no food to eat, all that day or night, other than the loaf of bread which each person had tied behind himself, as I told you, which was soaked with the horse's sweat. And we did not drink any beverage other than the running water of the river, except a few lords who had bottles; and so one can readily imagine that we were very thirsty, from the heat and the great labor which we had endured that day. Furthermore, all that night we had neither fire nor light, nor did we have any way to make one, except for some lords who had brought torches on their pack-horses. And in such misery we passed that night, without unsaddling or removing our armor.

When the eagerly awaited day arrived, which we thought would bring us some comfort for ourselves and our horses, either to set up camp or to fight with the Scots – which we much wanted to do, because of the great desire we had to escape from this discomfort and deprivation – just then it began to rain all day, and it rained so strongly and so ceaselessly that before noon had passed the river on which we were camped had become so swollen that no one could cross it. Therefore neither we nor anyone of the army could send out to discover what place we had come to, nor where forage and litter could be found for the horses, or bread, or wine, or other things necessary to sustain us. So we had to fast that day, and the night as well, and our horses had to eat dirt in order to get the green-sward of the heath, and leaves from the trees. And, all while it was raining, we had to use good swords to cut wooden stakes to tie our horses to, and sticks to make huts to cover ourselves.

Around noon, some poor men of the country were discovered, and they were asked where we had come to, since no one in our army knew this area well, nor could say for certain in what march we then were. So these poor men said that we were 14 English miles from Newcastle and 11 [leagues] from Carlisle; and there was no town any nearer where anything could be found to make us more comfortable.

This was announced to the King and the lords, and each immediately sent messengers on little horses and pack-horses to bring bread and wine (those who had bottles), and oats for his horses. And it was made known to the town of Newcastle, on behalf of the King, that whoever wanted to earn a profit should bring bread, wine and oats, and other supplies. They would be paid in cash and conducted safely to the army. Also, they were informed that no one would be leaving from around there until it was known what had become of the Scots.

The next day, around noon, the messengers whom the lords and the members of the companies had sent out returned, and brought with them as much bread, wine, and oats, and as many candles, as they could, along with other supplies for themselves and their households – which wasn't very much at all. With them some people came seeking to make some money, whose little horses and mules brought badly cooked loaves in baskets, poor wine in large barrels, and other goods to sell, which provided some relief for a large part of the army. And so it was the next day, and every day thereafter for as long as we remained around there, on the river, eight days among those mountains, always awaiting the arrival of the Scots, who did not know what had happened to us, just as we did not know any news of them.

And so, we had stayed for a day and two nights on that river without bread, without wine, without oats, without any supplies at all; and afterwards, for the space of four days, we had to pay six or seven English pennies for an ill-cooked loaf of bread, which was only worth a farthing, and to buy four gallons of wine,

which should have cost only 4 pennies, we had to pay 24 or 26. Even so, everyone was so eager for it because of hunger that one person grabbed it from
another out of the hands of the merchant, which led to many fights among some
people. In addition to all these miseries, it did nothing but rain that whole week,
so that saddles, cloths and girth-leathers were all rotted and ruined, and all our
horses, or most of them, injured on the back. And we had no way to shoe the
ones who had lost their shoes, nor anything with which to cover them except the
barrels for carrying our arms; and most of us had no coverings against the rain
and the cold except for our acquetons[4] and our armor. We also had nothing with
which to make a fire, except for green wood, which could not hold up against
the rain.

In such misery, discomfort and poverty we remained among the mountains on
the river all that week, without receiving any news of the Scots, who, we
thought, should have had to cross the river there, or pretty nearby, in order to
return to their country. This caused a great commotion to begin among the
English, for some of them wanted to accuse others, who had given the advice to
come there, of having done so in order to betray the King and his people. Therefore it was ordered, by the counsel of the lords, that we should move out from
there, and re-cross the river seven miles higher up, where it was smaller and
easier to cross. Immediately it was proclaimed that each should prepare to
decamp on the morrow and to follow the banners. It was also proclaimed on the
King's behalf that anyone who would undertake a difficult labor might earn a
good wage thereby: for the King would knight, and give 100 marks of heritable
rents to, the first person who brought him news of the Scots, and the specific
place where the King could find their army.

When this information was spread through the army, we rejoiced greatly.
Then some knights and squires of England, fifteen or sixteen of them, departed
from the army, desiring to win the promised rewards. They crossed the river at
great peril, and climbed the mountains there whence we had come, and then
split up, each from the others; and each ventured off on his own behalf.

In the morning the whole army decamped, and rode in a very leisurely
fashion all day: for our horses were weak and ill-furnished, and bowed- and
broken-backed, and badly shoed; our saddles rotted and ruined; and we ourselves had eaten a poor breakfast. And we managed to get across the river with
much discomfort and danger, for it was large and out of its banks because of the
rain, so that there were some who took a bath, and some of the English were
drowned – which didn't bother us too much.

When we had crossed, we encamped around there and found the land a bit
better, since we found enough forage, and later, to pass the night in, a small town
that the Scots had burned: so it seemed to us that we had entered into paradise.

The next day we departed from there and rode among mountains and valleys
all day, following the banners until between noon and evening, when we found

---

4   An acqueton is a form of quilted cotton armor, often worn under mail.

some burnt hamlets and some fields of wheat and other things nearby, so that we lodged there that night

The next day we rode just as on the day before, and camped in the same way. We did not know where we were being led, and heard no news of the Scots. On the fourth day, we decamped in the morning, and rode just as on the other days until mid-morning, and the weather was pretty good then, since the sun was shining.

Then an esquire arrived, riding hard towards the army, and said to the King: "Sire, I bring you news: The Scots are camped just four leagues from here on a mountain, and are waiting for you, as they don't dare to move, and they have been there fully eight days, and knew no more of you than you did of them. I make this known to you as a firm and definite truth: for I penetrated so close to them that I was captured and led before their lords, and I gave them news of you, and how you were seeking them in order to fight with them. And immediately the lords released me from captivity when I told them that you were supposed to give a hundred pounds sterling to the one who first brought you certain news of them, on condition that I would swear to them that I would not rest until I had told you this news. And understand that they say they have as much desire to fight with you as you have to fight with them; and there you will find them."

How the young King Edward besieged the Scots, who were devastating and burning his land, on a mountain

As soon as the King and his Council learned this news, he had the whole army stop, in a wheat field, to let the horses graze and to adjust their saddle-girths. This was at a Benedictine abbey which had been burnt by the Scots, which since the time of Arthur has been called Blanchland. There, each person took confession so as to be ready on the instant to live or die, and prepared his will. And the King had a great number of masses said there, in order to accommodate those making their devotions, and he immediately gave the promised hundred pounds reward to the esquire, and made him a knight during the mass, in front of everyone, and conferred great distinctions on him. When everyone had rested and eaten a little, the trumpet was sounded, everyone mounted, and the banners rode forward, with this new knight leading the way, and all the battles coming after him without breaking order for mountains or valleys, but always keeping rank as well as possible, as was ordered. We rode in this manner until, around the hour of noon, we came so close to the Scots that we could see them plainly, and they us.

As soon as they saw us, they sallied out of their lodgings, all on foot, and thus formed three good battles on the slope of the mountain where they were encamped. Below this mountain ran a strong and swift river, full of pebbles and such large rocks that one could not cross without great difficulty, even aside from their presence. And then, if we had passed the river, still there was no place between the river and their army where we could have arrayed our battles. And they had their first two battles established on two outcroppings of rock, where we could not well get up to attack them. And if we crossed the river, they would easily be able to stone us and smash us with rocks, and so we would not be able to retreat.

When the lords of our host saw how the Scots had posted themselves, they had us all dismount and remove our spurs, and form into the three battles which they had organized the other day. At that point, many men were knighted. When the battles were arrayed and put in order, some of the lords of England led the young King, on horseback, in front of all the battles, in order to embolden the men-at-arms. He asked them very graciously that each should concern himself with doing well and guarding his honor, and he commanded on pain of beheading that no one should put himself in front of the banners, or should move until commanded to do so. A little later, the order was given that the battles should go forward against the enemy, in good order, by the short step. Thus it was done; each battle advanced somewhat over a hundred yards, up to the slope of the mountain. This was done in order to see if the enemies would come down off their heights at all, and to see how they held themselves. But if they moved at all, it was not visible, even though we were so close to one another that some of their coats-of-arms could be recognized; and they could do the same with ours. Then we were ordered to halt, without engaging, in order to take different counsel. And so some companions were ordered to mount on coursers in order to skirmish and to check out the river-crossing and in order to examine their formation from closer up. Also, they [the Scots] were informed by heralds that, if they would cross over the river in order to come fight on the plain, we would draw back and leave them a place to draw up their battle, either immediately or the next morning; or if this did not please them, they should do the equivalent for us. When they heard this, they took counsel and answered that they would not do the one nor the other; but the King and all his Council saw well that they were in his realm, and had burned and devastated it; if this annoyed him, he might come and amend it, for they would tarry there as long as they liked. When the councilors of the King was that there was nothing else for it, they had it proclaimed and commanded that each person should encamp around there, without falling back.

Thus we lodged that night in very great discomfort, on hard earth and rough rocks, wearing our armor the whole time, and completely miserable. The grooms could not get any stakes or sticks to tie the horses, nor any forage, nor any bedding to comfort us or the horses, nor wood to make fires. And when the Scots perceived that we were setting up camp in such a way, they had some of their men stay where they had formed their battles, and the rest retired to their lodgings and made such great bonfires that it was a marvel to behold, and from dusk to dawn made such a great racket with their great horns blown all at once, and crying out all in one voice, that it seemed to us that these were the grand devils of hell who had come to strangle us.

Thus were we lodged that night, which was the night of St. Peter, the first of August, 1327, up until the lords had heard mass in the morning; and, when they had heard mass, we all armed ourselves and arrayed our battles, just like the day before.

When the enemy saw this, they came also to form up on the same piece of ground as the day before, and the two armies stayed thus up until mid-day, with the Scots never looking like they would come to us, and we unable to go to assail them without inviting disaster. Many of the companions who had horses to help them crossed the river, and some even did so on foot, in order to skirmish with them, and also some men from their army broke out of array, running out and back, skirmishing all the while, until there were some killed, wounded, and captured on both sides.

So in the afternoon the lords led it be known that everyone should return to his lodgings, for we were there for no purpose. We did so very willingly, for we clearly saw that there was nothing else that could be done. Thus we tarried there for three days, as did the Scots on the other side, on their mountain, without departing. Every hour of daylight there were skirmishes on both sides, and often men were killed or captured as a result; and the Scots customarily made such fires at midnight, that it was a great marvel; and they made such a clamor, by blowing horns and shouting in unison, that it seemed to us as if all of Hell was there, and that the devils had assembled there. The plan of the English lords was to hold these Scots in place as if they were besieged, since they could not do battle with them; and they thought they would be able to starve them fairly easily, since no supplies could reach them, and they could not leave from there, and the English knew well from the prisoners they had taken that they did not have any supplies of bread, nor wine, nor salt. Cattle they had in great plenty, having taken them from the countryside, so they could dine on water and roasts as much as they wished – but without bread or salt, so that it did not provide them very much nourishment. But they did have a small quantity of oats, of which they made use, as I told you about above. The same thing was practised by some of the English in our army, and they sold some of the oats to us as well, when we had no bread.

On the fourth day, when we got up in the morning and looked over towards the mountain, there where our enemies were encamped, we didn't see anyone, for the Scots had departed from there in the middle of the night. Our lords wondered greatly at this, and didn't have any idea what had become of them; so they immediately sent men on horseback and afoot to go see what had happened to them. Around six in the morning, they were found atop another mountain, two miles from the position they had vacated; and once again they were on the river, and in a rather stronger place than before, and they were encamped in a woods so as to be more comfortable and so that they could come and go more secretly, when they wanted to. As soon as they were discovered there, we were ordered to decamp and carry everything we had onto another mountain directly across from theirs. We were immediately drawn up and made to appear ready to move against them; but when they saw us, they issued out of their camp and took up their position so that they were quite close to the river, in order to meet us; but they would never cross towards us, and we could not go against them, or we would all have been lost, either killed or taken prisoner to our great harm.

Thus we encamped across from them, and stayed there until the eighteenth day, all told, on this second mountain. Every day we formed up in opposition to them, and they against us; but they would never cross over to us, nor give us space on their side, nor accept any agreement or any treaty we offered to allow them to come over to our side. During all this time, they had no bread, nor wine, nor salt, nor tanned or prepared leather to make leggings or shoes, so that they made shoes out of raw, hairy leather. Nor were we, for our part, especially comfortable, for we did not know where to take shelter, nor what to use to cover ourselves, nor where to go to forage except in the heath. So anyone can understand that we were very unhappy to think of our tents and carts and shelters, which we had purchased for our comfort, but had left unguarded in a woods, where we could not get them; we didn't even know where that was.

Thus we were for a full month in such misery and discomfort, as you have heard, that all our supplies failed us at our point of greatest need. Although supplies did come to us every day from all around for the whole time we were besieging the Scots and remained there opposite them, still they were never any great bargain, for a single loaf of bread, ill-cooked and made of bad wheat, which in town would only have cost one Parisian penny [about one quarter of a penny sterling], cost us threepence in sterling, and a gallon of bad overheated wine cost us twelve silver pennies, when a whole cask was only worth three! So we had to live, and to supply our servants, in a very strictly limited way; for we were constantly worried about even greater dearth of supplies, and that we would run out of money as a result of staying there too long.

The first night that our lords were lodged on this mountain, Sir William Douglas, who was very worthy, bold, and enterprising, took 200 men-at-arms and crossed the river around midnight, a good distance from our army, so that no one perceived him, and then struck the English army very valiantly, crying "Douglas! Douglas! You will all die, English lords!" And he and his company killed more than 300 men and spurred right up to the King's tent, always crying and shouting "Douglas! Douglas!" and cut two or three of the ropes of tent of the King.

Thus, in the way that I have described to you, we stayed twenty-two days on these two mountains in front of the Scots, always skirmishing (whoever wanted to skirmish), and nearly every day forming up, the ones against the others, one or two times; and very often, after we had drawn back and disarmed, once again came the cry "To arms! The Scots have crossed!" So we had to arm ourselves and then go to wherever that was. Furthermore, we had to keep watch every night, under constables, in the fields in three places on three sides of the host, after William Douglas made the incursion about which you have heard; and in each watch there were ordered to be 200 men-at-arms, for every day these lords of England led us to expect that the enemies were ready to come attack our army at night, for they could not stay as they were, nor endure such famine. These reports made us watch more attentively, which along with the poverty we endured, much exhausted and annoyed us: for we, the ones from across the sea, had a most troublesome task, namely to keep two watches every night: one, mounted, along with the lords of England, against the Scots, and the other, in our camp, against the archers, who hated us more than they did the Scots, and told us so, and often upbraided us for the battle we had had at York, as you have heard, and called us murderers. Thus we were, every day and night, in great fear of three things: in fear of the Scots, who were so close to us; of the archers, who were lodged among us and often threatened us; and also of famine, and of the prospect of even greater misery because of the long period of staying in one place.

On the last of the eighteen days, a knight was captured during a skirmish, who was most unwilling to tell our lords the state of their army, except that he said that their lords had agreed among themselves that morning, that each would be armed in the late afternoon, and that each would follow the banner of Sir William Douglas, to wherever he wanted to go, and that each would keep this secret; but the knights did not know for certain what he had in mind.

At this the English lords took counsel together, and said that perhaps the Scots might well come to strike our army on two sides, in order to take the chance of life or death, for they could not endure their famine any longer. So our lords ordered that each of our two battles be arrayed in three places in front of our camp, and that great bonfires be lit in each area, so that we could more clearly see one another, and that everyone should rest that night, fully armed, in place, so as to be more concentrated, and await God's will for the outcome. The servants were to remain in the camp to guard the horses. Thus it was ordered; thus it was done; and each man lay all that night on his arms in that place, in front of the fire and beneath the banners, [with his head] on the backside or the leg of his companion.

At the break of dawn, two Scottish traitors rushed up to one of the sentinels who was in the fields, and were taken and led before the lords and the Council of the King, and said: "Lords, why do you keep watch here? You are keeping watch for nothing, for, on our heads, the Scots all departed before midnight, and by now are four or five leagues away. They led us with them for a good league's distance, for fear that we would let you know about it, and then they gave us leave to come tell you." When the lords heard this, they held a council, and saw that they had been deceived by their expectations, and that it would profit nothing to chase after the Scots, because it would be impossible to catch up with them. But in any case, for fear of deceit, the lords quietly detained the two traitors, and had us stay in place until it had been light for an hour or so. Then everyone went to his lodgings to rest, and the lords went to a council to agree what to do.

Immediately some companions, including myself, mounted on our rouncies and crossed the river, and climbed up the mountain opposite, which was difficult and rough, and went to see the camp of the Scots. We found over 500 good, large, fat cattle, all quite dead, which the Scots had killed because they could not drive them in front of them, and didn't want to leave them alive for the English. And we also found over 400 cauldrons made of leather with all the hair still on, hanging over the fires and full of meat and water for boiling, and over a thousand spits loaded with meat to roast, and over 10,000 old worn-out shoes, made of crude, hairy leather, which they had left behind. In addition we found five poor prisoners whom the Scots had left in this woods, completely naked, tied to trees in spite, two of them with broken legs. But we did not know how to speak with them, so anyway we untied them and let them go, and then returned to our camp just in the nick of time, as everyone was striking camp in order to return to England by the counsel of the lords. We were very glad at that, but also extremely sad because we had endured so many evils, and yet were leaving with so little accomplished.

Anyway, we decamped and followed the banners that day until the late afternoon, when we made camp in a fine field and found plenty of forage, which was much needed by us and by our horses, who were so afflicted with runny noses, so starved, so broken down and rheumatic from bad saddles that one could neither drive them forward nor sit on them. We had no saddle pad, saddle-girth or counter-girth, crupper, bridle, nor breast harness which was not completely wrecked and spoiled; many of us had to make saddle-pads out of old doublets or old sheepskins, if we could get them, to put on our saddles and to belt beneath our saddle-girths. And on top of all this, the majority of our horses were entirely unshoed for lack of iron and blacksmiths. Many times I saw a single horse-nail sell for sixpence sterling. Thus one could certainly say, considering all the mischiefs, difficulties, and travails of the first ride and of this one, that never had so young a prince as our King undertaken two such hard, difficult, and dangerous rides as these two had been; and both were undertaken and completed in a single year; and he was only sixteen years old. So said all the most worthy in arms of our army, and those who had seen the most.

So we lodged that night in a fine field beside a fair park, and relaxed as much as we could, for we had great need of it, God knows. And so we slept a little more securely.

In the morning, we decamped and rode all that day in a leisurely way so as to rest our horses. In the evening we arrived at a large abbey two miles from the city of Durham. The King lodged in their court, and we, and all the army, encamped around the meadows, and we found plenty of forage: grass, beans, and wheat. The next day the King rested thereabouts without moving, and the King and the lords went to see the city and the church of Durham; and at that time the Bishop and the bourgeois did fealty to the King, for they had not yet done so. In this city we found all our wagons and carts, and all our gear that we had abandoned 23 days earlier in a woods at midnight, as you have heard recounted before. The bourgeois of the city had caused them to be brought in at their own expense in order to save them, and had them put in empty granges, each cart with its little pennon so that it could be identified. We rejoiced at this news, of course, for all our clothes and our possessions were on these carts. For we had not had anything to clothe ourselves with except our doublets, soaked with sweat and rain, and poor breeches, badly washed.

The next day we harnessed our little horses to our carts, and put ourselves on the road behind the King and the lords, and came after three days to the good city of York. The Queen was there, awaiting her son. Each of us went to the same lodgings from which we had earlier departed.

Once we had arrived in York, all the English left and returned to their homes and their lands, except for a few knights who stayed to keep [the King] company. We remained in the city for six days after our return. The noble knight Sir Jean de Hainault, and all those of his company, were highly fêted and honored by the King of the country, by the Queen, and generally by everyone, and especially by the ladies who were there. Each person made an account for his horses, dead and living, and for his costs. Then the King put himself into the debt of Sir Jean for that amount, and Sir Jean in turn obligated himself to all the companions, for the King could not so quickly put together as much money as the horses amounted to. But we were provided with a reasonable amount of money for our return to our own country, and thereafter within the year we were paid the total to which our horses had amounted.

When we had handed over our horses, we each bought some small hackneys to carry us back, and sent all our servants and our large gear which we did not need for the moment, tents, packs, tent-poles, and large coffers, and right there loaded them up in a vessel which the King had provided for us. And all our servants got on and traveled to Sluys. We and our lords took leave of the King, the Queen, and the other lords, and the King had us conducted to Dover by twelve knights, out of concern for the English and the archers, who hated us and had seriously threatened us at our departure: for which reason we rode fully armed through the kingdom up to Dover.

There we found vessels and ships fully ready, by the King's command, and we crossed over as quickly as we could to Wissant, for we were very eager to return, for fear of the English and considering the great discomforts which we had experienced and endured, just as you have heard.

Once we arrived at Wissant, we all took leave of one another courteously and humbly, and each went to the place he loved the best.

2. Political Consequences of the Failure of the 1327 Campaign: The "Cowardice Peace." [Source: Stones, *Anglo-Scottish Relations*, 161–2]

The complete failure of the campaign against the Scots in 1327 convinced Mortimer and Isabella to seek peace from Robert Bruce at almost any price, for it was clear that their somewhat tenuous hold on power could not withstand the political, military, and fiscal challenges of a sustained war in the North. In 1328, they agreed to a treaty with Scotland formally known as the Treaty of Northampton or the Treaty of Edinburgh, but at the time more commonly referred to in England as the "Shameful" or "Cowardice" Peace. The following text, taken from the preamble to the treaty, goes a long way to explain why the English government felt compelled to accept the Scottish demand for independence.

We, Edward, by the grace of God King of England, Lord of Ireland, and Duke of Aquitaine, give eternal greeting in the Lord to all who shall inspect the present letter. We, and certain of our predecessors as Kings of England, have tried to assert rights of rule, dominion, or superiority over the realm of Scotland, and in consequence a grievous burden of wars has long afflicted the realms of England and Scotland; therefore, considering the killings, slaughters, crimes, destructions of churches, and ills innumerable which so often befell the inhabitants of each realm, by reason of these wars, and the advantages which would accrue to each kingdom, to their mutual gain, if they were joined by the stability of perpetual peace, and thus enjoyed greater security against the evil attempts of those within or without desiring to rebel or attack them, we wish, and grant by the present letter, on behalf of ourselves, our heirs, and all our successors, with the common counsel, assent, and consent, of the prelates, magnates, earls, barons, and communities of our realm assembled in our parliament, that the realm of Scotland, defined by its true marches as they existed and were maintained in the time of Alexander, of worthy memory, the late King of Scotland, shall remain for ever to the eminent prince Lord Robert, by the grace of God illustrious King of Scots, our ally and dearest friend, and to his heirs and successors, divided in all things from the realm of England, entire, free, and quit, and without any subjection, servitude, claim or demand.

3. The Seeds of Future Wars. [Source: Maxwell, *Lanercost*, 259–60]

The following excerpt from the Chronicon de Lanercost *gives some more details concerning the treaty with the Scots, and also introduces a new issue which was to prove of great consequence in later years: Edward III's claim to the throne of France.*

The Lanercost Chronicle's main source for this period is a now-lost Franciscan chronicle probably composed in the years up to 1346, in Carlisle. The author was very interested in military history, and may have been a knight before becoming a friar. In any case, the chronicle is one of the best sources for the Anglo-Scottish wars of the period, and several excerpts from it are employed in this book.

In the same year [1328] died the King of France without heir born of his body, just as his brother had died before him. When the King of England heard of his uncle's death without an heir, he held himself to be the nearest rightful heir to the throne of France, but also feared that the French would not admit this, but would elect someone else of the [royal] blood (which they did, immediately, namely [Philip of Valois], the son of Charles, uncle of their deceased king).

Acting on the pestilent advice of his mother and Sir Roger Mortimer (they being the chief governors of the King, who was barely fifteen years of age), he was forced to release the Scots by his public deed from all exaction, right, claim or demand of the overlordship of the kingdom of Scotland on his part, or that of his heirs and successors in perpetuity, and from any homage to be done to the Kings of England. He restored to them also that piece of the Cross of Christ which the Scots call the Black Rood, and likewise a certain instrument or deed of subjection and homage to be done to the Kings of England, to which were appended the seals of all the chief men of Scotland, which they delivered, as related above, to the King's grandfather, and which, because of the multitude of seals hanging from it, is called "Ragman" by the Scots. But the people of London would no wise allow to be taken from them the Stone of Scone, on top of which the Kings of Scotland were customarily set during their coronations at Scone. All these objects the illustrious King Edward I, son of Henry, had caused to be brought away from Scotland when he reduced the Scots to his rule.

Also, the aforesaid young King gave his younger sister, milady Joan of the Tower, in marriage to David, son of Robert Bruce, King of Scotland, he being then a boy five years old. All this was arranged by the King's mother the Queen of England, who at that time governed the whole realm. The nuptials were solemnly celebrated at Berwick on [17 July, the] Sunday before the feast of Saint Mary Magdalene.

4. Enter Edward Balliol. [Source: *Cleopatra Brut*, fos. 177–177v]

One provision of the settlement of 1328 not mentioned above concerned the problem of Edward's subjects who claimed inheritances in Scotland, and Scots who claimed lands in England. In general, all such claims were declared invalid, but an exception to this provision was specified for several particular individuals, including a group of Englishmen who claimed extensive territories in Scotland. Their cases were left to be decided at some point in the future, but as time went by it became clear that despite the diplomatic efforts of the English government, the rulers of Scotland were not prepared to resolve the matter in favor of the Disinherited, as this group came to be called.

Meanwhile, in 1330, Edward III staged a coup against Roger Mortimer (whom he put to death) and the Queen Mother, and took power into his own hands. Thus, when Henry Beaumont (leader of the Disinherited and claimant to the Scottish Earldom of Buchan) sought help from the English government in 1332, it was to Edward III himself that he turned.

The description of Beaumont's arrangement with Edward III given below, which comes from a manuscript version of an English chronicle, the Brut d'Engleterre, *written only a year or two later, is somewhat controversial. Documents exist showing that Edward III actually issued orders for his sheriffs to prevent the invasion of 1332 from going forward, but it is impossible to know for certain whether these were prepared merely to provide diplomatic cover for a covert authorization of actions which might be seen as a violation of the treaty of 1328.*

The Brut *was one of the most popular chronicles of medieval England (well over a hundred manuscripts survive), and between 1350 and 1380 it*

was translated into English. The English version, which includes a series of con-
tinuations taking the narrative into the fifteenth century, has been edited by
F.W.D. Brie for the series published by the Early English Text Society, but the
French text has never been published.

And so it came about that lord Edward de Balliol, [the son of the John Balliol who had briefly been King of Scots in the time of Edward I] had with him an esquire of England who was born in Yorkshire, named John Barnaby, who was very close to his lord. This John of Barnaby, as it happened, was in a fight with a Frenchman in the town of Dampierre, and killed him. He hastily escaped out of the city to the castle, to seek refuge with his lord. The townspeople came into the castle to seize the said John Barnaby, but Sir Edward Balliol rescued him and slipped him out of the castle by night so that he reached England without suffering bodily harm. And when the King of France heard that the said Edward Balliol had rescued a felon he was very angry with him and had him arrested, and confiscated all his lands. Then the said Sir Edward Balliol remained in prison until the time when Sir Henry Beaumont came into France. This Henry Beaumont had formerly been Earl of Angus[5] in Scotland through his wife, but his county was adjudged forfeit when the accord was made between England and Scotland by Queen Isabella and Sir Roger Mortimer and their allies, through the marriage which was made between David, the son of Robert Bruce, and lady Joan of the Tower, King Edward's sister. And this Henry understood full well that he would never gain his rights unless it were by means of the said Sir Edward Balliol, who was the rightful heir of the realm of Scotland. This Henry was on good terms with Louis,[6] then King of France, and he decided to bring about the deliverance of the person of Sir Edward Balliol if he could in any way do so. So he asked the King if he, of his grace, would release the person of the said Sir Edward Balliol up until his parliament, and that he be allowed to live of his own rents in the mean time. The King granted his request and commanded that the said Edward be released from prison on those terms.

But as soon as he was out of prison the said Henry took him with him and led him into England and had him stay in secret in the manor of Sandhall on the Ouse in the county of York with the lady Vescy. While there he hired a great retinue of Englishmen and foreigners in order to reconquer his heritage in Scotland. So he gave great masses of silver to foreign soldiers to aid him; they promised him good succor, but they failed him in his hour of need.

At this time Sir Donald, Earl of Mar, heard that Sir Edward Balliol had arrived in secret in England; and he came to him and greatly rejoiced at his coming, and promised him that all the magnates of Scotland would be sympathetic to him and would consider him the rightful heir of Scotland; and they would

5　Beaumont's claim was actually to the Earldom of Buchan; another member of the Disinherited, Gilbert d'Umfraville, claimed Angus.
6　The King of France at this time was actually Philip VI.

do so much that he would be crowned King of the land. And in sign that he was King of Scotland, he did homage and fealty to him.

Then Sir Henry Beaumont came to the King of England and asked him, as a work of charity, if he would of his grace grant to Sir Edward Balliol that he might have his permission to go by land from Sandhall into Scotland in order to conquer his just heritage of Scotland. King Edward said that if he allowed Balliol to cross through his territory towards Scotland that people would conclude that he was in league with them. "Sire," said Sir Henry, "I ask you, by God, that you please give him leave to gather English soldiers, and that he be able to lead them safely through your land towards Scotland, according to the following arrangement: if, God forbid, they should be defeated in battle by the Scots, that I and Balliol's adherents should be disinherited forever of our rents in England." And the King granted his request on such terms, for him and for those of the quarrel who claimed to have lands and rents in the Kingdom of Scotland. And these were the lords of the quarrel: Sir Edward Balliol, who sought the realm of Scotland; Sir Henry Beaumont, Earl of Angus; Sir David Strathbogie, Earl of Atholl; Sir Geoffrey Mowbray, Walter Comyn, and many others of those who had been deprived of their heritage in Scotland in the way mentioned above.

5. The Campaign and Battle of Dupplin Moor, 1332: An English Account. [Source: Bridlington, 103–7]

The Deeds of Edward III, *a Latin chronicle composed by the canons of Bridlington, is one of the best narrative sources for the early fourteenth century, particularly for matters relating to the North of England. Although the surviving form of the chronicle was compiled near the end of Edward III's reign, the section covering the end of Edward II's reign and the start of Edward III's (to 1339) is derived from a now-lost work composed at the same time as the events it describes. The author is generally reliable, despite an anti-Scottish bias. The following description of the campaign of 1332, which culminated in the dramatic battle of Dupplin Moor, is taken from it.*

Even the best medieval chronicles can be wildly inaccurate in estimating the size of armies. As a rule of thumb, medieval chroniclers can be given some credence when they are reporting the size of their "own" armies, and when the totals they give are not too far out of line with the figures we know from pay records to have been assembled for particular campaigns (e.g. approximately 2,500 men-at-arms and 10,000 archers for the large English royal army which invaded Scotland in the summer of 1335, or 21,000 men-at-arms and 2,700 infantry in the French royal army at Arras in 1340). Reports of fourteenth-century armies in excess of 30,000 are probably never accurate, and estimates of "enemy" forces are often greatly exaggerated. Enumerations of the dead and the captured, particularly those contained in chronicles written by the victors, have at least the potential to be accurate, since corpses and prisoners could be actu-

ally counted off with relative ease. Thus, the Bridlington chronicler's estimates of the Scottish armies at Kinghorn and Dupplin are certainly much too high, but the figures given for English numbers and for Scottish losses at the battle may well be correct.

In the Year of the Lord 1332, the lord Edward, son and heir of John Balliol the former King of Scots, with the lords Henry Beaumont, Earl of Buchan, Gilbert d'Umfraville, Earl of Angus, and David Strathbogie, Earl of Atholl, and with Richard Talbot, Henry Ferrers, Fulk Fitzwarin, Nicholas de la Beche, Ralph Stafford, Thomas Ughtred, Alexander Mowbray, John Mowbray, Robert Winchester, and Walter Comyn, barons and bannerets, with a number of English soldiers, with horses, food supplies, and other necessaries, gathered into eighty-eight ships large and small, and on the last day of July, which is to say on the feast of St. Germanus the Bishop, began their journey over the waters from Barton and Kingston-on-Hull. For six consecutive days and nights they sailed towards Scotland, suffering more than a little from the rough seas. On the seventh day, however, namely on [6 August,] the day after the feast of Saint Oswald the King and martyr, they landed at Kinghorn in the county of Fife. While they were climbing up the beach, the Earl of Fife with 24,000 cavalry and infantry attacked them, in order to drive them off. The horses not yet having been led off the ships, it fell to the [English] infantry to fight. So they fought, and some of the Scots fell, among them Sir Alexander Seton the younger, who perished; the rest took flight. The Scots who thus turned their backs were followed by the English, until the difficulties of the mountains prevented the armored soldiers from pursuing the fugitives farther. Seeing that the Lord had granted them such a swift victory, they humbly and devotedly prayed to Him that He adorn the rest of their journey, and its end, with the same grace he had bestowed on its beginning.

Thus, after they had unloaded the horses and other necessaries from the ships, they came to the abbey of Dunfermline, where they stayed for two days. Then they marched farther into the realm, to the river Earn, where they fixed their tents and encamped. Across the river they saw a relatively large army of cavalry and infantry gathered. The leader and commander of this army was Donald, Earl of Mar, who had many times, by letters and messengers, promised aid and counsel to these lords. Coming to the river's edge on the other side, he exhorted them in words like these: "Presumptuous knights," he began, "tell us without delay from what part of the world you have come here, and what you seek in this region, and the name of the person who is accounted your leader." They answered: "We are the sons of the foremost of this land; and, putting our faith in his counsel and aid, we have come here with the rightful heir of this realm, lord Edward Balliol, claiming the lands and tenements which belong to us by hereditary right. We believe there is no need to announce our names to the person who was once the advisor of this undertaking, if indeed you are going to welcome and praise our arrival, as was often discussed between us beforehand."

To this he replied, "That is to no purpose, for fate and fortune have now transformed that agreement into something else. I sorrow for your loss, as your sudden invasion and arrival has stirred up the entire realm of Scotland, without any division; and, in your disorder, the more you show yourselves, the more you provoke them."

Each side having set out its position in this way, they departed one after the other. Seeing themselves to have been cheated out of any help from the Earl, and having held a council concerning these speeches, around sunset, guided by some people who knew the country and the fords of the river, they prepared to cross the river as soon as night fell. There on the river-banks they awaited the darkness of night, then crossed the water and, seeking out the tents of the enemy, they got in among their sleeping-places, and mercilessly cut down everyone who arose. At the screams of those who were thus killed, the others awoke. Not having space either to take up arms or to flee, the unarmed men ran around among the armored ones, who then struck them with blows as they fled hither and thither, none with a plan in mind. As the Englishmen rushed in, their wounded enemies fell continuously.

Thus, having spent the entire night in this way, and as a great ruin of killed people became visible in the light of dawn, they sent certain people out to examine how many of the fallen were footmen and how many were men-at-arms. And, returning, they announced that the dead were all footmen. And so it was. For all the men-at-arms and armored troops were, so to speak, besieging the bridge, presuming that the invaders were unaware of the ford. But with the sun leading in the new day, they sent out scouts to look around, so that they would not fall unaware into the hands of the enemy. And behold! immediately the aforesaid Earl of Mar, with a huge multitude of Scots arrayed in divisions according to their custom, came to meet them, marching on foot, around 40,000 infantrymen and men-at-arms. Then the English, who saw their own weakness, trusting not in their own virtue but in the mercy of God – exceedingly few, only five hundred knights and men-at-arms, and a thousand footmen and archers – lined up their formation against the enemy. The Scots joined the battle with spirit, but rashly, in truth. Having disposed their units and their archers in such a way that they attacked into the flanks of the enemy formations, these [English] men-at-arms overcame the great army. And, the battle having been joined, at first they could not withstand the impetus of the Scots, being forced to fall back a short distance; but inspired from Above they resisted, presenting their shields to the enemy's blows. The smaller units of the enemy, which were indeed very badly cut up by the archers, were compelled to join with the large army; and in a short time they crammed together into a single mass, pressed one against the other; thus, suffocated by their own men rather than struck by blows of the sword, they collected into an truly astonishing heap. Thus compressed, as if they were bound together by ropes, they perished in misery. The Earl of Fife, however, seeing himself and his men put in mortal peril, at that time ordered the enemy to retreat, rather than continuing to fight to their detriment; and in accordance with this wise counsel, he and a few others abandoned turned away from the fight.

Thus, with the Scots turning their backs, Lord Henry Beaumont with his cavalry followed and sought out the dispersed enemy, and determined to slaughter the fleeing enemies. The others, who remained behind, were ordered to surround the mass of the enemy described above, and to attack it unremittingly and finish it off. And indeed out of that heap, believed to have been miraculously piled together by divine vengeance, not a single survivor could be extracted. That day due to the pride of the Scots there fell three earls, namely Donald of Mar, the aforesaid Warden of Scotland, to whom the control of the business of the realm belonged, and the Earls of Moray and Menteith, along with 18 bannerets, 58 knights, 800 esquires, 1,200 well-armored infantrymen and many common footmen; not counting those in the aforesaid heap, whose number no one knows. Indeed the mass or heap aforesaid, miraculously piled together as was said above, reached a height of fifteen feet.

6. Dupplin Moor: A Second English Account. [Source: *Cleopatra Brut*, fos. 177v–179v]

It is often helpful to compare two or more independent accounts of the same events. The immediately following narrative of the 1332 campaign is taken from a manuscript of the strictly contemporary French-language Brut d'Engleterre; *after that the reader will find another description of the battle, this one from the Middle English verse chronicle of Andrew of Wyntoun, a Scottish cleric. Wyntoun's chronicle was not composed until the early fifteenth century, but in writing it he made use of more contemporary Scottish sources, now lost.*

Different manuscripts of the same chronicle sometimes have significant variations of the same text. Although the basic text from the Brut *below is taken from one manuscript of the chronicle, at a few points I have incorporated emendations from a different manuscript which seem to make more sense (as footnoted). Such variations are simply one more factor making the medieval historian's task more difficult.*

These lords gathered to them 500 men-at-arms and 2,000 archers and foot-soldiers, and took ship at Ravenspur and sailed by sea until they came to Scotland and arrived at Kinghorn, twelve leagues out of St. John's Town [Perth]. They sent their ships back to England so that they could not take refuge in them if they were presented with the need to flee; rather would they stand and fight to the death in order to maintain their quarrel.

The Earl of Fife, who is very cruel and a man of evil ways, heard that Balliol intended to conquer the land of Scotland, and came to Kinghorn with 10,000 Scots to prevent his landing; but Balliol and his company took the land despite his men, and defeated them. Sir Alexander Seton the younger and many others were killed in the defeat. And the Earl of Fife was very sorrowful that such a small company had defeated him and put him so shamefully to flight. Then Sir Edward Balliol took control of the surrounding land until he came to the abbey of Dunfermline, where he found food supplies for himself and his men, and he also found a good 500 large staves of oak with long, well-set iron heads. These he took and distributed to the strongest men of his company. From there he soon continued, and encamped in a field two leagues outside of Perth. And when the burghers of the town heard how the Earl of Fife had been defeated by the Balliol they were much afraid and broke the bridge over the river Earn so that Balliol could not cross. He therefore camped there all that night. Balliol had no care for rest, saying to his men: "Well you know, lords, that we have arrived in the midst of our enemies; and if they are able to capture us, there will be nothing more but death; so if we wait here all night in peace I do not doubt that it will turn out to our damage. For the strength of the Scots is multiplying, and we are but few men compared to them. Therefore I pray you, by God, that you embolden yourselves and that we make a strong assault on the Scots this very night. If they are over-come by your boldness, the other Scots who come against us in their aid will more dread to fight us; and we will fight with them all the more vigorously; and thus, with God's grace, all the world will speak of our chivalry."

Then Balliol and his allies followed this advice and accomplished a great deal by their boldness. They did great harm with their assault on the Scots, who had become fatigued and very weary, so that they were almost helpless. But they said among themselves: "What just happened to us, that so few men as the Balliol has, have so worked us over and harmed us? Certainly, it seems to us that he works by divine grace, for he is extraordinarily full of grace in his quarrel. But we shall all be dead before we submit to him, considering how his father left us cold."

First of all, Balliol and his men crossed the Earn. Sir Roger Swinnerton the younger drowned in the crossing, at which there was great sorrow, for he was a valiant knight. Then they encountered many of the Scottish men-at-arms and did mortal combat with them, and killed as many as they could lay hands on, and these were men of the countryside.[7]

During the assault, they had thought that they had struck the great army of Scotland. When it came to day, they rallied together and rested a little. And during this rest, Sir Thomas Vescy and the noble baron Stafford spurred their destriers here and there over the hills, keeping watch on the situation of the land. Thus they saw a great army in good array, in three divisions, with helms or shields gleaming, coming against them. So they returned to Balliol's men, and said to the lords "By God, be of good comfort, for you will have a battle any moment." Then said Sir Fulk Fitzwarin, a baron renowned in arms: "Know, lords, that I have been in various military formations, against Saracens as well as against Scotsmen, but never yet have I seen the fifth part of any formation fight. Therefore, if we have the will to fight and to stand against our enemies, we are enough to stop their force and to fight with them; but if we are not of good will to do this, then certainly we are too few for this encounter. And therefore let us

---

7   From *AM Brut*; *Cleopatra Brut* says they were "the most valiant men."

take strength and boldness into ourselves, and think neither on our wives nor our children, but only of winning the battle, and by the aid of God we will vanquish our enemies."

With that the great army of the Scots advanced in close order[8] against the Balliol, in three divisions, well equipped with armor; vigorously they rushed against the Balliol. But Sir Donald, Earl of Mar, who had done homage to him at Sandhall in the county of York as is said above, took pity on Balliol and his company and said to Sir Robert Bruce, Earl of Carrick, "Certes, sir, it displeases me much at heart that these men whom Balliol has led with him should die by the blows of Scotsmen's swords, since they are Christians as we are. Therefore it seems to me that it would be a work of charity to send to them to demand that they surrender to our grace, so that they should be ransomed for a severe ransom, considering that they have wrongly landed in our country."

"Certes, Donald," said Sir Robert, "now I know well that you are an enemy and traitor to Scotland, since you want to save our mortal enemies. Now it seems indeed that you are in accord with them."

"Certes, Robert," said Sir Donald, "you lie. I am not in league with them, and this I will show you in haste, for I will be the first of this army to fight with them."

"Certes," said Sir Robert, "I will attack them before you despite you." At which they pricked their horses with their spurs angrily over Gaskmoor, and their divisions followed in disorder.[9] So they met Balliol and his company on a downward slope at the edge of the moor in a narrow passage; and they came towards them in such haste that they piled up by their thousands, each on top of others. The Balliol and his men stood strong against them, and killed them and wounded them for such a long time that they stood on top of them and stabbed them through their bodies with their swords and lances; and struggled with them until they became so exhausted that they did not know what to do. And those on the other side who were left alive fled to save themselves, as best they could. And then Edward Balliol and his men pursued and killed them until it was night.

7. A Scottish Perspective on Dupplin Moor. [Source: Wyntoun, 2:387–9]

. . . That small band of people who were enclosed by their foes made themselves ready before day, and crossed the river secretly without noise or cry, so that none of those who sat on the rising banks knew it; for they so made mirth that they set no watch; for they had no fear of defeat. Men say that someone met them in the ford, and secretly without words led them up by the water, then, till they came to the Gask and Dupplin. There many were lodged to lie for the night: the majority of these they killed. Soon the great division kept higher up knew, by the noise

---

8   From *AM Brut*; *Cleopatra Brut* says "in poor order" [*espernelment*].
9   From *AM Brut* [*a randoun*]; but *Cleopatra Brut* has "in a row" [*sur un renge*].

and the cries of slain and stabbed men, whom they heard loudly cry and roar, that their foes had gotten past them. Therefore they quickly made themselves ready, and made their way to their foes; but they were so dispersed at that time that they were not then aught over eight hundred armed men. The Earl of Moray, young Thomas, was a leader in that division; Murdoch the Earl of Menteith also; Alexander Fraser the younger; with them in that group was Robert Bruce, who was King Robert's son.

The Earl of Mar, who was Warden, was nearby in another place. The first division made their way straight forward, and soon as it dawned day, they met their enemies head-on. Together they struck, but for a longer time were halted. Men say that the English there were pushed back a great space; that the baron of Stafford, on a height, bade them stand fast with a right sturdy word; but despite this, various men swore right firmly that if they had had leisure to fight, they would not have been defeated there. But Earl Donald came in haste. If he had joined them on their flank, they would have had the upper hand without doubt: but he with all his great division came on behind, and bore down all that he found before him there. There was the disaster so cruel, that whoever in that great throng fell, never had the chance to rise again. In this way a good two thousand men were smothered and slain, as men can guess. The Earl of Moray was slain there, the Earls Murdoch [of Menteith], Bruce, and Fraser, and one thousand, as I heard tell, and more, were smothered in that place, where not a drop of blood was drawn. The Earl of Mar died there also.

Hereby men may take example, that order is sometimes better in a fight than either strength or might. As Cato says: other things, men may often mend, when they have made a mistake; but in a fight, when men are not ruled aright, they shall not well mend it again, for in the neck follows the pain.

8. Balliol's Coronation and the Fruits of Victory. [Source: Maxwell, *Lanercost*, 271–4]

The Chronicon de Lanercost *describes the aftermath of the Scottish defeat at Dupplin Moor. The chronicler, who had little liking for the Scots, means Edward Balliol rather than David Bruce when he speaks of the King of Scotland.*

Now on the feast of St. Francis the Confessor, to wit, the fourth day of the month of October, my lord Edward [Balliol] was created King of Scotland at the Abbey of Scone according to the custom of that kingdom, with much rejoicing and honor. In which solemn ceremony it is said that this miracle took place, namely, whereas there were in that place an immense multitude of men and but slight means of feeding them, God nevertheless looked down and multiplied the victuals there as he did of old in the desert, so that there was ample provision for all men.

Meanwhile the Bishop of Dunkeld came to the King's peace, and undertook to bring over to the King all the bishops of Scotland, except the Bishop of St.

Andrews. The Abbots of Dunfermline, of Cupar-in-Angus, of Inchaffray, of Arbroath and of Scone came to his peace also; and likewise the Earl of Fife with thirteen knights, namely, David Graham, Michael Wemyss, David Wemyss, Michael Scott, John Inchmartin, Alexander Lamberton, John Dunmore, John Bonvile, William Fraser, William Cambo, Roger Morton, John Laundel and Walter Lundy. But the other chief men of Scotland, aside from those mentioned, seeing the King in the unwalled town of Perth, more or less in the middle of the kingdom with such a small force, assembled in great numbers and besieged him. When the people of Galloway, whose special chieftain was the King, heard this, they invaded the lands of these Scots in their rear under their leader Sir Eustace Maxwell, and thus very soon caused the siege to be raised. Upon this Earl Patrick, and the new Earl of Moray by the Scottish creation, with Sir Andrew Murray, and Sir Archibald Douglas, having collected an army, invaded and burnt Galloway, taking away spoil and cattle, but killing few people, because they found but few. And for this reason the Scots and the men of Galloway were long at war with each other.

Meanwhile the King strengthened and fortified Perth, appointing the Earl of Fife with his men as garrison there, while he with his army rode about and perambulated the country beyond the Firth of Forth, and then returned. But before he got back, the Scots, by stratagem and wiles, had captured the Earl of Fife and burnt Perth.

Now after the King's return and when he had arrived at Roxburgh on the feast of St. Calixtus, that is, the fourteenth day of the month of October, he dismissed his army in the town and went himself, for the sake of greater quiet, with a small retinue, to be entertained in the Abbey of Kelso, which is on the other side of the town bridge. But when the said Sir Andrew Murray heard this, with other knights and troops, he continually dogged the King and his people in order to harass them. They broke down the bridge between the King and his army by night, so that they might capture him with his small following in the abbey, or kill him if he would not surrender to them. But the King's army hearing of this repaired the bridge with utmost speed; and some of them, not waiting till this was done, plunged into the great river armed and mounted, swam across and pursued the flying Scots for eight miles, in which pursuit many were killed and others captured, among whom was the aforesaid Sir Andrew Murray, Guardian of Scotland since the death of the Earl of Mar, and a certain cruel and determined pirate called Crabbe, who for many years preceding had harassed the English by land and sea. Both of them were sent to the King of England that he might dispose of them according to his will. Howbeit this Crabbe, having been granted his life by the King of England, became afterwards a most bitter persecutor of his people, because of the ingratitude of the Scots of Berwick, who, at the time of the siege of that town refused afterwards to ransom him and even killed his son. But Sir Andrew Murray was ransomed afterwards for a large sum of money.

About the feast of St. Nicholas the Bishop [6 December], the King of England held a parliament at York, to which the King of Scotland sent my lord

Henry Beaumont, Earl of Buchan, and the Earl of Atholl, and many others with them, to negotiate and establish good peace and firm concord between my lord the King of England and himself; and this business, by God's ordinance, was carried to a prosperous conclusion, as will be shown anon.

9. Edward Balliol's Homage to Edward III. [Source: *Foedera*, II:2:847]

Edward III's assistance to the Disinherited had thus far been only covert, and there is some evidence that the English King at this stage gave serious consideration to backing his brother-in-law against the Disinherited, if King David would acknowledge English sovereignty over Scotland (see the excerpt from the Rolls of Parliament below). King Edward also seems to have contemplated an attempt to exercise direct lordship over the northern kingdom, which he could have claimed the right to do because John Balliol, at the time of his deposition, had surrendered his rights to the crown to Edward I.

On 23 November 1332, apparently in a bid to discourage the Plantagenet from abandoning his cause, Edward Balliol published a letter patent which seems to reflect the secret agreement made between the two Edwards before the invasion of Scotland by the Disinherited. The legalistic and convoluted prose of the letter (the French text of which can be found in the extremely valuable compendium of diplomatic documents, known as the Foedera, *collected by Thomas Rymer in the early eighteenth century) is typical of the official documents of the period. It begins with a summary of the Scots' acknowledgment of English suzerainty in the reign of Edward I, then continues as follows:*

As we now, by the sufferance of the most excellent prince, our very dear lord and cousin Sir Edward, King of England, Lord of Ireland, and Duke of Aquitaine, and by the aid of some of his good people, of his realm and dominion, who were and ought to be the inheritors of great territories in the realm of Scotland and the Isles, and who were by force dispossessed of them by the heir of Sir Robert Bruce, are come into our said realm of Scotland, as into our heritage, and as we now have been crowned King of the same realm and isles;

We, knowing the ancient right by which the realm of Scotland, and the Isles appertaining thereto, is, and has been, held of the Kings of England, as from a sovereign lord, have entered into the liege homage and fealty of the King of England, our very dear lord and cousin, by the following words, the said King holding our hands between his:

I, Edward, by the grace of God King of Scotland and of the Isles belonging thereto, become your liegeman [for] the said realm and isles, against all people who may live and die.

And the said King of England, as sovereign lord of the said realm of Scotland and the Isles, received our homage in the form said below: [blank.]

And then, next, we entered into fealty of the said King of England, sovereign lord of the said realm of Scotland and the Isles, touching the Holy Bible, by the following words:

> We will be faithful and loyal, and bear ourself faithfully and loyally towards you, our very dear lord King of England, and to your heirs, as to the sovereign lords of the said realm of Scotland and the Isles, against all people who may live and die.

. . . And, because of the great honors and profits which we have experienced and found in the sufferance of our said lord and cousin the King, and because of the great and good aid of his said good people, of his realm and dominion, as is said above, we wish and grant for ourselves, and for our heirs, that the said King of England be assigned, given, and delivered land, in suitable locations on the border of our realm of Scotland, adjoining the realm of England, worth two thousand pounds annually, by a reasonable survey, to be made by wise men, deputed by each side.

And, as part of that 2,000 librates of land, we give, grant, and assign, for ourselves and for our heirs, to the said King of England, the castle, town and county of Berwick . . .

10. Parliamentary Discussion of Intervention. [Source: *Rotuli Parliamentorum*, 2:67]

When Edward III received word of the battle of Dupplin Moor, he promptly summoned a parliament, for already parliamentary grants had become a necessary element of financing any major English military effort, and parliament was also the best venue for royal efforts to rally the political support which would be key to the success of any major undertaking. Fortunately for historians, a summary record of the proceedings of every parliament of Edward's reign was kept in writing, and many of these Rolls of Parliament *survive to this day. The following extract from the Rolls describes the deliberations of the parliament held in December of 1332 at York.*

On the appointed Friday [4 December] the King did not come, as he was, from close by, awaiting the arrival of the lords who had been summoned to the parliament; and so the parliament was put off until the following Monday. And on that Monday, in the presence of our Lord the King, the parliament was put off until the next day, Tuesday [8 December], because of the non-arrival of the lords, as stated above. And on Tuesday, thus, it was announced by Sir Geoffrey le Scrope, in the presence of the King and all the lords, in full parliament, how the immediately previous parliament had been summoned to Westminster because of affairs concerning the land of Ireland, the King having arranged a passage there in order to rein in the malice of the rebels against him there; and how the prelates, earls, barons, and other lords of the parliament and Knights of the Shires, had been charged to take counsel on the security of the land of England; and how the said prelates, by themselves, and earls and barons by themselves, and the Knights of the Shires by themselves, having deliberated, responded and advised that it would be best if the King were to stay in England, and, because of news coming from Scotland, move to the North country, because of the dangers to his people and his realm which might occur if the Scots were to enter there in order to do evil. And how he granted their request and thus came here; and how then, because of other news which came to him at York from Scotland, to the effect that Edward Balliol had caused himself to be crowned King of Scotland, the King and his Council then assembled had summoned this current parliament to York. And the cause of the summons was that the King wanted to have the counsel of his good people, and lieges of his realm, prelates and others, as to whether he should advance towards Scotland in order to claim the same land as his domain, or should get involved and take the favorable opportunity to have it in service, as his ancestors had done, or the equivalent.

And, by the mouth of the said Sir Geoffrey, in full parliament, on that same Tuesday, our Lord the King charged the prelates, earls, barons, and other lords, and the Knights of the Shires, and the men of the Commons, that they counsel him and give their advice, having regard to the honor and profit of him and his realm, and bearing in mind that at the time of the peace formerly made between the people of England and the people of Scotland that he was a minor, and not subject to his own will, but rather guided by others; and also taking into account that which the ancestor of this Balliol had forfeited to the grandfather of our Lord the present King.

The prelates and the clergy by themselves, and the earls and barons by themselves, and the knights and people of the shires and the people of the commons by themselves, thus discussed and took counsel up until the following Friday [11 December]. On that Friday, in full parliament, the prelates by themselves, the earls and barons by themselves, and the Knights of the Shires by themselves, and then all in common, answered that in such a great and weighty business, which touched so closely the King, his people, and his realm, they neither dared, nor knew how to, counsel without the advice of the prelates, who were, with three [sic] exceptions (the Archbishop of York and the Bishops of Carlisle and Lincoln, and the Abbots of York and Selby), not present, or the other lords of the realm who had not then arrived. And at that they asked the King if he would prorogue the same parliament until the upcoming octaves of St. Hilary [20 January 1333], to be held then in the same place, York; and to send weighty messages to the prelates and other magnates who were absent, that they should be there on the said day at the said place, so that affairs would not be delayed any longer by their failure to appear. These requests were granted by the King.

11. Balliol Cast Out of Scotland. [Source: Maxwell, *Lanercost*, 274–5]

Before the new parliament could gather, events took a dramatic turn in Scotland, as the Chronicon de Lanercost *explains.*

Meanwhile the new young Earl of Mar (by the Scottish creation),* and the Steward of Scotland, and Sir Archibald Douglas, having assembled a strong troop of men-at-arms, on the 17th of the kalends of January, that is, the ninth day [16 December] before Christmas, came secretly early in the morning to the town of Annan, which is on the march between the two kingdoms, where the King of Scotland aforesaid was staying with the small force he kept together, intending to remain there over Christmas. They found the King and his people in bed, like those who were too confident in the safety secured through many different victories already won, and they rushed in upon them, naked and unarmed as they were and utterly unprepared for their coming, killing about one hundred of them, among whom were two noble and valiant Scots, namely, Sir John Mowbray and Sir Walter Comyn, whose deaths were deeply lamented, but the King afterwards caused them all to be buried. Meanwhile the King and most of the others made their escape, scarcely saving their persons and a few possessions which they carried with them across the water into England. Of the Scots, as was reported, about thirty were killed in the brave defense offered by the naked men aforesaid.

The King therefore came to Carlisle, and there kept his Christmas in the house of the Minorite Friars, receiving money and gifts and presents which were sent to him both from the country and the town; for the community greatly loved him and his people because of the mighty confusion he caused among the Scots when he entered their land, although that confusion had now befallen himself.

12. The Siege of Berwick, 1333. [Source: *Melsa*, 2:367–9]

This description of the events following Balliol's expulsion from Scotland is taken from the Latin chronicle of Meaux Abbey, the earlier sections of which were composed by Thomas of Burton in the 1380s and 1390s. Although it is, thus, rather distant in time from the events in question, it includes one of the best and most detailed accounts of the siege of Berwick in 1333, apparently based on a lost Cistercian chronicle ending in 1334.

Edward Balliol therefore returned into England and anxiously begged for aid from Edward, King of England, promising him his homage and certain lands in Scotland if he would assist him in this hour of need. At this, Edward King of England granted him the right to pass through his territory into Scotland, and gave license to anyone willing to enter into his land along with him. Certain magnates, and many others, around 10,000 Englishmen, therefore entered into Scotland, and, after doing much damage to the Scots, reaching Berwick on the twelfth day of March, they opened the siege of that city, making a firm pact

* An error for the Earl of Moray.

among themselves that none would withdraw from there until the besieged town and castle either were surrendered, or were victoriously seized. Then they closed off all the entrances and exits of the town with ditches, and laid siege to it by land and sea everywhere . . .

Meanwhile, Archibald Douglas entered England with 3,000 Scots, and set fire to the entire country of Gilsland, that is to say for fifteen miles in length and six in breadth, even to the churches; and they began to lay waste to the country-side everywhere, believing that in this way they would break the siege of Berwick; but they did not succeed. At this time, Anthony Lucy and William of Lochmaben along with 800 Englishmen and Scots rode twenty miles into Scotland, pillaging the country. On their way they met William Douglas, returning along with his Scots. At the end of a long, vigorous struggle, William Douglas, William Bard, and a hundred others were captured, and Humphrey de Bosco and Humphrey Gardiner, knights, along with another 160, were slain, the remainder fleeing.

Meanwhile the English pillaged the goods at the Haddington fair, and killed the Scots they found there. When reports of Archibald Douglas' invasion of England were sent to Edward, King of England, he gathered his army and set out to defend the northern parts of his realm from the irruption of the Scots. Coming therefore to the siege of Berwick on the ninth of May, he ordered the construction of siege engines, and made a fierce assault on the town by land and water. But the besieged resisted manfully. The English of his army therefore dug a ditch all around the town, at the bottom of which they discovered four conduits which provided the town with fresh water. Breaking these, they entirely cut off the town's fresh water. Then they cast fire into the town, and burned a large part of it. In addition, the continuing assaults so exhausted the defenders, that, in exchange for a temporary truce, they promised to hand over to the King of England, Edward, twelve of the most noble among the besieged of the castle and the town; and they made a pact that, unless they were rescued by the magnates of Scotland or someone else before a certain fixed day, they would immediately on that day surrender the castle and town to the King of England, saving the lives, limbs, lands, tenements and goods, mobile and immobile, of all the besieged people.

13. A Scottish Relief Attempt. [Source: *Scalacronica* (Stevenson), 162–3]

From here the narrative is taken up by the Scalacronica, *an Anglo-Norman chronicle begun by the border knight Sir Thomas Gray during a spell in captivity in Scotland in the mid-1350s. The descriptions of warfare in the* Scalacronica *are particularly valuable because its author was himself an active soldier.*

Before the set time was up, all the forces of Scotland – an amazingly great multitude of people – crossed the river Tweed at dawn one day at Yair Ford, and presented themselves in front of Berwick on the other side of the Tweed, towards England, in plain view of the King and his army; and they sent men and supplies into the town, and remained there all the day and the night, and late on the morrow decamped and moved off through the country of Northumberland, burning and destroying the land in plain view of the English army. These people having thus departed, the Council of the King demanded the surrender of the town according to the conditions of the pact, the term of their rescue having passed by. Those inside the town said that they had been relieved, both with men and with supplies, and presented the new guardians of the town, and the knights who had entered the town from their army, of whom William Keith was one, along with others. And the said Council [of the King of England] was of the opinion that they had forfeited their hostages; so they had the son of Alexander Seton, the guardian of the town, hanged. When this hostage had thus been put to death, the others in the town, out of tenderness towards their children, who were hostages, renewed the surrender agreement by the assent of the knights who had come in from the army, who were of the opinion that their forces of Scotland exceeded the army of the King of England. So new conditions were agreed . . .

14. A Treaty for the Surrender of Berwick. [Source: *Foedera*, II:2:864]

The type of treaty mentioned in both the passages above, in which a hard-pressed garrison agreed to surrender by a certain fixed date unless rescued by a relieving army, was a regular element of medieval warfare. Although many such agreements were made, it is likely that few of them were put into writing, and fewer still survive. Thus, the treaty made between Edward III and the defenders of Berwick in 1333 is an almost unique document. The full text is substantially more elaborate even than the excerpt given here.

This indenture bears witness that the noble prince the King of England has granted a truce, by land and by sea, to last until sunrise on Tuesday [20 July], the upcoming day of Saint Margaret the Virgin, in the year of grace 1333, to the noble man, Sir Patrick of Dunbar, Earl of March, and to all those of the castle and town of Berwick-upon-Tweed who in any way are dependent on him, as follows:

So that the said Earl [of March], and all the aforesaid people, shall keep their lives and limbs, and they shall keep heritably all their lands, tenements, rents, fisheries, offices, fiefs, and possessions, whether purchased or inherited, of which they had possession the day that this accord was made, inside and outside of the said castle and town of Berwick, without other rights being denied, [except] through the laws of Scotland;

And that they will not be cast out in any way, except only by process of the common law of Scotland; nor denied any seisin or possession held, before the said day, by anyone whomsoever, in the time of any King of England or Scotland, with all their goods, castles, chalices, money, clothes, horses, armor, prisoners, and all other manner of goods, moveables and otherwise, spiritual as well as temporal, in England as well as in Scotland, and with all their franchises, usages, laws, and customs, as held and practiced in the time of King Alexander, entirely, quit, and freely, without being imprisoned or otherwise troubled . . . .

And the said King of England has given double safe conduct to Sir William Keith, warden of the town of Berwick, to go to the Warden of Scotland, and to return . . . .

And neither the King of England, nor any of his adherents, nor Sir Edward Balliol, nor any of his adherents, will do any harm to the said Earl, nor his afore-said people, nor to anything of theirs, inside or outside; nor will they approach their walls, nor their ditch, nor, without special leave by a person so empowered, will they enter inside their boundaries;

And the said Earl and his men shall, without fraud, maintain their defenses, which have been begun inside the castle, their walls, ditches, breastworks, and engines, in exactly the same state as they were on the day this agreement was made; and that they will not resupply the said castle with food, armor, or other items.

And if the castle should be rescued by the forces of Scotland . . . between now and the evening of Monday before the aforesaid Tuesday, by means of battle . . . or if a force including two hundred men-at-arms enters into the town of Berwick by day, that is to day between sunrise and sunset; then the castle shall be considered rescued, and the hostages . . . shall be surrendered to the said Earl on the said Tuesday at sunrise, without any longer delay or contradiction by anyone; . . .

And if the said castle is not rescued either by battle or by the entry of the said two hundred men-at-arms between now and the said Monday evening, the castle shall be surrendered to the said King of England on the said Tuesday at sunrise, without any longer delay or contradiction by anyone; in such a way that some magnates of the Council of the King of England shall receive the said castle, and protect the people in good faith, without oppression, injustice, or harm, so that they are kept safe in their persons and goods . . . .

15. The Scots Try to Break the Siege of Berwick. [Source: *Melsa*, 369]

We return to the narrative of the Meaux chronicle.

Now a certain Archibald, the Warden of Scotland, collected an army of 90,000 fighters. Divided into four parts, they came into England to the town of Tweedsmouth, on the other side of the river Tweed, sending word to the King of England that, if he would not lift the siege, they would destroy the greater part of England. To this Edward King of England responded that he would never lift the siege until the town had surrendered to him, or else fell by assault to his men. And so the Scots moved on, turning the town of Tweedsmouth into ashes, destroying the adjacent land all around, burning towns, slaughtering people, and perpetrating all the evils they could. In addition they besieged the castle of Bamburgh, where Queen Philippa of England was then staying, in order that they might thus perhaps dissolve the siege of Berwick.

16. The Scots Decide to Fight. [Source: Wyntoun, 399–401]

But those within Berwick soon sent to them, and told them that they could fight, for they were more numerous [than the English], and also seemed to be superior troops. Having faith in that representation, they then went to the park of Duns, and lay there all that night, thinking to meet their foes in the morning, expecting the town to provide some help. . . .

  They made their way from Duns Park to Halidon, where they could well see the town, and their foes also, and their encampment. They saw them ready for the fight; on St. Margaret the Virgin's day [20 July] they were all arrayed to fight. The Scotsmen arrayed themselves soundly, and advanced against them in open battle. But they had not considered the terrain: for there was a large, marshy creekbed between them, with steep rising ground on either side. They came together at that large valley, where they first had to go down the declivity, then climb up to their enemies up a slope where a single man might defeat three; but that they could not see beforehand.

17. An English Account of the Battle of Halidon Hill. [Source: *Cleopatra Brut*, fo. 182v]

The English minstrels sounded their drums, trumpets and pipes; and the Scots gave their hideous war-cry. Each division of the English army had two wings of good archers, who when the armies came into contact shot arrows as thickly as the rays in sunlight, hitting the Scots in such a way that they struck them down by the thousands; and they began to flee from the English in order to save their lives. But when the servants who were in the rear saw such a defeat, they pricked the horses of their masters with spurs in order to save themselves from peril, leaving their masters cold. With this the English mounted their horses and spurred them, and as they overtook the Scots they struck them right down, dead. There could one see the valiant and noble King Edward of England and his men: how vigorously they chased the Scots! There could one see many good men of Scotland dead and returned to the earth, their banners displayed on the ground, hacked to pieces, and many a good haubergeon[10] bathed in their blood. Many times they rallied in diverse companies, but always they were defeated. And thus it came about, as God willed, that the Scots on that day had no more numerical superiority against the English than twenty sheep would have against five wolves.

---

10 A short tunic of mail armor.

18. Another English Description of the Battle. [Source: *Lanercost* (Maxwell), 279–80]

After the mid-day meal, on the fourteenth of the kalends of August, that is, on the vigil [19 July] of St. Margaret, virgin and martyr, the Scots came up in great strength (to their own destruction) in three divisions towards the town of Berwick, against the two Kings and their armies occupied in the siege, who, however, were forewarned and prepared against their coming. Now the Scots marching in the first division were so grievously wounded in the face and blinded by the large number of English archers, just as they had been formerly at Dupplin Moor, that they were helpless, and quickly began to turn away their faces from the arrow flights and to fall. And whereas the English, like the Scots, were arrayed in three divisions, and the King of Scotland was in the rear division, the Scots diverted their course in order that they might first meet and attack the division of him who, not without right, laid claim to the kingdom. But, as has been explained, their first division was soon thrown into confusion and routed by his division before the others came into action at all. And in the same way as the first division was routed by him [Edward Balliol], so the other two were shortly defeated in the encounter by the other English divisions.

The Scots in the rear then took to flight, making use of their heels; but the English pursued them on horseback, felling the wretches with iron-shod maces as they fled in all directions. On that day it is said that among the Scots killed were seven earls, to wit, Ross, Lennox, Carrick, Sutherland, and three others; twenty-seven knights banneret; and 36,320 foot soldiers – fewer, however, according to some, and according to others, many more. Among them also fell Sir Archibald Douglas, who was chiefly responsible for leading them to such a fate; and, had not night come on, many more would have been killed. But of the English there fell, it is said [. . . blank in manuscript.]

19. The Results of the Battle. [Source: *Pluscarden*, 203]

The aftermath of the Battle of Halidon Hill is described here by the Book of Pluscarden, *a Scottish chronicle written in Latin in the late 1440s, based largely but not entirely on the slightly earlier fifteenth-century chronicle of Walter Bower. Bower, in turn, made use of various sources for his treatment of the events of the 1330s, probably including a now-lost St. Andrews chronicle composed in the 1370s or 1380s.*

Immediately after the battle was fought, as aforesaid, the lord Earl of the Marches and the lord Seton, being without hope of rescue, surrendered to the said King the aforesaid town of Berwick, together with the castle, the inhabitants being saved harmless in life, limb and property; and they tendered the oath of allegiance to him as their lord paramount. That Earl was compelled by the said King of England to rebuild at his own expense the castle of Dunbar, which had been previously battered to pieces. But within a few days afterwards Edward Balliol overran the whole kingdom with the forces of the King of England, subduing it and unsettling it and distributing offices, and placing in the hands of the English and of the Scots who embraced his cause all the castles and strongholds but four, namely Dumbarton Castle, the warden whereof was Sir Malcolm Fleming; Lochleven, the warden whereof was Alan de Vypont; Kildrummy, the wardenship whereof remained in the hands of Christian Bruce; and Urquhart Castle, of which Thomas Lauder, who was called the Good, had the wardenship; and there was also the stronghold of Lochdoun, the warden whereof was the venerable John Thomson.

20. Scottish Strategy. [Source: Froissart, *Oeuvres*, 6:288–9]

Jean Froissart, the most famous chronicler of the Hundred Years War, is not well informed of the details of Scottish affairs in this period (despite his service in the court of Edward III from 1361 to 1369, and his later visit to the court of David II) but the general statement of Scottish strategy below accurately reflects the general nature of the problem faced by Edward III after Halidon Hill.

When the Scots had departed from the mountain, as is described above, they rode on that day at their ease; for they understood well that the English did not have the ability to pursue them. At high noon they lodged along a small river which the locals call the Boée or the Bethe. All the lords of Scotland came there for a council to discuss what they should do, and how they could most honorably maintain themselves in this war against the English. Many speeches and remonstrations were prepared and delivered there. Some considered that this plan of fleeing before the English was a bad one, and likely to lead to their losing everything, their honor as well as their country. Then the wiser ones said that they did not see any way in which they were strong enough to do battle with the English King, who had 60,000 picked men with him; it was better for them to maintain themselves thus [by fleeing] than to risk everything and lose. They accepted this counsel; and that it would be best for the young King their lord to go to Dumbarton, a very strong castle at the edge of Gaelic Scotland, and stay there (he would be quite safe there), and the Queen with him. The young Sir William Douglas and the Earls of Moray and Sutherland and Sir Robert de Verssi and Sir Simon Fraser with as large a band of men as they could gather would keep themselves in the forest of Jedburgh, and shadow and harass the English. In this way they would make war on them wisely: on the one hand, they would inflict much damage on their enemies, and on the other hand they would preserve themselves as best they could. This counsel was accepted and held to; and their army split up, and each returned to his own place, without making or mustering any other defense of the country, other than in the manner that I have just described – except that they set large garrisons in Edinburgh, Perth, Aberdeen, Dundarg, Dalquist, St. Andrews, and in the fortresses, and they themselves laid waste to all the lowlands, and pulled the men and women and children back into the mountains and forests, who brought with them all their possessions, and gathered together there.

21. The Triumph of Edward III. [Source: *Lanercost* (Maxwell), 285–7]

The lands granted by Edward Balliol to Edward III in 1334 greatly exceeded, by any realistic measure, the 2,000 librates which had been promised to the English King in 1332, a fact which greatly undermined Balliol's credibility in Scotland thereafter.

On the nineteenth day of the said month [June, 1334], that is, on the feast of the Holy Martyrs Gervase and Prothasius, the King of Scotland came to Newcastle-on-Tyne, accompanied by the Earls of Atholl, Dunbar, Mar, and Buchan, and there in presence of the two English earls aforesaid, four Scottish earls, the Archbishop, the aforesaid bishops and an almost innumerable multitude of clergy and people, the same Edward Balliol, King of Scotland, performed his homage to my lord Edward the Third, King of England, in token of holding the kingdom of Scotland from him as Lord Paramount, and so from his heirs and successors for all time. And whereas the same King of England had assisted him in reclaiming and possessing his said realm of Scotland, whence for a season he had been expelled by the Scots, and had supplied large funds [for that purpose], the King of Scotland ceded to him the five counties of Scotland which are nearest to the English March, to wit, the counties of Berwick and Roxburgh, Peebles and Dumfries, the town of Haddington, the town of Jedburgh with its castle, and the forests of Selkirk, Ettrick and Jedburgh, so that all these should be separated from the crown of Scotland and annexed to the crown of England in perpetuity. Thus there remained to the King of Scotland on this side of the Scottish sea [i.e. the Firth of Forth] only the other five counties, to wit, Ayr, Dumbarton, Lanark, Stirling, and Wigtown in Galloway beyond the Cree. All these aforesaid things were publicly confirmed by oath, script and sufficient witnesses, and after they had been duly settled, the King returned to England.

Howbeit after a short lapse of time, to wit, about the feast of St. Mary Magdalene [22 July], the Earl of Moray newly created by the Scots, the Steward of Scotland, Lawrence of Abernethy and William Douglas, who had been taken by the English earlier and ransomed, having gathered a great force of Scots, raised rebellion against the King, and violently attacked the Galwegians, who adhered faithfully to him. Also they attacked others of Scotland who dwelt in the aforesaid five counties subject at that time to the King of England, and levied tribute from them.

Also a certain knight of Galloway, Dugald de Macdouall, who had always hitherto supported the King of Scotland's party, was persuaded for love of his newly-wedded wife to raise the Galwegians beyond the Cree against the King and against others on this side [of the Cree], who offered strong resistance; and thus they mutually destroyed each other.

22. Enter Philip VI. [Source: *Pluscarden*, 203–5]

Since the days of Edward I, Scotland and France had been bound together by a formal alliance. King Philip of France, thus, made repeated attempts to work out some sort of settlement between his ally King David and his vassal Edward III (who in 1330 had acknowledged Philip as his liege-lord for the lands of Guienne and Ponthieu in France).

Like other Scottish and French chronicles, the Book of Pluscarden *refers to David Bruce rather than Edward Balliol as King of Scots.*

In the year 1334 there came ambassadors from the King of France to Perth, to negotiate a peace between the Kings of England and Scotland by command of the supreme pontiff Pope Benedict XII, with his letters-patent to the two Kings, namely of England and Scotland; but the King of England would not deign to hear them, or even to see them. After this, when other ambassadors of King Philip of France were again sent over to the Kings of England and of Scotland, he would not hear of peace and concord between himself and the said [David Bruce,] King of Scotland. The same year, about the end of August, a dispute arose at Perth between Edward Balliol, who took the part of Sir Alexander Mowbray, and Henry Beaumont, David Earl of Atholl and Richard Talbot who were striving to thrust the aforesaid Alexander out of his inheritance and bring in before him his brother's daughters, the true heiresses by the law of succession. By reason of this dispute they parted and went their several ways, Edward to Berwick; Henry Beaumont to Dundarg in Buchan, the castle of which he repaired strongly, and he lorded it over the whole of Buchan; and the Earl of Atholl went to Lochindorb. Richard Talbot, however, made for England; and, when on his way through Lothian, he was there taken prisoner by Scottish supporters of King David on the 8th of September. But Edward Balliol, observing these things and wishing to be on the safe side, cast off the said Sir Alexander Mowbray; and, even as it is often said, "One man going out makes room for another coming in," the said Henry Beaumont and Earl of Atholl were restored to his good graces, and he invested the said Earl of Atholl in all the lands of the Steward of Scotland for ever. The said Alexander Mowbray, however, fearing the power and fierceness of the opposite party, became a hearty supporter of Sir Andrew Murray, who had shortly before been released from prison altogether on payment of a ransom. These, then, with their forces jointly besieged Henry Beaumont in Dundarg Castle for a time; but the said Henry, seeing that, for want of provisions, he could not long hold the said place, on a safe-conduct being granted to him, gave up the castle and retired to England with his wife and property, promising moreover to do his best to bring about peace and concord. Meanwhile Edward Balliol went about through the meadows and plains of Scotland, wherever he pleased, bestowing the lands and domains on his supporters, and securely roamed hither and thither at will. At length he came to Renfrew, and in royal fashion distributed domains, lands and offices to such of his supporters as he pleased, and received homage from many freeholders who took the oaths to him. Here were brought to him the keys of Rothesay and Dunoon, whereto he appointed as his lieutenants and wardens Thomas Wallor and the lord Lile, sheriffs of Bute and Cowell. But Sir William Bullock he appointed as his chamberlain, a man of great wisdom, cleverness and prudence, a priest; and he entrusted to him the charge of the castles of Saint Andrews and Cupar and many other strongholds. About the same time the young Robert Stewart, the designated heir to the throne . . . who was fifteen years old, was still, for fear of the enemy, lurking in concealment in Rothesay Castle aforesaid and was deriving great comfort from, and having frequent conversations with, two lovers of peace, friends of King David, namely John Gibson and William Heriot, then sojourning in the barony; and they found means to take him over to Dumbarton Castle, bringing with them the charters of Stewartland. The commandant of that castle was Sir Malcolm Fleming, and he received Robert with pleasure and gladness, and entertained him until he should hear better news.

23. A New Uprising in Scotland. [Source: *Lanercost* (Maxwell), 287–8]

There is no documentary evidence to support the claim that David Bruce did homage to the King of France during his exile, but it is certainly true that Philip went to great lengths to support David. In any case, the Lanercost chronicle's statement on the matter indicates what was commonly believed in England.

Meanwhile David, whom the Scots had formerly anointed as their King, and who had remained in the strong castle of Dumbarton, went to France, and did homage to the King of France, so that he should hold his realm from him as from a Lord Paramount, on condition that he should assist him in recovering his kingdom from the aforesaid Kings of England and Scotland. Rumour of this being spread through Scotland, the number of Scots in rebellion against their King [Edward Balliol] increased daily, so much so that before the feast of St. Michael [29 September], nearly the whole of Scotland rose and drove the King to Berwick, which belonged to the King of England. Even the Earl of Atholl, who had borne the chief part in bringing the King of Scotland to his kingdom, now deserted him, and the Earl of Dunbar did the same to the King of England, to whom he was bound by oath. Then the whole of Scotland rose as one man, except the Galwegians on this side of Cree and except the Earl of Buchan, who was not of Scottish birth and whom they kept in captivity. When the King of England heard this, he called parliament together in London, arranged for an expedition against Scotland, and before the feast of All Saints [1 November] arrived with an army at Newcastle-on-Tyne, where he remained until the feast of the holy Martyr and Virgin Katharine [25 November]. Then he entered Scotland, coming to Roxburgh, where he repaired the castle, which had been dismantled, as his headquarters.

24. The Start of the Roxburgh Campaign, Winter 1334. [Source: *Historia Roffensis*, fo. 76]

The as-yet-unpublished Historia Roffensis *was probably composed around 1350 by William of Dene, a clerk in the entourage of the Bishop of Rochester. Dene's short notice of the Roxburgh campaign of the winter of 1334–5 is particularly valuable for the light it casts on the reasons for Edward III's popularity among the martial elements of fourteenth-century English society. The letter which follows the excerpt from the* Historia Roffensis *dates to the same unsuccessful winter campaign; it too can contribute to an assessment of King Edward's character. The letter also illustrates both the sources and the limitations of the power of the crown in medieval England.*

In this parliament, an ecclesiastical Tenth and a Fifteenth from the people were granted to the King of England, in order to drive back the Scots from the English borders. And the King, in order to repel them, spent the winter at Roxburgh; the costs were great and the winter fierce. Other than the youths of the realm and the magnates, he had few people with him. No one bore the hardships and the harshness [of the winter] or labored more willingly than he; and all the time he greatly comforted his army by words, gifts, and deeds, saying that they would all drink from the same cup. And thus he inspired their resolve.

25. France, Scotland, and England. [Source: *Grandes Chroniques*, 9:142–3]

The following report on the growing Anglo-French diplomatic problems is drawn from the semi-official Grandes Chroniques de France, *this section of which was composed at the monastery of St.-Denys outside Paris around 1350.*

At or about this same time, the King of England took counsel with his barons. The Count of Hainault and Sir Robert d'Artois urged him to send to the King of France, in order to learn if he was willing to consider any accord. So he sent the Archbishop of Canterbury, Sir [William] Montague, and Sir Geoffrey le Scrope. When they came to Paris they found the court very inhospitable; but in the end the Count of Eu, master Pierre Roger the Archbishop of Rouen, and the Marshal de Trie were assigned to treat with them. The business was carried out so well that they came before the King; and there the peace between the two Kings was confirmed, and sworn to by the two parties. When the thing was done, the English left the King's chamber, and were conveyed by all the members of the royal Council, and peace was proclaimed throughout the town. But it was not long at all before things went differently, for they were not even to their lodgings when the King called them back and said to them that his intention was that

King David of Scotland and all the Scots be included in the peace. When the English heard this, they were greatly astonished, and said that no mention of the Scots had ever been made, and that they would not in any way dare to do or agree to this. When they saw that things could not be otherwise, they departed and went back to England, and recounted to the King and his Council how things had gone, at which the King of England swore that he would never stop until Scotland was brought low.

26. Edward III Attempts to Gather Stronger Forces. [Source: *Rotuli Scotiae*, 302]

The King to Nicholas de Meynil, greetings. We have been with our army in our lands in the march of Scotland for the safety and defense of the same [lands], and also of the marches of our realm [of England] and of our people of the said areas, against our enemies the Scots, who have risen against us in war and often entered as enemies into our said realm and lands, and have committed arsons and destructions, and still make themselves stronger from day to day, gathering to them all the forces they can to harm us and our faithful subjects who are with us, and our said people. Yet, although we have often sent to you by our letters that you should come to us provided with horses and arms, to help our said faithful subjects to repulse the malice of our said enemies, you, nevertheless, . . . willingly disobey our said orders, to our peril and in contempt of our commands, and to the delay of the success of our said business, to your great dishonor and shame. We marvel at this, and are very annoyed, as well we should be. So we order you once again, on pain of forfeiture of all that you can forfeit to us, making no excuses, to come to us with horses and arms and as strong a force as you possibly can, so that you shall reach us at Roxburgh, well arrayed and equipped, on New Year's Day at the latest, with supplies for fifteen days . . . . And we tell you that if you do not come to us on the said day in the aforesaid manner – considering the said disobedience, and the dangers which may come due to [your] default, and considering also the others of the country who take your example to hold back from our said service – we shall inflict on you such punishment that others will be taught a lesson by your example.

Given at Roxburgh, the fifteenth day of December.

By the King himself.

[Similar letters to 28 others]

27. End of the Roxburgh Campaign, 1334–5. [Source: *Lanercost* (Maxwell), 289]

On the third day after Christmas next following the King of England searched the forest of Ettrick with his men; but the Scots did not dare to give him battle, keeping themselves in hiding. Wherefore my lord the King of England sent the

King of Scotland, who was with him there, and the Earl of Warwick and the Earl of Oxford with their people, and certain barons and knights with all their people, to Carlisle, in order to protect that western district from the Scots. But on their march they turned aside to Peebles and those parts to hunt the Earl of Moray and other Scots who they were informed were thereabouts. Howbeit these [Scots] took to flight, so the English burnt and wasted everything on their march, and arrived thus at Carlisle.

After the Epiphany of our Lord [6 February], the forces of the counties of Lancaster, Westmorland and Cumberland assembled by command of the King of England at Carlisle under the King of Scotland and the earls and barons of England who were there; whence they all marched together into Scotland, destroying such towns and other property as they came upon, because the inhabitants had fled, and afterwards the King of Scotland returned to Carlisle.

28. Scotland Invaded Again, 1335. [Source: *Scalacronica* (Maxwell), 99–101]

The said castle of Roxburgh having been fortified, the said King of England moved to London and prepared for the coming summer, when he marched to Scotland in great force. He sent with Edward Balliol the Earls of Warrene [i.e. Surrey], Arundel, Oxford and Angus, the lords Percy, Neville, Berkeley and Latimer, and a great army, which entered [Scotland] by way of Berwick. He himself entered by Carlisle with all the rest of his chivalry, having with him the Count of Guelders, who afterwards became marquess and then duke, with a strong division of Germans. The two armies came near each other on the Water of Clyde, the King of England [being] in one place [and] Edward Balliol with his army at Glasgow, where there occurred a great conflict in the army on account of an esquire who carried the surname of de Gournay, whom the people of the Marches killed because it was alleged that one of that surname had been a party to the death of the King's father.

The two armies formed a junction at the town of Perth, and on their march thither they took the castle of Cumbernauld by assault. At the said town of Perth the Earl of Atholl, Godfrey of Ross, and Alexander Mowbray, with others, returned to the King's peace, and the Steward of Scotland there began to treat. At the same time, while the King lay at the town of Perth, came the Count of Namur to Berwick, with other English knights who had not been ready to march with the King. They now foolishly undertook to follow the King and to travel through the country to him at Perth, when they were surprised at Edinburgh by the Earl of Moray and forced to take [refuge on] the rock of the dismantled castle. There they defended themselves one night, and next day, until they received terms, [namely] that the said Count of Namur should swear that he would not bear arms from that time forward in the quarrel with David Bruce, and that the English there should remain prisoners held to ransom. The said Count of Namur returned to Berwick, whence he went by sea in company with the Queen of England to [join] the King at Perth. About the same time the Earl of Moray was captured by William de Presfen in a border skirmish . . . .

The King of England left the town of Saint John [i.e. Perth] and marched to Edinburgh, where he caused the castle to be fortified; and there Robert the Steward of Scotland, who was the son of Robert the Bruce's daughter, and nearly all the commons, came to his peace. The King caused a strong garrison to be placed in the castle, and repaired to England.

29. Peace in Scotland Agreed. [Source: *Historia Roffensis*, fo. 77v]

Then the King of France deceitfully sent ambassadors even more dignified than the last ones to Berwick, in the bitterness of winter, to treat concerning the Scottish peace. And an agreement was reached there that David Bruce should hold all the lands which had been held by his father in England, and should stay in England, and Edward Balliol should keep the realm of Scotland during his life. After his death the said David and his heirs and successors should hold it from the King of England in chief. The ambassadors and the Scots were given a date when they should appear to finalize the agreement, in the middle of the following Lent [c. 10 March 1336], in the King's parliament at London. On the assigned day, the lords and a great multitude of the commons came together to see the conclusion of the matters thus agreed, but without success: the agreement was turned back into the initial and normal state of discord. For, the French ambassadors having returned to their King and informed him of all that had been done, the King, as usual, transformed the proffered concord into discord. And thus the parliament closed, and each person returned to his own place.

30. The French Prepare to Intervene. [Source: *Original Letters*, 30–33]

The following report is as interesting for what it tells us about the English government's capacity to gather intelligence in France as it is for what it tells us about the course of events.

The King of France was in the [Papal] Curia in the middle of Lent [around 10 March 1336], and he met in secret with the Pope, such that no one could discover the content of their discussion; but at the instance of the King, the Pope granted grace to all those then in present at the Curia. And later, in Eastertide, the King stayed at Lyon, and there held talks with the Scots, and promised them all of his strength to conduct David Bruce into Scotland; such that there are said to be 2,000 sailors at Harfleur and Leure in Normandy, and 300 ships, each of which, according as they are larger or smaller, holds 120 men-at-arms. And there are 30 galleys strengthened with iron, such that no ship can resist them. Also at Leure there were skillfully manufactured crossbows, and broad shields to cover three soldiers; and there are around 10,000 crossbowmen, and around

14,000 cotton doublets reinforced with iron plates, which can hardly be penetrated by arrows, lances, or other weapons. In addition, on the day of the Annunciation of the Blessed Mary, two hundred ships full of arms arrived in Normandy, and five large casks of crossbow bolts. And the King of France has assigned the Constable of France, namely lord Matthieu de Trie, and lord Thomas de Bertram as the commanders at sea, and Jean le Mir in charge of horses and equipment. The citizens of Paris hold that one part of the army is to make its way to Portsmouth, and the other part towards Scotland, to land wherever Balliol is. Lord Alexander Seton, master Thomas of Twynholm, clerk, and John de Swecia, esquire, are to lead them from Scotland into England. The date assigned for their arrival is the feast of the Holy Cross, next May [third].

In addition all the skillful tailors of Paris were at Leure for fifteen weeks and six days in order to make banners, both English and French; and many of them were English, Irish, and French,* insofar as the spies could or would say. In addition many Germans, Brabançons, *Frandanciis*, and mercenaries have come to the King of France. A place and day has been assigned for the army of the Scots to meet the army of the King of France, and it is estimated that together they will have 40,000 men-at-arms . . .

The news of Scotland is as follows. Our men, immediately after the departure from Berwick, divided themselves into two armies: one went through the forests and mountains where William Douglas and his people were, and fought with them, putting him to flight and striking down his people, and capturing many food supplies both living [i.e. livestock] and dead. The army of the King of Scots made a transit through the lowlands, gathering at Stirling; and around there they had some battle-work with lord Andrew Murray, who also fled. And they captured many, who were put to the sword. And continuing on they came to the town of St. John [Perth], where they encountered the rebels and contrarians, and they seized it by force. They did not spare a soul; and it is reported for certain that they will meet no resistance from anyone else. Thomas Roscelyn was struck in the thigh by an arrow in a certain village; drawn out incautiously, it broke the veins and sinews, and he immediately died. The Scots fled, dispersed, and split up, although they were six times as numerous. Written at York, the 19th of July.

31. Edward III's Lochindorb *Chevauchée*. [Source: *Original Letters*, 33–9]

The political elites of England were kept informed of military and other developments by a variety of means; one of the most important was by the circulation of news bulletins such as this report of King Edward's dramatic ride to rescue the besieged Countess of Atholl (widow of David of Strathbogie, who had recently been defeated in battle and killed by the Scots) in 1336. Among other things, this letter is interesting for what it tells us about the speed of movement of small mounted forces, and of news.

---

* *Gallicana*, which properly means French, but the context suggests the author may have meant Welsh [Latinizing from the French *Galles* (Wales)].

Most reverend Father and beloved lord, the news of northern lands, written by our lady the Queen at Pontefract on the second of August, is as follows. Namely that our lord the King of England on the Friday [12 July] after the feast of the translation of St. Thomas the Martyr moved eight miles out of Perth so suddenly that no one was notified to arm himself. He fixed his tents in the fields that night, having with him 400 men-at-arms and as many archers. And on the morning of Saturday he rode to the castle of Blair-Atholl, a distance of 20 miles. On the following Sunday, through the middle of the great fastnesses of Atholl, he rode 30 miles that day, passing through the highest and most difficult [areas] of Scotland, spending the night at Fythewyn in Badenoch. The following Monday [15 July], in the morning, hearing that the Scottish siege force (20,000, including lord Andrew Murray) around Castle Lochindorb, where the lady Countess of Atholl was, had gathered at the church of Kynkardyn in Badenoch, he rode hell-for-leather for a distance of sixteen miles. And dismissing his baggage-train there, he advanced to two miles short of Lochindorb; and he saw the tents of those who besieged the castle. And with that their scouts saw ours, and thus they were forewarned, and all fled into Ross. And our same lord made his way directly to the castle aforesaid; and the sight of our lifted banners was the first news that the people in the castle had of the coming of our said lord. And indeed the said Countess, steering a small boat to the land, repeatedly thanked our said lord, expounding fully on the deprivation and adversity suffered by her and hers; and that for everyone in the castle there no longer remained any victuals, except for one cask of wine of little or no worth, and two bushels of grain; and they did not have any straw or cloaks or anything else on which they could lie down or take their rest. So our lord told them that he would return on the morrow, and send for them; and then he returned to his baggage-train. On that day he had ridden for forty miles with his entire army, over terrible paths; he lost many horses that day, and for himself and for all his army hardly a side of beef was to be had. But on the following Tuesday he sent his men a moderate day's ride, namely eight miles, up to Aberkarf in the highlands of Mar; they led a thousand and more animals back to our army. At this our men were refreshed, and rejoiced. And on that day the Countess separated from our said lord. And on Wednesday they reached the abbey of Kinloss in Moray, a distance of twenty miles. They burned the good town of Forres and all the countryside around. In the abbey they found wine, beer, salt fish, wheat, and other necessaries, by which our men were restored and more than a little comforted; and the castle of Lochindorb was thereby stocked sufficiently with food, by land. And on the following Thursday our said lord continued to Elgin in Moray, a distance of eight miles, so that he might destroy, around him, the best and most fertile [area] of Scotland, and burn it entirely by fire and flame. Out of reverence for the Holy Trinity, in whose honor the church there was built, Elgin was spared from burning. On Friday, our lord crossed the river Spee, continuing to the village of Colane on the sea, riding a distance of 18 miles. On Saturday he was in Doghwan after 16 miles. On Sunday, leaving the castle of Kildrummy off to the side, he continued on to arrive at the town of Aberdeen by night. The town's inhabitants, on the previous Thursday, had killed fifty or so of the men of our ships who had dared to land there, along with sailors from Flanders who had been detained in the port there until the arrival of the King. On Monday [22 July] the King caused the greatest part of the town, and Old Aberdeen, and the countryside all around to be burnt. A great quantity of goods was seized there. On Tuesday in the morning he had his wagons cross over the river Dee; he himself remained in the aforesaid town of Aberdeen so that it would be totally burned down, without the omission of any house whatsoever, be it the finest in Scotland. On Wednesday he was at Morton in Menris, the castle of Dunnotyr being in our said lord's hands; the march that day was 16 miles. On Thursday they rode 16 miles. On Friday to Forfar, eight miles away, where news came to him that William Douglas was hiding nearby in the forest of Platere with a thousand men; nor did he [William] at that time believe the head of the expedition to be anyone other than Henry of Lancaster. But with nightfall he learned of the presence of our said lord [the King] there, and fled towards the forest of Bronnan, and retreated to Stirling along with the garrisons of all the castles which they held in Scotland. At that, Father and Lord, you may know that on the Monday [29 July] after this was accomplished, the noble lord the Earl of Cornwall, with 400 men-at-arms (of whom 140, elegantly and well-equipped, are from his fiefs), along with 7,000 hobelars and archers collected from diverse lands, was led by God to proceed without any long delays into the country of Scotland; so that these days good news concerning the restraint of the malice of the enemies flows and overflows everywhere.

> . . . Written at York, the 3rd day of August.

32. Edward Announces His Efforts to Preserve Peace. [Source: *Foedera*, II:2:994; translation adapted from Ashley, 43–8]

The following document illustrates another medium by which the people of England received news relating to Edward's wars, and casts some light on contemporary attitudes towards war, and on Edward's reasons for going to war against his much more powerful neighbor. This text also marks the point at which the focus of the Plantagenet's military efforts shifted from Scotland to France.

The King to the venerable father in Christ, John, Archbishop of Canterbury, primate of all England, and to his trusty and well-beloved William Clinton Earl of Huntingdon, who have been appointed to declare in the county of Kent certain things touching the defense of our realm, of holy church, and of our other lands, greetings.

We send you a certain schedule, herein enclosed, of the promises which we and our ambassadors have made to prevent war with the King of France;

Commanding you, and each of you, that you cause what is contained in that schedule to be clearly and fully explained to the clergy and people of that county, on the day and at the place mentioned in the commission which has been issued to you;

Persuading them, by all the ways and means you can, to help us freely each of them, as far as their means permit, since that King threatens us with war, willing to consent neither to peace nor to negotiations for peace, whereby we are subjected to intolerable expense for public defense; So acting in this, that we may have to justly commend your diligence.

Witness the King, at Westminster, the 28th day of August [1337].
By the King.

A similar order was sent to the following persons appointed in the following counties to make the same announcement –

(Then follows a list of persons so appointed, e.g., in Oxfordshire and Buckinghamshire, the abbots of Abingdon and Osney and three knights.)

Schedule mentioned in the above order.

These are the offers made to the King of France by the King of England to prevent war.

In the first place, the King of England sent to the King of France diverse solemn embassies, requesting him to restore the lands that he withheld from him, willfully and against reason, in the duchy of Guienne; to none of which requests did the King of France consent; but at last he promised that, if the King of England would come to him in person, he would show him justice, grace, and favour.

Trusting to this promise, the King of England passed privately into France [in 1331] and went to him, humbly requesting the return of those lands, offering and performing to the King what he was bound to do and more; but the King of France gave him words only and not deeds, and, moreover, while the negotiations were going on, encroached wrongfully more and more on the rights of the King of England in that duchy.

Also the King of England, seeing the harshness of the King of France, in order to have his good will and that which he wrongfully kept from him, made him the great offers below mentioned; that is to say, when one was refused he made him another:

First, the marriage of his eldest son, now Duke of Cornwall, with the daughter of the King of France, without dowry;

Then, the marriage of his sister, now Countess of Guelders, with his son, with a very great sum of money;

Then, the marriage of his brother, the Earl of Cornwall, whom God absolve, with any lady of the blood royal of France;

Then, to make redemption for disturbance, he offered him as much money as he could reasonably demand;

Then, since the King of France gave the King of England to understand that he wished to undertake a crusade to the Holy Land, and greatly desired to have the company of the King of England, and that he would do him grace and favor therefor, the King of England, in order that the prevention of the crusade might not be attributed to him, offered to the King of France to go in force with him on the crusade; provided, however, that before going, he make full restitution to him of his lands;

Then, he offered to go with him on crusade, on condition that he made restitution of half or a certain part of his lands;

Then, afterwards, he offered, with still greater liberality, to go with him on condition that, on his return from the Holy Land, he made full restitution.

Then, to stay the malice of the King of France, who tried to put upon the King of England the blame of preventing the crusade, he declared himself ready to undertake the crusade, on condition that, on his return, he did him justice.

But the King of France, who endeavored in all ways that he could to injure the King of England and all his subjects, that he might keep what he unjustly withheld and conquer more from him, would not accept any of these offers, but seeking occasion to injure him, gave aid and support to the Scots, the enemies of the King of England, trying to prevent him, by the Scottish war, from seeking his rights elsewhere.

Also, then, from respect to the King of France and at his request, the King of England granted to the Scots a cessation of the war and a truce, with hope of bringing about the peace;

But, during the truce [in 1335], the Scots killed the Earl of Atholl and others, and took prisoner many nobles faithful to the King of England, and besieged and took castles and other places from the King and his subjects;

And, recently, at his request, he offered to the Scots a truce for four or five years, on condition that they restored what they had taken during the former truce, in order that the crusade might take place in the meantime;

To which restoration the King of France would not consent, but supported the Scots in their malice with all his power, and made open war without just cause on the King of England, and sent to sea his galleys and navy which he had prepared under pretense of the crusade, with a great number of armed men, to destroy the navy and subjects of the King of England;

Which men have taken in war and despoiled many ships of England and killed and taken the men who were in them, and have landed in England and the islands of the King of England, committing arson, as much as they could.

Also then the King of England by the counsel and advice of the magnates and wise men of the realm, wishing to prevent the war if possible, sent solemn embassies to the King of France, to offer him all he could without losing greatly of his inheritance, to obtain peace;

But the King of France, hardened in his malice, would not suffer these ambassadors to be brought before him, nor consent to peace or negotiations for peace; but sent a great and strong army to take into his hands by force the duchy before mentioned; declaring, untruly, that the duchy was forfeited;

Which army did great evils in the duchy, besieging and taking castles and towns as far as they could.

Also the King of France, to cover his malice, did try to misinform the Pope and the other great men of Christendom with regard to the King of England; aiming at conquering, as far he can, not only that duchy, but all the lands of the King of England.

These proposals and others the King of England and his Council could think of, have been made to the King of France to secure peace, and if any man can find any other suitable way, he will be bound and ready to accept it.

33. King Edward Seeks Allies on the Continent. [Source: Le Bel, 119–28]

At the time he wrote his chronicle (this section of it was composed between 1352 and 1356), Jean le Bel was a wealthy and popular canon of Liège, famous for the hospitality he gave to noble travelers. With friends on both sides of the conflict, he was well-positioned to gather information. Among his most important sources was his friend Jean de Hainault, who was one of Edward III's most important supporters through the 1340 campaign, and later one of Philip VI's advisors.

Le Bel is not really pro-English or pro-French, but he does clearly favor Edward III over Philip VI. As the chronicler says himself, though, his preference is the result of judgment, not prejudice.

How noble King Edward sent the Bishop of Lincoln to the Count of Hainault in order to have advice on the French war

After this noble King Edward of England had thus [in 1333], as you have heard, reconquered the good city of Berwick and laid waste all the lowlands of Scotland, and put his garrisons and his guards everywhere where it pleased him, and returned to rejoicing in his country, he was so beloved and so honored everywhere by great and small for the great nobility of his deeds and words, and for the very grand court and the great feasts and great assemblies of ladies and maidens, that everyone said that he was [the second] King Arthur.

Several times he took counsel and deliberated with those who were his most special counselors as to how he could deal with the great wrong which had been done to him in his youth regarding the realm of France; for, by succession to the nearest relative, it should by reason have come to him, as Sir Robert d'Artois had informed him. The twelve peers of France had given it to Sir Philip of Valois by agreement as if it were a legal judgment, without calling the opposing party, so he did not know what to think, for he was unwilling to leave it thus if he could amend it; and if challenged the judgment and began a dispute about it, and it was denied to him (as well it might be), and he then kept silent about it and did nothing to amend it, and had not increased his power thereby, he would be reproached for it. And on the other hand, he saw well that it would be difficult for him and the power of his realm to defeat the kingdom of France, unless he could gain by means of his treasures [the help of] some powerful lords, or an agreement with some of the twelve peers or other barons of France. So he often asked his special counselors to give him good counsel and advice about this, for he was not willing to undertake further action without counsel.

In the end, his counselors answered him in accord: "Dear lord, the matter seems to us such a great and lofty enterprise that we do not dare take it upon ourselves to give advice about it; but, dear lord, we counsel you, if it please you, to send certain ambassadors, well informed of your intentions, to the noble Count of Hainault, whose daughter is your wife, and to Sir Jean, his brother, who has served you so worthily, praying them, out of friendship, that they advise you concerning this; for they know better what is required for such business than we do; and also they are bound to guard your honor and your rights for love of milady your wife; and if they agree to your intent, they will know how to advise you well concerning which lords can help you most, and how you can best win them over." "With this advice," said the noble King, "I fully agree, for it seems fair and good to me, and it will be done just as you have said." Then the King requested the noble prelate the Bishop of Lincoln to undertake this embassy for him, and also requested two knights banneret who were there, but I have forgotten their names, and two lawyers as well, to accompany the said Bishop.

They did not want at all to refuse the request of such a noble king, so they agreed willingly and prepared themselves as soon as they could, and crossed the Channel, and put themselves on the road when they were ready, and managed things so that they came soon enough to Valenciennes in Hainault. They found the noble Count, who lay there so sick with gout and gravel that he could not move; and they found also Sir Jean de Hainault his brother. They were highly honored and feasted, as one would expect.

When they had been feasted very well, as befitted them, they recounted to the noble Count and his brother the message because of which they were expressly sent to them; and they conveyed to them all the doubts that the noble King had put forward, just as you have heard. When the noble Count heard why they had been sent there, and had heard the reasons and the doubts that the said King had put forth to his Council, he did not hear it at all unwillingly, so he said that the King was not without sense, when he had in such a way well considered these reasons and these doubts; for when one wants to undertake a great business, one should well consider how one can successfully complete it, and all the more, to his mind, how it might end up. And then the noble Count said: "If the King could achieve it, I would be very glad of it; and one can well imagine that I would prefer it for him, who has my daughter as his wife, than for the King who is not connected to me in anything, even though I have wed his sister, for he covertly disrupted the marriage of the young Duke of Brabant, who was supposed to espouse my other daughter, and kept him for one of his own. Therefore, I will not fail my dear and beloved son the King of England. If he shall find in council that he ought to undertake it, then I will loyally help him with counsel and aid as much as is in my power; and so will Sir Jean my brother, who has served him before. But know that he will well have need of other aid than ours, for Hainault is a little country in comparison to the realm of France, and England is too far from us to succor us."

"Certainly, Sire, you give us exceedingly good counsel and demonstrate very great love and good will towards us, for which we thank you on behalf of our lord the King," responded the noble prelate the Bishop of Lincoln for all the others, and then said: "Dear Sire, well, do advise us by which lords our sire could best aid himself and accomplish the most, so that we can report your advice to him." "By my soul," said the Count then, "I cannot suggest or think of lords who could aid him so well in this business as his first cousin the Duke of Brabant, the Bishop of Liège, the Duke of Guelders, the Archbishop of Cologne, the Marquis of Juliers, and the Lord of Fauquemont. Of all the lords I know of in the entire world, these are the ones who could have the greatest number of men-at-arms in a short time, and they are very good warriors, and if they should wish to, they could raise fully eight or ten thousand men-at-arms, provided that they were given money in advance; and they are lords and people who like to make money. So if my son the King retained these lords of whom I speak , and he were on this side of the sea, he would be strong enough to go seek out King Philip of France, all the way to Paris, to fight him." This counsel pleased the ambassadors of the King well; so they took leave of the noble prince and of Sir Jean, his brother, and returned to England, reporting the news and the advice which the gentle Count had given them.

When they had arrived in London, the King held a great feast for them, and they told him all they had learned from the advice of the Count of Hainault and of Sir Jean, his brother. The King gained much joy from it, and was much comforted. Therefore he immediately equipped ten knights banneret and forty other young knights, and sent them across the sea, at great cost, straight to Valenciennes with the gentle prelate, the Bishop of Lincoln, in order to negotiate with the lords whom the Count of Hainault had named to them, and to do all that he and Sir Jean, his brother, advised.

When they had come to Valenciennes, everyone esteemed them for the fine and grand state which they maintained, sparing nothing, no more than if the King had been there in person. No one could stop himself from marveling at this. And also there were some young men-at-arms who had each covered one eye with a piece of cloth, so that they could not see with it; and it was said that they had sworn, among the ladies of their own land, that they would never see except out of one eye, until they had done some deeds of arms in the realm of France, which thing they would not confess to those who asked them, so some people wondered much about it.

When they had been sufficiently feasted and honored at Valenciennes by the noble Count and some other lords and some bourgeois and ladies of Valenciennes, the said Bishop of Lincoln and most of the others drew towards the Duke of Brabant, by the advice of the noble Count, and the Duke entertained them well enough, and then they made themselves so agreeable to him that the Duke promised them to support the King his cousin and all his men in his lands, for it was fitting for him to do so, since he was his first cousin; so he could come and go, armed or unarmed, as often as he wished. In addition, he and all his Council made a covenant with them that if he [Edward] would sufficiently defy the King of France, then, for a certain sum of florins, he [Brabant] would defy him [Philip] and would aid him [Edward] to enter in force into the realm of France and would serve him with a thousand men-at-arms. Thus he promised to them on his faith, which he later cancelled and drew back from, as you will hear after this. These lords of England were very satisfied, for it seemed to them that they had managed very well with the Duke, so they returned back to Valenciennes and accomplished so much by their embassies and by the gold and silver which they had that the Duke of Guelders, the Marquis of Juliers for himself and for his brother Waleran, the Archbishop of Cologne, and the Lord of Fauquemont came to Valenciennes to speak with them in front of the noble Count of Hainault, who could not ride or travel, and in front of Sir Jean his brother; and in the end they so arranged matters that each of them should have great sums of money for himself and for his men, and that they should defy the King of France and that each should serve King Edward with a certain number of men-at-arms with crested helms.

At that time the great lords did not count men-at-arms if they did not have crested helms, whereas now [c. 1360] men with glaives, *panchiéres*, haubergons and chapeaux-de-fer[11] are counted. So it seems to me that the times have certainly changed from what I remember, for barded[12] horses, crested helms, with which one used to bedeck oneself, plates, and armbands with coats-of-arms have all disappeared, and the haubergeons, which are now called *panchiéres*, the gambesons, and the chapeaux-de-fer have come to the fore. Nowadays a poor servant is as well and as nobly armed as is a noble knight.

Then these abovesaid lords agreed that they would get help from other lords from beyond the Rhine who could lead a great number of men-at-arms, if they had sufficient reason to do so. Then they took leave of each other and returned to their own countries. The Bishop of Liège at the time, Adolphe de la Marck, was very properly sent for, and great embassies sent to him, and fine jewels presented, but he would never listen nor do anything against the King of France, whose man he had become and whose fealty he had entered. The noble King of Bohemia was neither asked nor sent for, for it was well known that he was so conjoined to the King of France by the marriage of their two children, to whom the realm was supposed to pass, that he would not go at all against him.

When these lords of Germany had departed with the promises that you have heard, these English lords remained at Valenciennes with great nobility and at great cost.

---

11 An open helmet.
12 I.e. armored.

34. The English Decide on War. [Source: *Scalacronica* (Maxwell), 102–4]

The King soon afterwards lost all the castles and towns which he had caused to be fortified in Scotland for want of good government in the prosecution of his conquest. The said King repaired to London for his parliament, where his eldest son, the Earl of Chester, was made Duke of Cornwall, Henry of Lancaster was made Earl of Derby, William de Bohun [was made Earl] of Northampton, William Montague [was made Earl] of Salisbury, Hugh de Audley [was made Earl] of Gloucester, Robert Ufford [was made Earl] of Suffolk, William Clinton [was made Earl] of Huntingdon. Upon which earls and other good men of his the King bestowed so liberally of his possessions that he retained for himself scarcely any of the lands appertaining to the Crown, but was obliged to subsist upon levies and subsidies, which were a heavy burden upon the people. He received a considerable share of the tithe of Holy Church, the fifteenth penny of the laity, and 47s. 8d. for every sack of wool. This subsidy was granted by the Commons for a set period, but it outlasted the time fixed. During two years he received the ninth sheaf throughout his realm.

At this same parliament it was decided by the King's Council, on the advice of the clergy, that he should no longer refrain from pressing his right and claim to the Crown of France, on which account war was declared, homage was renounced to Philip of Valois, King of France, who withheld the King's right, and defiance was also sent. Envoys were sent from the King of England to Germany to make alliance with the Emperor, the Bavarian, who had espoused the other sister of the Count of Hainault, and to retain the lords over there; this cost enormous treasure, without profit. The envoys were Henry Burghersh, Bishop of Lincoln, and the Earls of Salisbury and Huntingdon, who returned to the parliament of London with the reply to their mission . . . .

Soon afterwards, the Earl of Salisbury, who at that time was one of the most trusted of the King's Council, was of opinion that the alliance they had formed with the Germans was not likely to lead to profitable result, and that the King would not be able to bear the expense of the conditions which they demanded. Perceiving their greed, he explained his position to the parliament before the King and went off to Scotland in order to excuse himself from this Council.

35. The Siege of Dunbar. [Source: Wyntoun, 431–5]

Preparations for war with France were well underway by early 1337, and resources were consequently drained away from the effort to subdue Scotland, as we can see in this passage from Andrew of Wyntoun's chronicle.

Of the Siege of Dunbar, where the Countess was Wise and Wary

Sir William Montague, who had set up the siege [of Dunbar], quickly had a powerful and right stalwart engine constructed, and soon had it well prepared. They threw great stones, both hard and heavy, at the walls; but they did no damage to them. And once they had shot, a young lady, dressed prettily and well, wiped the wall with a towel so that they could see and be the more annoyed. They lay there at the siege quite a long time without gaining much advantage; for when they would skirmish or make an assault, their effort was largely wasted.

And now I shall tell you of a great shot made as they skirmished there one day, that caused them much wonder. The arrow pierced the blazon of William Despencer, and through three folds of mail armor, and through the three plies of the acqueton, and into the body, so that he lay there dead of the blow. At this Montague said: "This is one of milady's pins; thus her love runs to my heart."

While the siege continued in this way, it is said, several small conflicts took place. Lawrence of Preston, who was at that time considered one of the bravest men in all Scotland, saw a band of Englishmen ride by. They seemed good and worthy men, right richly arrayed. He attacked them there, with as few men as they had. But in the encounter he was struck in the mouth by a spear, which ran up into his brain. He withdrew to a ditch and died, for he could no longer live. His men did not notice his action, and fought stoutly with their foes until they utterly vanquished them. Thus was this good man, very respected, generous, and commendable, brought to an end. His soul is certainly in safety.

Also, Sir William Keith of Galstown, a man of good renown, met Richard Talbot by the way, and put him to so difficult a test that he forced him into a church and compelled him to make his defense there. But he [William] assailed him so keenly that in the end it behooved him to treat [for surrender], and offer to pay two thousand pounds' ransom. He left hostages, and went his way.

This, I trow, took place not three years after the Balliol and his folk arrived in Scotland, for I have heard men affirm that all the lords that were there [at Balliol's arrival] had fallen captive to Scotsmen within those three winters, except only Sir Ralph Stafford and the Balliol, who got away at Annan, as you heard me tell. It is a very wondrous thing to think that fighting great battles could not reach the same outcome which was accomplished by frequent small conflicts.

Montague was still laying siege to Dunbar stalwartly; and he had two Genoese galleys to besiege it by sea. And as he was thus maintaining the siege, he was put in a difficult situation. For he had bribed someone on the inside to leave the gate open, and set a certain time to come there. But the defenders were secretly informed of the whole thing. He came, and found the gate open, and would have stepped inside; but John Coupland, only a poor simple man, pushed him back and went inside. The portcullis came down immediately, leaving Montague outside. With a sturdy shout they cried "A Montague Forevermore!": then with the people he had there he retreated to his camp, acknowledging that he had been thoroughly tricked.

Soon Alexander Ramsay reckoned that the people besieged in Dunbar were in great distress, so one evening he and a few people with him took a boat out towards Dunbar. He went secretly, and slyly got by the galleys with all his company. The lady and all the others there were much comforted by his arrival. In the morning he sallied out in haste, and sturdily fought a bold, tough mêlée with the watch, and [re]entered Dunbar without loss.

While Montague was remaining there, King Edward of England purchased help and alliances, for he wanted to make war in France: and he sent for Montague, for he could not bring anything to a conclusion without him, since at that time he was the closest of his counselors. When he heard the King's bidding, he departed, dwelling there no more, when he had, I trow, lain there for a quarter of a year and more.

It was lucky for Scotland that they went to war in France: for had they fully undertaken to make war only in Scotland, after the great disasters of Dupplin and Halidon, they would have harmed it too greatly.

36. The Treaty with William of Hainault. [Source: *Foedera*, II:2:984]

Treaties very similar to the following one with William of Hainault were also made with a variety of other princes of the Low Countries. A roster of the main allies recruited for Edward III in this fashion, with the subsidy each was to receive and the contingent of men-at-arms he was to provide, follows the text of the treaty. Next comes a table of King Edward's revenues in the first decade of his reign, for purposes of comparison.

The "Emperor of the Romans" referred to, Louis of Bavaria, was of course the head of the German "Holy Roman Empire," which extended from Savoy to Silesia; the title of "King of the Germans" or "of Germany" was normally used for the ruler of the Empire in between his selection by the Imperial Electors and his coronation by the Pope. Since Louis was in the midst of a conflict with the Pope, he was under excommunication and had not been officially made Emperor, but used the title anyway.

Edward, by the grace of God King of England, Lord of Ireland, and Duke of Aquitaine, to all those to whom this present document may come, greetings.

We make it known to all that because the high and puissant man, our dear and beloved brother, Sir William, Count of Hainault, of Holland, and of Zeeland, and Lord of Friesland, has promised and covenanted to us that if the most high and powerful prince, the Emperor of the Romans, should undertake as principal chieftain (in person, or through his vicar or lieutenant) to retain, defend, acquire and recover the rights of the Empire; or if we should become King of Germany, or Vicar of the Emperor or of the King, or his lieutenant; or if someone else of our party should become lieutenant of the said, current, Emperor, or of his successor, whether King of Germany or Emperor;

Having full power to summon the princes, barons and men of the realm of Germany, by their fealties and their oaths, to aid, guard, retain, acquire and recover the said rights, such that one cannot make an expedition or repel an enemy without our will and leave; he, the aforesaid Count of Hainault, will aid and serve us with 1,000 men-at-arms, on that side of the sea, in order to retain, maintain, defend, acquire and recover the said rights, lordships, and heritages, of the said Empire, and of us the King of England, against any who have, or shall, put any impediment or disturbance in the way, as is more fully stated in his letters, given concerning this, sealed with his seal;

We, through the good deliberation and consent of our barons, loyal subjects, and councilors of our realm, have promised, and covenanted, in good faith, and by oath made and taken upon our soul, with hand on the Bible, in our presence, by our special procurator, assigned especially for that purpose, that we will have delivered to him, on that side of the sea, in a sure and certain place, 100,000 florins of Florence, or 15,000 pounds sterling, in place of the said florins, by the upcoming feast of St. Peter in August [1 August, 1338].

And furthermore, beyond that, another 100,000 florins of Florence, or 15,000 pounds sterling instead of the florins, by the next following day of Lent [14 February, 1339] our else within the octave of the said day [by 21 February], without duplicity. In addition we have promised and do promise, in the aforesaid manner, that we and our men-at-arms, and the others whom we shall bring with us, will be on the marches of Lower Germany, immediately at the opening of the month of August coming soon.

And furthermore, we have promised him and do promise him, that on the upcoming day of St. Lambert [17 September, 1337], we, and our men-at-arms, will be with the said Count or his lieutenant between Cambrai and Cateau-Cambrésis; and there we will pay and deliver entirely to him the wages for two months for his men-at-arms, namely, for 1,000 men-at-arms, whom the said Count or his lieutenant is supposed to have with us, 15 florins of Florence per man-at-arms per month:

Which month and wage will have their commencement and beginning on that day when he, the said Count of Hainault or his lieutenant, shall hold his assembly of the said 1,000 men-at-arms, and that he shall lead them from his country; in such a manner that if it should come about that the said Count should retain any foreign soldiers, for our profit, whether because they will not take an oath to us or otherwise, at the abovesaid wages, we will pay and deliver fairly to them, within the term that we have agreed to, the payment for the said two months.

And in addition we have promised to the said Count, that, if it seems good for the Empire, for us and for him, he can take and have as many as he wishes, up to 1,000, men-at-arms at our wages, as stated above, in order to aid, sustain, and guard the frontiers of the Empire, and to resist the enemies of the Empire, and our enemies, and the enemies of the lordships abovesaid; the men-at-arms may be whatever people he wishes, except that two or three hundred shall be of our men, if we wish.

And in case we do not send the two or three hundred men-at-arms of our people, the said Count, or his lieutenant, may complete the number up to 1,000 men-at-arms, of such men as please him, at our said wages;

Which 1,000 men-at-arms we will be obliged to support at our wages for the space of one year, on the frontiers of the Empire, if it seems good to the said Count.

And, if the King of France, or others on his behalf, because of these alliances, or treaties, comes with, or sends, against the Count such a powerful force that he is in need of more men-at-arms to defend himself and his supporters (concerning which we shall believe the oath of the said Count), he may raise another 1,000 men-at-arms at our said wages; in such a way that if he can get by with fewer, he shall in good faith do so.

These second 1,000 men-at-arms shall remain in the service of the said Count, at our said wages, up until our arrival, or our countermanding order.

Furthermore, we have promised to the said Count that we will not, nor will others on our behalf, make any treaties, friendships, peaces, truces, armistices, or respites of any sort with his enemies, against whom he has made war along with us and in aid of us, or on our behalf, without the full willingness and perfect consent of the said Count or his lieutenant;

And, if peace should be made, these present promises and alliances shall remain in force and retain their power so long as we and the said Count shall live.

In addition, we have promised and do promise to the said Count, that if he or any of his people should be captured in our aid or service, or because of our war, that we shall acquit and free them freely without cost to them, either by exchanging other prisoners for them, or by cash payment, or by some other way, as shall be the most convenient that can then be devised; on condition that the said Count shall render and deliver to us all the prisoners that he or his men shall capture in our service and aid.

Also, we have promised to the said Count, that if it comes about that he or his men should have their horses (that is to say, all the horses of the men-at-arms, not including baggage horses) killed or lamed in our service and aid, then the marshals of the said Count should report, by their faith and oath, the assessment of the worth and the compensation value that our brother the Count of Guelders, and our faithful subject the Earl of Huntingdon, have assigned to it; and we shall be bound to pay it without duplicity.

And, if it should occur – and may it not occur! – that the said Count of Guelders and Earl of Huntington, or one of them, should pass from life to death, then we, along with the said Count of Hainault, shall pick and elect another one or two, as necessary, to replace the one or ones who dies or die, within two months after he or they dies or die.

By the testimony of these letters, sealed with our seal.

And for bond and confirmation of all the abovesaid things, and that each of them shall be well and firmly held to, performed, and entirely accomplished, we have obligated and do obligate, towards the said Count our brother, all our possessions, mobile and immobile, present and future.

In testimony of which, we have caused to be made these, our letters patent, sealed with our great seal.

Done at Stamford, the 12th day of July, the year of Grace one thousand three hundred thirty seven, and of our reign the eleventh.

37. Roster of Allies and Subsidies [Source: *Foedera*, passim]

Main Allies	No. of Men-at-arms	Subsidy	Monthly Troops' Wages
Count of Hainault, Holland and Zeeland	1,000	£30,000	£2,250
Count of Guelders	1,000	£30,000	£2,250
Marquis of Juliers	1,000	£35,000	£2,250
Duke of Brabant, Lotharingia and Limbourg	1,200	£70,000	£2,700
Holy Roman Emperor	2,000	£60,000	£4,500

38. Chart of Edward III's Revenues 1327–1337. [Source: Sir James H. Ramsay, *A History of the Revenues of the Kings of England, 1066–1399* (Oxford: Clarendon, 1925), Table I, facing 2:292]

Edward's regnal year, counted from his coronation, ran from 1 February to 31 January.

Regnal Year	AD	Total Revenue (Pounds Sterling)
3	1328–29	39,625
4	1329–30	37,369
5	1330–31	37,597
6	1331–32	72,620
7	1332–33	n/a
8	1333–34	46,246
9	1334–35	111,630
10	1335–36	118,570
11	1336–37	179,642
12	1337–38	272,833
13	1338–39	167,039
14	1339–40	157,561
15	1340–41	35,641

39. Implementing the Wool Scheme. [Source: *Calendar of Patent Rolls, 1334–8*, 516, 580]

One of the primary instruments of government in medieval England was the "letter patent," a document "open" [patent] to any reader, rather than addressed to a specific individual (a "letter close"), and sealed by the Chancellor with the Great Seal of England. Copies of such letters patent were archived on large rolls similar to the Rolls of Parliament, and in the nineteenth century the British government published a mammoth "calendar" of translated summary transcripts of the entire contents of these rolls.

These two examples deal with a wool monopoly scheme concocted by Edward's ministers as a way to meet the huge cost of the alliances concluded in 1337. The idea for this scheme arose after the price of English wool rose to greatly inflated levels due to the imposition of an English trade embargo against Flanders (then part of the Kingdom of France) at the start of the war with King Philip. The basic idea was to take advantage of England's near-monopolistic position as a producer of fine wool for the mills of Flanders and Italy by having the royal government purchase the country's entire annual wool crop, at legally fixed standard prices, then re-sell the wool on the Continent at the new, inflated prices. The profit was to be shared with a consortium of English merchants who were to run the operation; Edward's half, along with £200,000 the merchants promised to lend him, was expected to be enough to fund his military operations against France.

August 20 [1337]. Westminster.

Commission to Walter de Mauny, admiral of the fleet from the mouth of the Thames northwards, to find by inquisitions in the counties of York, Lincoln, Norfolk, Suffolk and Essex, what persons after that the King had caused all the ships of ports and places of his realm to be arrested for the defense of the said realm by certain commissioners, and had inhibited under a heavy penalty all lords, masters and mariners of ships from taking any ships to parts without the realm or permitting any to go, until further order, have gone to foreign parts or to Scotland without license to succor his enemies, to what parts they have gone, and what merchandise, victuals and things they have taken with them, what ships arrested by the said Walter for the convoy of the fleet with the King's wool withdrew without license or came not to the King or to the places where he ordered them to be, the names of the masters and mariners who retired from his service without license, to arrest and imprison until further order all who shall be found guilty herein, and to seize their goods and ships into the King's hands to be dealt with as the Council shall advise. This commission is issued on information that ships of Kingston-upon-Hull and other ports have disregarded the said arrest and inhibition.

September 1 [1337]. Westminster.

Mandate to Reginald de Conductu, John de Grantham, John de Oxonia and Richard de Hakeneye, who were lately appointed to buy for the King 4,000 sacks of wool in the city and suburbs of London, and in the counties of Surrey, Sussex, Kent, and Middlesex, and afterwards, on account of some news sounded in the King's ears, rendering it necessary that he should have further wool, were appointed to make search for and buy all wools in the city and suburbs of London in the hands or custody of Englishmen, to be very diligent in the premises, and if, as is reported, some men not regarding the safety of the realm are scheming to remove and conceal their wools, to seize as forfeited to the King all wools so removed or concealed which they shall find in the said city and counties. They are to certify to the King from time to time of the names of those who have removed or concealed wools, and he will cause these to be punished as they deserve.

By the King and Council.

40. Edward and the Allies. [Source: Le Bel, 136–40]

The King was advised that he should cross to this side of the sea along with a grand company of earls, princes, barons, and knights, and he arrived directly in Antwerp in order the better to learn the arrangements and the specific will of the said Duke [of Brabant], his cousin, for himself rather than through someone else.

When it was known that he had arrived in Antwerp, people came to see him and the great state which he kept up. When he had feasted and honored them enough, he was advised that he should speak with the said Duke, his cousin; with the Duke of Guelders, his brother-in-law; with the Marquis of Juliers; with Sir Jean de Hainault; with the Lord of Fauquemont; and with the other lords with whom he had made treaties, in order to have their counsel concerning how and when they wanted to begin to accomplish that which they had undertaken.

Thus it was done, and they all came at his summons to Antwerp between the Pentecost [31 May] and the feast of St. John [24 June] in the year [13]38. There they were greatly feasted in the English manner. Afterwards the noble King Edward drew them into council, and laid his business before them very courteously in order to learn the intention of each one of them, and asked them if they would meet their commitments quickly, as it was for that reason that he had come there, and had equipped all his men. So it would turn greatly to his harm if they did not promptly do as they had agreed.

These lords came together for a grand council, for the matter caused conflict among them and they were not at all in accord with one another, and always they took into consideration the Duke of Brabant, who was not at all cheerful, and always kept his thoughts secret. When they had thus held council for a long time, they gave an answer to the noble King Edward and said: "Sire, when we came here, we came more to see you than for any other reason; so we are not ready, nor counseled, to respond to that which you have asked; so we will go back to our people, each to his own, and then we will return to you on a certain day, when it pleases you, and will give you so full an answer that no blame shall rest with us."

The noble King saw that he would not get anything else from them that time, so he made do with that much. And they agreed among themselves to reunite on a certain day, three weeks after the feast of St. John [i.e. on 15 July], in order to give their best opinion. But he let them know well the great expenses and costs which he bore every day because of their delay, because he had thought that they would be entirely ready, just as he was, when he arrived there; and he told them that he would never return to England until he knew their intentions fully, unless it were due to their default . . . .

The day on which the King awaited the response of these lords grew near, but they made excuses for themselves and sent to the King that they would be ready and equipped, as they had promised him, but that he should do something to ensure that the Duke of Brabant readied himself; for he was the closest to him, and yet he was making his preparations without enthusiasm. But, as soon as they knew that he would be ready to move, they would stir themselves, and would be as prompt to start the business as he would. The noble King arranged to speak with the Duke, and showed him the response which the lords had sent to him, and asked out of friendship, and requested by the bonds of lineage, that he consider this well, and that he not fail him in this; for he saw well that he exhibited no zeal in making himself ready; and unless he changed his ways, he worried greatly that he would lose the support and aid of these lords through his default. When the Duke heard this, he was entirely confounded and said that he would seek counsel on the matter. When he had taken counsel on the matter sufficiently, he answered to the King that he would be ready quickly enough when there was need, but he had already spoken to all these lords of a day when he would give an answer, farther in the future. When the King saw this, he well perceived that he would not get anything else from him, and that to anger him would not accomplish anything; so he agreed with the Duke that he would send to these lords and ask them to be at Hal for a stay with him on the day of Our Lady in mid August [the fifteenth], if they did not want to come somewhere closer to him, in order to come to an agreement concerning their enterprise. And he asked the Duke that he be there, and that in the interim he make sufficient preparations so that these lords would not be able to excuse themselves because of him. Thus it was agreed.

41. Edward Complains to His Council in England. [Source: Froissart, *Oeuvres*, 18:64–5]

Edward, by the grace of God King of England, Lord of Ireland and Duke of Aquitaine, to the Treasurer and the knights of our exchequer, greetings.

We make it known to you that, as things were before our departure from England, we expected that on our arrival at Antwerp we would find, already there, treasure, supplies and other things in the necessary quantities, as well for us and our people as for the expenditures owed on our behalf to our allies over here. However, when we got there we did not find resources of treasure, supplies, or other goods for us or for any of our people; and if it had not been for a loan which we secured with great difficulty since our arrival over here from one of our special friends – and that in the expectation of our wool coming quickly to our assistance – with which loan we were able to make a goodwill gesture to some of our allies [by paying] a portion of the amount we owe them, we would have been eternally dishonored, and we and our people and our realm of England in peril, God forfend! So we have sent to Saint-Gotulph and Kingston and Hull our well-beloved Nicholas Picard, Thomas of Sweetham and Richard Fill with 14 of our ships to bring us quickly wool, supplies, and other things, as we have commissioned them. Therefore we order you and charge you firmly, enjoining you by the faith and love that you owe to us, that you without delay pay to the said Nicholas, Thomas, and Richard money and supplies for their wages and expenses and those of the sailors on the said ships from the twenty-fourth day of July up to the day they reach you, and from that day for the three weeks next following, because we have ordered that from the hour that the ships shall come to us where we are and unload the wool, supplies, and other things which they will with the aid of God bring to us, they shall return to Sandwich, and from there will make their way to certain places where we have charged them to go. So we order and charge that you act in haste to send to Sandwich, against their return there, money and supplies in such an amount as will be necessary for their wages and sustenance for the following ten weeks, in a manner in accordance with the orders they will give you on our behalf. Take these matters as much to heart as you possibly can. Also, we command that you have sufficient money delivered to the said Nicholas, Thomas and Richard for the purpose of repairing our said ships . . . .

Given under our privy seal at Antwerp, the fourth day of August, in the twelfth year of our reign [1338].

42. The Allies Hesitate. [Source: Le Bel, 140–2]

The day [appointed for the conference] approached, and the said lords arrived there, but the noble prince, the Count of Hainault, was not there, for he had passed away the previous winter, and had with his own hand knighted his son, the young Count William – I forgot to mention that. This young Count was at this parliament with the others in place of his noble father; and Sir Jean de Hainault, his uncle, was there too. When these lords were all assembled, they held a very grand and long council, for the business made them uncomfortable. They were unwilling to carry through their agreements, and unwilling to break them for their honor's sake.

At last, when they had considered the matter, they reported their counsel to the King and his Council, and said: "Dear Sire, we have taken counsel together for a long time, for your business weighs heavily on us; for we cannot see how we have any grounds to defy the King [of France] at your instance unless you get the Emperor's agreement, and he commands us to defy the King of France on his behalf. He certainly has occasion and just right to do so, as we shall explain to you; and then nothing will remain to keep us from being ready, just as we have promised.

The cause that the Emperor might have to defy the King is thus: it is certain that long ago it was agreed and promised, sealed and sworn, between the Emperor of Germany and the King of France, that the King of France, whomever he might be, neither should nor might acquire anything within the Empire; and this King Philip has done, contrary to his oath, for he has acquired the castle of Crèvecoeur, the castle of *Labbel* in the Cambrésis and many other inheritances lying in the Cambrésis, which is Imperial land, and he holds them still. Therefore the Emperor has good cause to defy him, and to make his subjects do likewise. So we ask and require that you take pains to accomplish this, for the sake of our lands and honor; and for our part, we too will do what we can."

The noble King Edward was greatly downcast when he heard this report, and thought that this was in truth nothing but a delaying tactic, and that the language came from the Duke of Brabant, his cousin. In any case, he understood that he would get no other answer from them, and that anger would avail him nothing; so he put the best face on it that he could, and said to them: "Certainly, lords, I have not been advised of this point, and if you had advised me of it earlier, I would have taken counsel on it. Even so, I will act according to your advice on this matter, if you will aid me with good counsel, considering that I am in a foreign land across the sea. So you will want to give me good advice, for your own honor as well as mine: for know that if it turns out that I have stayed here for a long time, at great expense, without accomplishing anything, I will incur no blame, but you will gain no honor."

43. Edward Again Complains to His Council in England. [Source: Public Record Office, London, C49/File 7/7 and PRO 31 [Transcripts] 7/157.]

Edward's problems with his allies stemmed partly from his financial difficulties, for they were not eager to take action until they had actually received the sums promised to them. On the other hand, his financial problems also owed much to the delays of his allies, for his wage bills rose as time passed without progress towards victory in the war. The situation was extraordinarily frustrating for the King, and his anger at the situation was often directed at the administration back in England, which did not seem to be supporting his endeavors with sufficient drive and enthusiasm.

The articles reported to the Chancellor, the Treasurer, and others of the Royal Council in England by master Robert Askeby and Sir Renaud Donyngton, on behalf of our lord the King, from overseas, and the responses to the same articles.

– First, they should say [to the Council in England] how the King since his first arrival overseas has never received anything from the issues of his realm in aid or sustenance of him or of his men; at which he marvels greatly, as do all those who are around him.

The Response: Our lord the King is fully answered concerning this by Sir John Moleyns and the other messengers; and beyond this the Council of our lord the King should please consider the things contained in a cedule attached to this document.

Cedule: The overseas Council of our lord the King should please make understood to him that he has not had anything of the issues of his land due to the great payments and assignments which have been made to the merchants of the Bardi and Peruzzi; to William de la Pole; and to the magnates and others who are with our lord the King, for their wages and those of their men; for the fees of the earls created earlier; and to milady the Queen Mother, to milady the Queen Companion, to Sir Robert d'Artois, to the Countess of Ulster, and to others who receive their fees at the exchequer by the grant of the King; [to say nothing of] the expenditures which it is necessary to make for the guards of the isles of Wight and Jersey, for the guard of the town of Southampton and the castles . . . for the wages of the mariners in the King's ships, for the supplies and other courtesies which have been provided to the men of the fleets of the North and the South, for the wages and fees of the admirals and their men. In addition those for the land of Gascony, for the guard of the towns and castles of Scotland, for the wages of the King of Scotland, for the great costs and expenditures for canvas and the packing and carriage of the King's wool, and for other expenditures and costs which recur and grow every day, which have to be taken from the issues of the country and from the aids granted to our lord the King. So it is evident that he *has* been provided with a great sum from the profits of his said country.

. . . Another thing. They should say how the wools which have come to the King and to the merchants and others to whom they were assigned are so weak and of such small value and in such small sacks that three sacks of other wools weigh as much as four sacks of these; and it is notorious that, because of fraud by the collectors and lack of supervision of them, poor quality clippings and other unsellable wools are put inside the sacks marked for the King, more than good wools.

The Response. Collectors, surveyors, and receivers of the wools of the King throughout England, elected and named in parliament and in the Council of Northampton by the Lords and others of the Council there, received commissions to collect, survey, and receive the said wools, and in each commission express mention was made that no wool should be taken nor received for the King's use which was not suitable and of the best of the land, on pain of grievous fines; and the Council of the King was certified every day of the great harm done to the people by the selections made by the ministers; but no one who was assigned to survey the wools and to speed them to the ports has ever reported any default to the Council; and since it was ordered that each sack of the King's wool be marked with a certain mark of the royal arms and of the land from which the wool came, then it should be apparent over there in whom the default lay, for there was none here.

. . . Another thing. They should say how the King has set a definite day to go to the Emperor and to make payment to him and to his other allies; and has assigned a place where they will assemble in order to make a *chevauchée* against his enemies in order to win his rights by force of arms. All of this will be lost if he fails to make his payments, and he cannot make them without support and aid from his realm. Therefore they should energize themselves and put forth all the diligence they can that treasure, wool, and supplies come to him with all possible speed.

The Response: The Council has done everything that could be done; and the King is fully certified of this by the said messengers.

Another thing. They should cause the assignments and installments to be repealed immediately, and that the debts owed to the King by various people, and the aid for the marriage of his daughter, should hastily be collected, in accordance with the order of the King. And the Treasurer should quickly inform himself of all the aids which could be made, and make Sir Robert Saddington his lieutenant, and come quickly to the King so that he can learn his entire will and quickly return.

The Response. Concerning the aid for the marriage of the King's daughter, the messengers carry to the King the advice of his Council over here, and the Council will wait to make the collection until the King shall inform them of his will. And as to the repeal of the assignments, it is ordered in a covert manner that no payment should be made for the assignments except to the [persons specified] until our lord the King has sent his wishes concerning this a second time. But anyway it seems to the Council of the King over here that if this repeal should be known, that thereafter it could not be asked that anyone make a loan in the same way on the assignments, for each one would be worried about a similar repeal being made later; and there would be little advantage or profit in that. And as to the Lay Tenth and Fifteenth, the terms of two years of the three years are past, and the payments have been made . . . And concerning the clergy of the province of Canterbury, the terms of two years have passed . . . by an anticipation granted by the same clergy . . . so that there is nothing to pay from the two years except only the payments of a few prelates for the term of St. John next to come, which only amounts to a small sum; the which prelates will not change their terms of payment because they are paying the wools along with the laymen. And as to the third year of the said three years, no assignment has been made except to certain persons who were exempted from the said repeal, namely Sir William de la Pole and the merchants of the Bardi and Peruzzi.[13] . . . And the tenths and fifteenths of the clergy and the laypeople beyond the Trent are assigned to the Scottish war, wherefore the those of the Council of our lord the King over there should consider if the said repeal should be maintained, taking account of the small profit which our lord the King would have from it and of

[13] The Bardi and Peruzzi were Italian banking houses who provided the loans which financed much of Edward III's early war effort. Both houses eventually went bankrupt because of Edward's inability to pay all his debts to them.

the damage and shame which would result from it; and on this our lord the King should please command his will.

And as to the repeal of the fees of the ministers, they were paid out for the period up to the feast of St. A[ndrew] before the arrival of the said messengers; and they say openly that if their fees should be withdrawn, they will withdraw from their service . . . Concerning the installments . . . at the Council of Northampton, many of the greats answered, when the repeal of installments was made known to them, that in the memory of men installments have not been cut off, nor should they be changed; and they said that they would not by any means assent to the said repeal nor accept it insofar as lay in them. And also these things greatly concern the great people of the country, against whom the sheriffs do not dare execute their orders.

44. Edward Becomes Vicar of the Empire. [Source: Knighton (Luard), 2:5–6]

Henry Knighton, a canon of the abbey of St. Mary of the Meadows at Leicester, probably composed his chronicle c. 1390–1396. The section on the early reign of Edward III is thus of necessity derivative, but it does contain some passages not found in other surviving chronicles.

And when the King had come into those parts he found no one whom he could trust, excepting only the Duke of Guelders; so he told the Bishop of Lincoln and his other privy councilors that he had not been well advised. And so he made his headstrong way for seven days to Cologne, towards the Duke of Bavaria, who had made himself emperor and lived in High Germany. When the Emperor heard of the coming of King Edward, he came to meet him, journeying for four days to reach him, to a certain town named Coblenz, where he received the King with great honor. There one throne, decked with extraordinary richness, was prepared for the Emperor, another for the King, in the market place outside the residential area. There sat the Emperor and King Edward beside him; and there were waiting on them four dukes, three archbishops, six bishops, and thirty-seven counts; and of barons, bannerets, knights, and other comers, according to the estimate of the heralds, a good 17,000. The Emperor held in his right hand the imperial scepter, and in his left hand a round golden orb, which signifies the rule of the entire world. Above his head a knight held an unsheathed sword. There in the presence of all the assembled people the Emperor declared and made known to all the unnaturalness, disobedience, and wickedness with which the King of France had acted towards him; defied the King of France; and declared him and all his adherents to be under forfeiture.

Then the Emperor made King Edward his vicar, and gave him all the power he himself had, over Cologne and from there to the sea. In addition to this, with all the people looking on, he gave him a charter. On the morrow, at the metropolitan church, the Emperor and the King of England came together with the rest of the magnates, and they celebrated mass with the Archbishop of Cologne presiding; and immediately after mass the Emperor and all the other magnates swore to the King of England that they would aid and support him against the King of France, live or die, for the next seven years following, if the war between the said Kings should last so long. And likewise they all swore to the King of England that all the magnates from Cologne to the sea would quickly come to the King of England, and should be ready to join him against the King of France whenever they were summoned, either with him or in whatever place the King of England might wish to assign to them. And if it should happen that any of them did not obey the King of England in the aforesaid things, all the other [magnates] of High Germany would rise up against him and destroy him. With these affairs thus agreed and confirmed, the King took leave of the Emperor and returned to Brabant.

45. Edward III's Letter on the 1339 Campaign. [Source: Avesbury, 304–6]

The following campaign dispatch was preserved in the chronicle of Robert of Avesbury (died c. 1359), who was registrar of the court of the Archbishop of Canterbury. Many chroniclers based their narratives of military operations on similar campaign dispatches; Avesbury tended instead to incorporate the letters verbatim into his work.

Edward, etc., to our dear son, and to our honorable fathers in God, J[ohn] by the same grace Archbishop of Canterbury, R[ichard] Bishop of London, W[illiam] de la Zouche our Treasurer, and to the others of our Council in England, greetings.

The cause of our long stay in Brabant we have often made known to you before now, and is well known to each of you; but because lately hardly any aid has come to us out of our realm of England, and staying still was so damaging to us, and our people were in such dire straits, and our allies exceedingly malcontent with the business; and also [because] our ambassadors, who had stayed for such a long time with the cardinals and the Council of France in order to treat for peace, had not brought to us any offers except that we should have not one palm of land in the realm of France; and furthermore [because] our cousin Philip of Valois had always sworn, as was reported to us, that we would never spend a single day with our army in France that he would not give us battle; therefore we, trusting always in God and our right, had our allies come before us, and let them know for certain that we would not for any reason wait any longer, but would go forward in pursuit of our right, accepting whatever grace God should give us. They, seeing the dishonor which would have come to them if they had stayed behind, agreed to follow us. A date was set for all to be in the marches, inside France, on a certain day. We were at that place on that day completely ready, and our allies came thereafter, according as they were able.

Monday [20 September] on the eve of the feast of St. Matthew we left Valenciennes, and the same day began to burn in the Cambrésis, and continued to torch the area for the following week, so that that region is quite completely destroyed – wheat, cattle, and other goods.

The following Saturday [25 September] we came to Marcoign which is between the Cambrésis and France, and on the same day burning was begun inside France; and we understood that the said Lord Philip was drawing towards us, at Péronne, on the way to Noyon. So each day we held our way forward, our men burning and destroying commonly twelve or fourteen local leagues in breadth.

On the Saturday [16 October] before the feast of St. Luke we crossed the river Oise and encamped, and remained there that Sunday. On that day we had our allies before us, and they informed us that their supplies were nearly used up, and that winter was approaching with strength, so that they could not remain, but would be compelled to retreat to the border and return once their supplies were expended. In truth they had provided themselves with the fewer supplies because they understood that our said cousin would give us battle quickly.

On Monday morning [18 October], letters came to Sir Hugh of Geneva from the Master of Crossbowmen of France, mentioning that he wished to say to the King of England on behalf of the King of France that he should choose a place not strengthened by woods, marshes, or water, and that he would give him battle by the next Thursday [21 October]. On the following day [19 October], in order to wreak all the destruction we could, we moved on.

The next Wednesday [20 October] a messenger came to the said Sir Hugh and brought him letters from the King of Bohemia[14] and the Duke of Lorraine, with their seals attached, indicating that, concerning what the Master of Crossbowmen had sent on behalf of the King of France touching the battle, he would keep his agreement. Considering the same letters, on the morrow we immediately drew towards la Flamengrie, where we remained that Friday [22 October] all day. In the evening three spies were captured, and were questioned separately, and all agreed that Philip would give us battle on Saturday and that he was a league and a half from us.

That Saturday [23 October] we were in the fields a full quarter before daybreak, and took up our position in a place suitable for us and him to fight. Early in the morning some of his scouts were captured, who told us that his vanguard was out in the fields in order of battle, and would come out against us from there. This news come to our host, although our allies had earlier borne themselves very unenthusiastically towards us, surely they were now of such loyal intent that never were men of such good will to fight. Meanwhile, one of our scouts, a German knight, who had seen our entire array, was captured, and as it happened he disclosed it to our enemy; so that he [Philip] immediately drew back his vanguard and gave the order to encamp, and they dug ditches around

---

[14] Jean de Luxembourg, one of Philip's closest advisors, whose daughter married Philip's heir Jean.

themselves and chopped down great trees in order to prevent our coming to them. We stayed in battle-array on foot all day until, towards evening, it seemed to our allies that we had stayed long enough. So at evening we mounted our horses and moved towards Avesnes a league and a half from our said cousin, and let him know that we would wait there all Sunday [24 October], and so we did. And we had no other news of him except that on Saturday, at the hour when we mounted our horses in order to depart from our position, he thought that we were going to come towards him, and he made such haste to take a stronger position that a thousand knights at one time were sunk into the morass at his crossing, so that they came each on top of the other.

On Sunday the Lord of Faniels was captured by our men. On Monday morning [25 October] we received news that the said lord Philip and all his allies had scattered and retreated in great haste. So our allies would not thereafter remain. And so we will hold a council with them at Antwerp on [12 November,] the day after the feast of St. Martin, about what to do next. And after that we will quickly send word to you of that which has happened.

Given under our privy seal at Brussels, the first day of November.

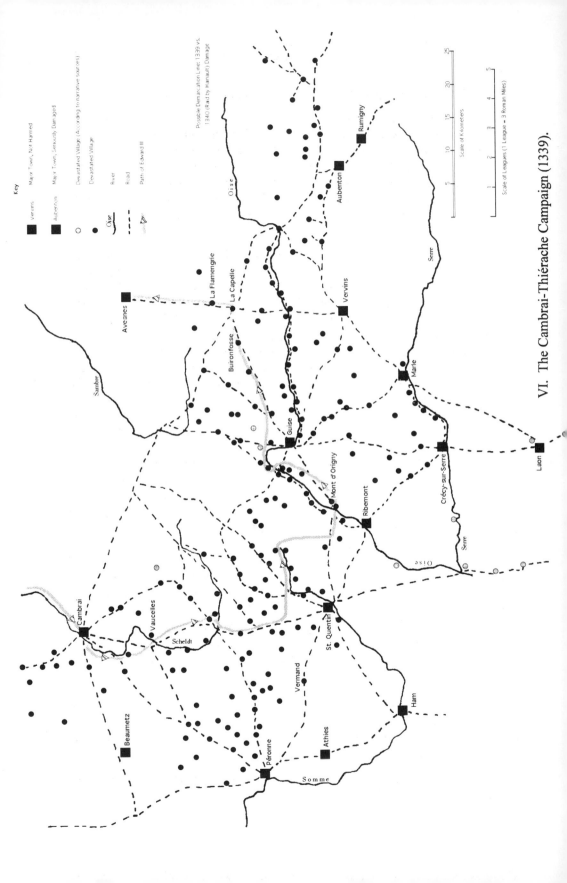

VI. The Cambrai-Thiérache Campaign (1339).

Labels on map: Rumigny, Aubenton, Oise, Serre, Vervins, La Flamengrie, Avesnes, Buironfosse, Guise, Marle, Mont d'Origny, Ribemont, Crécy-sur-Serre, Laon, Oise, Serre, Sambre, Cambrai, Vaucelles, Scheldt, St. Quentin, Vermand, Beaumetz, Ham, Athies, Péronne, Somme

46. The Details of Devastation. [Source: Carolus-Barré, 184–5, 222–7]

In the wake of the 1339 campaign, starting in September of 1340, Bertrand Carit, the Archdeacon of Eu, was entrusted by Pope Benedict XII with a sum of 6,000 florins, which he was ordered to disburse to the inhabitants of the devastated areas who had become paupers because of the war, rather than through any fault of their own. The following sections taken from the records of his mission give uniquely detailed and personal illustrations of the human misery encompassed within the chroniclers' catchphrase, "he laid the region waste by fire and sword."

The aforesaid deacons of Christianity of the said diocese of Laon, and many other worthy men of the said diocese, stated – first taking time among themselves for naming the people the most impoverished – that, in the said diocese of Laon, 78 parish villages large and small were completely or in large part burned, plundered, and laid waste by the enemy in the year [13]39, and up to the present have been devastated again and again.

For each and every one of the said villages, they also (individually and on many different occasions) named the people of the abovesaid villages who were the most impoverished and indigent because of the aforesaid cause, explaining their status and condition, and also that the named people were the ones of the said villages who most needed help and alms. Among those named were many craftsmen, farmers, merchants, and also people of the church, in addition to many noble women and wives. For all of these it was attempted to record their names, estate and condition, impoverishment, and the amount of money which each received, in registers, notarized books and cedulae given and written down by the aforesaid faithful men convened for that purpose, who were able to write down each town individually, thus overcoming the obstacle of the death of master R. de Estate, papal notary and associate of the said archdeacon.

Thus, after the ninth day of the said month of September, the said archdeacon, being in the city of Laon, having gathered information in the abovesaid fashion, began to give out, distribute, and disburse from the public treasure the said sums of money among the said destitute paupers, so that it could be done in the most discreet way, as ordered in the mandate.

Over the time just past, the above persons thus destitute and impoverished by the said cause, for just the diocese of Laon, have had and received from the hands of the said archdeacon, for particular reasons on many days and instances, 3,724 l. 10s. 6d.

There follow 85 entries for disbursements in the devastated villages and hamlets of the diocese of Laon, 12 in Reims, 60 in Noyon, and 30 in the portion of the diocese of Cambrai which fell inside the realm of France. One of these 187 entries, for the village of La Capelle, is as follows:

The first day in the diocese of Laon, in the deaconry of Aubenton, the village of La Capelle in Thiérache.

Petrus le Maistre, Lambinus Johins, J. le Maistre et J. Begins, from la Capelle in Thiérache, stated by their sworn testimony that:

The widow of Adam Denisart, an old woman of sixty years, having three children, was impoverished up to the sum of 100 livres, and thereby compelled to beg. She received in alms: 20s.

Item. J. d'Autreppes and his wife, old people, having four children, lost by reason of the war 150 livres. Of the said alms they had: 20s.

Item. Stephanus de Noermier and his wife, old people, having four children, were impoverished because of the war. They lost 90 l., and are forced to beg. Of the said alms they had: 20s.

Item. J. de Clouci and his wife, paupers, with three children, compelled to beg, lost 40 l. They had: 20s.

Item J. le Preus, impoverished cleric, having three children. He had: 15s.

Item J. Giles and his wife, having two children and his sister, an infirm woman, with him, forced to beg, lost around the value of 40 l.: 20s.

Item Nicaise Bauduin and his wife, although he does not beg, he lives exposed to very great poverty; and he lost around the value of 150 l.: 20s.

Item Colardus de Bray and his wife, having seven children; although he does not beg, he has been forced to seek his daily food by his own labor and hands; and he lost around the value of 200 l.: 20s.

The widow of J. Vaitte, elderly beggar, lost 10 l.: 15s.

Item Colinus des Brochars, his sister, orphans, beggars, lost 20 l.: 20s.

The widow of P. Bregier, whose husband was killed, and three children, beggar, lost 20 l.: 20s.

P. Cauce: 20s.

Colin Brochart: 20s.

Margarita, called la Hemarde, old, having three children: 5 l.

Johannes le Mestre, cleric, and his wife, having children, which at that time he did not have; they were able to live without help from the friends, from whom he is [now] forced to seek food for God's sake; and formerly he was of good estate, but does not dare, because of the wars, return to his possessions, which are near Hainault; and his losses are to the value of 200 l.: 50s.

Item Johannes Begin and his mother, 70 years old; he lost the clerical office, which was burnt along with all the rest of the town. The office was worth 20 l. per annum, and his mother is forced to beg and he himself to run to and fro in the countryside; and he lost in mobile property and a house around the value of 40 l.: 40s.

Item Massin le Mestre, orphan, fled to the place of his brother, whom he serves, and lost around the value of 100 l.p.: 20s.

Three sons of the late J. Symon, having wives and children; although they do not beg, they live most poorly; they lost around the value of 150 l.: 30s.

Johannes Cauce and his wife, both the old age of 70 years, live as paupers, though before they were content in good state; and they lost around the value of 100 l.p.: 20s.

Item J. Bourgne: 20s.

Johannes Viars and his wife, although they do not beg, live as paupers and are forced to serve others; and they lost around the value of 40 l.: 15s.

The entry for La Capelle goes on to list another 20 disbursements of alms, then:

And very many of these were cultivators of the land and lived decently by their lands, and [now] do not dare to return to their inheritances, as all their homes are burnt, and they lost all their mobile property, and the cattle which nourished them and with which they tilled the soil; and moreover they are next to the lands of lord Jean de Hainault, and men-at-arms come from day to day and seize whatever they come upon, and carry the torch; and just this last Thursday they seized two men nearby, and, unless God should provide some peace, they will have to die of hunger or to beg.

Fifty-two more entries for La Capelle, similar to the ones above, follow.

47. Assessments of the Campaign. [Source: Le Bel, 163–5]

On the following day, when the noble King Edward and the lords who were lodged in la Capelle [and] la Flamengrie in Thièrache learned that the King of France was encamped so close to them, they arose at the break of dawn and heard mass devoutly, and then stationed themselves in the fields, and arrayed their three battles all on foot, quite close to each other, all ready to await the strength of the King of France, and sent all their horses and their gear behind a nearby woodlet. There remained all these lords and their men, all on foot, until after noon, awaiting the arrival of the King of France and his great force.

The King of France, on the other hand, was at Buironfosse, and took counsel with his princes and barons in order to learn how he should handle the affair. In this council there was great strife and debate among the lords and barons of France, for some said that it would be a great failure and a great dishonor if the King did not fight them, when he saw so near at hand, in his country, the enemies who had so burned and devastated his realm in his sight and knowledge. The others said on the contrary that it would be great folly if he gave battle, for he did not know what each person thought, nor if he harbored treason; and besides, on the other hand, the game was not on even terms, for if Fortune turned against him so that he were defeated, he would lose his own person and all the realm; but if it turned out that it was the others who were defeated, he [Philip] would not have conquered the King of England or his lands, or the possessions of the other lords of England.

As they were fighting and arguing over these diverse opinions, the day drew on to nearly high noon without any definite agreement. On the other side, King Edward and the other lords who had been arrayed on foot in the fields up until noon without eating or drinking, saw well that the King of France and his men were not going to fight, and had no wish to do so; so they gathered together in order to discuss what they should do. There were many speeches and opinions expressed among them. In the end, it was agreed by common consent that they could not suffer blame nor reproach, from anyone who well understood the situation, for leaving: for at their entry into the realm of France they had offered battle to the King, before they had done harm to the land; and, since then, they had remained inside [France] for the space of seven days, burning and laying waste the countryside, within sight of the King [Philip] with all his power, of which no-one had ever seen the like. And they waited for him there all day in order to have battle, just two short leagues away from him, in a flat place, without a river or the impediment of fortifications, and still he neither came to them nor showed himself nor made any appearance that he was about to move. And besides, they were lacking supplies, wine and bread, and didn't know where they could get more. Therefore, taking all that into account, they all agreed to depart; so they moved off, and, quite late at night, came to rest around Avesnes, with all their baggage and their booty.

When they King of France and the French saw that the English had departed, they left too, and each went back to his own place. They maintained that their side had the honor of this mutual departure, for they had chased their enemies out, and, although [the English] had devastated and burned a large part of the realm, still they had not won it thereby, for the King still had plenty of it remaining to him; and if the King of England wanted to conquer the realm of France, he would need to make a large number of such *chevauchées*.

Thus said the Frenchmen who wanted to attribute the honor of this stand-off to themselves; and the English maintained the contrary for the reasons said above, so that each side claimed the glory for itself. Well, each one who hears these reasons can judge for himself and give the honor to the side which, by reason and the deeds of arms, ought to have it.

48. King Edward Takes the Arms and Title of "King of France." [Source: Le Bel, 165–8]

Ever since the start of the diplomatic preparations for the war, the English had been seeking to gain an alliance with the county of Flanders, which in this period was part of the realm of France, though its populace was not French by language or culture. The political situation of the county was complex; real power was in the hands of the demagogue Jacques van Artevelde and the municipal governments of Ghent, Ypres and Bruges, who were strongly influenced by English control of the wool needed to keep Flemish mills running, but young Count Louis was firmly in the French camp.

How and why the King of England took the name and the [heraldic] arms of France and titled himself King of France and England

Thus this great *chevauchée* ended for both sides, with each believing that his side had won the honor of it. The Duke of Brabant and the other lords of Germany returned, each to his own place, and the noble King Edward led his Englishmen through Flanders. They were received very favorably by Jacques van Artevelde, and also by all the Flemings; and he promised them that if they would aid him to carry on his war, he would help them recover Lille, Douai and other good towns which the King of France had seized from them and which he held by force and very wrongfully. The Flemings held a great council and deliberated much over this, forasmuch as they were obligated by a great sum of money at the Papal treasury, such that they could never begin a war nor do anything against the King of France without forfeiting the money. So in the end they agreed among themselves that if the King of England would style himself King of France in his letters, then they would hold him for King and obey him as their sovereign lord, from whom the county of Flanders ought to be held, and would help him to gain power in his realm. Thus, by this turn, they believed they could avoid forfeiting the sum of money, for he as King would quit them of it.

When the noble King of England heard this news, he was in great need of good counsel and advice, for it seemed to him a great and weighty thing to take the arms and the name of that which he had as yet conquered nothing of, and which he did not know if he could conquer; yet on the other hand, he was unwilling to refuse the aid of the Flemings, who could give him more help in his business than could all the rest of the world combined.

Finally, having considered and thought over everything, and weighed the good against the bad, he did take the arms of France, quartered with those of England, and from then on he styled himself King of France and England, and did everything that the Flemings asked of him, and as King of France quit them of any obligation that they had to the King of France; and from this point the Flemings continued to aid him during the rule of Jacques van Artevelde, as you will hear. And then immediately he returned to England in order to see how his men were doing against the Scots, leaving behind on this side of the sea the Earl of Salisbury and the Earl of Suffolk, with a hundred men-at-arms, in order to make war on those of Lille and Douai.

49. Edward's Proclamation to the people of France. [Allmand, *Society at War*, 147–9]

Immediately after assuming the title of King of France, Edward III issued a proclamation to the people of France which focused on promising to eliminate the various political vices indulged in by Philip VI, and thereby on wooing the French populace away from its obedience to the Valois.

Edward, by the grace of God King of France and England and Lord of Ireland, to all prelates, peers, dukes, counts, barons, nobles and commons of the kingdom of France, of whatever estate they be, these are the true facts.

It is a well-known fact that my lord Charles, of happy memory, formerly King of France, died legally in possession of the kingdom of France, and that we are the son of the sister of the said lord Charles, after whose death the said kingdom of France, as is well-known, came to and devolved upon us by right of succession; further, that Sir Philip Valois, son of the lord Charles's uncle, and thus more distantly related than we, seized the kingdom by force, against God and justice, while we were younger in years, and still holds it wrongfully.

We have now, after good and mature deliberation, and placing our faith in God and the good people, taken up the title to the government of the said kingdom, as is our duty. We are firmly intent upon acting graciously and kindly with those who wish to do their duty towards us; it is not in any way our intention to deny you your rights, for we hope to do justice to all, and to take up again the good laws and customs which existed at the time of our progenitor, St. Louis, King of France; nor is it our wish to seek our gain and your prejudice by exchanges and debasement of the coinage, or by exactions, or by raising taxes which were never due; for, thanks be to God, we have sufficient for our state and the maintenance of our honor. We also wish that our subjects, as far as is possible, should be relieved, and that the liberties and privileges of all, and especially of holy Church, be defended and maintained by us with all our power. We wish, further, when dealing with the business of the realm, to have and to follow the good advice of the peers, prelates, nobles and other of our wise and faithful subjects of the said realm, without doing or initiating anything with undue speed and only to satisfy our whim. And we tell you again that our greatest desire is that God, working through us and the good people, should grant peace and love among Christians, and especially among you, so that a Christian army may go in haste to the Holy Land to deliver it from the hands of wicked men; this, with God's help, we aspire to do.

And be informed that although we have, on several occasions, offered reasonable ways of peace to the said Sir Philip, he has been unwilling to make any such proposals to us, and has made war against us in our other lands, and is trying to defeat us utterly with his power; thus we are compelled by necessity to defend ourselves and to seek our rights. Yet we are not seeking the deaths, nor the impoverishment of the people, but we wish, rather, that they and their property be preserved.

For which reason we desire and decree, of our grace and kindness, that all people of the said realm, of whatever condition they be, who wish to approach us as our well-beloved and faithful people (as the good people of the land of Flanders have done), having regard to God and our right, thereby recognising us as their lawful King, and who shall do their duty towards us between now and the feast of Easter next to come, be received into our peace and our special protection and defense, and shall fully enjoy their possessions and goods, both movable and immovable, without losing anything or being hurt in any way for their resistance to us in the past; for we wish to save and protect them by all means open to us, as it is reasonable we should do.

And since the above-said things cannot be easily notified to each one of you individually, we are causing them to be proclaimed publicly and to be displayed on the doors of churches and in other public places, so that this may come to the notice of all, to the comfort of our faithful supporters and the terror of those in rebellion against us, so that no man, in future, may plead ignorance of these matters.

> Given at Ghent, on the 8th day of February, in the year of our reign of France the first, and of England the fourteenth [1340].

50. The Capture of Salisbury and Suffolk. [Source: Paris, Bibliothèque Nationale, MS Fr. 693, fos. 155–155v (a continuation of the *Manuel d'histoire de Philippe VI*)]

This previously unpublished story of the capture of the Earls of Salisbury and Suffolk is a nice example of the "chivalry" of the fourteenth century. The identity of the white knight remains a mystery.

A little after the last week of February, the King of England, leaving his wife in Ghent, returned with a small company to his country, via Bruges and Damme. And he always had a great fleet on the sea, and in truth he had more large ships than the King of France did; thus he could travel by sea in winter better and with less danger than was possible with galleys and small vessels. And so the King of England had the advantage of the sea in winter. So one night in January[15] his fleet suddenly descended on Boulogne and burned the majority of the houses which were on the harbor; but they received even greater harm than they inflicted, for they lost a good 200 men of their company who were killed there.

Also in this same month, and during the following Lent [5 March–15 April], the Lord of Vervins in Thiérache and the Bailli of Vitri were in Artois; they burned the greater part of the lands which lord Jean de Hainault held in Thiérache and thereabouts.

In this same year, on the Tuesday of Holy Week, which was the 21st day of April, around the hour of noon, 6,000 Flemings came within a half-league of Lille along with 40 English men-at-arms who were some of the King of England's best knights and esquires, including Sir William Montague, Earl of Salisbury, and another earl, and many others; and they dismounted along with the Flemings. And at that time the men of the garrison of Lille, who were about 500 men-at-arms and 2,000 infantry, were eating dinner; and as soon as the news reached the town, the men-at-arms armed themselves and around 26 of them went out in front and attacked them strongly. Their horses were killed and they

---

[15] The text says *ou mois de janiver ensuivant*, but this probably means the January following the 1339 campaign, not following Edward's return to England in February.

themselves were wounded. And then came the others, and there was a fierce struggle, and the exchange of blows lasted until night; finally the Flemings fled and all the English were killed except 12 knights, that is to say the two earls and ten others. And a knight who bore a blank, white shield was killed, for he refused to surrender or to name himself. And immediately his own men chopped up his face so that he would not be recognized. And he wore many rings, which could not be gotten off without cutting off his arms. And the said Earl asked where the white knight was; and someone answered that he was dead, and showed him the arms.[16] He was so enraged that he went three days without eating, and thus he was led to Paris to the King; but he would not name him even to the King. He said that he would let himself be burned alive before he would name him, which led some people to say that it was the King of England; others said it was the Earl of Arundel.

51. Edward Seeks Additional Subsidies from Parliament. [Source: *Rotuli Parliamentorum*, 112–13]

After the end of the Cambrésis campaign, Edward III returned to England to raise funds to enable him to continue the war, especially needed since he had promised the Flemings £140,000 in subsidies, on top of his earlier commitments. As usual when he needed large quantities of money, it was to parliament that he turned.

The petitions mentioned at the end of the document, which the King did grant, included a number of very important provisions. Among other things, the King effectively gave up his right to impose taxes within his demesne lands [i.e. the royal estates and boroughs] without parliamentary assent, and agreed to permit a parliamentary audit of collection and disbursement of the last subsidy granted. On the constitutional significance of these proceedings, see the article by G.L. Harriss, below.

On that day [29 May 1340] the causes of the summoning of the parliament were presented, first of all to the Prelates, i.e. the Archbishop of Canterbury, the Bishops of Lincoln, Durham, Chester, London, Salisbury, Ely, Chichester, Norwich, and Carlisle, and to the Earls of Derby, Northampton, Warenne, Warwick, Arundel, Huntingdon, and Angus, and to the Lords Wake and Willoughby, Baron Stafford, Sir Ralph Basset, and other great men; and then the same was done for the great men and commons of the land in general, in the following manner:

That is, how our Lord the King needed to be assisted by a great Aid, or he would be eternally dishonored, and his lands on both sides of the sea would be

---

[16] In English there is some ambiguity between the "arms" of the body and the "arms" (heraldic devices) of the knight, but no such ambiguity exists in French. According to the chronicle, it was the knight's limbs, not the devices on his shield, which were shown to the Earl.

in great peril; for he would lose his allies, and along with all of that it would be necessary for him to return personally to Brussels, and remain there as a prisoner, until the sums for which he was obligated should be fully paid. If, however, he were granted the Aid, all these ills would disappear, and the enterprise which he had undertaken would be brought, with the aid of God, to a good conclusion, and thus there would be peace and calm everywhere. And the prelates, earls, barons, knights of the shires, citizens and burghers of the cities and burghs were asked if they would consult among themselves between that day, Saturday, and the following Monday, and grant a suitable Aid, by which the King could be sufficiently assisted, and his business successfully completed, on both sides of the Channel.

To these requests the said prelates, earls, and barons, for themselves and for all their tenants, and the knights of the shires, for themselves and for the commons of the land, considering on the one hand the evils and perils which might come if, God forbid, the Aid should fail, and on the other hand the honor, profit, and peace which, with God's help, might come to the King and to the whole nation of England, should he be aided, did on that Monday grant to our Lord the King, for the reasons stated above, the following Aid: [every] ninth sheaf, ninth fleece, and ninth lamb, out of all their sheaves, fleeces, and lambs, from that point for the two years following. And the citizens and burghers of the realm [granted] a true ninth of their goods; and the merchants who do not reside in cities or burghs, and other men who dwell in forests and wastelands, and who do not live either by their wages or by their flocks of sheep, granted a fifteenth of their goods, according to the true value. This was granted under the condition, that our Lord the King, in his good grace, considering the great burden and subsidies with which they had already before now been loaded, and that this grant which was now being made seemed very burdensome to them, should grant the petitions which they put before him and his Council; which petitions are contained below, and begin in this way: "These are the petitions, etc."

52. The English Prepare a Fleet. [Source: Avesbury, 310–12]

Here we return to the chronicle of the well-informed Robert of Avesbury, who as the Archbishop of Canterbury's Registrar may well have been an eye-witness of the Archbishop's confrontation with Edward III before Sluys.

In the year of the Lord 1340, on a certain Saturday [10 June], a fortnight before the feast of St. John the Baptist, the King of England was at Orwell with 40 ships, or about that many, which he had prepared there for his passage to Flanders in order to see his wife and his two sons who were then staying in Ghent, and to treat with his overseas allies concerning the expedition of his war. At that time he was planning to make the crossing within two days. But the lord Archbishop of Canterbury, his Chancellor, warned him that lord Philip of Valois, his adversary of France, having cautiously foreseen his passage, had secretly sent over a great navy with a huge fleet of ships equipped for war in order to resist him in the port of the Zwin, and advised him to wait and provide himself with a greater force, lest by crossing then he lose himself and his [men]. The King, not trusting the dispatches, said that he would cross anyway. The Archbishop, in truth, immediately placed himself entirely outside the Council of the King, and, taking his leave, left his presence and returned the Great Seal to him. The King called to him lord Robert Morley, his admiral, and a certain sailor named Crabbe; seeking the truth, he consulted with them as to whether it would be dangerous to cross then; they answered him in the same way as the lord Archbishop of Canterbury had done earlier. At which the King said: "You and the Archbishop have collaborated in a premeditated sermon, in order to impede my passage." And, offended, he said: "I will cross despite you; and you who are afraid, where there is nothing to fear, you stay at home." Then the said admiral and sailor swore by their heads that, if the King were to cross over at that time, he and everyone coming with him would inevitably be cast into peril. They said, however, that if he wanted to make the crossing at that time, then they would go before him, even if they should die. Hearing this, the lord King immediately sent for the Archbishop, his Chancellor, and, speaking soothing words to him, returned to him the seal of the Chancellor. Immediately he had orders for the larger ships sent to each port to the north and the south and also to London, so that then within ten days he had enough ships and an unhoped-for number of men-at-arms and archers, more indeed that he wanted to have, so that he sent many back.

53. The Flemings Advise Edward to Wait. [Source: Villani, 377]

Thanks to the extensive mercantile and banking connections among England, Flanders and Italy in this period, the Florentine chronicler Giovanni Villani (d. 1348) had access to a surprising amount of information concerning the progress of the Hundred Years War.

That year, 1340, on the day of St. John the Baptist, the 24th of June, the good King Edward III, King of England, arrived in Flanders at the port of the Zwin with 120 armed ships, with 2,000 noble men-at-arms and an infinite number of common people, including many English archers; and he found the fleet of the King of France, which was 200 ships with 30 armed galleys and armed barges, of which the admiral was Barbanero di Portoveneri, a great pirate, who had done great harm on the sea to the English and Gascons and Flemings along their coasts, and seized the isle of Cadzant, which was opposite the Zwin, and pillaged and burned and killed over 300 Flemings. The people of Bruges, learning of the arrival of the King of England, sent their ambassadors to Sluys, begging him for God's sake and for his love of them that he not give battle against the armada of the King of France – which was as large again as his fleet, and moreover included the Genoese galleys – and that he wait for two days and rest his men, for at that moment they were arming a hundred ships of good men to aid him, and he could have a certain victory. The valiant King did not wish to wait, but had his men-at-arms and sergeants arm themselves.

54. The Battle of Sluys. [Source: French Chronicle of London, 76]

The French Chronicle of London *was written in or around 1343, and is an independent source for English history for the decade preceding that year. Its author may have been an official of the city of London.*

On Friday morning [23 June], our King saw his enemies on the sea, and said "because Our Lord Jesus Christ was put to death on a Friday, we do not wish to spill any blood this day." At that time the wind had been in the east, before the King took to the sea, for a whole fortnight; but by the grace of the Almighty the wind immediately turned to come from the west. Thus by the grace of God the King and his fleet had the wind and weather as they wished them. And so they sailed forward up until the break of day at sunrise [on Saturday]; and he saw his enemies so formidably prepared that it was too horrible to look at, for the ships of France were so strongly bound together with large chains, [and were equipped with] castles, wooden breastworks, and barriers. But nevertheless Sire Edward our King said to all those who were around him in the English fleet: "Good lords and my brothers, do not be at all dismayed, but be entirely of good comfort; and he who for me today gives battle will be fighting in pursuit of a just cause, and will have the blessing of God Almighty, and each shall keep whatever he may gain." And as soon as our King finished giving this speech, everyone was eager to seek to avenge him against his enemies. And then our sailors drew the sails to half-mast, and drew up their anchors as if they were going to flee; and when the navy of France saw this they unfastened their great chains in order to pursue us. And immediately our ships turned back against them, and the mêlée began with trumpets, nakers, viols, tabours, and many other musical instruments. And then our King, with 300 ships, vigorously attacked the French with 500 large ships and galleys; and eagerly all our men put forth great diligence in order to give battle to the French. Our archers and crossbowmen began to fire so thickly, like hail falling in winter, and our artillerymen shot so fiercely, that the French were unable to look out or to hold their heads up. And while this fight lasted, our Englishmen entered their galleys with great force and fought hand-to-hand with the French, and cast them out of their ships and galleys. And always our King, in the cog *Thomas of Winchelsea*, inspired them by fighting strongly with his enemies. And at the hour of mid-morning a ship of London, belonging to William Hansard, came to them; it did much good work in the battle. For the battle was so fierce and so dire, that the attack lasted from noon all day and all night, and the next day up until the first hour; and when the battle was won, no Frenchman remained alive except for Spaudefish, who fled with 24 ships and galleys.

55. Edward Informs Parliament of His Plans. [Source: *Rotuli Parliamentorum*, 2:118]

Edward, by the grace of God, King of England and of France and Lord of Ireland, to the dukes, archbishops, bishops, earls, barons and others, who shall be assembled at our next parliament at Westminster, greetings.

After our arrival in England, our parliament having been summoned and assembled in the aforesaid place on the appointed day [29 May], our business over here and the great necessity that we have to be aided for its good accomplishment was shown to those who were there. We found them to be of good will, which they well demonstrated to us by the large subsidy which they granted to us; but, because such an aid as was granted could not at that time be converted into money, and we and the other great men with us were bound to return to Flanders in order to keep our faith towards those who had lent us money in that country and elsewhere (which faith it was our fixed intention to keep; and which, also, the lords of our Council who were there advised us in council that we should keep), we were on the point of crossing, with a certain number of men-at-arms, at that time; after which other magnates would come to the other fleet, which had been ordered to be ready on the feast of St. John the Baptist [24 June], with all the lords and others, who were assigned to come there. And, just as we were about to make our crossing, with many of our horses having been led on board, news came to us that our enemy of Valois had arrayed a great armada of ships, which was before us in the river Zwin. Having heard this news, and considered the perils which might come if they left there in order to damage our realm of England or our people elsewhere, and what a comfort which it would have been to our enemies, and especially the Scots, if such a force came to them, we immediately decided to seek them out wherever we could find them, as is known to those of our Council who were there at our departure from England. And we found them, on the day of St. John, at the said port; and Our Lord Jesus Christ showed such grace to us against them on the said day, that we won the victory, as we believe has been told to you well enough by those who were there. We praise God for that grace and ask you all to thank Him for it.

After the said day of St. John, the country of Flanders, and also other lords, our allies, came to us, and informed us how our enemy was on the border, ready to enter Flanders or elsewhere against our allies, wherever he could most harm them and most effectively drive them to withdraw from our alliance.

Considering the pursuit of our right, and most importantly the keeping of our faith and the resisting of his malice, and by the assent of our said allies and of the lords of our realm and of the land of Flanders who were then around us, we decided to land and to split our host; one part going with us towards Tournai, where there would be 100,000 armed Flemings, and [the other with] lord Robert d'Artois towards St. Omer with 50,000. That is aside from all our allies and their forces. To govern and lead such a host requires a very great sum of money, on top of the debts that we must necessarily pay before our departure.

We pray you dearly, each one of you, that you first of all weigh the right that we have; next the great peril which will come, unless we are quickly succored with money and goods, in order to satisfy the said land [of Flanders] and our allies and the soldiers who have already been retained by us and who will withdraw if they are not paid. And also if our allies are not paid, they may even perhaps go over to our enemy; and considering his malice and their power rejoined to his, bear in mind that our land, ourself, our children and all the lords and others would be on the point of perdition. And [on the other hand] if we are quickly aided, we hope to take him at a disadvantage, and to triumph over him forever after – if only you will arrange that we should be hastily succored by money or by goods in such a way as to give satisfaction for our debts and to retain our forces.

The sum which we need quickly, and to whom it is to be paid and on what days, and more fully the decisions we have taken, will be made known to you by the mouths of the Earls of Arundel, Huntingdon, and Gloucester, and Sir William Trussell, who have borne themselves nobly and loyally towards us in this business and who are coming to you in order to explain to you our situation and our affairs. To them, and to each of them, give full faith and credence concerning that which they tell you on our behalf.

Given under our privy seal at Bruges, the 9th day of July, the fourteenth year of our reign over England, and the first year of our reign over France.

56. Robert d'Artois at St. Omer. [Source: *Grandes Chroniques*, 9:188–96]

Robert d'Artois, who led the Anglo-Flemish detachment which advanced to St. Omer (the capital of Artois), had been Philip of Valois' chief advisor until, in 1334, he fled from France after being implicated in a plot to gain by fraud the county of Artois, which rightfully belonged to Philip's sister-in-law. Robert found shelter in England, and it was generally believed in France that he was largely responsible for encouraging Edward III to go to war. Indeed, Edward's decision to shelter Robert was the official grounds given for Philip's confiscation of Guienne and Ponthieu in 1337.

After the outbreak of open conflict, d'Artois served as one of Edward III's principal captains.

Now I will tell you of lord Robert d'Artois, who was at Cassel, and there assembled an army to go to St. Omer. But the men of Veurne and Bergues, who were very numerous and good fighters, exited from their land and came to within a league of Cassel, to a town called Bambecque, and there announced that the would go no farther; for they had been led to St. Omer in the past, but had never benefited from it. When lord Robert d'Artois heard this, he took counsel with his knights and with the Brugeois, and then went to Bambecque and spoke with the people from Veurne and Bergues, and told them that they should go forward boldly, for he was very sure of the town of St. Omer, and had already received two pairs of letters saying that as soon as he came before the gate, the townsmen would let him in and would deliver the Duke of Burgundy to him; and he was fully confident about this. The unfortunate people believed him; so like fools they went forward. But they told him that they would still not go past the Neuf-Fossé, the ditch which separated Flanders from Artois, unless they were provided with better assurances. When lord Robert d'Artois saw that he had in this way got them to go forward, he was very happy about it, and immediately had his archers course through the land of Artois with torches in hand. When the Duke saw the flames in his land, immediately he had his trumpet sounded and sallied out of the town with his divisions fully arrayed. And when the archers learned that they were coming, they therefore decided to rally [back to the main force], but the Duke's men caught and killed fully 60 of them, right at a river-crossing called Le Pont-Asquin. The Duke stayed in the fields for a while, and when he saw that no one came, he therefore returned to the town. Then lord Robert d'Artois ordered his host to decamp and bind up the tents and move towards St. Omer. Those of Bruges, who formed the van division and led the baggage, came to a town near St. Omer called Arques. But the men of Veurne did not want to cross the Neuf-Fossé, as they had said earlier. When lord Robert saw that they would not go forward, he had a report sent to them that the Brugeois had been engaged, and for God's sake, they should come support them. When they heard this news, they abandoned their purpose and came forward towards the town by a long march. When they came to Arques, they found the men of Bruges, who had encamped.

While they were making camp, the archers advanced to the gate [of St. Omer] carrying a banner with the arms of lord Robert d'Artois, and they shot so thickly against the gate that it was a marvel to behold. When those who were at the gate saw them shoot thus, they sallied out all at once and charged against them; but they did not await them, fleeing instead, and the men from St. Omer chased them up to the hospital. They skirmished like this very often, but neither the Duke nor his men-at-arms took part. This skirmishing went on until the Flemings were entirely encamped, and then they torched the town of Arques and burned it completely. On this same day, the Count of Armagnac with his entire force entered the town [of St. Omer].

The King of France, who had assembled his host in order to go to Tournai, decided that it would be better for him to fight with lord Robert than to go to Tournai; so he put his army in motion to go to St. Omer in great haste. The Flemings who were outside Arques came nearly every day up to the suburbs of St. Omer in order to skirmish; and by night they made so much light in their host that the light shone up to the town. And also each day they made great assaults against a small fort belonging to the Duke of Burgundy, called Rihoult, but for all their assaults they could not take it.

When lord Robert learned that the King of France had left Tournai and was coming towards him, he therefore hastened his affairs greatly. On a Wednesday morning he summoned all the captains of his army, and said to them: "Lords, I have received word that I should go towards the town and that it will be immediately surrendered to me." Immediately they ran to arm themselves, and said to one another "Well now, comrades, we will yet this night drink the wines of St. Omer."

When the divisions were arrayed, they descended from their tents and took the highway through Arques towards the town of St. Omer. And in the first line went lord Robert, and he had with him two English banners, and all the men of Bruges, and the archers. And they did not stop until they had come to within a crossbow-shot of the hospital, and there they halted. They had ditches in front of them, so that it was impossible to reach them, and also they had placed in front of themselves some wooden constructions, which had great iron spikes, and were covered with linen cloth, so that they could not be perceived. And in the next division, which was very large, were the men of the Frank of Bruges. On the other side, on the hill next to [the house of St.-Bertin],[17] on the edge of Arques, were arrayed the men of Ypres, who were very numerous; and between these two divisions were arrayed the men of Veurne and Bergues and their castleries. And those of Poperinghe and the entire castleries of Cassel and Bailleul stayed to guard the tents. There was a traversing ditch which extended from the division from Ypres, which was on the hill, up to the division of lord Robert.

When the knights of St. Omer saw the Flemings ranged at the edge of the suburbs of the town, they sallied out by bands, without proper order; and all the banners went, except for the Duke of Burgundy and the Count of Armagnac and all their forces. And the reason the Duke did not sally out was because the King [of France] had ordered him not to fight against Robert d'Artois or his forces without him.

When these knights had arrived in the open fields where the Flemings were arrayed, they made many charges against them, but they could never make a dent in them. These attacks lasted from noon up to evening. When the Duke of Burgundy saw that his enemies were so close to him, he summoned the Count of Armagnac and his counselors and said to them: "Lords, how do you advise me? I do not see any way I can avoid being either dishonored or disobedient to the King today." Then the Count of Armagnac said, "Sire, with the aid of God and of your good friends, you will be able to come into the King's peace well enough." Immediately the Duke declared: "Well then, let us go arm ourselves for God and St. George." When he was armed, he issued out of the town, not having above 50 men-at-arms with him, and went straight to the hospital without halting; and there he found the division of lord Robert d'Artois to meet him.

After this, the Count of Armagnac sallied out with a good 800 men-at-arms, of whom fully 300 were perfectly armored, and this division drew towards the men of Ypres who were on the right. When the Burgundians saw the Duke in the field, they drew towards him, but the Artesians and the Flemings of the King's

---

[17] Supplied from the *Istoire et croniques de Flandres*, 1:388.

party held back in the fields just where they were. Then came the large divisions of Bergues and Veurne and of the Frank across the fields and attacked them; and the Flemings and Artesians defended themselves against them. But when they came to the traversing ditch, they were therefore unable to go farther. Immediately the banners reversed, and in turning back many nobles were cut down, and they fled on all sides, and would have left their lord in the field in the hands of their enemies, if he had not been saved by the grace of God. Immediately when the Flemings saw the banners retreat, they advanced beyond the ditch in large bands, and ran after them, thinking they had defeated them. But when the Artesians saw them beyond [the ditch], they turned their banners and charged them with tremendous courage; and there the battle began in such a way that in the end the Flemings were defeated. And the Count of Armagnac advanced against the men of Ypres, and they fled as soon as they saw him coming, so that no one is really sure where they went. And then the Count rejoined those who were pursuing the fugitives [from the defeated division of Bergues, Veurne, and the Frank]; and in this flight a great number of the Flemings on Robert d'Artois' side were killed. While the Artesians and the Count of Armagnac maintained the fight and chased the Flemings towards Arques, lord Robert d'Artois with his whole division saw the Duke of Burgundy stand in front of the hospital. So he had his engines moved to the rear, and with a great cry advanced towards the town of St. Omer. When the Duke's men saw him coming, they drew away from the road into the fields. Lord Robert thought he would catch them on the street of the suburbs, where the men-at-arms would not have been able to help against the infantry, but his plan failed. Immediately he [the Duke] retreated with his entire division towards the gate of the town of St. Omer, and once again the said lord Robert thought he had caught the said Duke of Burgundy. But, as God willed it, those who were in the gate recognized their banners, and immediately began to shoot and to cast [stones] at them; but the entry to the town was so packed with men that, because of those who were fleeing towards the town, no one could get in or out.

When lord Robert and his men saw that their plan had failed, they overtook some knights who were returning towards the town, and killed a few of them in front of the gate. And the Lord of Hamelincourt, Sir Froissart de Beaufort, another knight from Spain named the Lord of St. Vrain, and a knight of Burgundy named the Lord of Branges were killed there. And one English knight, whose arms were *argent* and *gules,* chequered, was killed there, shot through the brain.

Then they put their divisions in order and retreated towards Arques. But when they had exited the suburbs, the Duke, who had rallied his men and was waiting for them, wanted to attack them. But because it was night, his men would not stand for it. So the division of lord Robert d'Artois passed down the road, fully arrayed, shouting loudly "St. George!" The Count of Armagnac and the Artesians who had pursued the defeated [Flemings], and knew nothing of what had occurred in front of the town, encountered lord Robert and his entire division; but they did not recognize him, because it was so late; and therefore some of them were surprised and killed. A knight of Burgundy named Sir William de Jully was captured there. On that day, the Count of Monlezun, a new knight who was one of the Count of Armagnac's men, raised his banner [for the first time], and in the same way the Lord of Sainte-Croix raised his banner, and another knight of Artois called the Lord of Rely. And many men were made knights there.

The Duke of Burgundy, when he had rallied his people, went towards the town with great joy, and the townspeople came out to meet him with torches and led him into the town. There could the cries of many knights be heard, and they entered to such great rejoicing in the town that it would have been difficult to hear God's thunder there. Then the knights who lay dead outside the town were carried in, and on the morrow interred with great weeping. This battle took place on [26 July], the day after the feast of St. Jacques, in the month of July, the year of grace 1340.

When lord Robert d'Artois returned to his tents, the lights were still fully lit, but he did not find anyone there, for all the people had fled, and left their tents and armor and most everything else they owned behind them; and they were so thoroughly demoralized that they didn't really expect to reach Cassel successfully. A great number of them, all of whom had been shot or wounded, therefore died along the way. The host of Flemings who were with lord Robert was estimated by *connestablies*[18] at 55,000, not counting their baggage; and the killed were accounted at 3,000.

57. Edward Sends a Challenge to Philip. [Source: *Foedera*, II:2:1131]

Philip of Valois, for a long time we have importuned you, by embassies and all other reasonable ways that we know, to render to us our rightful heritage of France, which you have detained from us for a long time, and very unjustly occupied. And because we can see well that you intend to persevere in your injurious detention, without making a reasonable answer to our demand, we have entered into the land of Flanders, as sovereign lord of it, and passed through the country. And we signify to you that, with the aid of Our Lord Jesus Christ and our right, and with the forces of the said land [of Flanders] and with our own people and allies, considering the right that we have to the heritage which you wrongfully keep away from us, we are drawing towards you in order to bring our rightful challenge to a quick conclusion, if you will approach. And because such a great force of men as we have assembled (as we think you have as well) cannot long hold together, without causing harm and destruction to the people and to the land, something which every good Christian should eschew, and especially princes and others who hold themselves for governors of men; therefore we greatly desire that the matter be concluded soon, and that, to avoid the death of

---

[18] I.e. units commanded by a constable, probably of 100 each.

Christians, as the quarrel is between you and us, that the debate of our challenge be conducted by our two bodies. We offer this option to you for the reasons mentioned above, and considering that we can well see the great nobility of your person, as well as your good sense and wisdom. And, if you do not wish to do things that way, then we make the challenge that this battle should be brought to completion by yourself and 100 of the most suitable people on your side, against ourself and the same number of our liegemen. And, if you do not wish to pursue either of these ways, that you assign us a certain day to fight force against force before the city of Tournai, within ten days after the date of this letter. And we wish it to be known throughout the world that the above offers are what we desire, not because of pride or arrogance, but because of the reasons stated above, so that, the will of our Lord Jesus Christ having been shown between us, there will be able to be more and more peace among Christians, so that the power of the enemies of God can be resisted and Christendom made free . . . .

Given at Chin, 26 July 1340.

58. Philip's Reaction. [Source: Jan de Klerk (Delpierre), 20–1]

Suspended from this letter was the great seal with the quartered arms of France and England. Philip, on seeing this seal, took on a feverish appearance and examined it for some time in silence. After some moments of reflection, he answered that for many years he had possessed the crown in peace, that it was his legitimate heritage, that he had put it on his head by the unanimous consent of the Peers of France, and that no one but himself would have a single fleuron of it. Therefore, he did not think that he ought to accept a single combat; but, as soon as he thought fit, he would give battle, and perhaps sooner than his adversary would like.

59. Philip's Reply. [Source: Avesbury, 315–16]

Philip, by the grace of God King of France, to Edward King of England. We have seen your letters to Philip of Valois, brought to our court on your behalf, in which are contained certain requests made by you to the said Philip of Valois. And, because the letters are not addressed to us and the said requests are not made of us, as appears clearly from the content of the letters, we are not making any response to you. Nevertheless, because we have understood by the said letters and otherwise that you have entered into our realm of France, bringing much harm to us, to our realm, and to our people, willfully, unreasonably, and without considering the duty of a liegeman to look after his lord's interests – for you entered into our liege homage in recognizing us, as is right, as King of France, and promised obedience, just as one ought to promise to one's liege lord, as appears clearly by your letters patent, sealed with your great seal, which you sent to us, and [copies of] which you ought also to have in front of you – our intention therefore is, when it shall seem good to us, to cast you out of our realm, to our honor and that of our realm and for the good of our people; and that we shall do this we put our faith firmly in God, from whom all our power comes. For, by your undertaking, which is willful and not reasonable, the crusade overseas has been impeded, a great number of Christian men put to death, the divine service made less, and the reverence of the holy church reduced. And concerning what you have written, that you expect to have the Flemish army [with you], we think ourselves certain that the good people and the commons of the land will bear themselves in such a way towards our cousin the Count of Flanders, their immediate lord, and towards us, their sovereign lord, that they will guard well their honor and their loyalty. And that which they have done wrong up until now has been by the evil counsel of men who had no regard for the common profit or the honor of the country, but only for their own profit.

Done in the field, near the priory of St. Andrew, under our privy seal, in the absence of the great seal, the 30th day of July, the year of grace 1340.

60. Opening of the Siege of Tournai. [Source: "Tournai Bulletin"]

This dispatch from one of the men-at-arms in the English army was preserved in the Historia Roffensis.

Our lord the King entered the marches of France on the twenty-second day of July, accompanied by the power of the Flemings (around a thousand mounted men-at-arms and around 160,000 armored men on foot), and by his English men, to the number of 1,000 men-at-arms and 4,000 archers. And they came by a castle called Estaimbourg, which castle was so strong that it could not be taken by assault. And our said lord the King had a detachment of men remain before the said castle with engines, so that the castle was surrendered to them within five days. And then our said lord the King advanced up to the fair city of Tournai, in which there were a good three or four thousand men-at-arms, namely the Count of Eu, Constable of France; Marshal Bertrand; Marshal de Trie; the Count of Foix; and other great men. And the people of the town made a sortie against our men, and were defeated and cast back inside their gates, and lost some of their men and their horses, and in haste even dropped their portcullis on their own men, since otherwise our men would have entered the town with them. At which point Sir Reginald Cobham had a joust of war, and others of the Englishmen bore themselves very well indeed. And another time, a full 100 men-at-arms issued from the town, and our English archers defeated them, threw them back, and killed a portion of them and of their horses, and captured one esquire. And then afterwards the Count of Hainault came to our sire the King with half a thousand men-at-arms and around 8,000 armored infantrymen, and made a *chevauchée* to a town called Orchies, which was walled and strengthened with ditches and barriers. They took the town and burned it, and took many prisoners, and destroyed the neighboring countryside, and returned to base the same day.

And similarly, on Thursday the third day of August, the Count of Hainault, the Earl of Derby, and we other lords and companions made a *chevauchée* to the town of St.-Amand, which was strong, and well enclosed by walls and by a water-filled moat all around, and stuffed with men-at-arms, a good 200 of them, and 600 light troops, aside from the people of the town. And so we scaled the walls of the town on several sides, so that with the aid of God we captured it. And the people who were inside were all killed except for a few who escaped. And twenty fine destriers and coursers and many other goods were gained. And we had the town burned, the walls knocked down, and the moat filled, and we burned the countryside all around, and returned safely home. And none of our men were killed or wounded, except one knight and one esquire of the Count of Hainault.

And so on the 15th day of August the Duke of Brabant came to our lord the King with a good 5,000 men-at-arms and 150,000 armored infantrymen; and since his arrival our lord the King and all his friends and allies mentioned above have agreed for certain to lay siege to the said city of Tournai until they have conquered it, or until they have done battle with the King of France if he wants to come to rescue it. And they have decided to make *chevauchées* during the siege to devastate and destroy the land all around.

At the time when our lord the King entered the marches of France by the aforesaid coasts [of the Scheldt?] milord Robert d'Artois with certain men-at-arms and archers of England and 60,000 armored Flemings were sent to the region of St. Omer, and came before the said town, out of which the Duke of Burgundy issued with about 11,000 men-at-arms and fought with the said people, so that the Flemings fled. And the said Sir Robert, with the Englishmen and the men of Bruges who were with him, rallied themselves and fought with the French and killed fully 600 of their men, in addition to whom were killed many great lords of France, counts, baronets, knights, and others, in great numbers.

And in the same way on the 12th day of August the Count of Hainault, Sir Walter Mauny, and others made a *chevauchée* up to a town which is called Marchiennes, which was strengthened with walls and ditches, and took the town, and caused it to be burned; and they pillaged and burned the countryside all around and returned safe and sound the same day to the army with their company. And the Marquis of Juliers has also come to our lord the King with 1,000 men-at-arms, and Sir Jean de Hainault with a great number of people. And the Duke of Guelders with 1,000 men-at-arms. And they have made a definite agreement to lay siege to the said town of Tournai.

61. Two Days of the Siege: August 27th–28th, 1340. [Source: *Chroniques de Tournay*, in Froissart, *Oeuvres*, 25:355–7]

A local Tournai chronicle provides us with an extraordinarily detailed, day-by-day account of the siege. The extracts below give a sample of its contents. In reading it, consider the role of psychological warfare in the conduct of a siege.

On the 28th of August, some companions, both mounted and afoot, issued out of the Moreau Gate and went coursing; they captured two merchant women and fifteen horses and led them peacefully back into Tournai. . . .

On the Sunday before that, the 27th, some of the Count of Foix's men, around sixty men-at-arms, sallied out from the St.-Martin Gate at the sounding of the great drum and rode as far as the gibbet of Tournai. The whole English army was awoken by the alarm and took up arms. Foix's men returned, riding in fine form; they were followed up to the Valenciennes Gate by the English. There they dismounted and had their horses taken into the town; and a great assault took place. From there the English returned to the St.-Martin gate, in order to shoot and to make a great assault; and Locemens was shot in the eye by an arrow, causing him to die. And milord Godemar [du Fay] was shot in the plates of his armor, and the arrow remained stuck in it.

Item. When the English followed the men of the Count of Foix to the Valenciennes Gate, milord Pierre de Roussillon was with him, and fought against the English, and was killed along with one of his esquires. And a great lord of England, a knight, was also killed there, but his name was never known. And Walter Mauny was stuck down off his horse, and his banner knocked down beneath the bridge of the gate, and because of this there was a marvelous assault, the greatest which occurred during the entire siege. And Pierre de Werqinoeil was wounded, and Jacques Villains was wounded in an eye, and Lostart d'Englemoustier, who was entirely unarmored, up in the crennelations of the wall, watching the assault, was wounded in a leg; and Jehan le Musit was shot by an arrow there, so that he died. And the arrows shot over the crennelations and into the town were a marvel; the servant of the Lady de Leuse was shot in front of the hospital, so that he died.

The Count of Foix was at the turrets of the gate and shot plenty of quarrels against the English, and there continued to be a great amount of fire against the gate and the turrets; because of the arrows he had, perforce, to raise the drawbridge.

While this assault was taking place at the Valenciennes gate, the alarm was cried throughout the English army, and they all moved out of their camp. At that time they had a prisoner in a tent, and when he didn't see anyone around him, he set fire to his lodgings and burned it and others, and then returned into Tournai. The flames could be seen from the tops of the walls.

A Fleming came to the Ste.-Fontaine Gate and said: "Surrender, knaves, lest you die of starvation, and we take your women." And he said many bad things. So Lotin Mallart and Piérat Liégart sallied out by the wicket door of the said gate, and Lotin struck him from behind with a "woodpecker," which knocked him to the ground, and Piérart struck him with a dagger and left him for dead. And when he saw there was no one around him, he got back up. He was shot at, but he gathered up the quarrels and returned to his army.

There was not a single day when some companions did not issue out of Tournai and go to fight against their enemies, especially at the Prés-aux-Nonnains. And the enemies came each day to yell at the gates that they should surrender, and that they were being betrayed by the lords who were then in Tournai. Often they said: "Eat well tonight, for you will not eat at all tomorrow." And they said these things because they wanted to cause fighting among those manning the walls; but, God be praised, there was never any argument or fighting there; rather, they were very peaceable.

62. The Siege of Tournai. [Source: *French Chronicle of London*, 79–80]

And as long as the siege lasted, which is to say for a quarter of a year, our men made *chevauchées* into France every day, and burned and took plunder, captured knights and esquires of great renown, and seized cattle, wheat, and other supplies from the King of France, so that the land all around the siege was taken, burned, and destroyed. At that time, as long as the siege lasted, Sir Edward our King had the said city of Tournai assaulted six times per day with springalds, and mangonels firing great stones, and gunpowder weapons, and Greek fire, so that the engines with the large stones broke down the towers and the strong walls, churches, bell-towers, strong halls, fine dwellings, and rich habitations, throughout the said city of Tournai. And the people inside the town were after a little while destroyed by the great famine which there was in the city. For the water, running in a fine river, which normally ran through the city, was at that time blocked and held back, so that neither horse nor other living beast remained alive in all the city; for they were so strictly held inside the said city. And the famine was also great, since a quarter of wheat cost four pounds sterling, a quarter of oats two marks, a hen's egg six pence, two onions a penny. And our men outside in the besieging army, throughout the entire host of King Edward, had such a great plenty of supplies, wine, bread, and all sorts of meats, that nothing was lacking, Sweet Jesus be praised therefore.

And in the same time, those inside the city of Tournai had a letter written to their King Philip of Valois, saying that unless he aided them in force and quickly, they would be compelled to surrender the city to the King of England, for many of their men in the city were killed, dead, and destroyed, and their food supplies entirely eliminated, so that they had nothing left on which to live, nor with which to continue any longer the defense of the city against their adversary the King of England. And when their letters had been prepared, they took a servant, and dressed him in poor robes like a Dominican friar, and gave him their letters to carry to their King Philip of Valois, and sent him secretly at night through a postern gate. And when he had gone a good two leagues from the city, at the break of day Sir Henry of Lancaster, the Earl of Derby, encountered him on the road, and had him arrested and interrogated, and the servant vacillated in what he said. And immediately Sir Henry had him searched, and they found the letters on him, and immediately led this "Dominican" before the King of England. He was required on pain of life and limb to tell all the truth concerning the strong city of Tournai. And immediately the messenger began his account before the King: "Sire," he said, "I will not lie to you concerning anything. It is true that all their men-at-arms have been killed, and not over 200 fighting men remain; nor do they have supplies to sustain themselves for more than a fortnight."

On the same day the Count of Hainault took a great number of people with him and made a foraging raid a full twenty local leagues distant from the siege, and took a great amount of booty in the form of French cattle, and killed a great number of men-at-arms, and captured 26 knights who were among the most valiant in King Philip's service at that time, and led them as prisoners to the King of England. Innumerable cattle and immeasurable quantities of supplies were also brought to him, so that a good ox could be purchased for 40 pence, a pig for 18 pence, a sheep for 12 pence, and there was plenty of wine, God be praised! And when this news came to Philip of Valois, how he had lost his valiant knights, his men had been killed, his cattle and his supplies had been taken and carried to his enemy the King of England, he began to sigh and to display great unhappiness. For he did not dare to give battle to our King Edward, but like a coward and a defeated knight he made a woman, the Countess of Hainault, his messenger to our King and his Council . . . .

63. The Truce of Esplechin. [Source: Jan de Klerk (Delpierre), 23–7]

The Dutch chronicle Van den derden Eduwaert *was written by Jan de Klerk of Antwerp in 1347, based primarily on his own memories of events. The chronicler accompanied King Edward during much of the monarch's stay in the Low Countries.*

The text below is based on Octave Delpierre's nineteenth-century French translation of the work.

The dowager Countess of Hainault, a most generous and pious lady, who was the mother of the Count, the sister of Philip of France, and King Edward's mother-in-law, ardently desired that peace be made between these sovereigns. She made every effort to accomplish this, and finally obtained her son's consent to intervene. The old Countess then departed, and went to find her brother, reminding him how little advantage he had thus far gained from this campaign, and proclaiming that if he would follow her advice, the siege of Tournai would end soon enough; but that it would be impossible to bring about that result, as he well knew, except by the mediation of the Duke of Brabant. "It is true that he is your enemy," she added, "but for all that I hope that you will not refuse him as mediator, if you desire peace. It would certainly be better for you, that your domains not be ravaged much longer. Up to now you have had no success in repulsing your enemies. Famine reigns in the city, and if the defenders are forced to surrender, I greatly fear that you might lose your realm and your honor. The attackers are the best soldiers of Christendom. So I pray you, my lord, not to wait until it will be too late to follow good advice."

The King, after having listened attentively to his sister, answered "How could I so abase myself as to ask an enemy's grace? Never has such a thing happened to a King of France. Yet it is true that I am vigorously attacked, and that on many occasions my troops have been beaten. I know that I am in a critical position, and so if I should see a means of getting out of it with honor, I would submit it to my counselors, and I would follow their advice completely."

The King therefore summoned his Council, to which he added the King of Bohemia and the Bishop of Liège. The Council's advice was that it was urgent to bring an end to the war, and after deliberation, a unanimous decision was reached that the most fitting person to negotiate the peace was the Duke of Brabant, and that his wisdom could be trusted.

Jean, King of Bohemia, and the Bishop of Liège were sent to him, charged with presenting to him the things which appeared most necessary in order to arrive at the goal which it was proposed to reach.

The Countess of Hainault, guided by great wisdom, took herself before the King of England, her son-in-law, and with prudence began to discuss her projects with him. If he would consent to accept the mediation of the Duke, as her brother had done, she said, he would be well repaid thereby, for he would receive all that his ancestors had lost in Gascony and elsewhere in good will, and without war.

Edward reflected that this proposition was acceptable, especially as he was almost without means to pay the troops under his orders if the war continued, as his country had sent him neither men nor money. Thus necessity obliged him to follow the advice of the Countess.

A day was fixed when the parties were supposed to appear in the chapel of Esplechin, near Tournai, in order to agree on the conditions of the peace. Philip sent the King of Bohemia, the Bishop of Liège, and two counts; Edward, for his side, delegated the Bishop of Lincoln, a very skillful man, and two other lords.

64. An English Assessment of the Truce. [Murimuth, 115–16]

Adam Murimuth probably composed this section of his chronicle year by year as events unfolded. His position as a canon of St. Paul's in London gave him access to good information concerning the progress of the war, and his chronicle is generally very accurate and informed by good judgment.

The siege of the city of Tournai lasted until the feast of saints Cosimus and Damian [the 27th of September]; on which day, after many discussions concerning entering into a truce which the French had sought, a truce was agreed at the petition of the French, to last until the feast of St. John the Baptist next [June 24th], so that in the interim a peace could be negotiated. And the captives of both sides were released, under a sworn agreement that they would return [to captivity] on the said feast of St. John if a final peace were not agreed. And thus the abovesaid siege closed, and some of the nobles returned to England. There were many negotiations held concerning the truce while the said lord the King of England remained before Tournai conducting the aforesaid siege, and Philip of Valois with all his army was four leagues away; but Philip did not dare come to break the siege. Instead, through the King of Bohemia, who was with him, many discussions were held and offers made concerning the granting of a truce. Finally the Duke of Brabant, the Count of Hainault, the Marquis of Juliers and the Duke of Guelders and the other allies of the King of England agreed that an "honorable" (albeit unprofitable) truce should be made – unprofitable, I say, for the King of England and his people, not for the said counts, to whom the towns and castles of theirs which the King of France had long ago seized were returned. For a long time the King of England put off accepting this truce, expecting money from England which did not come; but because of the lack of money, he, who had only a few Englishmen with him, was finally compelled to follow the will of his confederates and consent to the truce. This he did unwillingly, and also against the will of the Flemings; but he could not do otherwise on this occasion.

65. Intervention in Brittany. [Source: Murimuth, 125–7]

The Truce of Esplechin effectively froze the war in place: for its duration, neither side was to harm the other, free trade and travel between the realms were to be restored, and sieges (including that of Tournai) were to be lifted, though the defenders were forbidden from increasing their stores of supplies or their defenses.

Edward agreed to this truce only because he was completely bankrupt, a fact which he blamed on maladministration by the Chancellor and the rest of the administration in England. On his return to England, he imprisoned most of his ministers and provoked a major constitutional crisis. For the next two years, the peace was maintained as both Kings sought to restore their finances and shore up their weakened domestic political situations. The truce was repeatedly renewed, and negotiations for a permanent peace began.

The course of events during the truce did not favor Edward III. French diplomacy drew the Emperor and some of the other Low Countries princes away from their English alliances; Pope Benedict XII died and was replaced by the much more pro-French Clement VI; David Bruce returned to Scotland, leading to a further deterioration of the English position in Scotland. Thus, when an opportunity arose in 1341 for Edward to gain some political ground by taking advantage of a succession dispute in the Duchy of Brittany, he did not hesitate to seize it, even though he had to skirt the edges of violating the truce to do so.

There were two claimants to the Duchy on the death of Duke Jean III in 1341: his half-brother Jean de Montfort, and Charles of Blois, the husband of the Duke's niece, Jeanne of Penthièvre. Since Charles was King Philip's nephew, while Montfort was suspected of pro-English leanings, it is no surprise that the King ruled that the inheritance should go go Charles. Jean, who had seized control of the treasury and much of the territory of the Duchy, was besieged and captured by a French army. Jeanne of Flanders, Montfort's wife, continued the war on behalf of her husband and her infant son, and sought help from England. Edward responded favorably, and sent assistance in three waves, as circumstances allowed: first a very small contingent under Sir Walter Mauny, then a little army under the Earl of Northampton and Robert d'Artois, and finally (after the expiration of the truce with France) by a full-scale military expedition under Edward III.

The story of the first two phases is told below by Adam Murimuth.

This year [1342] lord Walter Mauny, with sixty men-at-arms and two hundred archers, crossed over into Brittany by the King's leave, in order to help the Countess [of Montfort], who was at war with Charles of Blois and the Lord of Léon. He gained possession of three castles there, and captured the said Lord of Léon along with some other nobles. Then, making a truce with the said Charles until the feast of All Saints [1 Nov.], contingent on the approval of the King of England, he returned to England around the feast of the Translation of St. Thomas [7 July], bringing with him the said Lord of Léon and the other prisoners. And, as the truce did not please the King of England, the King arranged to send the Earl of Northampton, the Earl of Devon, Baron Stafford, and Sir William Kildesby, with five hundred men-at-arms and a thousand archers, to Brittany, in aid of the said Countess. They were at Portsmouth, ready to sail, on [2 February, 1343] the vigil of St. Laurence, where they awaited a favorable wind; and on the following vigil of the Assumption [i.e. on 8 May] they set sail . . . .

Around the octaves of the Assumption [i.e. 16 May], ships and letters sent to the King by the Earl of Northampton and his colleagues arrived. The letters stated that their entire fleet, which contained 260 ships not counting the smaller boats, had arrived off the coast of Brittany, next to the castle and town called Brest, on the previous Sunday [12 May]. The Duchess [sic] and her children were inside the said castle and town, under siege by sea and by land: more specifically, besieged by most of the power of the realm of France – on the sea by fourteen very large and well-equipped galleys, and on the land by the Counts of Blois, Savoy, and Foix. But, seeing the fleet of ships, and being themselves vigorously attacked from all sides, three galleys sought safety in flight before the ships were able to land. And eleven galleys, of which three were by far the largest, entered the water of a tight, narrow river emptying into this harbor; but, abandoning the galleys, they fled onto the land. In the same way, those who were besieging the castle and town by land left the siege and retreated, leaving behind, empty, a certain castle called Goy-le-Forêt, along with its supplies. The ships of the English, pursuing the said eleven galleys with small boats and barges, burned them. So all the English landed, and were received with joy and honor; and spreading out rapidly and recklessly through the countryside, they met resistance from no one.

Afterwards, reassembling, they arranged to ride more cautiously together through the country; and they appointed the lord de Say guardian of the said castle of Goy-le-Forêt. Most of the ships they sent back to England for the transit of the King . . . .

The Earl of Northampton later wrote to the King of England that, having taken counsel with those who knew the country, it was decided that for better subsistence they would draw towards the town and castle which in the vernacular are called Mons Relix [Morlaix]. And there they delivered an assault; many were wounded, and lord Jacob Lovel killed. So, expecting help from the allies of the King of England, who arrived after a fortnight, and hearing reports that lord Charles of Blois was coming in haste to break the siege of the aforesaid town and castle, the said Earl and his men waited there up until the evening on the feast of St. Michael, on Monday [29 September]. On that day the said lord Charles arrived with his large force, estimated at three thousand men-at-arms, 1,500 Genoese, and numberless common people, and around noon he approached the said Earl. And the Earl with his force drew nearer to them, going on foot at a quick step, and chose a position on which, with the aid of God, he fought; and he killed and captured at least two hundred men-at-arms, while the Earl himself did not lose a single person of note except lord Edward Despencer, who was killed there. So, the French having fled, the Earl of Northampton held the field.

And after the said Earl and his army returned towards Brittany, the King of England, with a great army of men-at-arms and infantry drew towards Sandwich, awaiting the return of the navy . . .

66. Edward III's Dispatch to Prince Edward on the 1342 Brittany Campaign. [Source: Avesbury 340–42]

Very dear and much-beloved son, we know well that you greatly desire to have good news of us and of our condition. Know that at the sending of this letter we are very well in body, God be praised, desiring only to hear and know the same of you. Very dear son, as to what has happened to us since our departure from England, we inform you that we have ridden a great ways into the duchy of Brittany, which land has surrendered to our obedience, with several good towns and fortresses, namely the town of Ploërmel, and the castle and town of Malestroit, and the castle and the town of Redon, which are good towns and well walled. And know that the Lord of Clisson, who is one of the greatest men of Poitou, and four other barons, namely the Lord of Loyat, the Lord of Machecoul, the Lord of Retz, and the Lord of Rieux, as well as other knights of the said country, and their towns and fortresses, which are directly on the borders of France and of our duchy of Gascony, have entered our peace: which is held to be a great success for our war. And, before the writing of this letter, we sent our cousin of Northampton, the Earl of Warwick, Sir Hugh Despenser, and other bannerets with a great number of men-at-arms, around 400, into the area of Nantes in order to achieve whatever success they can. And since their departure we have [received] news that the Lord of Clisson and the abovesaid barons have gone to the aid of our said cousin and his company with a good number of men-at-arms; but at the sending of this letter we have still not received any news of their success, though we hope to have good news soon, with God's help. Very dear son, know that, by the advice and counsel of the wisest men of our army, we have laid siege to the town of Vannes, which is the best town of Brittany after the town of Nantes, and even more able to harm the land and hold it to our obedience, for we have been advised that, if we had ridden farther without securing the said town, the lands which have surrendered to us would not in any way be able to hold to us. And also the said town is on the sea and is well walled, so that, if we can take it, it will be a great advantage in our war. And know, very dear son, that Sir Louis de Poitiers, Count of Valentinois, is the captain of the town, and it is said that there are good men with him; but we hope that, by the power of God, we will have a good result, for since our arrival in these parts God has given us a good beginning and enough success for the time, praise be to Him for it. And the land is very plentiful in wheat and meat. But always, dear son, it is necessary that you spur our Chancellor and Treasurer to send money to us, for they know well our state. Dear son, know that the third day that we were encamped at the said siege an abbot and a clerk came to us on behalf of the cardinals, with their letters asking us to send them safe conducts to come to us; and they told us that, if they had safe-conducts, they could be with us around eight days thereafter. And we had our Council respond to the said messengers and deliver to them our letters of safe-conduct for the cardinals only, so that they could come to the town of Malestroit, 30 miles from us, which had recently entered our peace; for it is not our intent that they should approach our army closer than the said town of Malestroit, for several reasons. And know that whatever situation that we are in, with the aid of God, it is always our intent to look favorably on a just proposal at whatever time it shall be offered to us. But, though it is fitting that the said cardinals come thus towards us, we do not intend to delay our plan by one day; for we can well think of delays that we have had before now because of their and others' negotiations. Dear son, as soon as we have any result of our siege or of other matters touching on us, we will send you the news, always as up-to-date as the messengers can manage. Dear son, have this letter shown to the Archbishop of Canterbury and to those of our Council near you. Dear son, may God watch over you.

Given under our privy seal, at the siege of Vannes, on December fifth.

Very dear son, after the writing of this letter news came to us that our cousin [the Earl] of Northampton, the Earl of Warwick, Sir Hugh Despenser, and the other bannerets and their company have besieged the town of Nantes, for they hope, with the aid of God, to have a quick success.

67. The End of the Breton Campaign. [*French Chronicle of London*, 92–3]

The narrative of the firmly patriotic French Chronicle of London *offers a rather slanted view of the end of the campaign, but the author's view of Philip VI's unchivalrous character was becoming more widespread in France as well as England.*

And so [King Edward] and his army advanced each day through Brittany, until he came to the city of Nantes; but he did no harm, for he did not want to destroy that city. But he turned towards Philip of Valois by another route, to see whether he would dare give battle on his own ground. Then Philip of Valois caused all the bridges in the country to be broken, so that neither our King nor his army could approach him any closer; but like a coward he sent letters to our King in order to seek a truce of three years. And then fourteen wise men of great renown were to be selected, that is to say seven for our King and seven for Philip of Valois, who were to go to the Pope to negotiate a peace between the two realms of France and England, and to reach an agreement. And if not, at the end of the truce, [he] [under]took to be prompt to the war, to give mortal battle, once and for all. Thus was the truce granted on both sides, by France and England.

The Truce of Malestroit to which the French Chronicle of London *refers above did not actually contain the last-mentioned provision, though it may have been informally understood. Concluded in January of 1343, the truce was intended to preserve the* status quo *pending the outcome of peace negotiations. Vannes was put into the hands of the papal mediators, where it was supposed to remain until the expiration of the truce in September of 1346, though in fact it was seized by English partisans later in 1343.*

The truce was badly kept in Aquitaine (especially by Edward III's Gascon subjects), and was not kept at all by Charles of Blois, who claimed that he was making war on his own behalf rather than as a partisan of Philip VI. The French King also committed a serious violation of its terms when he arrested and executed some of Edward's powerful supporters within the realm of France,who should have been protected by the armistice, most notably the great lord Olivier de Clisson, beheaded in August of 1343. Godfrey d'Harcourt, Lord of St.-Sauveur-le-Vicomte in the Cotentin peninsula of Normandy, who had joined the Plantagenet side to cover what was de facto *a private war against one of Philip's marshals, was driven from his lands in March.*

Under the circumstances, Edward III failed to take seriously the peace negotiations which the truce was supposed to make possible. Although he did the absolute minimum necessary to avoid a complete default, he declined to send a suitable embassy to Avignon (the Pope's residence in this period), and instead concentrated on raising the money and making the preparations necessary for another major expedition against France in 1344. It proved impossible, however, to assemble a parliament willing to finance a renewed war effort until June of 1344; this meant that, because Edward's ability to raise loans had declined greatly since the collapse of his Low Countries strategy, there would not be cash available for an army until the spring of 1345 at the earliest. The nature and terms of the grant are set out in the following passage from the Rolls of Parliament.

68. Parliament Advises Edward III on the Conduct of the War, 1344.
[Source: *Rotuli Parliamentorum*, 2:148]

On that day [26 June], the said Archbishop [of Canterbury], the Bishops of London, Chester, Chichester, Bath, Ely, Salisbury, Lincoln, Carlisle, the Bishop-elect of Hereford; the abbots of St. Alban's, Westminster, Abbingdon, Waltham, and Reading, the abbot of Hyde of Winchester, and the prior of Coventry; the Earls of Northampton, Warrenne, Huntingdon, Suffolk, Oxford, Pembroke, Devonshire, and Angus; the lords Wake, Percy, Berkeley; Sir Ralph Neville, Sir Hugh Despencer, and Sir Nicholas Canteloupe; and the Commons of the Realm, assembled in the White Chamber in the presence of our lord the King, having regard for the great mischiefs and perils which might befall our lord the King, and all his subjects and allies, if the malice of his enemy is not stopped; and considering the great burdens which the lords and commons of England have borne and sustained because of the war, which has lasted so long because of the false truces and armistices which have been made up to this time; and seeing clearly that if an end to this war with a good peace can be had, it can only be by means of a great force of men, and great strength; they therefore requested of our lord the King by unanimous assent, and each individual person of the Lords for himself, that he would make an end to this war, either by battle, or by a suitable peace, if he could get one; and that once our lord the King should be ready and equipped to cross [the Channel] in order to take whatever God might give him for the successful completion of the matter, that he should not abandon his expedition until he had brought matters to a conclusion in one way or another, not for letters or other commands or requests of the Pope or anyone else. The King gave his full assent to this request.

But because this could not be done without a great and suitable Aid, the said Archbishop, bishops, prelates, and representatives of the clergy of the province of Canterbury therefore granted to the lord King a Tenth for three years, to be paid in a certain manner, namely on the feasts of the Purification of Our Lady [2 February] and of St. Barnabas the Apostle [11 June], in aid of the performance of the said business. And the said Commons on the following Saturday granted to our lord the King for the same reasons two Fifteenths from the commons of the land, and two Tenths from the cities and boroughs, according to the form and conditions contained in a cedule which they delivered before our lord the King in parliament, of which the tenor is as follows:

Because of the great necessity which our lord the King has shown to his Commons through his Council, who have asked them for an Aid for the purpose of making an end to his war, with the aid of God, by one way or another; and having regard for his and the Lords' troubles, and the great danger of losing their lives which they are willing to suffer for the salvation of his people; and even though they have been put in great difficulties by the many Aids and burdens before this time; for the great affection they bear for their liege Lord, they willingly grant the fifteenth penny of their goods, and Tenths from the cities and boroughs, to raise the same sum and in the same manner as the last Fifteenth granted to him was raised, and not in any other way. Understanding, dread Lord, this sum to be more burdensome to your people than four Fifteenths would have been before these times, and reserving to your said commons their freedoms in all the points granted to them by your charters at your parliaments, your Commons makes this grant to you under these conditions: that the money thus raised should be expended for the said business brought before them in this parliament by the advice of the Lords; and that the petitions which they set forward at this parliament should be granted to them; and that all the Aid raised north of the Trent should be put towards the defense of the North; and that the Prince[,] Sir Edward de Balliol, or another close relative of the King should be in the Marches in order to act there in the best manner which can be ordained for the salvation of the land. And afterwards, the said commons, seeing the good intention of their liege Lord to bring an end to the said business, grant another Fifteenth on the condition presented to them: namely, that if the King crosses himself and makes an end to the said business, that then it should be raised: and if not, then the said Commons should be discharged of it. And the said commons request that the aforesaid Fifteenths and Tenths should be paid over two years, according to the conditions stated above: that is to say, on All Saints' Day [1 November] and at Easter, by equal portions; such that in any case the said commons should be discharged of all manners of earlier charges and Aids according to the contents of their charter: and that the passage of the sea should be opened to all types of merchants and merchandise; and that none of those who were summoned by letter to this parliament should be put on the commission for raising the aforesaid Fifteenths and Tenths.

And they asked our lord the King that these conditions should be held to. The King granted the request.

69. Derby's Gascon Campaigns. [Source: Froissart, *Chronicles*, 127–35]

In the fall of 1344 King Edward made at least some attempt to explore whether a "suitable peace" could be obtained without further war, finally sending a barely acceptable, if unimpressive, delegation to the Avignon peace talks. The ambassadors hinted that Edward might possibly be willing to accept the cession to him of Gascony in full sovereignty in compensation for his surrendering his right to the French crown, but since the Valois ambassadors were completely unwilling to acknowledge that Edward had any such right to surrender, no progress was made. By mid-January the negotiations had effectively broken off.

Despite the fact that the truce had over a year yet to run, the English government proceeded apace with preparations for a set of expeditionary forces to go to France in the early summer of 1345. The Earl of Northampton was to take 500 men to Brittany; Henry of Lancaster, the Earl of Derby, was to lead a contingent three times that size to Gascony, and the King was to lead the main army to somewhere in the north of France. In mid-June, Edward unilaterally abrogated the Truce of Malestroit, and small-scale campaigning began. Sir Thomas Dagworth won a minor victory in Brittany that month, while Derby's fleet was held up in England by contrary winds. In August, the Earl finally arrived in Bordeaux with 500 men-at-arms and 1,000 of the superb longbowmen who were such an important element of English military strength in this period. Combining these men with local Gascon soldiers, Derby immediately launched a series of stunningly effective campaigns into Poitou, the Agenais, and Périgord, displaying the boldness, judgment and skill which marked him as a truly great commander.

The chronicles which cover these operations are, unfortunately, quite confused. No one account is anywhere near complete, the stories they tell are often mutually contradictory, and none can be followed easily on a map. The following several documents can at least give a good sense of the elements of the campaigns, though the chronology and geography are not necessarily reliable. The great detail of Froissart's account is very valuable for its own sake; many of the details he describes were doubtless typical of many of the small actions which chronicles usually only record with a passing phrase or a name in a list of places captured.

St. George's day [23 April] drew near, when the grand feast was to be celebrated at the castle of Windsor. The King had made great preparations for it; and there were earls, barons, ladies, and damsels, most nobly entertained. The festivities and tilts lasted a fortnight. Many knights came to them from beyond sea, from Flanders, Hainault, and Brabant, but not one from France. During the holding of these feasts, the King received intelligence from different countries; particularly from Gascony. The lord de Lesparre, the lord de Caumont, and the lord de Mucident were sent there by the other barons and knights who at that time were dependent on the King of England, such as the lord d'Albret, the lord de Pommiers, the lord de Montferrat, the Lord of Duras, the lord de Curton, the lord de Grailley, and many others; and some were likewise sent by the cities of Bordeaux and Bayonne. These ambassadors were most courteously entertained and received by the King and his Council; to whom they explained the weakness of the country of Gascony, and that his good friends in that country and the loyal city of Bordeaux wanted aid: they therefore entreated, that he would send to there such a captain and force of men-at-arms, as he might think able to make headway against the French, who kept the field in opposition to all those who were sent to encounter them. The King soon afterward appointed his cousin the Earl of Derby leader of this expedition, and named the knights whom he had chosen to serve under his command: first, the Earl of Pembroke, the Earl of Oxford, the lord Stafford, Sir Walter Mauny, Sir Frank van Halle, Sir Henry Iam of Brabant, Sir Richard Fitzsimon, Sir Hugh Hastings, Sir Stephen Tombey, Sir

Richard Haydon, Sir John Norwich, Sir Richard Radcliffe, Sir Robert Oxendon, and several more. They were fully three hundred knights and esquires, six hundred men-at-arms, and two thousand archers. The King advised the Earl his cousin to take plenty of gold and silver with him, and to bestow it liberally among the knights and esquires, in order to acquire their good opinion and affection.

The King also, during the time of these festivals, sent Sir Thomas Dagworth into Brittany, to reinforce the Countess of Montfort, and assist her in preserving that country; for notwithstanding the truce, he had no doubt that King Philip would begin the war, on account of the message he had sent to him by Sir Hervé de Léon. He therefore dispatched to there one hundred men-at-arms, and two hundred archers, under the command of Sir Thomas. . . . Thus the King sent forth his people, and directed his treasurers to deliver out to the commanding officers a sufficiency of money for their own expenses, and to pay their fellow-soldiers; and each set out according to the orders he had received.

We will speak first of the Earl of Derby, as he had the greatest charge, which he conducted to Southampton, and embarking on board the fleet stationed there for him, sailed for Bayonne: it was a handsome city, and had always held out for the English. He arrived there, without incident, on the 6th day of June 1344, when he disembarked and landed all his stores: they were joyfully received by the inhabitants, and he remained there seven days, to refresh himself and his horses. The Earl of Derby and his army left Bayonne the eighth day after his arrival, and set out for Bordeaux, where a grand procession came out to receive him. The Earl was lodged in the abbey of St. Andrew, and his people within the city. When the Count de l'Isle was informed of the arrival of the English, he sent for the Count de Comminges, the Count de Périgord, the Count de Carmain, the Viscount of Villemur, the Count Duras, the Count of Valentinois, the Count of Mirande, the Lord of Mirade, the lord de la Barde, the Lord of Pincoraet, the Viscount of Châtillon, the Lord of Châteauneuf, the Lord of Lescun, the Abbot of St. Savin, and for all the other lords who were attached to the King of France. As soon as they were all assembled, he demanded their counsel on the arrival of the Earl of Derby. The lords, in reply, said they were sufficiently strong to defend the passage of the river Dordogne, at Bergerac, against the English. This answer mightily pleased the Count de l'Isle, who was at that time like a king in Gascony, and had been so since the commencement of the wars between the two Kings. He had taken the field, captured towns and castles, and waged war upon all who were of the English party. These lords sent immediately to assemble their dependents on all sides, and advanced to Bergerac, where they entered the suburbs, which are large, strong, and partly surrounded by the Dordogne. They had all their supplies brought to them there in safety.

Chapter CIII. The Earl of Derby Conquers Bergerac

When the Earl of Derby had remained at Bordeaux for about fifteen days, he was informed that the [French] barons and knights of Gascony were in Bergerac:

he therefore, one morning, marched that way with his army, and ordered his marshals, Sir Walter Mauny and Sir Frank van Halle, to push forward. The English marched that morning no more than three leagues, to a castle called Montcuq, which belonged to them, and was situated a short league from Bergerac. At this castle of Montcuq, they tarried that day and night. The day following, their scouts were sent as far as the barriers of Bergerac: and, on their return, they related to Sir Walter Mauny, that they had reconnoitered the position of the French, which did not appear to them anything very formidable. This day, the English dined early; and, during the repast, Sir Walter Mauny, addressing himself to the Earl of Derby, said, "My lord, if we were good knights, and well armed, we might, this evening, partake of the wines of these French lords who are in garrison in Bergerac." The Earl answered that it should not be his fault if they did not. When their companions heard this, they said, "Let us hasten to arm ourselves; for we will ride towards Bergerac." It was no sooner said than done: they were all armed, and mounted, in an instant. When the Earl of Derby perceived such willingness in his men, he was exceedingly joyful, and cried out, "In the name of God, and of St. George, let us march to our enemies." They then rode on, with banners displayed, during the greatest heat of the day, until they came to the barriers of Bergerac, which was not a place easily to be taken, for a part of the river Dordogne surrounded it. The French lords who were in the town, seeing the English coming to attack them, said they should be well received, and sallied forth in battle array: they had with them a multitude of foot soldiers, and country people badly armed. The English made their approaches in close order, so that they were plainly to be distinguished from the townsmen, and the archers began to shoot thickly. When the foot soldiers felt the points of the arrows, and saw the banners and pennons glittering in the air, which they had not been accustomed to see, they fell back upon their own men-at-arms: the archers continued to shoot with great quickness, doing much mischief to them. The lords of England then advanced, mounted on their excellent coursers, with lances in their rests, and, dashing into the midst of this infantry, drove them down at pleasure, and killed and wounded the French men-at-arms in abundance; for they could not in any way exert themselves, as these runaways had blocked up the road.

There was a severe engagement, and many were killed and unhorsed: for the English archers, being posted on each side of the road, shot so well together, that no one dared to venture upon it. Thus were those of Bergerac driven back again to the suburbs, but with so much loss, that the first bridge and bars were taken by storm, and the English entered with them. Upon the pavement were many knights and squires slain and wounded, and many prisoners made of those who came forward to defend the passage. The Lord of Mirepoix was slain under the banner of Sir Walter Mauny, who was the first to enter the suburbs. When the Count de l'Isle saw that the English had taken possession of the suburbs, and were striking down and killing his people without mercy, he and the other lords of Gascony made a handsome retreat towards the town, and passed the bridge with great difficulty. At this place the engagement was very severe, and lasted a considerable time: the noblemen of France and of England, named in the preceding chapters, combated most valiantly hand to hand: neither knight nor bachelor could there conceal himself. Sir Walter Mauny had advanced so far among his enemies, that he was in great danger. The English made prisoners of the Viscount of Bousquetin, the lords of Châtillon, of Châteauneuf and of Lescun. The French retreated into the fort, let down the portcullis, and, getting upon the battlements, began to throw stones and other things, to drive their enemies away. This assault and skirmish lasted until evening, when the English retreated, quite weary, into the suburbs, which they had won; where they found such quantities of provision and wine, that might, had there been need, have lasted them for four months most plentifully.

When the morrow dawned, the Earl of Derby had his trumpets sounded, and his forces drawn out in battle array, to approach the town, and make a mighty assault, which lasted until noon. They had little success; for they found that there were within it men-at-arms who defended themselves valiantly. At noon-tide, the English retreated, perceiving that they were only wasting their time. The lords then assembled in council, and determined to attack the town on the side next to the river; for it was there only fortified by palisades. The Earl of Derby sent therefore to the fleet at Bordeaux for vessels, which he ordered to come to him up the Dordogne: there were upwards of sixty barks and other vessels lying at Bordeaux that came to Bergerac. In the evening of the following day, the English made their arrangements, and at sun-rise, all those who were ordered to attack the town, and the fleet, were quite ready, under the command of the lord Stafford. There were many knights and squires who had requested to be on this expedition, in hopes of preferment, as well as a body of archers. They advanced in haste, and came to some large round piles placed before the palisades, which they flung down. The townsmen, seeing this, went to the Count de l'Isle, the lords, knights, and squires, who were present, and said to them, "Gentlemen, we pray you to take heed what you are about; for we run a great risk of being ruined. If the town be taken, we shall lose all we have, as well as our lives: it will therefore be much better that we surrender it to the Earl of Derby, before we suffer more damage." The Count replied, "We will go to that part where you say the danger is; for we will not consent to surrender it so easily." The Gascon knights and squires came, therefore, to defend the palisades; but the archers, who were in the barks, kept up so quick an attack with their arrows, that none dared to show themselves, unless they chose to run the risk of being killed or wounded. In the town, there were with the Gascons two or three hundred Genoese crossbowmen, whose armor shielded them from the arrows: they kept the archers well employed all the day, and many on each side were wounded. At last, the English who were in the vessels exerted themselves so much, that they broke down a large piece of the palisades; those of Bergerac then retreated, and requested time to consider, if they should not surrender the place. The remainder of that day and night was granted them, upon condition that they did not attempt to repair the breaches: and every one retired to his quarters. The [French] lords of Gascony held, that night, a long council; and, about midnight, having packed up all their baggage, they set out from Bergerac, and followed the road to La Réole, which is not far distant, whose gates were opened to them, and there they took up their quarters.

The English, the next morning, re-embarked on board their fleet, and came to the part where the palisades had been broken down: they found in that place great numbers of the townsmen, who entreated the knights, that they would beseech the Earl of Derby to have mercy on them and allow them their lives and fortunes, and from thenceforward they would yield obedience to the King of England. The Earl of Pembroke and the Earl of Oxford replied, that they would cheerfully comply with their request, and went to the Earl of Derby, who was not present, and related to him what the inhabitants of Bergerac had requested of them. The Earl of Derby answered, "He who begs for mercy should have mercy shown him: tell them to open their gates, and let us enter, and we will assure them of safety from us and from our people." The two lords returned, and reported what the Earl had said. Upon which the townsmen went to the market-place, where every one, men and women, being assembled, they rang the bells, threw open the gates, went out in procession to meet the Earl of Derby, and with all humility conducted him to the church, where they swore homage and fealty to him, acknowledging him as their lord, as the representative of the King of England, by virtue of a commission which he had with him.

Chapter CIV. The Earl of Derby Conquers Many Towns and Fortresses in Upper Gascony

The same day that the Count de l'Isle and the barons and knights of Gascony had retreated to La Réole, they held a council, and resolved to separate and withdraw into fortresses, to carry on the war from these garrisons, and to form a body of four or five hundred combatants, as a frontier guard, under the command of the Seneschal of Toulouse. The Count de Villemur was ordered to Auberoche; Sir Bertrand des Pres to Pellegrue; the lord Philip de Dyon to Montagrier; the Lord of Montbrandon to Mauduran; Sir Arnold de Dyon to Montgis; Robert de Malmore to Beaumont, in Lallois; Sir Charles de Poitiers to Penne in the Agenais. All these knights departed for their different garrisons; but the Count de l'Isle remained in La Réole, and had the fortress put in proper repair. When the Earl of Derby had taken possession of Bergerac, and stayed there for two days, he asked the Seneschal of Bordeaux what would be most advisable for him to undertake next, since he did not wish to remain idle. The Seneschal replied that he thought it would be best to go towards Périgord and upper Gascony. The Earl of Derby then gave out his orders to march to Périgord, and left Sir Jean de la Santé as captain of Bergerac. As the English advanced, they came to a castle called Langon, of which the Provost of Toulouse was governor: they halted there, not thinking it prudent to leave such a post in their rear, and the marshal's battalion immediately began the assault, which lasted all that day, but they gained nothing. Almost the whole army was employed against it the next day; and, with wood and faggots, they filled up the ditches, so that they could approach the walls. Sir Frank van Halle asked the besieged if they were willing to surrender, because they might delay until it was too late. Upon this, they requested a truce to consider it, which was granted to them. After some little time spent in counsel, they all set out for Monsac, which was under French control, but took nothing with them. The Earl of Derby appointed an esquire named Aymon Lyon as governor of the castle of Langon, and gave him thirty archers.

The Earl of Derby then rode on towards a town called Le Lac; but the townsmen came out to meet him, brought the keys of the town, and swore homage and fealty to him. The Earl passed on, and came to Mandarant, which he took by storm: after he had placed a garrison in the fortress, he came before the castle of Montgis, won it in the same manner, and sent the governor prisoner to Bordeaux. He afterwards advanced to Punach, which he took, and did the same to the town and castle of Lieux, where he stayed for three days, to refresh himself and his army. On the fourth day he marched to Fronsac, which he gained easily enough, and then the town of Pondaire. He next came to a town of considerable size, called Beaumont en Lallois, which was a dependency of the Count de l'Isle. The Earl was before it for three days, and many vigorous attacks were made, for it was well provided with artillery and with men-at-arms, who defended themselves as long as they were able. At last it was taken, with much slaughter on all those who were found inside. The Earl of Derby reinforced his troops there with fresh men-at-arms, and then advanced towards the principal town of the inheritance of the Count de l'Isle, which was under the command of the lord Philip de Dyon and the lord Arnold de Dyon. He invested it on all sides, and had his archers advance to the barriers, where they shot so well that none dared appear to defend them: the English, having taken the barriers, and everything even to the gate, retired in the evening. On the next morning, they renewed the attack in several different places at once, and gave those within so much to do, that they did not know which way to defend themselves. The inhabitants therefore requested two knights who were there to treat with the Earl of Derby for a peace, that their fortunes might be saved. They sent before them a herald, who obtained a short truce, to see if any agreement could be entered into. The Earl of Derby ordered his men to draw back, and came himself, accompanied by the lord Stafford and Sir Walter Mauny, to the bars, to confer with the inhabitants. The Earl at first would hear of nothing but unconditional surrender: at last it was settled, that the town should put itself under the dependency of the King of England, as Duke of Guienne, and that twelve of the principal citizens should be sent to Bordeaux, as hostages. The French knights and squires left the place with safe-conducts, and went to La Réole.

Chapter CV. The Earl of Oxford is Taken Prisoner in Gascony, but Set at Liberty by Exchange

After this conquest, the Earl of Derby left men-at-arms and archers there and went to Bonneval, and made a violent attack on it, in which many were killed and wounded. At last he took it, and showed mercy. After he had reinforced it with men-at-arms and another governor, he pushed forward, and, entering the country of Périgord, passed by Bourdeilles, but did not attack it, as he saw his efforts would have been wasted. He continued on until he came before Périgueux. The Count of Périgord, his brother the lord Roger de Périgord, the Lord of Duras, and fully six-score knights and esquires of that country were in the town. When the Earl of Derby came there, he considered in what manner he might most advantageously attack it, for he saw it was very strong. But, after having maturely weighed it, he thought it most prudent not to waste his time: he therefore retreated two leagues, and took up his quarters on the banks of a river, in order to attack the castle of Pellegrue.

Towards midnight, about two hundred lances, well mounted, sallied out of Périgueux: they rode so fast, that before daylight they came to the English camp, and falling upon it, killed and wounded many. They entered the tent of the Earl of Oxford, whom they found arming himself: he was immediately attacked and taken prisoner, as well as three knights of his household; otherwise he would have been slain. The Gascons, finding that they had awakened the whole army, retired, and made their way to Périgueux. It was time for them to do so: and fortunately they found the gates of the barriers open; for they were so closely pursued that they were thrown into confusion. But the Gascons, as soon as they could rally themselves, dismounted, and, sword in hand, fought with the English, and held their ground so well that they lost nothing.

The English returned to the Earl of Derby, who marched forward until he came before Pellegrue, where he remained for six days, and many an assault was made upon it. During the time he stayed there, the Earl of Oxford and his companions were exchanged for the Viscount of Bousquetin, the Viscount of Châtillon, the Lord of Lescun, and the Lord of Châteauneuf, and upon the condition that the lands of Périgord should remain in peace for three years – allowing, however, that any knight or esquire might take up arms without breaking the treaty; but nothing was to be burnt or pillaged in that country for that space of time. The English therefore departed from before Pellegrue, as it was part of Périgord, and rode towards Auberoche, where there is a handsome and strong castle, belonging to the Archbishop of Toulouse. The English took up their quarters round about it, as if they meant to remain there for a length of time, and sent word to those within, that if they did not surrender speedily, when the town was taken, they would all be put to the sword without mercy. The inhabitants of the town and castle were much alarmed; and, seeing no probability of any succor coming to them, they put themselves under the obedience of the Earl of Derby, on condition of their lives and fortunes being spared, and acknowledged him as their lord, for the King of England.

The Earl then made a handsome retreat towards Bordeaux, having left in Auberoche a sufficient garrison, under the command of Sir Frank van Halle, Sir Alain de Finefroide, and Sir John Lendal. On his way he came to Libourne, a fair and large town, twelve leagues from Bordeaux. He laid siege to it, and told those about him that he would not quit it before he had got possession of it. The inhabitants consulted together, and considering well the good and evil of being assaulted and vexed, they surrendered themselves to the Earl of Derby, and did homage to him during the three days he remained there. The Earl of Derby sent the Earl of Pembroke to Bergerac, and left the lord Stafford, Sir Steven de Courcy, and the lord Alexander de Haulfiel, with their men in Libourne. He himself, accompanied by the Earl of Oxford and Sir Walter Mauny, took the road for Bordeaux, where they arrived.

Chapter CVI. The Count de l'Isle, Lieutenant of the King of France in Gascony, Lays Siege to the Castle of Auberoche

The Earl was joyfully received on his return to Bordeaux: the clergy and inhabitants of the town came out to meet him, in a grand procession. They allowed him to take provisions, and whatever else he desired, according to his will and pleasure; and he and his army stayed in the town, entertaining themselves along with the citizens and their wives.

We will now turn to the Count de l'Isle, whom we left in La Réole. As soon as he was informed that the Earl of Derby had returned to Bordeaux, and had taken up his residence there, he did not think it probable that he would undertake any more expeditions this season. He therefore sent letters to the Counts of Périgord, of Carmain, of Comminges, of Bruniguel, and to all the barons of Gascony that were on the French side, to ask them to collect as many people as they could and come with them properly armed, by an appointed date, to meet him at Auberoche, as he intended to besiege it. They all obeyed his summons; for he was as a king in those parts of Gascony. The knights who were in Auberoche were not aware of this, until they found themselves so closely besieged on all sides that no one could go out of the garrison without being seen. The French brought from Toulouse four large machines, which cast stones into the fortress day and night; and they made no other assault. In six days' time they had demolished all the roofs of the towers, and none within the castle dared to venture out of the vaulted rooms on the ground floor. It was the intention of the army to kill all those within the castle, if they would not surrender themselves unconditionally.

News was brought to the Earl of Derby that Auberoche was besieged; but he did not realize his friends were so hard pressed. When Sir Frank van Halle, Sir Alain de Finefroide, and Sir John Lendal, who were thus besieged, saw how desperate their situation was, they asked their servants if there were not one among them who would, for a reward, undertake to deliver the letters they had written to the Earl of Derby at Bordeaux. One from among them stepped forward, and said he would cheerfully undertake the commission, not through lust of gain, but from his desire to deliver them from the peril they were in. The following night the servant took the letters, sealed with their seals, and sewed them up in his clothes. He was let down into the ditches: when he was at the bottom, he climbed up the opposite side, and made his way through the army; for he could not avoid passing through it. He was met by the first guard, but was not stopped, for he knew the Gascon language well, and named one of the lords of the army, as if he belonged to him; so he was allowed to pass on. But he was afterwards arrested, and detained under the tents of some other lords, who brought him to the main watch. He was interrogated and searched, and the letters were found on him. He was guarded until morning, when the principals of the army assembled in the tent of the Count de l'Isle, where the letters were read. They were overjoyed to find that the garrison were in such dire straits and that they could not hold out much longer; and, seizing the servant, they hung the letters around his neck, thrust him into one of the machines, and flung him into Auberoche. The valet fell quite dead amidst the other valets of the castle, who were greatly terrified by it.

About this time, the Count of Périgord, his uncle Sir Charles de Poitiers, the Count of Carmain, and the Lord of Duras, mounting their horses, rode as near to the walls of the castle as they could, and, calling out in derision to those within, said, "Gentlemen, inquire of your messenger where he found the Earl of Derby, and whether he is prepared to assist you, since your man was so eager to quit your fortress, and has returned equally quickly." Sir Frank van Halle replied, "By my faith, gentlemen, if we be so closely confined in this place, we will sally forth whenever it shall please God and the Earl of Derby. I wish to Heaven that he were acquainted with our situation; for if he were, the proudest of you all would be afraid of standing his ground; and, if you will send any one to give him this information, one of us will surrender himself to you, to be ransomed as becomes a gentleman." The French answered, "Nay, nay, matters will not turn out so: the Earl of Derby will be made aware of it at the proper time, but not until our engines have battered your walls level with the ground, and you shall have surrendered yourselves to save your lives." "That, for certain, will never happen," said Sir Frank van Halle, "for we will not surrender ourselves, even if it means we must all die upon the walls." The French lords then rode on, and returned to their army. The three English knights remained in Auberoche, quite confounded by the force of these engines, which flung such quantities of stones, that in truth it seemed as if the thunder from heaven were battering the walls of the castle.

Chapter CVII. The Earl of Derby Makes the Count de l'Isle and Nine More Counts and Viscounts Prisoners, before Auberoche

All these speeches, the treatment of the messenger, the contents of the letters, and the perilous situation of Auberoche were made known to the Earl of Derby by means of a spy he had in the French army. The Earl therefore sent orders to the Earl of Pembroke in Bergerac, to meet him at an appointed place and hour; and also the lord Stafford and Sir Stephen Tombey, who were at Libourne. Then the Earl of Derby, accompanied by Sir Walter Mauny and the forces he had with him, took the road towards Auberoche as secretly as possible; for he had guides who were acquainted with the by-roads. They came to Libourne, where they waited a whole day for the Earl of Pembroke; but, hearing not tidings of him and being impatient to rescue their friends who were in such difficult circumstances, the Earl of Derby, the Earl of Oxford, Sir Walter Mauny, Sir Richard Hastings, Sir Steven Tombey, the lord Ferrers, and other knights set out from Libourne: riding all night, they came on the morrow within two leagues of Auberoche. They entered a wood, and, alighting from their horses, they tied them to the trees, and allowed them to pasture, in expectation of the arrival of the Earl of Pembroke: they waited all that morning, and until noon, in vain, not knowing what to do; for they were only three hundred lances and six hundred archers, and the French were from ten to twelve thousand men. They thought it would be cowardice to allow their friends to be lost, when they were so near them. At last Sir Walter Mauny said, "Gentlemen, let us who are now here mount our horses, skirt this wood, and advance until we come to their camp: when we shall be close to it, we will stick spurs into our horses, and, with loud shouts, fall upon them. It will be about their hour for supper; and we shall se them so much cast into confusion, that they will never be able to rally again." The knights present replied, that they would all do as he had proposed. Each went to his horse, re-girthed him, and tightened his armor: they ordered their pages, servants and baggage to remain where they were.

They advanced in silence by the side of the wood until they came to the other end, where the French army was encamped in a wide valley, near a small river: they then displayed their banners and pennons, and, sticking spurs into their horses, dashed into the midst of the French and Gascon forces, who were quite confounded and unprepared for this attack, as they were busy with their suppers, many having sat down to eat. The English were well prepared to act, and crying "Derby, Derby forever!" they cut down tents and pavilions, and slew and wounded all that came in their way. The French were so surprised that they did not know which way to turn; and when they got into the plain, if there were any large body of them, the archers and crossbowmen made such good use of their weapons, that they were slain or dispersed. The Count de l'Isle was captured, in his tent, badly wounded; the Count of Périgord in his pavilion, and also Sir Charles, his uncle; the Lord of Duras was killed, and so was Sir Aymery de Poitiers, but his brother, the Count of Valentinois, was made prisoner. Everyone took to his heels as fast as he could; but the Count of Comminges, the Counts of Carmain, Villemur and Bruniquel, the lords de la Barde and de la Taride, with others, who were quartered on the other side of the castle, displayed their banners, and, having drawn up their men, marched for the plain. The English, however, who had already defeated the largest body of the army, fell on them most vigorously. In this engagement, many gallant deeds of arms were per-formed, many captures made, and many rescues accomplished. As soon as Sir Frank van Halle and Sir John Lendal, who were in Auberoche, heard the noise, and perceived the banners and pennons of their friends, they hastened to arm themselves, and all those that were with them; when, mounting their horses, they sallied out of the fortress, made for the plain, and dashed into the thickest of the combat, to the great encouragement of the English.

Why should I make a long story of it? All those who were of the Count de l'Isle's party were defeated, and almost all taken prisoners, or slain. Scarcely any would have escaped, if night had not closed so soon. Nine counts and viscounts were made prisoners, and so many barons, knights and esquires, that there was not a man-at-arms among the English that did not have two or three for his share. This battle before Auberoche was fought on the eve of St. Laurence's day [10 August], in the year 1344.[19] The English treated their prisoners like friends: they released many upon their promises to surrender themselves by a certain day at Bordeaux or Bergerac. The English retired into Auberoche; and the Earl of Derby entertained at supper the greater part of the prisoners, counts, viscounts, barons, and knights. They have thanks and praises to God, for having enabled them to overcome upwards of ten thousand men, when they themselves were not more than one thousand, including every one, and to rescue the town and castle of Auberoche, in which were their friends, who would necessarily have been captured in two days' time.

70. More on Derby in Guienne. [Source: *Chronique Normande*, 67–9]

The Chronique Normande du XIVe siècle *was probably composed (or compiled) by a Norman man-at-arms in the 1370s, though this is subject to debate. In any case, the chronicle includes a noteworthy amount of detail on military operations. The author may well have served in Gascony in 1345 or 1346.*

Then the Earl of Derby assembled his Englishmen and his Gascons and went to lay siege to Ste.-Foy. But Raymond Foucaut had gone to [seek help from] the King of France, and the castellan defended the place, and many times sallied out and inflicted substantial damage on the English. And the Lord of Château-Bayard came there with fully a hundred men-at-arms and two hundred infantrymen and, passing through the midst of the English army very valiantly and skillfully, and killing numbers of them along the way, he and his men entered into Ste.-Foy. And when the Earl of Derby learned that the Lord of Château-Bayard had thus gotten inside, he broke off the siege and went straight to Sauveterre, which he expected to conquer with little effort, since the Lord of Château-Bayard, its captain, and all his men were no longer inside it. But just as the Earl of Derby encamped before Sauveterre, the Lord of Château-Bayard, who had followed him very skillfully, passed through the end of his army, killed some Englishmen, and entered into the town. And immediately the Earl of Derby departed and went to beisege Montpezat. And when the townspeople saw the English, they killed the men of the King of France who were inside the town, then surrendered. The Earl received them, then went to the castles of Loury and Castelmoron and set up an ambush, and sent a large amount of booty to pass within the view of castle and of the town. Those of the town sallied out in order

---

19 Actually 1345.

to seize the plunder, but the Englishmen who were set in ambush surprised them, so that most of them were killed or captured, and the town and the castle were taken.

71. Derby at La Réole and Clairac. [Source: *St. Omer Chronicle*, fos. 255–6]

The chronicle contained in MS. 693 of the Bibliothèque Nationale in Paris, fos. 248 ff., which covers the years from 1342 to 1347, has never been published, nor even (so far as I am aware) been used by historians. The author was somehow connected to the French garrison of St. Omer, and may even have been a man-at-arms himself, or perhaps a herald. He was well informed concerning the war in Aquitaine and Brittany as well as the north-east of France.

Then a castle named Castelsagrat was surrendered to him [Derby]. From there he returned to Bordeaux with all his profit and his prisoners, but he did not rest there long at all, but gathered his host anew and went to the castle of La Réole and assailed it; but those within defended themselves very vigorously. Then he sent his miners to the wall, and in a short time they had undermined it, so that they brought down a large piece of it. And when those within saw that they had been uncovered, they decided to surrender, and sent to the Earl of Derby and negotiated, so that those within evacuated the place with their lives and their goods. The English rebuilt the wall and emplaced a garrison of good men. And from there he led his army before the castle of Clairac, which was guarded for the King of France by a prior. The Earl of Derby sent to inform the garrison of the castle that they should surrender themselves to him, or, from that day on, he would never receive them to mercy.

When the castellan heard this demand and saw the army was so large, he took counsel with his companions, and asked the Earl of Derby for a truce of eight days, after which he would surrender at his will. The Earl of Derby, who rejoiced at this promise, ordered his army to draw back to a suitable place, rather far from the castle. There they took their ease, waiting out the term of eight days; but those of the castle, who were not caught napping over this matter, collected a great number of laborers, rebuilt their gates and barbicans very well, and prepared their defense so well that they needed to fear no one. And when the eight days were past, the Earl of Derby and his entire army came before the castle in order to get what had been promised to him, but when those of the castle saw him approach, they launched a profusion of darts and quarrels and told him that he should go conquer other castles, for he had failed at this one. Then the Earl of Derby saw that he had been deceived, and moved towards Aiguillon, which belonged to the King of England. He had the town enclosed with a good palisade and deep ditches, then established a strong garrison, including the baron Stafford, the baron de Bustaree, Sir Bérard d'Albret, Sir Alexander de Caumont, Sir Walter Mauny and many other valiant men.

72. The Administration of an Invasion. [Source: Wrottesley, *Crecy and Calais*, passim]

While Henry of Lancaster (whose primary title changed from Earl of Derby to Earl of Lancaster on the death of his father in the autumn of 1345) was conducting himself so well in Aquitaine, King Edward's own expedition for 1345 was first held up by administrative delays, then side-tracked by the need for the King to lead a small army to Flanders to shore up his position there as Jacques van Artevelde was thrown out of power in the county. After returning from that operation in late July, Edward began preparations for another expedition to be sent in the fall of 1345. The following documents, taken from George Wrottesley's calendar of the French Roll entries relating to the expedition of 1346–47, illustrate the elements which went into the readying of King Edward's overseas expeditions, and also the delays and difficulties typical of them.

A writ to the Mayor, Bailiffs, and good people of Newcastle-upon-Tyne, to cause all captains of vessels of the said town to equip their ships of thirty tons burden and upwards, and to cause them to be sent to Portsmouth by [6 October,] the octaves of Michaelmas, and to aid Reynald de Donyngton, Lieutenant of Robert, Earl of Suffolk, Admiral northwards, and Richard de Cortenhale, the King's Sergeant-at-Arms, upon that duty; all vessels of the realm of thirty tons burden and upwards having been ordered to assemble there for the salvation and defense of the realm, and to succor the Earls of Derby and Northampton, who were in the King's service in Gascony and Brittany. Dated at Westminster, 26th August.

A writ to Edward, Prince of Wales, to cause trusty men to choose 100 archers of the best and ablest men in the county of Chester, and to bring them to Portsmouth. Dated 26th August.

A writ to Edward, Prince of Wales, commanding him to array 2,000 men of North Wales and 2,000 of South Wales, all of whom were to be Welshmen, one-half being spearmen and the other archers. Robert ap Griffith, Yevan ap Griffith ap Howel were to select them in the County of Carnarvon; David ap Rees ap Tudur, Howel ap Levelyn ap Griffith, in Anglesea; Eignon ap Griffith, Yevan ap Lewelyn ap Baron, in Merioneth in North Wales; and Res ap Griffith, Owen ap Oweyn, Thlewelin Eignon Vaghan, Res Dungan, in South Wales, and to lead them to Portsmouth. Dated 28th August.

A writ to the Mayor and Sheriffs of London commanding them to inform themselves, by inquisitions and other ways, of all able-bodied men-at-arms in the City aforesaid, between the ages of sixteen and sixty, that they, who were not of the retinue of the lords who were about to set out with the King, be with the King at Portsmouth with horses and arms on [20 October,] three weeks from Michaelmas next, ready to embark at the King's wages for the defense of the realm and Holy Church, and to make an end of the war in Gascony and Brittany. Witness the King, at Westminster, 28th August. [Like writs to 25 other ports.]

A writ to Richard, Earl of Arundel, Admiral of the Fleet from the mouth of the Thames westwards, ordering him to arrest all ships of thirty tons and upwards which he can find within in the ports and maritime places of his office of Admiral, and to send them to Portsmouth that they might be there, or within the water of Wight, by [6, October] the octaves of Michaelmas next. Dated at Westminster, 28th August.

Like writs were directed to the following on the same date –

To Robert de Ufford, Earl of Suffolk, Admiral of the Fleet from the mouth of the Thames northwards.

Reginald de Donyngton, Lieutenant of the Admiral of the said Fleet from the Port of Lynn to Berwick-upon-Tweed. To Philip de Whitton, Lieutenant of the Admiral of the Fleet from the mouth of the Thames westwards. To Robert Flambard, to arrest ships mooring in the Port of London.

A writ to the Mayor and Sheriffs of London to array 320 archers, and cause them to be brought to Portsmouth. Dated 28th August.

A writ to Henry de Wylyngton, John de Beaumont, and the Sheriff of Devon to array sixty archers in the said county; to provide them with bows, arrows, and other arms, and to cause them to be brought to Portsmouth by proper men, so that they might be there at [20 October] three weeks from Michaelmas. Dated 28th August. [Similar writs for the array of 120 archers in Somerset, 100 in Dorset, 200 in Wiltshire, 200 in Gloucestershire, 160 in Herefordshire, 160 in Oxfordshire and 120 in Berkshire, 60 in Bedfordshire, 100 in Surrey and 200 in Sussex, 200 in Shropshire, 160 in Warwickshire, 80 in Worcestershire, 80 in Leicestershire, 200 in the county of Norfolk, 100 in Suffolk, 60 in the county of Southampton, 280 in Kent, 200 in Essex, 100 in Hertfordshire, 100 in the county of Cambridge, 200 in Northamptonshire, 40 in Rutland, 100 in the county of Buckingham, 160 in Staffordshire, 60 in the county of Huntingdon, 60 in Middlesex, and 200 in the county of Lincoln].

A writ to all sheriffs, mayors, bailiffs, officers, and other faithful men in Kent, Surrey, and Sussex to aid Richard de St. Albans, the King's carpenter, in providing 200 cart wheels and 100 axles for carts. Dated at Westminster, 12th September.

A writ to aid William de Winchelsea in selecting forty competent carpenters to set out on the next overseas expedition. Dated Westminster, 20th September.

A writ to John de Clyvedon, Richard de Acton, and the Sheriff of Somerset to be ready to start with the men-at-arms between the ages of sixteen and sixty which they were assigned to array in the said county, on the morrow after they shall be warned, the King not wishing them to stay at Portsmouth due to lack of transport. Dated at Westminster, 29th September.

In the same manner the arrayers of the men-at-arms and archers in the other counties previously named were commanded on the same date.

A writ to Robert de Ufford, Earl of Suffolk, Admiral of the Fleet from the mouth of the Thames northwards, commanding him, that after taking security from the captains and masters of all the ships of England of thirty tons burden and upwards to have their ships at Portsmouth on [16 February 1346,] the Quindene of the Purification next at the latest, he should allow them to do as they like in the meantime. Dated at Westminster, 22nd October. [Like writs to the others assigned to arrest ships.]

A writ to John de Clyvedon, Richard de Acton, and the Sheriff of Somerset to array the men-at-arms between sixteen and sixty years and 160 archers of the county of Somerset, so that they be ready at Portsmouth on the 1st of March [1346] at the latest, as the King has appointed that day for his passage. Dated at Westminster, 12th November [1345].

A writ to the Sheriff of Lancaster to proclaim that all who have charters of pardon for felonies, homicides, murders and trespasses should prepare themselves, and hasten to Portsmouth so that they might be there on the 1st of March at the latest. Dated at Woodstock, 3rd January [1346].

A writ to John de Cylvedon, Richard de Acton, and the Sheriff of Somerset ordering them to array all the able-bodied men-at-arms between the ages of sixteen and sixty and 160 bowmen at Portsmouth on the Sunday in Mid Lent next [26 March] instead of the 1st of March, the King having postponed his passage till that date. Dated at Reading, 20th January.

Writ to the Mayor, Bailiffs, good men, and commonalty of Norwich to array 120 armed men in the city without delay, to provide them with suitable arms, and to cause them to be brought to Portsmouth so that they might be there on the Sunday in Mid Lent at the latest. Witness the King at Westminster, 10th February.

Like writs were directed to the Mayors, Bailiffs, good men, and commonalties of the following cities and towns, the same date, for the following number of armed men:

St. Edmund's	30	Lynn	50	Ipswich	15
Sudbury	5	Lincoln	40	Staunford	12
Grantham	10	Boston	10	Barton	10
Spaldyng	6	Cambridge	20	Ely	15

London: 100 men-at-arms, 500 armed men.

[And 128 other places, with contingents ranging from 2 (e.g. Hungerford) to 60 (Bristol), for a grand total of 1,837 men.]

Mandate to the Arrayers of men-at-arms, hobelars, and archers in the county of Leicester, for the passage abroad, not to compel Roger La Zouche, William Moton, and John Waleys, knights, John Maillore, William de Bredon, John de Lecure, and John de Herewyk to set out with the King nor to provide men-at-arms, hobelars, or archers, because they are of the retinue of the Archbishop of Canterbury, for the defense of England towards the Marches of Scotland. Witness the King at Westminster, 17th February.

Writ to the Sheriff of Kent postponing the array of the men-at-arms of the said county at Portsmouth from the Sunday in Mid Lent till [30 April,] the Quindene of Easter next, the expedition having been postponed on account of the storms. Witness the King at Westminster, 5th March.

Mandate to Robert de Ufford, Admiral of the Fleet northwards, to arrest all ships of twenty tons burden and upwards in his Admiralty, and to send them to Portsmouth so that they might be there on Palm Sunday [9 April]. Dated 8th March.

Writ to the Bailiffs and good men of Rameseye remitting to them four of the six armed men [formerly] ordered to be at Portsmouth on the Sunday in Mid Lent, and postponing the embarkation till the Quindene of Easter. Witness the King at Westminster, 9th March.

Writ to Richard, Earl of Arundel, Admiral of the Fleet westwards, or his Lieutenant, to arrest all ships, barges, and cutters of his Admiralty, great and small, which could be of use for carrying men and victuals beyond the sea, even if they are only of ten or twelve tons burden, boats of fishermen alone excepted, and to cause them to be brought to Portsmouth, before or on Palm Sunday at the latest. Witness the King, at Westminster, 18th March. [Similar writs to others commissioned to arrest ships.]

Writs authorizing all the Supervisors of Array to receive fines from men-at-arms, hobelars, and archers who wish to make fines for their passage and with the money to hire others. Dated 31st March.

Writ to all Sheriffs, etc., to aid Guy de Brian in choosing and taking forty miners in the Forest of Dene, four of whom should be master miners, who were to be brought to Portsmouth by the Sheriff of Gloucester for the next passage. Dated at Westminster, 1st April.

73. An Indenture of War. [Source: Wrottesley, *Crecy and Calais*, 192]

In all his campaigns, Edward III formed the core of his army around the knights and esquires of his own household and the retinues of the magnates and banner-ets who accompanied him, supplemented by archers and other troops arrayed from the towns and counties of England and Wales. The retinues of the lords, like the King's own household, were usually made up of a mix of men-at-arms and mounted archers in roughly equal numbers.

Heads of retinue operating independently of the King – e.g. as captain of a garrison in Scotland, or King's Lieutenant in Gascony or Brittany – often secured contracts or "letters of indenture" specifying their term of service, rate of pay and benefits, etc. The King rarely if ever provided such indentures for those serving personally with him, but nonetheless many soldiers in the royal host would be operating under letters of indenture, for it was often the case that the heads of retinues agreed on letters of indenture with those serving under them, at least down to the level of bannerets. The following is a typical example.

This indenture, made between the noble men Sir Ralph, Baron Stafford, on the one hand, and Sir Hugh fitz Simon on the other hand, bears witness that the aforesaid Sir Hugh is to remain as a banneret with the aforesaid Sir Ralph, along with four knights and eight esquires, for one year following the date of this document, to go to war with the said Sir Ralph wherever he wishes, receiving from the said Sir Ralph the customary wages, or else direct support at court, at the choice of Sir Ralph, which is to say for himself 4s., for each knight 2s., and for each esquire 12d. per day, and for his fee for the entire year, 100 marks. And the aforesaid Sir Ralph promises that he will pay to the aforesaid Sir Hugh, before his departure across the sea, half of his fee, which is to say 50 marks, and his wages, as specified above, for a quarter of a year in advance. And in case the said Sir Ralph wishes that he shall have direct support at court, he, his knights, and his esquires and their chamberlains, as is specified above, shall get hay and oats and stabling for forty-five horses, and eight baggage horses, and wages for their grooms. And Sir Ralph shall provide a mount for Sir Hugh, for his own person.

And in addition to the aforesaid, Sir Ralph promises that the great horses of the said Sir Hugh shall be appraised in the same fashion as his own great horses are by the King and his Council. And that the said Sir Ralph shall be bound to restore to the said Sir Hugh the loss of his said horses, thus appraised, if they should be lost in the service of the said Sir Ralph. And concerning the prisoners which may be taken by the aforesaid Hugh, or by his men, the aforesaid Sir Ralph shall have half the profits of their ransom, etc. In testimony whereof, etc. Written at London, the 16th of March, the year 21 Edward III [1347].

In total, eighty-eight men were listed in the records of the King's Wardrobe (the administrative department of the royal household which handled war-wages) as heads of retinues during 1346–7. The largest retinue was that of Henry of Lancaster, comprising 2 earls [himself and John of Kent, a minor], 11 bannerets, 193 knights, 512 esquires, 46 hobelars, and 612 mounted archers; the smallest was Sir Roger Lestraunge, who served as a retinue of one. Stafford's retinue, including himself and Sir Hugh, comprised 3 bannerets, 20 knights, 92 esquires, and 90 mounted archers, at 4s., 2s., 12d., and 6d. per day, respectively, the standard rates.

74. The Invasion of Normandy: A French Perspective. [Source: *Grandes Chroniques*, 9:270–4]

Lancaster's rapid conquests in the south-west made a major French effort there imperative. Not knowing where Edward III's own army would land in 1346, Philip could not concentrate all his forces in any single place, but he did dispatch a very substantial army to attempt to restore the situation on the Gascon frontier. Jean, Duke of Normandy, Philip's eldest son, led this army in a siege of Aiguillon which lasted throughout the summer of 1346.

According to a variety of sources, Edward III at first planned to lead his invasion force to Aquitaine, where he could aid Earl Henry to resist the powerful Valois forces arrayed against him and raise the siege of Aiguillon. Unfavorable winds, however, prevented the fleet from sailing south until mid-July. Then, con-

trary to the expectations of most, the English ships sailed not for Gascony but across the Channel to the small port of St.-Vaast-la-Hougue in the Cotentin peninsula of Normandy. Such may or may not have been King Edward's plan all along.

How the King of England came through Normandy and took Caen, and came through Lisieux, through Torigny to Vernon and to Poissy; and how the King of France followed him every day on the other bank of the Seine, and came to lodge at St.-Germain-des-Prés; and how the English passed the bridge of Poissy.

In this year, the King of France proposed to prepare a great armada of ships to cross over to England. At great expense, he sent to Geneva to seek these ships, but those who went to try to get them acted with little diligence, and were very late to arrive. In particular, one great ship which the King was having built at Harfleur in Normandy, said to be the fairest ship ever armed or launched, remained where it was until the King of England had landed at St.-Vaast-la-Hougue in Normandy with a very great force of men and a great multitude of ships, estimated at a good 1,200 large ships, aside from the small ships and other vessels. That was Wednesday July twelfth, and from then on the King of England called himself King of France and of England.

At the instigation of Godfrey d'Harcourt, who led and guided him, he began to burn and lay waste the country. First he came to the town of Neuilly, to which he could do no harm because of the strength of the castle; so he left there and came to Montebourg, where he halted for a time. Meanwhile, Godfrey d'Harcourt did all the damage that he could to the land of Cotentin. Next, the King of England came to the town of Carentan and captured the town and the castle; and he had all the goods which he seized there sent to England. He entrusted the guard of the castle to Sir Nicholas de Groussi and Sir Roland de Verdun.

When the King of England had left Carentan, some Normans, with lord Philippe le Despensier, gathered together and recovered the town and castle by force of arms, and captured and sent to Paris the two knights named above. In the interim, the King of England came to St.-Lô in Cotentin, where he caused to be solemnly buried the heads of three knights who, for their demerits, had been put to death at Paris. He captured and pillaged the town, which was very full of goods and supplies. From there he passed through the town of Torigni, burning and laying waste the country. It was commonly said that he sent to the bourgeois of Caen by his messengers and his letters, saying that if they would leave the King of France, and submit to the King of England, he would protect them faithfully, and give them many great liberties, and at the end the letters threatened them that if they did not do as he had instructed, they could be quite certain that he would assault them very soon. But the people of Caen, united in will and courage, defied him, saying that they would not obey the King of England. And when the King heard the answer of the bourgeois of Caen, he summoned them to give battle on the following Thursday; and this he did treacherously, because already in the morning of the day before, which was Wednesday the twentieth of August, he arrived before Caen. The captains established by the King were there: Lord William, Bishop of Bayeux and also his brother, Sir Robert Bertrand; the Lord of Tournebu; the Count of Eu and Guînes, at that time Constable of France; and lord Jean de Melun, then the Chamberlain de Tancarville.

When the English came before Caen, they assailed the town in four places, and shot arrows from their bows as dense as hail. And the people defended themselves as best they could, especially in the fields, above the butcher's shop, and also the bridge as well, because there the danger was the greatest. And it is said that the women, to help, carried the doors and windows of the houses to their husbands; and wine too, so that they would be stronger for the fight. Anyway, because the archers had a great quantity of arrows, the people had to retreat into the town; and so the English entered the town and fought from morning to evening. Then the Constable of France and the Chamberlain de Tancarville issued out of the castle and the strong part of the town, I don't know why, and immediately they were captured by the English and sent to England. But when the Bishop of Bayeux, the Lord of Tournebu, the Bailli of Rouen and many others with them saw that they had sallied out for nothing, and that it would be more harmful than profitable for them to make a sally, they retreated into the castle like wise men and held themselves behind the crenellations. Meanwhile, the English searched through the town very diligently and pillaged everything, and the King of England immediately sent the goods which they had plundered from Caen and the other towns to England in his ships. As he was leaving he burned a great portion of the town; but to the stronghold of the town he did no harm, nor did he halt there, for he did not want to lose any of his people. So he left there right away and advanced to Lisieux. And always Godfrey d'Harcourt, who burned and devastated the countryside, went ahead.

75. Letter of Edward III from Caen. [Source: Public Record Office, London, C81/314/17803, and Kenneth Fowler, "News from the Front: Letters and Despatches of the Fourteenth Century," in *Guerre et société en France, en Angleterre et en Bourgogne. XIVe–XVe Siècle*, ed. Philippe Contamine et al. (Lille: Centre d'histoire de la region du nord et de l'Europe du nord-ouest, 1991), 83–4]

At least eight variations of bulletins sent from the English army back to England during the Crécy campaign survive. Seven of them can be found in Richard Barber's Life and Campaigns of the Black Prince, *along with two excellent chronicle narratives from the English perspective. One last letter, recently discovered at the Public Record Office in London by Kenneth Fowler, is translated below. This letter is arguably the most important of the eight, because of the administrative instructions at the end. The narrative and the statement of intention in the letter, which were certainly intended for public consumption, could have been slanted for propaganda reasons, but it is safe to assume that Edward really meant for his orders to have been carried out as stated.*

Edward, by the grace of God King of England and of France and Lord of Ireland, to our dear and loyal Chancellor, Treasurer, and the others of our Council staying in London, greetings. To the honor of God and Our Lady Holy Mary, and to the comfort of you and of all our other loyal liegemen of England, we make known to you the grace and success of our affairs which God has granted to us in the time since our arrival at la Hougue near Barfleur (concerning the manner of our arrival at which place we informed you earlier). First, we moved out from la Hougue with our army on the Tuesday before the feast of St. Margaret and took the castle of Valognes, and then on our way we had the bridge over the Douve, which had been broken by our enemies, repaired, and crossed it and captured the castle and town of Carentan. And from there we made our way directly to St.-Lô. And we found the bridge of Pont-Hébert near that town had been broken in order to block our passage, [but] we immediately had it repaired, and on the next day captured the town. And we headed directly for Caen, without a single day of rest from the hour when we departed from la Hougue up to our arrival there. And as soon as we made camp there, our men began to assault the town, which was defended by a large number of men-at-arms, around 1,600, and the armed fighting men of the commons to the number of 30,000; and they defended themselves very well and skillfully, so that the mêlée was very fierce and lasted a long time. But, thanks be to God, the town was in the end taken by force without loss of our men. And there were taken prisoner there the Count of Eu, Constable of France; the Chamberlain de Tancarville, who was on that day proclaimed Marshal of France, and around 140 bannerets and knights, and a great number of esquires and rich bourgeois. And full many nobles, knights, and gentlemen were killed, and a great number of the common people. And our fleet, which has stayed with us, has burned and destroyed all the sea-coast from Barfleur up to the dyke at Colleville near Caen, and also they have burned the town of Cherbourg and the ships in the harbor, and a hundred or more of the great ships and other vessels of the enemy have been burnt, either by us or by our people. So we ask that you thank God devoutly for the success which he has given us up to now, and pray assiduously that he will give us a good continuance; and that you write under our great seal to our prelates and to the clergy of our realm that they should do so as well; and that you should make this matter known to our city of London and to our people in order to reassure them; for we have now, by the assent of all our people (who have shown themselves to be of good, loyal, and united will), taken the decision to hasten towards our adversary, wherever he may be from day to day, as well as we can; and we firmly trust in God that he will give us a good and honorable outcome to our emprise.

Also, we command you that you make every possible effort, in whatever way you can, to quickly raise a loan of money for our use, for although many of our people have been comforted by the profit they have made, we ourselves have gained nothing, but the whole burden rests on us, and our people press us much for their wages. And we also command that you have purveyed as many bows, arrows, and bowstrings as you can. And also we wish that you should arrange among yourselves that our ships which are over here, and which are now assigned to go to the river Seine . . .[20] after their return to England should be sent towards Le Crotoy, and with them all the money that you can raise in the mean time, [and with] as many men-at-arms and archers as possible, in order to restrain our enemies around there. And you will hear more full news of us from the mouth of our dear and loyal William, Earl of Huntingdon, whom we have caused to return to England because of a very severe and dangerous illness which he has contracted, even though his return was much against his will. We wish you to give faith and credence to him concerning what he will say to you from us, and to consult with him concerning the matters which touch upon us in our absence, for we have great trust in his knowledge and loyalty. Given under our privy seal at Caen, the 29th day of July, in the twentieth year of our reign in England and the seventh [of our reign] in France. Also, we command you that you immediately send on our letters, addressed to the Marquis of Juliers, to the Lord of Fauquemont, and to the good people of the three cities of Flanders and to our men who are in those parts, which we are sending to you by [the bearer of this letter].[21] And also send forward our letters addressed to the Bishop [sic] of York and to the other lords of the north.

76. From Lisieux to Paris. [Source: *Grandes Chroniques*, 274–82]

Next [after leaving Lisieux] they came to Falaise, but there they met vigorous resistance, so they turned towards Rouen. And when they heard that the King of France was assembling his army there, they went to Pont-de-l'Arche. Anyway, the King of France got there before them. And when he had entered the town, he sent to the King of England, saying that if he wanted to do battle with him, that he should set a day at his pleasure: he responded that he would fight with the King of France before Paris.

When the King of France heard this, he returned to Paris and took up lodgings in the abbey of St.-Germain-des-Prés. As the King of England approached Paris, he came to Vernon, which he expected to capture; but he was resisted vigorously, so the English departed from there, burning some of the suburbs. From there they came to Mantes, and when they heard it said that they were good warriors there, they did not want to stay at all, but continued to Meulan, where they lost some of their men. He was so angered by this that he put the closest town to there, called Les Mureaux, to the torch, and had everything there burned.

After that, he came to Poissy on Saturday the twelfth of August. Every day

---

[20] A few words here are illegible.
[21] This last phrase is a guess; the text of the letter here is illegible.

the King of France followed him continuously on the other bank of the river Seine, so that in many places and on many occasions, the two armies could see each other. And for the space of six days, while the King of England was at Poissy and his son was at St.-Germain-en-Laye, the outriders who went ahead carried the torch to all the towns around, even up to St.-Cloud near Paris, so that the people of Paris could, from Paris, clearly see the flames and the smoke, because of which they were very frightened, and for good reason. And although they many times set fire to our house in Rueil, which King and Emperor Charles the Bald gave to our church, it always remained without being damaged at all – through the merits of St. Denys, as we believe in good faith. And, so that I shall write the truth to our successors, the places where the King of England and his son were at that time were reputed and considered the principal residences and special solace of the King of France; so that it was a very great dishonor to the realm of France, and evident treason as well, that none of the nobles of France booted out the King of England, who was staying and residing for six days in the King's own houses, and in the middle of France besides, as Poissy, St.-Germain and Raye and Montjoye are, where he used up, wasted, and expended the King's wines and other goods. And there is another thing even more amazing, for the nobles had the boats scuttled and the bridges broken everywhere the King of England passed, when they should, quite the contrary, have crossed over to him over the bridges and in the boats, for the defense of the country.

Meanwhile, as the King of England was at Poissy, the King of France rode through Paris on Sunday [the thirteenth] and came to lodge with his army in the abbey of St.-Germain-des-Prés, so as to be at the meeting with the King of England, who was supposed to fight with him before Paris, as is said. And as the King was very eager and had planned to advance to Poissy against [King Edward] the next day, he was given to understand that the King of England had departed from Poissy and that he had repaired the bridge which had been broken, as God knows, so that the King of England could not escape without fighting the King of France. And when the King heard the news that the bridge at Poissy had been repaired and that his enemy had fled, he was very sorrowful about it, and left Paris and came to St.-Denys with his army on the vigil [14 August] of the Assumption of Our Lady. And no one living could recall any instance since the time of Charles the Bald, who was King and Emperor, that the King of France came to St.-Denys in the Ile-de-France in arms and entirely ready to give battle. When the King was at St.-Denys, he celebrated the feast of the Assumption [15 August] there most humbly and very devoutly; and he sent to the King of England, by the Archbishop of Besançon, to ask why he had not done what he had promised. The King of England responded fraudulently, as it appeared afterwards, that when he wanted to leave, he would direct his path [south] towards Montfort. Hearing the fraudulent answer of the King of England, the King received counsel which was not at all sound; for in truth there is no pestilence more capable of harming and injuring than that which is [in truth] an enemy and makes itself [appear] a familiar friend. So the King left St.-Denys and passed through Paris once more, sad and anxious, and came to

Antony beyond the Bourg-la-Reine, and lodged there on Wednesday [16 August]. And while the King of England had the broken bridge at Poissy repaired – and those who heard and saw it bear witness to it – there came to us at the church of St.-Denys, and into the room where the King was, a man who said that he had been captured by the enemies and then ransomed. He said openly and publicly, for the honor of the King and the realm, that the King of England was very diligently having the bridge at Poissy repaired; and this man would accept death if he did not speak the truth. But the nobles and knights nearest to the King said that he was clearly lying, and they made mockery of him, as of a poor man. Alas! Then was well verified that saying which goes: "The poor man has spoken, and it was said of him in mockery: 'Who is this?' The rich man has spoken and everyone keeps silent out of respect for him." Finally, when it was known truly that the bridge was being rebuilt, the commune of Amiens was sent to impede the business; but they couldn't resist the great number of arrows which the English shot, and were all put to death. And while the King was at Antony, that night news came to him that the English had definitely repaired the bridge of Poissy and that the King of England was expected to go across by it.

How the King of England left Poissy and put all the royal manors to the flames and fled towards Picardy; and how the King of France returned from Antony and passed through Paris saying with heavy sighs that he was betrayed, and pursued every day with great diligence his enemy, the King of England.

Then, the Friday [18 August] after the Assumption of Our Lady, around mid-morning, the King of England and his army, with uncovered arms and banners displayed, went onward without anyone pursuing them, which was a great sorrow to France. At his departure he set fire to Poissy, in the King's palace, without doing any harm to the church of the nuns which Philip the Fair, the said King of England's maternal grandfather, had built. St.-Germain-en-Laye, Raye, and Montjoye were also put to the flames, and in short all the places where the King of France was accustomed to relax were destroyed and burned. And when the King of France became aware that his enemy, the King of England, had departed so suddenly from Poissy, he felt great sorrow pierce his heart, and, greatly angered, he left Antony and returned to Paris. And in going along the highway, he was not ashamed to say to anyone who would hear that he had been betrayed; and the King doubted whether otherwise he could well have been led back and forth thus. The people murmured too, and said that such a way of going and returning would not be without treason, for which reason many wept, and not without cause. So the King left Paris and came directly to lodge at St.-Denys with his entire army.

In this year, the Duke of Normandy, who had gone to Gascony to besiege the castle of Aiguillon, and accomplished nothing there, heard some reports that the King of England made war on his father the King of France and had burned the houses of the King, and so was greatly troubled, and abandoned all his business [there] and departed. And when the King of England left Poissy, he came to the city of Beauvais. And because the people of Beauvais defended themselves nobly, and he could not enter the city, the English, full of evil spirit, burned some of the suburbs of the city and all the abbey of St.-Lucien, which was so fine and noble, so that nothing at all was left there. From there he entered into Picardy.

After this, the King of France left St.-Denys and followed his enemy the King of England up to Abbeville in Picardy, very courageously. And on Thursday, the feast of St. Bartholomew [24 August], the King of England was supposed to dine at Airaines; but the King of France, who very much wanted to follow his enemy with all his power, rode ten leagues that day in order to catch his adversary in the middle of his dinner. When the King of England heard the news, by letters from traitors who were in the court of the King, that the King of France was nearby and hastening against him, he abandoned his dinner and departed and moved to Saigneville, to the place called Blanchetacque. There he crossed the river Somme with all his host, and encamped near a forest called Crécy. And the Frenchmen ate and drank the food which the English had prepared for their dinner. Then the King returned, sorrowing, to Abbeville to assemble his army and to strengthen the bridge of the said town, so that his host could safely pass over it, for it was very weak and very old. The King stayed all of that day, Friday [25 August], at Abbeville, out of reverence for St. Louis, whose day that was. The next day in the morning, the King came to La Braye,[22] a town pretty near to the forest of Crécy. There it was said that the English host was a good four or five leagues away; but those who said these words lied falsely, for there was not more than one league between the town and the forest, or around that. In the end, around the time of evening, the King saw the host of the English. Being inspired by great boldness and fury, desiring with all his heart to fight with his enemy, he had "to arms!" cried immediately, and would not give credence to the advice of anyone who counseled him loyally, at which there was much sorrow. For he was advised that he and his army should rest that night; but he would not do it. Thus he went with all his men to attack the English.

77. King Edward's Own Account, from Caen through Calais. [Source: Coxe (ed.), *The Black Prince by Chandos Herald*. (Edinburgh: Roxburgh Club, 1842), 352–6]

The first part of the King's letter to Thomas Lucy (a Northern baron) is a variation of his letter from Caen (above).

. . . We remained at Caen four days in order to resupply and refresh our army, and from there, because we were positively informed that our adversary had

---

[22] Probably Sailly Bray; perhaps Brailly, or even Labroye, all near Crécy.

come to Rouen, we made our way directly towards him. As soon as he knew this, he ordered the bridge of Rouen broken, so that we could not cross there. Meanwhile, two cardinals met us in the city of Lisieux and made every effort to hold us up and hinder our expedition under pretext of negotiations; but we answered them briefly that we would not halt a single day for that reason, though whenever justice should be offered to us, we would make a fitting response. And, when we were informed that the said bridge of Rouen was broken, we encamped on the river quite close to the said town, on the river Seine towards Paris. And so we made our way up the said river, and we found all the bridges broken or fortified and defended, so that we could in no way cross over to our said adversary; nor was he willing to approach us, though he advanced parallel to us on the other side of the river each day, which much annoyed us. When we came to Poissy, near Paris, we found the bridge broken. At that time our said adversary was positioned with all his army and his strength in the city of Paris, and he had the bridge at St. Cloud knocked down, so that we could not cross to Paris from the part of the river where we were. So we stayed at Poissy for three days, as much in order to await our said adversary in case he wanted to give battle, as to repair the said bridge. And while the bridge was being repaired, a large force of enemies approached from the other side of the river in order to prevent the repair of the said bridge; but before the bridge was rebuilt some of our people crossed over on a plank and defeated them, killing a great number. And, when we saw that our enemies did not want to come and give battle, we therefore had the surrounding lands burned and laid waste. And each day our men engaged in skirmishes with the enemy, and always had the victory, God be praised. And we crossed the bridge with our army, and, in order to better draw our enemy to battle, we headed for Picardy, where our men had many good fights against our enemies. And when we came to the river Somme, we found the bridges there broken. So we headed towards St. Valery to cross at a ford where the sea ebbs and flows. At our arrival there, a great number of men-at-arms and men of the communes advanced to meet us, to defend the crossing, but we immediately took the passage from them by force. So, by the grace of God, we crossed a thousand people abreast, where before this time barely three or four were accustomed to cross. Thus we and our army crossed safely in a single hour, and our enemies there were defeated, and many captured, and furthermore a great number of the enemy were killed in the fight without loss to our people. And the same day, quite soon after we had crossed the river, our said adversary showed up on the other side with a great force of men so suddenly that we had no warning at all. So we halted there and took up our positions, and waited there all day, and the next day up to the evening. And in the end, when we saw that he did not want to cross, but turned towards Abbeville, we drew towards Crécy to meet him on the other side of the forest. On Saturday, the 26th of August, at our arrival at Crécy, our enemy showed himself quite close to us, at mid-morning, with a great number of men – for he had more than 12,000 men-at-arms, of whom 8,000 were noble knights and esquires. Immediately we arrayed our divisions, and thus we awaited on foot until a little before the hour of vespers [in the late afternoon], at which time the divisions met in the open field. The combats were fery fierce and long, for they lasted from before vespers until evening, and the enemies bore themselves most nobly, and very often rallied themselves; but, God be praised, they were defeated and our adversary fled. The King of Bohemia, the King of Majorca, the Duke of Lorraine, the Archbishop of [Sens], the Bishop of Noyon, the Grand Prior of the Order of the Hospital of France, the Abbot of Corbeil, the Count of Alençon, the Count of Flanders, the Count of Blois, the Count of Harcourt and his son, the Count of Salm, the Count of Auxerre, the Count of Montbéliard, the Count of Grandpré, the Viscount of Melun, the Viscount of Coucy, the Lord of Rosenberg, the Lord of Moreuil, the Lord of Cayeu, the Lord of Saint-Venant and many other counts, barons, and other great lords, whose names are not yet known were killed.[23] And more than 1,500 knights and esquires perished in a small place where the first clash took place, as well as a great many others who were killed afterwards all over the field. And after the defeat we remained all the following night without eating or drinking, and the next day in the morning conducted the pursuit, in which a good 4,000 men-at-arms were killed, counting both Genoese and other men-at-arms. And our adversary, after the defeat, went to Amiens, where he had a great number of his Genoese killed, saying that they had betrayed him. And it is said that he has summoned his forces again in order to give battle to us once more, and so we trust in God that He will continue to show His grace towards us just as He has up to now. And so we have now advanced to the sea in order to be resupplied and reinforced from England, with men-at-arms, military equipment and other necessary things, for the journey we have made has been long and continual; but anyway, we have no thought of departing the realm of France until we have made an end to our war, with God's help. Given under our privy seal before Calais, the 3rd day of September, the twentieth year of our reign in England [1346], etc.

78. The Battle of Crécy. [Source: Le Bel, 2:102–10]

The portion of Jean le Bel's chronicle covering the years after 1340 were composed after the death of his patron Jean de Hainault (who in 1345 transferred his allegiance from Edward III to Philip VI) in 1356. It is somewhat less sophisticated than the first section of the work, but still balanced and of high quality.

King Philip rode forward in order to overtake the English, and sent ahead some knights and esquires to scout out their position, for he thought that they surely were not far off. When he had gone three leagues [from Abbeville], these outriders returned and told him that the English were less than four leagues

---

[23] This list includes a few errors (e.g. the King of Majorca actually escaped and none of the clergymen listed were actually killed at the battle), but does not seem to be intentionally exaggerated.

ahead. Then the King commanded a knight who was very valiant and experienced in arms, and four others, to advance and go after the English, and consider their formation and their manner. These valiant knights very willingly did so, then returned towards the King. Meeting his banners one league away from the English, they had them stop to await the others; then they came to the King and said that they had seen the English less than one league from there, and considered their manner; and they were awaiting him in three battles. So, in council, he considered what was to be done. The King asked the aforesaid knight, [called] Monk, to give his opinion on the matter, since he was so worthy in arms. This knight, the Monk of Bazeilles, appeared unwilling to speak before the other knights; nevertheless, he agreed to speak. So he said to the King: "Sire, your host is very spread out over the fields, so it will be quite late before they are all assembled, for noon is already past; so I advise you to have your army encamp and then tomorrow morning, after Mass, array your battles and go against your enemies in the name of God and St. George, for I am certain that they will not flee, but, insofar as I have been able to determine, will await you."

This advice pleased the King well, and he would very willingly have followed it, so he had it proclaimed that each person should draw back his banners, for the English were arrayed nearby, so he wanted to encamp there until the next day. None of the lords wanted to turn back unless those ahead of them would turn back first, and those who were forward did not want to pull back, for it seemed shameful to them. So they held still without moving, and the others who were behind rode ever forward, and all this was through pride and envy, which destroyed them, for because of this the advice of the worthy knight was not followed. Riding thus, through pride and envy without order, one after another, they continued until they saw the English ranged in three battles, well arrayed, awaiting them. Then, when they had seen their enemies so close, the shame of retreating would have been even greater.

Then the commanders of the light infantry, of the crossbowmen, and of the Genoese had their men advance all the way to the fore, in front of the battles of the lords, in order to shoot at the English. They came so close that the two sides shot at each other. Very soon the light infantry and the Genoese were defeated and put to flight by the archers; but the battles of the great lords were so inflamed by envy, one against another, that they did not wait for one another, but attacked completely disordered and mixed together without any order whatsoever so that they trapped the light infantry and the Genoese between them and the English, so that they could not flee. Thus the weak horses fell over them, and the others trampled them, and they tumbled over each other like pigs in a heap.

On the other side the archers fired so marvelously that when the horses felt these barbed arrows (which did wonders), some would not go forwards, others leapt into the air as if maddened, others balked and bucked horribly, others turned their rumps towards the enemy, regardless of their masters, because of the arrows they felt. Some, unable to avoid it, let themselves fall. The English lords, who were on foot, advanced and pierced through these men, who could not help themselves, by their own efforts or by their horses.

This calamity for the French went on in this manner until midnight, for it was nearly nightfall when the battle began; and never could the King of France or those of his company come up to the melee that day. So it became necessary for the King to leave there, and his men led him away with great sorrow, against his will; and lord Jean de Hainault, who was retained to guard his body and his honor, made him ride on that night until they came to Labroye. There the King rested, greatly crestfallen. On the morrow he went to Amiens to await his men, what was left of them. The remainder of the French – lords, knights and others who had stayed behind – retreated like defeated men, and didn't know where to go, for the night was extremely dense, so that they could not perceive town or village, and they hadn't eaten all day. So they went in bands, three here, four there, like lost men; and none of them knew if their lords or relatives or brothers were dead or had escaped. Never had a greater misfortune befallen Christians than befell King Philip and his men then. This occurred in the year of Grace 1346, the morrow of the feast of St. Bartholomew, on a Saturday [26 August], in the evening, very near to Crécy-en-Ponthieu. All that night the French did not know that they had lost, so they passed the night in such misery as you have heard.

I have written this as close as possible to the truth, just as I have heard it recounted by my lord and friend Sir Jean de Hainault (whom God absolve), from his own mouth, and by ten or twelve knights and companions of his household, who were in the press with the valiant and noble King of Bohemia, and whose horses were killed beneath them; and so also I have heard it told in such a way by many English and German[24] knights who were there, on the other side.

Well, [now] I will explain how the noble King Edward had arranged his battles.

Know you that the valiant King of England knew well on Friday evening [25 August] that King Philip was at Abbeville, with a great number of knights. So therefore he made great cheer and said to his people that each should go rest, and pray to Our Lord that He would allow them to emerge from the affair with honor and rejoicing; for he was on his rightful heritage, so he would defend it, and not go further forward or back; if King Philip would come there, he [Edward] would await him.

The next morning, he had his men come out from their lodgings, and arm themselves, and, near to a woods, make all the carts and wagons of the army into a large enclosure with only one entrance, and he had all the horses put inside this enclosure. Then he ordered his battles in noteworthy fashion and assigned the first to his eldest son the Prince of Wales, with 1,200 men-at-arms, 4,000 archers and 3,000 Welshmen, and put him in the guard of the Earls of Warwick, Stafford, and Kent[25] and of Sir Godfrey d'Harcourt, and of many others whose names I do not know. And he assigned the second battle to the Earl of North-

---

[24] In this period including the Imperial sections of the Low Countries, Hainault, etc.

[25] In fact the young John of Kent did not join the royal host until the siege of Calais.

ampton, the Earl of Suffolk, and the Bishop of Durham, with 1,200 men-at-arms and 3,000 archers; and he kept for himself the third battle, which was to be between these two, with 1,600 men-at-arms and 4,000 archers. And know that they were all English or Welsh, for there were not six German archers there, of whom one was Sir Races Massures. I don't know the names of the others.

When the valiant King had thus arranged his battles in a fine field where there was neither pit nor ditch, he went all around and cheerfully admonished each to strive to do his duty. So sweetly he asked and admonished them that a coward would thereby have been made brave. He commanded, on pain of the noose, that none should break ranks, nor seek gain, nor despoil either living or dead, without his leave: for if the affair went in their favor, each would have enough time to pillage, and if fortune turned against them, then nothing they could do would gain them anything.

When he had arranged everything thus, he gave leave for each to go and drink and eat until the sound of the trumpet; then each should return to his position. Each so loved and dread him that none dared to violate his commands.

At the hour of noon, news came to the noble King that King Philip, with all his forces, was very nearby. Immediately he had the trumpets sounded, and without delay he got everyone in array. They waited until the French came, and acted so wisely and so perfectly that fortune turned in their favor.

When the affair was over, and the thick night closed in, the King had it ordered and proclaimed that none should pursue the enemy and that none should despoil or remove the dead until he gave leave, so that they could better be recognized in the morning; and he commanded that each should go to his lodgings to rest without disarming, and that all the lords should come to dine with him; and he ordered his marshals [to see that] the army was well guarded, and that a good watch was kept. Well, everyone can well understand in what joy the noble King and all his barons and lords dined and passed the night, thanking God for their good fortune, that such a small company had defended themselves and held the field against all the power of France.

In the morning there was a great din, so that a large number of English went into the fields with the King's leave, in order to see if they could find any Frenchmen who were re-assembling. Thus they found a great number of the commons, from the towns, who had slept in thickets, pits and hedges, and were asking each others' adventures, and what they could tell them, for they did not know what the outcome for their side had been nor where the King or their lords were. When they saw the English coming towards them, they awaited them, for they believed that these were their own people; and the English set upon them like wolves among sheep, and killed them at will. Another company of English went adventuring, and met another company of people advancing through the fields in order to see if they could hear news of their lords; others sought their masters, others their relatives, others their companions. The English killed all of these as they found them. Around the hour of mid-morning, they returned to their camp just as the King and the lords had heard mass, and told of their adventure. Then the King commenced to order Sir Reginald Cobham, who was a very worthy knight, to take a herald knowledgeable concerning [coats of] arms, and some lords with him, and all the heralds, and go through all the dead, and write down all the knights they could recognize, and have all the princes and great lords carried to one side, and on each one have his name written down. The said Sir Reginald did as he was ordered, and it was found that there were nine great princes lying there, and around 1,200 knights, and a good fifteen or sixteen thousand others – esquires, Genoese, and others – and they found only 300 English knights dead.

Well, there is good reason that I recount to you [only] the princes and high barons who remained there, dead; of the others, I could never reach the end. So I will begin with the most noble and most high-born, the valiant King of Bohemia who, entirely blind, wanted to be among the first to the battle, and commanded his knights, on pain of beheading, that they lead him as far forward as they could, so that he could strike a blow of the sword against someone of the enemy.

The next greatest prince was the Count of Alençon, the brother of the King of France. Next, Count Louis of Blois, son of the said King's sister. Next, the Count of Salm in Salmoire. Next, the Count of Harcourt. Next, the Count of Auxerre. Next, the Count of Sançerre. And it was said that for a long time no one had heard of so many princes killed in a single day, not at Courtrai, nor at Benevento, nor anywhere else.[26]

The following day, the valiant King Edward remained on the field the entire day in order to see if King Philip would bring his men into battle again, but he did not come. So the worthy King departed from there with his army, and he had the bodies of his dead people carried to a nearby monastery, and sent out his marshals to burn and devastate the country all around, just as he had done before. This they could do easily enough, for they did not find any one to defend it. So they came to Saint-Josse, and burned Beaurain and all the land around the town of Montreuil-sur-Mer, and all suburbs, which were very large. Then they departed from Saint-Josse and burned it, and Étaples, and Neufchâtel, and all the region of Boulognais around Boulogne, and then the noble King besieged the good town of Calais, which was held to be one of the strongest towns of the world.

79. Henry of Lancaster's Bulletin on 1346 in Gascony. [Source: Avesbury, 372–4]

When Philip learned of the landing of Edward's main army, he recalled the Duke of Normandy to join the main army. Duke Jean, even though he had sworn an oath not to depart the siege of Aiguillon until he had captured it, obeyed his

---

[26] This list includes only a fraction of the great lords slain in 1346; the two most noteworthy casualties left out of Le Bel's enumeration are the Count of Flanders and the Duke of Lorraine.

father's order, though he did not make it north in time to fight at Crécy. Henry of Lancaster, needless to say, took full advantage of the French retreat, as his own report shows.

Concerning the news from over here, know that, three full days before the feast of the Assumption of Our Lady [i.e. on 12 August], we moved from La Réole towards the area of Bergerac; and we had all the lords of Gascony, and other men from the garrisons, assemble there, with the intent of making a *chevauchée*. There we took counsel with the said lords. Before our departure from there some people, knights and others, came to us on behalf of the French who were still maintaining the siege before Aiguillon in order to ask for a truce. But, since we knew that my lord the King had arrived in Normandy, we would not agree to any truce. At this the enemies raised the siege the Sunday [20 August] immediately before the feast of St. Bartholomew, and departed from there very dishonorably, for they lost a large portion of their of their goods and of their people, and left behind their tents and all the best of their equipment. So, as soon as we knew of this, we made our way forward into the Agenais and came before Ville-Réal, which is a good town belonging to the King, which surrendered to us along with a great number of other towns and castles around there. And when we had secured this town and the countryside, we made a *chevauchée* through all the countryside and went directly to Tonneins and Aiguillon, and secured them and the surrounding area as well. And then we retired to La Réole, and remained there for eight full days, and we took counsel there, and we held the entire area. And we divided our host into three, and sent the Lord of Albret, Sir Bérard d'Albret, Seneschal of Gascony, Sir Alexander Caumont, and others towards the region of Bazadois; the lord Duras and the other lords of the Agenais we left in those parts; and we continued onward towards Saintonge with a thousand men-at-arms. And on the twelfth day of September we moved on, and spent the night in a good town, which had surrendered to us the same day, the town of Sauveterre. And the next day, when we had taken oaths from those of the town, we made our way forward for fully eight days, without attacking one town or castle, until we came to Châteauneuf, which is on the river Charente; and there we had the bridge, which was broken, repaired, for the water was so deep that it could not be crossed otherwise, and we crossed it the next day. And that day we had news that the men of Sir Walter Mauny, who had a safe-conduct from the French to go to the King by land, had been captured and imprisoned in the town of St.-Jean d'Angely; and so they had; and with much difficulty Sir Walter had escaped along with three others; so we made our way forward towards the said town and assailed it, and it was gained by force, thanks be to God, and the men freed from prison. And we remained there for eight days and secured the town, and those of the town made their oaths to us and became English; and they are obliged, at their own costs, to find 200 men-at-arms and 600 infantry to garrison the town for the duration of the war; and in time of peace they are to pay to the King each year 4,000 more écus in rents than they were accustomed to pay to the King of France. And on the day [30 September] after Michaelmas we rode towards the city of Poitiers, and spent a night before the town of Lusignan, which is a strong town, so that we went to assail it, and it was taken by assault, and the castle, which is one of the noblest and strongest of the castles which are defended in France or Gascony, was surrendered to us. And we secured the castle and the town and left fully 100 men-at-arms, and other footmen, with them. And we rode up to the city of Poitiers and called upon them [to surrender]; but they would not do anything, for it seemed to them their town was strong enough, and they had plenty of men. So it was assailed and taken by force on the Wednesday [4 October] next after Michaelmas, and all the people of the town were captured or killed. And the lords who were inside, one bishop and four barons, when they saw the capture of the town, departed on the other side. And we stayed there fully eight days. And, at the writing of this letter, we were at St.-Jean, and we hold a number of good towns around here which have surrendered to us. And so we have made a fine *chevauchée*, thanks be to God, and returned to St.-Jean; and from here we plan to make our way to Bordeaux, which will be hard to do, considering that the enemies are assembled in the country; but we hope to do well, with God's help.

80. The Scottish Invasion of 1346. [Source: "Neville's Cross," 72–76]

While Edward III was besieging Calais, Lancaster was making new conquests in the south-west of France, and Thomas Dagworth was carrying on the war in Brittany, the Scots renewed their conflict against England. The following account of the start of the Scottish invasion is taken from a manuscript that can tentatively be identified as an epitome of a chronicle prepared by William Pak-ington, Treasurer of the Black Prince's household in Gascony, in the mid-1370s.

When Philip of Valois knew that the King of England had arrived in Normandy and had made a *chevauchée* through the land, as is said above, he sent to David Bruce, King of Scotland, [to inform him of] how the King of England had come into his land, and brought the greater part of his men with him, and how he also had many of his people in Gascony and some in Brittany, so that the realm of England was left emptied of men-at-arms; and that no one worthy of concern of had stayed in the said realm – only clergymen and shepherds – and he requested of him, on they faith that he owed him and the alliance which existed between them, that he would make a warlike *chevauchée* and destroy the land of England, for now was the time; and he [Philip] would send some of his people by sea, as well, to destroy those whom they could, and to meet him. And the said David King of Scotland assembled all the force of Scotland and made a vow that he would hold the feast of Christmas at London, or at least at Northampton; and he entered the realm of England and came to the peel of Liddel Strength and took it by force. And he had a noble knight, Sir Walter Selby, guardian of the said peel, put to death in his own presence, spitefully; and would not allow him to take confession, for which God took vengeance, as will be explained hereafter. And then he made a *chevauchée* through all the March and the land of the North, robbing and pillaging, until he came to Durham. There he lodged in the Manor of Beaurepaire [or Bearpark], belonging to the Prior of Durham, which is set in a park. And the people of the country came and paid ransoms so that their lands and houses would not be burned. And they [the Scots] took such ransoms willingly, because their intent was to accept the surrender of the land at their entry, and yet nevertheless to burn it on their return, as the people learned afterwards from their own mouths.

81. The Battle of Neville's Cross. [Source: Froissart, *Oeuvres*, 5:490–1]

The following letter describing the rest of the Neville's Cross campaign was written by the clerk Thomas Samson almost immediately after its conclusion.

. . . And there [at Beaurepaire] they fixed their tents and their most noble, most rich pavilions, such as had never been seen in those parts, and these were well-stocked with all types of food supplies to last a long time. Having been made aware of these things, the honorable father in God, by His grace Archbishop of York, primate of England, and other great men of the North – the Earl of Angus, the lords Percy, Mowbray, Neville, Deyncourt, Maulay, Leybourne, Scrope, Musgrave, the Sheriff of York, Sir Robert Bertram the Sheriff of Northumberland and other nobles and bannerets assembled at Richmond and moved towards the enemies to Barnard Castle; and from there to the castle of Auckland; and there they encamped in the park. And, on the seventeenth day of the month of October of the year of the Incarnation of Our Lord Jesus Christ 1346, in defense of the realm of England and of the Holy Church and of the people, they moved towards the city of Durham against the enemies.

And the King of Scotland, with all his army, moved against them, and they arrayed and arranged their schiltrons and divisions on both sides. And in the first division on our side were the lords Percy, Neville, Maulay, Scrope, Musgrave, and the sheriff of Northumberland, and Sir Andrew FitzRalph as bannerets. And in the second division were milord the Archbishop, the Earl of Angus, the lord Deyncourt, Sirs Roger la Zouche and Ralph Hastings, the provost of Beverley and the banners of Turville, of Our Lady, and of St. John. In the third division and rear-guard were the lord Mowbray, lord Leybourne and the sheriff of York. And there were of our men a good 1,000 men-at-arms and over 1,000 hobelars and more than 10,000 archers, and of the commons fully 20,000, just from the region north of the Trent and the Humber. And they met and fought well and extraordinarily long, from the hour of noon to the hour of evening, before the enemies were fully defeated in the battle. Two times our archers and commons retreated; but our men-at-arms continued fighting very well until the archers and the commons rallied. And God by his grace and virtue gave us the victory. And King David and the Scots were defeated. And there were killed and captured in the battle: King David, wounded and captured by John Coupland;

the Earl of Moray; and other earls, nobles and barons of the chivalry of Scotland taken and killed, whose names are included and written more fully on the back [of this letter.] Lord Lucy, who came towards the battle as quickly as he could with a large number of men-at-arms, [but] wasn't at the battle, met the fugitives and pursued them eagerly and killed or captured many of them before they could reach the border of Scotland. The lord Tibetoft, guardian of the town of Berwick, and his force, very wisely held themselves within the town until he had news of the defeat; and then went in strength to encounter the enemies as far as the castle of Dunbar, and captured and killed many of them so that few worthies escaped. Thanks be to God!

82. Thomas Dagworth's Dispatch on the Battle of La Roche-Derrien. [Source: Avesbury, 388–9]

Edward III could only be at one place at one time, yet he had to oversee the war effort around Calais, in Brittany and Poitou, in Gascony, etc. Henry of Lancaster and the Black Prince often served as his lieutenants for independent campaigns, but Edward also made increasing use of professional soldiers to manage the war effort in certain areas, particularly Brittany. Sir Thomas Dagworth was one such man, who owed his position to his skill as a military commander, not to august birth. The dispatch below describes Dagworth's victory in the battle of La Roche-Derrien.

Very dear and much honored lord, you will wish to know the news from Brittany, that Sir Charles de Blois had besieged the town and castle of La Roche-Derrien, and had in his company 1,200 men-at-arms properly speaking, knights and esquires, and 600 other men-at-arms, and 600 archers of the country, and 2,000 crossbowmen, and men of the commons whose number I do not know. This Sir Charles had caused great entrenchments to be made around his position, and outside of his fortifications he had caused all manners of ditches and hedges to be filled or razed for half a local league's breadth around him, so that my archers could not find an advantage over him and his men, but had in the end perforce to fight in the open fields. And he and his people knew of my coming against them through their spies, and they were collected and in arms all the night. And we came against them, my companions and I, on the twentieth day of June, in the hours before dawn, and by the grace of God the affair went in such a way that he lost the field and was entirely defeated, God be praised therefor. And I had in my company around 300 men-at-arms and 400 archers, without counting Sir Richard Totesham and Hannekin of Ypres and the garrison of La Roche-Derrein, who sallied out when it was clear day and they could recognize us, and they came towards us against the enemy very chivalrously; and we fought with the enemies, before the sun rose, in four battles, each after the other. And that day were slain the Lord of Laval, the Viscount of Rohan, the Lord of Châteaubriand, the Lord of Malestroit, the Lord of Quintin, the Lord of Rougé, the Lord of Derval and his son and heir, Sir Ralph de Montfort, and many other knights and esquires (between 600 and 700 men-at-arms); and of the common people, I cannot tell you for certain. And Sir Charles de Blois, Sir Guy de Laval, son and heir of the Lord of Laval who died in the battle, the Lord of Rochefort, the Lord of Beaumanoir, the Lord of Lohéac, the Lord of Meillac, the Lord of Tinténiac, and a great number of other knights and esquires were captured at the said battle.

83. Philip Fails to Break the Siege of Calais. [Source: *St. Omer Chronicle*, fos. 275–276v]

While his armies won victories in England and Brittany, Edward maintained a very large force in his fortified camp outside of Calais, month after month, waiting for starvation to bring the defenders to terms, or for Philip to make an attempt to rescue the town.

This account, internal evidence suggests, was written shortly after the events it describes by someone attached to the garrison of St. Omer, near Calais.

The King of France was much distressed at heart, and didn't know what to do: for some said that he should go into Flanders against the Flemings, and that the King of England would break off the siege of Calais in order to rescue the Flemings; others told him he should go straight to do battle with the English, for if he could defeat them, he would win the whole war. Then some of his barons came to him and told him and said they were certain that he should boldly go towards the King of England, for they were positive that the Flemings would not send anyone from their country. And based on this assurance – which was not correct – the King went to Hesdin and there awaited his men, who joined him from all sides.

On the 15th of the month of June in the year 1347 the King of France departed Hesdin with all his forces, banners displayed, in order to go rescue the people in Calais . . . . It was proclaimed that all nobles and non-nobles who were on the frontiers should join his army, on pain of forfeiting whatever they had to lose; so great numbers came to him from all over. So his army was amazingly large . . . . Then the people of Calais knew for certain that the King of France was coming to save them; they rejoiced much at this, and forgot some of their misery. And all day the outriders of the King of England came, screaming and yelping around the army. There the King of France decided to advance further and went to encamp a single league from Calais on a height called Sangatte. From there the two armies could see each other; and it was a fine sight to see. But the Flemings, who in this war bore neither faith nor loyalty towards the realm of France, had assembled an army of 40,000 men and came to encamp before Calais in order to support the King of England against their just sovereign and lord, the King of France. And so it became quite apparent that what the King of France had been given to understand at Arras was not true. Between the two armies there were many jousts between young bachelors who wanted to advance themselves.

The two cardinals, who had been staying in Poitou, having heard the news concerning the King of France, who was so close to his enemies, came there and set up lodgings between the two armies. They spoke with the counselors of the two Kings until they assembled half-way between the two armies. The Duke of Athens, the Count of Armagnac, the Lord of Offémont and Sir Geoffrey de Charny represented the King of France, and the Earl of Lancaster, the Earl of Warwick, Sir Bartholomew Burghersh and another knight were there on behalf of the King of England. They set up two pavilions in the fields; there they conducted negotiations together for several days, but could not reach any agreement. Then the King of France was advised that he was wasting his time there, for he could only get supplies with great danger; and he would be better off to go straight to St. Omer and from there enter into Flanders and lay waste the country, which opposed him so much. When the King of France had heard this counsel he felt great sorrow in his heart, for he saw well, as the fire-signals of the defenders had indicated to him, that he would of necessity lose the town of Calais; but that was the best option he had. Then it was proclaimed that each should break camp and report to his division. Then you could have seen great tribulations, for some abandoned their carts, others poured out their wines, and a great portion of the military equipment was burned there. The King went to lodge at Audresselles. And the English, who saw the departure of the army, sallied out from their camp and went so far forward that they were surprised by the rearguard; so they were forced to retreat, and some of them were killed by the enterprise of the very valiant Lord of Montmorency.

Throughout the countryside raced the news that the King was going to go into Flanders; and already a great quantity of supplies arrived around the Neuffossé.[27] Then it was proclaimed in the army that everyone should follow the marshals; and most thought that they would go towards St. Omer. But the made their way elsewhere, and went straight to encamp at Lumbres. The lords were much dismayed when they saw which road was being taken, but they did not know what the King's intention was. From there he went straight to Hesdin, and there dispersed his army.

84. Edward III on the Negotiations outside Calais. [Source: Avesbury, 391–3]

Edward, by the grace of God King of England and France and Lord of Ireland, to the honorable father in God John, by the same grace Archbishop of Canterbury, primate of all England, and to our Chancellor and Treasurer, greetings. Because we know well that you will be glad to hear the news and state of affairs

---

[27] The trench which marked the border between Flanders and Artois.

over here, we make it known to you that, on this last Friday [27 July] immediately before the beginning of August, our adversary of France with all his forces came to encamp near us, on the opposite side of a morass, on a hillock. And on his arrival, some men of our army encountered his people and had a fight with them, and captured a fine company of knights and esquires. And the same day the cardinals came to the mouth of the causeway and sent their letters to our cousin of Lancaster and other great men of our host, asking to talk with them. Therefore, with our permission, our cousins of Lancaster and Northampton went there. The cardinals entreated them, very insistently, that negotiations might be held, and said that they knew well that our adversary would make such offers of peace as should by reason be acceptable. And at the instance of the said cardinals, as one who is and always has been ready to accept a reasonable peace whenever it should be offered to us, we fully assented to such negotiations. For this reason, our cousin of Lancaster had two pavilions raised in a place between the two armies. And there the cardinals met with the Marquis of Juliers, our said cousins of Lancaster and Northampton, Sir Bartholomew Burghersh, our Chamberlain, Sir Reginald Cobham, and Sir Walter Mauny, on our side; and the Dukes of Bourbon and Athens, the Chancellor of France, the Lord of Offémont, and Sir Geoffrey Charny, on our said adversary's side. They negotiated together, and the other side's delegates began to speak of the town of Calais, and proposed to surrender the town in such a way that those inside could go free, with their goods and chattels, and that, once that was done, they would treat of peace. And our people answered them that they had not been given authority to speak of the town, but to treat of peace, if they were shown a reasonable way [to achieve it]. And the negotiators of the other side held themselves entirely to the subject of the town, so that it was very difficult to get them to offer anything. But at last they offered the duchy of Guienne, in the fashion that his [sic] grandfather had it, and the county of Ponthieu; and our men responded that this offer was too small to compensate for such a major loss. And thus they negotiated for three days without any effect; for the negotiators of the other side stuck to talking about the town in order to rescue the people within by some subtlety. And then on Tuesday [31 July], towards [evening], certain great lords and knights came to the site of the discussions on behalf of our adversary, and on his behalf proposed a battle to our men, in such a way that we would come out of the morass, and he would give us a suitable place to fight at whatever time we pleased, between that time and the next Friday [3 August] evening. They wanted four of our knights, and another four of theirs, to select a site agreeable to both sides. And on this our men responded that they would present this offer to us, and give them an answer on Wednesday [1 August]. When this was presented to us, having taken counsel and advice with the magnates and other wise men of our Council and of our army, trusting in God and our right, we answered that we would accept their offer and would willingly accept the battle. We had letters of safe-conduct prepared for four knights of the other side, of whatever estate or condition they might be, to come to our army, so that we could pick another four of equal status, and equally so that the eight knights could take the oath to go examine and search out [potential] sites until they were in agreement. And when those of the other side heard this, they immediately began to change their offers, and to speak of the town entirely anew, leaving aside the battle, so that they would not stick to anything definite. And on that Thursday [2 August] before dawn, the aforesaid parleys notwithstanding, our said adversary departed, with all his men, as if defeated; and they were in such a hurry that they burnt their tents and a great portion of their equipment at their departure. And our men pursued them quite close on their tails, so that at the copying of this letter they have not yet returned. For that reason we have not yet decided for certain about what we will do about it later, but always we think to make a *chevauchée* in order to win our war as quickly as we can, with the aid of God.

85. The Surrender of Calais. [Source: *St. Omer Chronicle*, fos. 276v–277]

Let us return to those of Calais, who saw the departure of the King of France, as you have heard. So they were in great distress, and no wonder: for they no longer had any hope of rescue. They decided to send to the King of England; Sir Jean de Vienne and two knights and two bourgeois were chosen for this embassy. When they came before the King of England, they fell on their knees with great humility and begged him to have pity on the poor people who were in the town, as people who placed themselves entirely in his mercy. When the King heard their speech, he regarded them with a cruel expression. And then he said to them: "Oh you of Calais, where did you find the heart to dare to hold out so against me? And did you not realize that I am more powerful than you, and that I had made an oath to conquer you? You held out against me wrongly, and therefore I will not have any pity on you."

Then you might have seen the Queen with her ladies and a great number of knights go to their knees before the King, begging him to have mercy on them. The King was sufficiently moved to pity and by their prayers that he granted them their lives; and for everything else, they would be at his will. With matters thus agreed, they returned to the town; they explained the business to the knights and to the citizens, who all in common agreed to this arrangement. And then the councilors of the King of England took four knights and four bourgeois, who came to present themselves in front of the King, each knight with a naked sword in his hands, each burgher with a noose in his arms. When they had come before the King they went to their knees, and then told him that they had come on their own behalf and on behalf of all the townspeople to surrender to him, as those to whom he could do with as he wished. Then the King received them into his grace. Then it was proclaimed throughout the host that food should be carried into Calais. Those of the town rushed upon the food like madmen, so that it seemed that the King would never get his officials back from inside the town. The knights who were in the town were taken prisoner and sent to London until their ransoms should be paid. The citizens were made to depart the city without carrying any goods with them, then their houses were divided among the barons of England.

After some fifteen months of solid campaigning, Edward's troops and his finances were too exhausted to mount the major new chevauchée *mentioned in the close of his letter on the negotiations outside Calais. Philip's situation was even worse. When the ubiquitous Papal envoys once again appeared to propose a truce, both sides were ready to listen. In September of 1347 they sealed the Truce of Calais, which like earlier agreements effectively froze the war in place. By the time the first year of the truce expired, the Black Death had made its disastrous appearance, leaving little enthusiasm for renewing the fighting.*

In 1349 the war resumed, though without any operations on the scale of the Crécy-Calais campaign. Back in Gascony in 1349, Lancaster led a devastating chevauchée *to the very gates of Toulouse, capturing 42 towns and castles on his way. Shortly after the death of King Philip and the accession of his son as Jean II in 1350, the English navy defeated a French-allied Castillian fleet off Winchelsea, thereby convincing France's most important ally to bow out of the war. On land in the next year, the English won a small battle near Saintes, and conducted a short but destructive* chevauchée *in Artois and Picardy. In 1352 there were some minor successes on each side, but the new French King suffered a significant setback in Brittany, as the following dispatch from Sir Walter Bentley relates.*

86. Walter Bentley's Dispatch on the Battle of Mauron, 1352. [Source: Avesbury, 416–17]

Walter Bentley was, like Thomas Dagworth, one of the soldiers of modest birth who served Edward III very well as independent commanders.

Reverend father in God, it will please you to know that, since my arrival in Brittany, the men assigned to me and I, before entering any fortress, have made a *chevauchée* over here and have accomplished so much, thanks be to God, that the towns and castles of Ploërmel and of Fougères have been successfully relieved and resupplied; and we took by assault a small fortress which our enemies had constructed in front of Fougères. And, once that was done, my companions and I made a *chevauchée* against the land of our enemies, until the Marshal of France, with all the forces from France, Normandy, Anjou, Maine, Poitou, Touraine, Saintonge, and Brittany – a great number of men-at-arms and numberless other men – came to do battle with us, near a town called Mauron, between Rennes and Ploërmel, in the open fields, without woods, ditches, or other obstacles. There we fought with them, on the vigil [14 August] of the Assumption of Our Lady, between the hour of vespers [late afternoon] and sunset. By the grace of God, and the just right which He upholds, our enemies were entirely defeated, and with hardly any losses on our side, praise be to God. And the Seneschal of Anjou, the Seneschal of Benavent, the Viscount of Rohan, [eleven named knights and lords,] and up to 160 other knights were killed there, in addition to the esquires, who amounted to 500 dead on the field, all wearing armor, and common people without number. And the prisoners taken included the Lord of Briquebecq, son of Marshal Bertrand, Sir Tristam de Maignelay, the Lord of Malestroit, the Viscount of Coëtmen, [five more named lords], and many other knights and esquires, to the total of 160. Among the dead and captured are fully 45 Knights of the Star.[28]

87. The Town of Agen Seeks Safety from the English Garrisons. [Source: *Jurades de la ville d'Agen (1345–55)* (*Archives Historiques de l'Agenais, I*), ed. Adolphe Magen (Auch: Cocharaux, 1894), 328–9]

It was very common during the Hundred Years War for garrisons to sell "sufferances," "truces," "appatis," etc., to nearby enemy areas – the garrisons got cash and supplies, and in exchange promised not to burn or destroy the villages and towns which had made the payments. Since this enriched the enemy, and left those paying the protection money with little to give to their side's tax collectors, the practice was often forbidden. The minutes of a meeting of the Jurades *(town council) of Agen in 1353 reflect this.*

Session of 9 August 1353.

Item. That, after license from the King is received, milord the Bishop of Agen should be charged with negotiating a protection treaty for the lands between the Lot and the Garonne, and, if possible, after that one for the whole region; for all the other towns and places in the duchy [of Guienne] except for us already have them. Every day our people are harmed, captured and robbed, so that we do not dare work our lands, and the King does not defend us, nor can he defend us, from the bad men, and our people are abandoning the town every day. So it would be best for the King as well as for us.

88. The Treaty of Guînes. [Source: Avesbury, 420–1]

The Jurades of Agen, before they decided to seek a patis *from the English, had already written to the newly-elected Pope Innocent VI, describing the poverty to which they had been reduced by the war, and begging him to arrange a peace between the two Kings. During the Avignon negotiations in 1344, Edward's delegates had suggested a formula which might persuade the English King to surrender his claim to the French throne, and by 1353 the Valois government was willing to consider the possibility. In the fall of that year, negotiations began at Guînes, outside of Calais.*

---

[28] The Knights of the Star were members of a chivalric order founded in competition with Edward III's Knights of the Garter.

The Year of Grace 1354, after Easter, peace negotiations were held between magnates of the realms of England and France near Calais, and a certain form of peace was agreed between the parties. This was, as it is said, that the King of England and his heirs should have the Duchy of Aquitaine entirely, perpetually, free and quit, without making any homage to the King of France; and certain other things which this writer does not know [well enough] to speak of; and he [the King of England] would give up his right to the realm of France. It was agreed that, in order to get this peace agreement confirmed by the High Pontiff, solemn embassies would be sent to the Roman curia by each side. And at that time a truce was made between the two realms, to last up to the feast of St. John the Baptist [June 24], extending to the year following thereafter.

89. Secret Instructions Given to the Duke of Lancaster Regarding the Ratification of the Treaty of Guînes (1354). [Source: Bock, *Documents*, 94–6]

Throughout the war, Edward III proclaimed his willingness to accept an honorable and reasonable peace; what he meant by that phrase is made fairly clear in the following secret instructions given to the Duke of Lancaster on his departure for Avignon, where he was expected to finalize the agreement outlined at Guînes.

Although some historians (e.g. John le Patourel) have argued otherwise, the various forms of peace agreed upon between 1358 and 1360, including the Treaty of Brétigny, were all in principle similar to the terms set out below.

The charge given by our lord the King on the last day of October, the 28th year of his reign [1354], in the private chapel inside the palace of Westminster, in the presence of milord the Prince, the Archbishop of York, Chancellor, the Bishop of Winchester, Treasurer, the Bishop of Durham, the Earls of Warwick and Stafford, Sir Bartholomew Burghersh, Sir John Beauchamp, and Sir John Gray, to those noble men the Duke of Lancaster and the Earl of Arundel, dispatched as the King's ambassadors to the Court of Rome for the treaty of peace between him and his adversary of France

[1] Firstly they should commend our lord the King, milady the Queen, and their children to our holy father the Pope.

[2] Item. It pleases the King that they may agree, conclude, and finally confirm the things that were formerly agreed and treated of at Guînes: namely that the King should have freely and as an alod,[29] for himself and his heirs in perpetuity, in recompense for the crown of France, the entire Duchy of Guienne as fully as any King of England has ever held it, together with all the other lands

---

[29] An alod is a piece of territory owned outright and independently, rather than held as a fief provided by a superior lord.

named in the cedule then sent to the Pope by the confessor in the form which follows:

[3] Firstly the entire duchies of Aquitaine-Guienne and Normandy and the county of Ponthieu as entirely as any of the ancestors of the King ever held them; and with this Angers and Anjou, Poitiers and Poitou, Le Mans and Maine, Tours and Touraine, Angoulême and Angoumois, Cahors and Quercy, Limoges and Limousin, and all the other lands, castles and towns acquired since the beginning of the war; the King and his heirs to have and hold all the abovesaid things freely, and like neighbor and neighbor.

[4] And it pleases the King in honor of God and in order to avoid the perdition of Christians, and out of reverence for the Holy Father, if a good peace can be had, to release Normandy, Cahors, Quercy and the county of Angoulême. And all should be as included in the same cedule: that the King, in order to have peace, would release Cahors, Quercy and the county of Angoulême; however, it is not the intention of the King, nor will it ever be, to abandon the said lands, if they should be a portion of the duchy of Guienne of olden times; and this should be fully apparent from the form of the said cedule inasmuch as the said cedule names first of all the duchy entirely; and then says, after that, the other abovesaid lands with other different lands, not included in the said duchy.

And it is the intention of the King that the said lordships of Cahors, Quercy and Angoulême should be asked for in demesne, if one should learn that any of his ancestors, Kings of England, held them in demesne. And if his ancestors only held the homages and sovereignty, the King wishes that they should be asked for in the same manner that his ancestors held them.

[5] Item in case that one cannot come to have the said peace in the abovesaid manner, because of the cedule which speaks to the contrary, and namely [regarding] Angoulême and Angoumois, it pleases the King that in that case compensation should be made for the possession of the said lands out of other territories towards the high country where the thing can be done with the least damage to the King, and where the danger from the French in the future will be minimized. And if the other side will not agree to this at all, the King does not wish for the negotiations to be broken off for that reason, since it was written that way in the cedule.

[6] And as to the limits of the lands, and the borders of the duchy and of all the other lands, the King wills that the lords should treat first of all and agree in principle on the boundaries as near as they can before they show their authorization to make the Pope a mediator. And if it seems to them that the thing to do is that certain people should be assigned from each side to decide concerning the lands and the borders, [then] concerning this the King of definite knowledge and of his own initiative and will, desires and has commanded that the lords, if there should be debate concerning the limits or borders of the lands, may grant and give assent that the Pope, not as a judge but as an intermediary person or a mediator, should decide and conclude all debates concerning the limits of the lands and the aforesaid boundaries, within a certain time, for example within one month after the information concerning it should be acquired by the depu-

ties of the two sides. Also, they may grant that power to the Pope either before the sending of the commissioners for the determination of the boundaries, or after, and they have special power to do this.

And it is the intention of the King, that all this business should be taken care of and finally brought to a conclusion before the first day of April next, and that the King should be certified of the result within that time, if it is possible.

[7] Item, as to the guarantees which are to be made for the performance and keeping of the peace and the agreement, the King wills that the other side should make all the guarantees that anyone can arrange or think up, and he for his part will do the same in order to bind himself and his heirs and all his lands over there.

[8] Item, it is the King's will that the lords may extend the truce up to the Pentecost [1 June] if they see that it should be done, depending on how the business is progressing over there.

90. The French Renounce the Treaty of Guînes. [Source: Avesbury, 421]

In that same year [1354], around the feast of Christmas, at Avignon, in the presence of the Pope and of the ambassadors sent there for the purpose by King Jean of France, the terms of the said peace were pronounced by the noble lords Henry Duke of Lancaster, John Earl of Arundel, William Bishop of Norwich, and Michael then Bishop of London. The French ambassadors utterly refused this peace agreement, saying that this was not what had been arranged, and that they would not by any means consent to a peace such as that. Then, the said Bishop of Norwich having been there overtaken by death, the other English ambassadors returned to England without having accomplished the business.

91. Charles the Bad and the Expedition of 1355. [Source: Le Bel, 2:207–15]

When Edward learned of the outcome of events at Avignon, according to Froissart, "he declared that, since peace could not be made in Avignon, he would make war in France more strongly than ever before." While at Avignon, the Duke (as he had now become) of Lancaster had been secretly approached by Charles "the Bad," King of Navarre and one of the greatest lords of northern France, who also claimed to have some right to the crown of France through his mother. Charles proposed to help Edward oust King Jean in exchange for a portion of the kingdom for himself.

For the campaigning season of 1355, Edward planned two major expeditions. The first, under the command of his eldest son Edward the Prince of Wales (later known as the Black Prince), would go to Gascony and put an end to the French recovery begun there in the summer of 1354 by Count Jean I of Armagnac. The second army he himself would lead into northern France, where he would link up with Charles of Navarre.

King Jean of France unrelentingly hated the young King of Navarre and his brother Philip, because of the love he [Jean] had borne for Lord Charles of Spain, whom they had killed. This hate never left his heart, regardless of whatever appearances he might put on for them . . .

When the young King of Navarre and Lord Philip, his brother, saw that King Jean bore ill will towards them, though they did not for certain know why, they had all their castles and strongholds – of which they had quite a few, and still do, in the county of Evreux and elsewhere – well supplied and defended with men-at-arms and other needful things; and they always rode armed, with a great company of men.

Matters went from bad to worse, so that, it is said, an accord was reached between King Edward of England and the King of Navarre, with the intention that the King of England should come and land in Normandy, and the King of Navarre would open a path for him, and be his ally, and his brother Philip too.

And this became pretty clear, for it is a fact that in the year 1355 the noble King Edward provided himself with a very great number of men-at-arms and ships, and put to sea around the month of August, and remained at sea for a good month and more. King Jean was well aware of this, and sent to all the nobles and non-nobles that they should come to him at Amiens for the defense of the realm; for King Edward was at sea and was expected to land in France, no one knew where.

In this period some of the Council of the [French] King were aware of the agreements which were said to have been made between the King of England and the King of Navarre, and they considered that this accord could be the means of the destruction of the realm. So they spoke of it with King Jean and remonstrated with him with so many arguments that he was compelled to agree to their counsel, although his heart was against it. Treaties and negotiations were made until at last a day of reconciliation was set between King Jean of France and the King of Navarre; and the King of France had to come out of Paris to speak to the King of Navarre. It was agreed that arranged that King Jean should give to the King of Navarre all the lands which he had formerly given to Charles of Spain, who had been killed, which was the source of the hatred, and should hand over to him all the profits and arrears which he and King Philip [VI] had gotten from them over the space of twenty years, which might amount to 150,000 écus. And from then on the King of Navarre should be faithful and loyal to King Jean of France, and cancel his agreements with the King of England, if there were any. And furthermore, the King of Navarre and his brother would be allowed to ride through the realm of France with a total of 100 bascinets or lances without hindrance, if they wished. Thus was the King of England disappointed, and compelled to turn back without accomplishing anything, at great expense, which angered him greatly, so that he many times asked the King of Navarre to compensate him for his losses.

The noble King Edward did not leave matters so, but wanted to make use of his preparations in some way. "Go rest yourselves until I shall call for you," he said to his knights and men who had remained for a long time on the sea and were very worn out. "And I want it known throughout all of France that I will enter there shortly, and I will fight King Jean, and I will lay waste the land as far forward as I can." This news spread through France, and King Jean had all his men gather. So a marvelous number of great knights and commoners came to him. So he sent lord Louis de Namur and his marshal, lord Arnoul d'Audrehem, with 300 men-at-arms, to stay in St. Omer; and he sent to Boulogne, Hesdin, Montreuil, the bastide before Guînes, Ardres, Aire, and to all the fortresses, ordering that large garrisons be established.

The noble King Edward, thinking of the other half of his affairs, sent his son the Prince of Wales into Gascony with 1,200 men-at-arms and 4,000 archers. He himself came to Calais around six days before All Saints' [1 November] of 1355, remaining there for about four days to unload the ships and disembark the horses. When he understood that King Jean was at Amiens with a great army, he said that he would go there and show him [Jean] the flames and smoke of his country: if he wanted to come put out the flames, he should come [and do so]. So he departed from Calais one day, and went to stay between the bastide of Guînes and Ardres, where King Jean's men were. And in truth I have heard it said by the chevalier de Harduemont, and by the Lord of Bergues, and by many others that King Edward had no more than 3,000 men-at-arms and 6,000 archers on this *chevauchée*, and still he wanted to do battle with the King of France and all his forces on his own home ground. Also, he had brought with him three young children – two of the King's own children along with the son of the Countess of Montfort, who was supposed to be Duke of Brittany, and was so called – the oldest of whom was not yet fourteen years old, and each of them was well mounted and equipped for war.

The following day, the noble King moved off from near Ardres and advanced burning and devastating the country. He passed beyond St. Omer, drew near to Thérouanne, and encamped very near there.

There a valiant knight called Sir Boucicaut, the most renowned for his prowess of any man in France – who was not a free man, as he was the King's prisoner loose on parole – came to him. The noble King greeted him very pleasantly, and asked for news of his lord, the King [of France]. Sir Boucicaut answered that he thought that he was at Amiens. "Holy Mary," said the King, "why does he await me there, he who has such a great force and sees his land burned and laid waste by so few men?" – "By my faith," said Sir Boucicaut, "I do not know, Sire; I am not of his privy council."

The King immediately called over three of his knights and said to them: "I pray you that you lead Sir Boucicaut through all our divisions, so that he shall see what men we have, and tell his lord the King." Sir Boucicaut went there, and returned to the King and said to him: "Sire, you have fine men, but not as many as I believed." The King had him remain near him all that night, and on the morrow he rode beyond Hesdin, burning and devastating the country; and he did not hear any news of King Jean.

The next day he lodged in an abbey and called over Sir Boucicaut, then said to him: "Sir Boucicaut, do you know what you shall do? I know well that I could have more than 6,000 écus [ransom] from you, if I should wish to. You go say to your lord that I have burned his country up to here, because I thought that he would come to extinguish the flames; and tell him that I will await him here for three days, so that he will find me if he wants to come; and if he does not come, I will go the way that I came, for [otherwise] I could well remain so long that the Channel would become too difficult to cross. If you will give me your faith that you will deliver this message, just as I have said it to you, I will release you from your ransom."

The knight humbly thanked him and said that he would do it willingly, and that he was his knight in all cases except against the King of France.

Sir Boucicaut left King Edward, and went to King Jean at Amiens, and delivered his message well and sufficiently; but King Jean did not want to go to the meeting to which King Edward had summoned him.

So the King of England departed from the abbey, and returned towards Fauquembergues and through the county of Boulogne, burning, robbing, and destroying everything, until on the night of the feast of St. Martin [11 November] he came to Calais; there he joyously gave a supper for his knights in honor of St. Martin.

92. Back in Calais. [Source: Avesbury, 429–31]

On the morrow, which was Thursday [12 November], the Constable of France came along with other Frenchmen to the edge of the causeway of Calais bearing letters of credence. There, in the presence of the noble Duke of Lancaster, the Earl of Northampton, and the lord Walter Mauny, knights, they asked for battle with the King of England on the upcoming Tuesday [17 November]. The aforesaid English lords told the Frenchmen, by the command of the King, that the King had the desire to avoid the effusion of Christian blood as much as he could; and so he wished to expose his own body in pursuit of his rights and do battle with his adversary in person, such that all the rights which each of them held in the realm of France should be staked on the fight between just the two of them; or, if the adversary did not wish to fight alone, then each of them might add his eldest son; or further, if he did not wish to do that, that each of them might take two, three, or four noble knights, the closest in blood to him, combined with himself and his eldest son, so that thus the said rights might finally be decided, and the vanquished give up his right to the realm of France to the victor. The French rejected all these offers, and asked for battle on Tuesday, as before. Then the said English lords, ready for battle, suggested what was then the next day, that is to say Friday, or else Saturday. The French, forsooth, would not accept either day, sticking to their original proposal. Then the said English lords graciously accepted the aforementioned Tuesday, with a certain condition added: that the said Frenchmen would guarantee, on their own words of honor, that they would bring their King of France, Jean, ready for battle on the said Tuesday, to a certain place nearby to there, selected by knights wise in arms from both sides. And if not, then these Frenchmen at that time would surrender themselves as prisoners to the King of England and remain as captives just as if they had been taken prisoner in battle; and in equivalent fashion the said English lords would guarantee, on their own words of honor, that they would lead the King of England, ready for battle, to the said place on the said day, or else give themselves up as prisoners of King Jean of France and stay his captives. And the Frenchmen, not having a ready response for these words and offers, were speechless for a moment, and, after a delay to discuss it among themselves, said that they were by no means willing to act as guarantors in that way. Then the said English lords, thinking that the French planned by their tricks to deceive the King of the English, and to harm him through the useless expenses of staying there, proposed the morrow [25 June 1356] of the upcoming feast of St. John the Baptist for the date of this battle. Then both sides returned to their lodgings. And the lord King of England waited there until the said Tuesday [the seventeenth]; no Frenchmen came. And so he paid all of his foreign soldiers sums large or small, according to the status of the individuals, in addition to the wages owed them; and he returned to England much praised.

93. The Prince of Wales' Dispatch on His *Grande Chevauchée*, 1355. [Source: Avesbury, 434–7; translation adapted from Barber, *Life and Campaigns*, 52–5]

It has traditionally been believed that the great chevauchée *conducted by the Black Prince in Languedoc in 1355 was intended to inflict maximum damage on France, and hence on King Jean, while avoiding battle with the numerically superior French forces in the region by fast movement. Recent research, however, has cast some doubt on the proposition that the English were avoiding battle [see the article "Edward III and the Dialectics of Strategy, 1327–1360," below]. Prince Edward's own statements on the matter should be noted, but not necessarily taken at face value: only a careful study of the movements and relative positions of the two armies will enable the student to come to a firm conclusion on the matter.*

Reverend father in God and most trustworthy friend, as for news from these parts, this is to let you know that, since we last wrote to you, it was agreed by the advice and counsel of all the lords with us and the lords and barons of Gascony that we ought to march into Armagnac, because the Count of Armagnac was the leader of our adversary's troops and his lieutenant in the whole of Languedoc, and had done more damage to the liegemen of our most honored lord and father the King than anyone else in the region. So, in pursuit of this, we marched

through the country of Juliac, which surrendered to us, as did the fortresses in it. Then we rode through the country of Armagnac, laying waste the countryside, which greatly encouraged the liegemen of our most honored lord, whom he had earlier attacked. From there we went into Astarac, and then into Comminges, as far as a town called Samatan, the best town in the region, whose inhabitants left it empty as our men approached. Then we passed through the Count de l'Isle's lands, until we came within three miles of Toulouse, where the Count of Armagnac and other great men among the enemy were gathered. We stayed there two days and then continued on our march, crossing in one day the two rivers of Garonne and Ariège, three miles upstream from Toulouse, which are difficult enough to cross, with hardly any loss of men; and we encamped for the night about three miles beyond Toulouse. And we marched through the country round Toulouse where many good towns and fortresses were burnt and destroyed, because the region is very rich and fertile; and not a day passed without a town, castle, or fortress being taken by one or another of our divisions or by all of them. We continued to Avignonet, a large and strong town which we took by assault: all our divisions encamped in the town. Then we went to Castelnaudary, which we reached on All Saints' Eve [31 October] and remained there for the feast day [1 November], the entire army encamped inside the town. From there we marched to Carcassonne, a fine large town, held by important commanders, with numerous men-at-arms and common soldiers; the majority of the inhabitants of the country around Toulouse had fled there, but when we arrived they abandoned the town and retreated into the old town, a very strong castle. We stayed there two days, the whole army being inside the town, and spent the whole of the third day burning the town, so that it was completely destroyed. Then we rode right through the region round Carcassonne until we came to Narbonne, a noble town, and larger than Carcassonne. The inhabitants abandoned the town and took refuge in the castle, where the Viscount of Narbonne was, with a garrison of 500 men-at-arms, or so it was said. We stayed there two days; once again the whole army stayed in the town. Then the Pope sent two bishops to us, who sent for safe-conducts to us, which we did not grant them. For we did not want to enter into any treaty until we knew the wishes of our most honored lord and father the King, particularly since we had news that he had crossed into France with an army. So we sent letters back to them saying that if they wanted to negotiate, they should go to him, and we would do whatever he commanded; and so they went back. Then we held a council as to where it would be best to march next; and because we had news from prisoners and others that our enemy had gathered and was coming after us to give battle, we turned back towards them and expected a battle within the next three days. And when we turned back, they retreated to Toulouse. So we pursued them, making long marches to Toulouse: and then we crossed the Garonne at Carbonne three miles from Toulouse, where we rested for that day and the following night. Before midnight news came that the whole enemy army under the Count d'Armagnac, the Constable of France, Marshal Clermont and the Prince of Orange and other noblemen of the region had come out of Toulouse and were encamped about six miles from our rearguard, having lost some of their men and carts as they encamped. At this we marched towards them, sending on Bartholomew Burghersh, John Chandos, James Audley, Baldwin Botetourt and Thomas Felton and others, about thirty in all, to get definite information about the enemy. They rode on towards the enemy until they came to a town where they found 200 of the latter's men-at-arms, with whom they fought and captured thirty-five of them. This made the enemy retreat in great fear to their camp, and they marched to the towns of Lombez and Sauveterre, which are only half an English league apart. We encamped outside the towns that same night, so close that we could see their campfires. But there was between us a very large deep river, and that night, before we came, they had broken the bridges, so that we could only cross the next day after we had got our men to repair the bridges. From there the enemy moved to the town of Gimont, which we reached on the same day as them, and before they could enter the town our men captured or killed many of them. That same night we encamped outside the town, and waited there the whole of the next day, hoping that a battle might take place. And the same [next] day we and the whole army were in battle order before sunrise, when news came that before daybreak most of the enemy had left; only the commanders remained in the town, which was large and strong and could have been held against large numbers of men. So we returned to our quarters and had a council as to what to do. It was clear that the enemy did not want a battle, so it was agreed that we should return towards our own lands. Sir Richard Stafford will tell you about this more fully than we can in a letter; please give full credence to everything he has to say and to show to you. Revered father in God and most trustworthy friend, may the Almighty keep you always. Written under our privy seal at Bordeaux, Christmas day.

94. Excerpt From a Letter of Sir John Wingfield to the Bishop of Winchester. [Source: Barber, *Life and Campaigns*, 52]

The following passage, taken from a letter written by one of the Prince's captains to the Treasurer of England, repays very careful reading.

It seems certain that since the war against the French King began, there has never been such destruction in a region as in this raid. For the countryside and towns which have been destroyed in this raid produced more revenue for the King of France in aid of his wars than half his kingdom; and that is without the profits of recoinage and the profits and customs which he takes from those of Poitou, as I could prove from authentic documents found in various towns in the tax-collectors' houses. For Carcassonne and Limoux, which is as large as Carcassonne, and two other towns near there, produce for the King of France each year the wages of a thousand men-at-arms and 100,000 old écus towards the costs of the war. According to the records which we found, the towns around Toulouse, Carcassonne and Narbonne which we destroyed, together with Narbonne itself, produced each year, over and above this, 400,000 old écus as war subsidies; and the citizens of the larger towns and other inhabitants, who should know about such matters, have told us this. And, by God's help, if my lord had money to continue this war and to profit the King and his honor, he could indeed enlarge the boundaries of his territory and take a number of places, because the enemy are in great disarray. In order to do this my lord has ordered all the earls and bannerets to stay in different places along the border in order to raid and damage the enemy's lands. My lord, that is all the news for the moment, but please write to me and let me know your wishes, and I will do my best to help. Most honored lord, may God send you long life, joy and good health. Written at Bordeaux, Wednesday [24 December] before Christmas.

95. Sir John Wingfield to Sir Richard Stafford. [Source: Avesbury, 445–7; translation adapted from Barber, *Life and Campaigns*, 55–6]

Personal and place names in medieval documents can be very difficult to decipher, and it is often impossible to identify them with full certainty. This is especially true in the case of documents in which English writers try to incorporate the names of unfamiliar places in France, such as the news bulletin below. Translators of medieval documents can usually make an informed guess as to the identity of the people and places in question, but they will inevitably sometimes guess incorrectly, a fact of which the readers of translations should be fully aware. To highlight the significance and difficulty of this problem, the names of the places in this letter have been left in their original spelling. Serious students of medieval history may wish to make an exercise for themselves by trying to identify the locations in question by studying a good map (e.g. a 1:200,000 road atlas). A footnote gives two modern historians' versions of the same list of places.

Most dear lord and most trustworthy friend, as for news since you left, this is to tell you that five fortified towns have surrendered, namely Port seint Marie, Cleyrak, Tonynges, Burgh seynt Piere, Chastiel Satrat and Brassak and seventeen castles, that is, Coiller, Buset, Levynak, two castles named Boloygnes which are quite close to one another, Mounjoye, Viressch, Frechenet, Mountoundre, Pusdechales, Mounpoun, Mountanak, Valeclare, Benavaunt, Lystrak, Plasak, Contestablison, and Moun Ryvel. Sir John Chandos, Sir James Audley and your men who are with them, and the other Gascons in their company, Sir Baldwin Botetourt and his company, and Sir Reginald Cobham took the town called Chastel Satrat by assault, and the bastard de l'Isle, who was captain of the town, was killed as they attacked by an arrow which went through his head. Sir Reginald has turned back towards Lanedac and Sir Baldwin towards Brassac, with their troops; and Sir John and Sir James with their men have stayed at Chastiel Sacret, and have enough of all kinds of supplies to last until midsummer, except only for fresh fish and greens, according to their letters. So you need not worry about your own men. There are more than three hundred armed men in the town, three hundred foot soldiers and a hundred and fifty archers. And they have raided towards Agente, burning and destroying all their mills, and have burnt and broken all the bridges across the Gerounde, and taken a castle outside the town and garrisoned it. Sir Jean d'Armagnac and the Seneschal of Agenais, who were in the town Dagente, did not once poke their heads out, nor did any of their men; yet our people have been outside the town twice. Sir Boucicaut has come as has Sir Arnaut of Spain and Grismouton de Chambly, with three hundred lances and three hundred Lombard footsoldiers; they are at Musschak in Cressy, only a few miles from Chastiel Sacret and Brassak. There will be a good company there for each to try his comrade's worth. Sir Bartholomew is at Coinak with 120 men-at-arms from the Prince's household and 120 archers, and the Captal de Buch, the Lord of Montferrand and the Lord of Curton are with him with 300 lances and 120 archers and 200 footsoldiers, and there are men-at-arms at Tailborugh, Tanney, and Rocheforde, probably about six hundred lances in all. At the moment they are out on a raid towards Aungo and Peyto. The Earls of Suffolk, Oxford and Salisbury the Lord of Mussidan, Elie de Pommiers and other Gascons with more than 500 lances, 200 footsoldiers and 300 archers are at the moment in the area of Nostre Dame de Rochemade; they have been away for twelve days and had not returned when this letter was sent. Sir John Chandos, Sir James and Sir Baldwin and the men in their company are also out on a raid in their region. Sir Reginald and the men of the Prince's household and the Gascons who are with them are also out on a raid. The Earl of Warwick has been at Tonynges and at Clerak and has taken these towns; at the moment he is somewhere near Mermande, trying to destroy the enemy's provisions and other things. My lord (the Prince) is at Leybourne and the Lord of Pommiers at Frensak, a mile or two from Leybourne. The prince's men are at Seint Milioun and Leybourne, and Bérard d'Albret is with them. The prince is awaiting news which he expects to receive, and is going to decide what his best course of action is once he has heard the news. At the moment the Count of Armagnac is at Avinoun, as is the King of Aragon. As to the other reports about different places which you know about, I have no further information at the time of writing. Most dear lord, that is all I have to tell you; but please remember to send news to the Prince as soon as you possibly can. Written at Leybourne, 22 January.[30]

---

[30] The following list gives the places in the letter, as identified by Richard Barber, with differing identifications by Clifford J. Rogers given in brackets. Port Ste Marie, Clairac, Tonneins, Bourg St Pierre, Castelsagrat, Brassac, Quiller [Colleignes], Buzet [Buzet-sur-Baïse], Lavaignac [Lévignac], Boulogne [Bouglon], Montjoie, Virech [Vire-sur-Lot], Fresquenet [Frayssinet], Montendre, Pusdechales [unidentifiable], Montpon, Montagnac [Montignac], Vauclair [Vauclaire], Benevent [Bénévent], Listrac, Plassac, Crudestablison [La Contie], Montreal [Lamothe-Montravel], Castelsagrat, Lanedac [Lavardac; the manuscript of Aves-

96. The English Recover Berwick. [Source: Avesbury, 450–6]

One reason for the brevity of King Edward's Picardy campaign in 1355 was that, shortly before his return to England, he learned that the Scots had taken advantage of his absence to seize the town of Berwick by surprise, despite the desire of the captive King David II to reach a peace settlement with his brother-in-law, Edward III. The Plantagenet wasted no time in dealing with the situation.

On the thirteenth day of January, the aforesaid year [of 1356], the noble King of England came to the castle of Berwick which was guarded for the English by lord Walter Mauny, knight and captain of the place. Before this arrival, the said lord Walter had more than 120 men of the forest of Dene and other parts of England mining out a subterranean passage, by which the English could enter into the said town. On the morning it was completed, the lord King ordered that the Scots in the town should be assaulted from every direction, by sailors on the sea and by others overland. The Scots, perceiving this, were afraid, and immediately some of the greater among them called to the said lord Walter Mauny, then roaming the walls of the castle and preparing, with the others, to attack the Scots. And they asked him in humble supplication that he please take them into the castle into the presence of the King, so that they could speak personally with him. Afterwards the said Scots, introduced into his presence by permission of the lord King, prostrated themselves on the ground, acknowledging that the capture of the said town of Berwick had been foolishly done, and begging his grace and mercy, humbly made supplication that his Excellency deign to receive them into his grace, and they would promptly surrender the said town and its keys to him. Then the lord King, gracious as usual, allowed all the Scots to depart freely, and thus recovered the city from them and subjugated it to his authority speedily and easily, without the effusion of blood.

97. Surrender of Balliol's claim to Scotland to Edward III. [Source: Fordun, 363]

The Chronicle of the Scottish Nation *was composed by John of Fordun (d. 1384), a clerk of Aberdeen in Scotland. In reading this excerpt from it, consider why Edward III would have accepted (and indeed sought) Balliol's renunciation, when at the same time the Plantagenet had already persuaded the captive David II to seek his realm's approval for a peace settlement whereby if, as seemed likely, the Bruce king died without heirs of his body, the crown of Scotland would*

bury is unclear and the "Lanedac" in the printed version could be a "Lavedac"], Brassac, Castelsagrat, Agen, the Garonne, Agen, Moissac in Quercy, Castelsagrat, Brassac, Taillebourg, Tonnay, Rochefort, Anjou, Poitou, Rocamadour, Tonneins, Clairac, Marmande, Libourne, Fronsac, Libourne, St. Emilion, Libourne, Avignon, Libourne.

pass to one of his nephews by marriage (probably John of Gaunt), rather than his nephew by blood, Robert Stewart.

I must not omit to state that, the same year, immediately after the town of Berwick had been made over to the aforesaid King, and while he in person was at Roxburgh, before he had advanced further into the land of Scotland, Edward Balliol came, like a roaring lion, to meet him; and, scarce containing himself for wrath, he broke forth into these words, more bitter than death itself, and said: "O King, and best of princes, who art, I know, the mightiest of all mortals in the world in these days – I wholly, simply, and absolutely yield unto thee my claim, and all right I have, or may have, to the throne of Scotland, so that thou avenge me of mine enemies, the Scottish nation, a race most false, who have always cast me aside, that I should not reign over them." And as evidence that he did so he held forth unto him, as he spoke, the royal crown, and some earth and stones which he picked up off the ground with his own hand. "All these," quoth he, "I give unto thee as a token of investiture. Only, act manfully, and be strong; and conquer for thyself the Kingdom which ought formerly to have been mine."

98. The "Burnt Candlemas." [Source: Avesbury, 454–6]

On the twenty-seventh day of the month of January in the same year, the said lord King of England, having received the realm and crown of Scotland for himself, as noted above, in Roxburgh; and having with him there three thousand men-at-arms and ten thousand armored men and more than ten thousand horse archers and as many foot, began to ride into his new realm of Scotland, and, among his other banners, he had the banner of the realm of Scotland at his side, in his presence. Then William Douglas, a very wealthy lord of those parts, came to the same King and spoke words of peace to him, and fraudulently petitioned for a truce of ten days, so that in the interim he might speak with the magnates of the realm of Scotland and bring them over to the obedience and liegeance of this new King of Scots. The lord King, moreover, as one perfect in charity, believing everything, granted the truce to him as requested, and during the interval, though sparing him [Douglas], he devastated by fire all the lands of Patrick of Dunbar, Earl of March, who had on another occasion betrayed the said King. Thus did the army of the said lord King remain spread out over a breadth of almost twenty leagues. And while the said ten days slipped by, the aforesaid William Douglas and the other lords of those parts had everything possible speedily transferred to the other side of the Firth of Forth, to castles and other secret underground locations; and this done and the ten days lapsed, they fled from the face of the King and drew off to the flank, lying hidden in the woods and bogs. Many of them, however, met by chance in stony caverns, were captured by the English; and vice-versa, a few Englishmen wandering alone were captured by the Scots, and others killed. In truth the said King, seeing himself largely circumvented by the deceit of the said William Douglas, caused all his lands and those of other lords, as far as the Firth of Forth, to be destroyed by fire, so that nothing which could be found remained unburnt. They found very little food there; and what is more, many ships coming from England towards the King with victuals were horribly shaken by storms at sea, so that some of them perished, as is said, and some returned to various ports in England, compelled by the storm; and some of them were carried over to foreign lands. Thus it was that for lack of supplies the lord King, his plan frustrated for the time, returned to England. In returning, however, the English brought back great spoil and a truly huge booty in livestock. And the lord King sent the Earl of Northampton to Carlisle, with 500 men-at-arms and 1,000 archers; and in the region of Northumberland he sent the Bishop of Durham and the lords Percy and Neville, with other lords of those parts, a very sufficient force.

99. Further Progress of English Arms in Guienne. [Source: Avesbury, 449–50, 456–7]

Modern strategists (and military historians) tend to measure military success by the occupation of territory, or the destruction of enemy forces, but medieval generals, especially in wars like the Hundred Years War which had somewhat the character of a civil war, were often focused more on what Clausewitz recognized as the essentially political nature of war.

In the year of the Lord 1356, within a month after Easter (which fell on the 24th day of the month of April), the Lord of Caumont; Lord Jean Galard, the Lord of Limeuil; Lord Gaillard Durfort, the Lord of Grignols; and Lord Bertrand Durfort entered the allegiance of the King of England, bringing with them 30 castles, walled towns, and little forts. Also, a particular town named La Mas, lying on the banks of the Gironde, was surrendered to the Prince of Wales. Another thing: the Earl of Warwick subjugated to the commands of the King of England another walled town in Quercy, called Miramont, along with its extremely strong castle.

After the feast of the Purification of the glorious Virgin [2 February], in the said year of 1356, the Count of Périgord in Aquitaine, fearing lest the said lord the Prince, eldest son of the King of England, should conquer the city of Périgueux, wrote to his brother, a cardinal in the Roman curia, seeking his counsel and aid on the matter. At the instance of this cardinal, after taking counsel with other cardinals, the lord Pope Innocent sent letters to the Prince requesting that he please leave the said city in peace; and in exchange for his decision to grant toleration, he would give him a very large quantity of gold. To this the Prince responded in writing that his father, the lord King of England, was, by the grace of God, sufficiently wealthy, and had provided him with abundant gold and silver, so that he did not lack for money, nor would he accept gold or silver in exchange for granting such toleration. Rather, he would do everything he could to punish and discipline by force of arms the inhabitants of the

Duchy of Aquitaine who were in rebellion against his said lord and father, and, by means of his men, call them back into their original allegiance, and maintain in his justice those who were obedient to him. Within a few days thereafter, the said city of Périgord was captured by the English under the Captal de Buch and subjugated to the commands of the King of England.

100. Journal of Lancaster's 1356 Normandy *Chevauchée*. [Source: Avesbury, 462–5]

This campaign dispatch describes the chevauchée *undertaken by Lancaster in Normandy in support of Charles the Bad, who had once again fallen out with Jean II and been imprisoned by him.*

Of the movement of the noble Duke of Lancaster through the middle of the Normans in order to break the sieges of the King of Navarre's castles of Pont-Audemer and Breteuil.

These are the marches of the *chevauchée* through Normandy of milord the Duke of Lancaster, who had in his company lord Jean de Montfort (claimant to the Dukedom of Brittany, who had from infancy been raised with the King of England) and 500 men-at-arms and 800 archers. And lord Philip, brother of the King of Navarre, and Sir Godfrey d'Harcourt came to him with 100 men-at-arms of the country, and Robert Knolles brought 300 men-at-arms and 500 archers from the garrisons of Brittany, so that in all milord the Duke had 900 men-at-arms and 1,400 archers. And on the Wednesday [22 June] before the feast of St. John the Baptist, he advanced from the abbey of Montebourg on the Cotentin peninsula to Carentan, outside of the peninsula, five leagues of the country, each of which leagues is longer than two English miles, and there he remained on the day before the said feast. On Friday [24 June], the day of the said feast, he passed in front of the strong town of St.-Lô and moved up to Torigni, which is more than eight leagues from there. He stayed in the same place on Saturday, and on Sunday he advanced over seven leagues, to Evercy. And Monday he passed by Caen and advanced seven leagues to the town of Argences. And Tuesday he continued seven leagues up to the city of Lisieux, passing the bridge of Corbon, which is a very great fortress and the strongest passage in the realm, in a marsh. And on Wednesday he advanced six leagues until he came to the town and castle of Pont-Audemer, which belonged to the King of Navarre. The castle was being besieged by a great number of men-at-arms and crossbowmen, [but] when they heard that milord the Duke had passed the said bridge of Corbon, they fled at night in very great haste, leaving behind all their engines and artillery, crossbows, pavises,[31] and other various material. He stayed there that Thursday and Friday, in order to fill in the very fine and

---

[31] A type of large, roughly rectangular shield, used for infantry, particularly crossbowmen.

very strong mines which they had dug so close that they were only four feet from the walls of the castle, and he had the castle stocked with supplies for a year, and put a castellan, Sir Johann de Luk, a knight of Brabant, inside with 50 men-at-arms and fifty archers of his own men. And Saturday [2 July] he moved five leagues from there up to the abbey of Bec-Hellouin. And on Sunday he traveled from there up to the town of Conches, eight leagues away, where he made an assault on the castle and captured the outer ward of the castle by force and put it to the flames. And on Monday he went to Breteuil, which belongs to the King of Navarre, where there was a very strong castle, under siege by the enemies of the said King. But, before the arrival of milord the Duke, they departed from there. My lord had the castle stocked well with supplies, and then on the same day went two leagues to one side, to a large walled town called Verneuil, which belongs to the Countess of Alençon. My lord took the town by assault, and many prisoners and many goods were seized there. And immediately on the same Monday he made an assault on a tower in the said town of Verneuil, which was very strong, and the attack lasted all that day, and [continued] Tuesday, and Wednesday until the first hour of the day, when the tower was surrendered to him with all the goods within it, and the condition that [the defenders] should keep their lives, and not be made prisoners. Many Englishmen were wounded by quarrels and stones in that assault. My lord had the tower destroyed, and he acquired many goods there. And the said town of Verneuil is only 18 leagues from Paris, and is called the capital of Normandy.

On Thursday [7 July] my lord remained there to rest his men. And on Friday, returning back towards the Cotentin, the Duke moved to a town called l'Aigle, where Sir Charles of Spain was put to death by King Jean of France.[32] And his eldest son the Dauphin de Vienne, and his brother the Duke of Orléans, and many great men of the country, with 8,000 men-at-arms, [and of] crossbowmen and other commons 40,000, were next to the town, one mile away. And two heralds came to milord the Duke on behalf of the King, and said to him that the said King knew well that, since my lord had conducted a *chevauchée* into his realm for so long, and remained so close to him at Verneuil, that he had come in order to have battle; and he would willingly have it if he wished. To this my lord replied that he had come into these parts in order to do some particular tasks, which he had fully accomplished, thanks be to God, and was therefore returning to where he had business; and, if the said King Jean of France wished to disturb him on his way, he would be ready to meet him. But after this time he had no further news of the said King.

And on Saturday [9 July] he moved from l'Aigle to the town of Argentan. And on Sunday he continued to the town of Torigni. And on Monday he advanced to the abbey of St.-Fromond, where he crossed a very dangerous river, because the French had broken the bridge. In this area 60 men-at-arms and other sergeants had laid an ambush, in order to do what harm they could to our people.

---

[32] Actually by the Navarrese; Charles of Spain was one of King Jean's favorites.

Fifteen of our English men-at-arms had a fight with them, and killed every one of them, which was considered a miracle. And on Tuesday my lord moved to Carentan. And on Wednesday he came to the aforesaid Montebourg, in the Cotentin. On that day, when my lord first entered the peninsula, Robert Knolles with seven men-at-arms were riding in advance of my lord, to pick out lodgings for him and his men, and they suddenly met 120 men-at-arms, crossbowmen, light infantrymen, and Frenchmen, who had sallied out of a castle in those parts in order to plunder and burn a town which is in our obedience. And the said Robert and the seven men-at-arms killed all of them, except for four who were taken for ransom.

Each of the said towns where my lord stayed was a fair town, large and rich, and each day the men captured diverse fortresses and a very great quantity of prisoners and booty; and at their return they led with them 2,000 of the enemy's horses, so that in this *chevauchée* my lord has had great grace and great honor, for never before has anyone seen so few men make such a *chevauchée* in such a country, and without loss to our men, praise be to God. Written at Montebourg, the 16th day of July, the year of grace 1356.

101. The Prince of Wales Makes Preparations for a New Campaign.
[Source: MS CCC78, fo. 179]

Manuscript 78 of Corpus Christi College, Oxford, contains an independent continuation of the Brut *which may have some connection to William Pakington, one of the Black Prince's chief officers in Gascony in the 1370s. There is no documentary evidence to suggest that the tax mentioned below was ever collected, but that could be because it was cancelled as unnecessary after the extraordinary success of the 1356 campaign.*

The Prince called an assembly of the greatest lords of the land and of the commonalty, so that they might do him fealty and homage. And he showed them how he had been given possession of the land of Gascony, as his father's heir, by his letters patent, which were openly read before this assembly. And he informed them that he also intended, on behalf of his father, to demand the realm of France as his right and his heritage. On these points, he asked their counsel; many of them advised him to meet the King of France in arms. Hearing this, the Prince told them that he could not do so without their help, in arms as well as in goods, adding that if they would aid him with the fifteenth part of their goods according to the customs of England then he would willingly undertake the business. Immediately without contradiction it was granted to him. And the Prince assigned a day for everyone who was willing to go and to stand with him; and those who were not ready to come with him on that day, he would not consider his loyal friends.

102. Bartholomew Burghersh's Dispatch on the Poitiers Campaign.
[Source: Froissart, *Oeuvres*, 18:385–7]

Like the Crécy campaign, the Black Prince's chevauchée of 1356 is described in detail in a number of chronicles and campaign dispatches. Aside from those below, a number of translated sources can be found in Richard Barber's The Life and Campaigns of the Black Prince; *the chronicle of Jean Froissart is another valuable source. Modern historians dispute whether, in this campaign, the Prince was "eager for battle, because of the peace which usually accompanies it" (as the English chronicler Geoffrey le Baker claimed), or was simply seeking to inflict damage on the French while simultaneously avoiding battle with their much larger main army.*

Let it be remembered that the Prince departed from Bordeaux on the morrow [30 August] of the feast of St. John in August, the year of our Lord 1356, and made a *chevauchée* through Agenais, Limousin, Auvergne and Berry and beneath the river Loire from Nivers, which is the entrance of Berry, up to the city of Tours, in order to cross into the Ile-de-France; but all the bridges were broken, so that he could not cross. And all the way he did not encounter any army, until he came to a castle called Romorantin, which is in Berry. Before he came there, he had taken prisoner 120 men-at-arms. Inside the said castle were the Lord of Craon, one of the great lords of France, and lord Boucicaut, with fifty men-at-arms; and my lord the Prince besieged the said castle for eight days. The first day he captured all the fortifications of the castle except one great tower, and also captured forty men-at-arms. The Lord of Craon and Boucicaut entered the tower, and [then], compelled by fire, mine and engines, they rendered themselves prisoners.

Another thing. The Prince remained before the city of Tours, where the King of France's son the Count of Poitiers was with a great force of men, for four days, and no one from the city dared sally out.

On the Saturday immediately following, the Prince came to a castle called Chabotrie in Poitou, where the King of France had stayed the night before; and there the Count of Auxerre, the Count of Joigny and the Marshal of Burgundy, who were coming to the army of the King of France, were captured; and 240 men-at-arms were captured or killed there.

The next Monday, the 19th of September, the divisions of the two sides joined battle half a league from Poitiers, and there were captured the King of France; lord Philip his youngest son; the Count of Poitiers; the Count of Ponthieu, lord Jacques de Bourbon; the Count of Eu; the Count of Abbeville; the Count of Tancarville; the Count of Ventadour; the Count of Saarbrücken; the Count of Vendôme and his brother; the Count of Roussi; the Count of Vaudemont; the Count of Dammartin; the Count of Nassau; the Archbishop of Sens; the castellan of Amposta; Marshal d'Audrehem; the Count of Auxerre; the Viscount of Narbonne; [and eleven others of name]; and a further 2,500 persons, of whom 2,000 were men-at-arms.

At the same battle were killed the Duke of Bourbon, lord Robert Duras of the blood of France; the Duke of Athens, Constable of France; the Archbishop of Châlons; Marshal Clermont; the Viscount of Brosse; the Viscount of Rochechoauart; Sir Renaud de Pons; Sir Geoffrey Charny; Sir Geoffrey Matas: and a further 2,800 people were killed, of whom 2,000 were men-at-arms.

Of the said killed and survivors,[33] one thousand were knights bearing banners or pennons.

The King of France had at the battle 8,000 men-at-arms and 3,000 infantry; and the Prince had at the said battle 3,000 men-at-arms, 2,000 archers and 1,000 sergeants.

103. The Poitiers *Chevauchée*. [Source: *Anonimalle*, 35–39]

The portion of the Anonimalle Chronicle *of St. Mary's Abbey in Yorkshire dealing with the 1356 campaign was probably composed two or three decades later, but seems to have been based on eye-witness testimony.*

On the feast of Mary Magdalene [July 22] my most noble Prince of Wales began to move from Bordeaux towards Bergerac, where all his army assembled. And from there they rode towards [the Ile-de-]France, burning and devastating the counties of Périgord and Limousin and all the country of French Gascony; the county of la Marche, the city of Issoudun belonging to the King of France; and all the land of the duchy of Berry which used to be called the realm of desert, burning and destroying up to the town of Romorantin. There he found the Lord of Craon and Marshal Boucicaut and other great lords inside the castle of the said town of Romorantin, eleven leagues from Orléans where his adversary of France was with all the might of France. He besieged the said lords there, and in the end, at their request and prayer, he granted them respite and truce for eight days in order to see if his said adversary of France would do anything to rescue them. And when the eight days were past, the said knights inside the castle saw well that they could not have any succor from their lord of France and chieftain; for which reason they surrendered the castle, and life and limb, to the grace and mercy of the Prince; and the Prince granted them grace and allowed them to go on their faiths. Thereafter the Prince departed from the said town, burning and destroying it and all the countryside. And from there into the duchy of Touraine, as he could not find a bridge or crossing over the river Loire to attack his adversary of France, [they burned and laid waste] all the county up to a town with a fine castle called Montbazon, where he sojourned for two days. Meanwhile, the Duke of Lancaster came with all his forces before the cities of Angers and Tours in order to cross the Loire towards the Prince. But he found no bridge nor passage where he could cross, and so he turned back and besieged the

---

[33] The related letter to the prior of Winchester Cathedral makes it clear that this refers to the prisoners, not including those who fled.

city of Rennes in Brittany. During which time there were many moments of fine chivalry; and in the end he gained [the city] through the nobility of his chivalry.

At this time the cardinal of Périgord came for the first time to the most noble lord the Prince, in order to treat of peace between him and his adversary of France. And the Prince advanced burning and destroying the land until he came to a town called Châtellerault seven leagues from Poitiers, and there he stayed with all his army for four days.

On Friday night, September 16 of 1356, the Prince had the first news from his scouts that his adversary the King of France had come to the town and castle of Chauvigny with all his army, without knowledge of the Prince, in order to be first to Poitiers in order to fight with him. A quarter before dawn on Saturday, the Prince sent for the Earls of Warwick, Suffolk and Salisbury and for the other earls and lords and captains of his host and told them the news that he had heard of his enemies from his scouts; and immediately the said lords armed themselves and heard mass, devoutly kneeling and praying to God for aid and succor; and they had their armor laced up and then mounted their horses and crossed the bridge of Châtellerault. They left the highway to Poitiers and turned their path towards Chauvigny. Suddenly, on the said Saturday the [17th] day of September, they saw [the] adversary of France with his divisions going towards Poitiers, the men's heads covered by chaplets with ostrich plumes or other caps rather than bascinets. Seeing the army of the Prince coming suddenly against them, they made a great cry of "Treachery! Treachery!"

The Prince attacked them vigorously, striking and defeating one division of the French. The Counts of Auxerre, Sancerre, and Joigny were captured there, along with a good eight hundred men-at-arms, knights and esquires. The adversary of France fled with his division towards Poitiers along with two other divisions; the fifth division took flight back towards Chauvigny. That night the Prince encamped with all his army in a woods on a little river near the site of the defeat. His adversary of France remained on the hill before Poitiers with all his army, and on the same night had it proclaimed that no man of worth should be so bold as to remain in Poitiers, but all should gather to him, on pain of life and limb.

On Sunday morning, the very noble Prince and all his army heard mass, armed themselves, and moved off from there, to a place where they saw all the great forces of France come. During this time the cardinal of Périgord went between the two hosts, begging for truce and peace negotiations between them, in reverence of Our Lord: to which they assented. So they chose from the two sides 24 of the wisest men of the two armies, bishops, dukes, barons, counts and knights, twelve from each side. And so they negotiated for a truce all that Sunday, being in the open field all day as well as the following night, a bow-shot's distance between the two armies. The adversary of France sent word to the Prince on Sunday evening that if he would offer assurances on his faith that he would stay in place all night until sunrise, that he [Jean] would grant peace and truce without deceit to him and all his people, so that they could sleep and relax as they wished. And to this the very noble lord the Prince replied furiously that he had not come there on his behalf nor by his assent, but against the wishes of him and all his supporters; and he [the Prince] would stay and go at his own pleasure despite him and all his men, and in spite of all his well-wishers; and if he [Jean] were afraid of him and his men, *he* [the Prince] would willingly grant *him* truce and respite. And so they departed without agreement. And the Prince remained in the field all night.

On Monday morning, the Prince and the great lords of his army with him heard mass in reverence of God, and then moved off towards Poitiers at dawn. And the Earl of Warwick crossed a narrow causeway over a marsh where he found a French town with a castle. The press of the carriage of the English army was so great, and the causeway so narrow, that they could hardly pass, and so they remained up through the first hour of daylight. And then they saw the vanguard of the French come towards the Prince with two large divisions of men-at-arms, shield-bearers, and crossbowmen. And so the Earl of Warwick turned back with his men and crossed the marsh, finding a good passage which had never before been found. All on horseback, they struck and defeated the shield-bearers. Dismounting, he arrayed his division, the vanguard striking the front of his enemies. And immediately the Earl of Salisbury with the rear-guard came to the aid of the Earl of Warwick, hitting and striking down the vanguard of the French so that between these two the enemies were defeated. And the noble Prince of England joined his division with the division of the Dauphin of Vienne and the two brothers, the Dukes of Anjou and Berry, striking and fighting with them, and in the end defeating them. And in such a way the Duke of Orléans with his great division was defeated. Next came the King of France with his grand division and with all those who would rally to him (the estimated number of his men-at-arms was 8,000 bascinets, along with a great number of shield-bearers, crossbowmen, and other infantry, the Dauphin and his two brothers having fled); they found the Prince standing together with 160 bascinets and 40 archers. To him came the Earl of Warwick with twenty bascinets and twelve archers. And soon afterwards the other English and Gascons rallied to him from all over the field. The prince and his men attacked the French and for a long time fought with them hand-to-hand, where many were killed and wounded. In the end, by divine grace and not by human power, the French were defeated and put to flight, and the English pursued them. In the pursuit, a great number of the enemies were taken. And at the battle, the King of France was captured, and along with him, his son Philip and many great lords, counts, barons, and knights, to the number of 92 banners. And so the Prince returned to Bordeaux in Gascony, bringing with him his adversary of France, his son, and many prisoners, thanking and praising Our Lord for the grace of his victory.

104. France Begins to Collapse. [Source: *Scalacronica* (Maxwell), 130–2]

This passage from the Scalacronica *briefly describes the beginnings of the Free Companies, the famous uprising known as the Jacquerie, and also the revolt of the Parisians under Etienne Marcel, as well as the war between the Dauphin and the King of Navarre, all of which were symptoms of the near-collapse of French political institutions in the wake of Poitiers.*

Since there was a truce in this period between the realms of England and France, English soldiers who kept plundering France could not claim to be fighting in pursuit of Edward III's claims. Some, therefore, continued to make war on their own account (making them no different from brigands according to medieval laws of war); others declared themselves partisans of the King of Navarre, who as an independent sovereign had the legitimate right to wage war.

In the same season, a truce having been agreed [to resume peace negotiations after the capture of King Jean at Poitiers] as aforesaid, numbers of Englishmen who lived by the war invaded Normandy, plundered castles, seized manors, and carried on such warlike operations in the country by help of those of the English commonalty, who flocked to them daily against the King's prohibition. It was astonishing how they went in bands, each on their own account, without an appointed captain, and wrought much oppression in the country. They levied tribute from nearly all Normandy and the marches of the neighboring lands, securing for themselves good fortresses in Poitou, Anjou, and Maine, and into fair France [itself] within six leagues of Paris. They were scattered in so many places over different parts of the country that no one could recount the combats and deeds of arms which befell them during this time; but they so acted that all Christian people were filled with astonishment. And yet they were but a gathering of commons, young fellows who hitherto had been of but small account, who became exceedingly rich and skillful in this sort of war, wherefore the youth of many parts of England went to join them.

The villagers and laborers of the commonalty of France gathered in crowds after their King Jean was taken at Poitiers, despising the nobility and doing violence to those whom they could reach, throwing down their houses and declaring that noble people were of no use except to oppress the commonalty and poor people by their extortions. They slew in some places the wives and children of gentlemen, wherefore the gentlemen gathered together and defeated them and put them to flight, and put down this rising.

In the same season the commonalty of Paris, having chosen themselves a leader, and named him Provost of the Merchants, rose suddenly and went to the palace of the King, where the King's son, who was called Duke of Normandy and Dauphin of Vienne, was in council. They broke open the doors of his chamber, killed in his presence the Marshal de Clermont, brother of him who died at Poitiers, and beheaded sundry others there, accusing them of having wasted by living in great towns the treasure of France taken from them [the commonalty] without any intention of making war upon the enemy, notwithstanding that the said Marshal in that very season had inflicted a defeat upon the English in Normandy, where Godfrey d'Harcourt was killed, who in former times had adhered to the English.

The said Provost of the Merchants clapped a cap of his colors on the head of the King's son and brought him before the commons, where he [the Dauphin] entered into a covenant to conduct himself according to their wishes; which promise he did not keep, but escaped as soon as he could, and raised forces against them.

105. The Anglo-Navarrese at Paris. [Source: *Scalacronica* (Stevenson), 179–80]

For that reason, the said Commons retained the King of Navarre and some Englishmen who were staying in Normandy. The King of Navarre had [formerly] been imprisoned by the King of France, as stated above, but in this same season had been rescued by the Lord of Picquigny and his other friends, who by night seized the place where he was imprisoned and took him to Normandy. The said King with many Englishmen joined with the said Commons of Paris and stayed inside the city. From there the English sallied out and by surprise captured a bridge of boats which the Dauphin had recently constructed across the Seine two leagues above Paris, so as to block supplies [from reaching the city]. At the ambush his marshal was captured along with four of his knights, who were led into Paris by the English, where the latter were well received and held in much esteem until they caused disorderly riots by their extortions in the city. Because of these, the commons rose up against them, and chased them out of the town, pursuing in battle array those who escaped through the fields.

The English who had captured and strengthened Poissy and other fortresses in the area were making a sally towards St. Cloud. Hearing the news, meeting the fugitives, they made their way towards the Parisians who had sallied out, and attacked and defeated them, contemptuously driving them back into their city, many of them being killed and drowned in the Seine. The King of Navarre [who was allied with these English] escaped out of Paris. Because of this conflict, the Commons on that very night returned to allegiance of the Dauphin, the son of the King [of France], who was nearby with his army. At that time they beheaded their Provost of Merchants, whom they had raised to be their chieftain, and many others of his supporters with him. So the said King of Navarre with the Englishmen who were occupying Normandy mustered their army in front of Paris, offering battle to the Dauphin, who however would not come out. And in their departure from there they captured by assault the castle of Creil . . . .

The English seized and garrisoned many fortresses, including one called Mauconseil between Beauvais and Picardy. The Bishop of Noyon and the Lord of Aunay besieged it, so four hundred men-at-arms of the said English and the Lord of Picquigny went to rescue the place, capturing the said bishop and with him four barons and fifty knights, defeating the rest. Many fine deeds of arms befell the English in this time in diverse places in the realm of France, which are not recorded here . . . These Englishmen, on their own accounts, had set themselves up in many places in the realm of France during this war – common people, young, unknowns from various regions of England, many of them starting as archers and then becoming knights, some even captains.

106. The Ravages of War. [Source: Venette, *Chronicle*, 93–4]

Written by a Parisian Carmelite, Jean de Venette's chronicle has an unusually strong sympathy for and interest in the common people of the realm of France. The picture he paints of his home village may seem melodramatic, but the war had in fact reduced wide areas of France to near-wastelands.

The English destroyed, burned, and plundered many little towns and villages in this part of the diocese of Beauvais, capturing or even killing the inhabitants. The loss by fire of the village where I was born, Venette near Compiègne, is to be lamented, together with that of many others near by. The vines in this region, which supply that most pleasant and desirable liquor which maketh glad the heart of man, were not pruned or kept from rotting by the labors of men's hands. The fields were not sown or plowed. There were no cattle or fowl in the fields. No cock crowed in the depths of the night to tell the hours. No hen called to her chicks. It was of no use for the kite to lie in wait for the chickens in March of this year nor for the children to hunt for eggs in secret hiding places. No lambs or calves bleated after their mothers in this region. The wolf might seek its prey elsewhere and here fill his capacious gullet with green grass instead of rams. At this time rabbits and hares played freely about in the deserted fields with no fear of hunting dogs, for no one dared to go coursing through the pleasant woods and fields. Larks soared safely through the air and lifted their unending songs with no thought of whistling attacks of eyas or falcon. No wayfarers went along the roads, carrying their best cheese and dairy produce to market. Throughout the parishes and villages, alas! went forth no mendicants to hear confessions and to preach in Lent but rather robbers and thieves to carry off openly whatever they could find. Houses and churches no longer presented a smiling appearance with newly repaired roofs but rather the lamentable spectacle of scattered, smoking ruins to which they had been reduced by devouring flames. The eye of man was no longer rejoiced by the accustomed sight of green pastures and fields charmingly colored by the growing grain, but rather saddened by the looks of the nettles and thistles springing up on every side. The pleasant sound of bells was heard indeed, not as a summons to divine worship, but as a warning of hostile incursions, in order that men might seek out hiding places while the enemy were yet on the way. What more can I say? Every misery increased on every hand, especially among the rural population, the peasants, for their lords bore hard upon them, extorting from them all their substance and poor means of livelihood . . . .

Yet, their lords did not, in return, repel their enemies or attempt to attack them, except occasionally.

107. The First Treaty of London. [Source: R. Delachenal, *Histoire de Charles V* (Paris: Picard, 1909), 2:400–407]

While France descended into chaos and misery, Jean II, from his comfortable captivity in England, conducted peace negotiations with the Plantagenets on the basis of the 1354 draft treaty of Guînes. An initial agreement in principle was reached by December of 1357, and presented to the Dauphin and his council the next month. Although the French government was pleased with the terms, Edward's own parliament refused to ratify them until King Jean had used his influence with his kinsman Pope Innocent VI to secure a set of concessions from the papacy on several points of contention between England and the Curia. While an embassy was sent to Avignon to try to resolve those issues, the two royal Councils continued to meet. By May of 1358, the details of the so-called "First Treaty of London" had been agreed.

According to the terms of this agreement, Jean II was required to make tremendous political and territorial concessions to Edward III. Furthermore, the French were to pay, by instalments, the astronomical sum of 4,000,000 écus (£666,666) for King Jean's ransom. What exactly the English were supposed to give in return is subject to debate, particularly since only a draft of the agreement has survived. Professor John le Patourel argued that "there is nothing in the surviving documents, so far as they go, to suggest that Edward made any concessions whatever" beyond the release of King Jean, and that the First Treaty of London was, therefore, a mere "ransom treaty" rather than a true peace treaty. A case has recently been made, however, that the draft treaty does implicitly include major concessions by the English, which can be inferred from a careful reading of the following provisions.

The Traittié[34] *and Discussion of Peace between Our Sire the King and the French Side.*

Firstly, that along with all the lands, regions and places which our lord the King holds at present in the duchy of Guienne and in Gascony, and also in the isles . . . he, and all his heirs and successors as kings of England, will have and hold entirely and perpetually all the cities, counties, regions, lands, and places named below, viz.: [Saintes and Saintonge, Angoulême and Angoumois, Poitiers and Poitou, Limoges and the Limousin, Cahors and Quercy, Périgueux and Périgord, Tarbes and Bigorre, Guarre, Agen and the Agenais, Montreuil and Ponthieu] . . . with all the rights, homages . . . services, jurisdictions both high

---

34 "Traittié" in Old French can refer either to the process of negotiation or to the final agreement produced by such negotiation.

and low, sovereignties, towns, castles, fortresses, and all other appurtances [belonging thereto] . . . as fully as . . . any of his ancestors, kings of England, held them, since the time of the reign of King Richard of England . . . along with all the other lands, castles, fortresses, towns, places and lordships whatsoever, which the adversary of France held within the . . . places aforesaid . . . which the said adversary shall render to our said lord the King as entirely as he held them on the day of the battle of Poitiers . . . so that neither the said adversary nor any other king of France will hold anything within the boundaries and borders of the regions, lands and places aforesaid . . .

And also the said lord the King shall have and hold for himself and for all his heirs, kings of England, perpetually, the town and castle of Calais and all the neighboring lands . . .

And also the said adversary, for himself and for all his heirs, kings of France, will render and deliver for all time to our said lord the King, and his heirs, kings of England, all the honors, regalities, obediences, homages, allegiances, vassals, fiefs, services, recognitions, oaths, rights, jurisdictions, resorts, safeguards, and all manners of lordships and sovereignties which belong or might in any way belong to the king and crown of France within the Duchy of Guienne and in the entire land of Gascony . . . without holding back for himself, his heirs or successors, or the crown of France, in these people . . . and places, anything because of which he, his heirs or successors, kings of France, might in times to come claim, pretend to, or ask for anything from the King of England, his heirs or successors, or from any of the vassals and subjects aforesaid . . .

And that the said our lord the King, and his heirs, will have and hold all the aforesaid lands . . . and other things aforesaid perpetually, in perpetual and entire freedom and liberty, as sovereign, liege, and direct lords, and as neighbors to the kings and the realm of France . . .

And beyond all the things said above, the said adversary will, for his deliverance from captivity, pay to our said lord the King 4,000,000 gold *écus*, . . . each *écu* valued at 40 pence sterling. Of this he will pay £100,000 . . . before his departure from England, and another £66,667 after his departure, in the same year, and from then each following year £100,000, until the total sum has been paid.

And also the said adversary of France and the entire French side will henceforward depart from all the alliances they have with the Scots, and then shall be made final accord and peace, and perpetual alliance and friendship, between the Kings and the realms of France and of England . . .

108. Rejection of the Second Treaty of London. [Source: Le Bel, 2:287–90]

The First Treaty of London was never implemented. The French proved unable to secure the concessions from the Pope which parliament demanded before ratification of the treaty, and the Dauphin (as Charles of Normandy, Jean's heir and regent, was now known) likewise was unable to raise the money for his father's ransom according to the stipulated schedule. The French government also failed to deliver the hostages who were supposed to go to England as securities for the treaty's full implementation.

When it became clear that the French were unable or unwilling to fulfill the terms of the First Treaty of London, Edward III began preparations for a new expedition to France in 1359. Jean, afraid that the new English invasion might enable the Plantagenet to finally make good his claim to the French throne, desperately negotiated a new agreement, the Second Treaty of London, which was even more generous to the English than the First Treaty. By its terms, Edward III was to receive the entire western half of France, all of Henry II's old "Angevin Empire," including Normandy, Maine, Anjou, Touraine and Brittany, in exchange for his (this time explicit) renunciation of his claims to the remainder of the kingdom.

How the peace between the two Kings of France and England was agreed and sealed by them themselves, but the French would not keep [their agreement]; so the King of England prepared himself to enter France immediately.

Well, now it's time to return to the story of the noble King Edward, from which I have digressed for quite a while [to discuss the ravages of the Companies]. He held the King, Jean of France, in captivity along with the greatest barons of France, and let these pillagers of whom we have spoken work over and lay waste the entire realm, in hope of bringing an end to the war, or of having a peace in accordance with his will. So it came about in the year 1359, around Pentecost [June 9] – after the two cardinals whom the Pope had sent into England in order to make peace between these two Kings, because of whom all Christendom was in a state of torment, had departed from England without accomplishing anything, even though they had been there for two years and more, at their ease, at great expense – that the two Kings drew apart one day in the city of London, and they had no one with them but the Prince of Wales, the eldest son of King Edward, and the bold Earl of Lancaster; and they made a certain agreement, sealed with their seals, and sent it to the princes and barons of France and to all the communities, by means of the chamberlain de Tancarville (Count of Melun) and Sir Arnoul d'Audrehem, who was considered the most worthy knight of France, who were both prisoners of King Edward.

As these two lords were coming into France, the Duke of Normandy and the King of Navarre were reconciled, as you have heard, and returned from Melun to Paris. So, at the request of the aforesaid knights, they summoned all the barons, all the nobles and the commons of the good towns. When they were all assembled, the two knights delivered their message and caused the letters which they carried, and all the points of the peace which had in good will been agreed by the two Kings, to be read out in front of everyone. When everything had been read, they drew off to take counsel, and when they had taken counsel for a good long time, yet they were not all in agreement, for the said peace seemed to some to be too damaging for the realm of France in several ways, and they would rather continue to endure the misery in which they found themselves, and which

King Jean suffered, and await the pleasure of God, than to consent that the noble realm should by thus lessened and divided by the said peace. When the knights heard this, they took their leave and returned to England, and recounted to the two Kings what they had found out.

When the noble King Edward heard these reports, he was made very angry by them; so he said, in such a loud voice that everyone could hear him well, that before August was gone by he would enter into the realm of France with such great forces that he would stay there until he had brought an end to the war with an honorable peace; and he began to make the greatest preparations that anyone had ever seen, in that country or elsewhere.

109. Languedoc in 1359. [Source: A. Germain, "Projet de descente en Engleterre . . . ," *Publications de la société archéologique de Montpellier*, 26 (1858), 425–6]

The following is taken from the text of a document setting out the arguments to be used before the Estates of Languedoc by a representative of the Regent seeking their financial support for a plan to pay the King of Denmark to invade England and rescue King Jean. Nothing ever came of the effort, but the portion of the document translated here gives a remarkable picture of the condition of the kingdom of France in 1359, and the state of mind of her people.

First, he should recall the great honors, goods, riches, and great abundance of merchandise which used to be found in the realm of France, more than in any other realm, by which each person was, and could again be, rich.

Item. Of the great reputation which the said realm and its inhabitants had; for in all places and in all lands they were the most honored and esteemed people in the world.

Item. And how, by the wars which have been going on, the people of the realm have suffered a decline in their goods and their estates, to such an extent that, unless they provide a remedy for it with God's help, they are likely to lose all their goods, estates and reputation.

Item. And considering the state in which they are at present, they and the realm are in danger of experiencing and suffering more evils and inconveniences than they have up to now.

Item. And the great worthiness, goodness and loyalty, sweet goodness and love of our lords the kings of France, predecessors of our very dear and right dread lord the present King, Jean, should not be forgotten; and how they have always been sweet, good friends, and full of pity and mercy towards the good people of the realm and to its inhabitants

Item. And especially the people of the said realm should remember and hold in perpetual affection our said lord King Jean, and call to mind his very great valor, and how, because of the very great desire which he had to bring his people out of their current misery, he personally fought so worthily, as each person knows, that all people, even his enemies and ours, hold him for the most valiant of Christians, and do as much honor as they can to such a prince, even though he is their prisoner.

Item. And also it should be noted how he has borne himself during [his] long imprisonment; for no prince has ever displayed such great constancy in such a situation.

Item. And how the people have always said and maintained that they were willing to put their bodies, estates and wealth towards his delivery, not just the men, but the ladies as well; and that they did not want to spare anything, not jewels, nor robes, nor any others of the things which God has lent to them.

Item. And the evils, harm, and inconveniences which have been inflicted on the realm by the enemies, who continue to do the same from day to day, such as the burning and violation of churches and towns; the killing and murder of men, women, and children; the deflowering, corruption and dishonoring of ladies and maidens.

Item. And when they capture the men, they hang them for two or three days, without drink or food, by the arms, some by the genitals, others by the fingers of their hands, others by their feet, and torture them and beat them to make them talk, so that many of them die; and those who escape from their clutches by paying ransom cannot survive, and if they do live, they are driven mad or maimed in their limbs; and they [the enemies] will not even ransom them for as much as they are worth, but rather [demand] as much as the loans of their friends will bring.

Item. And also that the amount we spend on the war inside the realm is only enough to nourish and appease the war, and always has been and will be lost to it; for the enemies live off us, and our realm is broad and spacious; and therefore the good warriors say that one should distance warfare as far as possible away from oneself; and that there is more peril and loss to be found in awaiting the enemies in our realm than in fighting the enemies far from here; and also people are bolder when they are far from their homes, than they are at their own doors, where they may retreat as soon as they see that they can thus save themselves.

Item. And anyone can see what a situation the people and the realm would be in, if they King of England or the Prince of Wales should enter into this kingdom; for we have enough to do to save our lives from the enemies who are here already.

Item. How the lands of Brittany, Normandy, Picardy, Beauvaisis, the county of Valois, Vermandois, and the Ile-de-France used to say that they were not worried by the enemies, and that, let them come when they wished, they would meet them and fight with them; and nevertheless everyone knows how they have been devastated and despoiled.

Item. And the people of Languedoc should consider and think on the fact that there are more nobles in the said lands [than in Languedoc], and that the other inhabitants are men capable of defending themselves, and that they were not caught napping, but had provided for the defense of their lands, just as the people of Languedoc have done; and nevertheless they have been brought low.

Item. And it should be a matter of concern that if the King of England, the Prince of Wales, or other enemies come from Bordeaux, where they can land without difficulty, they will be able to lay waste the country in the same way, or at least it is a great worry that they might, since they have and hold many garrisons and fortresses between Toulouse and Bordeaux. . . .

110. The Start of the 1359 Campaign. [Source: *Anonimalle*, 44–5]

The initial target of Edward III's invasion of 1359 was the cathedral city of Reims, where the Kings of France were traditionally anointed and crowned.

In the year 1359, before the feast of St. Michael [29 September], the King of England gathered his host in order to cross the sea to France, intending to reclaim by force of arms his rights and his heritage. It was arranged by common consent of the Council that Duke Henry of Lancaster should make the passage first; and so he made a good, safe crossing without any disturbance and arrived at Calais. The Marquis of Meissen and Sir Henry, the Count of Flanders, were lying there with a great multitude of soldiers in order to besiege the said town; but at the arrival of the Duke of Lancaster, the enemies, aware of his coming, departed covertly and headed for Flanders. When his men were assembled, the Duke of Lancaster departed the town of Calais for the realm of France. Arriving there, his divisions rode through and destroyed the land of Picardy, coasted the county of Flanders up to the city of Arras in the county of Artois, and then rode further, destroying up to the city of Cambrai in the Cambrésis, and from there rode, laying waste, up to the city of St. Quentin in the Vermandois. There the King of England sent word by his messengers to the Duke of Lancaster that he should return to him as quickly as he could, for various reasons; and the said Duke returned by way of the head of the Somme, destroying the land all around.

And on the feast of St. Michael the King of England and the Prince crossed the sea with their entire army and arrived at Calais; and from there they split into two divisions, the King by himself, and with him the Duke of Clarence, the Earl of Cambridge, the Duke of Montfort, the Earl of Warwick, the Earl of Suffolk, the Earl of Salisbury, the Earl of Oxford, and other great lords, and a great number of the common soldiers; and they divided themselves into three battles, riding through and destroying the land of France. And the said lord the Prince made his *chevauchée* through another portion of the country, and with him he had his brother the Earl of Richmond, the Earl of Northampton, the Earl of Stafford, and other great lords and commoners. Dividing themselves into three battles, they rode through and devastated the said land of France; and thus they encountered the good Duke of Lancaster, coming towards the King with his said force, twenty miles from Calais. There they took counsel together, as to what course of action would be the most profitable, and to which land they should make their way. So they divided into three parts, the King commanding one part, the Prince another, and the Duke of Lancaster the third, all with their battles well arrayed; and each of them kept twenty or thirty miles apart from the others, riding and destroying the land. And so they passed through Picardy into Artois, and through Artois into the Cambrésis, and through the Cambrésis into the Vermandois, coasting Flanders, Brabant and Hainault and the Empire; and thus, through Vermandois up to the noble city of Laon in the Laonnois. They crossed the fair river Aisne and came up to the noble city of Reims in Champagne. And there the said King of England held the feast of Christmas two miles outside of the city; and there the other two armies assembled, namely those of the Prince of England and the Duke of Lancaster with all their men; and they encamped and found lodgings and solemnly held the feast of Christmas. Thus they remained together and encircling the city for three weeks or more, making many *chevauchées*, laying waste and destroying the land all around.

111. From Reims to Paris. [Source: *Scalacronica* (Maxwell), 148–59]

Sir Thomas Gray, the northern baron who wrote the Scalacronica, *served as one of the captains in the Black Prince's division.*

From the division of the said prince the town of Cormicy was taken by escalade and the castle won, the keep being mined and thrown down by the Prince's men. On the challenge of the French in Reims, Bartholomew de Burghersh, a captain in the the Duke of Lancaster's division, engaged there in jousts of war, by formal arrangement, where one Frenchman was killed and two others wounded by lance-point.

From the King's division, the Duke of Lancaster and the Earls of Richmond and March captured two fortified border towns, Autry and Cernay, on the river Aisne and the border of Lorraine. Lords and knights of the King's division made a raid from Reims nearly to Paris. They set themselves in ambush and sent their scouts up to the gates of the city. They made such an uproar in the suburbs that those within the city did not have the courage to come forth.

The bands of English, those who had been staying there on their own account before the coming of the King, were scattered in various places. They were in diverse bands; one band, called the Great Company, had remained in the field throughout the year in Burgundy, in Brie, in Champagne and in Berry, and wherever they could best find provender. This Great Company had taken the city of Châlons in Champagne by night escalade; but the people of the said city rallied in the middle of their town on the bridge of the river Marne, which runs through the city, and kept them by force out of the best part of the city; wherefore they [the Great Company], finding it impossible to remain, were compelled to evacuate [the place]. This company disbanded soon after the coming of the King, and sought refuge for themselves. There were other bands of English, some of which took by escalade the town of Attigny in Champagne at the time of the arrival of the said King before Reims.

The said King of England afterwards broke up from before Reims, and marched towards Châlons, where he made a treaty with the people of Bar-sur-Aube; once it was completed, he distanced himself from their lands. An English knight, James Audley, took the fortress of Chancu in the vale of Saxoun from the Bretons under Hugh Trebidige. The said James came from his castle of Ferté in Brie to the army of the said Prince near Châlons, in company with Captal de Buch, who came from Clermont.

The said King having caused the bridge over the river Marne to be repaired, and over other very great rivers also, marched to the neighborhood of Troyes. From there the Marquis de Metz and the Count of Nidau, and other German lords who had come with the King, went off to their own country, partly because of scarcity of victuals and partly from respect for the approach of Lent. Due allowance was made to them for their expenses.

The King crossed the river Seine near Méry-sur-Seine, and made his way near Sens and through Pontigny into Burgundy. His son the Prince followed him, and the Duke of Lancaster also; but for want of forage for the horses his said son left the route of his father, and quartered himself at Ligny-le-Châtel, near Auxerre, where the said Prince's army suffered more from the enemy than in any other part of this expedition up to then. Several of his knights and esquires were killed at night in their quarters, and the servants out foraging were captured in the fields, although the country was more deserted before them than in all the other districts, so that they scarcely saw a soldier outside the fortresses.

Five English esquires belonging to the army of the said Prince, without armor except their bascinets and shields, having with them only one [soldier in a] coat of mail and three archers, were in a mill near les Régniers, a fortress held by the English near Auxerre, in order to grind some corn. Fifty men-at-arms, the troop and pennon of the Lord of Hangest, came to attack them; but the five defeated the fifty, taking eleven prisoners; wherefore even the French of the other garrisons called this in mockery the exploit of fifty against five.

The said King remained at Guillon near Montréal in Burgundy, to negotiate a treaty with the duchy of Burgundy; and here Roger Mortimer, Earl of March and marshal of the army and most in the confidence of the King, died of a fever on the 24th day of February.

Three years' truce was made with Burgundy, on payment to the said King of England, at three terms, the sum of 200,000 florins *moutons*, the florin being reckoned at 4s. sterling.

The town of Flavigny in Burgundy, strong and well-fortified, which had been taken by the Englishman Harleston, was restored by the hands of Nicholas Dagworth, because it had been surprised at the time the negotiations for a truce had just begun. Near this town of Flavigny, the said Dagworth in the previous season had fought a skirmish with his thirteen English against sixty-six French lances. The English had occupied a narrow street at the end of a village, having drawn carts across the road before and behind them. They sallied from their shelter at their pleasure, wounding, killing and capturing some of the French. Norman Leslie, who had come from Scotland to help the French, was captured; the others were put to flight.

At the same time William de Aldborough, captain of Honfleur in Normandy, was taken by the French in a sortie, and his people were defeated. An English knight, Thomas Fogg, who was in a fortress of his in the neighborhood, hearing of this affair, threw himself into Honfleur, found it emptied of provender, and rode forth with other English garrisons in the neighborhood, foraging in the country for supplies for the said town. They came suddenly upon 210 French men-at-arms and 200 archers and crossbowmen, who were set in ambush on the English line of march, Sir Louis d'Harcourt and Baudric de la Heuse being in command of the French. The English, numbering forty men-at-arms and one hundred archers, had the protection of a hedge. Both sides dismounted and engaged smartly. The French were defeated, their two leaders being captured, and with them several knights and esquires, and several were killed in the mêlée. Louis d'Harcourt soon afterwards was released by the same English who had captured him, and they became Frenchmen with him.

At Fresnay, an English fortress on the march of Beauce, a French knight who bore the name of the Chevalier Blaunche, challenged the constable of the said place to a personal encounter of two Englishmen against two Frenchmen. The encounter was arranged at a place agreed on. The Chevalier and his esquire were defeated by the two Englishmen, who were arrayed in scarlet, and were taken prisoners into the aforesaid English fortress.

About this time the English knight John Neville, with thirteen lances, defeated near Étampes fifty French men-at-arms, of whom several were taken prisoners. Beyond the Cher, in Berry, the Gascons and English of the garrison of Aubigny met with a defeat, several of them remaining prisoners of the French.

At this time French, Norman and Picardese knights, with others of the commonalty, 3,000 fighting men, made an expedition into England at the expense of the good towns of France, with a show of remaining there so as to cause the said King of England to withdraw from France, in order to rescue his own country. These Frenchmen arrived at Winchelsea on Sunday in mid-Lent [15 March] of the aforesaid year [1360], remained in the said town a day and a night, set fire to it on leaving, and, in going off in their ships, they lost two ships which were left grounded, and about 300 men [killed] by the commonalty who attacked them.

Near Paris Robert le Scot, a knight on the English side, was taken and his people were defeated by the French, and his forts were taken just when he had fortified them.

As the Prince of Wales, son of the said King of England, was marching through Gâtinais,[35] five knights of the country with 60 men-at-arms and one hundred others, people of the commonalty, had fortified anew a country house in front of Fournelis, a fortress which the English held. The said Prince suddenly

---

35 An area south-west of Nemours.

surrounded these knights, bivouacking in the woods, and directed siege engines and assaults; wherefore the said knights, Sir Jacques de Gréville and Hagenay de Bouille, with the others, surrendered unconditionally to the said Prince.

The said King of England, coming from Burgundy, lost two or three German knights from his army. They were killed in their quarters at night by Ivo de Vipont, a French knight, and his company. And as the said King was marching through Beauce, near Toury, that castle chanced to be set accidentally on fire by those within it; wherefore most of them rushed out and threw themselves on the mercy of the said King. The castellan held the keep for two days and then surrendered to the said King, who caused the walls of the said castle to be razed. . . .

This chronicle does not record all the military adventures which befell the English everywhere during this war because of the [great] variety of them; but [it records] only the more notable ones. To relate everything would be too lengthy a business.

Be it known that, in Passion week of the same season [29 March–4 April], the said King of England marched through Beauce, where the monasteries were almost all fortified and stocked with the provender of the country, some of which were taken by assault, others were surrendered so soon as the siege-engines were in position, whereby the whole army was greatly refreshed with victuals.

At this time the Captal de Buch went by permission of the said King of England to Normandy with 22 English and Gascon lances, to interview the King of Navarre to whom he was well-disposed. Near Dreux he fell in suddenly with four and twenty French men-at-arms, knights and esquires, who were lying in ambush for other English garrisons. Both sides dismounted and engaged smartly; the French were defeated, and Bèque de Villaines their leader was taken with four of his knights, the others being taken or killed.

The said King of England took up his quarters before Paris on Wednesday in Easter week [8 April] in the year of grace 1360, [namely] in the villages adjacent to the suburb of St. Cloud, across the Seine above Paris. He remained there five days, and in departing displayed himself in order of battle before the King of France's son, who was Regent of the country and was in the city with a strong armed force. The Prince of Wales, eldest son of the said King of England, who commanded the vanguard, and the Duke of Lancaster with another division, held the fields in front of the suburbs from sunrise till midday and then set them on fire. The King's other divisions kept a little further off. A French knight, Pelerin de Vadencourt, was captured at the city barriers, where his horse, being wounded by an arrow, had thrown him. Some knights of the Prince's retinue, newly dubbed that day, concealed themselves among the suburbs when the said divisions marched off, and remained there till some [Frenchmen] came out of the city, then spurred forth and charged them. Richard de Baskerville the younger, an English knight, was thrown to the ground, and, springing to his feet, wounded the horses of the Frenchmen with his sword, and defended himself gallantly till he was rescued, with his horse, by his other comrades, who speedily drove back into their fortress the Frenchmen who had come out.

Then the Count of Tancarville came out of the city demanding to treat with the Council of the said King of England, to whom reply was made that their said lord would entertain any reasonable proposal at any time.

The said King marched off, spreading fire everywhere along his route, and took up quarters near Montlhéry with his army round him. On Sunday the 13th of April it became necessary to make a very long march toward Beauce, by reason of want of fodder for the horses. The weather was desperately bad with rain, hail and snow, and so cold that many weakly men and horses perished in the field. They abandoned many vehicles and much baggage on account of the cold, the wind and the wet, which happened to be worse this season than any old memory could recall.

About this time the people of Sir James Audley [namely] the garrisons of La Ferté-sous-Jouarre and Nogent in Brie escaladed the castle of Dhuisy in Valois, near Soissons, after sunrise, when the sentries had been reduced. This [place] was very well provisioned and full of noble ladies.

And some men-at-arms, knights and esquires, along with eight Welsh archers of Lord Despencer's retinue, had a pretty encounter in Beauce while the said King's army was billeted in the villages. While outside the army, near Bonneval, keeping watch on the millers in a mill, to have some grain milled, they were espied by the French garrisons in the neighborhood, who came to attack them with 26 lances and 12 French Breton archers. Both sides dismounted and engaged smartly; the French were defeated, three of their men-at-arms being killed and nine made prisoners, every man on both sides being wounded nearly to death. Some of the said English had surrendered on parole to the said enemy during the mêlée, but were rescued by the said Welshmen, who behaved very gallantly there.

The said King of England remained in Beauce, near Orléans, fifteen days, for peace negotiations which the Council of France proposed to him, the Abbot of Cluny and Sir Hugh of Geneva, envoy of the Pope, being the negotiators. The English of the said King's army had encounters, some with loss and others with gain. Certain knights in the following of the Duke of Lancaster, disguising themselves as pillagers, servant foragers, without lances, rode in pretended disarray in order to give the enemy spirit and courage to tackle them, as several of their foragers had been taken during the preceding days. Some of whom, the knights Edmund Pierpoint and Baldwin Malet, overdid the said counterfeit to such an extent in running risks from the French that it could not be otherwise than that they should come to grief; thus they were taken and put on parole.

Sir Brian Stapleton and other knights of the Prince's army and the Earl of Salisbury's retinue, while protecting foragers, had a skirmish with the French near Janville, and defeated them, capturing some of them . . . .

112. Negotiating the Treaty of Brétigny. [Source: Froissart, *Chronicles*, 282–4]

Modern historians tend to emphasize Realpolitik *explanations of Edward III's conduct of his war, but, as his own letters suggest, it would be unwise to ignore religious feeling when assessing his motivations. Thus Froissart's claims concerning the impact of the fearsome (and well-attested) hailstorm of Black Monday on the King deserve to be taken seriously.*

The intention of the King of England was to enter the fertile country of Beauce, and follow the course of the Loire all the summer, to recruit and refresh his army in Brittany until after August; and as soon as the vintage was over, which from all appearances promised to be abundant, he meant to return again and lay siege to France, that is to say, to Paris (for he did not wish to return to England, as he had so publicly declared, on setting out, his determination to conquer that kingdom), and to leave garrisons of those who were carrying on the war for him in France, in Poitou, Champagne, Ponthieu, Vimeu, Valguessin, in Normandy, and throughout the whole kingdom of France, except in those cities and towns which had voluntarily submitted to him.

The Duke of Normandy was at this time at Paris with his two brothers, their uncle the Duke of Orléans, and all the principal councilors of state, who, well aware of the courage of the King of England, and how he pillaged and impoverished the whole realm of France, knew also that his situation could not last, for the rents both of the nobles and clergy were generally unpaid. At this period, a very wise and valiant man was Chancellor of France, whose name was Sir William de Montague, Bishop of Thérouanne: by his advice the kingdom was governed: every part of it profited from his good and loyal counsel. Attached to him were two clerks of great prudence; one was the Abbot of Cluny, the other friar Simon de Langres, principal of the predicant monks, and doctor in divinity. These two clerks just named, at the request and command of the Duke of Normandy and his brothers, the Duke of Orléans their uncle, and of the whole of the Great Council, set out from Paris with certain articles of peace. Sir Hugh of Geneva, Lord of Autun, was also their companion. They went to the King of England, who was overrunning Beauce, near to Gallardon.

These two prelates and the knight had a parley with the King of England, when they opened peace negotiations with him and his allies. To this conference the Duke of Lancaster, the Prince of Wales, the Earl of March, and many other barons were summoned. However, this treaty was not concluded, though it was discussed for a long time. The King of England kept advancing into the country, seeking for those parts where the greatest abundance was. The commissioners, like wise men, never quitted the King, nor suffered their proposals to drop; for they saw the kingdom in such a miserable situation, that the greatest danger was to be apprehended if they should suffer another summer to pass without peace. On the other hand, the King of England insisted on such conditions as would have been so very grievous and prejudicial to France, that the commissioners, in honor, could not assent to them: so that their treaties and conferences lasted seventeen days, the two prelates and the Lord of Autun constantly following the King of England: this last was much listened to at the court of the King. – They sent every day, or every other day, their treaties and minutes to the Duke of Normandy and his brothers at Paris, that they might see what state they were in, and have answers thereto; as well as to know in what manner they were to act. All these papers were attentively examined and considered privately in the apartments of the Duke of Normandy, and then the full intentions of the Duke were written down, with the opinions of his Council, to these commissioners; by which means, nothing passed on either side without being fully specified and examined most cautiously. These aforesaid Frenchmen were in the King's apartments, or in his lodgings, as it happened, in the different places he halted at, as well on his march towards Chartres as otherwise; and they made great offers, to bring the war to a conclusion; but the King was very hard to treat with: for his intention was, to be in fact King of France, although he had never been so, to die with that rank, and also to put Brittany, Blois and Touraine in the same situation as those other provinces where he had garrisons. If his cousin, the Duke of Lancaster, whom he much loved and confided in, had not persuaded him to give up such ideas, and advised him to listen to the offers of peace, he never would have come to any terms. – He very wisely remonstrated with him, and said: "My lord, this war which you are carrying on in the kingdom of France is a cause of wonder to all men, and not too favorable to you. Your people are the only real gainers by it; for you are wasting your time. Considering every thing, if you persist in continuing the war, it may last you your life; and it appears to me doubtful if you will ever succeed to the extent of your wishes. I would recommend therefore, whilst you have the power of closing it honorably, to accept the proposals which have been offered to you; for, my lord, we may lose more in one day than we have gained in twenty years." These prudent and sensible words, which the Duke of Lancaster uttered loyally, and with the best intentions, to advise the King of England to his good, converted the King to his opinion, through the grace of the Holy Spirit, who also worked to the same effect: for an accident befel him and all his army, who were then before Chartres, that much humbled him, and bent his courage.

During the time that the French commissioners were passing backwards and forwards from the King to his Council, and unable to obtain any favorable answer to their offers, there happened such a storm and violent tempest of thunder and hail, which fell on the English army, that it seemed as if the world was come to an end. The hailstones were so large as to kill men and beasts, and the boldest were frightened.

The King turned himself towards the church of Our Lady at Chartres, and religiously vowed to the Virgin, as he has since confessed, that he would accept of terms of peace. He was at this time lodged in a small village, near Chartres, called Brétigny; and there were then committed to writing, certain rules and ordinances for peace, upon which the following articles were drawn out. To follow up this, and more completely to treat of it, the counselors and lawyers of the King of England also drew up a paper called the Charter of Peace, with great deliberation and much prudence . . .

113. King Jean's Letter on the Treaty of Brétigny. [Source: A. Bardonnet, *Procès-verbal de l'delivrance à Jean Chandos, commissaire du roi d'Angleterre, des places françaises abandonnées par le traité de Brétigny* (Niort: 1867)]

The terms of the treaty negotiated at Brétigny were very similar to those of the First Treaty of London, except that King Jean's ransom was reduced to 3,000,000 écus [£500,000], while the valuable county of Rouergue was added to the lands to be ceded to Edward III. In the following letter, variations of which King Jean sent to all the regions which were to be handed over to English rule, the Valois King explained why he felt it necessary to surrender so much.

The wars which have lasted for a long time between our very dear lord and father formerly King of France, during his life, and after his decease between us on the one side and the King of England our brother, who claimed to have a right to the said realm, on the other side, have brought great damages not only to us and to you, but to all the people of our realm and of neighboring realms and to all Christendom, as you yourselves well know: for because of the said wars many mortal battles have been fought, people slaughtered, churches pillaged, bodies destroyed and souls lost, maids and virgins deflowered, respectable wives and widows dishonored, towns, manors and buildings burnt, and robberies, oppressions, and ambushes on the roads and highways committed. Justice has failed because of them, the Christian faith has chilled and commerce has perished, and so many other evils and horrible deeds have followed from these wars that they cannot be said, numbered or written . . . therefore, considering and thinking on the evils abovesaid – and that it seemed in truth that even greater [evils] could have followed in time to come – and that the world suffered so many anguishes and sorrows because of the said wars, and having pity and compassion on our good and loyal populace which so firmly and so loyally has held itself in true constancy and obedience towards us, exposing bodies and goods to all perils and without avoiding expenses and outlays, which we ought never to forget; we have therefore recently undertaken discussions and negotiations of peace . . . In order to put an end to the wars and the evils and sorrows spoken of above, which have led to so much evil for the people, as is said above, more than for the deliverance of our person, and for the honor and the glory of the King of Kings and the Virgin Mary and for the reverence of the holy Church, of our holy father the Pope and his said nuncios, we have consented and do consent to, ratify, will and approve [this treaty of peace] . . .

The draft treaty negotiated at Brétigny was later ratified at Calais, with one major difference. The Brétigny agreement called for King Edward to renounce his claims to Normandy, Touraine, Maine, Anjou, Brittany and Flanders, and to the crown of France; in return, King Jean was to release sovereignty over wide territories in south-west France (comprising about one third of the entire kingdom) to the Plantagenet, so that this expanded duchy of Aquitaine would be separated from the Kingdom of France and held in sovereignty by the English monarchy. This exchange of rights and claims was still envisioned in the Treaty of Calais, but was extracted from the body of the main treaty and placed in a cedule, which called for Jean to complete the transfer of territories before Edward renounced his claim to the French throne, at which point the French King would also make his renunciation. Due to wrangling over the implementa- tion of the treaty, this final exchange never took place, leaving the door open for the resumption of the war in 1369.

English soldiers participated in a great deal of fighting between 1360 and the death of Edward III in 1377. Even before the French war resumed, the Black Prince led a large force into Castile in 1367, where he won his third great battle- field victory at Nájera. Pedro "the Cruel" of Castile, who was temporarily restored to his throne by the English intervention, was supposed to have borne the costs of the expedition, but he failed to meet those obligations. This led the Prince to impose heavy taxation within the Principality of Aquitaine; rather than allow the new taxes to be levied in their lands, the Count of Armagnac and his nephew the Lord of Albret appealed to the new French King, Charles V, for relief.

Charles chose to accept the appeal, thus reasserting his claim to sovereignty over Aquitaine and launching the war anew. For this new phase of the war, the English chronicles are much less common and less detailed than in the earlier periods, so aside from the Anonimalle Chronicle, *we must turn mainly to French chroniclers, and to Froissart, to carry the narrative forward.*

114. The Resumption of the War. [Source: *Quatre premiers Valois*, 200–205]

The Chronique des quatre premiers Valois, *written at the end of the fourteenth century by a cleric of Rouen, is less biased in favor of Charles V than most of the French chronicles of this period.*

Here is told the story of the war recommenced between the King of France and the King of England. The English, acting for the King of England, raided into Picardy and suddenly seized Nesle. The King of France and his Council heard the news of this, and so Sir Hugh of Châtillon, master of the crossbow- men, was sent to the frontiers. Then, by the order of the King of France, the Count of St. Pol and the Constable and Sir Jean, called "Mouton" [the sheep], Lord of Blainville, Marshal of France, went into Picardy to take back Nesle, which they captured and won from the English.

At Easter in the year 1369, the bourgeois of Abbeville turned French. And the English there were ejected from the town without doing any harm in any way. And those commissioned on behalf of the King of France entered therein and were joyfully received by the people of the said town.

The King of France deliberated long in council, and by the advice of the barons, the prelates, and the good towns, defied Edward, King of England. The officers of the King who were at Abbeville seized the county of Ponthieu by themselves and took the castle of Montreuil, which the King of England had caused to be built. The King of England, who considered himself one of the most powerful princes of the world, made an alliance with the King of Scotland, his brother-in-law, and delivered a great sum of gold to him. But the Scots, in particular those of the good towns, were unwilling to go against the King of France or against the French in any way.

Here it is told that the King of France held a great Council at Paris and caused it to be shown to the people how, by their counsel, he had defied the King of England. And for that reason a loan was imposed on the rich people against the salt tax; and the King affirmed that he would send milord the Duke of Burgundy, his brother, into England. And for this the said King made a great summons of noblemen. And in order to provide for his deed, the King of France came to Rouen. And then milord Philip of France, Duke of Burgundy, went to espouse the daughter and heiress of the Count of Flanders. And when he had done so, he immediately departed and came to Rouen where the King his brother was. While the King was at Rouen, an army of the men of the Seine, of the coast of the Caux, and of the Somme was gathered, and they raided into England. And on the other side, the King of England prepared an armada of barges, and they came to the coast of the Somme and captured around a dozen vessels, Norman and Picard.

Edward the King of England, in order to disrupt the effort and the undertaking of the King of France, so that the French would not enter his lands, sent his son the Duke of Lancaster to Calais with over 4,000 fighting men, and they attacked the land of the King of France. The King, who was then at Rouen in order to make preparations for the expedition to England, held a parliament of the good towns of his realm, where he had some bourgeois from each large town and city in order to get loans and money. And then the Abbot of Fécamp, named de la Grauche, from Burgundy, asked on behalf of the King for a tax of six pence for each six bushels of wheat; and the sixth penny on all beverages, whether wine, cider or beer – over and above all other subventions, including both gabelles and taxes. For this reason the Abbot earned the ill-will of the people of the entire realm of France, and was in very great danger of death. And this would have been imposed on the people, but the said prelates, clergy, nobles and bourgeois did not advise it, nor consent to it, so that they were completely refused.

Meanwhile, news came to the King of France that the Duke of Lancaster was in Picardy and invaded the land of the King. And then counsel was given to the King that it would be better first to go to fight the Duke of Lancaster; but the King willed that the crossing to England be made. And anyway, the King wished that it should be determined by the people of the good towns which would be better and the most expedient. And for this, four prelates, twelve barons and twelve bourgeois were selected, who reported to the King, to the prelates and clergy, and to the other nobles and bourgeois that it would be better to go first against the Duke of Lancaster. Then the summons of the army was proclaimed for the nobles and those holding lands in the manner of nobles, to go under the Duke of Burgundy to Abbeville. There the French assembled, namely the Duke of Bourbon, the Count of Perche, the Count of Eu, the Count of Harcourt, the Constable Sir Moreau de Fiennes, the Count of St. Pol, the Bishop of Troyes, the Viscount of Narbonne, the Count of Dammartin, and many high and noble men with them in the company of milord the Duke of Burgundy. The said lords rode with their men against the Duke of Lancaster and his host.

Meanwhile the King of France heard news from the Duke of Brittany that the English had come to St.-Sauveur-le-Vicomte. And, therefore, the Marshals of France, Sir Louis de Sancerre and Sir Jean de Blanville, called Mouton, milord de la Ferté and Sir du Melle. These assembled in great crowds of men-at-arms, especially from Normandy. And Sir Olivier de Clisson joined with them, and laid siege to St. Sauveur-le-Vicomte [in the Côtentin, western Normandy] . . . .

Now we return to speak of milord of Burgundy, who was going to take an army against the Duke of Lancaster, who had occupied a position in the valley at Tournehem. And the Duke of Burgundy went to his brother the Count of Flanders, then came to his army. And the Frenchmen encamped directly in front of the English in order to have a battle. But the Duke of Lancaster and the English, who were very subtle and crafty in war, fearing the great chivalry and the strength of the French, had fortified themselves in such a way that none could approach them. The Duke of Burgundy sent to the Duke of Lancaster to offer battle; and the Duke of Lancaster granted it to him, in such a way that the place should be selected four days before the battle. And knights were chosen from each side to pick the place. But thus matters remained, because the English wanted to fortify themselves.

While the Duke of Burgundy was at Tournehem in front of the army of the Duke of Lancaster and his host, there was a brawl between the French and the Flemings. And the Duke of Burgundy came to break up the fight. And if he had not been present there, one of the Flemings would have killed the Count of Perche. Milord of Burgundy remained in front of the English more than a month, he and his army, and the soldiers were owed the greater part of their wages. And the people of the region, the Picards, were unwilling to provide them with any credit. Therefore the Duke of Burgundy sent to his brother to ask for money to pay the said soldiers, but no cash was brought to him. And it was commonly reputed that this was the fault of the Abbot of Fécamp. And because there was no money, the French army decamped; the great lords could not keep their men-at-arms there. Thereby did the realm of France suffer great shame and great harm . . . .

115. Lancaster Moves On. [Source: *Anonimalle*, 59–61]

It is fascinating to compare the French version of the 1369 campaign, above, with the description in the English Anonimalle Chronicle. *As is often the case the events are much the same (with different omissions), but the interpretation of their significance and motives varies substantially.*

So [King Edward] assembled his army, sending milord John of Gaunt, Duke of Lancaster, and the Earl of Hereford and the Lord of Mauny and other great lords, along with a powerful force of valiant men, beyond the sea to Calais around the feast of St. Peter ad Vincula [1 August]. And when they were all assembled at Calais, they rode towards Ardres and broke the French siege of it, burning and destroying the environing lands, chasing their enemies up to the city of Thérouanne, in which were the bishop of the city and the Count of St. Pol. The following night the said Count escaped out of the said town, fleeing to the town of St. Pol; and the Duke of Lancaster, learning from a spy of his flight, chased after him, burning the land up to the town of St.-Pol-sur-Ternoise. The next night the said Count fled to the town called Pernes, where his wife the Countess lay in childbirth inside the castle of the said town; and the Duke of Lancaster, learning by means of a spy of his flight, chased after him, destroying and burning the countryside up to the said town of Pernes. Immediately on his arrival there he launched an assault on the said town, and by force of lance and sword the town was captured; and he stayed there for two days. At that time the castle of Audruicq was captured by the Earl of Hereford, and the castle of Estrée-Blanche by Sir Walter Hewitt. And when the Duke of Lancaster and his men saw that the castle of Pernes was so strong that it could not be taken, they returned to the valley of Guînes and Ardres and there they rested. And in this *chevauchée* more than 90 towns, castles and small fortresses were captured and won.

Afterwards, on the vigil [23 August] of St. Peter the Apostle, the Duke of Burgundy, who is called Sir Philip the Bold, came suddenly against them with all the forces of France as the said Duke of Lancaster and the other lords were eating. And when the news of the arrival of the French was brought to them, they rushed out in all haste, crying "to arms!," and, arming themselves, taking to horse, rode towards the mountain of Baligate and took their position on the said mountain, arraying their divisions and units skillfully. And when the said Frenchmen saw them make their exit and their array, they therefore turned back towards a mountain near the forest of Boulogne, two English leagues away, and there they lodged and encamped, preparing great ditches between them. And thus they remained for five entire weeks. And the Duke of Lancaster, hearing of this, sent to them Sir Walter Mauny and Sir Richard Pembroke to offer battle, and to choose a suitable place by the assent of both sides. But the Duke of Burgundy and the other lords of France sent the Lord of Fiennes, Constable of France, and a knight of the said Duke of Burgundy in order to choose a place along with the English so as to have the battle. And when the French had returned to their army, the said lords of France by common assent completely refused the battle and the preselected place.

In this time there were many good deeds of war in the same place between the English and the French. After this the King of England sent another force beyond the sea to Calais, namely the Earl of Warwick and the Earls of Salisbury, March, and Oxford, with a great multitude of ships and a great strength of men. And on the Wednesday [12 September] after the feast of the Nativity of Our Lady Holy Mary, the Earl of Warwick rode secretly with six lances to the host of the Duke of Lancaster, sitting on the said mount of Baligate, asking of the said Duke and the Count of Hereford how long they would thus lie there at their ease, when the enemies were not two English leagues away from them, badly arrayed. And he swore by a great oath that if the said enemies stayed in their position two whole days more, he would have them, either alive or dead. And a French spy, hearing of these words, hastily went to the Duke of Burgundy and to his men, bringing word to them how the "devil Warwick" had come with a large army from England in aid and support of the Duke of Lancaster, and how he had promised to take them within two days, by God's help; and therefore it would be better to leave than to stay. And the following night the Duke of Burgundy and the other Frenchmen fled towards France out of fear. The next day in the morning, hearing of this, the said Duke of Lancaster and the Earl of Warwick and the other lords armed themselves and rode towards the mount where the French were lodged. But all had escaped; and so they found inside the camp a good sixty tuns of wine, and as many of beer, and plenty of bread, and a great plenty of fresh and salted meat and of fish.

116. Lancaster's Campaign Continues. [Source: *Quatre premiers Valois*, 205–6]

After the Duke of Burgundy and the French broke camp from before Tournehem, the Duke of Lancaster and his army of English coursed through Picardy, and came to cross the Somme at Blanchetacque. And then they rode on until they came to the Clos de Caux and laid siege to Harfleur, and conducted a strong assault against it, but without accomplishing anything thereby. For the town was well defended, and the Count of St. Pol was inside with a great number of knights of Caux and with the townspeople, who defended themselves well. But while the Duke of Lancaster was at the siege of Harfleur, he sent one of his marshals to attack Montivilliers. But Baudric de la Heuse with a hundred men-at-arms, along with the townspeople, defended themselves very well. And then when the Duke of Lancaster saw that he was wasting his time by laying siege to Harfleur, he broke camp and passed again through Caux, burning and setting fires, and recrossed at Blanchetacque. And by means of an ambush which he had one of his marshals set, the Master of Crossbowmen of France was captured, and was taken as a prisoner to England.

117. Sir Robert Knolles' Campaign, 1370. [Source: *Chron. Jean II et Charles V,* 143–4]

The Chronique des regnes de Jean II et Charles V *is essentially a continuation of the* Grandes Chroniques, *prepared by Charles V's Chancellor, Pierre d'Orgemont. It is discernibly more biased than the portions of the* Grandes Chroniques *composed at St.-Denys (covering the period to 1350), but nonetheless generally reliable in the facts it presents.*

In the following month of July [1370], on behalf of the King of England, Sir Robert Knolles and Sir Thomas de Grandson, Englishmen, along with a company of about 1,600 men-at-arms and 2,500 archers, departed Calais, and rode to St. Omer, and from there to Arras, and burned a great portion of the suburbs of Arras and of the wheat, which was standing in the fields. Then they went in front of Noyon through the Vermandois, and burned a great number of houses. They did not, however, burn anything for which a ransom was paid.

118. The French Shadow the English. [Source: Froissart, *Chronicles*, 449]

The English continued their march in battle array, intending to enter the Laonnois, and to cross the rivers Oise and Aisne. They committed no devastation in the county of Soissons, because it belonged to the Lord de Coucy. True it is, they were followed and watched by some lords of France, such as the Viscount of Meaux, the Lord de Charny, lord Raoul de Coucy, lord William de Melun, son of the Count of Tancarville, and their forces; so that the English, not daring to quit their line of march, kept in a compact body. The French did not attack them, but every night took up their quarters in castles or strong towns; while the English encamped in the open plains, where they found provision in plenty and new wine, with which they made very free.

119. Knolles Advances to Paris. [Source: *Chron. Jean II et Charles V,* 145–6]

Then they passed the rivers Oise and Aisne, and came before Reims, and then crossed the river Marne, around Dormans, and then went up to around Troyes, and crossed the rivers of Aube and Seine in advancing to St.-Florentin. From there they went to cross the river Yonne, around Joigny, always burning the lands which would not pay ransom. And next they passed through the Gâtinois, and descended by Château-Landon and Nemours, through the countryside up to Corbeil and Essonne. And on Sunday, the 22nd day of September 1370, they encamped around Mons and Ablon and the vicinity.

On the following Tuesday, the 24th day of the said month, they were in battle array between Villejuif and Paris. And there were a good 1,200 men-at-arms, aside from those of the town, in the King's pay inside the city; and that day some skirmishes took place in front of the town of St.-Marceau, and the said English lost around six or eight of their men there. And, that day, the said English set fire to a great number of villages around Paris, such as Villejuif, Gentilly, Cachant, Arcueil, and to the hall of Bicêtre; and the King was advised, for the better, that they should not then be fought with. And that evening the said English went to lodge at Antony and around there, and on the following Wednesday they broke camp and departed for Normandy, and then returned within four days, and went to Étampes, to Milly, and through Beauce and the Gâtinois, always doing the things that enemies ought to do.

120. The English Break Up. [Source: *Anonimalle*, 64–5]

In this period the said Sir Robert took all the ransoms of diverse countries for himself; because of this great envy and great rancor of heart developed between the lords and commons and the said Sir Robert Knolles. And there they arrayed their divisions in order to give battle to their enemies, but the latter would not issue out of the city nor give battle. And afterwards the English passed through the Ile-de-France through a great forest up to Beauce, and from there up to the forest of Orléans, and into the county of Perche and the counties of Blois and Anjou and the country of Maine. And then into Brittany, and took up positions there, etc. And they split up for the towns of Josselin in Brittany, etc., Le Conquet, Becherel, and St. Omer.

And before the feast of Christmas, the chief men of the army, out of envy and self-importance, split it into four parts, to the great harm of England, and great comfort of the enemies: that is to say, the Lord of Grandson with his men in one part, the Lord FitzWalter in another, and Sir John Minsterworth in the third part, and Sir Robert Knolles in the fourth.

Soon after this, Sir Bertrand du Guesclin and the Lord of Clisson, hearing of their disarray and their splitting up, hastily assembled the French and their men and came against the Lords of Grandson and FitzWalter and Sir Matthew Redman where they were lodged, and captured them and killed their men, and then led the said lords in carts, shamefully and to the great despite of the English, to Paris, and there put them in a strong prison. And the said Sir John Minsterworth, hearing of this affair, put to sea with all his men and crossed safely and arrived in England. But the said Sir Robert Knolles retreated with his men towards Le Conquet, to his own castle, and commanded all the other men-at-arms and commons to come with him; and when they had arrived, he caused them to issue out of the town with their horses and gear, and then he had the gates locked, and had it proclaimed throughout the host, deceitfully, that all those who wanted to take ship for England should immediately go to the sea, where they would find a sufficiency of large ships. And so they left the town, deceived, and found only two small ships; and therefore not more than 200 men went on board, and the others returned to the said town and castle, and found the gates closed and were unable to enter. They therefore made their way to St.-Mathieu to take ship there; but there they were killed and chased by their enemies into the sea and drowned, a good five hundred or more men-at-arms and commons, to the great desolation and dismay of the English.

121. A French View of the End of the Campaign. [Source: *Quatre premiers Valois*, 207–8]

At the time the said Knolles and his army departed from before Paris, Sir Bertrand du Guesclin, who returned from Spain at the order of the King of France, arrived at Paris and was made Constable of France; and Sir Moreau de Fiennes resigned from the office of Constable.

The said Sir Bertrand, the new Constable, summoned the nobles and pursued Sir Robert Knolles, but the said Knolles had already entered Brittany. And Sir Hugh Calveley had remained behind from Knolles' army. And as soon as he perceived that the said Constable was pursuing them, he departed from a strong town where he was and fled. Sir Bertrand ordered an assault on the said town and took it by storm. And the day after the Constable captured the said town, he took an abbey which the English had fortified near Le Mans. Sir Thomas Grandson, who was the marshal of the King of England, conducted the rearguard of the English along with six hundred fighting men. He was in a valley named Mayet. Sir Bertrand learned by means of a spy that the English were there. Immediately he departed from Le Mans with a few men-at-arms and rode all night. And when the Frenchmen knew that he was riding, immediately and hastily they followed the said Sir Bertrand. And as day was breaking, they perceived the English. And then they put themselves in their units and in battle array, and fought with them and defeated them. And the said Marshal of England was taken prisoner, and the Constable sent him to the King of France at Paris.

122. A French Offensive in the Agenais. [Source: Froissart, *Chronicles*, 445]

The Duke of Anjou left the city of Toulouse with a great and well ordered array. He was attended by the Count d'Armagnac, the Lord d'Albret, the Count of Périgord, the Count of Comminges, the Viscount of Carmaign, the Count of l'Isle, the Viscount of Bruniguel, the Viscount of Narbonne, the Viscount of Talar, the Lord de la Barde, the Lord de Pincornet, Sir Bertrand Tande, the Seneschal of Toulouse, the Seneschal of Carcassonne, the Seneschal of Beaucaire and several others, amounting in the whole to upwards of two thousand lances, knights and squires, and six thousand footmen, armed with pikes and shields. Sir Bertrand du Guesclin was appointed to the command of all this force. They directed their march through the Agenais; and being joined by more than a thousand combatants from the Free Companies, who had waited for them all the winter in Quercy, they made for Agen.

The first fort they came to was that of Moissac. The whole country was so frightened at the arrival of the Duke of Anjou, and the large army he had brought, that they trembled before him, and neither towns nor castles had any inclination to hold out against him. When he arrived before Moissac, the inhabitants instantly surrendered and turned to the French. They then arrived before Agen, which followed this example. They afterwards marched towards Tonneins on the Garonne; and the French went on unmolested, following the course of the river Garonne, in order to have plenty of forage. They came to Port St. Marie, which was immediately surrendered. The French placed men-at-arms and garrisons in all these towns. The town and castle of Tonneins did the same, in which they placed a captain and twenty lances to guard it. They afterwards took the road to Montpezat and Aiguillon, burning and destroying all the country. When they came before Montpezat, which is a good town and has a strong castle, those within were so much frightened by the Duke of Anjou that they immediately opened their gates. The French then advanced to the strong castle of Aiguillon, where they only remained four days; for then the garrison surrendered to the Duke, not being such men as Sir Walter Mauny had commanded, when he had defended it against Jean, Duke of Normandy, who afterwards became King of France.

123. The English Riposte. [Source: *Quatre premiers Valois*, 208–10]

The King of England sent his son the Duke of Lancaster to Guienne with a great number of English men-at-arms. And as soon as he arrived in Bordeaux, he summoned the nobles of the land, then went to besiege Montpon, and pressed the town very strongly. And he had the food supplies of the surrounding countryside carried to his army; and so for a half-day's journey around his position the countryside was emptied and cleared out, out of concern for the new Constable, Bertrand du Guesclin, and the French. Sir Jean de Vienne, who was in Guienne, and the other lords made this known to the King of France, who sent Sir Bertrand to them. But before the said Sir Bertrand could arrive there, the Duke of Lancaster had already captured the town and the Frenchmen who defended it.

The Prince of Wales and the Captal de Buch, with a great number of men, went to besiege the city of Limoges. And the Duke of Lancaster joined them with his men, and swore to maintain the siege. Sir Jean de Vinemeur, who was inside the city, defended it very vigorously. And the English had a large number of engines which they fired day and night. The Duke of Lancaster had the town mined, and was with the miners, and personally watched over them. The said Sir Jean de Vinemeur had a countermine made, and so it came about that the miners encountered one another and attacked each other. Then it happened that the Duke of Lancaster and Sir Jean de Vinemeur fought with one another very valiantly. Then the Duke of Lancaster said: "Who are you, who fights so strongly against me? Are you a count or are you a baron?" "Not at all"; said Vinemeur, "I am but a poor knight." Then said the Duke of Lancaster, "I pray you, tell me your name, since you are a knight, for it might be such that I would gain honor for having tried myself against you, or not." Then said Vinemeur: "Know, Englishman, that never in arms would I withhold my name. It is Jean de Vinemeur." Then the Duke of Lancaster said: "Sir Jean de Vinemeur, I rejoice that I have tested myself against so fine a knight as you are. So know that I am the Duke of Lancaster." And the battle resumed between the two of them. And the others came forward, and the struggle lasted until night. And the Duke of Lancaster was injured by one of the supports, which crumpled.

After that, the Prince of Wales and the Duke of Lancaster caused the city of Limoges to be assailed vigorously and continuously, and pressed it so hard that by force they captured it. And they put many of the citizens to death, because they had turned French. But Sir Jean de Vinemeur and some of the people of the city retreated into a church, where they held out and kept fighting for a long time. There the said Vinemeur bore himself most valiantly, but they were captured by the force of the Duke of Lancaster.

After the city of Limoges was captured, the Prince of Wales, because of his illness, was carried in a litter to Bordeaux, and the Duke of Lancaster overran the countryside.

124. The English in Normandy. [Source: *Quatres premiers Valois*, 226–30]

Some Englishmen who were at St.-Sauveur-le-Vicomte in the Cotentin, around forty men-at-arms and some archers, went to Nôtre-Dame de Tombehelaine and seized it. . . And in this church and place, which was in a very strong position, they set themselves up and began to fortify it. The Frenchmen who were in this area on the frontier, namely the Besgue de Faiel, Sir Guillaume Martel, Sir Guillaume de Flamencourt, and others, to the number of 2,000 men-at-arms, went to Tumbehelene and fought with the English. And the English were defeated; the majority killed, the others captured.

After this deed, another band of Englishmen from the said stronghold of St.-Sauveur-le-Vicomte, in the Cotentin, went to escalade the castle of Bricquebec. And they only barely failed to capture it. Those of the castle perceived the English and cried the alarm, and knocked down the ladders, and caused the English to tumble down into the ditch. And some of the Englishmen were already in the castle; they were put to death. When those outside saw that they had failed to take the castle, they turned back.

Sir Bertrand du Guesclin, Constable of France, and Sir Olivier de Clisson made a *chevauchée* in Guienne and captured a stronghold named Montmorillon near Poitiers. And there the Frenchmen seized some good men-at-arms. But in this *chevauchée* the Frenchmen lost many of their horses, who perished of hunger.

125. The Battle of La Rochelle, 1372. [Source: *Quatre premiers Valois*, 232–4]

The account of the naval battle of La Rochelle given in the Chronique des quatre preimers Valois *differs substantially from the more familiar story given by Froissart, but it seems quite credible.*

King Enrique of Spain prepared a fleet of twenty galleys, and put them under his admiral, who was a very valiant and worthy man. He departed Spain, and failed to find the navy of France, and sailed towards La Rochelle and Poitou. At that time the Earl of Pembroke, coming from England with a very large army of Englishmen, had arrived at La Rochelle and had summoned the great men of the land, Sir Guichard d'Angle and others. Then the Spanish navy appeared. And the English, seeing this, were marvelously pleased, for they did not think much of the Spanish. And the Englishmen boarded their ships. The Earl of Pembroke, who was a good knight, put himself with his best men in his largest ships, and put to sea to fight the Spanish. The Admiral of Spain, who was very wise in matters of the sea, came to his galleys in order to attack the English, and skirmish with them, and draw them out. And he kept to the open sea. Then the Admiral of Spain ordered his galleys to draw back. And then the English raised a hue and cry: "Go! Go! You weak Spaniard, miserable recreant!" Then the Earl of Pembroke said to them: "We shall not move. Tomorrow the Spanish will come at high tide, and we will enclose them and combat them. For they will not long withstand us, if it comes to a battle." So the English did as the Earl of Pembroke said, and the Spanish withdrew.

Then their admiral said: "Dear lords, if you trust me, tomorrow I will give you the English, defeated. They expect us at high tide. If you believe me, we will attack them at low tide. And here is the reason. Our galleys are light, and their large ships and large barges are heavy and fully loaded. And they will not be able to move when the water is low, and we will attack them with fire and projectiles. If we are good men, we will defeat them." Thus it was done, as the Admiral of Spain had set it out for them. The next day, at the break of dawn, as the tide was just starting to go in, the sea being still so low that the English ships were not floating, the Spanish came back to attack them, strongly and fiercely, and commenced to fire strongly against the English ships, shooting fire and oil. The fighting there was extremely hard and heavy. The English defended themselves very vigorously, but they could not protect themselves when they saw their ships entirely engulfed in flames. It was a horrible thing there to hear the din and the noise, from the fire and the clamoring of the horses who were burning in the holds of the ships. The said Admiral of Spain and six of the galleys approached the ship of milord the Earl of Pembroke and Sir Guichard d'Angle, a good knight of Poitou. And there was an extremely great and fierce battle. And the English fought very valiantly, and shot strongly against the Spanish. But the latter cast and shot fire and oil into the Earl of Pembroke's ship so that it was totally in flames. And when the horses who were in the hold of the ship felt the flames, they smashed and crumpled the ships entirely. Then when the Earl of Pembroke saw that he could no longer hold out, because of the flames, he surrendered, as did Sir Guichard d'Angle. There was there great destruction and death of men and of horses, whether burned, drowned, or killed by shot. For many leapt into the sea, maddened by the fire which they felt. Many of the people of La Rochelle, who put themselves into little boats in order to rescue the English, were killed and drowned. Then, after the Spanish had defeated the English and captured the most important of them, they burned the greater part of the fleet of the English; then they decided to return to Spain.

126. The Implications of the Defeat. [Source: Froissart, *Chronicles*, 475]

You must know that when the King of England heard of the defeat of the fleet he had sent to Poitou, and that it had been overcome by the Spaniards, he was greatly afflicted; so were all those who were attached to him; but fore the moment he could not amend it. The wisest in the kingdom imagined that this unfortunate business would cause the loss of the countries of Poitou and Saintonge; and they stated this as their opinion to the King and Duke of Lancaster. They had many councils upon it. The Earl of Salisbury was ordered thither with five hundred men-at-arms. However, notwithstanding this order, he never went; for other affairs concerning Brittany came up, which prevented it from taking place. The King repented of this afterwards, when it was too late.

The loss of the fleet at La Rochelle – which was so important in part because the Earl of Pembroke had been bringing a substantial sum of cash to pay the wages of King Edward's troops in the Duchy – was only the first in a series of disasters for the English in Aquitaine. Du Guesclin led an active French army which overran Poitou, capturing Montmorillon, Chauvigny, Lussac, and Moncontour with little opposition. Sir Thomas Percy, Seneschal of Poitou, and the Captal de Buch managed to assemble a small army of some 900 men-at-arms and 500 archers, but they were unable to prevent the capture of St.-Sevère and Poitiers (the latter betrayed to the French by its wealthier inhabitants). The Plantagenet army split into three elements, the Englishmen occupying Niort, the Captal based in St.-Jean-d'Angély, and the Poitevins holding Thouars.

The French sent a detachment to besiege the strong castle of Soubise; the Captal, learning of this, led a small force to attack the besiegers by night. Though this was initially successful, the French were reinforced by another large detachment, and this carried off the victory, and took the Captal prisoner. Following up this success, the French rapidly captured Soubise, St.-Jean-d'Angély, Angoulême, Taillebourg, Saintes, and La Rochelle.

127. Du Guesclin Harries the English. [Source: Froissart, *Chronicles*, 483–6]

When Sir Bertrand du Guesclin had resided four days in La Rochelle, and had pointed out to the inhabitants in what manner they should conduct themselves henceforward, he set out on his return to the lords he had left at Poitiers, with whom he instantly marched off to conquer other strong places in Poitou. They were full three thousand lances. On their departure from Poitiers, they laid siege to the castle of Benon, and declared they would not leave it until it had changed masters. A squire from the county of Foix, named William de Pau, was governor of the place, under the Captal de Buch: he had with him a Neapolitan knight, called Sir James, but without any surname. Many violent assaults were made, which were well repulsed by the garrison.

Not far distant was the town of Surgères, which was garrisoned with English, by orders of the Captal, then a prisoner, who said one evening they would beat up the French quarters. They therefore marched out, according to an agreement with those of Marans, and mustered in the whole about forty lances: they fell upon the quarters of the Constable of France, wounded many, and particularly slew one of his own squires. The army was roused, and the French collected together as fast as they could; but the English, who had performed all they intended, re-entered their fortresses unhurt. The Constable was so enraged at this, that he swore he would never quit the spot where he was without conquering the castle of Benon, and putting to death all within it. He gave orders that very morning for every one to be ready for the assault, and had large machines brought, so that for a long time such an attack had not been seen. The men-at-arms and the Bretons did not spare themselves: they entered the ditches with shields on their heads, and advanced to the foot of the walls with pick-axes and iron crowbars, with which they worked so effectually that a large breach was made, through which they might easily enter. The castle was taken, and all within put to the sword. The Constable had it repaired and garrisoned anew. He then advanced towards Marans, the garrison of which surrendered on having their lives and properties saved. He next came to Surgères, which also put itself under the obedience of the King of France, for the English garrison had gone away, being afraid to wait the arrival of the Constable. He marched after this to the castle of Fontenay-le-Comte, where the lady of Sir John Harpedon resided. He assaulted both town and castle frequently: at last, the garrison left it on capitulation, and retreated to Thouars with the lady, under passports from the Constable. The French therefore took possession of the castle and town, and halted there to rest themselves.

Sir Bertrand and the lords of France marched to besiege Thouars, whither the greater part of the knights of Poitou had retired, namely, the Viscount of Thouars, the Lords de Partenay, de Pousanges, de Cors, de Crupignac, Sir Louis d'Harcourt, Sir Geoffrey d'Argenton, Sir James de Surgères, Sir Percival de Cologne. They had large engines and cannons manufactured at Poitiers and at La Rochelle, with which they much harassed these lords of Poitou in Thouars;

who, having mutually considered their situation, proposed a treaty, the terms of which were, that there should be a truce for them and all that belonged to them until Michaelmas ensuing, [29 September] 1372: during which time, they should let the King of England, their lord, know the state of the town and country: and if, within that period, they were not succored by the King of England or some of his children, they were, for themselves and their territories, to swear obedience to the King of France. When the treaty was agreed to, some of the knights returned to Paris. The Captal de Buch was conducted thither, and imprisoned, under a good guard, in one of the towers of the Temple. The King was so much pleased with this prize, that he gave to the squire that had taken him twelve hundred francs.

The messengers from the lords of Poitou arrived in England, to acquaint the King, the Prince of Wales (who at that time had pretty well recovered his health) and the Council with the situation of Poitou and Saintonge. The King, learning that he was thus losing all the territories which had cost him so much to conquer, remained pensive and silent: at last he said, that in a very short time he would go to that country with such a powerful force as would enable him to wait for the army of the King of France, and never return to England before he had regained all that had been conquered from him, or lose what remained.

At this period, the army under the command of the Duke of Lancaster was completed. It was very numerous, and had been ordered to Calais; but the King and Council changed its destination, having determined it should go to Poitou, Saintonge and La Rochelle, as the places where the business was the most pressing. The King of England issued a special summons throughout the realm, ordering all persons capable of bearing arms to come properly equipped to Southampton and its neighborhood by a certain day, when they were to embark. None either wished or dared to disobey the command, so that numbers of men-at-arms and archers of all sorts marched towards the sea-coast, where there were about four hundred vessels of different sizes ready to receive them. The principal nobility waited on the King and his family, who resided at Westminster. It had been settled between the King and Prince, that if either of them should die in this expedition, the son of the Prince, named Richard, born at Bordeaux, should succeed to the crown. When therefore all the nobles were assembled about the King before his departure, the Prince caused them to acknowledge that in case he should die before his father, his son should succeed as King of England after the decease of his grandfather. The earls, barons, knights and commonalty of the country were so much attached to the Prince for his gallantry at home and abroad, that they cheerfully assented to his request; the King first, then his children, and afterward the lords of England. The Prince put them upon their oath, and made them sign and seal to observe this arrangement before they separated.

Matters being thus settled, the King, the Prince, the Duke of Lancaster, the Earls of Cambridge, Salisbury, Warwick, Arundel, Suffolk and Stafford, the Lord Despencer (who was but lately returned from Lombardy), the Lords Percy, Neville, Roos, de la Warre, and all the principal barons of England, with about three thousand lances and ten thousand archers, arrived at Southampton, when they embarked on board the fleet, which was the largest that ever a King of England sailed with on any expedition whatever. They steered for La Rochelle, coasting Normandy and Brittany, and had various winds. The King of France, in the meantime, was collecting a great army in Poitou, to maintain his pretensions to Thouars: so that the whole country was full of soldiers. The Gascons, on the other hand, were as actively employed in raising men under the command of the Lord Archibald de Grailley, uncle to the Captal de Buch, who had come forward at the entreaties of Sir Thomas Felton, Seneschal of Bordeaux: they amounted to full three hundred lances. In this number were the Lords of Duras, de Curton, de Mucident, de Rosen, de Langoren, and de Landuras, Sir Peter de Landuras, Sir Peter de Curton, and Sir William Farrington, an Englishman.

This body of men left Bordeaux, and advanced to Niort, where they found Sir Walter Hewitt, Sir John Devereux, Sir Thomas Gournay, Sir John Cresswell, and several others. When they were all assembled, they amounted to about twelve hundred combatants. Sir Richard de Pontchardon arrived there also, and brought with him twelve hundred more. The King of England and his children, with his large army, were beaten about on the sea, and could not land at La Rochelle, nor any where near it, for wind and weather were against them.

They remained in this situation for nine weeks; and Michaelmas was so near at hand that he found it was not possible for him to keep his engagement with the Poitevin lords in Thouars. He was severely disappointed at this, and disbanded his troops to go whither they wished. The King, on his return, said of the King of France, "that there never was a king who had armed himself so little, nor one who had given him so much embarrassment."

Thus did this large fleet steer to England, when it had as favorable a wind as could be wished. After they were disbanded, there arrived at Bordeaux upwards of two hundred merchant ships for wines.

When Michaelmas was nearly arrived, the barons of England and Gascony, who had advanced to Niort in order to attend the King of England at Thouars, were very much surprised that they heard not any tidings of him. In order, therefore, to acquit themselves, they sent messengers to the Poitevin lords in Thouars. The messengers said to them: "Very dear lords, we are sent hither by the lords of Gascony in the dependence of the King of England, and by those English lords now in company with them, who have desired us to inform you, that they have collected all their forces, which may amount to about twelve hundred fighting men, ready and willing to serve you. They entreat you to inform them, if, in the absence of the King of England and his children, they can assist you, and if the relief may now be accepted, for they are eager to adventure their lives and fortunes in your company." The barons of Poitou replied: "We will call a council on what you have said; and we return our kind thanks to the barons of Gascony and England for sending to us, and for being so well prepared and willing to assist us."

The knights of Poitou assembled; but at the first meeting they could not agree on any determination, for the Lord de Partenay, who was one of the principal barons, thought they should defend themselves, as if the King of England had been present: but others maintained that they had given under their seals a declaration, that if neither the King of England nor any of his children were present, they would surrender themselves to the obedience of the King of France. The Lord de Partenay returned to his hostel in a very ill humor; but he was afterwards so much talked to that he consented to agree with the others. They therefore sent word, that according to their treaty, it was absolutely necessary for the King of England or one of his sons to be present. The English and Gascons at Niort were much vexed on hearing this, but they could not prevent it.

The Dukes of Berry, Burgundy, Bourbon, the Constable of France, the Lord de Clisson, the Viscount of Rohan, the Dauphin of Auvergne, the lord Louis de Sancerre, the Lord de Sully, and the barons of France: in all, about ten thousand lances, without reckoning the others, advanced from Poitiers, and drew up in battle-array before Thouars on the vigil [28 September] of Michaelmas, and also on the feast-day until evening, when they retired to their quarters. On the morrow, the two brothers of the King of France and the Constable sent to the knights of Poitou in Thouars, to remind them of what they had sworn and sealed. They returned for answer, that they should very soon retire to Poitiers, when they would put themselves and their dependencies under the obedience of the King of France. The lords of France, satisfied with this answer, departed from before Thouars; and the Dukes disbanded the greater part of their men.

On this separation, the Lord de Clisson, with a large body of men-at-arms, of whom the Constable had given him the command, came before Mortaigne-sur-mer, which at that time was attached to the English. An English squire, called James Clerk, was governor of the place, and might have had with him about sixty companions. When the Lord de Clisson came before Mortaigne, he assaulted it very vigorously: but, though he did not spare himself on the occasion, he gained nothing; upon which he retreated to his quarters. The governor, who found he should be hard pushed, sent off secretly to those knights of Gascony and England who were at Niort, to desire they would come that night to Mortaigne; that he would lodge them in his hôtel; and that they might easily pass through the quarters of the French forces, who were but two hundred fighting men. These lords set out from Niort, with five hundred lances, and rode all night to arrive at Mortaigne, for they had a great desire to catch the Lord de Clisson. But a spy, who had left Niort with them, having overheard some part of their intentions, made as much haste as possible to the Lord de Clisson, whom he found sitting at his supper. He informed him that the enemy had marched from Niort with five hundred combatants, and were advancing fast towards him. Upon hearing this, the Lord de Clisson pushed the table from before him, and hastily armed himself. He mounted his steed, and set off suddenly, with all his men, leaving the greater part of what belonged to them on the field. He never stopped until he arrived at Poitiers. The English were much vexed at their disappointment. They returned to Niort, where they left in garrison Sir John Devereux, the Earl of Angus and Cresswell. Sir Walter Hewitt went to England. All the others went back to Bordeaux, burning in their way the whole of the territories of the Lord de Partenay. Thus was all Poitou conquered, except the fortresses of Niort, Eliseth, Mortemer, Mortaigne, Lusignan, Chastel-Accart, La Roche-sur-Yon, Gauzar, La Tour de l'Arbre, Merxis and others. These castles however, held out, and made frequent inroads and attacks on their neighbours; sometimes invading, at other times chased back again.

128. The French Carry the War to Brittany. [Source: *Quatre premiers Valois*, 245]

In this year, 1373, Sir Bertrand du Guesclin, Constable of France, with a great number of barons, went into Brittany against the Duke of Brittany, because the said Duke, Jean de Montfort, had betrayed his homage and fealty to the King of France. And the said Duke did not dare await the said Constable, but crossed over to England, taking his treasure with him. And he complained to the King of England of the said Sir Bertrand, Constable of France, who had entered Brittany with the aforesaid baronage of France. And the good towns of Brittany and all the castles surrendered, except Le Conquet, which was taken by assault, and Derval and Brest, where the Duchess and Robert Knolles were.

129. The English Riposte: Lancaster's *Grande Chevauchée*. [Source: *Chron. Jean II et Charles V*, 2:171–2]

In that month of July [1373], John, Duke of Lancaster, son of the King of England, and he who had been Duke of Brittany, who at that time showed himself manifestly to be the enemy of the King and of the realm [of France], came from England to Calais, accompanied by a great number of men-at-arms and of archers. And, after they had remained for some time at Calais and on the frontier, they set off and rode straight to Hesdin, where they remained for several days, inside the park, without assailing the town or the castle. After that they rode to Doullens, without attacking, and next to Beauquesne, and from there towards Corbie. And they crossed the river Somme and continued their *chevauchée* to Roye in Vermandois, and stayed in the town 7 days, and could not take the church, which was strong. So they burned the town and went to the Laonnois and to Vailly-sur-Aisne, and burned many towns, and also lost many of their men, for wherever the Frenchmen, who shadowed them on horseback, found any of them separated from their divisions, they defeated them, without the Frenchmen suffering any losses, and so they gained a great deal from the English. In particular, on Friday, the 9th day of September, in the morning, Sir Jean de Vienne and his company found near Oulchy-le-Château 50 lances and 20 archers of the English, who were all defeated. And there ten knights of great status and 22 esquires were captured. And always the English continued their *chevauchée*, and crossed the rivers Oise, Aisne, Marne and Aube, and rode through Champagne, through Brie, right to Gyé-sur-Seine, and crossed the river Seine, continuing straight to the river Loire, to Marcigny-les-Nonnains, and crossed the said river Loire. All the time the Duke of Burgundy and the other men of the King of France rode nearby them, pressing them so closely that they had little to eat, and did not capture any notable fortress; and they lost many of their people and the majority of their horses. And from there, the English crossed the river Cher and went to Bordeaux, but they lost many of their men, and were in such a state that they had more than 300 knights on foot, who had abandoned their armor, some having cast it into the rivers, others broken it up, since they could not carry it, and so the French would not have the benefit of it. And although the said *chevauchée* may have been very honorable for them, it was very damaging for them.

130. The Unhappy Conclusion of Lancaster's *Grande Chevauchée*.
[Source: *Anonimalle*, 74]

After that, the said Duke moved with his host towards Guienne, where they did not find sufficient victuals for them or for their horses; nor did the common soldiers have any gold or silver to spend. At that time the Duke of Lancaster had it proclaimed throughout the host that, on pain of life and limb, none should be so bold as to take any supplies for themselves or for their horses without making payment for them to the suppliers of victuals of the country; and for that reason a great number of the common soldiers perished due to famine and want, and the horses of the lords and of the commoners died in great numbers. And therefore the commons, at that time, asked of the Duke of Lancaster that he return into France where they could find supplies, and live instead of dying from want, or else give them leave to go to their own lands. And to this the Duke would not agree, but pressed on to Bordeaux, to the great dismay and detriment of many men. And there the Duke broke up his army, intending that it should remain in the country, but the commons, who were in distress, crossed the sea to England (those who had enough to pay for their passage). And many knights and esquires and commons were on foot, without horses, badly arrayed and equipped; they stayed in Bordeaux and other areas in order to save their lives, and a great number of esquires and of the commons of the small garrisons, who had nothing to spend or to pay for their food, perished. And some had alms, given for the love of God and the saints by the citizens and burghers and other good people of the city and of the country, to comfort them in their distress until more could be done.

Thus ended the last major campaign of Edward III's fifty-year reign. The lands gained at Brétigny had nearly all been lost, though the core of Guienne which had been under English control at the start of the Hundred Years War remained. The captains who had accomplished so much for King Edward earlier were gone. The Earls of Northampton, Oxford and March had all passed away in 1360, Henry of Lancaster in 1361, Warwick, Suffolk and Bartholomew Burghersh in 1369, Stafford in 1372. Huntingdon and Salisbury were long gone.

Chandos was killed in a skirmish in 1369; in 1372, the Captal de Buch was captured, and Walter Mauny died. In 1377, King Edward himself died, a year after his eldest son. Despite the failures of the end of his reign, his subjects remembered him as a great warrior and chivalric figure, as "Arthur come again."

131. An English Chronicle's Eulogy for Edward III. [Source: *English Brut*, 2:333]

This King Edward was forsooth of surpassing goodness, and very full of grace even by comparison with all the worthy men of the world: for by his virtue and the grace given to him by God, he surpassed and shone above all his predecessors, who were themselves noble and worthy men. And he was of hearty courage, for he never dread any mishaps, nor harms, nor evil fortune that might befall a noble warrior . . . . And in all battles and engagements, with surpassing glory and honor, he had ever the victory.

PART II: INTERPRETATIONS

1

ENGLAND, SCOTLAND AND THE HUNDRED YEARS WAR IN THE FOURTEENTH CENTURY[1]

James Campbell

Geoffrey le Baker says that in 1333 Edward III, like the apostle, put away child-ish things.[2] He means that when he intervened to help Edward Balliol displace David Bruce from the Scottish throne Edward broke the treaty of Northampton, concluded in his minority. His motives are not far to seek. Robert Bruce had inflicted on England the worst humiliations it had suffered since the loss of Nor-mandy. But when he died he left an infant heir and a kingdom that did not seem likely to be able to maintain what he had won. Scotland's resources were inferior to those of England and the Crown's control over them less. It is, at least, sym-

---

[1] W.C. Dickinson, *Scotland from the Earliest Times to 1603* (1961) is the most recent general account of medieval Scotland, with a good bibliography, J.H. Ramsay, *The Genesis of Lancaster*, 2 vols (Oxford, 1913) and E.W.M. Balfour-Melville, *Edward III and David II* (1954), contain the best accounts of Anglo-Scottish relations; see also E. Miller, *War in the North* (Hull, 1960). The most relevant printed record sources are *Foedera*, ed. T. Rymer, 20 vols (1704–35), new edn, 4 vols (Record Commission, 1816–69) – all references below are to the latter edition unless otherwise stated – *Rot[uli] Scot[iae]*, ed. D. Macphearson, J. Caley and W. Illingworth, 2 vols (Record Commission, 1814–19); *The E[xchequer] R[olls of] S[cotland]*, vols i–iii, ed. J. Stuart and G. Burnett (Edinburgh, 1878–80); *C[alendar of] D[ocuments] R[elating to Scotland]*, ed. J. Bain, 4 vols (1881–88); *[The] A[cts of the] P[arlia-ments of] S[cotland]*, vol. i, ed. T. Thomson and C. Innes (Record Commission, 1844); and *[The] Parl[iamentary] Rec[ords of Scotland in the General Register House Edinburgh]*, ed. W. Robertson (Record Commission, 1804) – this work, which contains valuable and otherwise unprinted documents from the manuscript in H.M. General Register House, Edinburgh, known as the Black Book, was withdrawn and few copies exist. The principal Scottish chroni-cles are those of Fordun, *Chronica Gentis Scotorum*, ed. W.F. Skene, 2 vols (Edinburgh, 1871–72); Bower, *Joannis de Fordun Scotichronicon cum Supplementis et Continuatione Walteri Boweri*, ed. W. Goodall, 2 vols (Edinburgh, 1759); and Wynton, *The Original Chron-icle*, ed. F.J. Amours, 6 vols (Scottish Text Society, 1903–14). Froissart gives much informa-tion on Scotland; all the references below are to the edition of S. Luce, G. Raynaud, L. Mirot and A. Mirot (in progress, first 13 vols, Paris, 1869–1957), unless that of Kervyn de Letten-hove, 25 vols (Brussels, 1867–77), is specifically cited.
[2] Ed. E.M. Thompson (Oxford, 1889), 50.

bolic of the power of the Scottish nobility that the Gough map of c.1360 notes in Scotland, not, as it sometimes does in England, the administrative counties, but the *comitatus* of the earls. Bruce's triumph had been not only in a struggle against England but also in a long civil war which had accompanied it. Much land had changed hands and much resentment remained. Scotland was vulnerable, yet rich enough to offer more than the opportunity for revenge. Her wealth derived largely from foreign trade and above all from the export of wool. This averaged at least 5,500 sacks annually between 1327 and 1333 and was nearly all from the eastern and especially the south-eastern ports. Berwick was the most important of these. Its average annual export was over 1,800 sacks in these years and its customs revenue, at an average of about £640 a year, was the largest single regular item in the revenue of the Scottish Crown.[3] The area which England could most easily conquer was also that most worth conquering.

After his victory at Halidon on 19 July, 1333, it seemed that Edward III, at the age of twenty, might dispose of Scotland as best suited him. He imposed a settlement whereby much of the south, including Edinburgh itself, was to be joined to England and the rest ruled by Balliol under strict conditions of vassalage. The next four years were devoted to the consolidation of his success. He moved his central administration to York and led an army into Scotland every year, that of 1335 one of the largest he was ever to raise.[4] But by the time the French war began in 1337 he was far from having defeated the supporters of David Bruce. He held the main fortresses as far north as Stirling and Perth and from them controlled some, but by no means all, of southern Scotland. The Highlands were inaccessible; the violent campaign of 1336 had failed to secure the area between the Dee and the Moray Firth, where David's followers retained the vital port of Aberdeen and kept some kind of administration going; there was considerable resistance elsewhere. Sir Andrew Moray and the other Scottish leaders controlled wide areas and considerable forces and were able to take the offensive.[5]

The English failure is easy to explain. There was no chance of avoiding resistance. Those whom Edward sought to expropriate were too numerous and too powerful.[6] The geography of Scotland favoured those who chose to resist and the devastation and opportunities of war made it easy for them to find followers. Edward lacked the means to suppress the guerrilla war they waged. He could hold towns and fortresses at a price: by 1337 garrisons in, and repairs at, Edin-

---

3 *ERS* i, nos. III, IV, X, XIV, XVI, XIX, XXII.
4 A.E. Prince in *The English Government at Work*, ed. J.F. Willard and W.A. Morris (Cambridge, Mass., 1940), 332–76; R. Nicholson, 'An Irish Expedition to Scotland in 1335', *Irish Hist. Studies* xiii (1963), 197–211.
5 For the scanty records of the administration of David's lieutenants, see *ERS* i, 435–68; *Handlist of the Acts of David II*, ed. B. Webster (Edinburgh, 1962, duplicated).
6 David Dalrymple, Lord Hailes, *Annals of Scotland*, ii (Edinburgh, 1797), 159–62; R.C. Reid, 'Edward de Balliol', *Trans. Dumfriesshire and Galloway . . . Antiquarian Soc.*, 3rd ser., xxxv (1956–57), 59–62; *Chronicon de Lanercost*, ed. J. Stevenson (Bannatyne and Maitland Clubs, 1839), 276; *CDS* iii, 318–47.

burgh, Roxburgh, Perth and Stirling were together costing about £10,000 a year while his income from Scotland probably did not exceed £2,000.[7] Large areas and a wide allegiance could be won by the use of big armies, but were lost when they left. As the French had found in Flanders, and Edward was again to find in France, the relation between the income of a king and the pay of a soldier was not such as to permit the permanent occupation of a country in the face of widespread resistance from its inhabitants. Edward's efforts in Scotland created conditions which made pacification harder to achieve. Power on the Scottish side lay with leaders who were often doing well from plunder and ransoms and who did not spare their own countrymen.[8] According to Fordun Sir Andrew Moray did much for the freedom of Scotland, but 'all the country he passed through he reduced to such desolation and distress that more perished afterwards through starvation and want than the sword devoured in time of war.' Like Robert Bruce after 1306 such men built up their power by having booty won within Scotland to offer. It was to be feared that they might turn south of the border as he had done after 1311. If Edward's grip on southern Scotland were to slacken, the conditions he had created there could generate attacks against England on a much larger. scale than those which had been in progress since the war began. In so far as there was a risk that northern England might be devastated as it had been under Edward II, his son's position in 1337 was one, not only of expensive frustration, but of danger.

Thus the war with France began at a time when Edward was heavily, or even inextricably, involved in Scotland. Its immediate cause was quite probably the help which Philip VI gave, or threatened to give to the Scots. The links between France and Scotland were old and numerous.[9] Kings of Scotland had married French wives. Some of the Scottish nobility had special connections with France: Edward Balliol was in private life a French landowner with whom Philip VI had a quarrel of his own.[10] There was a considerable trade between the two countries. Many Scots settled in France: a possible originator of the idea of applying the Salic Law to the French succession was called Jean Lescot. Trade and settlement need have had little political effect. Scottish entrepreneurs are to be found all over Europe in the fourteenth century. They appear selling cloth in Pomerania and perpetrating religious frauds in Italy. There were probably more Englishmen settled in France and more Scots in England than there were Scots

---

[7] These rough figures are based on *CDS* iii, app. iii–vi and nos. 1240, 1241, and *Rot. Scot.* i, 489b–490a.

[8] *Fordun* i, 362–3; *Lanercost*, pp. 278, 288; *Murimuth*, ed. E.M. Thompson (1889), 75; H.S. Lucas, *The Low Countries and the Hundred Years War* (Ann Arbor, 1929), 183.

[9] Francisque-Michel, *Les Écossais en France: les Français en Écosse*, 2 vols (1862); the catalogue by B. Mahieu and N. Gand de Vernon of the exhibition at the Archives Nationales, Paris, 'France-Écosse' (Paris, 1956), indicates some of the materials from which this outdated work may be supplemented.

[10] *The Brut*, ed. F.W.D. Brie, i (Early Eng. Text Soc., 1906), 273–4; *Inventaire d'anciens comptes royaux*, ed. Ch.-V. Langlois (Paris, 1899), 45.

in France. The important consideration was the value of an independent Scotland to French policy. This had been clear since the time of Philip the Fair and had most recently been recognized by the treaty of 1326 whereby Robert I and Charles IV bound themselves and their heirs to mutual aid against England in war and peace. Philip VI de Valois was not the most imposing of French kings, but he ruled a state whose power was all and more than all than that of the France of Louis XIV was to be in Europe, and he was well capable of protecting a friend or a client.

Philip began by bringing David to France in May 1334, established him at Château Gaillard and gave him a pension to help maintain his little court, which included some of the Scottish bishops, many of whom had gone into exile.[11] In June Philip broke up an Anglo-French conference which seemed just to have reached an agreement on Gascony by saying there could be no settlement in which Scotland was not included.[12] Thereafter he involved the Scottish issue with the other disputes between France and England, claiming the role of mediator. Philip was in a position where he could bring great pressure to bear. Edward was seeking to improve his position in Gascony, where he was very vulnerable and where, having admitted that he owed liege-homage, he had no substantial *quid pro quo* to offer in return for concessions. There was little to deter Philip from adopting David's cause. There were dangers within France but hostility towards England might help rather than hinder him in dealing with these. Edward's continental alliances did not present a serious threat until 1337. Edward had to take Philip's stand on behalf of David very seriously. At the same time he was not willing and may not have dared to make concessions sufficient to satisfy him. English discontent with the treaty of Northampton had helped Edward to establish his power in and after 1330. It had been one of the causes of Lancaster's rebellion, in which most of the leaders of the Disinherited, Beaumont, Wake, Atholl, and Henry Ferrers were, in different degrees, implicated. After the failure of the revolt Beaumont and Wake had retired to France, returning after the coup at Nottingham in the company of other exiles with Scottish claims, Richard fitzAlan and Fulk fitzWarin. There are indications that Edward was not altogether secure in England in the mid-thirties and the support of these men may have been important to him.[13] His prestige was in any case heavily committed to the Scottish war. He played for time. A series of conferences in which French, English, Scottish and papal representatives participated were held

---

11 *ERS* i, 448–54, 464–8; P[ublic] R[ecord] O[ffice, London], French Transcripts, 8/138, fols 12, 14, 15.

12 E. Déprez, *Les préliminaires de la Guerre de Cent Ans* (Paris, 1902), 97. For the diplomatic position, see also H.S. Lucas, op. cit., H. Jenkins, *Papal Efforts for Peace under Benedict XII* (Philadelphia, 1933) and R. Cazelles, *La société politique et la crise de la royauté sous Philippe de Valois* (Paris, 1958).

13 G.A. Holmes, 'The Rebellion of the Earl of Lancaster 1328–9', *Bull. Inst. Hist. Res.* xxviii (1955), 84–9 and the works cited there; *Lanercost*, 266–7, 279; cf. R. Nicholson, 'The Last Campaign of Robert Bruce', *E*[ng.] *H*[ist.] *R*[ev.] xxvii (1962), 234.

at intervals up to the end of 1336. Nothing is known to have come of them apart from a certain number of truces between the English and the Scots.

From the beginning the French gave the Scots more than diplomatic support. Scotland depended upon imports for most manufactured goods and, to some extent, for food. In this, as in all wars with Scotland in the fourteenth century, the English tried hard to prevent the Scots importing the arms, harness and food upon which their ability to resist must largely have depended.[14] Almost as soon as the Anglo-Scottish war began Philip sent ten ships laden with arms and food. These almost certainly did not arrive, but others which followed probably did.[15] French influence helped to prevent the efforts of English diplomacy to cut the Scots off from Flanders, their chief market and – with the possible exception, even in wartime, of England and Ireland – their main source of supply. France did much to further the naval activities of the Scots. English commerce depended on the safety of the narrow seas; the south coast was open to raids; the garrisons and armies in Scotland depended on sea-borne supplies. The Scots took the opportunity to carry on a *guerre de course* with French and Flemish help. Although the scale of this is uncertain it is clear that, together with the need to blockade Scotland, it forced Edward to maintain a considerable and continuous naval effort.[16]

From the beginning of the war with Scotland it was the possibility that Philip might go so far as to send an army to Scotland or to England which did most to make his intervention formidable. Edward ordered extensive precautions against invasion from the sea by the Scots and their foreign allies during the campaigns of the summer of 1333 and of late 1334. The danger seems to have been thought even greater in the summer of 1335. Orders were issued that all ships over forty tons capacity were to be held ready to intercept the invaders. Beacons were to be prepared on hills to warn of their arrival. The fortresses of Wales and the south-east were put in a state of defence. Arrayers were appointed to levy men all over England should the need arise. These precautions were repeated during the campaign of 1336 when, from July, fears centred on the presence of Philip's erstwhile crusading fleet in the Channel ports. At the beginning of 1337 orders were issued for the collection of another great fleet to resist invasion.[17] These were the first of the invasion-scares which were to occur in every decade of the French war in the fourteenth century. They were burdensome, especially in so far as they led to the arrest of shipping, and expensive. It is unlikely that there was much to justify Edward's fears in 1333 and 1334 and it is not clear how strong they were. In 1335 and 1336 there was real cause for alarm. On 31 July,

---

[14] R. Stanford Reid, 'Trade, Traders and Scottish Independence', *Speculum* xxix (1954), 210–22; 'The Scots and the Staple Ordinance of 1313', ibid. xxxiv (1959), 598–610; 'Sea-Power in the Anglo-Scottish War 1296–1327', *The Mariner's Mirror* xlvi (1960), 7–23.

[15] C. de la Roncière, *Histoire de la marine française*, i (Paris, 1899), 388–9; Lucas, op. cit., 142–3; *Rot. Scot.*

[16] De la Roncière, i, 388–98; *The English Government at Work*, i, op. cit., 376–93.

[17] For precautions against invasion see especially *Rot. Scot.*

1335, the archbishop of Rouen, preaching before the French court, said that Philip intended to send 6,000 men-at-arms to help the Scots, though this was not, so he is said to have said, to interfere with the crusade.[18] At some time in the same year the Constable of France, the count of Eu, was appointed to command such an expeditionary force. A scheme exists, probably drawn up in 1335 or 1336, for the despatch of 1,200 French men-at-arms and 20,000 serjeants to Scotland.[19] A letter of 19 June, 1336, written by someone close to Edward's court, shows what was thought to be known of French plans in England. It contains detailed and alarming information on the collection of a strong fleet and army to be sent to England or Scotland.[20] Some French troops may have been sent to Scotland at this time.[21] It is not known how far Philip went towards putting his project for large-scale intervention into effect, to what extent it was one among several alternative plans, or how far he was himself frightened by Edward's diplomatic and naval activity. But there is quite enough evidence to show that during the campaigns of 1335 and 1336 Edward was rightly frightened of what Philip might do. He took the risk, played for time in his negotiations with France, and made a great and very expensive effort to crush Scottish resistance. He failed and found himself still involved in a war which he could neither win nor abandon and still faced with the possibility of French invasion. Those chroniclers who thought that his intervention on the Continent was a direct response to Philip's threat of intervention in Scotland may well have been right.[22] Edward's reaction was not only characteristically aggressive, but even, perhaps, prudent. Whatever may be said against his activities in the Low Countries from 1337, they did at least ensure that England was not invaded.

Until the summer of 1338 Edward concentrated his war-effort on Scotland. He had about 4,000 troops there at the beginning of the year and a considerable army besieged Dunbar, in vain, until June.[23] Its departure marked the beginning of a defensive war in the north which dragged on, despite abortive negotiations for peace and ill-kept truces, until Neville's Cross was won in October 1346.[24] The English fortresses in Scotland fell quickly. Edward's preoccupations pre-

---

18 *Chronique parisienne anonyme*, ed. A. Hellot (Soc. de l'hist. de Paris, xi, 1884), 164–5.

19 De la Roncière discusses much of the evidence for French invasion plans, i, 347n, 391–3. He may well be right in dating the scheme in Bibliothèque Nationale, MS Français 2755, fols 216–21 to 1336 and it is almost certainly for an expedition to be commanded by the Constable (fol. 221) but it could be rather earlier or later.

20 Cf. *Lanercost*, 286; *Knighton*, ed. J.R. Lumby, i (1889), 477.

21 *ERS* i, 451, 453; R. Cazelles, *La société politique . . .*, op. cit., 148–9 (the de Garencières involved was probably Yon, not Pierre).

22 E.g. *Grandes chronique de France*, ed. J. Viard, ix (Paris, 1937), 158.

23 A.E. Prince, 'The Strength of English Armies in the Reign of Edward III', *EHR* xlvi (1931), 358–60.

24 A truce was concluded for a year in 1338. It is uncertain whether the Scots exercised their right to accede to the truce of Esplechin (1340) as they did to that of Malestroit (1343). It is likely that only shorter truces made on the Marches had much effect, cf. *The Priory of Coldingham*, ed. J. Raine (Surtees Soc., 1841), Appendix, cvii.

vented their being adequately supplied with food or money and neither he, nor his grandfather, had spent enough on their fortification. After the fall of Stirling in April 1342 the English retained nothing in Scotland but Berwick, some lands around it, Lochmaben, and the occasional allegiance of some of the weather-cock gentry of the south-west.[25] England's greatest advantage in war against Scotland lay in her capacity to bring her superior wealth and organization to bear by sending armies into the Lowlands so large that the Scots dare not face them in the open field. This was not done between 1338 and 1347, although northern forces did invade Scotland and Edward himself led a considerable army to the border at the end of 1341 and the beginning of 1342. As the English weakened and proved unable to retaliate in great force so Scottish raiding increased in strength. David's return home in 1341 – probably in June – was followed by powerful raids in the autumn and in 1342; at least one of them reached the Tyne. Heavy raiding recommenced in 1345 after something of a lull, culminating in the great expedition which came to grief at Neville's Cross. This was one of the rare Scottish armies to include forces from nearly the whole of the kingdom. As in the later campaigns of Robert I and in those of 1384–89, border warfare snowballed into something more as the prospect of plunder attracted Scots from beyond the Marches. The damage done in northern England in the years before 1346 was considerable, though not so great as it had been in Edward II's reign or as some applicants for financial relief made out. Cumberland, which suffered most, had its assessment for the tenth and fifteenth reduced by more than half between 1336 and 1339: by 1348 ninety-two places in the county had to be exempted altogether. Northumberland suffered considerable harm even, in 1346, in the far south.[26] Perhaps the most convincing evidence of the power of the Scots is that by 1344 the bishop of Durham had reverted to the ways of Edward II's reign and was raising a tax to buy them off for a few months.[27] The difficulties caused by raiding were exacerbated by the disorderly state of northern England. English and Scottish brigands co-operated and on both sides there were men who were beyond the control of their rulers. In 1339 an attempt to suppress violence in north-west England had to be abandoned because it gave offence and those offended threatened to join the Scots – as many Englishmen had done under Edward II.[28]

In spite of all, the March was defended, and in the end triumphantly.[29] The

---

25 B. Webster, 'The English Occupation of Dumfriesshire', *TGDS*, 3rd ser., xxxv (1956–57), 64–80.

26 J.F. Willard, 'The Scotch Raids and the Fourteenth Century Taxation of Northern England', *Univ. of Colorado Studies* v (1907–8), 240–2; *Cal. Close Rolls 1346–9*, pp. 30–1, 87–8; *CDS*, iii, no. 1441; *Cal. Inquis. Misc.*, ii, nos. 2037, 2051.

27 *Registrum Palatinum Dunelmense*, ed. T.D. Hardy, iv (1878), 273–7; cf. *The Anonimalle Chronicle*, ed. V.H. Galbraith (Manchester, 1927), 24, 26; and *Coldingham*, Appendix, xvi.

28 *CCR 1339–41*, 94.

29 For the following paragraph see especially *Rot. Scot.*, *Rot. Parl.* ii (1783), and J.E. Morris, 'Mounted Infantry in Medieval Warfare', *Trans. Roy. Hist. Soc.*, 3rd ser. viii (1914), 98–102; cf. M. Powicke, *Military Obligation in Medieval England* (Oxford, 1962), 182–212.

triumph was partly that of the northerners themselves, partly of the English administrative system. After 1338 Edward left England north of the Trent to look after itself to a large extent. Very few of its levies or magnates were summoned to serve abroad, apart from the bishop of Durham and a few others in 1346. Conversely, few troops from south of the Trent were sent north, except for the campaigns of 1341–42. The taxation of the north was largely appropriated to its defence and was kept under special officers at York. A lieutenant or *capitaneus* was put in command for particular campaigns or crises but much power lay with commissions of northern magnates. Most conspicuous of these were Henry Percy and Ralph Neville, particularly in regard to the control of expenditure. An important part seems to have been played by northern assemblies which were held in most years. Commissions were sent to these to announce decisions, usually taken in parliament, on the defence of the north and to make arrangements accordingly. Their most important function was probably the conclusion of indentures with the northern lords. The eight counties north of the Trent had considerable military resources. Something of the order of 8,000 archers and hobelars were available for array; 500 or more men-at-arms and a similar number of archers could be raised in the retinues of the magnates, usually, perhaps always, by indenture. Small raids were left to the levies of the March counties and to the magnate retinues which were probably kept on the March for part of most years. If a more dangerous invasion threatened, more troops were summoned from further south. That an army sufficient to defeat the Scots was collected in time and at the right place in 1346 was the result, not of fortunate improvisation, but of the orderly working of a system of defence much of which was at least as old as the reign of Edward I. It worked, admittedly with much default and delay, because the northerners were used to it, because it was to their interest to make it work, and because Edward ensured the co-operation of the magnates by giving them power and money.

The relatively successful defence of northern England and the victory of Neville's Cross are to some extent to be accounted for by the weakness of the Scots. The limited resources and unfortunate history of the Scottish monarchy rarely permitted the king adequate control over the nobility. Little is known of the internal history of Scotland in the years following David's return, but it is clear that he had to face serious disorder. The incidents of which we know most are connected with William Douglas of Liddesdale – who must be distinguished from the future earl.[30] This man was in high favour after 1341 and received many grants. But his anxiety to extend his lands on the March led him to murder Alexander Ramsay in 1342 and, perhaps, to engage in some kind of treasonable negotiation with the king of England. The internal weakness of Scotland may help to account for the relative peace on the border in 1343 and 1344. Its effect

---

[30] For the Douglases see W. Fraser, *The Douglas Book*, 4 vols (Edinburgh, 1885); H. Maxwell, *History of the House of Douglas*, 2 vols (1902); R.B. Armstrong, *The History of Liddesdale* (Edinburgh, 1883).

on the conduct of war is clearly to be seen in the campaign of 1346. Scottish armies were not paid by the king.[31] A large army to attack England could be gathered only by a French subsidy or the hope of plunder; and the gathering took time. The main invasion of 1346 did not take place until October, but the English suspected before the end of August what was afoot.[32] Once gathered such Scottish forces were hard to control. Most of the men of the isles and the west who mustered for this invasion went home before it began. When it did begin, the army spent four days besieging the peel of Liddel in the interests of William Douglas of Liddesdale. He had already quarrelled with the earl of Moray while it was being besieged earlier in the year and so had forced the Scots to retire.[33] This time it fell and he at once suggested that the army should return home. Had less time been spent in besieging this minor fortress, David need not have been intercepted at Durham. In short, while the Scots could easily, almost naturally, keep the borders in turmoil, their effectiveness for war on a grander scale was impaired by the weakness of the Scottish Crown.

Satisfactorily though the war ended Edward had had to pay a heavy price in the north after 1337. He lost his dearly-bought chance of gaining southern Scotland. A major recruiting-ground and a considerable part of his income had to be devoted to the Scottish war. He had to spend or owe £30,000 or more on the fortresses of Edinburgh, Perth, Stirling and Roxburgh between the beginning of the war with France and their loss.[34] The campaign of 1337–8 was very expensive. Expenditure through the wardrobe on the winter campaign of 1341–2 and on the maintenance of troops on the March in the following summer amounted to nearly £11,000.[35] The cost of the defence of the north to the king may have diminished in subsequent years but he by no means bore the whole burden of war, especially within England. Many of the parliamentary grievances of the period related to the means whereby he sought to transfer part of it elsewhere – array, purveyance, excessive pardoning – and can be amply illustrated in the north. It is true that complaint and evasion often indicate not so much the oppressiveness of exactions as the opportunities for resistance to them in a society which was for many a very free one. Nevertheless, some of these demands, perhaps array especially, imposed heavy burdens. The counties were supposed to pay their levies to the muster, or even beyond, and sometimes to provide them with arms and uniforms. It is not yet clear how much money was involved or who actually provided it but the cost was certainly considerable. On the other hand some nobles and merchants were enriched by the Scottish war and Neville's Cross brought profit to many.

---

[31] D. Hay, 'Booty in Border Warfare', *TDGS*, 3rd ser., xxxi (1952–53), 158.
[32] *Rot. Scot.* i, 673b.
[33] *Murimuth*, p. 202.
[34] This estimate is based on *CDS*, iii, *Rot. Scot.*, i, *CCR 1337–9*, 525 and *Rot. Parl.* ii, 115a–116b.
[35] PRO, E.36/204, fols 102r–105v.

It is difficult to determine how far Scottish attacks were coordinated to suit French strategy. Certainly the main invasions were launched when Edward was involved on the Continent. Conversely, the only occasion on which he seems to have contemplated a big attack upon Scotland was in 1344. Concern for the north may have made him more willing to conclude truces with France. In both 1337 and 1341 the conclusion or extension of such a truce was followed by the despatch to Scotland of troops originally intended for the Continent. The only Scottish attack which we can be fairly sure to have been directly instigated by France was that which ended at Neville's Cross. Philip wrote to ask David for help in June 1346 and, more urgently, in July.[36] Philip did the Scots some service when, in 1342, he released the earl of Salisbury from captivity in exchange for the earl of Moray, who was in English hands. It does not seem that he sent much material help. Ships which the English captured in August 1337 were said to have been taking arms, treaties, and a large sum of money from France to Scotland.[37] If so, this interception was very important since this was just the kind of assistance needed to induce the Scots to launch a major attack. French ships and troops, though probably not many of either, took part in the siege of Perth in 1339.[38] According to le Bel and Froissart a certain number of French troops – Froissart says 200 – fought with the Scots in c.1340–42.[39] There is no evidence that French aid came to Scotland in 1346, apart from Baker's statement that Philip sent a large force.[40] In general it seems that the French received a great deal of useful help from the Scots at small cost.

Neville's Cross left David and many Scottish noblemen in English hands. Edward now held the initiative. Much of southern Scotland was immediately overrun – roughly the modern counties of Berwick, Roxburgh, Dumfries, Peebles and Selkirk. In May and June 1347 Edward Balliol invaded Scotland and penetrated as far as Glasgow with a powerful army. This expedition may have been a serious attempt to establish him on the Scottish throne. If so, it was the last. Another, lesser, incursion was made into Scotland in October and thereafter Edward III's policy on the March was defensive.[41] Until 1355 the truces were nearly continuous, though ill-kept. Little effort seems to have been made to hold the newly-won lands, a large part of which the Scots had regained by 1356.

---

[36] There seems no reason to doubt the authenticity of the letters from Philip to David given in Latin translations in the continuation of Hemingburgh, ed. H.C. Hamilton (1849), ii, 420–423. Their form is the appropriate one of letters missive (cf. R. Cazelles, *Lettres closes . . . de Philippe de Valois* (Paris, 1958), 6–17, esp. 9–10) and there is a near correspondence between the places from which they are dated and Philip's itinerary (J. Viard, 'Itinéraire de Philippe VI de Valois', *Bibl. de l'éc. des Chartes* lxxiv (1913), 569.

[37] *Cal. Pat. Rolls 1334–8*, 513 and *CCR 1337–9*, 172 nearly resolve doubts on the date of this incident, cf. F. Lennel, *Calais au Moyen Age*, i (Calais, 1909), 79.

[38] *Fordun* i, 363–4; *Wynton* vi, 124–7; *ERS* i, 507.

[39] Discussed by J. Viard and E. Déprez, *Chronique de Jean le Bel*, i (Paris, 1904), 274n.

[40] Op. cit., 86: Philip does not seem to have used his strong fleet to aid Scotland, Bibl. Nat., MS Franç. nov. acq. 9241, fols 48r–94v.

[41] PRO, Various Accounts (E.101), 25/10 gives details of the campaigns of 1347.

The English kept Roxburgh and considerable areas in Berwickshire and Roxburghshire. They had never lost Berwick and Lochmaben. Edward Balliol exercised what sway he could in the south-west from Hestan Island and Caerlaverock.

In every year from 1347 negotiations went on for David's release. Great problems and opportunities faced Edward here. He did not recognize David as king of Scotland but if he was to profit from his great prize it was very necessary that the Scots should do so. David was childless. Robert Stewart, his half-sister's son and eight years his senior was heir presumptive and ruled Scotland as guardian in his absence. Robert may not have been over-anxious to redeem his uncle. The English did not cause enough trouble after 1347 to make a settlement imperative. David had been badly wounded at Neville's Cross, still, maybe had an arrow-head in his head and needed frequent medical care. Were he to be ransomed Robert would be displaced from power. If he were to die soon after being freed the ransom would be wasted. If he were to live he might outlive his heir, or engender another one.

Whether or not such considerations weighed with Robert he had every reason to resist the kind of settlement which Edward at first sought. In a letter of 1350 to the pope, David said that Edward required that he or one of his sons should be recognized as David's heir and that England should have the fullest feudal superiority over Scotland.[42] This would have involved the abandonment of Balliol. Edward was ready for this – as he seems to have been ready to abandon de Montfort in 1353 – but Balliol was not. In 1349 Edward was already seeking to bring pressure to bear on him to accept a settlement which seems to have been agreed with David and which was thought to have some support in Scotland.[43] By 1351 Balliol may have been looking towards France; for John II then stated that if Balliol abandoned the English cause, as he heard he proposed to, then his French property would be restored.[44] But Balliol had no support worth the name and David was probably willing to accept Edward's terms *faute de mieux*. Robert and the Scots presented the chief difficulty. Edward's chief agent in Scotland appears to have been William Douglas of Liddesdale, who virtually entered his service after being captured in 1346. He was sent, probably in 1351, to offer the Scots David's return and the restoration of the Scottish lands held by England in return for £40,000 and the recognition of the right of one of Edward's sons to succeed to Scotland.[45] The offer was rejected. David was himself sent home in 1352 to put similar terms. These too were rejected. Yet another vain effort was made at a conference at Newcastle in 1353. There are indications that Edward thought he might have to participate in a Scottish civil

---

42 E.W.M. Balfour-Melville, 'David II's Appeal to the Pope', *Scott. Hist. Rev.* xli (1962), 86.
43 C. Johnson, 'Negotiations for the Release of David Bruce in 1349', *EHR* xxxvi (1921), 57–8.
44 *Froissart*, ed. de Lettenhove, xviii, 336–7, cf. 216, n. 47 below.
45 E.W.M. Balfour-Melville, 'Papers Relating to the Captivity and Release of David II', *Misc. of the Scott. Soc.* ix (1958), 1, 3–4, 37, 44–5.

war to gain his ends and that the Scots themselves feared they might have their king returned to them by main force. On 1 February, 1352, Edward warned his followers in Scotland to be ready to assist William Douglas to maintain David's cause should any rise up against him when he attempted to get an agreement with Edward confirmed.[46] A letter from John of France, probably of September 1351, envisages David's invading Scotland with English support and offers to pay for 500 men-at-arms and 500 archers in that eventuality.[47] Knighton has a story that after the abortive conference at Newcastle in 1353 the Scots threatened not to ransom David but to elect another king unless he pardoned all that had been done in his absence and stood up to Edward. He adds that the English council then ordered Northampton, the northerners, and all who claimed lands in Scotland to accompany David there.[48]

In 1354 an agreement was reached on a different basis. An indenture was concluded on 13 July by which it was agreed that David should be released for £60,000, guaranteed by hostages and payable in nine annual instalments, a truce to last meanwhile. A meeting for the performance of the agreement was to be held on 25 August. It does not seem to have been held. But in early October the English prepared the documents necessary for the ratification, David was sent to the north and it seemed that he was about to be released. He was not. Instead another indenture in almost the same terms as the first was drawn up on 12 November. The chief differences from that of July were, firstly that David, who had not been referred to as king of Scotland in the earlier document, was accorded that title when first mentioned – but not thereafter – in this, and secondly that a clause providing for three captured Scottish knights, who may have played some part in arranging the earlier agreement, was omitted. It was agreed that there should be another meeting on 14 January to confirm the agreement if the king of England approved.[49] This meeting may have taken place, but the agreement was not ratified. The most likely explanation of these events is that the July indenture was a consequence of the proposed treaty of Guînes between

[46] *Rot. Scot.* i, 748a.
[47] *Parl. Rec.* 100. I have assumed that the Black Book rightly records all four letters on fols 15–16 as the same date, but wrongly gives it as 1361. Alternative texts of the first two printed by de Lettenhove (xviii, 336–8) are dated 1351 which accords better with their contents, and especially with the address of the second. The text of the letter cited above is at least slightly corrupt. Philip had sent a little help to Scotland – 20 suits of armour – in 1348 (*Les journaux du trésor de Philippe VI de Valois*, ed. J. Viard (Paris, 1899), no. 1278). See also, for what it is worth, Francisque-Michel, op. cit., p. 64, n. 2.
[48] Op. cit., ii, 75–6.
[49] The indenture of 13 July is PRO, Scottish Documents, Exchequer (E.39), 2/36, printed *Foedera*, III, 281–2 – wrongly stated there to be the text from the Scotch Roll. The ratifications of 5 October and the documents indicating the preparations for David's release are printed *Rot. Scot.* i, 768a–774a. The indenture of 12 November is E.39/2/35, inaccurately described in *Foedera*, III, 291. The alleged ratifications dated 5 December of the indenture of 13 July printed in *Foedera*, III, 293 do not exist. Rymer appears to have misread 'd'Octobre' in the ratifications of 5 October as 'Decembre' and to have printed them twice, under both the right date (III, 285) and the wrong one.

England and France, drawn up in the previous April.[50] In this John II granted Edward III good terms and agreed, by implication, to renounce the Franco-Scottish alliance. This would have left the Scots hopelessly exposed and bound to come to terms. But the ratification of the treaty of Guînes was not supposed to take place until a meeting was held at Avignon towards the end of the year. It seems likely that the Scots delayed the ratification of the July agreement with the English until they knew whether or not the Anglo-French treaty was to be ratified. That the delay came from their side and not from the English is suggested both by the fact that the November indenture was marginally more favourable to Scotland than that of July, though this is anything but a conclusive argument, and by the apparent completeness of the English preparations to put the agreement into effect in October. It looks as if by 14 January the Scots either knew that the negotiations at Avignon were vain, or were still awaiting news. The French may have already been urging them towards war and in any case were soon to do so.

On 5 March, 1355, the Sire de Garencières received orders from the king of France to go to Scotland with fifty men-at-arms and, more important, 40,000 *deniers d'or a l'escu* to induce the Scots to attack England.[51] He left Paris on his way to Scotland on the 16th. The English had been uneasy about the March since February, although their keeping David in the north until towards the end of that month suggests that they still hoped for an agreement. By June they were aware that there were French in Scotland and feared their participation in an attack by 'the whole Scottish army'. A considerable army was summoned to Newcastle in July and August to be ready to oppose them. Then, probably about Michaelmas, a truce was concluded. Relying on this, Edward took many of the northern magnates with him to Calais at the end of October, including, of all people, the keeper of Berwick. This proved imprudent. De Garencières had not brought his money with him, but by 15 September he had reached a sufficiently firm agreement with some at least of the Scots for it to be handed over at Bruges on that day to Walter Wardlaw, acting in the name of 'the lords and barons of Scotland'.[52] The Scottish nobles seem, in fact, to have been divided on whether to attack: it may be that only some of them, in particular William Douglas – the future earl – had agreed to the truce. On 6 November the earl of Angus, supported by the earl of March, took the town – but not the castle – of Berwick by surprise. Edward III learned of this either just before or just after he left Calais for England on about 19 November. He went to the north almost at once, summoning a very large army to him. Berwick was quickly recovered. He went on to

[50] F. Bock, 'Some New Documents Illustrating the Early Years of the Hundred Years War', *Bull. John Rylands Library* xv (1931), 60–99; cf. J. Le Patourel, 'Edward III and the Kingdom of France', *History* xliii (1958), 177.
[51] The main sources for the events of 1356 are the Scottish chronciles, *Scalacronica*, ed. J. Stevenson (Maitland Club, 1836), *Rot. Scot.* and the French records for which see de la Roncière, i, 505–6 and R. Delachenal, *Histoire de Charles V*, i (Paris, 1909), 108.
[52] Bibl. Nat., MS Clairambault CIX, no. 141, cf. LX, no. 6.

Roxburgh, where, on 20 January Edward Balliol ceded to him the kingdom of Scotland. Edward entered his new realm with its banner borne before him and advanced to Edinburgh. Although he did a great deal of damage – the 'Burnt Candlemas' was remembered long after – the failure of his victualling ships to arrive compelled him to leave after an active campaign of little more than a fortnight.

Negotiations recommenced almost at once. Edward's victory at Poitiers in September 1356 strengthened his already strong position. He sought to use it to separate the Scots from the French. His instructions to the Black Prince of 17 December, 1356, for the forthcoming negotiations with France said that the Scots were to be excluded from the negotiations, and if possible from the short truce which was to be made with the French. The French were to be told that the Scots had made truces for themselves and had negotiated for peace in the past without the French being represented and were about to do so again.[53] France was not, in any case, in a position to help the Scots, who, left to themselves, concluded an agreement with England at Berwick in October 1357. David was freed on heavy terms which settled no issue but that of his release. The ransom was fixed at 100,000 marks, to be paid in ten annual instalments, a truce to last meanwhile. David was referred to as king of Scotland in the treaty, but nothing was said specifically about the recognition of his claim and in later documents the English avoided giving him the royal title. On the other hand nothing was said about the recognition of English territorial claims in Scotland: the nature of some of the references to Berwick suggests that the possibility of its return to Scotland – probably in connection with a settlement of the succession in Edward's favour – was contemplated. The Franco-Scottish alliance was not mentioned. The Scots had made no concessions affecting their dynasty, their territory, or their international position, but Edward had at last coerced them into buying back their king. There are many parallels between the negotiations for David's release and those for that of John of France. In both cases the heir, who was left in power at home, had little reason, sentiment apart, to negotiate a ransom, particularly since either king might soon have died. Both captives were willing to grant more generous terms than their countries could stomach. Each ransom was agreed after Edward had made an intimidating military demonstration before or in the enemy's capital. While it is true that in neither case did Edward obtain his full demands, it is equally true that he might never have obtained a ransom at all from either Scotland or France. From a purely military point of view the 1356 campaign in Scotland and that of 1359–60 in France were doubtfully successful. Their political results place them amongst the most effective Edward ever launched.

David remained at peace with England for nearly twenty years after 1357.[54] In June 1359 he tried to escape from the heavy obligation imposed at Berwick

---

[53] *Bull. John Rylands Library*, xv, 99.
[54] E.W.M. Balfour-Melville, *Edward III and David II* gives the best account of Anglo-Scottish relations 1357–77. The more important documents are printed in *Foedera*, *APS*, *Parl.*

by offering to join in a Franco-Danish attack on England provided that France helped him to pay off the ransom and so to regain the hostages. (The alliance with France was still in force, the 'first treaty of London' of May 1358, which required France to sever it, having come to nothing.)[55] The Dauphin offered him 50,000 marks and an agreement may have been concluded.[56] If so, the English invasion of France in October made it abortive. The Scots continued to pay off the ransom, completing the second instalment in January 1360. Thereafter they paid no more until Candlemas 1366. This default left them in a very weak position. Edward held their hostages and the conclusion of a peace between England and France in October 1360 meant that there was small chance of French help, even though the provision requiring the abrogation of the alliance between France and Scotland did not become effective.[57] Edward took his opportunity to press again for the succession to Scotland for his house in negotiations which lasted at least until 1365. David was willing to defer or to appear to defer to him, but the Scottish nobility were not. Robert Stewart must have opposed it. Patriotic sentiment no doubt had some effect. Other considerations are suggested by a tract purporting to describe a discussion of the succession issue in a Scottish council.[58] The opponents of an English succession are represented as maintaining that the English had shown in Wales and Ireland that they were not to be trusted, that an English king would be bound to favour his countrymen and the Disinherited, and that the English lacked the will or the means to attack Scotland. The first two points were sound and the third defensible. How little the Scots accepted it is shown by their readiness to accept almost any terms other than the succession of an English prince and by the new and onerous agreement made in 1365. This raised the amount still to be paid for the ransom from 80,000 marks to £100,000, payable in instalments of £4,000 during a twenty-five-year truce, which Edward could terminate at the end of four years at the cost of reducing the ransom to the old figure. As France became stronger the Scots became less accommodating, and the English started to take fright. But the agreement of 1365 was observed until 1369, when the renewal of the Anglo-French war greatly strengthened the Scottish position. In June of that

Rec., *Rot. Scot.* and by C. Johnson, 'Proposals for an Agreement with Scotland', *EHR* xxx (1915), 476.

55 Delachenal, ii, 407. The 'second treaty of London' (March 1359) left the question of the Franco-Scottish alliance for later discussion, E. Cosneau, *Les grands traités de la Guerre de Cent Ans* (Paris, 1889), 26.

56 Arch. Nat., J.677, 7 and 8; Delachenal, ii, 94–105; *ERS* ii, 52.

57 The fate of the hostages is obscure. The last reference to one of the twenty heirs of noblemen remaining a hostage appears to be *Rot. Scot.* i, 930a (1369); two certainly and probably more died in the plague of 1361–62. It may be that releases were made as the ransom was paid. Of the three magnates Angus and Thomas Moray died in 1361 and do not seem to have been replaced and Sutherland is last mentioned as a hostage in 1367 (*Rot. Scot.* i, 911a) and died before 19 June 1371.

58 'Papers relating to the Release and Captivity of David II', op. cit., 36–56.

year, the total of the ransom, paid and payable was reduced to the former figure of 100,000 marks. David returned from concluding the new agreement in London to find Charles V's ambassadors awaiting him in Edinburgh. Their and later French offers were unsuccessful in inducing Scotland to make war on England while Edward III lived. Robert Stewart, who succeeded as Robert II in February 1371, lost no time in concluding an agreement with Charles V. But this provided for mutual aid only when the Anglo-Scottish truces should end, or be broken by the English. Another agreement was prepared at the same time which provided that the pope should be induced to annul the Anglo-Scottish truce and that Charles should give 100,000 nobles to pay off the ransom and should send 1,000 men-at-arms to Scotland for two years together with arms and pay for another 500 knights and 500 serjeants. The first agreement was ratified by Robert in October; the second, so far as is known, was not, and was certainly not acted upon.[59] Robert maintained the ransom payments. The last was made on 24 June, 1377, before the Scots had heard of the death of Edward III two days before. After that they paid no more, while war flared up in the Marches.

The years of peace after 1357 brought a certain prosperity to Scotland. The exchequer rolls show the collection of a surprisingly large revenue.[60] The heavy burden of the ransom was met by doubling, trebling, and finally quadrupling the customs. The mere capacity to raise the sums needed is an indication of the wealth of the country and the power of the state. The flow of money into the exchequer, for whatever purpose it was intended, helped the king. David was able, for instance, to rebuild Edinburgh Castle and, in 1363, to put down a rebellion with the aid of paid troops.[61] The period saw the reform of the Scottish currency and to some extent of the law.[62] A good deal of church-building went on and the first important work of Scottish literature, Barbour's *Bruce*, was completed in 1375. There were repeated rebellions against David, but all were more or less successfully repressed. Rebellion was normal in later medieval Scotland, which in this, as in other respects, resembled Anglo-Norman England. Much remains to be done before knowledge of David's later years reaches its limit. But it is likely that Wynton's judgment, that his rule was effective and he kept good order, is more nearly true than is suggested by the strictures of more modern Scottish historians, to whose high standards of political and personal conduct

[59] *Foedera*, III, 925–6, Register House, French Treaties 2, Black Book, fols 64–9, *Parl. Rec.*, 120–4, Arch. Nat., J.677, 9–13. The more aggressive agreement is known only from letters of Charles copied into the Black Book (fols 68–9); it may be that the considerable sum of money which Charles had deposited in the monastery of St Catherine in Paris by May 1378 'pour certaines besoignes qui sont entre nous et le roy d'Escoce' and which he was then drawing upon for other purposes had something to do with this, or a similar agreement, *Mandements [et actes divers de Charles V]*, ed. L. Delisle (Paris, 1874), nos. 1712–14.

[60] The account of Scottish finances and exports below is largely based on *ERS* ii. Burnett's valuable introduction gives some account of the Mercer family (xlii–iii, n. 4), cf. p. 221 below.

[61] *ERS*, ii, 64.

[62] I.H. Stewart, *The Scottish Coinage* (1955), 25–31; T.M. Cooper, *Select Scottish Cases of the Thirteenth Century* (1944), p. lxvii.

David notably failed to measure up. That he enjoyed the success he did was due largely to his keeping the peace with England, and his ability to restrain the Marchers and so to keep the peace is an indication of his strength in Scotland.

Burgesses were more prominent in Scottish politics after 1357 than ever before. Their regular summons to parliament begins in the sixties.[63] In 1364 David granted a general charter which seems to have given the burghs a new degree of monopoly in trade.[64] John Mercer of Perth, probably the greatest Scottish merchant of his day, acted as the chief financial agent of the Crown in the organization of the ransom payments and in other matters and was prominent in a way that no member of his class is known previously to have been. He appears much like a Scottish equivalent of William de la Pole. These things reflect the importance of foreign trade. The exports of wool recorded between 1359 and 1377 averaged about 5,000 sacks annually and the customs on them constituted a high proportion of the royal revenue. Scotland carried on a considerable trade with England, exporting chiefly fish and hides and importing manufactured goods and food. There was a constant demand for English grain in Scotland in the later fourteenth century. Licences to export it were used as diplomatic presents to Scottish ambassadors; English prisoners sometimes paid their ransoms in it. Between 1357 and 1377 licences were issued for the export to Scotland of just over 20,000 quarters.[65] Their issue sometimes had a diplomatic purport. None of the exceptionally heavy exports of 1365 were issued until the new ransom agreement was drawn up on 20 May, while about half of them were licenced on that day. In some ways the most remarkable English export to Scotland was wool. From 1361–2 the custumars' accounts record the export from Scotland of English wool at a rate of custom lower than that normal in either England or Scotland. The most reasonable explanation of this is that the Scots sought to enhance their revenue by encouraging the smuggling of English wool over the border for export from Scotland. The constant efforts of the English authorities to stop such smuggling are thus explained. Between 1362 and 1377 6,619 sacks of such wool were exported from Scotland, 1,800 of them between February 1373 and February 1374. War was almost certain to harm Scottish trade. It could, indeed, lead to circumstances – such as an embargo on English wool-exports to Flanders – which benefited it. But such advantages were outweighed by the vulnerability of the Scottish route to Flanders, running along the east coast of England. As soon as tension increased in the late 'seventies the English started to seize Scottish cargoes. It is probable that even in time of peace most of the English exports of food to Scotland were illicit. For instance, in 1378 a Louth merchant was pardoned for the unlicensed export of 3,260 quarters of grain to Scotland.[66] The Scots nevertheless considered the opportunity to import

63 W.C. Dickinson, *Scotland from the Earliest Times to 1603*, ch. xx.

64 *Early Records of the Burgh of Aberdeen*, ed. W.C. Dickinson (Scott. Hist. Soc., 1957), xcviii.

65 Nearly all the licenses which were enrolled are in *Rot. Scot.*

66 *CPR 1377–81*, 140; cf. *Some Sessions of the Peace in Lincolnshire*, ed. R. Sillem (Lincoln Record Soc., 1933), 99, 138–9.

food from England as one of the advantages of peace.[67] (Such trade was of some importance to the English also; a parliamentary petition on 1394 maintained that many would be unable to pay their rent if they were not allowed to export grain.[68]) Even the smuggling of wool seems to have been affected by war. Recorded exports of English wool from Scotland drop after 1377 to a total of 1,524 sacks between then and 1399. In short, foreign trade was very important for Scotland and its interests were best served by peace with England.

Good relations with England had other attractions for the Scots. For some they were financial. In 1359 the earl of Mar did liege homage to Edward III against all men but David, in return for a promise of 600 marks a year.[69] In the same year the earl of Angus, one of the hostages, agreed to serve him in France with a retinue, though it is doubtful whether he went.[70] Edward seems to have been at some pains to court his more important Scottish hostages, as he later courted those from France. Many lesser Scots entered his service when the French war began again. In 1369–70 the garrison of Calais contained about 140 Scots, though some of these probably came from English Scotland.[71] Edward seems to have been short of trained troops at this time and glad to get them from anywhere. Many Scots simply liked to be able to come to England. The attractions of Edward's court must partly account for David's three known visits after his release. The Scottish nobility were very isolated in wartime and many may have already spoken no language but English. After 1357 many of them obtained safe-conducts to come on pilgrimage to England. Scotland had no university until 1413. Her aspiring clerks had to look southwards. Between 1357 and 1377 two general and sixty-eight individual safe-conducts were issued to enable Scots to attend the English universities. A Scottish gentleman is found coming to London to consult a doctor and a lesser man to learn a craft.

These advantages were not enough to prolong the period of peace into Richard II's reign.[72] In the last years of Edward III Scottish pressure on the *terra irredenta* of English Scotland exacerbated the usual hostility between the English and Scottish Marchers. In particular, Percy and Douglas disputed Jedworth Forest. The wardens of the Marches were hardly able to maintain the truce when the chief among their own number sought to break it. Edward repeatedly

---

[67] N.H. Nicolas, *Proceedings and Ordinances of the Privy Council*, i (1834), 32.

[68] *Rot. Parl.* iii, 320.

[69] *Rot. Scot.* i, 836ab.

[70] Ibid., i, 840b.

[71] *Issue Roll of Thomas of Brantingham*, trans. F. Devon (1835), 83–5, 162; cf. 282, 337, 410–11; cf. *Froissart*, vii, 232, 235–7, viii, 138, 148; G.S.C. Swinton, 'John of Swinton', *Scott. Hist. Rev.* xvi (1918–19), 261–79.

[72] The usual sources for Anglo-Scottish relations are supplemented in Richard II's reign by the important diplomatic material in British Library, MS Vespasian F vii. Most of it has been printed, but in many different places. All the major English chronicles pay more attention to Scottish affairs after the outbreak of war. There is no reliable modern account of Robert II's reign apart from Burnett's introductions to *ERS*, ii and iii and E.W.M. Balfour-Melville, *James I, King of Scots* (1936), 1–21.

sent commissions of conservators, some, and, towards the end, all of them non-Marchers, to hold March-days and to restrain his Marchers. Robert sent his sons, Carrick and Fife, to restrain his.[73] These efforts were in vain. Raiding and counter-raiding by important men and large forces started in 1376 and the Marches were soon reduced to a state such as they had been in during the early 1340s. The central authorities still hoped to maintain the truce and sent embassies to the border every year to attempt to do so.

The English had every reason to be conciliatory. They did nothing to enforce the payment of the remainder of the ransom. Offers were made for permanent peace: in 1378 and 1379 the marriage of Richard to a Scottish princess was discussed.[74] Efforts were made to force the English Marchers to break the vicious circle of reprisals. At the same time considerable garrisons were kept on the border and large forces sometimes accompanied the conservators to remind the Scots of the power of England. That sent with Gaunt to hold a day in 1380 was intended to consist of 14 bannerets, 162 knights, 1,492 esquires, and 1,670 archers and to cost over £5,000.[75] These efforts resulted in the conclusion of a truce within a truce, a *specialis securitas*, in November 1380 which was extended in June 1381 to last until February 1384, when the truce of 1369 was due to expire.

There were strong forces making for war. Frequent negotiations had not saved the English border from serious damage. The *securitas* was badly broken, especially in 1383. The Marchers were resentful and half-rebellious, above all when efforts were made to make them keep the truce. Those of Gaunt as lieutenant on the March contributed to his great quarrel with Northumberland in 1381. The defence of the March had become a serious burden and there were bitter disputes as to whether the whole of it should fall on the Marchers. Richard must have been tempted to launch a major attack on Scotland on the model of 1356 and so seek to put an end to these troubles. On the Scottish side it seems that while the Marchers, and above all the earl of Douglas were for war, Robert still wanted peace. French influence must have been for war and France may have had powerful friends in Scotland. William Landallis, bishop of St Andrews from 1342 to 1385, had lived in France and John II had at least professed to think that he had been active on the French behalf during David's captivity.[76] Sir Nicolas Erskine was in receipt of a pension of 300 gold francs a year from France.[77] William, earl of Douglas, had been partly brought up in France, had fought on

---

[73] For attempts to maintain the truce, see *Rot. Scot.*, *Wynton*, and the accounts for March-days in *ERS*, ii and PRO, Foreign Accounts (E.364).

[74] PRO, Diplomatic Documents, Exchequer, 1527.

[75] Advance payments were made on 7 September, PRO, Issue Rolls, 478 mm. 26, 27. The arrangements were subject to some alteration but a very large force certainly went north, *Historia Anglicana*, ed. H.R. Riley (1864), i, 446–7, E.364/15 mm. F and M, 16 m. F.

[76] *Parl. Rec.*, 90.

[77] Arch. Nat., J.621, no. 77; *Comptes du Trésor*, ed. R. Fawtier (Paris, 1930), no. 1469; H. Moranvillé, 'Extraits de journaux de Trésor', *Bibl. de l'éc. des chartes* xlix (1888), 384; cf. *Froissart*, vii, cv, n. 2.

the French side at Poitiers and, according to Froissart, had been given a pension of 500 livres a year by John II.[78] In 1377 Charles V spent 500 gold francs on a present of armour for him, his son James and Robert Erskine.[79] At least one Scot was high in the French royal service. A 'Johannes le Mercier, de patria Scotie' was in receipt of an annuity of 400 *livres parisis* as *consiliarius regis* in 1384. He had probably been in the French service since at least 1377 and may well be the John Mercer whom Walsingham describes as a trusted adviser of Charles V on matters concerning England.[80] There is thus little reason to doubt that the French were well-informed on Scottish affairs or that they were in direct communication with those Scottish magnates who wished for war with England. In spite of the pressure upon him, from within Scotland and without, Robert II had held aloof from the Anglo-French conflict, content to make his profit by ceasing after 1377 to pay off the ransom. He may have concluded some agreement with Charles V before May 1378 for, aggressive action.[81] If so, if did not come into effect. All that he is known to have done before 1384 to help France is to support Clement VII, the French claimant to the papacy. This seems to have had no effect on Anglo-Scottish relations, although the bombastic Clementist propaganda of Thomas of Rossy, bishop of Galloway, may have caused a certain stir in England.[82] But in 1383, probably through fear of what might happen when the truce expired, Robert made an agreement with France. If Scotland and England were to be at war he was to be sent 1,000 men-at-arms, 1,000 suits of armour and 40,000 gold francs before May 1384.[83]

A somewhat obscure series of events followed. On 26 January, 1384, England and France concluded a truce until October, in which the Scots could join if they wished. Scotland was not represented at the conference. This was commonly so, partly because it was often the case that neither side wanted it, partly because she could not afford the expense. Big conferences were in more ways than one the clerical equivalent of campaigns.[84] After the old truce expired on 2 February open war broke out between England and Scotland. It seems that the Scots attacked and took the most exposed of the English fortresses, Lochmaben,

---

[78] *Froissart*, iv, 194.

[79] *Mandements*, no. 1564.

[80] *Comptes du Trésor*, no. 1440; *Mandements*, no. 1414; and *Chronicon Angliae*, ed. E.M. Thompson (1874), 198, where Walsingham probably confuses the John Mercer in the French service with John Mercer of Perth; they can hardly be identical because he of Perth died before 14 March 1381 (*ERS* iii, 652); it is, however, conceivable that more than one Scottish John Mercer served the kings of France. A French Jean le Mercier very prominent in the financial administration of the French Crown at this time must also be distinguished.

[81] Above, 220, n. 59.

[82] H. McEwan, ' "A Theolog Solempne", Thomas de Rossy, Bishop of Galloway', *Innes Review* viii (1957), 21–9; E. Perroy, *L'Angleterre et le grand schisme d'Occident* (Paris, 1933), 71–6.

[83] Ratified by Charles in June and by Robert in August, Black Book, fols 69–70; *Parl. Rec.*, 131–2; *Foedera* (1st edn), vii, 406–7, cf. 391.

[84] *ERS*, ii, passim for the high proportion of the royal income spent on diplomacy.

before reports of the new truce could arrive. This probably decided the English, who were hesitating between peace and war, to launch a major attack. They may have taken the opportunity to delay the French ambassadors who were taking word of the new truce to Scotland via England. In April Lancaster led an army on a very short campaign to Edinburgh, which he ransomed. Robert wished, nevertheless, to accept the new truce. He was overborne by the Marchers who retaliated in great force with some French freelances in their company.[85] Thereafter the Scots did accept the truce, and its extension until May 1385, agreed at the Boulogne conference, at which they were represented.[86] Their Marchers did not observe it.

The Scots blamed the French at Boulogne for not having sent troops in 1384. The reproach would not have been deserved in 1385 when it was through Scotland that for the first and last time in the Hundred Years War a major French army invaded England. At the end of May Jean de Vienne, Admiral of France, set sail for Scotland with at least 1,300 men-at-arms, and 250 crossbowmen, together with armour and 50,000 gold francs for the Scots.[87] He was intended to attack from the north while another French army invaded England from the south. The southern force never set sail but in July Vienne and Douglas invaded England on the East March. Richard collected the biggest army of his reign, probably nearly 14,000 men, drove the French and Scots north and advanced to Edinburgh.[88] The enemy, who had been there not long before him, moved south-westwards to harry the West March almost undisturbed. The French went home in November ill-pleased with their experiences. They seem to have found only the Marchers and the earl of Moray well-inclined and the chief object of Robert and his subjects to take as much money as they could from them. Richard's invasion, though it lasted less than three weeks, had its effect. A truce was concluded in September, which was probably extended until June 1388.[89] It was in force during the period when the French armada of 1386, fully as dangerous as the Spanish armada of 1588, was threatening England. In 1388 the Scots, tempted by English weakness during the Appellant coup, refused to renew the truce and attacked with forces gathered from the whole kingdom, probably their largest army since 1346. Fife invaded on the West March, Douglas on the East, where he penetrated beyond the Tyne, defeating Hotspur and meeting his death at Otterburn on the way home. Heavy fighting continued until the next year, when the Scots were given the opportunity to join the three-year truce concluded by France and England in June. The English appear to have been reluctant to

[85] *Froissart* xi, 164–75 is the chief authority for the division between the king and the Marchers. His account is partly borne out by English record evidence.

[86] E. Martène and U. Durand, *Voyage littéraire de deux religieux bénédictins* (Paris, 1724), 332–40.

[87] Terrier de Loray, *Jean de Vienne* (Paris, 1877) gives the best account of this expedition and prints many of the abundant documents.

[88] N.B. Lewis, 'The Last Medieval Summons of the English Feudal Levy', *EHR* lxxiii (1958), 1–26.

[89] *Rot. Scot.* ii, 75b, 85b–86a, 91b, 93b, E.101/73/35.

agree to the inclusion of the Scots. It was to Scotland's advantage that she should adhere; she had been extremely fortunate in the preceding two years and could hardly hope to stand alone against England. Nevertheless, Robert and Fife, who was ruling for him, seem to have hesitated before they agreed to join, which they did before 27 September. Walsingham plausibly says that whiie the Scottish nobles wanted peace the *vulgus* did not, because they had impoverished themselves to buy equipment for raiding in England.[90] Some of them may have found employment for it in France, where considerable numbers of Scottish archers are found in 1391.[91] The Scots adhered to the extensions of the truce up to and including that from 1394 to 1398. The war was at an end.

The Anglo-French war of 1369–89 covered a wider area and was more dangerous and burdensome to England than any she was to fight until the Anglo-Spanish war of 1585–1604 – which it resembles in many ways. Scotland contributed largely to the burden and the danger. In the last year of Edward III's reign the defence of the March cost less than £1,000.[92] In 1384 Northumberland was paid £4,000 for defending it for forty-two days. In 1385 and 1386 the cost of the garrisons on the March ran at a rate of about £16,000 a year in war and £8,000 in truce.[93] At the same time Calais, Cherbourg and Brest together cost not less than £25,000 a year while Richard's annual income was of the order of £125,000.[94] A defensive policy was the royal road to ruin. Besides garrisons it required fortifications. The Scottish threat in the north, like that from France in the south, led to the building or rebuilding of many royal and private castles. Roxburgh, Dunstanburgh, Carlisle, Castle Rushen, Durham and Warkworth are only the most conspicuous examples from Richard's reign and the later part of Edward's.[95] Numerous smaller works were built by lesser men. The value of lands on the March was greatly reduced by the fighting. That of one of the most exposed manors, Burgh-by-Sands, went down, according to the *inquisitiones post mortem*, from £21 15s. 4d. in 1339 to 12s. 2d. in 1384.[96] Otterburn must have ensured that the balance of ransoms went against the English.

[90] *Hist. Ang.* ii, 182–3.

[91] *Copiale Prioratus Sanctiandree*, ed. J.H. Baxter (Oxford, 1932), 220–2.

[92] E.101/68/140 and 142, 73/21, E.364/9 m.O, 13 m.E, 25 m.C; J.L. Kirby, 'The Keeping of Carlisle Castle before 1381', *Trans. Cumberland and Westmorland Arch. and Ant. Soc.*, new ser., liv (1955), 131–9.

[93] *Rot. Scot.* ii, 62, E.101/68/239 and 242, 73/29–35, E.364/22 m.E, 23 m.G, 32 m.E, 33 m.C; R.L. Storey, 'The Wardens of the Marches of England towards Scotland', *EHR* lxxii (1957), 593–603.

[94] E.101/68/244, E.364/20 m.A, 23 m.F (Cherbourg); E.101/68/237, E.364/20 m.G (Brest); E.364/22 m.H (Calais); A. Steel, *The Receipt of the Exchequer* (Cambridge, 1954), 49–57, 446; cf. E. Perroy, *Compte de William Gunthorpe, Trésorier de Calais 1371–2* (Arras, 1959), 5–10.

[95] *The History of the King's Works*, ed. H.M. Colvin and others, ii (Oxford, 1963), 567–9, 599, 818–21; W. Douglas Simpson, 'Further Notes on Dunstanburgh Castle', *Archaeologia Aeliana*, 4th ser., xxvii (1949), 1–28; B.H. St J. O'Neill, 'Castle Rushen, Isle of Man', *Archaeologia* xciv (1951), 1–26; cf. B.H. St J. O'Neill, *Castles and Cannon* (Oxford, 1960), 1–21.

[96] R.L. Storey, 'The Manor of Burgh-by-Sands', *TCWAS*, new ser., liv (1955), 126.

But in Richard II's reign the English often did better on sea than on land and the war against Scotland was not an exception. Considerable fleets were maintained on the North Sea, partly for use against the Scots. For instance, between December 1383 and Martinmas 1384 Northumberland, as admiral of the north commanded a force whose wages cost, he maintained, £2,186 16s. and which comprised at its maximum 2 knights, 297 men-at-arms and 544 archers and mariners.[97] Such fleets, the numerous privateers of the east-coast ports and the position of the main Scottish trade-route ensured that many Scottish ships and cargoes fell into English hands when the two countries were at war or when relations between them grew tense. The captures were sometimes very valuable; some ships taken in 1380 or 1381 were said to have been worth £10,000.[98] Robert II had to spend over £500 in 1380 on fitting out ships to defend Scottish trade.[99] It is likely that the gains or losses by sea were on at least the scale of those by land, as may well have generally been the case during the Hundred Years War. It is impossible to know exactly how much the English gained since only a proportion of their captures are recorded in the public records. They certainly suffered some losses to the Scottish privateers who were active in the north and Irish seas. But there is little reason to doubt that, on balance, the advantage was theirs.

War between England and Scotland was not to the advantage of the kings of either country. England could, by an effort, overrun southern Scotland, but lacked the resources to occupy it permanently. The Scots had the power to reduce the March counties of England to misery and three times in the fourteenth century they did so. The Marches were not the only part of England to bear the burden of home defence. The not infrequent threat of invasion required garrisons, fortifications and the gathering of ships and men from the maritime counties too.[100] It was thought that the value of a man's arms might well exceed that of the rest of his property if he lived either on the Marches or on the coast.[101] Nevertheless it was only the north which felt the full weight and savagery of war. Its defence diverted men and money that were needed, or could be used more gainfully, elsewhere. Neville's Cross was very profitable for Edward III – David's ransom alone produced 76,000 marks in one form or another – but it was the great exception. Otherwise the English Crown consistently spent far more in the north than it gained. War with England had attractions for the Scots; raiding England was for them what raiding France was for the English. But Scottish trade was vulnerable and Scotland lacked the military power to prevent the king of England marching straight to Edinburgh when he chose and was able to exert his full strength. Each side had more power to harm the other than to profit itself. In the earlier part of the period neither king recognized this. Edward

---

97 PRO, Memoranda Roll, K.R., 165 Communia E.T., mm. 24–5.
98 *CPR 1381–5*, 83–4.
99 *ERS* iii, 55, 651.
100 E.g., *Records of Norwich*, ed. W. Hudson and J.C. Tingey, i (1906), 272.
101 *Rot. Parl.* iii, 82.

endeavoured to conquer Scotland. David attacked England when he need not have done. Each learned his lesson. Neither Edward, after 1347, nor Richard made war on Scotland until he was driven to it, although the claim to suzerainty over Scotland was always kept alive. David tried hard to keep the peace in his later years. As Robert Bruce had been willing to pay £20,000 for peace when Scotland was strong and England weak, so did Robert II continue to pay off David's ransom for six years, while England was at war with France and doing badly.

Two forces made for war, French pressure on Scotland and that of the Marchers on either side. It was to the interest of the French to be loyal allies to the Scots and so they proved, though they were nearly driven to abandon them between 1356 and 1360. Philip VI saved Scotland during David's minority. The French observed their obligation to include the Scots in their truces with England, while the Scots did not – could not, in fact – observe the reciprocal obligation on them. It was not from France but from the papacy that there came the suggestion, in 1344, and perhaps again in 1375, that Edward should be given Scotland, abandoning his French lands, where the king of Scotland might be compensated.[102] At the same time the French alliance had disagreeable consequences for the Scots. Accounts of what Scottish ambassadors said in negotiations with France reveal a certain rancour and suggest resentment of a subordinate position. Once England and France were at war the interests of the kings of Scotland and of France diverged. It was to the advantage of the one to maintain at least formal peace with England while extorting what concessions he could the position of Robert II from 1377 to 1384. The other required that the Scots should go to war, as David did up to 1346. On two later occasions the Scots could be induced to intervene only by a subsidy, all of it paid directly to the magnates in 1355 and most of it in 1385. There are indications that on each occasion some Scots were doubtful of the prudence of the venture. They were right to be so, for the king of England was in Edinburgh at the head of an army within three months of each attack. The ability of the king of France – and of the king of England – to patronize Scottish notables weakened the power of the Crown. In 1371 Robert II even feared that the French might intervene in the succession dispute which could follow his death. In short, because Scotland was dependent almost for her existence on its value to France she was subject to pressures which threatened to impair her freedom of action. Portugal was in much the same position in regard to England and presents many parallels. For example, Edmund of Cambridge's expedition to Portugal in 1381–82 met almost exactly the same difficulties and followed very much the same unsatisfactory course as that of Jean de Vienne to Scotland in 1385. It was easy for great powers to gather clients and promises in such relatively poor and feeble states. But the political divisions and institutional weaknesses which made this easy

---

102 E. Déprez, 'La conférence d'Avignon (1344)', *Essays . . . Presented to T.F. Tout*, ed. A.G. Little and F.M. Powick (Manchester, 1925), p. 312; E. Perroy, 'The Anglo-French Negotiations at Bruges 1374–7', *Camden Misc.* xix (1952), xvi.

made it equally difficult to induce the small states to give more than passive and ambiguous help. They were capable of effective action on a large scale only under the stimulus of great danger or great opportunity. But however ungrateful an ally Scotland proved it was always in the interest of France to support her against England and her kings were never in a position where they had simply to obey those of France.

It was the Marchers rather than the French who did most to bring about war between the kings of England and Scotland in the later part of the century. March society had had to live through so much war that it had come to live by it. Continued war had much the same effect on the border that it did in parts of France. Bodies very like free companies appeared on the Scottish side as they had, in Edward II's reign, on the English. It was impossible to prevent petty warfare on such a frontier and difficult to prevent its escalation into something worse. Faced with this problem, which was as much one of regulating a society as of defending a frontier, the English authorities had, characteristically, developed an institution to deal with it; the wardenship of the Marches reached under Edward III and Richard II what was to be very nearly its final form. The English wardens – little is known of their Scottish counterpart – were fairly effective, especially in so far as they were backed by the power of the central government in enforcing the payment of compensation to the other side.[103] They could just about keep the peace provided that the Marcher magnates on either side were not inclined towards war. But the magnates often were so inclined. They disputed lands on the border – which were sometimes surprisingly valuable – with rivals on the other side, feuded with them and were often tempted to raid or retaliate. It was very difficult for kings to check such men. The effect of war between England and Scotland was to increase the power of the Marcher houses, above all of those of Douglas and Percy. Neither was of the first importance at the beginning of the century. By its end they were not far from being dominant within their respective states. At the beginning of Richard's reign his government had the greatest difficulty in controlling the earl of Northumberland, as did Robert II in controlling Douglas. At the end of Richard's reign the Percies played a principal part in toppling him from his throne. They did so for reasons very much connected with the March. The war of 1384–89 had left them more powerful than ever. After about 1397 there was renewed tension on the March. It had the same causes as that in the last years of Edward III's reign and the king tried to deal with it in the same way, by taking the conduct of March affairs out of the hands of the Marchers. Lancaster was again appointed lieutenant. Commissions of conservators, full of Richard's friends and servants, were again sent to the March. The Percies, who had other grievances connected with the tenure of March offices, were again displeased.[104] But this time their displeasure had more serious consequences for the Crown. The forces and circumstances that

---

[103] R.R. Reid, 'The Office of the Warden of the Marches', *EHR* xxxii (1917), 479–96 is the fullest but no altogether a reliable account.
[104] E.g. *Wynton* vi, 379–81.

had helped temporarily to humiliate Gaunt in 1381 did much to put his son on the throne in 1399. War in the north had left the Percies too powerful to be overborne. In this, as in other respects, the Scottish wars of Edward III and Richard II resemble the whole Hundred Years War as it used to be seen.[105] In his attack on Scotland Edward merited Stubbs' strictures; it was an ambitious, unscrupulous and extravagant venture. The ensuing wars were cruel and destructive and chiefly to the advantage of the northern nobility, whose power was so far enhanced as to become a danger to the state. Much is rightly said of the profits of war in the fourteenth century. These wars remind us of the profits of peace.[106]

---

[105] For recent views on the Hundred Years War, see e.g. M. McKisack, 'Edward III and the Historians', *History* xlv (1960), 1–15.

[106] I am much indebted to Professor M. McKisack and to Dr P. Chaplais for reading this paper and making helpful suggestions; the responsibilty for any errors is mine.

2

EDWARD III AND THE BEGINNINGS
OF THE HUNDRED YEARS WAR

G. Templeman

Historians have long been concerned with the circumstances in which the Hundred Years War began, and their interest shows no sign of slackening. During the present century not a little has been added to our knowledge of the matter through the labours of scholars in this country, in the United States and on the continent. This means that by now a formidable array of evidence bearing on the subject has been brought to light, while numerous books and articles, packed with comment and explanation, lie ready to hand. It is true that important sources still remain unprinted, although not unused, but the scholars of the eighteenth and nineteenth centuries made available most of the chronicles and some of the records, while more documents have steadily found their way into print during the last fifty years.[1]

The present century has also seen the publication of some important studies of particular problems connected with the outbreak of the struggle. Eugène Déprez has examined the complicated dealings of the French, English and Papal courts with one another in the years 1328 to 1342.[2] Professor Lucas has carefully scrutinized the affairs of the Low Countries between 1326 and 1347 in order to show how considerable an influence they exercised upon the course of events which led to the beginning of the war.[3] The French historian Viard died without producing that great study of the reign of Philip VI which was to have crowned the labour of a lifetime. Nevertheless his many articles shed a flood of fresh light upon the working and policy of the French government in the crucial years before 1337.[4] Our knowledge of English diplomatic practice in these years

---

[1] There is a full bibliography of all but the most recently printed material in H.S. Lucas, *The Low Countries and the Hundred Years War, 1326–1347* (Ann Arbor, 1929).

[2] *Les préliminaires de la Guerre de Cent Ans* (Paris, 1902).

[3] Lucas, *op. cit.*

[4] The following are of particular importance: 'La France sous Philippe de Valois', *Revue des Questions Historiques* lix; 'Itinéraire de Philippe de Valois', *Bibliothèque de l'École des Chartes* lxxix, lxxxiv; 'Philippe de Valois, début du règne', *ibid.*, xcv.

has been much enlarged by Mr Cuttino's scholarly work.[5] The part played by the Papacy has also received particular attention, not only in Mollat's general work on the Avignonese popes, but also more recently in papers by Miss Helen Jenkins and M. Renouard.[6] These and other similar modern studies bear directly upon the political, diplomatic and military circumstances which attended the start of the war, but much other modern work, not written with this immediate purpose in view, does contribute usefully towards a better understanding of these issues.[7]

Although it is probable that economic motives played little or no part in provoking the conflict, economic considerations in one form or another could never be entirely thrust aside even by those deeply immersed in the absorbing business of political intrigue and military preparation. Alliances had to be paid for, and, particularly in the Low Countries, they were apt to prove worthless if the commercial interests of those concerned were not taken properly into account. Economic historians have of late done a great deal to illuminate these matters. There is Laurent's study of the cloth trade in the Low Countries, de Sturler's work on the duchy of Brabant, and the contributions of our own Eileen Power and George Unwin, to mention only a few of the most important.[8] Finally much more is now known of the complicated social and economic background against which the political manoeuvring of the years 1327–37 was conducted. It is clear that the English kingdom was but poorly endowed by contrast with the great material resources of its French neighbour. The historian, who cannot lightly set aside these considerations of material strength which are the solid foundations of military power and political influence, is now able to form at least a rough estimate of their significance.[9] In short, the pattern of events in the years 1327–37 is now more fully revealed, and the general situation of those soon to be at grips is much better known.

Yet this considerable enlargement of knowledge, contrary to what has happened in so many other cases, has not wrought any striking change in the answer given by historians to the question why the conflict started at all. That answer,

---

[5] *English Diplomatic Administration, 1259–1339* (Oxford, 1940).

[6] G. Mollat, *Les papes d'Avignon* (6th edn, Paris, 1930); H. Jenkins, *Papal Efforts for Peace under Benedict XII, 1334–1342* (Philadelphia, 1932); Y. Renouard, 'Les papes et le conflit franco-anglais en Aquitaine de 1259 à 1337', *Mélanges d'Archéologie et d'Histoire* li (1934).

[7] A case in point is the American symposium, *The English Government at Work, 1327–1336*, vols i–iii, edited by J.F. Willard, W.A. Morris, J.H. Strayer, W.H. Dunham (Medieval Academy of America, 1940–50).

[8] H. Laurent, *Un grand commerce d'exportation européen au Moyen Age; La Draperie des Pays-Bas en France et dans les pays méditerranéens* (Paris, 1935); J. de Sturler, *Les relations politiques et les échanges commerciaux entre le duché de Brabant et l'Angleterre au Moyen Age* (Paris, 1936); E.E. Power, *The Wool Trade in English Medieval History* (Oxford, 1941); G. Unwin (ed.), *Finance and Trade under Edward III* (Manchester, 1918). See also R. Boutrouche, *La Crise d'une société. Seigneurs et paysans du Bordelais pendant la Guerre de Cent Ans* (Paris, 1947).

[9] There is a brief but masterly sketch of these matters in E. Perroy, *La Guerre de Cent Ans* (Paris, 1945), pp. 12–56.

put shortly and rather crudely, is this. The French possessions of the English kings were the real root of the trouble. Ever since the agreement of 1259, constant disputes about these lands had poisoned the relations between the English kings and their French overlords. Edward III decided to have done with the interminable skirmishing and haggling over these matters in which his predecessors had involved themselves. Where argument had failed, force was now to be tried.[10]

This view of the matter has been slowly and not very systematically built up over the last two hundred years or so. Its elements have been there all the time, but, as knowledge of the problem has increased, they have been more carefully dovetailed together, and their setting has been made more elaborate. The notion was formulated by Hume, albeit somewhat roughly, for he did not look much beyond the immediate circumstances of Edward III's own time. Indeed, he was more concerned to lament the effects of the war than to search out its causes.[11] Nevertheless he did recognize that the dispute over Gascony, which 'lay so much exposed to the power of Philip', acerbated by French interference in the Scottish war, was at the root of the matter, and disposed Edward to press his claim to the French throne, something he would otherwise never have bothered to do.[12] Hallam was of much the same opinion. Here is what he says on the point:

> Probably Edward III would not have entered the war merely on account of his claim to the French crown. He had disputes with Philip about Guienne, and that prince had, rather unjustifiably, abetted Bruce in Scotland.[13]

Longman, following Sismondi, gave this same idea a further twist:

> The resolve of Philip to wrest Aquitaine from the rule of the king of England, and Edward's determination to keep it were, seemingly, the main and true cause of the War.

Then, probing a little more deeply, he goes on:

> Philip wished to destroy feudalism; and to reduce Aquitaine to the same state of dependence on the throne of France as that to which he had reduced all the other great fiefs held of the French crown, and thus to consolidate France into one homogeneous kingdom. His object was a wise one; but, it was not to be

---

[10] Like most folk who have wrestled with this subject, I have found myself in a difficulty over the use of the terms Gascony, Guienne and Aquitaine. Although the purist may shudder, these terms are in fact, almost of necessity, used very loosely. There is a comfortable if not very scholarly precedent in the practice of the Chancery. There the clerks often used these terms interchangeably to denote the English lands in south-western France, and that is what I have done.

[11] 'From this period we may date the commencement of that great animosity which the English nation has ever since borne to the French, which has so visible an influence on all future transactions, and which has been, and continues to be, the spring of many rash and precipitate resolutions among them', *History of England* (1841 edn), ii, 143.

[12] *Ibid.*, ii, 140–1.

[13] *Middle Ages* (edn 1868), i, 53.

expected that Edward would quietly submit to occupy the comparatively degraded position destined by Philip for him.[14]

Stubbs tackled the problem rather differently, for he was concerned to divide the guilt of starting the war rather than to explain why it began. Moreover, since he had previously condemned the retention of Gascony by Edward I as inconsistent with the national interests of the English kingdom, he was not likely to summon up much sympathy for Edward III's difficulties in France. Nevertheless his verdict was not substantially different from that of his predecessors. Edward's claim to the French crown was frivolous. On the other hand

> the breach of the peace came from Philip who, not content with protracting a series of irritating and unmeaning negotiations about old quarrels, had conceived the notion of using the Scots as a thorn in the side of England and of winning Gascony by battles fought on British ground . . . Philip thus made the war inevitable; Edward by assuming the title of king of France made the quarrel irreconcilable.[15]

Scholars who have re-examined the whole matter during the present century have found no reason to challenge the older view that the English possessions in Aquitaine were at the bottom of all the trouble. They have, however, done a great deal to search out the ramifications of this fact, and to mount it on a better understanding of what had gone before. In particular they have contrived to show that the problem was of such a kind that there was little hope of solving it by peaceful means. It was not merely that the English kings were required to behave towards their French suzerains in a manner ill suited to the power and dignity they enjoyed elsewhere. No successor of Philip Augustus could number the English king among his vassals with anything but anxiety and foreboding. Memories of Angevin greatness were deep rooted and tenacious. Small wonder, then, that ever since the treaty of 1259 constant friction, flaring at times into open strife, had marked the dealings of those who ruled in England and France with each other.

The successors of St. Louis, moved by fear as well as by hope of gain, matched interminable negotiations with efforts to vex and harry their English vassals whenever they had the chance. Thus they thrust a meddlesome finger into the affairs of Scotland, but their most rewarding opportunity for trouble-making came in Aquitaine itself. There they regularly used legal process as a handy instrument to prise away small bits of the English lordship, and also to loosen the joints which held the rest together. Then, from time to time, they would insert the crowbar of military force. Hitherto its action had always been stayed at the moment when the weakened structure was threatening to topple over in ruins, but obviously the end could not be long delayed.

Henry III, his son, and his grandson found themselves in a position of extraordinary difficulty. They might have cut their losses and abandoned their

[14] *The Life and Times of Edward III* (London, 1869), i, 94.
[15] *Constitutional History of England* (1896 edn), ii, 396–7.

French lands altogether, but there is no evidence that such a step was ever contemplated, except when rumours that this might happen were circulating in Bordeaux just before Edward II was deposed.[16] Instead they chose to stand firm for their rights, and their problem was how to do it. A strong ruler, like Edward I, tried to tighten his grip in Aquitaine by overhauling his government there. He also deliberately stirred up trouble for the French elsewhere, particularly in the Low Countries, in order to relieve the pressure in Aquitaine. But his efforts met with only moderate success, for his French opponents were astute men not easily fooled. Edward II fumbled with Gascon affairs as he did with so much else, and his faltering led inexorably to a further weakening of the English situation there. It was thus a very dilapidated and troubled inheritance which came to Edward III.

Modern scholars have looked more closely into the immediate circumstances in which the war began than their predecessors were able to do. Déprez concluded that, from the outset, Edward III was intuitively aware that the problem of Gascony could not be solved except by force. He also thought that the fumbling, tortuous policies of Philip VI gave Edward every encouragement to violent action, while papal diplomacy, though well intentioned, failed to keep the peace because it never probed the real causes of the trouble.[17] Vickers held that war was inevitable between Philip and Edward because 'feudal ideas could not solve a problem of such complicated relationships as existed between the two sovereigns.' All the same, he thought that Edward did his best to postpone the struggle so that he might promote his Scottish plans without hindrance, and that her persevered in this intention until the autumn of 1336, when Philip's meddling had shown it was no longer possible.[18] Professor Perroy, who has made the most recent examination of what he rightly calls this thorny problem, thinks rather differently. He is concerned to emphasize the slow and haphazard way in which the situation that generated the war was shaped. He does not think that the struggle was carefully premeditated by Edward III or anybody else. To begin with, the pressing of Edward's claim to the French throne in 1328, a chance too good for the English to miss, superimposed a dynastic conflict upon the festering problem of Gascony. That action provoked an immediate and unhesitating response from Philip and his advisers. They put relentless pressure on the English king in the matter of his French fief, pressure that was harder than it would have been in ordinary circumstances, pressure which Edward was in no position to resist. He was compelled to do homage, and, by 1331, he was to all appearances as tightly enmeshed in that same web of troubles with his French overlord as ever his father and grandfather had been. There was then no threat of a great armed conflict, nor did those most concerned appear to have considered it a likely possibility.

[16] E.C. Lodge, *Gascony under English Rule* (London, 1926), pp. 73–4.
[17] *Les Préliminaires de la Guerre de Cent Ans*, pp. 400–6.
[18] *England in the Later Middle Ages* (London, 1913), pp. 156–8.

Yet, Perroy argues, in the course of the next few years the whole prospect was completely altered for the worse. Nor is he content to lay most of the blame for this, as Déprez and other modern writers have done, on Philip VI. He holds that Philip was anxious to do his duty as he understood it, but that he was constantly tempted to imprudent action by a lack of political common-sense. Thus he did not deliberately arouse the implacable hostility of Edward III. His fault lay elsewhere. It lay in his failure to realize that the things he did could have no other result. Philip's scrupulousness in refusing to abandon the Scots wrecked the agreement with Edward over Gascony, which was on the verge of being concluded in 1334. Acts of this sort gave rise to fear and resentment on the other side of the Channel, which Philip's conduct over the projected crusade and in the later stages of the Scottish war did nothing to allay. As for Edward, he required little persuading to believe that he was the chosen victim of deliberate French provocations, which thwarted his policies at every turn, threatened to destroy his Gascon inheritance, and were nourished by every concession he made. So by the autumn of 1336 he seems to have come to the conclusion that force was the only remedy for this intolerable state of affairs. When the struggle did begin in earnest, Edward and the others were soon caught in its tentacles, from which they never contrived to escape, and which squeezed their original purposes into a variety of strange new shapes.[19]

From all this it is clear that the salient facts of the matter have been established with reasonable certainty, and their causal relationships carefully and exhaustively tested. In particular, it is generally recognized that Edward III bestrides the scene, for he made the war, even if others helped to provoke it. He stands a portentous figure, who not only gathered up in his own person the suspicions and resentments of many years, but who, feeling himself thwarted by Philip VI, deliberately reached for the sword. By no means all historians have shared Hume's opinion that Edward was a genius, or agreed with Hallam about what he called the splendour of Edward's personal character.[20] Some have thought with Stubbs, who described him as ambitious, selfish, unscrupulous, extravagant and ostentatious, and added that, had be been without foreign ambitions, he might well have risen to the dignity of a tyrant or sunk to the level of a voluptuary.[21] Others, like Professor Perroy, feel that Edward's powers were only slowly unfolding and his intentions were only gradually hardening in the years before the war began. But at least they are all agreed on one thing; namely, that by the end of 1336 Edward had become convinced that war with Philip was inevitable. He had realized that the hand that was choking his ancestral power in Aquitaine and disarranging his Scottish plans could never be persuaded to relax its grip by any other means.

There are, however, two further considerations which have a direct bearing on

---

[19] Perroy, *op. cit.*, pp. 57–86.
[20] D. Hume, *History of England*, ii, 219; Hallam, *Middle Ages*, i, 51.
[21] Stubbs, *Constitutional History*, ii, 393.

Edward's part in shaping the circumstances in which the war began, and which have not hitherto received perhaps quite the attention they deserve. The first is a general point. It concerns the nature of politics in that age, and the importance which should be ascribed to it in this particular connection. The second is more specific. Edward III inherited a considerable body of painfully acquired experience of how to deal with the French kings. Did he make us of it, and, if he did, did he learn from it? A casual glance would suggest that these matters have little connection the one with the other. But in fact they were linked, and, together, they were not without influence on the course of events.

When probing these things, it is worth remembering how speculative many of our judgments of Edward's purposes must, in the nature of the case, remain. It is true that, in the years before the war began, the king often went out of his way to explain to those most interested what he intended to do and why he intended to do it. He had a very shrewd eye for the value of what we should now call Public Relations, and he, or at any rate those who served him, were thoroughly skilled in the gentle art of retrospective justification. But such pronouncements, as cynics have frequently observed, were not always meant to be as informative as they seem to be. Nor, in Edward's case, did his actions always tally with public declarations.[22] Thus historians have usually and wisely preferred to judge what Edward intended from what he regularly did rather than from what he occasionally said. Yet this is no easy task, for however skilfully it is performed a residue of doubts and uncertainties is left behind. For this reason it is useful to look more closely than has customarily been done at the nature of politics in that age with the particular purpose of discovering something about the conventions which governed the outlook on affairs possessed by those in authority. It may be difficult to establish the precise motives of a man like Edward III, and his personality may, to a large extent, be hidden from us, but if we can grasp the system of assumptions, the framework of accepted notions, within which his political thinking was conducted, that will be of some help at least in understanding more exactly what he was really about.

That the politics of the age had a distinctive character is clear from what happened in Aquitaine and Scotland, in the Low Counties, in Italy and the Empire. However, Aquitaine will serve as a convenient example, since events there had an immediate bearing upon the beginnings of the Hundred Years War itself. The point at issue in Aquitaine was clearly something more than a territorial dispute

---

[22] Before 1337 Edward III wrote on many occasions to individuals and to groups explaining and justifying both what he had done and what he intended to do. The recipients of these confidences included the pope, the king of France, the people of London, his vassals and his officers in Gascony, and the English bishops and clergy. A representative selection of these documents can be found in T. Rymer, *Foedera* (edn 1707), iv, 449, 529, 540, 553, 557, 568, 650, 658, 705, 742. An example of the economical use made of the truth on these occasions is to be seen in the letters written between August 1332 and May 1333, when Balliol's invasion of Scotland was in progress. At first Edward III strove to represent himself as a disinterested and somewhat shocked spectator, and then to justify his intervention on the ground that the Scots had first attacked him (*ibid.*, iv, 529, 540, 553, 557).

of the kind which has become familiar in European politics during the last few centuries. The modern student can, if he chooses, say that what was at stake was whether these Gascon lands were to be included in the kingdom of France, or whether they were to remain under the rule of the English king. Yet it is very likely that such a statement of the case would have seemed almost meaningless to those who were actually busied in the dispute. They certainly thought of the matter in very different terms. They would have said it was a quarrel about the adjustment of some peculiarly tangled jurisdictional and tenurial relationships in which the rights of both parties were deeply embedded. To explain why it proved so difficult to find an acceptable solution they might well have pointed to two other facts. First, two kings were involved in the delicate relationship of lord and vassal, a consideration which did not make the handling of the problem any easier. Second, the dispute had already been smouldering for the best part of seventy years when Edward III appeared on the scene, while bad faith and suspicion on both sides had inflamed the controversy to an alarming extent. At the same time, the contemporaries of Edward III and Philip VI did not find it strange that they should wrangle over things of this kind. Indeed, such disputes were the very stuff of politics as they knew them; of politics among princes, and of politics between princes and their subjects. Rights of this order, rights which conferred status and jurisdiction, were the sinews of power in that age, because they were the only effective means by which authority and profit could be acquired. As such they were coveted and schemed for unceasingly. They could be bought, sold and gained by marriage. They might involve no more than the temporary custody of a tiny estate, with the perquisites and pickings to be had from it, but they could also bestow the hereditary possession of that great bundle of privileges annexed to the dignity of count, duke, king or emperor. Often such rights were ill defined. Then the powerful could seize upon them and, while pretending to reassert them in what was alleged to have been their original form, could pull and twist them in ways they themselves desired.

In a sense these rights can be described as feudal, but such a description needs to be carefully hedged about with explanation. They had, it is true, been shaped, often in minute detail, by the strict feudal practice of earlier centuries. In many cases the legal forms in which they were originally cast had been toughened by the passage of time and by regular use. Nevertheless, by the beginning of the fourteenth century, although their form remained unyielding, the spirit in which these rights were used, and the circumstances in which they had to operate, were both vastly different from what they had been in the twelfth century. In particular, the eroding action of political, social and economic change had stripped away those characteristically feudal notions of personal loyalty and dependence. Now, therefore, such rights had become in fact what they had always threatened to become; nothing more than elaborate property rights regulated by feudal conventions. The politics of the age which saw the beginnings of the Hundred Years War were almost wholly concerned with the manipulation of the more important of these kinds of rights. In itself, this is a fact which has a direct bearing upon our understanding of the acts and policies of Edward III, but lying behind it is something else not less significant. The kings of this period were in no real sense sovereign princes in the modern meaning of the term. Of course a high doctrine of monarchy had already been impressively proclaimed by some of the great lawyers of the thirteenth century. Bracton had written of the king as one without peer in his own realm, as the vicar of God, subject to no man but only to God and the Law. Beaumanoir held the same opinions, and expressed them in even more practical terms, while the Castilian jurists were no less emphatic.[23] Moreover, the king's person had long been invested with peculiar sanctity; a notion which owed much to Christian teaching, but which was also deeply rooted in ancient Teutonic custom.

Yet it is possible to attach undue importance to these things by themselves in studying the age in which the Hundred Years War began. It was not simply that then the theory of sovereignty marched ahead of the practice of sovereignty. The actual situation was more subtle and complicated than that. The kings of the period were quite well aware of the dignity and uniqueness of their regality, but they were content that it should be manifest in familiar and accustomed ways. They could and did subscribe to what Bracton and Beaumanoir had taught, but as yet this had not led them to grasp after new and strange forms of authority. This point is aptly illustrated by the practice of the French kings in the making and receiving of homage. When it was owed to them they sought to exact it in full, since it constituted their title to exercise rights over those who rendered it. This is plain time and again in their dealings with the English kings over Aquitaine after 1259, and not least in the pertinacious efforts of Philip VI between 1328 and 1331 to compel Edward III to render liege homage without equivocation. When the French kings themselves owed homage, as they some-times did, the situation was significantly different. They desired to exercise the rights to which the act of homage admitted them, but they felt it was inconsistent with their kingship to be another's vassal. As early as 1185 Philip Augustus had declared that, as king, he was neither able nor willing to do homage to anyone. His successors in the thirteenth century felt the same, and they gradually elaborated the convention that homage owed by the king should be rendered through a substitute, a practice which was formally recognised in an ordinance of March 1303.[24] The English kings never quite brought themselves to this point, although they often boggled at the homage they were required to render for Gascony, trying every dodge they knew to diminish its significance and whittle away its implications.[25] The truth is that at this time kingship was first and foremost a matter of exercising the rights belonging to a particular kind of

---

[23] R.W. and A.J. Carlyle, *A History of Medieval Political Theory in the West*, v, 359–64.
[24] L. Halphen, 'La place de la royauté dans le système féodal', *Revue Historique* clxxii, 249–56.
[25] Henry II, Edward I and Edward II tried the experiment of transferring their Gascon rights and obligations to their eldest sons. It is probable that in the circumstances of the time this kind of solution was the one best calculated to secure general acceptance. However, it was not persisted with. Perroy, *op. cit.*, pp. 47–8.

dignity. These rights were similar in character to those enjoyed by a host of other lords, lay and ecclesiastical, but different from them in that the king's rights were usually more extensive and more secure. Successful kings, men like Philip the Fair and Edward I, were those who exercised their rights to the full and even contrived to enlarge them, usually by setting stricter limits to the rights exercised by other people. With these things in mind it has been said that the kings of the late thirteenth and early fourteenth centuries still retained much of the mentality of the great feudal magnate. Conversely it has been argued that in the minds of folk like Philip VI and Edward III the modern idea of sovereignty rubbed uneasily against the feudal notion of proprietary right. Yet all this in some measure distorts the situation of that age. These men did no more, and no less, than share an attitude of mind, an outlook on affairs, which was then common to all who wielded authority in church and state. It was an attitude which did not distinguish between the modern idea of sovereignty and the feudal notion of proprietary right because the need for that distinction was not yet generally apparent.

There is solid evidence that Edward III regarded politics in this kind of way. That it was his principal business to assert what he regarded as his undoubted rights against all and sundry was the unquestioned assumption on which he acted. This is manifest in document after document where stereotyped phrases about asserting, recovering and maintaining his rights occur with monotonous regularity.[26] Such was also the constant preoccupation of that procession of ambassadors who hurried to and from the papal court, or busied themselves in those interminable negotiations on the king's behalf in Scotland and France, in the Low Countries and Germany. For it was with this that his diplomacy was habitually concerned.

But it is in Scotland, and particularly in his dealings with Balliol, that Edward III's attitude to politics and his political methods are most clearly to be seen. There he had more freedom of action than in Gascony, and his purposes were less hindered in finding practical expression. A series of grants made by Balliol to Edward between November 1332 and June 1334 aptly illustrate the point.[27] It is true that they were all wrung from Balliol's necessities, but that makes them even more valuable here because they show what Edward did when he had the chance. Taken together, they demonstrate that the purpose of Edward's policies towards Scotland was to grasp after rights which conferred substantial power and profit in that kingdom. But their acquisition was governed by well-established conventions, and these Edward observed with such scrupulous care that it is hard to believe that he regarded them as of only formal significance. Thus the grant of November 1332 opens with an unequivocal statement that Edward was suzerain, *dominus superior*, of Scotland, and Balliol his undoubted vassal. This had to come first because this right underpinned everything else.

---

[26] *Foedera*, iv, 344, 345, 346, 347, 354, 367.
[27] *Ibid.*, iv, 536, 539, 548, 590, 614.

Yet it could not remain a mere assertion, Edward's title to possess it had to be properly displayed. Hence there next follows a carefully phrased justification designed to show three things. First, that this privilege had always belonged to the English kings, and came to Edward III by hereditary right. Second, that it had been effectively exercised by Edward's predecessors, notably by his grandfather, Edward I. Thirdly, that for a time Edward himself, and his father, had been unlawfully deprived of their right by Bruce. Yet even this did not suffice, for the title, properly authenticated though it was, had to be solemnly recognized by Balliol in his Parliament.

Edward's title as suzerain established, Balliol's duties as vassal were then set out, together with the pains and penalties which failure to perform them would involve. He undertook to support Edward's privileges in Scotland, and, significantly, in Gascony. One other concession made by Balliol is even more revealing. To explain what was to be done the charter makes mention of the affection and duty Balliol owed to Edward, and of his very proper desire that his overlord should not be out of pocket on his behalf, for, it was said, Edward had involved himself in great expense and run great risks for the sake of his vassal. Accordingly Balliol handed over to Edward all his rights in the town and county of Berwick unconditionally, and promised even more. That promise was fulfilled in June 1334 at Newcastle-on-Tyne, when Balliol handed over to Edward absolute possession of all his rights, which are carefully listed, in the counties from Linlithgow to the Solway. Edward's intentions here are plain enough. His right as overlord was the essential and valuable thing, to be secured at any cost, but, if opportunity offered, it could and should be made to yield even larger benefits. Properly used, it could be the means by which a proportion of the vassal's most valuable rights were transferred to the permanent and direct use of his overlord.

In the light of all this we may look again at Edward III's problem in Gascony. It has sometimes been said that from the beginning Edward was convinced of his overlord's determination to deprive him of his French lands altogether, and that his policy towards Philip VI was governed by this assumption. Those who hold this view usually point to the persistent efforts of Philip's predecessors to encroach by force and fraud upon the English lands in Gascony. These, it is said, argue a fixed purpose, a deliberate intention, which only waited upon time and opportunity for its complete fulfilment, and all the signs were that this would not be long delayed. It was something which no man as alert as Edward III could possibly overlook. Yet it is not altogether clear either that the evidence will bear this interpretation, or that Edward might reasonably have been expected to draw this conclusion from it.

If we first take into account what has just been said of the character of early fourteenth-century politics, it is obvious that Edward III's problem in Gascony was of a type then very familiar. It also bore a remarkable resemblance to his problem in Scotland immediately after the death of Robert Bruce, with, from Edward's point of view, one very significant difference. In Gascony he himself had to sustain the part Balliol filled in Scotland. The importance of this fact is greatly enlarged when it is also recognized that Edward's political ideas and his political methods were highly conventional. On the face of it, he was much more likely to have regarded Philip VI in Gascony as a domineering overlord, rather than as one bent on naked expropriation. There are a number of other considerations which lend further support to this reading of the situation.

First among them is the behaviour of Philip VI and his immediate predecessors towards their English vassal. The acid test of their real intentions is provided by the extreme, though still conventional, measures they often felt bound to adopt. Before Edward III's time the duchy of Gascony had been confiscated twice, by Philip IV and again by Charles IV. It is perhaps not without significance that on both occasions the actual conduct of operations had been entrusted to Charles of Valois, father of Philip VI. Each time the French kings, had they been so minded, could have held fast to their conquest and made an end of the English dominion without further argument. Instead they made restitution on terms of such a kind as to argue that their real intention coincided with their declared purpose; namely to bring a recalcitrant vassal to his senses, and to what they considered a proper appreciation of his duties. Philip VI, for his part, seems to have viewed the matter in much the same light. He was understandably anxious to press Edward III in the matter of his homage, for the claim to the French crown still rankled, but that difficulty was resolved, although not without the accustomed menaces on both sides, in April 1331. Then Philip accepted Edward's homage as satisfactory, released him from the penalties he had incurred because of the imperfect homage he had previously rendered at Amiens, and took a number of other steps designed to put his relations with his vassal on a better footing. As a mark of his particular esteem he also presented Edward with a choice selection of relics, derived, so it was said, not only from the Holy Innocents, but from St Silvester, St Laurence and St John Baptist as well.[28]

Second, there is that constant bickering over smaller matters; things like the precise boundaries of the English lordship in Aquitaine, the payment of damages in settlement of earlier disputes, and the adjustment of jurisdictional rights as between vassal and suzerain. Too much importance can be attached to these things by themselves, particularly by arguing that their very existence proves the intention of successive French kings to destroy their vassal's power altogether. In part, at any rate, such frictions were the ordinary and accepted accompaniment of the type of relationship which existed between Philip and Edward in Gascony. They were often matters over which the principals themselves had little or no direct control. Edward III found great difficulty in keeping his Gascon officers and vassals in order, and there seems little doubt that Philip's seneschals were more zealous in forwarding their master's interests than he intended them to be.[29] Nor is it so surprising to find that it proved difficult to settle these matters, to quieten this groundswell of Gascon politics. That the will

[28] *Foedera*, iv, 481, 482, 483, 485, 486.
[29] Perroy, *op. cit.*, pp. 43–4; Lodge, *Gascony under English Rule*, p. 74.

to make a settlement was frequently lacking on both sides is plain enough, for often, as Knighton remarked, Philip and Edward were friends only according to the outside of their faces.[30] But there were other reasons too. The machinery for adjusting such differences was cumbersome and inefficient, its procedures were highly technical and of their nature dilatory. What is more, even in the ordinary course of things, these disputes multiplied with surprising rapidity. Finally, common experience showed that it was a grievous temptation to a suzerain to encroach on his vassal's rights when opportunity offered. Edward III did this with brutal directness to the hapless Balliol. He cannot have been altogether surprised to find that his own overlord in Gascony was prone to do likewise, particularly because as vassal there he had shown an undutiful readiness to wriggle out of his obligations.

This raises a third point. It is obvious that Edward III recognized his position in Gascony as somewhat precarious. It is equally clear that he understood the intricacies of his legal relationship with Philip VI there very thoroughly. Mr Cuttino and Professor Rothwell, between them, have made us aware of the great mass of legal opinion about this matter which had been built up since the treaty of 1259 for the use of the English government, and carried forward as a sort of diplomatic stock in trade down to Edward III's own time.[31] Nor, in the years before the war began, did Edward seem to regard the obligations he owed to Philip as of themselves either antiquated or specially degrading. That they were often irksome needs no emphasis, nor does the fact that Edward, as was common among vassals, did his best to make the least of them. Homage could be postponed, and that technically put his duties in suspense, but it might also put his rights in jeopardy. Edward III tried this dodge as his predecessors had done. Like them, he had to come to heel eventually, and his submission, when it came, was even more complete than theirs had been. Again, like a prudent vassal, Edward did not neglect any unusual opportunity of interfering with his suzerain's authority, of putting it even temporarily out of gear, or of hindering its operation. It is not unlikely that this was one of the objects in view when his claim to the French throne was first pressed in 1328. Here there was a useful precedent to hand from his father's time, for Edward II had apparently contemplated similar action in 1317, when Louis X died.[32]

There is, however, one other side of the Gascon problem which calls for special mention here. For purposes of study it is convenient to treat Gascon affairs separately; apart, that is, from the other dealing of the French and English

---

30 Quoted *ibid.*, p. 75.
31 H. Rothwell, 'Edward I's case against Philip the Fair over Gascony in 1298', *English Historical Review* xlii, 572–82; Cuttino, *op. cit.*, pp. 73–83.
32 E. Déprez, 'La Conference d'Avignon (1344)', in *Essays presented to T.F. Tout*, p. 306. At the same time, as Professor Perroy reminds us, Edward was in no sense a foreigner in the French kingdom. He spoke the language, he was the son of a French princess, and himself a peer of the kingdom as duke of Gascony and count of Ponthieu. He was also married to a daughter of William of Hainault, herself the niece of Philip of Valois.

kings. Yet it is worth remembering that those who bore responsibility for these matters were unable to make any such neat division. For them the Gascon problem was only one thread in the highly complicated political web they had to manipulate. It was spun from the interests of the French and English kings in the Low Countries, on the Narrow Seas and, after 1295, in Scotland, as well as from the marvellously intricate relationships they each maintained with the princes of Germany, the pope, the emperor and the rulers of the Netherlands. This pattern of politics, which was already firmly established long before either Philip VI or Edward III appeared, was continually subject to violent strains and tensions, while disturbance to one part of it was almost certain to produce trouble elsewhere. Unless it was firmly handled this in turn was always likely to boil up into a general crisis, which invariably affect Gascony severely. This was precisely what happened between 1333 and 1337. It was no deep-laid scheme on the part of Edward III or anybody else. On this occasion the troubles of Scotland acted as the wind which blew the smouldering French and English discords in Gascony and the Low Countries into flame.

The intricate and often confused diplomacy of these years has already been carefully examined by others,[33] but there are some things about it which need further emphasis here.

There is the fact that it was Philip's meddling in the Scottish business which precipitated the general crisis from which the war emerged. The situation which developed in Scotland after the death of Robert Bruce in 1329 was something no one could have foreseen, but Edward III would not have been the kind of man he was had be not done his best to profit from it. From the end of 1332 all the signs were that he intended to devote himself to forwarding his Scottish interests. Not only was he often personally present there, but the transference of so many of the departments of state to York also argues strongly for this purpose. Equally Philip could not resist the temptation to interfere. By the summer of 1334 his anxieties about the course of events in Scotland were clearly reflected in his actions towards Gascony, for he put an end abruptly to some most promising negotiations designed to settle outstanding differences in the duchy because David Bruce and the Scots were not to be included in the agreement. From then on the crisis widened and deepened as others, like Robert of Artois, took a hand in the business. All the same, it was not until the autumn of 1336 that Edward III and his advisers recognized the full extent of the mischief, when they saw that the confiscation of Gascony was clearly impending. Philip VI had moved slowly with many hesitations and changes of direction, while the shuttle of papal diplomacy had been hurried busily to and fro, spinning a web of compromises, which for a time veiled the real situation from all concerned. Even when an open breach could no longer be avoided, both parties proceeded by well-tried methods. Philip VI ordered the confiscation of the duchy, and Edward III cast

---

[33] Déprez, *Les Préliminaires de la Guerre de Cent Ans*, pp. 83–169; Lucas, *op. cit.*, pp. 167–203.

around for allies who might help by diversionary manoeuvres to relieve the pressure in Aquitaine. The re-assertion of his claim to the French crown seems to have been no more than a tactical move, designed to quieten the consciences of some of his allies and to cause embarrassment to his opponents. Again, when they argued that Gascony was an allodial possession of the English crown, Edward III and his advisers had a precedent to guide them. This doctrine had been strongly pressed by the English envoys on Edward I's behalf when Boniface VIII had arbitrated over Gascony in 1298.[34]

Finally, so far as Edward III is concerned, it looks as if he was considerably influenced by the experience of his predecessors in handling the crisis in his relations with Philip VI. That he might well have been disposed to avail himself of this experience is suggested by the fact that his attitude to politics was closely akin to theirs, and especially to that of his grandfather, Edward I. But there are other and stronger reasons to clinch the point. Mr Cuttino has shown how this experience was carefully gathered up, meticulously sorted and arranged for further use in the office of the Keeper of the Process. Here, in what was really a special secretariat for French affairs, the material of policy lay ready to hand, and there is plenty of evidence to show that constant and intelligent use was made of it by the capable men who served Edward III. Among them was Elias Joneston, whose tenure as Keeper stretched from 1306 to 1336, and who was, in many ways, the living embodiment of the great Edward's experience.[35] Again, the situation with which Edward III had to grapple from 1333 onwards was, in some crucial respects, remarkably like that which had confronted Edward I in the closing years of the thirteenth century. This was simply because the issues of Scotland and Gascony were firmly hooked together once more.[36] Later, when the peak of the crisis was reached, Edward I's experience was again relevant. Under the spur of necessity he had improvised a northern coalition against Philip IV through his connections in Holland and Brabant. Edward III and his helpers also rapidly constructed an alliance against Philip VI, but their work was far more elaborate and widely based, for they could build across the strong links Edward III already had with the Low Countries and the princes of the Rhineland through his father-in-law, William of Hainault.

There is thus something to be said against the accepted view that Edward III deliberately made the war because he desired to have done with ancient bickerings and old methods in his dealings with the French king. The crisis which led to the Hundred Years War was, in itself, only one of those recurring periods of acute tension which had marked Anglo-French relations since the collapse of

34 Rothwell, *op. cit.*
35 Cuttino, *op. cit.*, passim. He also notes that when Philip's intentions towards Scotland were becoming more obvious, Edward III's counsellors instinctively looked back to his grandfather's time, for, as they saw it, he had known how to get himself out of tight corners with some agility (*ibid.*, p. 70).
36 The first French agreement with the Scots dated from 1295, and what the Scots later called 'the auld alliance' had already become a tradition of French policy by the time of Philip VI.

the Angevin dominion under John. It bore a particularly close resemblance to the clash between Edward I and Philip IV at the close of the thirteenth century. In his handling of it Edward III relied heavily on his predecessors' experience and on their well tested methods. The reason why the crisis which came to a head in 1337 had a different outcome from those which had preceded it lies elsewhere. It lies in the fact that Edward III, Philip VI and Benedict XII were not men of the stature of Edward I, Philip IV and Boniface VIII.

3

EDWARD III AND THE KINGDOM OF FRANCE[1]

John Le Patourel

While the causes of the Hundred Years War have given rise to a great deal of discussion, the war aims of the kings of England and France have generally been
taken for granted rather than discussed.[2] It has been too easily assumed that the
deeper causes of the conflict, what ever they were, determined the objectives of
the contestants; and, since it now seems to be agreed that the problems of
Aquitaine in some way lay at the root of the trouble,[3] it is argued that Edward's
aim was no more than the defence of his duchy, if necessary by enlarging it or at
least recovering its ancient limits, and that his claim to the throne of France was
rather a tactical device, never taken really seriously, and easily thrown over for
territorial concessions.[4] In this paper it will be argued, first, that Edward's claim
to the throne of France was meant more seriously and deserves to be taken more
seriously than it has been by historians during the present century, both as to its
merits and as to its place in his war aims; and second, that his chances – and
indeed his achievement – up to the winter of 1359–60 were a great deal better
than they are generally reckoned to have been.

---

[1] This paper represents, not a mature statement of conclusions, but an airing of ideas, substantially as they were presented at a Director's Conference in the Institute of Historical
Research (November 1957). I am indebted to my audience on that occasion for the discussion
that followed, and to Dr Pierre Chaplais who has read and criticized the typescript.
[2] For a convenient discussion of the origins of the war, see G. Templeman, 'Edward III and
the Beginnings of the Hundred Years War', *Transactions of the Royal Historical Society*, 5th
series, ii (1952), pp. 69–88 and above, pp. 231–276; cf. Ph. Wolff, 'Un problème d'origines:
La Guerre de Cent Ans', *Eventail de l'histoire vivante: homage à Lucien Febvre*, ii (1953),
pp. 141–8.
[3] E. Déprez, *Les Préliminaires de la guerre de Cent Ans*, 1902. Cf. E. Perroy, *The Hundred
Years War*, trans. W.B. Wells (1951), p. 69, and the same writer's valuable article 'Franco-
English Relations, 1350–1400', *History* xxi (1936–37), pp. 148–54.
[4] Perroy, *op. cit.*, pp. 69, 116, 129, 139; Templeman, p. 87.

I

In any discussion of the French succession problems of the early thirteenth century, the fundamental consideration is that the situations of 1316 and 1328 were without precedent.[5] A monarchy which had been more elective than hereditary in the tenth century had become unquestionably hereditary in the fourteenth; but it had become so not by enactment or by a series of disputes leading to clear decisions, but by the fact of a continuous succession from father to son, uninterrupted through three centuries. There was therefore no rule to which appeal could be made when, as in 1316, the king's only son was a posthumous infant who died within a few days of his birth or, as in 1328, when the king left no son to succeed him. Every question was wide open. Had the royal succession a rule of its own, or could analogies be adduced from neighbouring kingdoms, from royal appanages in France, from the great fiefs, from manors in the Ile de France?[6] Could females succeed in default of males, or, if they could not succeed in person, could they transmit their rights to their own heirs? All these points were argued over and again; and perhaps all that can be said on the question of absolute right is that no word was breathed in 1328 of a Salic Law and that analogy, for what it might be worth, on the whole told in favour of female rights in the succession. Indeed, as recently as 1314, when the future Philip V had applied to his brother King Louis X for a ruling on the succession to his appanage of Poitou, the king had said, 'Reason and natural law instruct us that in default of male heirs females should inherit and have succession to the goods and possessions of the fathers of whom they are procreated and descended in legal marriage, in the same way as males.'[7]

The issue of 1316 was decided, not by discussion, but by the ambition and ruthlessness of the man who became Philip V; and the opposition he had to face, interested though it may have been, is testimony to the strength of the feeling that women had a place in the succession, just as the many bargains which he struck implicitly recognized their rights. No serious objection seems to have been raised, in 1322, when his brother Charles thrust aside Philip's daughters; but in 1328, the fact that Philip VI allowed Jeanne, daughter of Louis X, to

5   P. Viollet, 'Comment les femmes ont été exclues en France de la succession à la couronne', *Mémoires de l'Institut, Académie des Inscriptions et Belles Lettres* xxxiv (1895), ii, pp. 125–78, for the most part reproduced in the same writer's *Histoire des Institutions politiques et administratives de la France*, ii (1898), pp. 52–86. Cf. Déprez, *Préliminaires*, chs. II, VI; J. Viard, 'Philippe VI de Valois, la succession au trône', *Moyen Age* xxxii (1921), pp. 218–22; J.M. Potter, 'The Development and Significance of the Salic Law of the French', *English Historical Review* lii (1937), pp. 235–53.
6   The general uncertainty is well shown by the judgements given in the king's court on succession problems in the great fiefs during the fourteenth century: see the editor's notes in *The Chronicle of Jean de Venette*, ed. R.A. Newhall (1953), pp. 151–3, 160–1, and authorities there cited.
7   Quoted by Potter, *op. cit.*, p. 237; Viollet, p. 58.

succeed to Navarre, and made generous compensation for Champagne, shows that the possibility of a queen regnant cannot have been entirely ignored.

Now it is certainly true that, in a general sense, 'le fait crée le droit'; but in 1328 there were only two precedents for the exclusion of women, they were recent and they did not entirely meet the case. In view of the general feeling in favour of women's rights to succeed (to property certainly, though not necessarily to the functions of monarchy) there was still room for argument, particularly on Edward's thesis that, even though his mother might not be able to succeed, she could transmit her rights to him and that, through her, he was in fact the nearest male heir to the late King Charles IV. What we know of the discussion in the great assembly which met in Paris during the spring of 1328 shows that there was some substance in this argument. Edward, as duke of Aquitaine and peer of France, was rightly represented there, and well represented it would seem, for, according to one manuscript of the *Grandes Chroniques*, his proctors convinced some of the doctors of civil and canon law of the validity of his argument.[8] If this is so, then Edward already had some support in France.

There is no need to bring in considerations of national feeling, which may or may not have existed at the time, in order to explain the final decision. It is true that the chronicler known as the First Continuator of Nangis states that some French barons said openly that they could not contemplate subjection to English rule with equanimity;[9] but before building too much on that remark, we must remember that it applies to the year 1328, when a decision in favour of Edward would have meant the rule of Isabella and Mortimer in France, a prospect which it might well have been difficult for the French to face with equanimity. Edward, after all, was no alien in France. His ancestry was as 'French' as Philip's; he was duke of Aquitaine, count of Ponthieu and a peer of France; he spoke French; and the case of Navarre provided a good and recent precedent for the rule of two kingdoms by one king. More revealing, perhaps, is the remark preserved in the *Chronographia*,[10] that Philip of Valois was preferred to Philip of Evreux (another possible candidate) because he was of more mature age. Philip of Valois was in fact 35 at the time, and Philip of Evreux 23; but Edward was still only 15 and in no sense his own master. There were thus good and practical reasons for preferring Philip of Valois to Edward, in 1328; and Philip was regent, well thought of and presumably in command of the situation. But while such considerations may explain what actually happened, they do nothing to weaken the merits of Edward's claim.

It was, indeed, opposed not by a rule of law but by a *fait accompli* or, perhaps one should say, by a short series of *faits accomplis* – unless it be argued, in face of the evidence, that the throne of France could be regarded as elective in the fourteenth century. Since, in the abstract, there was much to be said for it, there

---

8 *Grandes Chroniques* (ed. J. Viard), ix (1937), pp. 72–3, note 2. Cf. *Chronique latine de Guillaume de Nangis . . . avec les continuations* (ed. H. Géraud), ii (1843), pp. 82–4.
9 *Ibid.*, p. 83.
10 *Chronographia regum francorum* (ed. H. Moranvillé), i (1891), p. 292.

was no reason why Edward should not believe in his cause; and if the circumstances of the first ten years of his reign in England made it impossible for him to do much more than state his claim at that time[11] (and circumstances, indeed, had forced him to do homage for Aquitaine, an act which was taken to imply, and was intended by the French to imply, a renunciation of his claim to the throne of France, though he was still under age and in no position to resist the demand for homage), it was not unnatural that he should take it up again when circumstances were more favourable. Indeed, if the claim meant anything to him he had no choice, for an inherited right implied a duty. Authority came from God. Edward made this point very clear in his manifestos of 1340:

> Whereas the kingdom of France has fallen to us by most clear right, by divine disposition and through the death of Charles of famous memory, late king of France, . . . and the lord Philip of Valois . . . intruded himself into the said kingdom by violence while we were still of tender years and occupies it in defiance of God and of justice; we, lest we should seem to neglect our right and the gift of celestial grace, or appear unwilling to put our will into conformity with divine pleasure, have put forward our claim to the said kingdom in due form and, trusting in the support of the heavenly kingdom, have undertaken the government of it, *as we ought to do.*[12]

This is too easily dismissed as common form or fine phrases. It rings true. Considerations of this sort tend to establish Edward's good faith in his claim to the throne of France; they do not, by themselves, establish the point that the throne was his real war aim. This, perhaps, can best be argued from his military and political strategy, and from the whole manner in which he fought his war; but first it is necessary to consider the opposing thesis – that the claim and his assumption of the French royal title were simply a manoeuvre and that his real objective was a secure and sovereign Aquitaine.

On the face of it, the war, up to 1360, does not look like a war in defence of Aquitaine. The campaigning started in the north-east of France and then moved to Brittany; only after six years or so was there any military activity of any consequence in the south. Although such a thing is difficult to measure quantitatively, it is perhaps reasonable to say that the greater part of Edward's military activity, until 1369, was in the north; and he himself led no campaign beyond the Loire. If all this activity in the north was a diversion, it was a very big diversion – too big to believe in, for it seems far-fetched to speak of defending Aquitaine on the moors of Brittany or the plain of Flanders.

More specifically, however, it is argued that Edward's real objective could not have been the throne of France because he showed himself ready, on more than

---

[11] But the claim was formally made in 1328, and some attempt to apply military pressure: Déprez, *Préliminaires*, pp. 35–6; *Foedera* (Rec. Comm.), ii, pp. 736–7, 743, 744, 749, 750–1.
[12] *Foedera*, ii, pp. 1108–9; quoted by Avesbury (*De gestis mirabilibus*, ed. E. Maunde Thompson, RS, 1889), pp. 309–10.

one occasion, to abandon his claim in return for territorial concessions – in fact, for a sovereign Aquitaine. This argument needs closer examination. The incidents quoted in support of it are the discussions at Avignon in 1344, the negotiations leading to and developing out of the draft treaty of Guines in 1354, and the ratification of the treaty of Brétigny in 1360.[13]

The discussions at Avignon during the autumn of 1344 are known to us in some detail owing to the survival of letters sent back by the English envoys and a journal written by one of them.[14] From these documents it is clear that they began by stating Edward's claim to the throne of France without qualification, that they returned to it again and again, and that although they could be persuaded to put it aside, as it were, in order to discuss other proposals that might tend towards a peace, they never retreated from their position that their king's demand was for the kingdom of France, as his right. It was the French delegates who insisted that the origins of the war lay in Aquitaine, and that the way to a settlement lay through a discussion of disputes arising in the duchy.

The treaty of Guines was drawn up in the spring of 1354.[15] According to the text printed by Bock, it would have given Aquitaine, the Loire provinces, Ponthieu and Calais to Edward, all in full sovereignty, in return for his renunciation of the throne of France. There is no mention of Brittany where Edward's forces and those of his Breton allies were well established. Final renunciations and ratifications were to be made at Avignon. A meeting duly took place there in the autumn, but no treaty was made. There is no direct evidence to show which side was responsible for this breakdown; most English chroniclers blame the French, but Knighton, whose information may ultimately have come from Henry of Lancaster, the leader of the English delegation, says that Lancaster refused specifically to give up Edward's claim and title to the kingdom of France.[16] Such a stand would have wrecked the treaty at once; and if he was at the same time negotiating with Charles of Navarre for a joint conquest and partition of France,[17] as he seems to have been, it may be that he came to Avignon with no intention of ratifying.[18]

[13] Perroy, *Hundred Years War*, pp. 116, 129, 139.

[14] Froissart, *Chroniques*, ed. Kervyn de Lettenhove, xviii (1874), pp. 202–56; E. Déprez, 'La Conférence d'Avignon (1344)', *Essays in Medieval History presented to Thomas Frederick Tout* (ed. A.G. Little and F.M. Powicke), 1925, pp. 301–320.

[15] G. Mollat, 'Innocent VI et les tentatives de paix entre la France et l'Angleterre (1353–55)', *Revue d'histoire ecclésiastique* x (1909), pp. 729–43; F. Bock, 'Some new Documents illustrating the early years of the Hundred Years War (1353–1356)', *Bulletin of the John Rylands Library* xv (1931), pp. 60–99.

[16] *Chronicon Henrici Knighton* (ed. J.R. Lumby, RS), ii (1895), p. 78. But this part of the chronicle may have been written many years after the event, see V.H. Galbraith, 'The Chronicle of Henry Knighton', *Fritz Saxl, 1890–1948, A Volume of Memorial Essays . . .* (1957), pp. 136–48.

[17] R. Delachenal, 'Premières négociations de Charles le Mauvais avec les Anglais (1354–1355)', *Bibliothèque de l'Ecole des Chartes* lxi (1900), pp. 253–82.

[18] But see the secret instruction printed by Bock, *Bulletin of the John Rylands Library* xv, pp. 94–6.

However, the treaty of Brétigny does seem at first sight to destroy the argument, for here is a treaty in which Edward unquestionably renounced the throne of France in return for territory – an enlarged Aquitaine, Ponthieu, Calais and the county of Guines, all in full sovereignty. But, to divine Edward's intentions, the treaty must be considered in relation to the earlier drafts of 1358 and 1359 and the ratification at Calais in October 1360. The text of the first draft, which Delachenal discovered and which he called the 'First Treaty of London', would have given to Edward all that the treaty of 1360 gave him, together with suzerainty over Brittany.[19] Neither he nor other commentators seem to have noticed, however, that it demanded nothing whatever from Edward in return. The French territorial concessions would have been part of the price to be paid for King John's conditional release; nothing more. The second draft, produced rather more than a year later, in March 1359 ('the Second Treaty of London'),[20] demanded far greater territorial concessions from France, the whole of the old Angevin Empire, together with the counties of Ponthieu, Boulogne and Guines, and the town of Calais, all in full sovereignty and completely detached from the kingdom of France; but this time Edward promised to renounce his claim. However, if the seemingly casual way in which this promise is made is compared with the elaborate securities demanded of the king of France for the performance of his part in the treaty, and if one tries to visualize what France would have been like (shorn of all her western and northern provinces) if the treaty had been carried into effect, it is difficult to believe that it represents a sincere proposal for peace on Edward's part or, if it does, then his price for a promise to renounce the claim – a promise unsupported by any security – was the kingdom virtually delivered into his hands. This is how it must have seemed to the French Estates when, with superb courage, they rejected the treaty as 'ni passable ni faisable'.

If, a year later, Edward was prepared to give up his claim and his title for considerably less territory,[21] this was due to the overwhelming defeat he had suffered in the winter of 1359–60. The great campaign which was to have brought him to a coronation in Reims Cathedral petered out in the suburbs of Paris. Even so, the renunciation that he undertook to make was never actually made. French historians have seen in the detachment of the renunciation clauses from the ratification of the treaty at Calais, and their embodiment in a separate document to be put into force at a later date, a great victory for French diplomacy.[22] It may have been so. But the evidence which Dr Chaplais has now put together suggests

---

[19] R. Delachenal, *Histoire de Charles V,* ii (1927), pp. 59–77, 402–11.

[20] Text in E. Cosneau, *Les grands traités de la Guerre de Cent Ans* (1889), pp. 1–32. Cf. Delachenal, *op. cit.*, pp. 77–88.

[21] Texts of the treaties of Brétigny and Calais with subsidiary documents are printed in *Foedera* iii, pp. 485–547. They are most conveniently studied in Cosneau, *op. cit.*, pp. 33–68, 173–4.

[22] Petit-Dutaillis and Collier, 'La diplomatie française et le traité de Brétigni', *Moyen Age* x (1897), pp. 1–35; E. Perroy, 'Charles V et le traité de Brétigni', *ibid.* xxxviii (1928), pp. 255–81.

that it was Edward, not King John of France, who defaulted on the renuncia-tions;[23] and if that is so, we may ask whether, having brought his army safely home in the summer, he no longer felt that the military situation was quite so desperate in October 1360 as it had appeared to those negotiating on his behalf in May. Had he given away more than he had any need to do?

It is difficult to be sure that Edward would never have renounced the title, short of military necessity, for a 'good peace'; but in fact no peace ever was good enough. Though he gave up the use of the French title for nine years, he never actually renounced the claim. The burden of proof still lies with those who maintain that Edward's aim was anything less than the throne of France.

II

Edward III was no fool. If he had really made the throne of France his war-aim, he must have felt that he had some chance of success. It is possible that recent historians have played down the dynastic issue, which a French writer has dis-missed as 'preposterous',[24] because it seemed to them that Edward had no chance whatever of making himself effectively king of France, and therefore his real aim must have been something different. Now that the evidence can be seen to support the seriousness of Edward's claim, his chances must be re-examined.

In part, clearly, this is a matter of military organization. A good deal is now known about the organization of the English armies at this time,[25] but it is still difficult to compare it in detail with the French.[26] In part, similarly, it is a matter of personalities. England was favoured in the 'forties and the 'fifties with a rare constellation of military leaders, from the king himself, the Black Prince, and great nobles like Lancaster and Northampton, to men of much humbler origin such as Thomas Dagworth, Walter Mauny and Walter Bentley. No one can say, as yet, whether the presence of so much ability was a lucky chance, or whether there was something in the system that enabled the talent available to he used to the best advantage; and it would be good to know, more specifically than we do at present, how military and political policy was worked out and who was responsible. These questions become all the more interesting when it begins to appear that Edward's campaigns were not simply a matter of sending an army to France to look for a battle. There appears to be a pattern in these campaigns –

---

23 P. Chaplais, 'Some Documents regarding the Fulfilment and Interpretation of the Treaty of Brétigny, 1361–1369', *Camden Miscellany* xix (1952), p. 7.
24 Perroy, 'Franco-English Relations, 1350–1400', *History* xxi (1936–7), p. 154.
25 A.E. Prince, 'The Army and the Navy', in *The English Government at Work, 1327–1337*, ed. J.F. Willard and W.A. Morris, i (1940), pp. 332–76, and works cited there; N.B. Lewis, 'The Organisation of Indentured Retinues in Fourteenth-Century England', *Transactions of the Royal Historical Society*, 4th series xxvii (1945), pp. 29–39 etc.
26 Cf. F. Lot and R. Fawtier, *Histoire des Institutions françaises au Moyen Age*, ii, *Institutions royales* (1958), pp. 511–35.

perhaps it would be too much to call it a 'higher strategy' – a pattern that was closely related to political conditions.

The starting-point in this discussion must be Edward's assumption of the title 'King of France' at Ghent, on 26 January 1340. This was no impulsive and ill-considered act. The idea that Edward should assume the title is known to have been suggested by a deputation from Bruges as far back as 1328.[27] He actually used it in letters patent dated 7 October 1337;[28] and although its use on this occasion seems to have been for one particular purpose only,[29] it implies an intention to assume the title definitively at some suitable moment. The assumption of the French title had been under discussion between Edward and his allies for some months at least before January 1340,[30] and the decision must have been taken well before the date of the ceremony, for the new seal was used on that day.[31] Was it merely a coincidence that the ceremony took place so near to the anniversary of Edward's accession to the throne of England that his regnal years could be dated from the same day in both countries?[32] Moreover, as Jean le Bel pointed out,[33] Edward must have expected a great deal from this act if he was prepared to face the ridicule that would fall upon a ruler who called himself king of a country that he did not possess. It is quite possible that Edward's need for an alliance with Flanders provided the occasion; but the assumption of the French title could solve so many problems[34] that it is hard to believe that no considerations other than those directly affecting the Flemings were taken into account.

That much wider possibilities were in fact taken into consideration is shown by Edward's letters of reassurance to the people of Gascony[35] and the people of England,[36] and still more by the manifesto which he addressed to the people of France.[37] This last is a most important document which has not received the attention it deserves. It begins by stating the basis of Edward's claim and accuses Philip VI of usurping the kingdom of France while Edward was under age 'against God and against justice'. After long and mature deliberation, Edward had undertaken the government of the kingdom and had assumed the

---

[27] H. Pirenne, *Histoire de Belgique*, ii (4th edn, 1947), pp. 94–5.

[28] *Foedera* ii, pp. 1000, 1001.

[29] Letters were issued on the same day without the French title (PRO, Treaty Roll ii, m. 2).

[30] H.S. Lucas, *The Low Countries and the Hundred Years War, 1326–1347*, pp. 358 ff.

[31] *Foedera* ii, p. 1107; letter dated 'apud Gandavum, xxvi die Januarii, anno regni nostri Franciae primo, Angliae vero quartodecimo'. This formula would not have been compatible with the old seal.

[32] A matter of considerable convenience: compare the complexities in the regnal years of Philip and Mary.

[33] *Chronique de Jean le Bel* (ed. J. Viard and E. Déprez), i (1904), pp. 167–8.

[34] Cf. the letter of summons addressed to the archbishop of Canterbury, 21 February 1340 (*Foedera* ii, p. 1115): 'Non mirantes ex hoc quod stilum nostrum consueteum mutavimus & Regem Franciae nos facimus nominari; nam diversae subsunt causae, per quas hoc facere necessario nos oportet.'

[35] *Foedera* ii, p. 1127.

[36] Froissart, ed. Kervyn de Lettenhove, xviii, pp. 129–30.

[37] *Foedera* ii, pp. 1108–9, 1111.

title, as he was in duty bound to do. It was not his intention to deprive the people of France of their rights; on the contrary, he was resolved to do justice to all 'and to re-establish the good laws and customs that were in force in the time of his progenitor St Louis'. Nor was it his intention to seek his own gain at their expense, by variations in the currency or by unlawful exactions and maltolts because, he thanked God, he had enough to support his estate and his honour; indeed, he hoped to ease their burdens and to maintain the liberties and privileges of everyone, especially those of Holy Church. In all matters affecting the kingdom of France he would seek the counsel of peers, prelates, nobles and other *sapientes* who were faithful to him; and he would never act capriciously or arbitrarily. All men of the kingdom of France who should recognize him as their lord and king before Easter following (as the people of Flanders had already rightly done) would be received into his especial peace and protection and would continue to enjoy their property undisturbed. The manifesto was ordered to be affixed to church doors so that all might take notice.

No doubt historians have taken little notice of this document because it seems, at first sight, so commonplace, the sort of appeal that any invader might put out. But in fact it is very carefully drafted. Whoever composed it knew a great deal about the history of France during the previous fifty years or so, for point by point it meets the grievances of the politically effective (or at any rate politically articulate) French against their government, as these were expressed, for example, in the provincial charters of 1314–15 – taxation which was held to exceed the bounds of legality and which was regarded as an attack upon the rights, property and privileges of churches, nobility and townsmen: debasement of the currency: arbitrary acts of kings and their officials.[38] Edward does not merely denounce these evils; he offers himself as a 'constitutional' king, prepared to act always with the counsel of magnates and learned men; above all he undertakes (this is a direct echo of nearly all the provincial charters) to return to the customs 'of the time of the good St Louis', that is, to the time when, as it was generally thought, these objectionable practices were as yet not prevalent.

What this really amounted to is that Edward might represent what we should call 'an alternative government', with a readily comprehensible political programme which was all the more telling because, though there had been opposition to royal centralization in France since the beginning of the century, it had so far failed to find effective political expression. Henceforward, however, any Frenchman who might find it convenient or profitable to change his allegiance, or who might be driven to it; anyone who might come to feel, as the result of defeats or disasters, that the Valois succession had not been blessed by God; all who were alienated by those arbitrary acts of cruelty and violence to which the early Valois kings were occasionally prone (such as the execution of the Breton seigneurs in 1343, of the count of Eu and Guines in 1350 and of the friends of

[38] On the provincial charters, see A. Artonne, *Le mouvement de 1314 et les chartes provinciales de 1315* (1912).

Charles of Navarre in 1356) – all such could look for protection and comfort to one who was already acknowledged as the rightful king of France in Flanders (and presumably in Aquitaine) and who had solemnly taken the title and assumed the responsibility of government; and they were provided with a legal pretext for so doing.

That there must have been some such calculation in the minds of Edward and his advisers, however vaguely, is shown by what followed. The leagues of 1314–15, and the provincial charters they produced, were the work of the nobility of the second order, not the dukes of Brittany or Burgundy or their peers, but nobility of provincial importance. This was shown clearly in Artois where the leaguers were as much concerned with the oppressions of the officers of the Countess as with the aggressions of the king's officers; and the really significant thing about these leagues is the most immediately obvious. In contrast to baronial movements in England during the thirteenth and fourteenth centuries, they were organized on a provincial basis and their aim was a charter of provincial liberties. This by itself shows that national consciousness, if indeed it existed in early fourteenth-century France, was still a very tender plant; and Edward, if he were prepared to conduct the conquest of France province by province, while not neglecting more traditional methods altogether, was provided with a fine opportunity which, as duke of Aquitaine, he should know how to exploit. His action in Normandy, during the years 1356–60, offers a very good example.

The duchy, though incorporated into the royal domain after 1204, had preserved much of its individuality.[39] Its administration, staffed though it was by royal officers from Paris, remained distinct; nobles and prelates still attended the exchequer of pleas which, though no longer sovereign, continued to administer the custom of Normandy. This distinct legal system, so often described simply as 'the laws and customs of the country' – in practice, the liberties and privileges of individual churches, barons and communities quite as much as details of legal precepts and procedure – gave to the Normans the basis of their 'provincial consciousness'. To the Norman seigneurs and churchmen, the vast development in the activity of royal government during the thirteenth century appeared as a threat to their 'laws and customs', otherwise their properties and liberties. They objected to the practice of encouraging appeals from the exchequer to the parliament, because that endangered the custom; they objected to the methods and indeed to the fact of royal taxation as an assault upon their liberties and property; they objected to the activities of the royal *baillis* who strove continually to exalt royal jurisdiction against private rights of justice. They stood out for traditional feudal decentralization against royal centralization.

These grievances were given an opportunity to express themselves, and thereby to grow and be organized, in the assemblies which the king summoned

---

[39] A. Coville, *Les États de Normandie* (1894); J.R. Strayer, *The Adminstration of Normandy under St Louis* (1932). R. Besnier, *La Coutume de Normandie, Historie externe* (1935), pp. 70 ff.

from time to time to consent to his demands for taxation, particularly since such meetings were often called as assemblies of the duchy. One result was the 'Charte aux Normands' of 1315 which because of its background was a more effective document than any of the other provincial charters of the time. Among other things it restored its sovereignty to the Norman exchequer, thus safeguarding and, as it were, sealing the custom; and it offered some protection against taxation without consent, making it more difficult for the king to raise taxes in Normandy without calling a provincial assembly. The important implication of these concessions is that they made Normandy a distinct, privileged and quasi-political entity. But this did not end the Norman grievances, for the movement of 1314–15, as a whole, hardly affected the development of royal policy; though now, and for some time, the Normans were able to make consent to taxation conditional upon a confirmation of their privileges, and on one occasion the king had to associate himself with an extraordinary scheme for a new 'Norman Conquest of England' to divert their indignation away from himself.[40]

Edward's opportunity to turn all this to his own account came in 1356, when King John surprised a dinner-party that was being held by his son, the duke of Normandy, in Rouen Castle, took Charles of Navarre prisoner and executed four of his associates out of hand.[41] One of these was John, count of Harcourt, who, with his uncle Godfrey of Harcourt and Charles of Navarre himself, was among the leaders of the Norman opposition. Now although there may well have been an element of personal feud in this incident, there can be little doubt that the Norman grievances were at the bottom of it. Already, in 1354, Charles of Navarre had assured Edward that the Norman nobility was behind him to a man;[42] and now Philip of Navarre, Charles's brother, having failed to obtain satisfaction from King John, sent in his *défi* and opened negotiations with Edward. Godfrey of Harcourt did likewise; and both did homage to him as 'King of France and duke of Normandy',[43] for that was the condition which Edward imposed before he would give them assistance. It is easy to see that the simple title 'King of France' would not raise much enthusiasm in Normandy, for the Norman quarrel was with the king of France, his violence and his centralizing policy; but Edward could offer himself to the Normans as their duke, pledged to act in all things 'selon les lois, coutumes et usages du pays'. In the Cotentin, where the barony of St Sauveur-le-Vicomte was bequeathed to him by Godfrey of Harcourt, he was able to put this principle into practice by appointing officers to the traditional posts of local government with such authority as pertained to their offices 'according to the custom of our duchy of Normandy'.[44]

[40] Coville, *op. cit.*, pp. 47–50. A copy of the agreement was found, presumably in the archives of the town, during the sack of Caen in 1346. It was sent back to England and read at Paul's Cross – a superb gift to Edward's war propaganda (Avesbury, *De gestis mirabilibus*, pp. 363–7; cf. Murimuth, *Continuatio Chronicarum, ibid.*, pp. 205–12, 257–63).

[41] On this incident, see Delachenal, *Histoire de Charles V*, i, pp. 134–56.

[42] Froissart, ed. Kervyn de Lettenhove, xviii, pp. 354–6.

[43] *Foedera* iii, pp. 332, 340.

[44] L. Delisle, *Historie du château et des sires de Saint-Sauveur-le-Vicomte* (1867). Le

It is difficult to measure the degree of support that was given to Edward's cause in Normandy; but after Lancaster's brilliant campaign in the summer of 1356, the co-operation of his forces with those of Philip of Navarre brought English troops to the gates of Paris and even into the city, and established a number of English garrisons in Norman strongholds. Politically, Edward's action gave him recognition as king of France by a group of Norman seigneurs and their followers, which, whether large or small, was important simply because it existed. Edward had a foothold, perhaps more than a foothold, in the strategically vital duchy of Normandy.

Behind the opposition of this provincial nobility, however, there lurked, already in 1340, the beginnings of a still more dangerous reaction to royal centralization in France. The nobles of the front rank, the counts of Flanders, the dukes of Brittany and Burgundy – and the duke of Aquitaine – had been building up the structure of government in their duchies and counties just as the king had been building up the government of his kingdom, sometimes in advance of the king, as in Normandy and Flanders during the twelfth century, sometimes in imitation, as in Brittany and Burgundy during the thirteenth century when both were ruled by dynasties of Capetian origin. Each 'principality' had a *curia* in a more or less advanced state of specialization into *conseil*, *parlement* and *chambre des comptes* (though the names varied from one to another), and each had an organized system of local government. In Flanders the count's *baillis* can be seen pursuing precisely the same policy of disintegrating seigneurial autonomies as the king's *baillis* were pursuing in the kingdom at large; and each of these princes was building up a system of judicial appeals within their territories on the same principles as the king in his kingdom.[45]

Sooner or later the royal and princely governments were bound clash for both were moving towards the same end. No doubt the princes felt the effects of royal centralization in their pride and in their pockets as much as the nobility of the second rank; but they also resented it as interference in their governments, as a threat to their authority, as a menace that might at any time throw their administration completely out of gear or bring it to a standstill. It is likely that this was felt as strongly by his officials as by duke or count himself – before the end of the century the lawyers were saying, both in Normandy and Brittany, that 'le duché n'est pas du royaume'.[46] Besides, most of the principalities had strong interests in countries outside the kingdom, Flanders in the Empire and in England, Brittany in England, Aquitaine in England and in Spain; and liege

---

Patourel, 'Richard III, "roi de France et duc de Normandie", 1356–1360', *Revue historique de droit français et ètranger*, 4e ser., xxxi (1953), pp. 317–18.

[45] F. Lot and R. Fawtier (eds), *Histoire des Institutions françaises au Moyen Age*, I, *Institutions seigneuriales* (1957). This volume gives much of the information, but it is not the comparative constitutional history of the grear French fiefs which is so much needed.

[46] E.G. Léonard, *Histoire de la Normandie* (1944), p. 69; B.A. Pocquet de Haut-Jussé, *Les papes et les ducs de Bretagne*, i (1928), p. 420.

homage as it was being interpreted in the fourteenth century made it difficult or impossible for the princes to pursue the 'foreign policies' that their interests demanded.

The beginnings of a princely reaction can already be seen before 1310. It can be seen most clearly in Aquitaine, where Edward I had done all that careful organization could do to restrain or prevent appeals in Paris, to anticipate royal legislation and evade royal taxation, to build up a complete provincial govern-ment[47] and ultimately to set up a theory of English sovereignty in Gascony over against the French king's sovereignty in his kingdom.[48] The possibility of ducal sovereignty was hardly envisaged as yet in Brittany, where the duke was, in general, a very loyal vassal like his brother of Burgundy at this time; but he too could get it established that there should be no appeals to Paris from his duchy until all the resources of his own hierarchy of courts had been exhausted, and secure acknowledgement that he performed military service of his own free will and not as an obligation.[49] In Flanders the position was vastly complicated by the precocious economic and social – as well as political – development of the county, so that King Philip IV's demands led to what was in effect a war of inde-pendence in which England had been involved as far back as the 1290s.

Thus Edward's difficulties in Aquitaine, whatever their place may be in the origins of the war, were by no means peculiar to him. However loyal the princes might be personally, these same difficulties were present in all their duchies and counties to a greater or less degree. If one were to say that the first phase of the Hundred Years War was a civil war, a rebellion of the princes against royal cen-tralization which threatened to reduce them before very long to mere landlords – a rebellion led by the duke of Aquitaine because of his great resources outside the kingdom – it would be an exaggeration of one aspect of the matter, but there would be a good deal of truth in it. There can be no doubt, at least, that the war greatly assisted the process which was raising these duchies and counties into real principalities that were independent *de facto* and all but sovereign *de jure* in the fifteenth century.[50]

However this may be, the situation offered great possibilities to a prince who, having a claim to the throne of France, might think of pursuing it province by province, adjusting his methods to the individual circumstances of each. The traditional alternative of a single decisive engagement failed, as it was bound to

[47] Unpublished theses, P. Chaplais, 'Gascon Appeals to England, 1259–1453' (University of London), and J.P. Trabut-Cussac, 'L'Administration anglaise en Gascogne sous Henri III et Edouard Ier' (École des Chartes); cf. Sir Maurice Powicke, *The Thirteenth Century, 1216–1307*, ch. vii.

[48] P. Chaplais, 'English Arguments concerning the Feudal Status of Aquitaine in the Four-teenth Century', *Bulletin of the Institute of Historical Research* xxi (1948), pp. 203–13.

[49] B. Pocquet du Haut-Jussé, 'Le grand fief breton', in *Histoire des Institutions françaises au Moyen Age*, ed. Lot and Fawtier, I, *Institutions seigneuriales*, p. 277; E. Durtelle de Saint-Sauveur, *Histoire de Bretagne*, i (3rd edn, 1946), pp. 214–15.

[50] E. Perroy, 'Feudalism or Principalities in Fifteenth-century France', *Bulletin of the Insti-tute of Historical Research* xx (1947), pp. 181–5. B. Pocquet du Haut-Jussé, *Deux féodaux*

do, for there was no reason why the king of France should risk all on such a judgement by battle. Edward tried it in 1339–40,[51] and even sent his personal challenge to Philip; but though his actions in the Low Countries and north-eastern France did not give him his battle and failed to win over the count of Flanders, it did give him some recognition and support in the great Flemish cities. That was so much gained; and it might have suggested a 'provincial strategy', for the essence of the agreement he made with those who would support him in Flanders was that he should give them those things which they could not obtain from King Philip – not economic facilities only, but release from ecclesiastical penalties imposed at the instance of King Philip, the restoration of the 'western provinces' lost in the wars of the past 150 years, a common currency for Flanders, Brabant and France, and protection in their persons and their property particularly from impositions and exactions laid upon them by the king of France[52] – and the campaign of 1340 was fought ostensibly to redeem his promise. Whatever his ultimate aim, the immediate objective then was of provincial significance.

This 'provincial strategy' is well seen in Edward's handling of the succession dispute in Brittany which arose on the death of Duke John III in April 1341.[53] In a sense Edward was following a policy which may perhaps be traced ultimately to the ambitions of the dukes of Normandy in the tenth and eleventh centuries, certainly to the time when the sea route from London and Southampton to Bordeaux and Bayonne came to have some importance for the kings of England. Their need to maintain a friendly Brittany is well shown in the use which John, Henry III and Edward I made of the earldom of Richmond, traditionally a possession of the ducal house of Brittany.[54] During Edward II's reign it seemed as though Richmond and Brittany might go to different branches of the family; but when John of Brittany died in 1334, Edward III restored Richmond to Duke John III, and followed this up with marks of signal favour.[55] Not only were Breton possessions in England specifically exempted from the general seizure of French property at the beginning of the war,[56] but the earldom of Richmond

---

Bourgogne & Bretagne (1363–1491), 1935. It would be interesting to know how much the Breton principality of the fifteenth century owed to Edward's administration in the duchy from 1342 until 1362 and Duke John IV's upbringing in the English court.

[51] And again in 1355? – Delachenal, *Histoire de Charles V*, i, p. 108.

[52] *Calendar of Patent Rolls, 1338–1340*, pp. 511–16; H.S. Lucas, *The Low Countries and the Hundred Years War*, pp. 362–3.

[53] The best account of the Breton war of succession, though it stands in need of considerable amendment both in detail and in general interpretation, is still A. Le Moyne de la Borderie, *Histoire de Bretagne*, iii (1899). Cf. Durtelle de Saint-Sauveur, *Histoire de Bretagne*, i, pp. 237–52; E. Déprez, 'La "Querelle de Bretagne" . . .', *Mém, de la Soc. d'histoire et d'archéologe de Bretagne* vii (1926), pp. 25–60.

[54] S. Painter, *The Scourge of the Clergy: Peter of Dreux, Duke of Brittany* (1937); G.E.C., *Complete Peerage*, art. 'Richmond'; Victoria County History, *York, North Riding*, pp. 1–9.

[55] E.g. *Cal. Close Rolls, 1339–1341*, p. 450 – and note the date, 18 February 1340.

[56] *Foedera* ii, p. 982. Cf. e.g. *Cal. Patent Rolls, 1340–43*, p. 73 ff.

was left in Duke John's hands to the day of his death, notwithstanding the fact that he had taken part, on the French side, in the campaigns of 1339 and 1340.

It had long been known that his death would lead to a succession dispute, and that, of the two candidates, the king of France favoured Charles of Blois. His rival, John of Montfort, was likely therefore to turn to Edward on general grounds, and also because the earldom of Richmond, if he could persuade Edward to grant it to him, would make a welcome addition to his meagre resources. Nevertheless, in the negotiations of the spring and summer of 1341, it was Edward who took the initiative, or so it seems.[57] These negotiations resulted in an alliance, a conditional grant of Richmond to John of Montfort and the promise of military assistance.[58]

Before the end of the year, John of Montfort was a prisoner, and his cause might well have foundered then and there but for the energy and determination of his 'lion-hearted' duchess. Fresh negotiations, conducted in her name, produced two agreements, one in the spring and the other in the summer of 1342; and this time, in return for military help, Edward was given recognition as king of France and suzerain of Brittany, the right to collect such ducal revenues as could still be levied and the use of such castles, towns and ports as he might require for his troops.[59] After John of Montfort's death in 1345, Edward acted as guardian of his heir and namesake (who was brought up in England), and governed the duchy, or such of it as he controlled, both as suzerain and as guardian. The civil administration which he set up there was as near normal as, in the circumstances, it could be. He set up courts and appointed officials according to the laws and customs of the country, and was able to maintain some degree of

[57] This point can hardly be said to be established, but it is strongly suggested by Edward's policy up to the time of John III's death and by the time-table of events, so far as we know them, in the weeks immediately following. John III died on 30 April, 1341. A letter patent dated 10 May refers to him as though he were still living (*Cal. Patent Rolls, 1340–43*, p. 185), though his lands were committed to custody by an order dated 16 May (*Cal. Fine Rolls, 1337–47*, p. 255). This suggests that the news reached the English court at some time between those dates. Now Richard Swaffham and Gavin Corder, who were sent on an important mission to John of Montfort 'super aliquibus eidem Duci ex parte Regis exponendis & ad audiendum & recipiendum & reportandum Regi super hiis deliberacionem & voluntatem dicti ducis', left London on 6 June (Swaffham's expenses account, Pipe Roll, 16 Edw. III m. 48r). The terms of their commission, as paraphrased in this account, suggest that it was Edward who was making proposals; and, seeing that the Council had to decide its policy and the English envoys had to prepare for their journey, this time-table hardly allows for the reception of a Breton mission before Swaffham's departure. This same account makes it quite clear that John of Montfort did not visit England during the summer of 1341.

[58] *Foedera* ii, p. 1176. Great preparations were made for an expedition in the autumn of 1341, but Murimuth was probably right when he said 'Super quo fuit diu deliberatum, sed nihil factum hoc anno': *Continuatio Chronicarum*, p. 121.

[59] The text of these agreements does not appear to have survived; but their substance is preserved in the commissions given to Sir Walter Mauny and the earl of Northampton. Some of these commissions are printed in *Foedera* ii, pp. 1189, 1205.

continuity in the forms and institutions of government.[60] He never attempted to occupy the duchy as a whole, though opportunities were presented to him in 1346 and 1352. His objective was to maintain a strong military foothold there, sufficient to give confidence and security to the supporters of John of Montfort who recognized him as king of France and suzerain of Brittany, to encourage their loyalty and to win new adherents by grants of castles, lands and revenues seized from those who refused their allegiance. The objectives of Lancaster and the Black Prince in Aquitaine were fundamentally the same.

The Breton episode has been treated as something of a sideshow in the wider conflict of the fourteenth century; but when it is seen that Edward was doing in Brittany just what he was doing in Flanders, Normandy, Aquitaine, and elsewhere – gradually extending the 'area of recognition', bidding for the allegiance of seigneurs and towns – it assumes as much importance as any part of Edward's war. Indeed, it is beginning to appear that this competition for provincial allegiances, with its often sordid trade in 'confiscations', represents the way in which the war was being waged quite as much as the campaigns and the battles, and that many of the campaigns were designed as much to impress provincial opinion and provide 'confiscations' for distribution as any thing else. The Valois throne was indeed at stake.

The purely military side of the war becomes more comprehensible when these provincial considerations are borne in mind. The campaigns in Brittany in 1342–43 seem to have been intended to do no more than establish a foothold in the duchy, though Edward was no doubt ready to take any opportunity that might present itself. Likewise, when it is suggested that he had nothing to show for the Crécy campaign and the exhausting siege of Calais but 'one battle and one town',[61] it is forgotten that, at the same time, Northampton and Dagworth had not only strengthened and extended his hold on Brittany so that it would have needed a tremendous effort on the part of the French to drive out his garrisons there, but they had also secured the person of Charles of Blois. Moreover there can be little doubt that these Breton campaigns were planned as a combined operation[62] with Lancaster's campaigns in Aquitaine, which completely restored the English position and prestige there. The king's invasion of Normandy may, indeed, have been secondary, designed to divert French forces from their counter-attack in Aquitaine. The notion of simultaneous and related campaigns in several provinces had produced excellent results; and Neville's Cross was thrown in for good measure.

The outcome, when the similarly related campaigns of Lancaster in Nor-

---

60 Le Patourel, 'L'Administration ducale dans la Bretagne montfortiste, 1345–1362', *Revue historique de droit français et étranger*, 4e série, xxxii (1954), pp. 144–7.

61 Perroy, 'Franco-English Relations, 1350–1400', *History* xxi, p. 140.

62 This seems to follow from the terms of the commissions, *Foedera* iii, 34–5, 37. Northampton was to operate in Brittany and France, Lancaster in Aquitaine and (as documents issued by him and enrolled on the Gascon rolls show) Languedoc. Cf. *Cal. Patent Rolls, 1348–50*, p. 541.

mandy and the Black Prince in Aquitaine[63] had culminated in the battle of Poitiers, was impressive. Consider the situation early in 1359, irrespective of the internal dissensions which had been tearing France apart. Edward was recognized as king of France in his own duchy of Aquitaine, secured and enlarged by the successes of Lancaster and the Black Prince; in a large part of Brittany, where allegiance was supported and maintained by English garrisons and by the later campaigns of Bentley and Lancaster; in Normandy likewise, thanks to the alliance with Philip of Navarre and the establishment of English garrisons there; in Calais and the surrounding country; and in large parts of Flanders.[64] Add to that one unlooked-for result of the indenture system and the static garrison warfare in Normandy and Brittany – the formation of what were in effect free companies that were now spreading almost unchecked far into the Loire provinces, into Picardy, Champagne and even into Burgundy[65] – and it will appear that Edward had some reason to think that the time had come for a 'coronation in force'. What the effect of such a coronation might have been is shown by a clause in the treaty of Guillon by which the duke of Burgundy agreed to accept Edward as king of France if he were duly crowned in Reims Cathedral.[66]

This methodical provincial strategy, this striving for local recognition, tend to confirm the evidence quoted earlier in favour of the thesis that Edward's objective was the crown of France and nothing less; and the situation of 1359, which explains and in a sense justifies the terms of the 'Second Treaty of London' (since nearly all that he demanded in that treaty was in some sense his already), suggests that he had come a great deal nearer to this objective than has commonly been thought.

The spring of 1359 saw the climax in his fortunes. Thereafter things soon began to go wrong. He ignored Charles of Navarre in his plans for the final campaign, with the result that that slippery prince remained neutral and non-participant when he might have been useful – or did Edward think that the time had come to throw him over since he, too, had claims to the throne of France? In addition, Edward's security was very bad in 1359. It was known so well in advance that he would make for Reims that the citizens had time to complete and strengthen the new defences of their city.[67] On this occasion it was the future

---

[63] H.J. Hewitt (*The Black Prince's Expedition of 1355–1357* (1958), pp. 101, 105–7) is doubtful if there was co-ordination between them; but if there was not, Lancaster's march to the Loire is hard to explain. Cf. Delachenal, *Histoire de Charles V,* i, pp. 129, 203, 266, and the indenture calendared in *The Black Prince's Register,* part iv (1933), pp. 143–5.

[64] By the Treaty of Brétigny, Edward undertook to renounce 'homagio, superioritati & dominio ducatuum Normannie & Turonie, comitatuum Andegavie & de Mayne; et superioritati & homagio ducatus Britannie; superioritati & homagio comitatus & patrie Flandrie . . .', *Foedera* iii, 489.

[65] Delachenal, *Histoire de Charles V,* ii, pp. 21–45; S. Luce, *Histoire de Bertrand du Gueslin . . . La jeunesse de Bertrand* (1876), pp. 458–509; A. Denifle, *La Guerre de Cent Ans et la désolation des églises . . .,* I. i (1899), pp. 217–316.

[66] *Foedera* iii, p. 473; cf. Delachenal, *Histoire de Charles V,* ii, p. 170.

[67] Delachenal, *Histoire de Charles V,* ii, pp. 154–7.

Charles V who directed the defence of his country; and his strategy of avoiding an engagement at all costs, whatever the invading armies might be doing, won its first great victory. The treaty of Brétigny-Calais registers Edward's defeat; for although he might repent of his concessions and shirk the fulfilment of its terms, he had shot his bolt.

4

EDWARD III AND THE DIALECTICS
OF STRATEGY, 1327–1360

Clifford J. Rogers

He that will fraunce wynne, must with Scotland first beginne.[1]

When I tell people that I'm studying English strategy in the Hundred Years War, the response is very often something to the effect of 'did they really have "strategy" in the Middle Ages?' This idea, that strategy was absent from the medieval period, remains deeply embedded in the historiography of the subject. Sir Charles Oman, probably still the best-known historian of medieval warfare, wrote of the Middle Ages that 'the minor operations of war were badly understood, [and] strategy – the higher branch of the military art – was absolutely nonexistent'.[2] Professor Ferdinand Lot said much the same. Other scholars have argued that the medieval commander 'had not the slightest notion of strategy', or that 'never was the art of war so imperfect or so primitive'.[3] But the truth is that most medieval commanders did not show 'a total scorn for the intellectual side of war' nor ignore 'the most elementary principles of strategy';[4] nor is it fair to say that ' "generalship" and planning" are concepts one can doubtfully apply to medieval warfare'.[5]

If medieval commanders have in general received little credit for their strate-

---

[1] 'The old auncient proverbe used by our forfathers', according to Edward Halle, *The Union of the Two Noble Families of Lancaster and York* (1548), sub Henry V, folio 39v.
[2] He first made this comment in 1885, but as late as 1953 John Beeler, then among the foremost medieval military historians, wrote that 'this is still the generally accepted view of the medieval concept of war'. C.W.C. Oman, *The Art of War in the Middle Ages*, revised and edited by J.H. Beeler (1953), 61, 61n.
[3] Ferdinand Lot, *L'art militaire et les armées au Moyen Age* (1946), ii, 449: 'la grande stratégie est inexistante' in the Middle Ages. Napoleon III and I. Favé, *Études sur le passé et l'avenir de l'Artillerie* (1846), 31; R. Van Overstraeten, *Des principes de la guerre à travers les âges* (1926), quoted in Philippe Contamine, *War in the Middle Ages* (Oxford, 1987), 209.
[4] Lynn Montross, *War Through the Ages* (New York, 1960), 135.
[5] John Keegan, *The Face of Battle* (New York, 1984), 336. Cf. Sir Michael Howard, *War in European History* (Oxford, 1977), 27.

gic understanding, Edward III in particular has been singled out as, in Oman's words, 'a very competent tactician, but a very unskilful strategist'. Oman argued, indeed, that 'the details of the campaign which led up to the battle of Creçy are as discreditable to his generalship as those of the actual engagement are favourable'.[6] J.F.C. Fuller agreed that 'what his strategic aim was, it is impossible to fathom . . . Edward's conduct of the campaign of Crécy shows no proof of any rational scheme.' Major-General George Wrottesley, an amateur historian of some distinction, wrote that the campaign was conceived 'against every principle of the military art'.[7]

H.J. Hewitt's study of the organisation of war under Edward III, which appeared in 1966, put forward a new interpretation of the strategic rationale for Edward's campaigns of devastation in France.[8] He argued that these great English *chevauchées* of the fourteenth century served two purposes: to undermine the political support of the Valois monarchy by showing its military weakness in comparison with English might; and, as part of a war of attrition, to destroy the resources with which the Valois fought the war. Hewitt argued further that the aim of the *chevauchée* 'was not, as might have been supposed, to seek out the enemy and bring him to decisive combat'; indeed, according to his analysis, the English actively sought to avoid battle.[9]

This new interpretation of the *chevauchée* has become the dominant one, adopted by C.T. Allmand, Kenneth Fowler, Michael Prestwich, and Maurice Keen, among others.[10] It comes much closer to the truth than the older ideas of Oman and his school; but it still misses the mark in important ways which have led to serious misinterpretations of some of the English campaigns, notably the

---

6   C.W.C. Oman, *A History of the Art of War in the Middle Ages* (1924), ii, 111, 126; cf. 160. This view remains pervasive: the best general textbook on medieval history, Brian Tierney and Sidney Painter's *Western Europe in the Middle Ages, 300–1475* (New York, 1983), 495, claims that Edward 'had too little grasp of reality to be a competent strategist'.

7   J.F.C. Fuller, *The Decisive Battles of the Western World and their Influence upon History*, ed. J. Terraine (1970), 311. G. Wrottesley, *Crecy and Calais from the Public Records* (1898), iii; cf. Michael Powicke, 'The English Aristocracy and the War', in *The Hundred Years War*, ed. Kenneth Fowler (1971), 127.

8   Although Hewitt himself was unwilling to acknowledge it as such – he considered it part of the 'practice of war' as distinct from the 'art of war', thus separating it from the realm of strategy. H.J. Hewitt, *The Organization of War under Edward III 1338–62* (Manchester, 1966), 111. Cf. H.J. Hewitt, *The Black Prince's Expedition of 1355–1357* (Manchester, 1958), 13, 105.

9   Hewitt, *Organization*, 99; H.J. Hewitt, 'The Organisation of War', in *The Hundred Years War*, ed. Kenneth Fowler (1971), 86–7. Cf. Christopher Allmand, *The Hundred Years War* (Cambridge, 1988), 54–5.

10   C.T. Allmand, 'The War and the Non-Combatant', in *The Hundred Years War*, ed. Fowler, 166; Allmand, *The Hundred Years War*, 54–5. Kenneth Fowler, *The Age of Plantagenet and Valois* (New York, 1967), 152. Michael Prestwich, *The Three Edwards* (1980), 177–8, 180, 186. Maurice H. Keen, *England in the Later Middle Ages* (1973), 135. Scott L. Waugh, *England in the Reign of Edward III* (Cambridge, 1991), 17.

1346 'Crécy' *chevauchée*. The most important error made by Hewitt and his followers is to portray the *chevauchée* as a battle-*avoiding* rather than a battle-*seeking* strategy. In this paper, using the Crécy *chevauchée* as my primary example, I will put forward the opposite case. I will then proceed to a deeper analysis of what Hewitt correctly perceived to be the other important components of the *chevauchée* strategy: political destabilisation and economic attrition. First, though, I will address the origins of the English version of the *chevauchée* in the Scottish campaigns of the earlier fourteenth century, and also the tactical basis on which the English method of war rested: for without the 'Halidon' tactics, there could have been no strategy of *chevauchée*.

Historians now generally accept that Edward's war-aims in 1337 were first and foremost to secure sovereignty over his continental possessions, and so to put an end to the interference of the French royal bureaucracy in his government of Guienne.[11] Doubtless, Edward would have preferred to have made good his claim to the French throne, but he was realistic enough to know, even after his triumphs in the 'year of miracles', 1346, that this was practically beyond his reach. Still, it did remain a secondary goal, to be pursued if opportunity arose, as his negotiations with Burgundy in the course of the 1359–60 Reims campaign show.[12]

It is striking that Edward, when he began the war, had already seen equivalent goals accomplished by others. In 1326–27, his mother Isabella and her lover Roger Mortimer succeeded in defeating and deposing Edward II, and replacing him on the throne with the young Edward III himself. Then, just a year later, Robert Bruce of Scotland wrested from the English exactly what Edward himself would later seek for his duchy of Aquitaine: *de jure* acknowledgement of long-held *de facto* sovereignty. A smaller, weaker, poorer country had forced its larger, richer, more populous neighbour to renounce its claim to feudal superiority in order to put an end to devastating mounted raids. If this sounds familiar, it is for good reason: there is more than a coincidental relationship between the 'Shameful Peace' of Northampton (1328) and the Treaty of Brétigny which Edward imposed on the French in 1360. Edward won that latter treaty precisely by doing unto the French as the Scots had done unto him in 1327.

The experiences of the English in their Scottish wars, especially from Bannockburn to Halidon Hill, led Edward III and his advisors to develop new tactical and strategic conceptions that decisively shaped the first half of the Hundred Years War. Tracing Edward's military evolution through these Scottish campaigns serves two important purposes: it enhances our understanding of English

---

[11] But see J. Le Patourel, 'Edward III and the Kingdom of France', *History* xliii (1958), and above, pp. 247–264.
[12] For a concise but informed treatment, see Kenneth Fowler, *The King's Lieutenant* (New York, 1969), 205–6.

strategy during the first phase of the Hundred Years War; and it provides a valuable paradigm of the dialectical process by which a commander's understanding of the craft of war develops.

In 1314, not long after Edward's birth, his father, Edward II, led a large English army to the relief of Stirling castle, which was under siege by the Scots. The English were attacked under unfavourable circumstances near Bannockburn and decisively defeated. The military reputation of the English sunk so low as a result that, as Knighton commented, 'two Englishmen were hardly a match for one feeble Scot'.[13] Bannockburn, by far the most important battle fought during Edward III's childhood, showed clearly the difficulty of disrupting a tight infantry formation by cavalry charges alone, a lesson Edward was later to use to good effect.

Over the succeeding years, the triumphant Scots used the threat of further devastating raids to extort large sums of money from the northern counties, in the process almost totally eliminating the revenues which the Exchequer received from the region.[14] In 1327, the year of Edward III's coronation, with England weakened by internal dissension arising from the deposition of Edward II, Robert Bruce decided to try to extort a much greater prize from the English: acknowledgement of his independent sovereignty over Scotland.

A large group of Scottish mounted infantry (soldiers who rode from place to place, but fought on foot in pike phalanxes called 'schiltrons') raided deep into English territory that year 'with a strong hand, and laid it waste with fire and sword'.[15] An English army under Edward III's nominal command set out after them, but could not match the speed of the highly mobile Scots. Eventually the English abandoned all their excess baggage and tried to outmanoeuvre the Scots instead of out-marching them. Their intention, explains Jean le Bel (who took part in the campaign on the English side), was to pin the Scots against the Tyne and force them 'to fight at a disadvantage (*à meschief*) or to remain in England, caught in the trap'.[16] But they failed, and in the end were only able to find the Scots because the raiders sent a captured English esquire to inform the English of their location. The Scots were quite eager to give battle, so long as they could do so on their own terms.[17] The English host found the Scottish schiltrons deployed in an unassailable defensive position, across a swift river (the Wear)

---

[13] Knighton, i, 452. Cf. Petrarch's comment to the same effect, quoted in R. Boutruche, 'The Devastation of Rural Areas During the Hundred Years War and the Agricultural Recovery of France', in *The Recovery of France in the Fifteenth Century*, ed. P.S. Lewis (New York, 1972), 26.

[14] For tax revenues, see Public Record Office, London: E359/14 mm 13, 13d. For extortion, see J. Stevenson (ed.), *Chronicon de Lanercost* (Edinburgh, 1839), 222, and *Calendar of Close Rolls, 1318–23*, 274.

[15] John of Fordun, *Chronica Gentis Scotorum*, ed. W.F. Skene (Edinburgh 1871), 351.

[16] Jean le Bel, *Chronique de Jean le Bel*, ed. Jules Viard and Eugène Déprez (Paris, 1904), i, 55.

[17] le Bel, *Chronique*, i, 63.

and atop a steep hill, without enough room between the water and the slope for the English to form up.[18] The English tried to persuade the Scots to fight on a more even field, but the raiders declined. 'The king and his council saw well,' they replied, 'that they were in his kingdom, and had burnt and devastated it; if this annoyed the king, he might come and amend it, for they would stay there as long as they liked.'[19]

This left the English in a lose-lose situation. To attack would be to invite a repetition of Bannockburn, which is clearly what the Scots hoped for; on the other hand, not to attack would be to allow the enemy to escape unpunished; the massive effort and expense put into mounting the English expedition dissipated without result; and the royal government's prestige once again sent to rock bottom. Opting for the lesser of the two evils, the English declined the assault. As a result, their enemies escaped – Scot free, as it were – after having committed such destruction that, because of it, for the Twentieth granted in the fall of 1327, Cumberland, Westmoreland, and Northumberland contributed nothing at all, and even Yorkshire and Lancashire contributed only about 40 per cent of their 'peacetime' levels.[20] The young king returned to England 'in great desolation and sorrow because things hadn't gone better for him at the beginning of his reign; and, stricken with shame, he grieved much',[21] as Knighton tells us. The Brut adds that 'when the Kyng wist that the Scottes were ascapede, he was wonder' sory, and ful hertly wepte with his yonge eyne'.[22] Murimuth describes him as returning to York 'sorrowing and without honor'.[23] The point I want to make here is that this expedition was deeply engraved on the consciousness of the young king, and did much to shape his understanding of the craft of war. The more so, since the end result of his military failure was the *turpis pax* or 'Shameful Peace' of 1328, which required Edward to renounce his suzerainty over Scotland.[24] However, he learned well the lesson of the power of a mobile raiding force relying on the tactical defensive when brought to battle. In his later conflicts with France, he would use this lesson extremely well.

First, though, England had to quell the menace to the north. When Robert Bruce died in 1329, leaving an infant son to be king after him, the opportunity

---

[18] This was just what the English Council had anticipated. See *ibid.*, i, 54.

[19] *Ibid.*, 66.

[20] J.F. Willard, 'The Scotch Raids and the Fourteenth-Century Taxation of Northern England', *University of Colorado Studies* v, no. 4 (1908), 238–40. Cf. *Rotuli Parliamentorum*, ii, 176.

[21] Henrici Knighton, *Chronicon*, ed. J.R. Lumby (Rolls Series, 1895), i, 445.

[22] *The Brut, or the Chronicles of England*, ed. F.W.D. Brie (1906), 251. Cf. Thomas Gray, *Scalacronica*, ed. Joseph Stevenson (Edinburgh, 1836), 155: 'Le roy, vn innocent, plora dez oils'. The *Chronicon de Lanercost*, ed. J. Stevenson (Edinburgh, 1836), 260, also supports the story.

[23] Adam Murimuth, *Continuatio Chronicarum*, ed. E.M. Thompson (1889), 53.

[24] It is worth noting that Edward personally objected to the Treaty of Northampton, agreeing to its terms only under pressure from Mortimer and Isabella. Ranald Nicholson, *Edward III and the Scots* (Oxford, 1965), 51.

soon presented itself. In 1332 Edward Balliol, a pretender to the Scottish throne, mounted an invasion of Scotland with an army composed largely of English men-at-arms and archers. Balliol's tiny army defeated two larger Scottish forces in succession, the second one probably ten times the size of his own.[25] He then had himself crowned as king of Scots at Scone – another important precedent showing Edward III the political potential of a battlefield victory.

Balliol's successes encouraged Edward III to grant him more overt support, and in 1333 the English king led a large army into Scotland. The Plantagenet monarch forced his opponents into open battle by threatening Berwick, much as the Scots had drawn Edward II to battle by besieging Stirling in 1314, and as Edward later sought to draw the French into battle by besieging Cambrai in 1339. The Scottish army of 1333, which far outnumbered the English force, was pressured into taking the tactical offensive, even though Edward had the advantage of a powerful defensive position atop Halidon Hill, one not utterly unlike the site held by the Scots in 1327. Using the same tactical formation as he was later to employ at Crécy, with dismounted men-at-arms in the centre flanked by archers equipped with the immensely powerful yew longbow, Edward utterly routed the attacking Scots, inflicting outrageously unequal casualties.[26] For the moment, at least, Balliol was restored to power in Scotland and the 'Shameful Peace' of 1328 completely overturned.

Let us briefly consider the tactical system which made this dramatic turn of events possible. Strategy is the art of using available military means to achieve desired political goals, and the strengths and limitations of the tactical means employed by a commander can have a powerful effect on shaping his strategy. The precise formation employed by the English is not entirely clear, and varied slightly from battle to battle, but its basic characteristics remained constant from Dupplin Muir to Agincourt and beyond. The English men-at-arms, using their lances like pikes, drew themselves up on foot in a dense phalanx, often subdivided into three divisions or 'battles', one of which might be held back in reserve. On the flanks of this core of dismounted men-at-arms were ranged the English archers, protected by such natural barriers or improvised field works as could be prepared before a battle. The archers' arrows, coming 'thicker than rain', wounded or killed men and horses before they could close with their enemy, throwing an attacker's formation into disarray and driving it onto the lance-points of the men-at-arms.[27] An immobile formation of pikemen is diffi-

---

[25] Bridlington Chronicler, *Gesta Edwardi Tertii Auctore Canonico Bridlingtonensi*, in *Chronicles of the Reigns of Edward I and Edward II*, ed. W. Stubbs (1883), ii, 102–3, 106; *Scalacronica*, 159; *Lanercost*, 267; Andrew of Wyntoun, *Orygynale Cronykil of Scotland*, ed. D. Lang (Edinburgh, 1872), ii, 383–5.

[26] For Halidon Hill, see Bridlington, *Gesta Edwardi*, 114–16; Wyntoun, *Orygynale Cronykil*, ii, 401–2; *Lanercost*, 273–4; *Brut* i, 283–9; Walter of Hemingburgh, *Chronicon* (1849), ii, 308–9; Thomas Burton, *Chronica Monasterii de Melsa* (1867), ii, 369–70.

[27] For an explanation of the effectiveness of the longbow, and an analysis of the broader

cult to disrupt under the best of situations,[28] and by the time the attacker reached the English men-at-arms, his situation would be very far from the best.

The key point about this tactical system is that it proved extraordinarily effective so long as the enemy could be provoked to attack, but it was not well suited to taking the tactical initiative, especially against the heavy cavalry for which the French were renowned. The strategic implications of this fact will become clear, I hope, in the forthcoming examination of the Crécy *chevauchée*.

Edward's original objectives in launching the Hundred Years War in 1337 were to establish full sovereignty over his Continental duchy of Aquitaine, and put an end to French interference in Scotland, though his goals later grew with his successes. The first strategy employed by Edward to this end, initiated in 1339, was to attempt to do to the French what he had already done to the Scots in 1333: ravage the lands of the French king, besiege an important city, and thus draw his enemy into battle[29] where he could be decisively defeated. Of course, France was a far greater enemy than Scotland, so Edward prepared for this initial expedition by securing substantial Imperial and mercenary contingents to supplement his own forces. Indeed, English supporters of the Continental alliances claimed that Edward 'need not bring anyone with him except [his chamber servant], as he would be strong enough with his allies over there alone to conquer his heritage of France'.[30] The plan did not work, however: the two hosts met at Buironfosse, but Philip VI, as Edward had at Stanhope Park in 1327, chose the lesser of two evils and declined to initiate a battle, despite the '*trop grant blasme*' this occasioned.[31] Much the same happened the next year when, despite Edward's siege of Tournai, Philip refused to give battle.

Edward had made his bid for a decisive confrontation, but without success. In the wake of the 1339 and 1340 campaigns, his finances in complete disarray, he fell back on a less costly war of opportunity in Guienne and Brittany, where he enjoyed substantial success. At the conference of Avignon in the fall of 1344, Edward tried to turn these military successes into the political result he desired: the cession to him of Guienne in full sovereignty. Philip was willing to return the duchy as a fief, but not as an independent territory. Edward began to realise that France was too big for his gradualist strategy to be successful, given the limited resources of manpower, money and time available to him; he needed a big victory to force the peace terms he desired. The means he employed to this end was the *chevauchée*.

social implications of the English infantry-based style of war, see Clifford J. Rogers, 'The Military Revolutions of the Hundred Years War', *Journal of Military History*, lvii (1993), 249–57.

[28] Except by an enemy with missile superiority.

[29] *Chronica Monasterii de Melsa*, iii, 73; cf. 41, 50, and John of Reading, *Chronica Johannis de Reading et anonymi Cantuariensis, 1346–1367*, ed. J. Tait (Manchester, 1914), 122.

[30] *Scalacronica*, 168. Cf. Froissart, *Oeuvres*, ii, 353 and iii, 16.

[31] Froissart, *Oeuvres*, iii, 44.

*

Beginning with the campaign of 1346, Edward sought to put Philip of Valois into the same position Edward himself had been in after 1327. He would ride through Philip's territory as Robert Bruce had ridden through England, destroying and burning as he went. This destruction, which Hewitt has effectively described, did not result from the indiscipline or poor pay of the English troops,[32] nor from the need to live off the land: none of those factors could account for the degree of devastation reported in chronicles and records of the period. Houses, windmills, orchards, ships, fields, vineyards: all were plundered, destroyed, and burnt in this 'werre cruelle and sharpe'.[33] This was clearly an intentional element of Edward's military policy:[34] the destruction would damage Philip's tax revenues, just as the Scottish raids of 1327 had eliminated Edward's revenues from the northernmost counties of England; it would threaten Philip with the same kind of popular and baronial discontent that had made possible the deposition of Edward II; and, most importantly, it would place strong political pressure on Philip to attack Edward's army and thus give Edward the chance to win a decisive victory like the one he had gained at Halidon Hill but been denied at Buronfosse. Philip would thus be faced, as Edward had been in 1327, with the choice of either forcing a battle under unfavourable conditions, or accepting the dishonour and political destabilisation – as well as the loss of taxation revenue – that would result from his failure to defend his vassals and subjects. Edward, as we shall see, was hoping that Philip would choose the former alternative – battle. The Plantagenet king knew, however, that even if his enemy declined battle it would be a major political victory for England, and it would be the Valois monarch left 'sorrowing and without honour'. During the Middle Ages, perhaps more than at any other time, war was intimately intertwined with politics. It could not be otherwise when the men who formed the most important part of every army also composed the political élite. Since the nobility and gentry who provided the king with his men-at-arms were directly tied to their land, to such an extent that they usually took their

---

[32] Allmand, 'The War and the Non-Combatant', 169–70, attributes the destruction to lack of regular pay, although this seems to be inconsistent with his overall argument. But if the lack of regular pay were the reason for the devastation, then we would expect to see little or no destruction at the outset of a campaign, since most indentures specified that one quarter or more of the total wages be paid in advance; yet there is no evidence for an increase in the amount of destruction inflicted as the campaign went on. Furthermore, le Bel comments repeatedly on how well paid Edward's armies were.

[33] The phrase is from Sir John Fastolf's 1435 report advocating a return to the *chevauchée* strategy, in *Letters and Papers Illustrative of the Wars of the English in France during the Reign of Henry the Sixth, King of England*, ed. J. Stevenson (1861–4), ii, 581.

[34] Despite Hewitt's contention, which I find quite mystifying considering the overall direction of his argument, that 'looting arose neither from military policy nor from military necessity' ('Organisation', 37; cf. *Organization*, 96). Compare Fastolf on military policy of 1435, in *Letters and Papers*, ed. Stevenson, ii, 581.

names from it, an attack on the land was equally a political, economic, and military assault.

The feudal system, even in its 'declined' form of the fourteenth century, rested on the contract of homage, whereby a vassal pledged support and military service to his lord in exchange for land (theoretically) and protection and 'good lordship' (practically). This contract was replicated down the social ladder from king to magnates to simple knights and gentry to (implicitly if not literally) the peasants themselves, who provided their lords with food and labour service in exchange for tenure on the land and protection. The king who willingly failed to provide protection to his vassals, rear-vassals, and subjects violated the contract which enabled him to demand taxes and military service from them, and seriously undermined the basis for his claim to legitimacy.[35] As the count of Foix put it, 'all landed lords are duty-bound to guard their people; it is for that that they hold their lordships'.[36]

So in 1346 Edward landed in Normandy and began a *chevauchée* – destructive mounted raid designed to ravage rather than to conquer, 'burning, devastating and driving away the people; then did the French greatly sorrow, and loudly cried: where is Philip, our king?' – in that poorly defended land.[37]

Up to now, it has been unclear whether Edward III wanted to do battle with the French in 1346, or whether he was forced to do so when caught by Philip. Despite the claims of Edward himself and his contemporaries to the contrary, those modern authors who give their position on the matter, including Edouard Perroy, Philippe Contamine, Michael Prestwich, Richard Barber, Barbara Emerson, Jim Bradbury and Maurice Keen, unanimously agree that, in Perroy's words, 'Edward did not dream of measuring himself against this imposing enemy, too numerous for him.'[38] Most descriptions of the campaign interpret all of Edward's actions with this assumed, and when this does not fit the English actions, merely comment that 'at this point Edward's tactics seem obscure'[39] or that they are 'surprising'.[40] Statements of those involved which contradict this

---

[35] John Fortescue, *De Laudibus Legum Anglie*, ed. and trans. S.B. Chrimes (Cambridge, 1942), 33: 'a king . . . is obliged to protect the law, the subjects, and their bodies and goods, and he has the power to this end issuing from the people, so that it is not permissible for him to rule his people with any other power'. Cf. 35, 89.

[36] Froissart, *Oeuvres*, xii, 109. Philip's repeated failure to prevent the English from ravaging his realm led Jean le Bel to denounce him as unworthy of the appellation 'noble' – in contrast with Edward III, who 'cannot be too much honoured'. *Chronique*, ii, 65.

[37] Chandos Herald, *Life of the Black Prince*, ed. M.K. Pope and E.C. Lodge (Oxford, 1910), 7.

[38] Edouard Perroy, *The Hundred Years War* (New York, 1965), 119. Cf. Philippe Contamine, *La Guerre de Cent Ans* (1972), 29; Prestwich, *The Three Edwards*, 177–8, 186; Jim Bradbury, *The Medieval Archer* (Woodbridge, 1985), 105, 111; Maurice Keen, *England in the Later Middle Ages* (1973), 135, and citations to other authors named, below.

[39] Richard Barber, *Edward, Prince of Wales and Aquitaine* (1978), 58, re Edward III's decision to wait for Philip at Poissy.

[40] *Ibid.*, 62, re his not attempting to escape Philip after the crossing of the Somme.

assumption are considered to be jokes,[41] propaganda for distribution in England,[42] or attempts at deceit[43] which 'cannot be taken seriously'.[44]

The conviction that Edward was unwilling to risk a general engagement seems to come from two sources: the 'inherent military probability' idea that no commander so outnumbered would wish to fight; and the fact that Edward was moving rapidly northwards, towards Flanders, before Philip 'overtook' him. Before we turn to the primary source evidence which suggests that the English were indeed willing, even anxious, to do battle, these contrary arguments must be addressed. Neither is convincing when subjected to close examination.

The 'inherent military probability' idea, always risky, necessitates particular caution when applied to the mind of the medieval commander. Edward probably believed – and indeed had many good reasons to believe, since his earlier successes from Halidon Hill to Sluys had been phenomenal, and his claim to the French crown was a strong one – that God was on his side.[45] Both this belief and the complementary secular ethos of chivalry, which held that a good knight should *'fais ce que dois, adviegne que peut'*[46] would have discouraged him from placing too much emphasis on the smaller size of his army. Furthermore, deficiency in numbers can be compensated for by superiority in tactics, equipment, discipline, leadership and morale. The English soldiers and captains were largely experienced veterans, many of whom had participated in the glorious victories of Halidon Hill, Morlaix, or Dupplin Muir. At Halidon Hill they had overcome odds of, perhaps, 3:1; at Dupplin Muir, they won against odds of about 10:1. Clearly the victors of such engagements would not see a disadvantage in numbers as an insurmountable obstacle.[47] As Froissart says, the English

---

41 Barbara Emerson, *The Black Prince* (1976), 34.
42 *The Life and Campaigns of the Black Prince*, ed. Richard Barber (1979), 13.
43 A.H. Burne, *The Crécy War* (1955), 154.
44 Barber, *Edward, Prince of Wales and Aquitaine*, 59.
45 See his letter to Clement VI, in Robert of Avesbury, *De Gestis Mirabilibus Regis Edwardi Tertii*, ed. E.M. Thompson (1889), 380–81; his earlier letter to Simon Boccanegra, quoted in Jonathan Sumption, *The Hundred Years War: Trial by Battle* (1990), 380; and also his letters cited in notes 63 and 68, below.
46 That is the version of the saying, which translates roughly as 'do the right thing, come what may', in Guillaume de Machaut's *Le confort d'ami*, a near-contemporary text on chivalry. François de Montebelluna also gives the same admonition. See Françoise Autrand, 'La déconfiture. La bataille de Poitiers (1356) à travers quelques textes français des XIVe et XVe siècles', in *Guerre et société en France, en Angleterre et en Bourgogne. XIVe–XVe Siècle*, ed. Philippe Contamine et al. (Lille, 1991), 95–96. Edward's personal character was well in accord with this motto, for 'he dred neurer of none myshappes, ne harmes ne evyll fortune, that myght falle a noble warryour'. *The Brut or the Chronicle of England*, ed. E.W. Brie (1906–8), ii, 333.
47 Among the leaders of the English army at Crécy, for example, Richard Talbot, Ralph Stafford and Fulk Fitzwarren had fought at Dupplin Muir, while Edward III, Bartholomew Burghersh, Ralph Basset, John Willoughby and the earls of Warwick, Oxford, Arundel and Suffolk had fought at Halidon Hill. The earl of Northampton had been the commander at Morlaix, where lord Stafford and Reginald Cobham also fought. It is significant that the four veteran soldiers assigned to choose the ground for the English formations at Crécy – Warwick, Staf-

'never worried about it if they were not in great numbers'.[48] To paraphrase a contemporary poem on the battle of Halidon Hill, if the French outnumbered them by 3:1 it would be like 'fifteen sheep against wolves five'.[49]

Edward was in a much better position than are we to evaluate his own army in comparison with that of his enemy. The Valois host was relatively incohesive, lacking in missile capability, and had no tactical doctrine to match that of the English. Edward could not have expected to win as overwhelming and total a victory as we know with hindsight that he did; yet it seems equally unlikely that victory *per se* came as any great surprise to him. Philip's reluctance to force battle early on in the campaign indicates that he, too, was less than certain of a French victory. Indeed, Jean le Bel specifically states that the Valois monarch 'had neither the boldness nor the courage to fight'.[50] With God and his veteran army fighting for him, Edward was confident enough to risk battle, at least if he could fight it on his own terms.

The English movement towards Flanders may at first appear to be an attempt to slip away northwards, hoping to reach the coast before being overtaken, and thus to avoid battle;[51] in fact, however, this movement was intended to help keep the army fed and to secure the best possible situation before the sought-after confrontation. Edward had hoped to link up with his Flemish allies, who were supposed to be marching to meet him, to counter the endless stream of reinforcements to the Valois host, and also wanted to fight with his back to friendly territory in case of defeat.[52] Furthermore, Calais had been his destination from early in the campaign, so his path would have been sensible even if Philip had not had any army in the field at all.[53] But most important of all, Edward had to

---

ford, Cobham and Godfrey d'Harcourt – thus included at least one of the leaders from each of these three battles.

[48] Froissart, *Oeuvres*, vii, 333: 'ne n'ont pas ressongné pour ce se il n'estoient point moult grant fusion'.

[49] *The Brut*, i, 288.

[50] *Chronique*, ii, 86–7. See Sumption, *Trial by Battle*, 514, for the concessions offered by Philip early in the campaign in hopes of avoiding battle.

[51] This is the interpretation in Perroy, *The Hundred Years War*, 119, for example.

[52] For Edward's desire to meet his allies, and the English army's need for food, see the *Chronique et Annales de Gilles le Muisit, Abbé de Saint-Martin de Tournai*, ed. H. Lemaître (1906), 158–9. The northward movement after crossing the Somme led to the capture of 'graunt plente du vitailles' on the eve of the battle of Crécy. Avesbury, *Gestis Mirabilibus*, 368.

[53] Jean le Bel's statement that Edward, after crossing the Seine and reaching Beauvais, 'did not want to stop to drive out the local people nor for any other reason, because he had no other intention but to besiege the strong city of Calais, since he could not be attacked [estre combastu] by king Philip, as he desired' (*Chronique*, ii, 89), like Froissart's indication that Edward had already decided to march to Calais before his capture of Caen (*Oeuvres*, iv, 412) would seem to be distortions of hindsight, were it not for the support offered by PRO C81/314/17803, in which Edward orders from Caen that supplies be sent to Le Crotoy, which is north of the Somme on the way to Calais. Edward probably hoped that a siege of Calais would be enough to provoke Philip into an attack if the ravages of his *chevauchée* proved insufficient.

avoid the trap which Philip was trying to set for him, a trap precisely similar to
the one the English had tried to set for the Scots in 1327. Philip wanted to pin
his enemy in place against an impassable barrier – the sea, the Seine or the
Somme – just as Edward had earlier sought to trap the Scots against the Tyne.[54]
Edward would then presumably do what he had done at Buironfosse, and what
he indeed did do at Crécy: draw up his army in a Halidon-style array. But, as you
will remember from the above discussion of the tactical strengths and limitations of this formation, it was a purely defensive one. If the English were pinned
between the French army and a natural barrier, however, Philip would have no
need to take the tactical offensive. Earlier, at Buironfosse, after waiting for the
French to attack, Edward had run out of food and been forced to move off back
towards his base.[55] In 1346, too, he would have been unable to stand on the
defensive for long without supplies. Then Edward would have had his battle –
but on Philip's terms, not on his own.[56] Given that the French army was much
larger and, indeed, better prepared for such an 'open' battle, the outcome would
not have been a Crécy or a Poitiers, except perhaps in reverse. But Edward
managed to avoid this trap by crossing the ford at Blanchetacque. When he had,
thus, secured his line of retreat, he quickly found a good defensive position and
halted to wait for Philip's army.

In addition to these negative arguments, there are three positive reasons to
believe that Edward wanted an engagement. First, Parliament had advised him
to seek battle. Second, he claimed at the time that he had actively sought to
engage the Valois forces, and those with him said the same. Third, and most
important, some of his actions, which are difficult to explain otherwise, support
his words.

The Parliament of 1344, the last before the battle, was requested by Edward
to advise him concerning the war. They responded by requesting that he 'make
an end of this war, either by battle or a proper peace, if such might be had';[57]
indeed, they made the collection of the second year of the subsidy they voted
conditional on his going in person to France with that aim.[58]

The taxpayers of England, 'that with their chattels and their goods/ maintained the war both first and last',[59] as a contemporary poem had it, were nearly
exhausted, and wanted the king to end the war quickly. He had tried to secure 'a
proper peace' at the 1344 Conference of Avignon and failed: battle was the
remaining alternative for a rapid settlement – or so he thought.

---

[54] Froissart, *Oeuvres*, v, 3, 7, makes this explicit.
[55] *Scalacronica*, 169.
[56] Just as the English tried to do to the Scots along the Wear in 1327. Froissart, *Oeuvres*, ii, 166–7.
[57] *Rotuli Parliamentorum*, ii, 148.
[58] G.L. Harris, *King, Parliament, and Public Finance in Medieval England to 1369* (Oxford, 1975), 320. The writs of summons for the expedition specified that it was being undertaken 'to make an end of the war'. Wrottesley, *Crécy and Calais*, 53.
[59] John Barnie, *War in Medieval English Society: Social Values in the Hundred Years War 1337–99* (Ithaca, New York, 1974), 21.

Now to the second point. None of the seven surviving English campaign letters from 1346 indicate that the English wished to avoid battle. Froissart says that Edward 'desired nothing more than to meet his enemies in arms'.[60] Geoffrey le Baker, one of our best sources for the campaign, describes the king as 'always ready for a battle'.[61] Edward III himself, in his letter to Thomas Lucy, says that after leaving Caen

> because we were assured that our enemy had come to Rouen, we made our way directly to him; and as soon as he knew this, he had the bridge at Rouen broken so that we could not cross . . . We found all the bridges broken or strengthened and defended, so that in no way could we cross over to our adversary; nor would he approach us, although he paced us from day to day along the other bank, greatly annoying us . . . So we stayed for three days at Poissy, as much to await our enemy in case he wanted to give battle as to repair the [broken] bridge . . . And when we saw that our enemy did not want to come to give battle, we therefore (*sy*) had the country burnt and devastated all around . . . And to better draw our enemy to battle, we headed towards Picardy.[62]

Nor can these accounts be dismissed as mere propaganda for public consumption, since another private letter by the king to his Council in London, outlining his plans after leaving Caen, states that he intended to 'hasten towards our adversary, as well as we can, wherever he may be from day to day, with firm hope in God that He will give us a good and honourable outcome to our emprise'.[63]

The *Acts of War of Edward III*, written from a campaign diary, notes that after crossing the border of Normandy the vanguard of the army 'drew themselves up in battle array against a possible enemy attack which, *they hoped*, was imminent'; that after leaving Cormolain 'they burnt the town and the surrounding country *so that the enemy should know of their coming*', and that since 'although the enemy were opposite the English army, and could have chosen various places at which to cross the river, they never showed themselves nor offered battle . . . the English armed themselves and raised fire-signals everywhere *to encourage the enemy to attack*'. 'On the 14th,' continues the account, 'rumours ran through the army that the enemy were lurking in the very strong city of Paris, and the king remained where he was on that day and the next waiting for the appearance of

60 *Oeuvres*, iv, 381–2: 'ne désiroit fors à trouver les armes et ses ennemis'.
61 Geoffrey le Baker, *Chonicon Galfridi le Baker de Swynebroke*, ed. E.M. Thompson (1889), 82.
62 Printed in the notes to the Roxburgh Club edition of Chandos Herald's *The Black Prince* (1842), 351–5, here at 352–3. An English translation of the letter is easily available in Barber, *Life and Campaigns*, but it should be used with caution, because the (usually reliable) editor has at one point left out four lines of text. Cf. the *Anonimalle Chronicle, 1333–1381*, ed. V.H. Galbraith (1927), 21, and *Chronica Monasterii de Melsa*, iii, 57.
63 PRO, C81/34/17803; cf. Froissart, *Oeuvres*, xviii, 287. Compare the letter of Bartholomew Burghersh to Archbishop Stratford, written at the time: 'et [le roi] pense de sui trere tot dreit devers soun adversere, de faire tiel fyn coom Dieu luy ad ordeyne'. Murimuth, *Continuatio Chronicarum*, 203.

the enemy, which *he heartily hoped to see*.'[64] Indeed, he did more than just wait: according to the *Chronica Monasterii de Melsa*, Edward 'in particular burnt the manor of Montjoye, the most pleasant of all the manors of the king of France, *in order better to provoke Philip to fight*'.[65] Then, explains Jean le Bel, he advanced towards Calais, intending to besiege the town 'since he could not be attacked [estre combastu] by king Philip, as he desired'.[66]

The famous letter sent by Edward to Philip just before the English crossed the Seine has been described as 'disingenuous' and intended 'chiefly for consumption in [Edward's] own army',[67] but I believe that it is a serious and important statement of Edward's aims in 1346:

> we have come without pride or presumption into our realm of France, *making our way to you to make an end to war by battle*. But although you could thus have had a battle, you broke down the bridges between you and us, so that we could not come near you nor cross the river Seine. When we came to Poissy and had the bridge there which you had broken repaired, and stayed there for three days, waiting for you and the army which you have assembled, you could have approached from one side [of the river] or the other, as you wished. Because we could not get you to give battle, we decided to continue further into our realm, to comfort our faithful friends and punish rebels, whom you falsely claim as your subjects; and so we will remain in the realm without leaving to carry on the war as best we can, to our advantage and the loss of our enemies. Therefore if you wish, as your letters purport, to do battle with us and protect those whom you claim as your subjects, let it now be known that at whatever hour you approach you will find us ready to meet you in the field, with God's help, which thing *we desire above all else* for the common good of Christendom, since you will not deign to tender or accept any reasonable terms for peace. But we would not be well advised to [allow ourselves to] be cut off by you, nor to let you choose the place and day of battle.[68]

Once again the parallel with the Weardale campaign of 1327 is striking. When Edward requested that the Scots descend from their position and give battle on a fair field, they declined and told him that they would tarry in his

---

[64] I use here the readable translation of Richard Barber, in *Life and Campaigns*, with emphasis added. The relevant pages in Barber are 30, 31, 37. The original Latin can be found in J. Moisant, *Le Prince Noir en Aquitaine* (1894), 162–3, 163, 168–9. On the use of fire and smoke to provoke the enemy, see also le Bel, *Chronique*, ii, 85–6.

[65] *Chronica Monasterii de Melsa*, iii, 57 (emphasis added). Cf. ii, 73, and the *Anonimalle Chronicle*, 21.

[66] *Chronique*, ii, 89.

[67] Sumption, *Trial by Battle*, 520.

[68] Emphasis added. *Calendar of Patent Rolls (1345–48)*, 516–17; dated August 15 (the day before Edward crossed the Seine), at Autes(?). It is quite possible, however, that 'Autes' is Auteuil, which Edward did not reach until the 17th. The more often used version given in the *Acts of War of Edward III* (Moisant, *Le Prince Noir*, 171–2; reprinted in Froissart, *Oeuvres*, iv, 497, and in English translation in Barber, *Life and Campaigns*, 38) is nearly identical to the enrolled form of the letter (which I have checked), but misses out one key phrase in the first sentence of the text given above: it has 'to make an end to the war' omitting the 'by battle' immediately following.

kingdom as long as they liked, unless he dared to do something about it. Nineteen years later, Edward responded to Philip's similar offer with a more elaborate but essentially equivalent response.[69]

Richard Wynkeley's campaign letter, and indeed all the sources, agree with Edward's challenge that Philip 'neither wished nor dared to cross the Seine, as he could have, in defense of his people and his realm, even though all the land was wasted and burnt for twenty miles around, and to within a mile of his position'.[70] Moreover, Philip did break or strengthen all the bridges along the Seine to prevent the English from crossing, showing his equal unwillingness to fight on the northern side of the river either. Even Jean de Venette, a loyal Frenchman and particularly well-disposed towards Philip, remarks that even when flames from the raiders' fires could be seen from Paris itself, 'no one interfered with what the English were doing, and King Philip of France passively awaited their withdrawal'.[71] According to the *Valenciennes Chronicle*, 'all the people of Paris wondered greatly that . . . [Philip] did not hasten against (*courir sur*) the King of England, who was camped in the middle of France, with so few men that the King of France had five men for his one'.[72] These testimonies hardly support the contention that Philip was the hunter and Edward a fugitive. Quite on the contrary, they present a clear portrait of the Plantagenet's eagerness for an engagement, provided he could provoke Philip into assuming the tactical offensive; and of the Valois' desire to avoid doing so.

This portrait of words is supported by the louder voice of actions. Philip *did not* cross the Seine to engage Edward. The English *did* burn as they went to make it easy for the enemy to find them and to encourage him to attack.[73] The English did linger and await their adversaries at Poissy – if we believe the *Acts of War of Edward III*, which is probably our single best source for the campaign, Edward stayed there three days even though the bridge could be crossed with horse and cart by the end of the first day[74] – and then again at Crécy after crossing the Somme, just as the Scots had awaited the English on the Wear in 1327. Indeed, Edward reportedly even offered the Valois army free and peaceful passage over the Somme so that Philip could choose a fitting place for a battle.[75]

Those who hold to the theory that, in 1346, Philip was the pursuer and

---

[69] Cf. le Bel, *Chronique*, ii, 106, 212.

[70] Avesbury, *Gestis Mirabilibus*, 363. The author of the *Grandes Chroniques* considered it a great marvel that 'the nobles [of France] sank the boats and broke the bridges everywhere the king of England passed, when they should, quite the opposite, have used the boats and bridges to cross over against him in order to defend the country'. *Grandes Chroniques de France*, ed. J. Viard (1937), ix, 276.

[71] This version, from *The Chronicle of Jean de Venette*, trans. J. Birdsall, ed. R.A. Newhall (New York, 1953), 41, is more complete than the Latin version in the *Société de l'histoire de France*'s 1843 edition, 199, which omits the adverb 'taciter'.

[72] In Froissart, *Oeuvres*, iv, 495. Cf. the *Grandes Chroniques*, ix, 276.

[73] Cf. le Bel, *Chronique*, i, 53, for the English using the smoke from fires set by the Scots in 1327 to find their enemy.

[74] In Moisant, *Le Prince Noir*, 170–171.

[75] According to le Baker, *Chronicon*, 82.

Edward the prey find many of these actions difficult to explain. A.H. Burne, in his book *The Crécy War*, remarks that the French failure to attack at Poissy is 'hard to understand', and that the slowness of the English retreat (they continued to burn and plunder all the way up to Crécy) at times 'reminds one of a hunted fox stopping in the course of its flight to rob a hen roost'.[76] Barber comments that the English tactics at Poissy 'seem obscure', and that it is 'surprising' that, though in the two days following the English crossing of the Somme Edward could have easily outdistanced his French pursuers, he did not.[77] All of these puzzles become clear at once if we abandon the assumption that Edward was simply trying to escape, and Philip attempting to catch him.

The English strategy of 1346 was a battle-seeking one, and battle they got. Surprisingly, to the French at least, the battle resulted in a total victory for the English. The reasons for the English success are beyond the scope of a paper on strategy; suffice it to say that they benefitted from superior organisation, cohesion, and leadership; from a good defensive position and an extraordinarily effective tactical doctrine; from the presence of a large contingent of longbowmen, by far the most effective missile troops of their day; and from the indiscipline of the French. In any case, the English strategy was proven as valid as their tactics.

So much for the campaign of 1346. It is only one specimen of the genre I am analysing here: to what extent, then, do the other great *chevauchées* of Edward's reign share its characteristics? All of them were essentially the same in operational terms – they moved fast, with troops spread out usually in three parallel columns so as to devastate a broad swathe of territory along their march, and inflicted maximum damage as they passed to fields, other elements of the economic infrastructure and – when these could be taken without long investments – castles and towns. Let us consider in somewhat more detail the Black Prince's *grande chevauchée* of 1355. In Edward III's 1346 response to Philip of Valois' challenge to do battle at an appointed place, Edward said that he was continuing his *chevauchée* 'to comfort our faithful friends and punish rebels, whom you wrongly claim as your subjects; and . . . to carry on the war as best we can, to our advantage and to the loss of our adversaries'. It is clear that the Black Prince, in his great expedition of 1355, had these same four objectives in mind.

First, 'to comfort our faithful friends'. The initial target of attack was the territory of the count of Armagnac, the general who had led the French forces in assaults on English supporters in Guienne. 'He had more harmed and damaged the liegemen and land of our most honoured lord and father the King,' said Prince Edward in his letter to the Bishop of Winchester, 'than anyone else in those parts. . . So we rode through the country of Armagnac, ruining and destroying the land, which much comforted the liegemen of our most honoured lord.'[78]

[76] Burne, *The Crécy War*, 152, 157.
[77] Barber, *Edward, Prince of Wales and Aquitaine*, 58, 62.
[78] Avesbury, *Gestis Mirabilibus*, 434.

Second, 'to punish rebels'. Having acted to support his father's vassals on the borders of Guienne, the Prince reinforced his message by contrasting treatment at Carcassonne of those who held to King John. The inhabitants of the *bourg* of that city offered him 250,000 gold *écus*, a very substantial sum indeed, to spare it from the flames. 'Offered the gold,' says Geoffrey le Baker's chronicle, 'the Prince responded that he had come to seek justice, not gold; to take cities, not sell them. Since the citizens remained in fear of the French king (*coronati*), did not wish to obey their natural lord, or indeed did not dare to because they feared the revenge of the aforesaid French king, the Prince therefore ordered that the town be burnt.'[79]

Third, 'to carry on the war to our advantage'. 'They seized' le Baker tells us, 'no small wealth from the land of the enemy, enriching their own country.'[80] Froissart agrees that the Black Prince and his men secured a 'very great profit' from the expedition, acquiring 'so many goods, fine supplies, and so much good wine, that they didn't know what to do with it all'.[81] According to Jean le Bel, they found an unbelievable amount of wealth, so that even the common troops paid no attention to silver coins, goblets, tankards or furs, being interested only in gold florins, brooches and jewels.[82]

Fourth, and most interesting of all: 'to the loss of our adversaries'. The key document for this aspect of the *chevauchée* is the letter written by Sir John Wingfield to the bishop of Winchester, who, significantly, was then Treasurer of England. It is worth quoting at length:

> I am certain that since the beginning of this war against the king of France, there has never been such destruction in any region as on this *chevauchée*. For the countryside and good towns which were destroyed in this *chevauchée* found more money each year for the king of France in support of his wars than did half his kingdom (excluding the annual devaluation of the money and the profits and customs which he takes from Poitou), as I could show you from good records found in various towns in the tax-collectors' houses. For Carcassonne and Limoux, which is as large as Carcassonne, and two other towns besides Carcassonne, find each year for the king of France the wages of a thousand men-at-arms and, in addition, 100,000 old crowns, in support of the war. And I know, by the records we found, that the towns which we destroyed around Toulouse and Carcassonne, along with Narbonne and the Narbonnais, found each year an additional 400,000 old crowns in aid of his wars, as the citizens of the large towns and other men from the area, who should be familiar with the matter, have told us.[83]

---

[79] le Baker, *Chronicon*, 133. There is a similar story concerning Périgueux (for the 1356 *chevauchée*) in Avesbury, *Gestis Mirabilibus*, 457.

[80] le Baker, *Chronicon*, 138–9.

[81] Froissart, *Oeuvres*, v, 353, 351. Cf. 347.

[82] *Chronique*, ii, 221–2.

[83] Avesbury, *Gestis Mirabilibus*, 442. The *Anonimalle Chronicle*'s claim (page 35) that the English destroyed eleven *bonnes villes* and 3,700 villages on this *chevauchée* is doubtless an exaggeration, but it is certainly evocative.

Note that the prince and his advisers were so concerned with this aspect of the *chevauchée* that they went to the effort of confirming the tax records they collected with a second source – the testimony of influential citizens. And Wingfield's figures are not as incredible as they might seem. In 1329 the king of France had a document prepared to estimate how much a war in Gascony would cost him, and where he could find the necessary money. The clerks who prepared that document expected to get more money from Carcassonne alone than from Champagne, Anjou, Maine, Touraine, Valois, Chartres, Senlis, Vermandois, Amiens, Bourges, Sens, and Tours combined. Toulouse was expected to provide even more than Carcassonne,[84] and then there was Narbonne, which Wingfield described as 'only a little smaller than London'!

From all of that, it is clear that the importance of the economic attrition aspect of the *chevauchée* can hardly be exaggerated. And what about the third aspect I emphasise in my analysis of the *chevauchée*: the desire to bring the enemy to battle? That, too, is borne out by the testimony of the participants of the 1355 *chevauchée*. Wingfield writes: 'my lord had news that the French forces had come out of Toulouse towards Carcassonne, and he wanted to turn back on them suddenly; and so he did. And the third day, when we should have come upon them, they had news of us before dawn; and they retreated and disappeared . . .'[85] Prince Edward himself wrote much the same to the bishop of Winchester: how the English repeatedly sought to come up with the French forces, 'intending to have a battle', and then returned to their own lands only after it became clear that the French did not want to fight.[86] The *Anonimalle* chronicler, similarly, writes that when Prince Edward encountered a French army under the count of Armagnac and the constable of France, 'he eagerly prepared to encounter them and to give battle . . . [But] they fled without giving or taking a blow of the lance or the sword.'[87] Geoffrey le Baker writes that the French were in effect defeated, since they 'fled from their adversary in terror', when the English had 'made a long and hard journey in search of them'.[88]

So at every point, the 1355 *chevauchée* fits my model exactly. If space allowed, I could provide similar evidence for the 1356 Poitiers campaign and for the 1359–60 Reims campaign, when for nine months the English traversed as much of France as they were able 'seeking battle to maintain the right of their lord, but not finding any takers anywhere'.[89]

It took those two latter *chevauchées*, along with the battle of Poitiers, to fully

[84] M. Jusselin, 'Comment la France se preparait à la guerre de cent ans', *Bibliothèque de l'école des chartes* lxxiii (1912), doc. ii (Touraine and Sens in doc. iii). Froissart (*Oeuvres*, v, 344) points out that Toulouse was not much smaller than Paris.

[85] Avesbury, *Gestis Mirabilibus*, 441–2.

[86] Avesbury, *Gestis Mirabilibus*, 435–6.

[87] *Anonimalle Chronicle*, 35.

[88] le Baker, *Chronicon*, 137.

[89] *Scalacronica*, 196 ('ne trouerount nul. part countenaunce a ceo faire'). Cf. 194. I intend to argue this case more fully in a book to be entitled *War Cruel and Sharp: English Strategy under Edward III, 1327–1360* (Woodbridge: Boydell Press, forthcoming).

drive the message home. Then, with the 1360 treaty of Brétigny, the English strategy faithfully pursued since the Crécy campaign bore full fruit, and Edward gained territories comprising a full third of France, to be held in full sovereignty, along with a huge ransom for the captive King John – his original war aims and much more. His effective use of a sophisticated strategy involving political destabilisation, economic attrition, and open battle shows that Edward III, far from being the general of 'scant strategical skill' described in the standard reference work of military history,[90] was probably the finest commander of his day.

---

[90] R. Ernest Dupuy and Trevor Dupuy, *The Encyclopedia of Military History* (New York, 1970), 357.

THE ORGANIZATION OF WAR

5

THE ORGANISATION OF WAR

H.J. Hewitt

The aim of this essay is to describe the extensive and co-ordinated preparations for landing armies in Flanders or France, and the activities of such armies on the very many days when they were not fighting battles. With leadership, skill in arms, victories and defeats, spoils and ransoms we shall not attempt to deal. It is neither the Romance of War nor the Art of War, but some aspects of the Practice of War that we seek to explain. And the Practice of War involved 'civilians' far more closely than has hitherto been noted.

The neglect of the civilian's involvement in the Hundred Years War is fairly easily explained. War had been considered, to cite the dictionary, as a 'contest between states carried on with arms'. It was, therefore, an activity of men who wielded arms, a class whose function was the defence of the realm. Creditable performance in arms brought honour and renown, and led to a literature in which noble conduct in war was among the highest virtues and, therefore, worthy in Froissart's words 'to be enregistered and put in perpetual memory'. The narratives in verse and prose of real or imaginary adventures seldom referred to the subsidiary activities – mere crafts? – which make knightly deeds possible: the provision of arms without which there could be no 'feats of arms', or the provision of ships without which there could be no campaigns beyond the sea, or the sources of food without which – since 'an army marches on its stomach' – there could be no army!

Military historians, basing their studies on the chronicles which wrote of the Art of War, pictured the long conflict as the activity of soldiers isolated from the life and work of the nation in England or in France. It is, however, now recognised that an adequate history of any war should include an account of the roles and experiences of the civilians of the warring nations. The field of study is no longer the army-at-war, but the nation-at-war. It should, therefore, cover the work of all who directly or indirectly aid or hinder the nation's effort and the experiences of all whose lives are affected by the war.

If this wider conception of the field of study is applied to the Hundred Years War, it leads to some homely but indispensable aspects of war work, to the discovery of civilian suffering, and to episodes unpictured in the illuminated manuscripts and unmentioned in the chronicles. But it reveals some of the fundamentals of the war.

I

One fundamental was the defence of England. The circumstances of the time made it impossible to conceal preparations for the dispatch of troops to the Continent. The French, therefore, could seek to take counter-measures in their own land, or attack English ports, or plan an invasion of England. The Scots could foresee an opportunity for extensive raiding which the French encouraged them to exploit to the uttermost. Before, therefore, a single English soldier set foot on French soil, the defence of England had to be assured.

From Wales, except during the Glendower period, no danger was to be expected. Cheshire, once the main source of archers for war in the Principality, could provide troops for wars in France; the native Welsh could now be recruited for that purpose. But the northern counties must be ever prepared for attacks by the Scots, and the southern counties ready to repel invasion by the French.

The situation was brought home vividly by a series of French attacks on the southern ports in 1338–40. Harwich was burnt, Southampton plundered and burnt, the Isle of Wight raided and several other places damaged. The distribution and severity of these attacks and the frequent appearances of French fleets off the southern coast revealed the French capacity for menacing, and it might be invading, England. From the Isle of Wight and neighbouring regions and especially from Southampton, the population fled inland. Though prompt measures were taken to rebuild and fortify the town, it was only with great difficulty that the former inhabitants could be induced or compelled to return. Till Henry V's conquest of Normandy, there was a widespread view that the southern counties were never wholly safe from invasion.

That the French would attempt an invasion of England was repeatedly declared by proclamation; it amounted to a kind of news service to the people. Sometimes it was a simple prediction: the French are about to invade England. Sometimes it was more specific: the French intend to land in Kent (or another county). Sometimes it was horrifying: the French are about to attempt a landing; if they succeed, they will perpetrate horrible deeds. The assertions were not wholly groundless, for each side knew a good deal of the other's plans and, indeed, in 1346 an authentic copy of a French scheme for an invasion of England was discovered, brought to London and made known to the nation.

Defence measures, therefore, were taken on a scale and with a thoroughness greater than the nation had hitherto known. On the principle that 'all men must be compelled to repel enemies if they invade the realm', the men of the coastal counties, especially those bordering the Channel, were called on to fulfil their military obligation to defend their localities. The spheres of operations were the 'maritime lands' in their own counties, a strip deemed to extend inland for six leagues from the coast. All men living in these coastal counties were liable for service in this coastal area. Their function was the *garde de la mer.*

Keepers or wardens were appointed for the maritime lands in each county. Their duties were to guard the coast, to be responsible for the beacons and to take whatever action was necessary in their several counties. The sheriff (after due warning) had to parade the posse for their inspection; arrayers had to lead fencible men as the keepers directed; the public were ordered to give the keepers every assistance.

In some instances, the same men acted as keepers for adjoining counties (e.g. Norfolk and Suffolk) and in 1346 a scheme was drawn up under which, at the request of the keepers, men of certain inland counties had to be sent to aid the men of the coastal counties (e.g. the men of Hertford and Middlesex might be sent to Essex). Moreover, as the century advanced, the sheriffs of the coastal counties became associated with, rather than subordinate to, the keepers.

The principles underlying the *Garde de la Mer* had been understood for centuries. Though there were occasional murmurs about the burden of the *Garde*, petitions that it should operate 'at the king's cost', and, of course, efforts to avoid it, the obligation did not violate age-old principles, but its application did impose greater burdens than earlier generations had borne. There arose also the awkward problem of ensuring that men liable for service were actually resident in their counties for, as already mentioned, from the areas in which French attacks had occurred or been predicted, the inhabitants tended to move inland. Time after time proclamations were issued commanding all men holding lands in coastal counties to live on their estates.

When the war was resumed in 1369, the defence system was modified; the keepers of the maritime lands were replaced by the arrayers who were directed to raise men and lead them to the coast or elsewhere within their counties where danger threatened. But warnings about invasion and strict orders for residence in coastal counties continued to be issued. There were stern warnings in 1386, for a large French army and fleet were assembled in Flanders for many weeks with the declared intention of invading England. Additional defence measures were, therefore, taken and there were strong precautions in 1404, 1415 and 1416.

At times, French fleets swept up and down the Channel. Lightning raids could not be prevented but they were few. Winchelsea had been burned in 1360; Rye and Hastings were sacked and Gravesend burned in 1377; the Isle of Wight threatened, Plymouth and other southern ports plundered in 1404. In all, the damage sustained was trifling compared with the damage inflicted in France.

Warnings of Scottish intentions to invade the northern counties were fewer, but there were serious incursions into Cumberland, Northumberland and Durham.

II

Though the chroniclers deal at length with the armies – their leaders, marches and battles – they throw very little light on the methods by which armies were raised, the wages the fighting men received, the ships in which they were taken overseas or the victuals and other stores the ships carried. On these and allied topics much research has been concentrated during the last few decades. Perhaps the most important result has been the clarification of the change which took place in the fourteenth century from obligatory service to contractual service, that is from the compulsory to the voluntary. The change was not introduced as a single stroke of policy, but gradually as circumstances revealed its advantages or even its necessity.

Under the earlier system, when it was necessary to raise an army for service outside the kingdom, commissioners were appointed in each county and directed to 'choose, test and array' a certain number of the best (or it might be the fittest, or strongest or most skilled) men within the county. To these terse instructions there was usually added an order to provide for each man a suit and 'competent arms'. In some instances the arrayers had also to provide horses. It cannot be assumed that they were able to apply uniform standards of selection in their various counties, or that the weapons supplied were uniform in pattern, or that the ratio of men demanded to the population of a county was uniform, though there was evidently a desire to make demands proportional to population.

In practice, the arms supplied were commonly a bow, a sheaf of arrows and some kind of knife or lance. As for the clothing, there is very little evidence of its nature, colour or manufacture except the articles supplied to the Cheshire archers and the lancers of Flintshire. For these groups the material was woollen; the clothing consisted of a short coat and a hat; the colour was green and white with green on the right side, white on the left.

Thus selected, equipped and clothed, the 'civilians' were converted into soldiers and available for service. In some instances they had to be sent to a port immediately. In others, they were to be held in readiness till further instructions were received. There may have been twenty from a small county, forty from another, fifty from a larger county and, though among their number there were probably a few craftsmen, by the time they reached the port, they were likely to fall in with a group recruited specifically for their skill or experience as miners, carpenters or smiths.

Before following them to the coast, mention must be made of a two-fold controversy surrounding the county levies. The principle of obligatory service had been extended from the defence of the locality to the defence of the realm and was now extended to service on the continent of Europe. The legality of this step was warmly disputed. Even if one allowed necessity or loyalty to triumph over principle, there remained the practical question of paying wages for service outside the county. It must suffice here that large numbers of archers were raised by this method for service in France, and that in practice the county provided wages for the men till the day they reached the coast. From that day, even if they waited – as they usually did – a week or sometimes a month for ships, they were 'at the king's wages'.

The distance of the port of embarkation from the county boundary was therefore calculated. The sheriff made his estimate of the number of days needed for the journey – on foot, of course – published a date and place for the assembly of the archers – say Bridgwater, Lichfield or Shaftesbury – held a review, and paid out wages according to his estimate or handed wages to a leader who could pay out as the march proceeded. Many journeys began in summer, but some men had to set out in December or January. Within a year a similar contingent might be required for reinforcements. Men of Cheshire, Derby or Nottingham might walk down to Plymouth (or proceed northward to Carlisle or Newcastle upon Tyne for service in Scotland), but levies from the northern counties normally only served in Scotland. How they fared, where they rested is not known.

The other method of raising armies is now commonly known as the 'indenture system', because contracts of service were drawn up in the form of indentures. In essence it was a system of double contracts: individual lords agreed with the king to supply given numbers of knights, men-at-arms and archers who, on their part, undertook to serve for a certain period at a fixed daily wage. Earls received 6s 8d, bannerets 4s, knights 2s, men-at-arms 1s, mounted archers 6d. The king handed over in advance to the leaders a large part (sometimes a half) of the total sum needed for the payment of the troops for the agreed period, and gradually it became possible to extend the period as circumstances required. As examples of the leaders and their companies, we may cite the earl of Warwick who in 1341 contracted to raise 2 bannerets, 26 knights, 71 men-at-arms, 40 armed men and 100 archers;[1] John de Lisle who went out with the Black Prince in 1355 taking 20 knights, 39 esquires and 40 mounted archers;[2] and Michael de la Pole, who raised in 1418, 3 knights, 56 esquires, 40 men-at-arms and 120 mounted archers.[3] Like the county levies, these men proceeded to the port, and it was at the port that the muster was held – sometimes on the ships – payment dating from the day of the muster and in some instances being made on the ships.

The indenture system proved effective. Under the terms of the contract the king provided ships for the transport of both men and horses, guaranteed compensation for loss of horses lost in his service, and often arranged that he should have a share in the ransoms received for prisoners captured during the forthcoming campaign. In addition to the fixed wages, there was a kind of bonus called a 'regard'. The terms proved very satisfactory. Obligatory service was superseded by voluntary service.

For the great noble bound by family tradition of service, for the lowest outlaw anxious to gain a pardon, for the gay young squire seeking fame or honour, for the ne'er-do-well or the sulky malcontent – for all these, military service offered

---

[1] *CPR 1340–1343*, pp. 264–7.
[2] PRO, Pipe Roll E.372/200, m. 7.
[3] PRO, E.101/46/24.

advantages of companionship, good pay and, particularly in France, opportunities for enrichment by spoils and ransoms.

III

The organisers of the supply of victuals for an army about to be shipped beyond the sea had to accumulate at the port of embarkation enough food and forage to sustain the troops, the horses and hundreds of mariners during the period of waiting at the port, during the voyage, and during the first few days the army spent on foreign soil. The normal problems were increased in the fourteenth century by the fact that never before had such large armies been assembled for service overseas, and never had it been necessary to sustain a large force from English sources for so long a period as that needed for the siege of Calais in 1346–47.

The pattern of operations was broadly as follows: estimates of the total requirements were made, and then estimates of the quantities of this and that commodity various counties might reasonably be expected to supply. The commodities demanded were beef, mutton, pork (usually salted), oats, beans, peas, cheese, fish (commonly dried and for use in Gascony), wheat (usually ground into flour before being shipped) and ale. Transport was, of course, effected mainly by water and eastern England afforded both more foodstuffs and better waterways than western England. Depots for the accumulating stores were planted alongside the rivers and at the ports. Very many containers were needed. Tuns, therefore, cleaned and dried, were in demand.

Agents were sent to the counties to get the quantities of goods laid down. These men, called 'purveyors', were armed with two powers – the right to buy in advance of competing buyers or of the market (pre-emption) and the right, in co-operation with the sheriff, to 'take carriage' (wagons, horses, boats) for the conveyance of the goods acquired to a chosen destination. For carriage by land, some of the vehicles needed might be drawn from monastic granges, though the monks' stocks might be protected. It was necessary also to achieve some measure of co-operation with the admiral in order that river-borne supplies might be transferred at the port to sea-going vessels.

The extensive preparations for King Edward's expedition of 1346 illustrate the operation. Down the tributaries of the Yorkshire Ouse to York, down the valley of the Trent to Hull, from the rivers emptying into the Wash via Boston and King's Lynn, through Norwich to Yarmouth, through Ipswich to Orwell, through Chelmsford to Maldon, the goods were sent, loaded into ships and taken to Portsmouth. From Oxfordshire and Berkshire, the stores were sent via London; from Kent via Sandwich, while some of the western counties sent their supplies by way of Bristol.[4]

---

4   H.J. Hewitt, *The Organization of War Under Edward III*.

For smaller armies, the resources of fewer counties, of course, sufficed. The needs of the Channel Islands were commonly supplied from Hampshire and the stores of Gascony augmented from several southern counties while, after 1347, the constant and considerable needs of Calais were met partly by purveyance (that is to say the government ensured the supplies), partly by free enterprise.[5]

In view of the circumstances of the period, it is not surprising that occasionally some small part of the stores purveyed proved to be 'surplus to requirements' or unfit for consumption. More serious were the complaints made against the purveyors and in some measure against the system under which they worked. That they did not carry large sums of money with which to make immediate payment – they gave tallies – was part of the common practice of the period, but the delays in payment caused hardship. That they spared the rich and were harsh with the poor, that under the guise of purveyance they bought cheaply and sold for their own advantage, that they demanded 'heaped measure' (as contrasted with 'rased measure') – these and other bitter complaints led to a great outcry and demand for changes in 1362. The purveyors, it must be allowed, were obliged to obtain their various quotas within limited areas and within limited time, and they acted high-handedly. On the other hand, some of them lacked integrity. As for dilatoriness in payment, an example may be cited from the southwestern counties where in the summer of 1355 large quantities of victuals were hastily gathered for the army of the Black Prince waiting at Plymouth. They were paid for in the spring of 1357.[6]

For his expedition of 1415, Henry V made important changes in the mode of getting victuals. After a preliminary warning to the people of Hampshire that he desired them to 'bake and brew' in preparation for the arrival of his troops,[7] the king departed from preceding practice by issuing orders for hundreds of live oxen, cows and stirks to be driven from neighbouring counties to depots near Southampton.[8] He tried also to avoid the malpractices of the purveyors; the cattle were to be sold 'as may be with the owners agreed'[9] and if any men felt aggrieved over the matter of purchase and payment, they were to lay their cases before officers of his household. The king promised, on his arrival, that he would show them justice.[10]

The first action of the English army after landing in France was the siege and capture of Harfleur. In order to maintain the garrison in this town, and to extend his operations, the shipping of large quantities of corn, bacon, peas, beans and malt was necessary. The work was carried through (as such work was normally done in the preceding century) by granting commissions to merchants to gather

---

5   S.J. Burley, 'The Victualling of Calais', *BIHR* xxxi (1958), 49-67.
6   Hewitt, op. cit., pp. 168–72.
7   *CCR 1413–1419*, p. 214.
8   Ibid., pp. 217, 218.
9   Ibid., p. 218.
10 Ibid., p. 278.

specified amounts of this or that commodities in given counties and dispatch them through named ports.[11]

Notwithstanding the copious evidence for the victualling of English armies, research is needed on the arrangements for sharing (or dividing) and cooking the accumulated stores. Indentures of retainer of men serving the king or, say, the duke of Lancaster provided in some instances for wages *with* board, in others for wages *without* board. As for the archers, we know nothing yet of their 'messing arrangements'. But the fact remains that the first and indispensable step towards a victorious campaign in France was the accumulation of supplies of food in England by organising collection and transport even in regions as remote as the dales of Yorkshire.

The Tower of London was the great arsenal for the manufacture and storage of bows and arrows. These arms were also, of course, made in all counties and could be sent to the Tower or a port of embarkation as required. Supplies were accumulated by instructing the sheriffs to obtain certain quantities within their bailiwicks. These they bought – usually at standard prices – at various places and gathered to their chief towns where the bows were packed in canvas and the sheaves of arrows corded (or sometimes placed in tuns) and dispatched to London in hired wagons. Bowstrings also were bought, and from the areas in which iron was worked, such as Salop, Staffordshire and the Weald, iron or steel arrow heads were obtained.[12]

In the earlier part of our period, 'engines' were widely used for attacks on walled towns, but they served also for defence. They might be constructed on the spot (as at Romorantin in 1356), but some were made in England and had to be conveyed to a port and got on board. Long ladders for scaling walls were taken overseas, and from the 1340s onwards orders for quantities of saltpetre, sulphur and charcoal point to the increasing use of gunpowder.

Many carts were taken on the ships and a wide range of miscellaneous goods were indispensable: tools for carpenters, woodcutters, diggers, miners, blacksmiths; horseshoes and nails, forges; tents for the great leaders; arms, armour and clothing for the knights; harness; parchment for the king's secretaries. In the campaigns of Edward III, the king and the prince of Wales had physicians, but there is scarcely any reference to medical stores (though Chaucer mentions narcotics, drugs and opium).[13] Henry V, however, took to France a group of 'surgeons' with their 'instruments' and stores.[14]

---

[11] *CPR 1413–1416*, pp. 361, 412; *CPR 1416–1422*, pp. 1, 7, 8, 173.
[12] H.J. Hewitt, op. cit., pp. 63–71.
[13] *Canterbury Tales* (Everyman edition), pp. 35, 64.
[14] *Foedera* ix, 252 (1415); *CPR 1416–1422*, p. 31 (1416).

IV

The assembly of sufficient suitable ships for the transport of an army, its horses and supplies formed one of the most difficult tasks of executive government. Scattered between the Baltic and Bayonne or along English coasts between Berwick and Bristol, unaided by charts and lighthouses, imperfectly equipped both for direction-finding and for navigation, ships ran grave risks from pirates, from their nation's enemies and even at times from their own countrymen, for the sea was no-man's-land; they remained beyond call till they touched port and it was impossible to predict arrival dates. Coasting vessels sailed from port to port, but the wine ships on their annual journeys to Bordeaux were repeatedly directed to assemble at Sandwich, the Isle of Wight or Plymouth and proceed in convoy for their own safety.

Merchant ships were, of course, used for the transport of armies. They might be adapted for combat by having castles built on deck fore and aft, so that from an elevated position archers might achieve a longer range. They had to be adapted for carrying horses. For a typical expedition hundreds of hurdles were made, brought to port and fitted into the ships to make 'stalls'.

A fleet assembled for the transport of troops from an English port to the Continent consisted of ships varying widely in size – from 30 to as much as 300 tons – and drawn from almost all the ports in the country. A hundred vessels and in some instances more than two hundred might be needed. One chronicler[15] even states (and reputable historians[16] have followed him) that Henry V had 1500 ships for the army he led to France in 1415, but the figure should be treated as intended to impress the reader. Judged by modern standards, the crews were very large. In the early part of our period, it is not clear that owners were paid for the use of their vessels, but a practice grew of paying 3s 4d per ton for each quarter-year they were in the king's service.[17]

Once a port of embarkation had been chosen, a broad estimate of the necessary shipping determined, and a date proposed (rather than fixed) for assembly, the admirals took in hand the work of getting the ships and crews. Armed with powers to requisition all vessels of over a given tonnage, to impress sailors for manning them, and to order masters to sail their ships to the appointed rendezvous, the two admirals and their deputies rode from port to port along the stretches of coast in which they were authorised to act (namely from the mouth of the Thames towards the north and from the Thames towards the west), seeking suitable ships. No English vessel of above the required minimum tonnage was exempt. Even a ship laden with cargo destined for a distant port and calling solely for water was liable to seizure; it had to be unloaded and sailed to

---

15 Thomas Walsingham, *Historia Anglicana* (2 vols, Rolls Series, 1863–64), ii, 307.

16 E.F. Jacob, *The Fifteenth Century* (Oxford, 1961), p. 148. Christopher Hibbert: *Agincourt* (1964), p. 27.

17 *Rot. Parl.*, iii, 213, 223; ibid., iv, 79, 104.

the port of embarkation. Occasionally, a vessel of a foreign merchant was taken though this was acknowledged to be irregular.

Many weeks might elapse between the issue of orders to the admirals and the arrival of ships at, say, Southampton or Plymouth; weeks might pass while ships and crews lay in harbour waiting for the complement to be made up; and in some instances troops had to wait for weeks on land near the port. Seldom, if ever, did an expeditionary force leave England on the appointed date. Deplorable though such delays might be, it would be an error to attribute them to administrative incompetence. The convergence of the ships on the port, the adaptation of the horse boats, the transport of supplies and the marching dates of knights and men were as well co-ordinated as the circumstances of the period permitted.

Two factors appear to have governed the choice of a port of embarkation, namely the distance to the port of disembarkation and the need for a suitable roadstead in which a very large number of miscellaneous ships could ride in safety and be manoeuvred with reasonable speed to the water's edge for loading and back into mid-stream or mid-harbour. Little is known of the harbour installations and facilities. A few ports had quays; some had windlasses; in the mid-fourteenth century, Sandwich had a dock; new gangways – some of them very wide – were commonly ordered in the fourteenth century for the expeditions; warehouses are very seldom mentioned though their existence might be inferred. Lodemen (pilots) were employed fairly often, not only for entering and leaving harbours but also for long journeys.

London formed the starting-point for only one expedition – that of Henry of Lancaster in 1355. Orwell (near Harwich) was used for the departure of troops for Flanders; Sandwich was the port of embarkation of troops moving to Calais; Portsmouth and Southampton were suitable for landings in Normandy or the mouth of the Seine; Plymouth was used for expeditions to Brittany and Gascony and for the considerable traffic of the 1360s, when men and arms were being sent to Aquitaine to the prince of Wales. Reinforcements and supplies were sometimes sent from smaller ports, and at intervals troops sailed to Ireland from Milford Haven and from Chester.

In the days preceding departure, the leader was at hand at Portchester or Plympton or Northbourne by Sandwich. The roads leading to the port were crowded with horse- or ox-drawn wagons bearing victuals, forage, siege material, supplies of many kinds and empty tuns (for drinking-water). Horses were appraised (in order that in the event of their being 'lost in war', compensation might be based on their estimated value before they left England). A proclamation (cried locally) announced that knights and men must be in the port by a certain day. Mariners and archers were paid their wages and a review of the troops was held. This was a formal inspection in which two or three knights, appointed for the purpose, reported to the Council concerning the 'sufficiency of the array'.

At last, with supplies on board, tuns filled, horses led up the wide gangways and leaders and men in their appointed ships, the expeditionary force sailed away, the destination being undisclosed in 1346, 1415 and 1417. The Black

Prince took about eleven days for the voyage from Plymouth to Bordeaux in 1355; Edward III made the journey from Sandwich to Calais in a single day in 1359 (but most of his troops had preceded him); Henry V left Portsmouth on 11 August 1415 and dropped anchor near Harfleur on 14 August; two years later, on a similar journey, he set sail on 30 July and landed just west of the mouth of the Seine on 1 August.

V

After a few days spent in disembarkation and the sorting of men, horses and transport into a column of route, the army was ready to set about its business. This was not to seek and defeat the enemy army, but to bring military pressure on the enemy's country. Moreover, since men and horses had to be fed, victualling was of great importance; and as looting was commonly permitted, that constituted a third regular practice. These three activities were carried on week after week in a period when hastily assembled troops were not fully accustomed to restraint, and when the inhabitants of those towns which preferred siege to surrender expected no mercy should their towns be taken.

Military pressure consisted in inflicting *damnum* (loss), or working havoc by the destruction of the means by which life was maintained – houses, barns, stables, mills, stores, vehicles, boats, and such food and forage as was needed by the victuallers. Fire was the chief agent of destruction. It was widely used and wholly effective, for almost all houses, vehicles, implements and domestic utensils (such as vats and pales) were of wood. It was, of course, difficult to control, and though leaders usually directed that churches and church property were to be spared, they were often engulfed in the general conflagration.

Victualling called for organisation, promptitude and foresight. Wagons had to be taken several miles to right and to left of the line of march, eatables of all kinds requisitioned, cattle driven to a central point, dressed or cooked or boiled.

Looting arose neither from military policy nor from military necessity, but it was gratifying to the troops as well as an incentive in recruiting. The property of the Church was understood to be sacrosanct, but in the exciting episodes following the capture of a town, sacred vessels and altar hangings were often stolen. None of these three activities called for the virtues and skills associated with chivalry.

Constantly needing supplies of food, the invaders seldom spent more than two nights in one place. In many instances at the approach of an English army, the inhabitants fled taking such valuables as they could carry. In other instances, however, towns offered resistance. A few (such as Carcassonne and Périgueux) tried – unsuccessfully – to negotiate immunity from pillage and destruction;[18] a

---

[18] H.J. Hewitt, *The Black Prince's Expedition of 1355–57*, pp. 59, 60, 89.

few (Cambrai, Tournai, Rheims)[19] endured sieges and, by the fortune of war, escaped destruction; while in others (Calais,[20] Limoges,[21] Harfleur[22]), the inhabitants suffered very seriously after their town was captured.

The dire conflict of pitched battle was a rare occurrence. The invaders had days of profitable plunder, days of frustration, days of ample food and wine, days of scarcity, and in no campaign did they wholly escape the rigours of war: food ran very short as Edward III approached Crécy and Calais; the Black Prince's army had to swim or ford swollen rivers in November 1355; the king's army marched in appalling weather from Calais to Rheims in November 1359 and spent Christmas in the snow outside that city; the Black Prince led his troops through the bleak pass of the Pyrenees in February 1367; during John of Gaunt's *chévauchée* through central France to Bordeaux in November and December 1373, many men and horses died of cold and starvation; it was a disease-smitten army that marched to Agincourt in 1415.

Far worse was the fate of the French people. Though English soldiers were at least as well disciplined as any of the period, their routine activities struck at the deepest feelings of their victims; foreign troops insolently seized the whole of their stores of food and wine, carried off their hay and corn, drove their cattle from the fields, entered their houses, ransacked their cupboards and coffers of treasured possessions, sat down to feast and spend the night in their town and the next day set it on fire. From miles away, refugees saw the smoke by day and the red glow in the sky by night. Returning a fortnight later, they could not even locate the sites of their former homes. This was 'the desolation'. Here indeed was housing shortage, increased cost of food, inability to pay rents, landlords' losses, decline of public revenues and general social and economic dislocation.

Though there is so much written evidence of devastation, pillage and burning, it is noteworthy that the illuminators of the chronicles avoided these aspects of the war. Men rich enough to pay such artists desired pictures of more valorous episodes and got them in abundance.

Broadly the military historians also have ignored these non-fighting aspects of the conflict. They have described selected incidents, commented on strategy, tactics and military organisation, and led readers to confuse war with battles. Battles were few and brief. War was the continuous exertion of military pressure – mainly, as we have seen, on the civilian population. It was not for the seizure of food or the looting and destruction of towns that knights had trained themselves in the jousts and archers at the butts. Nor was it by working havoc in a fertile land that men gained fame for chivalry. Nor indeed did they need to 'summon up the blood' and 'lend the eye a terrible aspect' in order to fling burning matter on the thatched roofs of wooden houses. Such things do not fit into the Art of War. Yet they are the outstanding features of the Practice of War,

---

19 H.J. Hewitt, *Organization*, pp. 104, 110–11, 119, 130.
20 Ibid., pp. 59, 85, 119. *The Chronicles of Froissart*, ed. Macaulay (1924), pp. 107–9, 114–16.
21 H.J. Hewitt, *Organization*, pp. 120–1; *Froissart*, ed. Macaulay, pp. 107–9, 114–16.
22 Jacob, op. cit., pp. 150–1.

not regrettable by-products but willed and planned operations. They require explanation.

Writing of Edward III's campaign in the Cambrésis in 1339, Colonel A.H. Burne found it 'difficult for us to understand the military object to be achieved by this systematic burning'.[23] Of King Edward's work in 1346, he experienced a 'slight feeling of embarrassment when trying to excuse or explain the burnings in the Normandy campaign',[24] although he allowed that the Black Prince's 'work of destruction' in the campaign of 1355 had a 'clear military object',[25] Sir Charles Oman dismissed that campaign as 'a destructive but rather objectless raid'.[26] Ferdinand Lot regarded it as a 'typical martial undertaking . . . in which pitched battles are avoided and the troops are occupied in pillage, devastation and burning houses and standing crops in order to ruin the enemy'. Here Lot unconsciously mentioned the truth; the operations which he regarded as lying outside his study of the Art of War came to a climax in the 'ruin of the enemy', the very aim of the Practice of War!

R.C. Smail summarises more modern views thus:

> Historians have not yet fully interpreted the precise purpose and value of these raids. To Oman, as to French scholars, they appear to be entirely aimless and lacking in real military value, contributions to the sum of human misery but failing to apply military means to secure political ends. This verdict has more recently been challenged. The raids have been seen as part of a long-term military plan, designed to provoke the enemy into offering battle and, if he refused, to weaken him materially and to destroy his will to continue the war. They have been seen, too, as part of an ambitious plan for striking at the heart of the enemy's territory from a number of points on his borders . . . (simultaneously as in 1346 and 1356).[28]

An explanation closely related to the evolution of the French State deserves consideration. Though the means used by Edward III were military, his aim was political, namely the establishment of a Plantagenet monarchy in France or at least the recognition of his unqualified sovereignty over a large part of France. He, therefore, needed to weaken the hold of the Valois monarchy on the French people or, more correctly, the Gascons, Bretons, Normans . . . who were gradually coming to regard themselves as members of a French nation, for France was not yet an integrated kingdom. Provincial loyalties remained strong – in some places as strong as national loyalties. Edward, therefore, sought to impress French provincial opinion by demonstrating his might – as he did with impunity – and, by contrast, the feebleness of the French king. Instinctive feeling and expectation was that a ruler who lacked the will or the power to protect his own

---

[23] A.H. Burne, *The Crecy War*, p. 45.
[24] Ibid., p. 252.
[25] Ibid., p. 252.
[26] *The Art of War in the Middle Ages*, 160.
[27] *L'art militaire*, i, 352.
[28] *Medieval England*, ed. A.L. Poole (1958), i, 157.

subjects must forfeit their allegiance. Edward was competing for that allegiance.[29]

The terseness of the chronicles concerning the three recurrent activities of the invaders might leave doubt about the severity of the damage inflicted during a campaign. However, there are more precise sources for an assessment, for apart from the large sums offered by Carcassonne and Périgueux for exemption from destruction, in 1359 the duke of Burgundy actually paid a very large sum in order that his country might be freed from the presence of the English army before it caused further damage.[30] Another source lies in a report in the Close Rolls following an incursion by the Scots in 1345. Many inhabitants of Cumberland had protested that owing to the losses sustained, they were unable to pay taxes. An official investigation revealed that more than fifty (named) towns and villages had been 'totally burnt and destroyed'.[31]

A still more precise statement is found in a very long report on relief work in the region south of Cambrai, where King Edward's troops had spent a week in the work of devastation in 1339. The report throws a flood of light on the homelessness, the poverty, the personal sufferings, and the material damage caused in no less than 174 parishes (all of which can be identified today). It mentions the names of scores of the victims and the sums awarded to relieve their immediate needs.[32] Both here and in Cumberland (above), it is clear that human suffering was accompanied by very considerable loss of public revenue; it was this kind of loss that John Wengfeld, the personal assistant of the Black Prince, emphasised in a statement about the prince's *chevauchée* of 1355.[33]

During the period 1369–96, English invasions of France were on a smaller scale but they followed the same pattern as those of 1338–59. In particular, the *chevauchée* of John of Gaunt in 1373, was marked by pillage and burning. After the battle of Agincourt, however, Henry V modified the character of the operations. At the beginning of his first campaign he had issued disciplinary rules for the troops which had been published only occasionally during the campaigns of his predecessors. The official aim of his expedition of 1417 was the reconquest of lands unjustly detained by the French. The people inhabiting these lands he considered his own subjects. However, it was not for their sake that he was determined to enforce control in his army, but to make it an efficient instrument of his policy. The lives of French non-combatants and the Church's vessels and ornaments were now safer. The wanton destruction of food was stopped. Once a region was gained and peace proclaimed, pillage had to cease. The burning of houses without the king's explicit orders was forbidden on pain of death.

---

[29] J. Le Patourel, 'Edward III and the Kingdom of France', *History* xliii (1958), 188 also above, p. 262.
[30] H.J. Hewitt, *Organization*, p. 131.
[31] Ibid., pp. 126–30.
[32] Ibid., pp. 124–6.
[33] H.J. Hewitt, *Black Prince's Expedition*, p. 73; Robertus de Avesbury, *De Gestis Mirabilibus Regis Edwardi Tertii*, ed. E.M. Thompson (Rolls Series, 1889), p. 443.

It would be an error to infer that Henry had changed the Practice of War. His purpose and that of his successors in France was to occupy territory rather than to inflict damage on it. Moreover, he did not live many years, and though the duke of Bedford strove to maintain the discipline of English armies, the heterogeneous French army (made up of Scottish, Italian, Bretons and Castilian troops) supported itself by plundering the people of France.

VI

Intelligence (in the sense of information about the enemy) was, of course, needed, if not for the direction of operations, at least for the timing and point of attack of the expeditions. Concerning the sources and collection of information, there is need for research. For Froissart, the presence of spies was commonplace; he repeatedly states that the intention and preparations of this or that kingdom or province were known outside it. Much information might, however, have been obtained from watchers on the coast, fishermen in the Channel, merchants and masters of ships trading in Sluys and the French ports, from churchmen, diplomats and messengers travelling to and from Avignon, even from pilgrims returning to England. Further, one of the purposes of a fleet assembled in 1359 was 'to bring back to the Council news of the king and his army'. One way or another, 'tidings came', and it is probable that the courteously treated noble prisoners who spent years in England revealed sidelights on their and their neighbours' loyalty to the French throne or on the separatism of the various regions of France.

But we are not concerned solely with secret information reaching the king and Council. It is necessary to consider the information which reached the people as a whole and helped to form the national outlook. The arraying of archers, the passage of troops, the assembly of shipping in the ports, the making of arms, the strengthening of castles, the purveyance and transport of foodstuffs, border warfare in the north, attacks on ports in the south, obligatory residence in the counties bordering the Channel, watches on the coast – all these 'facts' pointed to a state of war. And the Englishman in his homeland gradually developed the attitudes with which, during continental wars, later generations have become familiar: distrust of all foreigners (including alien monks and friars), suspicions about spies and credulity concerning enemy intentions. Later, when the soldiers returned, there was added the gossip of the market-places and the inns. In short, people everywhere had the fruits of local observation mingled with hearsay and prejudice.

A combination of military precaution, administrative policy and enlightened publicity tended in the first part of the war towards an elementary news service which might engage the interest and develop the convictions of the mass of the people. First – as already shown – came the warnings about the invasion: that it was impending, that it would begin in a certain county, and that it would be accompanied by great evils. The news was sent out through the sheriffs and published by 'criers' in seaports, markets, fairs and other public places. If and when invasion occurred, the news would be spread by the well-manned beacons.

More news about the war was sent out for administrative purposes, but it was accompanied – as was common at the period – by explanation of the grounds for action. Mayors and bailiffs of seaports, for example, were directed to prevent the export of horses, or of arms, or of the good English specie; travellers entering or leaving the country were subjected to rigorous search for letters 'prejudicial to the interests of the king'; markets might be closed for a period in given areas; cellars might be searched for hidden stores of wine or arms. Officials explained their actions and the public became aware that such measures were taken in the national interest for the purposes of war.

Parliament was given such news as was available. The Commons were not critical of the aims or conduct of the war. They made large grants for its further-ance, drew attention to grievances (such as the losses of shipowners and the mal-practices of purveyors) and expected and often received a statement on the situation at the time of their meeting.[34]

But the clearest examples of communication between ruler and nation lie in letters sent to the sheriffs expressly for publication (i.e. by criers) on the widest scale. It was by this means that English people learned that King Edward had assumed the title 'king of France', that he had won the battle of Crécy, that he had captured Calais and that a peace treaty had been concluded in 1360.[35]

The Church also aided the spread of news, for requests to the bishops to cause the people to invoke divine aid for the success of English arms drew attention to the course of events. The machinery may appear cumbrous: a communication passes from the king to the archbishop; it is forwarded to all the bishops in the province; they turn the message into mandates addressed to the archdeacons and other executive officers, who pass the instructions to the parochial clergy. The instructions are not, of course, uniform throughout a province, but broadly they order 'prayers, processions [litanies] and preaching [sermons]'. Usually, the requests refer to specific expeditionary forces and their leaders. They were sent out in almost every year between 1338 and 1351, and again in 1355, 1356 and 1359. (The Black Prince sent a similar request from Bordeaux in June 1356.)[36] Nor was the king lacking in gratitude; through the same channels, he asked that thanks be offered to God for the victories gained at Sluys (1340), in Gascony (1346) and at Poitiers (1356).

The practice of requesting the Church to offer prayers for the armies may be traced in some of the episcopal registers down to the end of the war[37] (though in 1439 the special intention was for a peace mission of Cardinal Beaufort). It is

---

34 H.J. Hewitt, *Organization*, pp. 175–7.
35 Ibid., p. 159.
36 *Hereford Episcopal Registers*, John de Trillek, i, 243.
37 *Exeter Episcopal Registers*, John de Grandison, i, 66, 11, 1173; ibid., ii, 120–2; ibid., *Thomas de Brantingham*, i, 186–7, 199, 299, 342, 432; ibid., *Edmund Lacy*, i, 38, 39, 85, 109, 116, 149; ibid., ii, 15, 156, 237, 283, 311, 375.

doubtful whether there is sufficient evidence for an investigation of the zeal with which the clergy carried out their instructions – Archbishop Chichele[38] referred three times in 1416–18 to their 'growing tepid in their devotions for the success of the king' – but it is probable that in very many places the litanies served to focus worshippers' attention not on war in general but on the nation's latest military effort.

The maintenance of the war depended not only on the military qualities of the leaders and troops in the field, but also on the ability of the 'civilians' at home who organised the defence of the realm, the recruitment of soldiers, the collection of victuals, the production of arms, the assembly of shipping, the transport of the expeditionary (and later, the occupying) forces and even a rudimentary service of news.

By far the greater part of the time of the men serving abroad was used in the seizure of food and in systematic devastation. Both operations had very serious effects.

BIBLIOGRAPHICAL NOTE

E. Perroy, *La guerre de Cent ans* (Paris, 1945; English trans., *The Hundred Years War*, 1951), is a comprehensive survey, useful for the general background.

Concerning the Art of War, the following may be consulted: C. Oman, *A History of the Art of War in the Middle Ages* (1924); F. Lot, *L'art militaire et les armées* (Paris, 1945); A.H. Burne, *The Crecy War* (1955) and *The Agincourt War* (1957). In these works, war is treated as an activity of soldiers only. Lot gets down to the real sizes of armies. Burne's volumes are the studies of a soldier rather than of a historian, and they are not free from errors, although they make lively reading.

A.E. Prince, 'The Indenture System under Edward III', in *Historical Essays in Honour of James Tait*, ed. J.G. Edwards, V.H. Galbraith and E.F. Jacob (Manchester, 1933), forms a guide to one aspect of recruiting, while M. Powicke, *Military Obligation in Medieval England* (Oxford, 1962), though an advanced study of legal aspects, is helpful for the transition to the contractual system of raising armies. R.A. Newhall, *The English Conquest of Normandy, 1416–1424* (New Haven, 1924), throws light on the later period of the war.

Three books go much further than their titles might suggest; while necessarily giving full accounts of battles, they also deal with transport and victuals: H.J. Hewitt, *The Black Prince's Expedition of 1355–57* (Manchester, 1958); E.F. Jacob, *Henry V and the Invasion of France* (1947); C. Hibbert, *Agincourt* (1964; Pan Books, 1968). H.J. Hewitt, *The Organization of War under Edward III, 1338–1362* (Manchester, 1966), omits battles, deals with shipping, supplies, victuals, etc. and the involvement of 'civilians' in the war.

---

[38] *Registrum Henrici Chichele*, ed. E.F. Jacob (1947), iv, 158–9, 167–8, 176.

Froissart's *Chronicles* throw light on several aspects of the war. His figures for the sizes of armies are usually wide of the mark, but his narrative breathes the spirit of the age: the chivalry and challenges to single combat alongside the looting, devastation, sieges and attempts to capture rich nobles for ransoms. The *Chronicles* were translated by Lord Berners in 1521–53 and reprinted by W.P. Ker (6 vols, Tudor translations, 1901–3), and there are single-volume selections such as *The Chronicles of Froissart*, ed. G.C. Macaulay (1924) and *Froissart: Chronicles*, ed. and trans. G. Brereton (Penguin Classics, 1968).

6

ENGLISH ARMIES IN THE FOURTEENTH CENTURY

Andrew Ayton

On 12 April, the Sunday after Easter, 1360, an English army led by Edward III stood fully arrayed for battle outside Paris.[1] After two decades of intermittent war, the stage was set for a decisive confrontation between Plantagenet and Valois. The gauntlet had been thrown down, but much to Edward's chagrin the dauphin declined to take up the challenge. Despite the anticlimactic turn of events, the spectacle of an English army before Paris, with several columns marching, like Joshua's host, 'close under the faubourgs from sunrise till midday', would linger long in the memories of those who were there. Sir Thomas Gray harked back to these events in his military memoirs.[2] Many of the deponents in the Court of Chivalry cases of the 1380s recalled that they had been participants in what the deposition of that old veteran Sir Adam de Everingham described as the 'great voyage when the late king and his army had been before Paris.'[3] To have been arrayed with their king in this display of military might outside the French capital was clearly a source of lasting pride – and it is easy to understand why, for this particular army was indeed a formidable fighting machine. An excellent set of pay accounts suggests that its effective strength at the start of the campaign was approaching 10,000 men.[4] This would make it one of the largest English armies fielded during the Hundred Years War, surpassed in size during the fourteenth-century phase of the war only by the hosts assembled for the Normandy campaign of 1346 and for the subsequent siege of Calais in 1347. But Edward III's army in 1359–60 was formidable in more ways than just its size. It was exceptionally well equipped; and it was led by a glittering array of military talent, headed by the king's most trusted lieutenants,

---

[1] *The Anonimalle Chronicle, 1333 to 1381*, ed. V.H. Galbraith (Manchester, 1927), p. 46. All documents cited in the footnotes are in the custody of the Public Record Office, London. I am grateful to my colleague Dr J.J.N. Palmer for comments on a draft of this paper.
[2] *Scalacronica*, ed. and trans. Sir H. Maxwell (Glasgow, 1907), pp. 156–7.
[3] *The Scrope-Grosvenor Controversy*, ed. N.H. Nicolas (2 vols, London, 1932), i, pp. 240–1.
[4] E101/393/11 fos. 79–16v. The total excludes non-combatants, as well as the contingents of continental men-at-arms, Welsh infantry and others who left the king's pay during the first few days of the campaign.

including the Prince of Wales, Henry, duke of Lancaster, the earls of Northampton and Warwick and Sir Walter Mauny: men who had been responsible for many of the English military successes of the preceding two decades. In the autumn of 1359, as this army landed in France, the reputation of English arms was as high as it had ever been. In the view of the Liègeois chronicler, Jean le Bel, the English were 'les plus nobles et les plus frisques combastans qu'on sache'.[5] The transformation since the dark days of Edward II's reign, since the débâcle of Bannockburn in 1314 and the series of dismal campaigns in Scotland and Gascony during the following decade, had indeed been astonishing. At the heart of England's rise as a front-rank military power in the middle decades of the fourteenth century were changes in military organisation, in the composition of armies and in the conduct of war: changes which, when taken as a whole, amount to a major overhaul of the military machine at the disposal of the English crown. Some historians, indeed, have called it a 'military revolution'.[6]

It has become customary in discussing the Edwardian military revolution to focus particular attention on changes in methods of recruitment and forms of remuneration: in short, on the emergence of paid contract armies. The provision of pay on a large scale has been seen as a catalyst for wider developments, with the 'indenture system', the raising of armies by means of short-term, written contracts between the king and his captains, as the most effective way in which paid armies could be put in the field. In broad brush-stroke terms, the feudal host, based upon the compulsory, unpaid provision of companies of men-at-arms by tenants-in-chief in fulfilment of their military obligations, had been superseded by contract armies, consisting of paid volunteers. Seen from the perspective of the later fourteenth century, a radical change in recruitment practice had taken place, but the transformation occurred only gradually and the seeds of change had long been sown. English kings had been employing paid contingents for several centuries prior to the Edwardian period. What we see in the first half of the fourteenth century is the establishment of *wholly* paid armies. Hitherto, complexity of recruitment practice had prevailed. A typical royal army of Edward I's reign, such as that which fought the Caerlaverock campaign in 1300, consisted of a mixture of feudal, voluntary unpaid and paid elements. Magnates, concerned that their retinues should properly reflect their status, supplemented their shrunken feudal quotas with additional men-at-arms and met the extra expense themselves. Even when pay was available, some magnates, like Thomas, earl of Lancaster, resolutely refused to accept it for their men. Turning to those who did receive the king's pay, we should not imagine them all to be volunteers. Many had been pressured into the performance of military service. In the case of the aristocracy, this pressure might involve a personal – though non-feudal – summons, or a general invitation addressed to those possessed of a particular level of landed wealth (in 1300, £40 *per annum* landholders). For

---

5   *Chronique de Jean Le Bel*, ed. J. Viard and E. Déprez (2 vols, Paris, 1905), i, p. 156.
6   M. Prestwich, *The Three Edwards: War and State in England, 1272–1377* (London, 1980), p. 62.

lowly foot-soldiers, the pressure would come from the operation of commissions of array: the high rates of desertion from the shire levies during Edward I's Scottish campaigns suggest that many of those arrayed were anything but enthusiastic volunteers. Armies including both paid and unpaid elements persisted into the 1320s. Troops serving in fulfilment of the feudal obligations of tenants in chief were still in evidence in the hosts raised in 1322 and 1327.[7] By the time of Edward III's campaigns in Scotland in the mid 1330s, royal armies were wholly paid, even though, for the moment at least, many captains bringing contingents did so in response to individual mandatory – though non-feudal – summons from the crown. Paid service, then, was not necessarily voluntary service. Even when we find captains contracting freely with the crown, as many did during the Hundred Years War, we may be sure that *they* would often need to turn the screws of obligation and exploit ties with local communities when recruiting their retinues, calling upon the services of indentured retainers, tenants and members of a wider affinity. English armies were held together, albeit loosely, by threads of obligation; wholly freelance sub-contractors provided only a proportion of the manpower of a contract army.

It is usual to speak of 'paid armies', but it is important to remember that for the rank and file of these armies pay was very often only one element in a 'package' of terms of service, involving both benefits and obligations. One benefit *not* related to the receipt of pay was the letter of protection: a document, issued by Chancery, which gave the recipient security from a wide range of legal actions for the duration of a specified period of service. A man knowing that court proceedings were pending at the time of his departure for war could secure a letter of protection and thereby halt the process of law until he had returned to England; but it is likely that most letters of protection were obtained as precautionary measures, to deal with unexpected legal actions. Since the traditional warrior class was also the landowning class, with a great deal to lose at the hands of litigious neighbours and rivals, it is not surprising to find that often at least a third, and sometimes as many as a half, of the men-at-arms serving in a mid fourteenth-century army secured the issue and enrolment of protections before leaving the kingdom. In a very real sense, the availability of protections, along with the development of enfeoffment to use, allowed the aristocracy a degree of freedom to perform, if only intermtittently, their traditional martial function at a time of regular, heavy recruiting demands. Mention should also be made at this point of charters of pardon, granted as reward for spells of service in the king's armies, since the government used them as an even more blatant recruiting device. Here was a means of securing legal redemption, of wiping the state clean, and many criminals seized the opportunity with both hands. During the Scottish and French wars large numbers of war-service pardons were issued

<hr/>

[7] N. Fryde, *The Tyranny and Fall of Edward II, 1321–1326* (Cambridge, 1979), chapter 9; N.B. Lewis, 'The Summons of the English Feudal Levy, 5 April 1327', *Essays in Medieval History Presented to Bertie Wilkinson*, ed. T.A. Sandquist and M.R. Powicke (Toronto, 1969), pp. 236–49.

(including, for example, several thousand during and after the Crécy-Calais campaign in 1346–47), the great majority to non-aristocratic combatants.

The issue of pardons was not connected specifically to the receipt of pay (indeed, for some campaigns, those seeking a pardon were obliged to serve 'at their own expense'); but the other terms of service which affected, in particular, men-at-arms were all related in one way or another to the receipt of the king's wages. Firstly, there was the bonus payment known as *regard*. This was introduced for continental expeditions in the mid-1340s and appears to have been intended as a supplement to men-at-arms' pay to help cover the ever growing cost of plate armour. At the usual rates, paid as a lump sum to captains, *regard* represented a supplementary payment of about 6d. per day for each man-at-arms. This was a significant bonus, since the usual daily rates of pay – 2s. for knights and 1s. for ordinary men-at-arms – remained unchanged right through the fourteenth century. A man-at-arms receiving the king's pay for continental campaigns would also benefit from the appraisal of his principal war-horse, so that, in the event of its loss, he would be able to claim from the crown an appropriate cash payment as compensation (*restauratio equorum*). The sums involved were not insignificant, since a man-at-arms' war-horse was his most expensive item of equipment. Drawing on the evidence of surviving appraisal lists, we can see that the average value of war-horses taken by Englishmen to France at the start of the Hundred Years War was about £15; with esquires of modest means often being content with £5 mounts and great captains, like the earl of Northampton, serving with magnificent *destriers* valued at £100. To put these figures in perspective, a knight serving in the king's army for one year would receive, in theory at least, about £45 in pay and *regard*. Horse appraisal and compensation was, therefore, a most welcome dimension of paid service. It was a privilege for those taking the king's pay, but also, in the earlier fourteenth century at least, a prerequisite of receiving pay. From the crown's point of view, the horse appraisal process was an integral part of muster and review, a means of checking that men-at-arms were serving with horseflesh of respectable quality. This, at the start of the Hundred Years War, meant horses worth at least 100s.

The last element in the standard package of terms of service accepted by men entering the king's pay concerns the division of the spoils of war. In taking the king's pay, a man accepted that he owed the crown a proportion of the profits, from booty and ransoms, which he might accumulate whilst on campaign. In practice, men-at-arms and archers would deliver this portion of their winnings to their captain, and he in turn would render the same proportion of his overall takings to the crown. The long-established view has been that the king's portion was a third;[8] but recent research has established that until the early 1370s, provided the full package of benefits was on offer – normal rates of pay and regard, and horse appraisal – then the senior contracting party would expect to receive

---

[8] D. Hay, 'The Division of the Spoils of War in Fourteenth-Century England', *TRHS*, 5th ser., 4 (1954), pp. 91–109.

half of the value of his subordinates' profits. As with most aspects of military organisation during this era of war, the package of terms of service was by no means fixed in granite. There were occasional experiments and, in the early 1370s, a major and permanent reform. The records for the campaigns of 1372 and 1373 reveal the nature of the changes that were made.[9] Horse appraisal was abandoned and to compensate for this, *regard* was paid at double the former usual rate and the king's portion of the winnings of war was reduced from a half to a third. Horse appraisal was administratively expensive, but cost-cutting was probably not the only motive behind the reforms; the government appears also to have been aiming to provide more favourable terms of service. In this they achieved a measure of success: the typical man-at-arms *was* likely to be better-off under the new arrangements. The mechanism for horse compensation had always been an imperfect method for covering campaign costs. Only one of a knight's several war-horses would be appraised and thus eligible for compensation at any one time; and horse compensation payments were often hopelessly in arrears. Moreover, with war-horse quality declining perceptibly as the century progressed, the need for appraisal and compensation may have seemed less pressing than before; and, under the reformed package of terms, double *regard* offered a larger assured lump-sum payment to cover the costs of campaign preparations.

Paid military service, then, was actually service which involved a range of benefits and obligations. These terms of service are perhaps most readily seen in indentures of war, but the package of terms would operate perfectly well when no written contracts were employed. Bearing in mind the prominence accorded to the 'indenture system' in many discussions of the Edwardian military revolution, it is worth emphasising that indentures of war were scarcely employed at all for the major expeditions led personally by Edward III during the first phase of the Hundred Years War.[10] Take, for example, the army with whose parade outside the walls of Paris in April 1360 this chapter began. Its personnel were certainly subject to the normal terms of service. The pay-rolls reveal the operation of most elements of the package; and, as we shall see shortly, this army was not at all backward-looking in its structure and composition. Yet, as with the army which fought the Crécy-Calais campaign, no formal written contracts between the king and his English captains were deemed necessary, for both of these armies were led personally by the king and administered directly by the royal household's financial department, the Wardrobe. The army of 1359–60 was still, as it had been in Edward I's day, 'the household in arms', although the household division – the companies brought by royal household bannerets and knights, which under Edward I might provide a third or more of paid heavy cavalry – was smaller by the mid to late fourteenth century, contributing about a

---

[9] For example, E101/68/4 nos. 92–94; E101/32/26 mm. 3–4.

[10] The use of contracts for a cancelled expedition in 1341 was necessitated by the crown's reliance on wool assignments to finance recruitment: M. Prestwich, 'English Armies in the Early Stage of the Hundred Years War: A Scheme of 1341', *BIHR* 56 (1983), pp. 102–113.

sixth of men-at-arms in 1359 and a similar proportion to armies later in the century.[11]

The 'indenture system', then, was a mechanism designed to fill the administrative vacuum which appeared when the king was not leading the army in person and the clerical staff of the royal household were not on hand to supervise the distribution of wages and deal with related matters, such as horse appraisal. Indentures of war had shown their potential in this respect during the reigns of the first two Edwards, when they had been used to recruit troops for garrison service and for spells of duty on the Scottish border and in Gascony. In the early summer of 1337, on the eve of the continental war, about 500 men-at-arms were raised by contract for a Scottish expedition which the king did not intend to lead in person.[12] Indentures of war emerged as a distinctive feature of the first phase of the Hundred Years War because the struggle was fought simultaneously on several fronts, with most of the expeditionary forces being led, not by the king himself, but by his lieutenants. For example, in the spring of 1345, as the king contemplated a campaign in northern France, Henry of Grosmont, earl of Derby contracted to take 2,000 men to Gascony, whilst the earl of Northampton agreed to serve with about 500 men in Brittany.[13] The 'indenture system', with captains accounting for their periods of service directly at the Exchequer, became the invariable method of raising armies during the second phase of the war, from 1369, because the king, increasingly inactive during the 1370s, was no longer directly involved in the struggle. By the time of the Agincourt campaign in 1415, all armies, whether or not they were to be led by the king in person, were raised by means of indentures of war.

The establishment of wholly paid armies, whether recruited by means of informal agreements between king and captains or formal written indentures of war, greatly enhanced the quality and effectiveness of the military resources at the disposal of the English crown. The size of armies and the duration of their service could be pre-determined and adjusted to suit particular military requirements; and appropriate budgeting and administrative provisions could be made. Numbers of personnel and quality of equipment could be checked by regular muster and review. It would not be true to say that 'control was lax' in the fourteenth century; a great many pay accounts, muster rolls and other documents confirm the regularity of personnel checks. With paid, contract armies, a king had at his disposal the means of waging war on an ambitious scale, of executing coordinated strategic plans, such as the multi-pronged attacks on France in the 1340s and 1350s, when expeditionary forces operated simultaneously in Brittany, Gascony and northern France. A strategy of this kind, depending as it did

---

[11] C. Given-Wilson, *The Royal Household and the King's Affinity. Service, Politics and Finance, 1360–1413* (New Haven and London, 1986), pp. 63–4.

[12] N.B. Lewis, 'The Recruitment and Organisation of a Contract Army, May to November 1337', *BIHR* 37 (1964), pp. 1–19.

[13] K. Fowler, *The King's Lieutenant: Henry of Grosmont, First Duke of Lancaster, 1310–1361* (London, 1969), pp. 230–2; E 101/68/4 no. 72.

upon the work of a team of lieutenants, offered great opportunities to the militarily talented members of the aristocracy, whether from the higher nobility – like Henry, duke of Lancaster and William de Bohun, earl of Northampton – or of more modest gentry stock, like Sir Thomas Dagworth and Sir Walter Bentley. The captains relieved the crown of much of the burden of recruitment and military administration, and at the same time acquired considerable influence in the direction of the war. These responsibilities were potentially costly; indeed, the functioning of the military machine *depended* upon contracting captains making full use of their own financial and manpower resources. The mobilisation of feed retainers speeded up the process of recruitment, as well bringing a degree of stability to a contract army. Magnate money eased the cash-flow problems with which military expeditions were invariably beset. Timely injections of a captain's own cash would help to get expeditions underway, keep them moving and hold them together. Of course, privatisation of the war effort also brought opportunities for gain. Apart from those princely ransoms much-discussed by historians, some captains found that 'margins of profit' could be secured by recruiting men at pay rates below those offered by the crown. Perhaps most important as an attraction, if as elusive in fulfilment as ransom-hunting, was the prospect of enhanced political influence and personal honour which successful war leadership could bring. But profits of whatever kind could not be relied upon. Altogether more certain was that war leadership would eat into a noble captain's personal resources. Dependence on the wealth and social authority of the nobility ensured that command of major field armies was rarely given to the 'professional' captains, but remained in the hands of senior members of the titled nobility. For example, of the major expeditions from 1369 to 1380, four were led by one or more of Edward III's sons, whilst the only non-noble captain to be an army commander during this period, Sir Robert Knolles in 1370, found it difficult to exercise authority over his lieutenants. This is not to suggest that the 'professional' captains were of little value to the English war effort, for they certainly performed an invaluable service as independent commanders in *secondary* theatres of war. For example, maintaining the sometimes precarious English foothold in Brittany, often with no more than a handful of paid troops, was the responsibility of a series of experienced, resourceful soldiers of gentry stock: men like Sir Thomas Dagworth, Sir John Hardreshull and Sir Walter Bentley.[14]

Paid service, and particularly the 'indenture system', did much more than merely enable a group of captains to advance their ambitions in the king's war; it also created an environment which allowed the latent military potential of the whole aristocracy to be harnessed more effectively. Baronial suspicion had first to be overcome: some magnates under Edward I found the subordinate status which receipt of the king's pay implied intolerable. But given the cost of cam-

---

[14] M. Jones, 'Edward III's Captains in Brittany', *England in the Fourteenth Century*, ed. W.M. Ormrod (Woodbridge, 1986), pp. 99–118.

paigning in Scotland, this reluctance was unlikely to endure and paid service became firmly established as the norm during the course of the Scottish wars. By the start of the French war, the aristocracy had been eased into a new way of thinking; war, a social responsibility, an 'honourable obligation', but costly and sometimes bitterly resented, had become paid, contract work. Pay, along with letters of protection and enfeoffment to use, had made it easier for the aristocracy to fulfil their military potential, to perform their function as a warrior élite; and, from the king's point of view, a major continental war had become a realistic proposition. Yet, accepting the king's wages was one thing; being willing to serve overseas was quite another. It is important to remember that the English aristocracy's enthusiasm for the French war at the time of the great expedition of 1359–60 represented a complete transformation of outlook from their lukewarm, sometimes downright hostile, attitude to overseas military service during the reigns of the John, Henry III and the first two Edwards. The knightly class in England, it was said, 'did not give a bean for all of France'. It is hardly surprising, then, that the government considered it necessary to offer pay at double the usual rates for the early campaigns of the continental war (1338–40) and to employ foreign mercenaries in large numbers. Yet within a few years there had been a major shift in attitudes and a marked increase in the level of military participation within the English aristocracy. How had this change come about? Part of the explanation is to be found in the eagerness of the nobility, following the political crisis of 1341, to be reconciled with the king;[15] but the aristocracy needed a push in the right direction if it was to be induced to take up the sword *en masse*. That there may have been as many as 4,000 (and possibly more) English men-at-arms at the siege of Calais in 1347[16] was largely the result of heavy royal pressure exercised through a new military assessment based on landed wealth. This experiment met with opposition in the Commons and was soon abandoned; but it had forced the secular landowning community to face-up to their traditional military responsibilities and it had involved many of them, either directly or by substitution, in an enterprise which led to the triumphs at Crécy and Calais. The process of aristocratic 're-militarisation' had, then, required a kick-start; but campaign successes, exploited by royal propaganda and consolidated by the encouragement of chivalric *esprit de corps* through such inspired *coups* as the appropriation of the soldier martyr St George as patron of the Order of the Garter, kept up the momentum. The army which Edward III assembled in the autumn of 1359 included more than 3,000 English men-at-arms[17] (of whom over 700 were bannerets and knights). This was a most impres-

---

15 W.M. Ormrod, *The Reign of Edward III* (New Haven and London, 1990), pp. 100–103.

16 On the interpretative difficulties of the 'Calais Roll', see A. Ayton, 'The English Army and the Normandy Campaign of 1346', *England and Normandy in the Middle Ages*, ed. D. Bates and A. Curry (London, 1994), pp. 253–68.

17 The earl of Arundel's retinue, which included 2 bannerets, 25 knights and 108 esquires, didn't sail (E101/393/11 fo. 80): these men would bring the overall total near to 3,500 men-at-arms.

sive figure for post-plague England, an aristocratic recruitment level which, apart from the siege of Calais, had probably not been attained since the battle of Falkirk in 1298. Although a proportion of these men would have been professional soldiers, men like John Hawkwood, whose origins were less than aristocratic, the great majority would have been drawn from the gentry – that is, from about 9,000 to 10,000 families.[18] In fact, the pool of potential men-at-arms for the French war in 1359 was rather smaller than this, since by no means all of the English nobility and gentry were available for continental service. England was a patchwork of local military communities and those of the northernmost shires and of the 'maritime land' of southern coastal counties were often preoccupied with defence responsibilities, a preoccupation which extended to the whole kingdom in 1359 in the face of a serious threat of invasion. All things considered the 'military participation ratio' of the aristocracy at the time of the show of force outside Paris in April 1360 was indeed impressive. If pressed for a view on Edward III's continental enterprise, the great majority would no doubt have echoed the Garter motto: 'shamed be he who thinks ill of it'. Small wonder that the king in 1359 could afford to turn away many of the foreign mercenaries who had flocked to join his army, for 'he had brought enough men from his own country to complete his task'.[19]

The recruitment level of 1359–60 represents a landmark in the English aristocracy's new-found appetite for continental campaigning. The scale of the gentry's response in 1359 was not repeated until Richard II's campaign in Scotland in 1385, the next expedition to be led by the king in person.[20] The field armies during the period 1369–80 were of more conventional size, numbering from 4,000 to 6,000 fighting men, with proportionately scaled down, but still substantial, numbers of men-at-arms: several of the armies fielded more than 2,000 of them, which suggests an enduring aristocratic commitment to the war in France. But the 'remilitarisation' of the gentle-born was not to be long-lasting, not least because campaigning opportunities thinned out significantly at the end of the century. Nor, for some, had it ever been particularly profound. Among the knights and esquires who accompanied their king to France in 1359 were many for whom this would have been the highlight of an intermittent career in arms: intermittent because of their commitments in England, the management of their estates and the governmental and judicial responsibilities which arose from the possession of land. This is not to suggest that such 'occasional' soldiers contributed little to the functioning of the English war machine. If the king was periodi-

---

[18] C. Given-Wilson, *The English Nobility in the Late Middle Ages* (London, 1987), pp. 69–83.

[19] *Chroniques de Jean Froissart*, ed. S. Luce et al., 15 vols, Société de l'Histoire de France (Paris, 1869–1975), v. p. 197.

[20] There were perhaps as many as 4,500 men-at-arms in this army: N.B. Lewis, 'The Last Medieval Summons of the English Feudal Levy, 13 June 1385', *EHR* 73 (1958), pp. 5–6. Cf. A.L. Brown, 'The English Campaign in Scotland, 1400', *British Government and Administration. Studies Presented to S.B. Chrimes*, ed. H. Hearder and H.R. Loyn (Cardiff, 1974), pp. 40–54.

cally to mount large-scale expeditions, such as those of 1346 and 1359, and yet to avoid dependence upon foreign mercenaries, the service of large numbers of 'occasional' soldiers was essential. Moreover, a strategy which relied primarily upon the employment of short-service contract armies actually made optimum use of the native aristocracy's military potential. For heads of gentry families and others with domestic commitments in England, long periods of service were effectively ruled out. As the century progressed and the French war entered a particularly intensive phase (1369–89), the numbers of county knights taking up their swords, even for short expeditions, diminished steadily. Captains contracting with the king had difficulty finding the numbers of knights stipulated in their indentures. To some extent the smaller proportion of *strenui milites* in later fourteenth-century armies mirrored a general decline in the numbers of knights in society: a fall from perhaps 1,500 in 1300 to well under 1,000 in 1400, as knighthood became a more burdensome estate, administratively and financially; but the numbers of *fighting* knights may have declined at a more rapid rate. By the 1370s and '80s, typically, fewer than 10% of an army's men-at-arms would be knights, as compared with about 20% or more for armies of comparable size earlier in the French war; and the shrinkage in the numbers of *strenui milites* continued further during Henry V's reign.

In spite of diminishing numbers of militarily-active knights, the English military community in the mid to late fourteenth century did not suffer from a shortage of men-at-arms. On the one hand, there were expanding numbers of non-aristocratic professional soldiers, men drawn to war by the prospect of profit rather than by birth (to whom we shall return later). On the other, there were men of gentle blood with time on their hands: men awaiting inheritances or younger sons expecting to inherit very little, perhaps reconciled to the fact that a military career was their best chance of making their way in the world. Many of them never advanced beyond the status of esquire. Some specialised in garrison service, such as the military professionals involved in the protracted defence of Aquitaine during the last decades of the century, many of whom were from Cheshire or Lancashire. Some were fortunate in finding regular service with one of the more bellicose members of the higher nobility, such as Edward, prince of Wales or the two dukes of Lancaster, Henry of Grosmont and John of Gaunt – magnates whose military responsibilities necessitated the maintenance of a permanent retinue of reliable men. Feed retainers, together with the men in their companies, provided a nucleus around which the less stable, more transitory elements in a magnate's war *comitiva* could be assembled. Important as such retainers were in providing a backbone to a contract army, probably far larger numbers of men in the pool of regularly serving personnel had no such permanent commitment to a single magnate. They enlisted for one expedition after another in a variety of theatres of war under a series of different captains. Their restlessness certainly contributed to that unsettled appearance which English armies exhibited during this period; but, in effect, an old, much used pack of cards was simply being reshuffled. The Nottinghamshire knight Sir Nicholas de Goushill illustrates well the life of the committed, yet restless soldier. During an eventful career, which began with the battle of Halidon Hill in 1333 and lasted thirty-five years, he served in Scotland with William, Lord Deyncourt, in Ireland with William of Windsor, in several parts of France with Henry, earl of Derby, two earls of Salisbury and Sir Robert de Herle, ending with service in William, Lord Latimer's retinue on John of Gaunt's *chevauchée* in 1369. The intensity with which Goushill followed a life in arms appears to have been prompted by the extraordinary longevity of his parents, who lived into their eighties; he didn't inherit his family's property until he was an old man. William de Thweyt's problem was that, as a younger son of a minor Norfolk gentry family, he stood to inherit very little. His response was a career which spanned exactly the same period as Goushill's, though in his case he combined involvement in the great expeditions – he was at Halidon Hill, Sluys and Crécy – with several spells of garrison duty, at Corfe castle in Dorset and in Ireland. Men like Goushill and Thweyt formed the seasoned, dependable backbone of the Edwardian military community. For such veterans as these, lacking prospects at home and drawn by birth to the martial life, regular paid service in a war with many dimensions represented perfect employment. They, just like Dagworth, Bentley, Chandos and the rest of the notable captains were beneficiaries, and products, of the Edwardian military revolution.

Historians considering the transformation of the English war machine during the second and third quarters of the fourteenth century have devoted a good deal of attention to the emergence of paid armies and the 'indenture system'; but in addition to these developments, and in part bound up with them, the years separating the battle of Bannockburn from Edward III's expedition to France in 1359–60 also witnessed profound changes in the structure and general character of English armies. The host which Edward II led to the relief of Stirling castle in 1314 and which was heavily defeated by the Scots at Bannockburn probably consisted of about 2,500 men-at-arms serving in companies of various sizes and 15,000 infantry, raised in the shires by commissions of array. The two sections of the army – the men-at-arms and the foot soldiers – were numerically unbalanced, they were recruited separately and they fought separately. The contrast with the army with which Edward III embarked upon the march to Reims in 1359 is striking indeed. This consisted, as we have seen, of nearly 10,000 men, of whom the most important elements were about 4,000 men-at-arms (including perhaps 700 continental mercenaries) and over 5,000 mounted archers. This was a large army by the standards of the French war (logistical constraints usually restricted armies to half this size), but it was also notable for the predominance of mounted troops and the rough equality between the numbers of men-at-arms and mounted archers – a balance which was, moreover, reflected in the composition of individual retinues making up the bulk of the army's strength. Those retinues were very varied in size: one thing that the Edwardian military revolution did not bring about was the establishment of military units of uniform size, such as we find, for example, in the standing armies of some continental states in the fifteenth century. The retinues in an English field army were temporary establishments, their size usually reflecting, in broad terms, the rank and social

status of their captains. In 1359 the Prince of Wales landed in France with a
retinue which had the proportions of a small army: the pay-rolls suggest that it
was nearly 1,500 men strong. At the other end of the scale, King Edward's army
in 1359 also contained dozens of very small companies led by knightly captains.
Sir Richard Pembridge, for example, was accompanied by no more than nine
fighting men. Between these extremes, a typical knight banneret might have a
retinue consisting of sixty to seventy men; and an earl would usually have
several hundred men in his. But whether large or small, the retinues in the army
of 1359–60 were often composed of roughly equal numbers of men-at-arms and
mounted archers. The earl of Warwick, for example, served with a retinue consisting of 120 men-at-arms and 120 mounted archers, whilst the banneret Sir
Robert de Morley was accompanied until his death by thirty men-at-arms and
thirty horse archers.

The structure of the army which arrayed outside Paris in April 1360 high-
lights, therefore, two of the crucial developments in the transformation of the
English fighting machine in the mid-fourteenth century: the emergence of the
mounted (or 'horse') archer; and the establishment of the 'mixed' retinue, consisting of men-at-arms and mounted archers. The transformation of the military
machine, as witnessed by the army raised in 1359, was only gradually achieved.
There had been a number of unsuccessful experiments following Bannockburn
and only after the battle of Halidon Hill in 1333 is it possible to see lasting
changes in the character and organisation of English armies. The mounted
archer appears for the first time in significant numbers in the surviving records
in 1334. In the summer of 1335, there were about 3,350 of them in the army of
rather more than 13,000 men which Edward III led to Scotland. Yet of these
mounted archers, only about a third were serving with men-at-arms in mixed
retinues and the greater part of the king's army in the summer of 1335 was still
being raised in the shires by commissions of array.[21] The onset of the war with
France gave added impetus to the process of change in English military organisation, to the rise of the mixed retinue and the declining contribution of shire
levies. The transformation was admittedly not achieved overnight. County and
urban levies continue to figure prominently in the pay-rolls of some English
armies until at least 1360 – as witnessed, for example, by the major contribution
of arrayed infantry to Edward III's army at Crécy and the siege of Calais. But
the direction of change is unequivocal. Particular stimulus was given to this
movement by the 'indenture system'; but the process of change can be seen
equally well in those armies which were not raised by means of formal written
contracts. Take, for example, the army which conducted the campaign in Brittany in 1342–43.[22] The main body of this army, which arrived in the Duchy with
the king in the autumn of 1342, appears from the pay-rolls to have included
1,700 foot soldiers raised by commissions of array. But these men served for

---

[21] R. Nicholson, *Edward III and the Scots* (Oxford, 1965), pp. 199–200.
[22] For the pay-roll, see E36/204 fos. 105v–110v.

only a short period and some infantry contingents never actually arrived in Brittany. So, the effective strength of the king's army was formed by about 1,800 men-at-arms and 1,800 mounted archers, with the great majority of retinues being composed of balanced numbers of each. Seen in this light, then, the army of 1342–43 begins to appear a smaller version of the great army of 1359; indeed, it is not dissimilar in overall proportions to those armies, now raised almost exclusively by indentures of war, which fought in France after the resumption of hostilities in 1369. The English expeditionary forces during the years from 1369 to 1380 were dominated by mixed retinues, very often composed of roughly equal numbers of men-at-arms and mounted archers. A planning document headed *Pur le viage de Portugale*, showing the contingents expected to comprise Edmund, earl of Cambridge's expeditionary force of 1381, lists ten retinues, ranging in size from 40 to 1,000 men, each with exact parity of men-at-arms and archers.[23] This one to one ratio may well have represented the perfect balance of complementary personnel; but if it was the optimum arrangement, it had but a brief heyday. In the last years of the fourteenth century, as the numbers of fighting knights declined, so we also find a larger proportion of archers in royal armies. At 6d. per day, mounted archers were relatively inexpensive (and, given their tactical importance, very cost effective), but their increased numbers *vis-à-vis* men-at-arms also no doubt reflected the growing prosperity of the yeoman farmer in the decades following the Black Death. Archers outnumbered men-at-arms by 2 or 3 to 1 in many of the retinues in Richard II's army of 1385 and by the time of the Agincourt campaign in 1415, the optimum ratio of archers to men-at-arms was deemed to be 3 to 1.

The emergence of the mounted archer as associate of the man-at-arms in mixed retinues brought about a significant shift in the social composition of the military community. Compared with the poor-quality infantry of Edward I's armies, the mounted archers of the mid to late fourteenth century were more expensively equipped and, consequently, drawn from a wealthier social group; they were men of yeoman stock, 'men of some standing in local society'. So, with the diminished role for infantry and the rise of the mounted archer, military service in the king's armies was now becoming the preserve of a smaller section of society; the military community had a narrower social base. Moreover, the gap between the chivalrous and non-chivalrous of the military community had also narrowed, for just as the heraldic separation of knights and esquires was becoming blurred during the fourteenth century, so the social and economic distinctions between archer and man-at-arms were also becoming less pronounced. This process may have been more marked in some parts of England than others. In Cheshire, for example, as Philip Morgan has shown, there were many archers 'whose standing, within the confines of county society, was analogous to that of men-at-arms raised elsewhere in England'.[24] A single family might contribute both men-at-arms and archers to a royal army; a man might serve in both capaci-

---

[23] C47/2/49 m. 2.
[24] P. Morgan, *War and Society in Medieval Cheshire, 1277–1403* (Manchester, 1987), p. 109.

ties during the course of his career, perhaps as a consequence of a change in fortune. Social mobility was possible; the opportunities for enrichment and social advancement were frequently mentioned by contemporary writers. Admittedly, the extent of Sir Robert Knolles' rise from archer to wealthy knight was not often emulated, but there must have been many amongst the swelled numbers of English men-at-arms in the later fourteenth century, serving in royal armies and garrisons, as freebooters, mercenaries or crusaders, who had not been born into the chivalric class. It is clear that Sir Thomas Gray, a product of an old northern family and thoroughly imbued with traditional values, did not entirely approve. At one point in his *Scalacronica* he draws attention to the swarms of young men from all over England who descended upon France in the 1350s: 'young fellows who hitherto had been of but small account, who became exceedingly rich and skilful in this [kind of] war . . . many of them beginning as archers and then becoming knights, some captains'.[25]

The emphasis on mounted troops and recruitment on the basis of individual retinues consisting of roughly equal numbers of men-at-arms and archers greatly enhanced the effectiveness of the English fighting machine under Edward III. Mounted expeditionary forces could operate with speed and flexibility. The *chevauchée*, the destructive, mounted raid, which was used so frequently in the war in France, had been influenced by the experience of the protracted Scottish wars, in which both sides had recognised the importance of mobility. In 1336, on the eve of the French war, Edward III himself led a small-scale raid into the Scottish Highlands and gained first-hand experience of the effectiveness of a wholly mounted force of men-at-arms and archers. The *chevauchées* in France were often on a larger scale, audacious challenges to the authority of the Valois kings and sometimes, as with the Prince of Wales' raids in 1355–56, spectacularly successful. If brought to battle, an English army consisting of balanced numbers of men-at-arms and archers could offer an effective and flexible tactical response. In a series of hard-fought battles during the first phase of the French war – Morlaix (1342), Crécy (1346), Mauron (1352), Poitiers (1356) to name only the most notable – dismounted men-at-arms and archers combined in defensive formation to repulse the attacks of numerically superior opponents. The massed hitting-power of the archers thinned-out the enemy at a distance, blunting their impetus, thereby giving the English men-at-arms, fighting shoulder to shoulder in disciplined formations, the edge in the hard-fought mêlées which these battles invariably involved. As with the development of the *chevauchée*, the origins of the distinctive English tactics of the Hundred Years War can be traced to the Anglo-Scottish wars earlier in the fourteenth century. Although large numbers of foot archers had been recruited in Edward I's reign, they were not well equipped, nor well disciplined; nor were they yet employed in a coordinated fashion. The real tactical turning point was not the battle of Falkirk (1298), but the battle of Bannockburn, when the flower

[25] *Scalacronica*, pp. 131, 134.

of English chivalry, fighting in the traditional fashion on war-horses, were routed by a Scottish army consisting in the main of pikemen. It was this humiliating defeat which seems to have brought about a major shift in tactical thinking in England. A combination of dismounted men-at-arms and archers in defensive formations reminiscent of Scottish schiltroms was the basis of Sir Andrew Harcla's success at Boroughbridge in 1322 and was later employed to devastating effect against the Scots at Dupplin Moor in 1332 and Halidon Hill in 1333. It was entirely natural that these tactics should also be used in France where numerical inferiority usually obliged the English to adopt a defensive posture. Occasionally, of course, we do find the English launching a mounted charge, as at Auberoche in 1345; but even when the tactical situation required that an offensive stance be adopted, the attack was as likely to be conducted by men-at-arms and archers on foot, as for example at La Roche Derrien in 1347. To appreciate the completeness of the tactical revolution, the extent to which the English aristocracy had abandoned fighting on horseback, we should focus attention not so much on the comparatively few major battles of the period, but rather on those numerous small-scale encounters which abound in the pages of the narrative sources: minor skirmishes in which we find the English showing great consistency in their tactical methods. In the Scottish border country, as well as France, the English dismounted to fight as a matter of course; whilst by the early 1360s, Englishmen serving in the White Company had introduced their distinctive tactical methods into Italian warfare as well.

The tactical revolution affected the character of English armies in several ways. The aristocracy's abandonment of mounted combat in favour of fighting on foot had a number of practical consequences. The man-at-arms' equipment had to be modified to allow for maximum mobility out of the saddle. Plate armour was developed to accommodate combat on foot and the flowing surcoat was replaced by the short jupon. The lance, the cavalry weapon par excellence, was used by dismounted men-at-arms as a pike in bristling 'hedgehog' formations.[26] More intriguingly, the relegation of the war-horse to a secondary battlefield role (pursuit or flight) appears to have had a significant effect on the quality of horseflesh taken on campaign. The average value of appraised English war-horses dropped from £16 for the first major campaign of the French war in 1338–39 to about £9 for the 1359–60 expedition. The effect of the tactical revolution on the collective mentality of the English aristocracy cannot be measured in such precise terms, yet the blow to the aristocratic sense of identity can easily be appreciated. The war-horse had been, after all, the *sine qua non* of chivalrous combat, It was, as much as anything, what distinguished a man-at-arms at muster from his social and military inferiors. In commenting on how the English at Halidon Hill 'fought on foot, contrary to the old habits of their

---

[26] See Sir Thomas Gray's description of the battle of Lunalonge: *Scalacronica*, pp. 136–7. Cf. T.F. Tout, 'Some neglected fights between Crécy and Poitiers', *EHR* 20 (1905), pp. 727–8.

fathers', the chronicler, Geoffrey le Baker,[27] would have been expressing the thoughts of many of the knights and esquires in Edward III's army. In fact, the English aristocratic warrior appears to have reconciled himself to the tactical revolution rather quickly and a clear distinction soon emerged in English military circles between deeds of chivalry, which were most appropriately performed on horseback amongst his peers – on the tournament field and in those individual combats and small-scale encounters which often occurred on campaign – and the practical business of battlefield fighting which was most effectively done on foot in disciplined tactical formations, in combination with archers. But the rise of the archer, his tactical importance underlined in the later fourteenth century by his numerical predominance, undoubtedly left the aristocratic combatant with a greatly altered military status. No sooner had the provision of pay and a major continental war provided him with an opportunity to convert the ideal of a warrior class into a functioning reality, than he found himself no longer the only really important component of the military community. If not exactly a mere supporting battlefield player (as he has sometimes been portrayed), the aristocratic fighter had become the partner of the bowman in a tactical system which depended upon them both. Moreover, he was now increasingly likely to find himself fighting shoulder to shoulder with *parvenu* men-at-arms, men who were certainly not of gentle blood. War was no longer an activity which set the minor aristocrat apart from his social inferiors. The fading of the gentry's interest in war, which is only too evident during the fifteenth-century phase of the Hundred Years War, may well be as much connected with this change in military status, as with the heavier demands of shire administration and local justice.

These, then, were the principal developments in English military institutions in the fourteenth century: the emergence of wholly paid armies and the 'indenture system'; the restructuring of armies around wholly mounted retinues of men-at-arms and archers recruited by a re-invigorated class of aristocratic captains; and the narrowing of the social base providing manpower for the military community. These developments, combined with the changes in strategy and tactics which stemmed from them, contributed in no small degree to the dramatically improved performance, and correspondingly enhanced reputation, of English arms on the continent in the mid-fourteenth century. Underpinning this overhaul of the military machine, fuelling the more effective mobilisation of the realm's manpower, was the exploitation of the kingdom's economic resources through national taxation; the revenues from direct taxation of the laity and clergy and from customs duties on exported wool were the lifeblood of the contract armies which conducted the war in France.

All this may well amount to a 'military revolution', but we should not be blind to the limits of the transformation that had occurred. There were no centrally planned, highly structured institutional reforms to compare with the *ordonnances* of the Valois kings of France and the dukes of Burgundy. What

---

[27] *Chronicon Galfridi le Baker de Swynebroke*, ed. E.M. Thompson (Oxford, 1889), p. 51.

fourteenth-century England experienced was a 'quiet revolution', involving institutional evolution, gradual development with occasional bursts of rapid change, frequently as much a consequence of the interplay of circumstances as of royal planning. The military institutions which emerged were not without faults and limitations. Contract armies were well-suited to a strategy of free-moving *chevauchées*, but there was more to the French war than *chevauchées*. 'Siege warfare', as Anthony Goodman has noted, 'was not an English military speciality; English forces were more at ease on *chevauchée*, unencumbered by elaborate siege trains'.[28] The fourteenth-century phase of the Hundred Years War was punctuated with unsuccessful sieges: Tournai (1340), Vannes (1342–43), Rennes (1356–57), Reims (1359), St-Malo (1378). The ultimately successful investment of Calais, 1346–47, was a triumph of endurance rather than ingenuity or superior military technology. Although gunpowder weapons made their first appearance during the period under review – primitive cannon were employed at Crécy – they did not contribute significantly to English military enterprises until the reign of Henry V. Nor was a military machine based upon short-service contract armies particularly well-suited to those strategic commitments which required long-term occupation, garrisons rather than flying columns. In the fourteenth century, such commitments stretched England's financial and manpower resources to their limits. In Aquitaine, the English relied heavily on the Gascon nobility.[29] In Brittany, and indeed elsewhere in France, the English 'presence' was more often based upon private enterprise, garrisons living off the country, than upon royal pay – with all the disciplinary problems which inevitably resulted from such an unsatisfactory arrangement. The Lancastrian conquest of northern France would in due course necessitate the adaptation of the 'indenture system' to meet the demands presented by a strategy of steady territorial expansion and long-term occupation. But already in the later fourteenth century a proportion of military expenditure had become a permanent commitment: the security of Aquitaine, Ireland, the Scottish Marches and Calais were accepted financial responsibilities in peace as well as war. As John Gillingham has observed, the Calais garrison was 'the nearest most English kings ever came to having a standing army'.[30]

---

[28] A. Goodman, *John of Gaunt. The Exercise of Princely Power in Fourteenth-Century Europe* (Harlow, 1992), p. 235.

[29] See, for example, M. Vale, *The Angevin Legacy and the Hundred Years War, 1250–1340* (Oxford, 1990), p. 262.

[30] J. Gillingham, 'Crisis or Continuity? The Structure of Royal Authority in England, 1369–1422', *Das spätmitterlalterliche Königtum im europäischen Vergleich*, ed. R. Schneider (Sigmaringen, 1987), p. 67; and see p. 74.

7

WAR AND THE EMERGENCE OF
THE ENGLISH PARLIAMENT, 1297–1360

Gerald L. Harriss

Although the opening of the Hundred Years War led the kings of France and England to make similar demands upon their subjects, the effect on the monarchy and on the Estates was markedly different in the two countries. In England taxation gave parliament a central role in the medieval polity while in France it strengthened first local autonomy and then absolute monarchy. Because parliament had an inescapable obligation to grant taxation for common defence, the Commons sought to limit this to periods of open war, and to criticise and control the handling and expenditure of the tax. The character of taxation at levied by common assent and for the common profit, likewise permitted resistance to the extension of prerogative rights and the assertion of parliament's right to grant the tax on wool. In these matters the Commons were forced into a defensive dialogue with the Crown over their obligations which educated them in political argument and the techniques of parliamentary opposition. The power to levy taxation on grounds of 'necessity of state' strengthened both monarchies; but in England this was subject to the assent and authority of parliament which thereby emerged as a political institution concerned with the common needs of the realm.

Historians have long been aware that in the first half of the fourteenth century the feudal monarchies in France and England began to exhibit divergent trends until in the next century they would be regarded as different types of government. This did not reflect different views of kingship. Indeed the dominant Aristotelianism of the late thirteenth and fourteenth centuries ensured a remarkable consensus about the duties of kingship and the obligations of subjects (Dunbabin 1965:73–9; Keen 1965:121–4; Lewis 1968:78–110). The divergence was rather in the institutions of government and reflected the influences of geography and of inherited political and administrative traditions. Thus A.R. Myers argued (1961:141–53) that the distinctive prestige of the French monarchy which enabled it to become the focus of unity after the three Estates had been discredited by defeat and dissension, and the size and regionalism of

France, together thwarted the creation of a central assembly able to represent and bind the whole nation. In England by contrast the monarchy was weakened and humiliated by the limitations imposed on John and Henry III and the depositions of Edward II and Richard II, while the greater unity of the realm was reflected in the frequent assembly of representatives from traditional units of local government in a national parliament.

These are valid points, yet it is doubtful whether such differences would have manifested themselves so quickly, or so profoundly have affected political mentalities, had it not been for the pressures of war. From 1297, and then more evidently from 1337, war began to acquire a national character. It was no longer merely the king's war, waged for the preservation of his honour and the recovery of his rights, but a war which touched the safety of one and all. In both kingdoms the reality of this was borne home to ordinary subjects by the Crown's attempts to mobilise their services and goods for defence and by the actual dangers and destruction of enemy raids. There was in consequence increasing reference to and debate upon the obligations which subjects owed to the king for the preservation of the realm. In both realms such debates were conducted in terms of the legal and scholastic – one might say the 'constitutional' – doctrines of the age. We must therefore ask how it was that in England these doctrines became entrenched in the procedures of parliament and even in the law of the land as constitutional limitations while in France they did not. With regard to the French side the answer is being given by the work of J.B. Henneman (1971). In this article I want to ask how war compelled Englishmen to acknowledge certain public obligations, how they were led to define these by reference to current political ideas, and how they contended for them in dialogue with the king in parliament. It will be argued that the emergence of parliament as a political institution was vitally influenced by the strains of war.[1]

From their different standpoints the king and his subjects both treated parliament as an instrument of government for the common profit of the realm, the king requiring parliament to recognise the needs of the realm and subjects using it to present the ills of the realm. Parliament thus became the vehicle of the whole political community, enshrining its conflicts as much as its common assumptions. This was important, for it was not so much the existence of representative institutions as the work which they were made to do which distinguished English and continental practice.

We can best begin by examining how the English Crown obtained taxation, for there the parallels and contrasts with France are most striking. Gaines Post and Ernst Kantorowicz have shown how, during the thirteenth and fourteenth centuries, civil and canon lawyers popularised the legal principle of state authority (Kantorowicz 1957; Post 1964). For obvious reasons the power to tax attracted immediate and widespread attention from rulers. The Romano-canonical doctrine of 'necessity' stated that, for a necessity of the realm which

---

[1] This paper was read at a conference of England and French historians at Bristol in 1973 and draws on the arguments in my book (Harriss 1975).

touched the common safety and good of the kingdom, the realm could legitimately demand taxation from its subjects which they were obliged to give. The doctrine comprised safeguards for the subject as well as obligations. The 'necessity' had to be one which touched the welfare of the realm, and not merely its ruler; hence it could not be proclaimed by the king alone without some kind of adjudication or acceptance of it rendered by subjects on behalf of the realm. Since the tax was asked for a specific purpose the obligation was limited to the achievement of that purpose. Finally, since free subjects were thereby deprived of their goods, they had to give their free assent. This was, therefore, a doctrine of political obligation. It postulated a political society of free men, who agreed that the preservation of the state was to their common profit and acknowledged a fundamental and inescapable obligation to contribute their wealth for this purpose. The inspiration for this doctrine came partly from Aristotle, partly from Roman law, while it could be grafted on to the customary feudal obligation to render aid to a lord in his time of need. But what made it such a formidable weapon in the hands of monarchs was the beginning of national wars and the efficiency of administrative methods which permitted them to control and exploit the resources of their kingdoms.

Even during the light and occasional warfare of Henry III's reign, the doctrine of 'necessity' was used to justify the demand for national taxation, but both in England and France it was in the last decade of the century that the obligation on all subjects to contribute to a war waged for their common defence was firmly stated (Harriss 1975:27–74; Rothwell 1945:18ff; Strayer 1948:289–96; Bisson 1966:75–102). In France the almost annual levy of taxes for the defence of the realm, without consent, produced a reaction after 1300 to safeguard local rights against the doctrines of the royal lawyers. The successors of Philip IV were never able to press the case of 'necessity' with such authority: at most they could hope to win general acceptance from a central assembly of the case for taxation, being compelled thereafter to secure actual grants by local negotiations which often involved exemptions, local choice of the tax, and local control over its use. The idea of national danger could only be aroused at moments of exceptional crisis, as in 1346 and 1356. Neither the nobility nor the towns were willing to countenance taxation on a national basis, being too distrustful of each other, and of the military capacity of the king, to submit their particular interests to the demands of common safety. Philippe de Mézières advocated local control of taxation on grounds of both convenience and efficiency (Coopland 1969:392–400). In fact French kings found it more effective to proclaim the *arrière ban* and negotiate taxation as a commutation of traditional military obligation, or to trade their fiscal prerogatives for grants. Not until after the battle of Poitiers did the French crown begin to develop a routine system of tax collection on a national basis. This lack of a legal or institutional basis for national taxation was an undoubted French weakness at the beginning of the Hundred Years War (Strayer 1938:45–6; Henneman 1971).

In England, by contrast, the forty years between 1297 and 1337 saw fourteen lay subsidies granted by fully representative assemblies, eleven of which fell in the thirty years after Edward I's death. Taxation was thus frequent enough to be a normal act of government, but it was not sufficiently persistent or continuous to threaten its occasional, emergency character. Only from 1294 to 1296 and in 1315–16 was it levied in consecutive years. Moreover during this period every tax with one exception was for the war against Scotland. Each grant was made for a particular emergency, presented as a threat to the realm and Church, and often accompanied by graphic propaganda about the murder and devastation wrought by Scottish raids (Nicholson 1965:1–3; Keeney 1947:534–49; Willard 1908:237–42). Correspondingly, during periods of truce on the border from 1322 to 1327 and 1328 to 1332, taxation ceased. Parliament was in this manner accustomed to the notion of an obligatory tax for a defensive war which constituted a 'necessity' of the whole realm. Already in the *Modus tenendi parliamentum* (1321) its essential character is clearly defined. Aids, the author says, must be asked in full parliament, they must be for actual war, request and response must be in writing, and each estate must give its assent. Thanks in no small measure to the recurrent threat from Scotland, Edward III entered the larger war with France possessed of a firm tradition of parliamentary grants for a defensive war which could be collected as a matter of administrative routine.

In the next twenty-three years he put this to good effect. For thirteen of these England was engaged in open hostilities with either France or Scotland, the remaining ten being short periods of truce. Most of the fighting consisted of aggressive raids on foreign soil. For seventeen of these years the realm was paying direct taxation specifically asked and granted for a necessity of the king and kingdom involving the safety and defence of the realm. As the state of war was prolonged, taxation thus became continuous and apparently permanent. This marked a vast increase in the resources and authority of the Crown and enabled Edward to plan and fight a war over a period and on a scale hitherto unconceived, without the disruption which truces caused to French finances.

In England, therefore, the practice of taxation conformed with great fidelity to Romano-canonical teaching. The 'necessity' became identified with national war and was explained and justified before the realm in parliament; parliament adjudicated and accepted the case of 'necessity' and to meet it granted taxation which the whole realm was obliged to pay. To explain the anomaly that such doctrines were more effective in the land of the common law than under the lawyers of the late Capetian and early Valois kings, we can point to the greater unity of political society and the long tradition of central government and local answerability to it within the smaller, more easily controlled realm. If the English monarchy lacked the peculiar prestige of the French, its executive authority had always been greater.

Although we should not be surprised that notions of state authority found fertile ground in England, this raises problems for our accustomed interpretation of the relations between the Crown and its subjects in parliament. For historians have been unanimous in holding that Edward III's dependence on parliament for war taxation both strengthened the Commons and eroded the royal prerogative. In McKisack's words (1959:221), 'Edward's wooing of the

Commons depended for its success largely on his readiness to concede their demands and abandon most of his extra-parliamentary resources'; and more recently M.H. Keen has concluded that the pattern of the reign was concession. He needed money and soldiers and was prepared in return for them to relax royal control. He was pliant at home in order to permit adventure abroad' (1973:158–9, 163). Implicit in such judgements is the assumption that taxation was a matter of free bargaining in which the Crown's needs placed it at a perpetual disadvantage. But is it true that it was 'within the Commons' power to give or withhold supplies', as A.R. Myers believed (1961:147); or was Stubbs right when he declared that 'as to taxation, parliament found itself able to give but not to withhold' (1887, 2:421)? Our interpretation of the concessions which the Commons secured depend not a little on our answer. For if the Commons were obliged to grant taxation then their main concern must have been to define the limits of their obligation rather than to erode the royal prerogative. Hence one should first ask how far the Commons were able to restrict the king's demands for taxes and control his expenditure of them. How was it that the king could seek taxation in the name of common defence whilst conducting devastating attacks overseas for personal gain? Did the continuance of war threaten the Commons with permanent taxation, and how was taxation justified in time of truce? Until we have defined the rights and obligations of the king and his subjects in respect of taxation it is hardly possible to assess their political relationship or their disputes over prerogative rights. For such a relationship evolved out of their direct confrontation and debate over these matters.

Let us begin with the limitation of taxation to a defensive war. In the canonists' view the plea of 'necessity' could only be invoked in the defence of the realm and for the recovery of just rights, not for an aggressive attack on alien territory. Boniface VIII had condemned Edward I's Flanders campaign in these terms and the doubts he raised found echoes amongst the baronial opposition of 1297 (Rothwell 1945:21). There is no doubt that in 1337 parliament supported the war with France as an ineluctable extension of the threat from Scotland rather than as a prelude to a generation of imperialist conquest and profitable venture (Campbell 1965:184–216; Fryde 1969:250–69). Thereafter French coastal raids and projects for invasion lent credibility to the king's plea that his continental strategy was essentially defensive. Edward's claim to the French throne gave further legality to the war while it enabled him to merge the feudal concept of war as fought for the king's honour and rights into the new one of national survival. He asserted that the rejection of his claim would 'overthrow him and his realm of England', and his pleas that he was fighting 'to recover his rights overseas and defend his realm' found echoes in the patriotic verses of the time (*Rotuli parliamentorum* 2:237, 157).

Although the Commons never questioned their obligation to grant taxation in these terms, theirs was a heavy burden, and as the war was prolonged the threat of perpetual taxation to meet a continuing necessity became a grim prospect. In the canonists' view, 'necessity' should be invoked only to meet a dire and exceptional emergency; yet the war with France had brought a state of emergency from which a final peace offered the only escape. The Commons indeed bemoaned the 'false truces' which deprived them of the decisive battle which would bring conclusive victory; in 1344 they granted the second year of the subsidy on condition that the king went in person 'to make an end to the said business' and in 1354 voiced their eager assent to the peace terms proposed (*Rotuli parliamentorum* 2:147–8, 200, 237, 264). But it was only in the nine years of peace following the Treaty of Brétigny, when the case of 'necessity' could no longer be pleaded, that they were finally released from demands for direct taxation.

Were there any ways in which parliament could challenge or limit the king's demand for taxation while this state of war persisted? In France the monarchy was forced to recognise that the plea of 'necessity' could only be pressed in situations of actual danger: that where a region was not directly threatened by invasion it could not be made to pay, and that when a truce intervened taxation should cease and what had been collected should be repaid (Henneman 1971:30, 117, 130, 155). Such regional opposition to taxation did not occur in England. Taxation was consistently granted and levied on a national basis, though it was not always spent thus. Both king and Commons recognised that the north of England was a theatre of war on its own and from 1337 to 1349 the taxes from north of the River Trent were appropriated to its defence. A closer parallel with regional control of taxation as practised in France was the use of the subsidy of 1359 to pay for local defence forces on a county basis. This was not, in fact, a parliamentary subsidy and stands unique as an experiment in England.

J.B. Henneman has pointed to the very considerable difficulties which the French monarchy suffered from being unable to obtain taxation before the expiry of a truce in order to meet the cost of preparations for war and the permanent charges for defence, as well as from a sudden truce which might deprive it of taxation needed to meet war expenditure already incurred. Edward III dealt with this problem more successfully. To secure taxation in time of truce – in 1344, 1348 and 1352 – he was able to adduce evidence that the enemy planned to resume the war and thus establish that a grant was necessary to forestall this. By this means he secured biennial and triennial subsidies which underpinned his finances, although the Commons sought to limit their obligations by restricting their grants to the purposes for which they were sought. In 1344 they asked that the subsidy be safely stored until it was used for the proposed expeditions; in 1348 that the aid be assigned solely for current war expenses and not for the payment of ancient debts; in 1352 that it should be kept for the war according to the king's intention. By ensuring that the tax was not spent before it was needed the Commons hoped to avoid a renewed demand when the emergency finally came. They also sought to cancel the tax should the emergency cease. In 1346 and 1348 they stipulated that the final year of the tax should not be levied if truce or peace had by then been achieved (*Rotuli parliamentorum* 2:148, 201, 252). None of these conditions which the Commons made was illegitimate for they merely elaborated the purpose for which the tax was asked. Nor, by contrast with French practice, were they very effective. Edward did, in fact, collect the final years of the subsidies granted in 1346 and 1348 despite more than usual opposition in the shires; he was technically within his rights in so doing as in both cases the truce briefly expired before being renewed. Nevertheless the Commons' reiterated limitation of their grants to open war prepared the ground for their later attempts to free themselves from direct taxation in time of truce. In 1356 they managed to break the pattern of continuous triennial subsidies by granting the wool subsidy for six years, thus initiating its development as a recurrent tax for the permanent charges of defence.

Equally, the Commons could exercise no control over the king's use of the subsidies. Before the capture of Calais taxation was wholly consumed by the needs of war; but from September 1347 to early in 1355 although there were only eighteen months of active warfare the king received lay subsidies for practically the whole period. Much of this taxation was spent on repaying the debts of previous campaigns, but from 1352 onwards Edward was able to apply a large proportion of it to his household.

If one safeguard against permanent taxation lay in emphasising the temporary, emergency quality of 'necessity', another was to insist that a common obligation needed common assent. The divergence of French and English traditions was to be most marked in the requirement of assent to taxation. This was the result less of different views of its nature than of the different ways in which taxation was negotiated. In both countries the assent of representatives was rendered not primarily to the grant of taxation but to the 'necessity' which justified and required taxation. Proclaimed as it was by the king and attested by the council, the 'necessity' had also to receive the assent of the realm if the king's free subjects were to be deprived of their goods. The 'full power' with which representatives were invested to render such assent did not give them any right of free or unrestricted refusal if the necessity was urgent and evident; yet at the same time they rendered something more than the legal assent given by suitors and attorneys to the judgement of a court (Post 1964:91–162). It was rather a political assent, the free acknowledgement of an obligation, following consultation and issuing in agreement. In France, as in England, such assent was at first rendered centrally; but whereas in England the agreement between monarch and subjects on a specific tax to meet the necessity was negotiated in parliament, in France such bargaining took place in local assemblies where local interests were paramount and often overrode the needs of the kingdom. The fact that the real negotiation over the terms of taxation took place locally had led by the end of the fourteenth century to the atrophy of the estates general as an assenting body, leaving merely the assent of the council as necessary for authorising an aid (Lewis 1962:4, 9; Henneman 1971:325–7). Writing in 1389 Philippe de Mézières deplored the decline of representative assent in France (Coopland 1969, 2:390) and in the following century Sir John Fortescue treated assent to taxation as the key distinction between mixed and absolute monarchies (Plummer 1885:113). Yet here again the contrast with England should not be overstressed for it was only extremely rarely that the Commons successfully challenged the king's plea of 'necessity' in the later middle ages. Perhaps the most notable occasion was when they resisted the demand for a lay subsidy in 1376. Even so they could adduce 'sufficient cause', not merely on grounds of poverty, but because the tax was demanded in time of truce. Moreover they coupled their refusal with the renewal of the wool subsidy and a promise to aid the king when the need arose (*Rotuli parliamentorum* 2:322).

The distinctive development of parliament in the later middle ages was indeed related to assent to taxation, but it sprang from the responsibility of the Commons as representative of the whole realm to negotiate the terms of the tax. For this purpose they were informed of and involved in royal policy; and as a corollary they became, in some degree, the Crown's agents in the shires. Empowered by their constituents to grant a tax and negotiate its conditions, they had an equal responsibility to the king to ensure that what they granted was collectable. This meant that they had to strike a perpetual balance between the king's needs and the grievances of their communities. For as representative of the whole realm they were empowered not merely to adjudicate its common needs but to attest its common ills.

The Commons' dual responsibility was manifested in 1311, 1344, and 1348 when they sought to appease their constituents by securing letters patent which recited both the king's plea of necessity and the concessions which they had secured by their grant. Only in 1339 did they not dare to meet the king's demands for fear of local opposition, asking to refer back to their constituents and thereby threatening the cornerstone of the edifice of representation, their *plena potestas*. Formal assent in parliament was thus dependent on actual assent in the shires. Except in moments of acute political crisis, when they acted in concert with the Lords, it was this threat of opposition in the shires rather than the ability to refuse the king's legitimate demands which gave the Commons their most effective bargaining counter with the Crown. Even when, as in 1348, they incorporated their grievances and demands for redress as conditions in their grant, these were binding only in so far as the king freely accepted them. The Commons could not dictate conditions as the price of taxation, for while they were bound by obligation to meet the king's demands, the king was only bound to meet theirs by his free grace. Their right of assent required their participation in matters which touched the whole realm; it involved them in political responsibilities and political dialogue; but it did not give them a veto over the legitimate demands of the Crown.

It was thus of prime importance that the Commons' adjudication of and assent to these demands was made in terms of the common profit. Appeal to the common profit had underlain the baronial opposition to Henry III and was made explicit in the Remonstrances addressed to Edward I in 1297. In consequence the principle that taxation should be levied for the common profit as well as by common assent was enshrined in *Confirmatio cartarum* (1297) and this invited a direct association between taxation and the presentation of grievances. For while in demanding taxation, the king interpreted common profit as common peril, the Commons judged the effects of taxation in terms of common welfare. Taxation for the profit of the realm should not impoverish it, for it was the mark of a tyrant to impoverish and enslave his subjects. That was the message of the Remonstrances of 1297, passed on by the Ordainers, and eventually assimilated by the Commons. Thus the fact that taxation was freely given for the common good made it the natural vehicle for criticism of royal government, and the terms of such criticism were frequently similar in France and England (Henneman 1971:254, 258, 284, 321, 324; Coopland 1969, 2:364–6). Complaint was most immediately aroused by the burdens of prerogative levies, which were the inevitable accompaniment of war, and by the exactions of royal officials. The king had a general obligation to heed complaint and to redress illegalities, but there was no inherent connection between these and the grant of taxation. More directly it might be alleged that the tax had not been used to defend the community of the realm, or that it had been used for the profit of individual subjects. Although once the tax was granted to the king it became legally his and he could not be required to render account, such criticism implied that subjects had a legitimate concern with the expenditure of the tax. Debate over these matters helped to establish the character of taxation as public revenue and was profoundly educative for the middling landholders who granted the tax and represented the communities who shouldered its burden.

The general success of English arms in the first phase of the Hundred Years War meant that there was little occasion for criticism over the expenditure of taxation. It is true that in 1297 the barons had questioned the wisdom of Edward I's aggressive expedition in Flanders and that the Ordainers were critical of Edward II's defence of the northern border, but it was the combination of burdensome taxation and military setback in 1340 that brought the most specific attack on the handling of taxation by the king and his ministers. In their petition the Commons did not directly question Edward III's strategy but claimed that the taxes which had so impoverished the community had failed to reach the king, ascribing this to the ministers and merchants who had handled them. They demanded that these should be brought to account and sought to place the expenditure of all future grants under the control of a committee of peers who would in turn be answerable in full parliament. Thus the king would be aided and his people's burdens lessened. Edward, under pressure, conceded all this and more (Harriss 1975:253–69, 518–20). This marked the Commons' first attempt to enforce changes in the structure of royal government by using their authority to grant taxation. Their success owed much to the exceptional political situation in 1340; even so it revealed their impressive grasp of the dialectical and tactical opportunities for criticism in terms of the common profit.

The diversion of taxation for private gain was one reason for hostility to the privileges or the king's merchants in the decade following 1340 (Unwin 1918:179–255; Fryde 1959:1–17). Although this primarily related to the wool trade (which we shall discuss presently) the merchants' contracts with the king frequently embraced the lay subsidies as security for loans and provided opportunities for buying discredited royal bonds on which full payment was secured from the lay subsidy. This brought a protest from the Commons in March 1348, which they coupled with another against the handling of the forced loan of

20,000 sacks of wool. Recalling that divers aids had been granted to and taken by the king from his poor Commons in aid of his war, to be used entirely for his profit, the Commons complained that the king's merchants were handling the levy in wool to their own profit and the king's loss. There was some substance in their allegation, for the king had sacrificed to the merchants a substantial proportion of the profit theoretically accruing from the sale of wool to secure an immediate if much smaller advance. As in 1340 the Commons demanded a commission of enquiry (on which they were to be represented) to ensure 'that the goods of his subjects should reasonably and fully come to the king's profit'. But Edward, now in a much stronger position than eight years before, repudiated any obligation to answer for his employment of the tax (*Rotuli parliamentorum* 2:170, 200–1; *Calendar of patent rolls, 1348–50*:104).

The same grasp of the public nature of taxation – that what was levied from the goods of subjects for their common safety should be used for their common profit – informed the Commons' efforts to establish their right of assent to the wool subsidy, the *maltolt*. The view of B. Wilkinson, broadly shared by E. Power, was that the Commons' primary object was to abolish the *maltolt*; that they went on demanding this up till 1348 and that it was only between then and 1350 that they came to accept it as inescapable and (in Wilkinson's words, 1937:72–6) 'fearfully and reluctantly offered in future to vote the tax themselves'. If recognition of the king's needs was one reason for this, recognition of the true incidence of the tax was another. In their petitions of 1343, 1348 and 1351 the Commons complained that the merchants passed on the tax to the growers, to whom they paid correspondingly lower prices for the wool. As they came to understand that it was not the merchants but the community who paid the tax, so they came to demand that they, who represented the community, should grant it. By then, too, the internal dissensions of the estate of merchants and the consequent support given by the lesser merchants to parliament had strengthened the demands of the Commons. Eventually the king was brought to accept these as the greater merchants proved broken straws in supplying his needs. Thus Eileen Power (1941:74–5, 82) was led to the conclusion that 'if the Commons fought the issue on abolition and not consent it was because they were more interested in the economic consequences of taxation than in constitutional theory', a judgement that certainly reflected her own interests. But there are grounds for thinking that the Commons were neither ignorant of nor indifferent to the principles of public taxation.

What, to begin with, was the nature of the *maltolt*? If it was an imposition, levied at the will of the king, then parliament had good reason to seek its abolition and, failing that, to try to make it legal by consent. But if the *maltolt* was an aid for a necessity of the realm, as was the lay subsidy, then it was by definition obligatory, impermanent, and dependent on assent. It is not difficult to show that from its inception in 1294 up till the grant of 20 shillings the sack in September 1336 the *maltolt* conformed to all these requirements. It was granted by merchant assemblies for limited periods to meet an acknowledged necessity of the realm, and was paralleled by grants of lay subsidies by parliament. The merchants were expected to endorse or adjudicate the necessity and assent to a tax on mercantile wealth as the Commons did on lay and the clergy on clerical wealth. It is not surprising therefore that in 1340, 1343, 1348, 1351, 1353 and 1356 assent was received for the levy of the *maltolt* for a limited period and for a necessity of the realm. What is remarkable is that on all these occasions it was the Commons who authorised it, coupling this with a firm rejection of the claims of either the merchants or the great council to give assent. It is certainly not true that the Commons were only won over to assent after 1348. It is true that they continued to demand the abolition, or rather cessation, of the tax in 1340, 1343, 1346, 1348 and 1351, but these demands related to the grants made by other bodies and were frequently accompanied by offers from the Commons to grant it themselves.

What made the Commons so dissatisfied with the earlier tradition of assent by the merchants, and on what grounds did they claim an exclusive right of assent for themselves? The grant of 20 shillings in September 1336 had all the characteristics of its predecessors, but by May 1338 this had been raised to 40 shillings as part of the king's agreement with the Contract Merchants whose monopoly of export would enable them to recover their loans to the Crown from the additional subsidy more speedily. The tax was to continue until these loans were repaid and it was still being taken when parliament met in October 1339 and demanded its cessation. That parliament, as we have noted, saw a bitter outburst against the king's merchants who were widely suspected of embezzling and mishandling the taxes. Their privileged position rested, of course, upon the prerogative preemption and export of wool under monopoly, which was designed to benefit both merchants and king (Fryde 1952:8–24). As originally conceived, the Contract scheme had extended the monopoly widely, it had the assent of the merchants, and it aimed to provide the growers with acceptable minimum prices. There was some attempt to go back to these conditions in 1342, but the general tendency of such schemes in 1338–40 and in the next decade was towards a narrow monopoly which excluded the lesser merchants from the trade, which probably enabled the king's merchants to depress prices paid to the growers, and which, even if it did not ruin these two classes by the disruption of the market, effectively excluded them from the large profits which the king's merchants were – in intention at least – enabled to secure.

These economic effects of the monopoly schemes are well established and in so far as the wool growers and lesser merchants were represented in parliament undoubtedly explain the bitter hostility of parliament to the king's merchants for the next twenty years. But the Commons' protests over the *maltolt* rested on a broader basis than outraged sectional interests, for as negotiated with the merchants in 1337 and 1342 and sanctioned by the council in 1346 and 1347, the *maltolt* lost its public character as an aid and formed part of an economic bargain for the mutual profit of the parties. Although one of those parties was the king acting in the public interest, the other represented the particular or 'singular' interests of individual merchants. Moreover, since the purpose of this agreement was the profitable exploitation of the wool trade, there was no reason why it should be confined to financing a war or why it should not continue to operate as long as it proved profitable. As granted by the merchants after 1336, the *maltolt* thus violated all the principles of the aid: it was for 'singular' not common profit, it was not restricted to an emergency, and the assent rendered to it was no longer part of the common assent of the realm. After 1340, in the Commons' view, common assent meant assent by parliament. This they reiterated persistently, until in 1351, after the bankruptcy of the farmers of the customs, it was secured along with safeguards for free trade.

The Commons then asked that 'such singular grants of the *maltolt*' by the merchants should be void, remarking in the same breath 'in case it pleased the king in this his great necessity to have the 40 shillings subsidy for a half year or a year, let him show his wishes to the Lords and Commons'. Thereupon 'for great necessity . . . by common assent' they granted the subsidy for two years (*Rotuli parliamentorum* 2:229). Five years later, in 1356, by granting the *maltolt* for an unprecedented period of six years they were able to interrupt the Crown's continuous demand for lay subsidies and initiate the long history of the wool subsidy as a renewable tax for the safeguard of commerce and the recurrent charges of defence. Direct taxation could be increasingly restricted to periods of open conflict or particular expeditions. Thus by 1360 the character of direct and indirect taxation had been established for the following centuries with momentous consequences for English political development. The demands of war had forced Crown and subjects to define their rights and obligations in the context of common safety and common profit.

The twin criteria for public taxation – that it should be levied by common assent and for the common profit – likewise served the Commons in their struggle against taxation by extensions of the Crown's prerogative rights. The most burdensome were the levy of war supplies through purveyance and the demand for unaccustomed military service.[2] The first had become a major grievance in 1296–7 when in the fourteen months preceding July 1297 three great prises covering many counties had been ordered to provision the royal army. These did not differ in nature from the ancient prises for the king's household, but they did differ in degree. On what basis could they be opposed? The baronial Remonstrances gave the lead by asserting that such tallages and prises had reduced the people to poverty so that they could not aid the king: such levies were by definition contrary to the common profit. *Confirmatio cartarum* identified such national prises as war taxes, acknowledging that they had no basis in custom and requiring them to be levied for the common profit and by common assent. It thus encouraged subjects to expect that taxation should be used to pay for supplies taken for war. Payment was at the heart of the issue, for if the subject received satisfaction for his goods he was not being taxed. In the years immediately following 1297 prises for the Scottish war do seem to have been authorised

---

[2]   The effects of these on the peasantry during this period have recently been explored by J.R. Maddicott (1979).

by assent, centrally in the council and locally in the shires, and payment for them provided from the taxes granted for it.

With the opening of the French war large-scale prises were again needed, particularly in 1337–40 and for the siege of Calais in 1346–7. Much of the protest in parliament centred on the illegal actions of royal purveyors as defined by existing legislation. It elicited promises of redress and stricter control of officials from the king, and eventually issued in the elaborate code governing purveyances in the great statute of 1362. Alongside this the Commons castigated purveyances which were not paid for as a form of taxation without common assent. In 1339 they asked that purveyors who had taken goods without payment and had assessed and levied sums of money from communities in respect of victuals should have their commissions repealed 'so that no free man be assessed or taxed without common assent of parliament' (Richardson and Sayles 1935:269).[3] In the parliaments of 1346 and 1348 they went further and asked that commissions to take prises should be issued only by assent of parliament, and in 1351 when purveyors had been scouring the country for corn to supply the garrison at Calais they protested that 'no such charges or prises be made without the assent of parliament' (*Rotuli parliamentorum* 2:227). Though in no doubt about the extent of the abuses or the unpopularity of these levies, Edward never conceded the right of parliament to authorise them. But by 1350 he was ready to welcome a means of removing a contentious issue from the political arena. In the second half of the century widespread purveyance by sheriffs to supply royal armies declined as the practice of contracting for supplies from merchants, perhaps first applied at Calais, became more widespread (Burley 1958:49–57). It was from London merchants whose patents specifically permitted them to make profit from such transactions that the Black Prince's army for Gascony and the royal army of 1360 was supplied.

Complaint against unaccustomed military service was roughly coterminous with that against purveyances, was pressed in the same terms, and produced similar claims (Powick 1962). For his campaigns in Flanders and Scotland Edward had begun to extend the obligation to military service. At the lower end of the social scale he invoked the Statute of Winchester to array men for long periods of service on or beyond the borders of the realm as part of the royal army. These demands were made more acceptable by the offer of pay, usually from the point of leaving the county boundary. But service on the Scottish border remained unpopular and the high rate of desertion and heavy cost had led Edward I to abandon large scale levies by the end of his reign. To continue the war Edward II had to resort to compulsory unpaid service on the plea of necessity or secure quotas of soldiers from the shires and towns by some form of assent locally or in parliament. This provoked the Commons' first attempt to define military obligation at the beginning of Edward III's reign. In answer to

---

3 E.B. Fryde (1969:259) assigns this petition to 1337 but I have preferred the dating by Richardson and Sayles.

their petition the king asserted his right to compulsory service on the borders of
the realm, leaving unspecified whether this should be at his wages, but dis-
claimed any right to compulsory service overseas (*Rotuli parliamentorum* 2:8,
11; *Statutes of the realm* 1:255–7; Prince 1940:360–2). By virtue of his prerogative and on the plea of necessity, the king could usually command service when
he paid wages; it was when support costs were borne by local communities or
charged on a national scale that the demand for common assent in parliament to
such levies became vocal. In France local communities often preferred to grant
soldiers rather than money, as giving them greater control over local defence.
The readier acceptance in England of the obligation for national defence, and
the established tradition of parliamentary taxation for this, effectively prevented
such a development. On the eve of the French war attempts to secure quotas of
troops from cities and boroughs in 1335–6 were commuted to money grants
when parliament met. Parliament's only initiative in organising military defence
on its own authority occurred in 1340 when, during Edward's absence abroad, it
drew up an extensive scheme of military service for the defence of northern
England, levying quotas of troops from each county and providing payment
from the lay subsidy reserved for northern defence.

This experience must have emboldened the Commons to protest against the
large scale arrays of men at arms, hobelars, and archers for the expeditions of
1344 and 1346–8. Yet the Commons' reiterated demands that commissions
which were in any manner a charge on the community should not be issued
without assent of parliament were not aimed at securing parliamentary control
of arrays but were a means of denoting their illegality as a form of taxation. The
statute of 1344 produced a further definition of the limits of obligation. It provided that for service overseas wages should be paid by the king from leaving
the county boundary, while for service on the borders there was by now a well
established tradition that wages were paid from the point of muster (*Statutes of
the realm* 1:300–1). By 1360 therefore the king exercised his prerogative to
require communal military service for defence of the realm free from any form
of parliamentary assent; as a corollary he respected the inviolability of his subjects' property in laying no charge on the community beyond that defined in
statute.

The other attempt to enlarge the scope of military obligation centred on the
class of non-feudal middling landowners. In the years 1295–7 Edward I made
determined efforts to enlist the service of those holding £20–£40 annual value
of land on the basis of their common fealty and allegiance. For the Flanders
expedition of 1294 the writs emphasised that service was to be in the king's
presence and was for the safety and welfare of the realm, but no wages were
promised and a heavy financial burden was thus imposed on the plea of 'necessity'. So strong were the protests in 1297 that Edward I never repeated his
demand, and even the sole attempt in his son's reign to require service at their
own expense from all holding fifty librates of land, in August 1318, met determined opposition although it had been endorsed by the magnates. Not until
1334–5 was there a further attempt to compel service from those with lands and

rents up to £40 per annum. None of these incidents had produced a definition of the subject's obligation. As a means of raising troops for an unpopular campaign and one which could clearly be represented as in defence of the realm, the enforcement of service on this section of the landholding class still had some value, but for the French war contract proved more reliable and more popular.

When late in 1344 Edward revived the idea of an assessment for military service proportionate to landed income on a scale between 100 shillings and £1,000, it was as a form of taxation. In the summer of 1346, individuals and towns were induced to commute their assessed obligation for fines. In reply to the Commons' protests in the parliament of September 1346 the king justified the levy by the general assent given by the Commons to the war and their promise to support his quarrel with their goods and bodies, and by the specific assent of the Lords on account of the great necessity of providing for the defence of the realm. This answer revealed the essential flaw in the king's case. He had acknowledged that the levy was a form of taxation which needed assent of some kind, but by analogy with taxation this could not be derived from the initial assent to the war; it had to relate to this particular levy. When the Commons returned to the charge in 1348 they stipulated in making their grant that no form of taxation (*imposition, taillage, ne charge d'apprest*) should be levied by the *Prive Conseil* without their grant and assent in parliament (*Rotuli parliamentorum* 2:160, 166, 170, 201). Four years later, when the urgent military demands of 1345–7 had passed and the social repercussions of the plague were beginning to draw king and gentry together, Edward accepted without dissent a petition that no man should be compelled to find soldiers unless by assent and grant in parliament (*Rotuli parliamentorum* 2:239; *Statutes of the realm* 1:321). National prises and novel forms of military service thus evoked a similar response. Both were extensions of customary royal right justified as necessary to meet the demands of national war; both were opposed by the Commons as a charge or burden on the subject which deprived him of his property and could impoverish him. In both cases the Commons defined their illegality by reference to the principle that burdens imposed on them for the common profit needed common assent of parliament which alone represented the realm. In general the king refused to accede to the principle of parliamentary authorisation of either prises or arrays, preferring – as did parliament – to resolve the dispute in terms of guarantees of payment. Eventually such issues ceased to be contentious as the Crown came to prefer contract to compulsion in both cases.

Edward III exploited the Crown's rights as a means of taxation in two other spheres. Firstly he used judicial enquiries as fiscal levies. At the beginning of the French war in October 1337 Edward had authorised enquiries into the liabilities of communities for the escapes of felons and their chattels, with the avowed purpose of raising fines for his expedition, and on his return in December 1340 he launched the notorious trailbaston commissions which provoked widespread condemnation in the parliament of April 1341 (Hughes 1915:167–8). Since the legality of both of these was unchallengeable, their withdrawal had either to be purchased by the grant of taxation (as in 1340) or secured by concerted political action (as in 1341). But the king did not surrender his right to the trailbaston which was again vigorously pressed by Chief Justice Shareshull between 1344 and 1348 and again intermittently from 1351 to 1358. The Commons' complaints in the parliaments of 1344, 1348 and 1354 listed them among their burdens: they were 'to the destruction of the people and little for the keeping of law and the peace' (*Rotuli parliamentorum* 2:148; Putnam 1950:64–8, 72–3, 209–11). Although the Commons made some attempts to ensure that the commissions were submitted to parliament before they were issued, they chiefly resorted to buying their remission by grants of taxation, even making this one of the conditions of their grants in 1348. This had the defect of being an inherently recurrent remedy. In 1357 – only a year after they had broken the sequence of lay subsidies by granting the *maltolt* – they were induced to grant a whole subsidy to secure release from amercements under future eyres and the remission of fines due from felons' escapes and chattels. In the following decades they were repeatedly induced to repurchase such release. Yet the king's willingness to commute judicial penalties for parliamentary grants also signified the Crown's reluctance to penalise the knights who were emerging as allies in the judicial government of the shires, enforcing labour laws and keeping the peace.

Edward also exploited his prerogative right to feudal aid. The Commons had purchased release from this among other burdens with the grant of the ninth in 1340, but in 1346 the king knighted his eldest son on landing at La Hougue and at the end of the September parliament the Lords authorised the collection of an aid of 40 shillings from each knight's fee to be levied not only on tenants-in-chief but on mesne lords and demesne tenants. There was opposition to its collection, and in the parliament of March 1348 the Commons alleged that the levy was contrary to the release given in 1340 and that its rate and incidence were contrary to the Statute of Westminster I. Edward seems to have interpreted the concession of 1340 as a remission of his rights solely on that occasion and not as a renunciation of his prerogative. Although the Statute of Westminster had fixed the aid at 20 shillings on each fee, in 1290 the magnates on behalf of the realm had sanctioned it at 40 shillings and had done likewise in 1306 when the aid was commuted for a tax. There is no doubt that in 1346 they were consciously following these precedents and supported the king in holding that he was entitled to the aid and that their assent was sufficient to increase its rate. Yet the Commons clearly felt that its incidence was sufficiently broad to require their assent, while they may also have been aggrieved at the lack of opportunity in the September 1346 parliament to negotiate or protest about it, the aid having been authorised by the Lords after the Commons had voted their subsidy and perhaps after they had gone home. Despite the substantial objections which the Commons could raise, most of the aid had been collected by the time parliament met again in March 1348 and it was not until 1352 that, in response to a petition, the king agreed to observe the statutory limitations with the implication that any demand beyond these would require their assent (*Rotuli parliamentorum* 2:201, 240).

Any assessment of the effects of these political conflicts must start from the realisation that war enormously enlarged the fiscal resources of the English

Crown, strengthened its authority through the introduction of regular taxation, forced it to develop new techniques of persuasion and administration, and thus extended the political basis of its support. With its emphasis on common need and common profit war also brought to fruition a traditional sense of geographical unity and common identity to form the concept of the realm as a community, and this received institutional expression in the Crown in parliament. Parliament became the instrument through which the Crown governed for the common profit.

Taxation did much to focus and bring these developments to fruition. For while 'necessity of state' brought a new dimension to the authority of the medieval monarchy, making the Crown the symbol of the political identity of the nation and the guarantor of its safety, in England the case of necessity was habitually submitted to and accepted by parliament. It was never left to the sole discretion of the monarch. The Crown became dependent on parliament for taxation, but this was because of the dependability of parliament when called on to meet the Crown's legitimate demands. Because the Crown was assured of receiving taxation for a necessity of the realm by grant of parliament it did not, as in France, seek to obtain taxation by other means. Thus Philippe de Commynes could later remark on the strength which this brought to the English Crown, for although taxation was restricted to war, for expeditions against the enemies of the realm parliament granted money very willingly and liberally (Calmette 1925:8; Jones 1972:225).

Parliamentary assent was no real barrier to continuous taxation in time of war, but it did force the Crown into a dialogue with its subjects over their respective political obligations. Although broadly they shared a common purpose and outlook, their interests were at times inevitably in conflict. In their differences over taxation the room for manoeuvre was limited and the rules largely favoured the Crown. The case of 'necessity', if proved, imposed an inescapable obligation; in the business of parliament, taxation preceded the Commons' complaints, remedy for which was at the king's grace, while the prerogative rights could not be challenged; the tax once granted became the king's property for which he could not be called to account. Against such bastions of royal authority frontal assault by the Commons was pointless, nor could they conduct a war of attrition by withholding supplies. They could defend their interests only by establishing the legal limits of their obligations. They might parry the king's demands by distinguishing between open war and truce, emphasise the restriction of the grant to the purpose to which it had been demanded, define illegalities by the need for consent, petition and negotiate for redress of grievances, purchase release from burdens. In substance they had achieved little by 1350. By 1360 their gains were greater: some cessation of continued taxation in time of truce; the recognition of parliamentary assent to the *maltolt*; strict statutory control of purveyors and a decline in war purveyances; statutory payment for arrays and the proscription of assessments of the wealthy to military service; the beginning of a tradition of purchasing exemption from the penalties of the eyre, and a right of assent of extensions of feudal aids. Even so these were essentially defensive achievements. The Commons had not eroded any of the Crown's prerogative rights nor had they been able to resist or limit its legitimate financial demands as had their contemporaries in France.

The very rigours of the Commons' predicament proved fruitful in educating them in the language and practice of politics, and thus preparing their incorporation into the political community. In their debates with the Crown they were forced to evolve parliamentary techniques, to achieve a degree of political maturity, and to develop a corporate political identity. Moreover because parliament adjudicated the common profit of the realm not merely in terms of the common peril which it was obliged to meet, but of the common welfare of subjects which the king was obliged to promote, the dialogue over taxation gradually extended to a critical concern with many other aspects of government. The power of the Commons to grant taxation from their communities for the needs of the realm came to be paralleled by their duty to present the ills of their constituents and of the realm at large. The Crown became the symbol of the realm but parliament became the most authentic voice for its common concerns.

But to fully understand the political development of the Commons in this period we must remove our gaze from the parliamentary scene and briefly take note of three external forces which contributed to this. First there is what we may conveniently call the Lancastrian critique of royal government, particularly during the period from the Remonstrances to the Ordinances. However opportunist the purposes of the magnates were, their appeal to the burdens and grievances of the realm to attest royal misrule and justify the imposition of baronial restraints on royal power was a powerful stimulus to the political awareness of the Commons. They were made partners and heirs of the tradition of constitutional opposition to the Crown in its more radical manifestation. The effect was visible in the Commons' petitions of 1340 where the programme of the Ordinances provided them with their own remedies for royal abuses. But we should also not forget that it was because Edward III succeeded in dissolving this tradition of baronial appeal to popular grievance that the Commons were themselves encouraged to emerge as its political representatives.

Secondly we must take account of the relations of the parliamentary classes with both the king and the magnates in war itself. As companions in arms, respected for their proved abilities to lead and fight in the contract companies, the shire gentry were more readily embraced by their political and social superiors in the work of parliament.

Although during the half century after 1297 both these factors were slowly modifying the relations between the traditional leaders of society and the shire gentry, in the sphere of parliament they were largely held in check by the demands of war. Feudal war was aristocratic in purpose and outlook, and even while it was acquiring a national dimension king and Lords were intent on exploiting the Commons for their military ambitions. The Commons in turn still saw parliament as the instrument of the Crown and magnates, in which their role was to protect the community of the shire, including the poor, from misgovernment and impoverishment by royal officials. But from the middle of the fourteenth century the relationship between the Crown and the parliamentary Commons subtly changed. The 1350s saw a marked lessening of the Crown's demands, a greater readiness to concede legal safeguards against abuses and to acknowledge the need for parliamentary assent. This was due partly to the victories of 1346–7, partly to the declining involvement of Edward himself in the war. More immediately it reflected the third of these external factors, the change wrought in society by the Black Death.

The sudden opportunity given to the poorer classes to secure higher wages and personal and tenurial freedom rallied all ranks of landlords to a policy of legislative suppression. Almost overnight the Commons became the allies of the Crown and the Lords and their necessary agents for the enforcement of this policy in the shires. Recruited into the political government of the shires, and increasingly identified with the aims and assumptions of royal government, they began to adopt the proprietary attitude to parliament of the king and the Lords, to see themselves as rulers as well as ruled. Correspondingly, from being protectors of the shire poor against royal demands they became exponents of forms of taxation which would tap the new found prosperity of the lower classes. The first signs of this change of emphasis were the rebate of taxation from the fines under the Statute of Labourers and the concession of fines from felons and fugitives in 1357 'on account of the various adversities which the king knows the middling men of the realm to have long undergone' (Putnam 1908:98–149; 149; *Calendar of fine rolls* 1356–88:44). It bore fruit, as E.B. Fryde has pointed out, in the revolt of 1381 (1970:77–9).

In all these ways the parliamentary Commons and the classes from which they were drawn were becoming part of the 'establishment' within the shires and within the nation as a whole. By the second half of the fourteenth century there had formed a political society whose community of interest and common assumptions were to ensure the stability of English political life until the seventeenth century. Parliament, which served to ritualise the conflicts and attest the unity of this society, had acquired its character and role under the pressure of national war and the consequent disputes over financial obligation.

Literature

Bisson, T.N. 1966. 'Negotiations for taxes under Alphonse of Poitiers'. XII *Congrès internationale des sciences historiques. Études presentées à la Commission Internationale pour l'Histoire des Assemblées d'États*: 75–102. Paris and Louvain.

Burley, S.J. 1958. 'The victualling of Calais, 1347–65'. *Bulletin of the Institute of Historical Research* 31: 49–57.

Calendar of fine rolls, 1356–68. 1922. London.

Calendar of patent rolls, 1348–50. 1905. London.

Calmette, J. (ed.) 1925. 'Philippe de Commynes, Mémoires', 2. Les classiques de l'histoire de France au moyen âge. Paris.

Campbell, J. 1965. 'England, Scotland and the Hundred Years War'. In *Europe in the later middle ages*. J.R. Hale, J.R.L. Highfield, and B. Smalley (eds.), 184–216. London. [And above, pp. 205–230.]

Coopland, G.W. (ed.) 1969. *Philippe de Mézières. Le Songe du vieil pèlerin*, 2. Cambridge.

Dunbabin, J. 1965. 'Aristotle in the schools'. In *Trends in medieval political thought*. B. Smalley (ed.), 65–85. Oxford.

Fryde, E.B. 1952. 'Edward III's wool monopoly of 1337'. *History* 37: 8–24.

Fryde, E.B. 1959. 'The English farmers of the customs, 1343–51'. *Transactions of the Royal Historical Society*, 5th series 9: 1–17.

Fryde, E.B. 1969. 'Parliament and the French war, 1336–40'. In *Essays in medieval history presented to Bertie Wilkinson*. T.A. Sandquist and M.R. Powicke (eds), 250–69. Toronto.

Fryde, E.B. 1970. 'The English Parliament and the peasants' revolt of 1381'. In *Liber memorialis Georges de Lagarde*, 73–88. Paris and Louvain.

Harriss, G.L. 1975. *King, parliament and public finance in medieval England*. Oxford.

Henneman, J.B. 1971. *Royal taxation in fourteenth-century France*. Princeton.

Hughes, D. 1915. *The early years of Edward III*. London.

Jones, M. (trans.) 1972. *Philippe de Commynes, Memoirs*. London.

Kantorowicz, E.H. 1957. *The king's two bodies*. Princeton.

Keen, M.H. 1965. 'The political thought of the fourteenth century civilians'. In *Trends in medieval political thought*. B. Smalley (ed.), 105–26. Oxford.

Keen, M.H. 1973. *England in the latter middle ages*. London.

Keeney, B.C. 1947. 'Military service and the developement of nationalism in England, 1272–1327'. *Speculum* 22: 534–49.

Lewis, P.S. 1962. 'The failure of the French medieval Estates'. *Past and present* 23: 3–24.

Lewis, P.S. 1968. *Later medieval France*. London.

McKisack, M. 1959. *The fourteenth century*. Oxford.

Maddicott, J.R. 1975. 'The English peasantry and the demands of the Crown, 1294–1341'. *Past and present*, supplement 1.

Myers, A.R. 1961. 'The English parliament and the French Estates General in the middle ages'. In *Album Helen Maud Cam. Études presentées à la Commission Internationale pour l'Histoire des Assemblées d'États*, 23: 139–54. Paris and Louvain.

Nicholson, R. 1965. *Edward III and the Scots*. Oxford.

Plummer, C. (ed.) 1885. *Sir John Fortescue, The governance of England*. Oxford.

Post, G. 1964. *Studies in medieval legal thought*. Princeton.

Power, E. 1941. *The medieval English wool trade*. Oxford.

Powicke, M.R. 1962. *Military obligation in medieval England*. Oxford.

Prestwich, M.C. 1972. *War, politics and finance under Edward I*. London.

Prince, A.E. 1940. 'The army and navy'. In *English government at work,*

1327–36, 1. W.A. Morris and J.F. Willard (eds.), 332–93. Cambridge, Massachusetts.

Putnam, B.H. 1908. *The enforcement of labourers*. New York.

Richardson, H.G., G.O. Sayles (eds.) 1935. 'Rotuli parliamentorum hacentus inediti'. *Camden Society*. 3rd Series. 51.

Rothwell, H. 1945. 'The confirmation of the charters, 1297'. *English Historical review* 60: 16–35, 177–91.

Roututi parliamentorum, 2. 1767. Ed. J. Strachey and others. London.

Statutes of the Realm, 1. 1810. London.

Strayer, J.R. 1948. 'Defence of the realm and royal power in France'. In *Studi in onore di Gino Luzzato* 1:289–96. Milan.

Stubbs, W. 1887. *Constitutional history of England*, 2. Oxford.

Thomson, W.S. (ed.) 1944. 'Lincolnshire assize roll for 1298'. *Lincoln Record Society* 36. Lincoln.

Unwin, G. 1918. *Finance and trade under Edward III*. Manchester.

Wilkinson, B. 1937. *Studies in constitutional history of the thirteenth and fourteenth centuries*. Manchester.

Willard, J.F. 1908. 'The Scotch raids and the fourteenth-century taxation of northern England'. *University of Colorado studies* 5: 237–42.

8

WAR AND FOURTEENTH-CENTURY FRANCE*

Michael C. Jones

The effects of the Hundred Years War on France in the fourteenth century can be discerned in almost every sphere besides the strictly military: political and institutional, economic and social, religious and intellectual. Attention can only be directed here to a few aspects of an enormous subject. It was one which already fascinated contemporary writers, for example, Froissart or Jean de Venette in their contrasting appreciations of the martial events which fill their chronicles. In more recent times the war has engaged the energies of several generations of outstanding historians and resulted in a formidable literature. Among recent additions one need only mention Jonathan Sumption's splendid narrative account, 250,000 words of text for the war's first decade, or there is Philippe Contamine's yet more massive study of the composition of French royal armies, which may be conservatively estimated at some half a million words.[1] Even when in the late twentieth century it is often the indirect consequences of warfare that come under scrutiny because of a primary concern with broader institutional, economic and social matters rather than with military affairs *tout court*, the *histoire événementielle* of the war continues to grow almost exponentially as investigation of previously untapped archival sources reveals, for instance, the movements of soldiers, the response of rulers and administrators to perceived danger and the impact of war on combatant and non-combatant alike. In particular, local or regional contexts have been illuminated by a series of major monographs.

Here a pattern set with exemplary clarity by Robert Boutruche's study of the Bordelais, first published in 1947, has been followed with further notable success for other provinces like the Ile-de-France, Normandy, Auvergne and

---

* This chapter is offered as a brief and partial synthesis, deliberately based on a limited number of modern, chiefly detailed French studies; its only claim to originality is in presenting some results of this work to a more general English readership and in providing a guide to other important recent literature.

1 J. Sumption, *The Hundred Years War, i. Trial by Battle* (London, 1990); P. Contamine, *Guerre, état et société à la fin du moyen âge. Etudes sur les armées des rois de France, 1337–1494* (Paris, 1972).

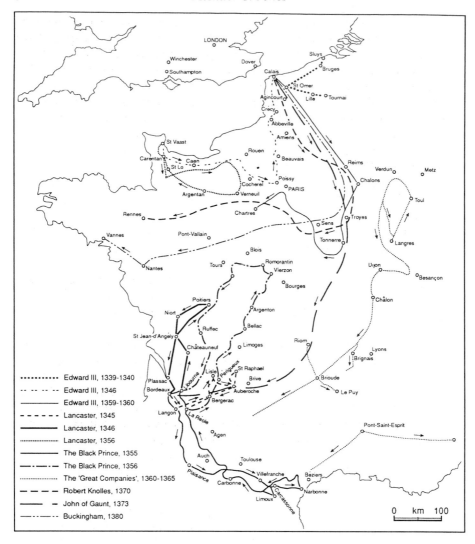

Fig. 1. The main campaigns in France, 1339–1381 (after Fowler, 1969)

Anjou,[2] or by taking a particular town as the main focus and putting local military events in a broader context. Among outstanding studies in which the effects of war on urban society are clearly seen are those of Toulouse, Tours, Périgueux,

[2] R. Boutruche, *La crise d'une société. Seigneurs et paysans du Bordelais pendant la Guerre de Cent Ans* (Strasbourg, 1947; revised edition, Paris, 1963); G. Fourquin, *Les campagnes de la rigion parisienne à la fin du moyen âge* (Paris, 1964); G. Bois, *La crise du feodalisme* (Paris, 1976) [*The Crisis of Feudalism. Economy and society in Eastern Normandy, c. 1300–1550*, trans. Jean Birrell (Cambridge, 1984)]; P. Charbonnier, *Une autre France. La seigneurie rurale en Basse Auvergne du XIVe au XVIe siècle*, 2 vols (Clermont-

Poitiers, Reims and St-Flour, to mention but a selection.[3] The result is that both the diversity of experience and more general patterns within France at large during this 'temps d'épreuves' can be fully appreciated. Whilst there are clearly still problems in disengaging the exact contribution of warfare, as opposed to that of the two other major scourges of the period, disease and famine, in the overall pattern of demographic decline and social and economic dislocation that characterizes the fourteenth century, war's importance in that triad, sometimes questioned on the grounds that medieval armies were usually modest, devastation localized and hostilities intermittent, is assuredly undeniable. Here I simply want to evoke some thing of the atmosphere war created in this period, its particular characteristics and some responses to it. The wider political and institutional effects – the fragmentation of Capetian France with emerging principalities and appanages challenging the crown, and the creation of the administrative and taxation system that later served the monarchy during the Ancien Régime – must largely be neglected.[4]

We may start with some maps and then by quoting one of the most poignant contemporary descriptions of how warfare impinged on ordinary people as a commentary upon these. Fig. 1 shows the principal English campaigns in France fought between 1339–81, the brief apogée of the classic *chevauchée*. Many remarks could be made, including two obvious ones. First, the route taken by most English invasions of France, by entering or exiting via Calais and its Pale, inevitably meant that north-eastern France – Artois, Picardy, Champagne, the Ile-de-France – suffered directly on numerous occasions. We might expect to find evidence from these regions for some of the worst destructive and long-lasting effects of late medieval warfare. The other area of France which *prima facie* may have suffered to a comparable degree is in the south-west. Here during the lieutenancies of Henry of Lancaster and Edward, Prince of Wales, regions under French control facing Guyenne were the scene of much serious fighting,

Ferrand, 1980); M. Le Mené, *Les campagnes angevines à la fin du moyen âge (vers 1350–vers 1530)* (Nantes, 1982). *L'Histoire médiévale en France, Bilan et perspectives*, ed. Michel Balard (Paris, 1991), is a valuable guide to work since c.1970 on all the themes touched upon in this paper but I have not yet seen his companion volume *Bibliographie de l'histoire médiévale en France (1965–1990)* (Paris, 1992).

3 P. Wolff, *Commerce et marchands de Toulouse (vers 1350 – vers 1450)* (Paris, 1954); B. Chevalier, *Tours, ville royale (1356–1520)* (Paris and Louvain, 1975); A. Higounet-Nadal, *Périgueux aux XIVe et XVe siècles. Etude de démographie historique* (Bordeaux, 1978); R. Favreau, *La ville de Poitiers à la fin du moyen âge. Une capitale régionale*, 2 vols (Poitiers, 1978); P. Desportes, *Reims et les Rémois aux XIIIe et XIVe siècles* (Paris, 1979); A. Rigaudière, *Saint-Flour, ville d'Auvergne au Bas Moyen Age. Etude d'histoire administrative et financière*, 2 vols (Paris, 1982); J-P. Leguay, *Un réseau urbain au moyen âge: les villes du duché de Bretagne aux XIVe et XVe siècles* (Paris, 1981) also pays considerable attention to the impact of war.

4 C. Allmand, *The Hundred Years War. England and France at War c.1300–c.1450* (Cambridge, 1988) is the best brief introduction; L. Henneman, *Royal Taxation in Fourteenth Century France*, 2 vols (Princeton and Philadelphia, 1971–6), exhaustively deals with this central theme.

whilst the recovery of French military fortunes after 1369 was marked by swift inroads into the greater Aquitaine established by the treaty of Brétigny-Calais (1360). This ensured that Guyenne and neighbouring regions in the often neglected Midi, remained a major theatre of warfare in the late fourteenth century just as Sumption's ambitious narrative underlines the scale of fighting in the south during the first decade of the war.[5]

Secondly, however, we should remember that regions which seem to have been spared full-scale invasion (apparent blanks on the map like Brittany and its Marches, especially those south of the Loire towards Poitou, parts of central France, Languedoc and the south-east) were by no means free from warfare. Some of this was generated by local causes but then prosecuted under the cover of the general Anglo-French war. The feuding of great lords, most obviously the long-term though intermittent rivalry of the houses of Foix and Armagnac and the often conflicting interests of other great Gascon noble families like the Albret, Comminges, Durfort and L'Isle Jourdain added to the mayhem.[6] Examples of shorter violent interludes, since in many parts of France the nobility still exercised the right to make private war, may be widely found. That in the county of Burgundy between the duke and the lords of Chalon-Arlay in the early years of the war is a good example, and that between the vicomte de Polignac and the sire de St-Ilpize in the Auvergne in the early 1360s is another; while the family of Mirepoix was deeply divided around 1360.[7] In the case of the duchy of Brittany there was for over twenty years from 1341 a civil war for possession of the ducal throne, a war of siege and counter-siege, attrition and guerilla actions, though one not entirely devoid of more significant encounters: Morlaix (1342), La Roche Derrien (1347), Mauron (1352) and Auray (1364), in the event a high ratio of battles to other forms of warfare for the period [fig. 2]. Even after the victory of Jean de Montfort and his English allies at Auray, the duchy was far from peaceful. It witnessed further extensive military activity between 1372–81

---

5   H.J. Hewitt, *The Black Prince's Expedition 1355–57* (Manchester, 1958), K.A. Fowler, *The King's Lieutenant. Henry of Grosmont, First duke of Lancaster 1310–1361* (London, 1969) and A. Goodman, *John of Gaunt* (London, 1992) provide accessible accounts of most important fourteenth-century campaigns in the Midi.

6   Malcolm Vale, *The Angevin Legacy and the Hundred Years War, 1250–1340* (Oxford: Blackwell, 1990) provides much detail on the Gascon nobility; R.W. Kaeuper, *War, Justice and Public Order: England and France in the Later Middle Ages* (Oxford, 1988), esp. pp. 225–60 for private war.

7   Dom U. Plancher, *Histoire générale et particulière de Bourgogne*, 4 vols (Dijon, 1739–81), ii. *Preuves*, no. cclxi for letters of Philip VI announcing terms of peace between Duke Eudes IV and Jean de Chalon, sire d'Arlay, 13 June 1337, and cf. R. Cazelles, *La société politique et la crise de la royauté sous Philippe de Valois* (Paris, 1958), pp. 116 and 121n; Dom Cl. Devic and Dom J. Vaissete, *Histoire générale de Languedoc* [cited as *HL*], ed. A. Molinier et al., 16 vols (Toulouse, 1872–1904), x, *Preuves*, 1083–4, 1096–9, 1180–1 (Mirepoix), 1300–1 (Polignac).

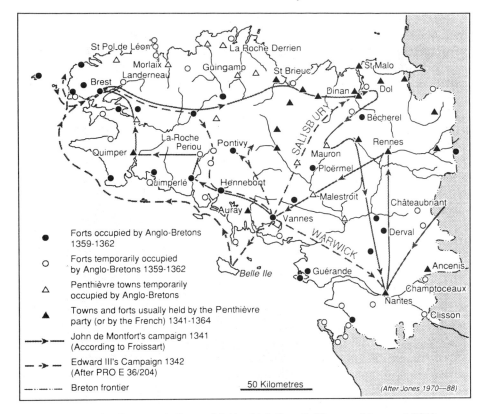

Fig. 2. The Breton civil war 1341–64 (after Galliou and Jones, 1991).

and again intermittently to the mid 1390s, whilst from 1342–97 an English garrison held Brest in a hostile fashion despite an Anglo-Breton alliance.[8]

Brittany was one of the first regions in which bands of free-booting adventurers, *routiers*, absent from France since the defeat of John Lackland by Philip Augustus early in the thirteenth century, began to proliferate again. Individual captains seized strongholds from which to exploit and terrorize the surrounding countryside by levying *rançons* and *patis*, demands for money and provisions, often raised on a regular basis at set times of the year; such captains frequently paid only the loosest lip-service to their nominal sovereign, the king of England or France.[9] Such behaviour, even in a country which knew noble lawlessness, was deeply atavistic, a reversion to far-off days before the Capetians had estab-

---

8   Michael Jones, *Ducal Brittany, 1364–1399* (Oxford, 1970); idem, *The Creation of Brittany* (London, 1988).
9   S. Luce, *Histoire de Bertrand du Guesclin et son époque. La jeunesse de Bertrand 1320–1364* (Paris, 1876) is a classic account; K.A. Fowler, 'Les finances et la discipline dans les armées anglaises en France au XIVe siècle', *Les Cahiers Vernonnais* 4 (1964), pp. 55–85, for a good modern discussion of 'ransoming'.

lished their dominance and ensured that, at least in northern France, the majority of the population normally lived in peace. By the 1350s other provinces like Poitou (plate I), the Limousin and Normandy witnessed a similar development. Mounting their own unofficial *chevauchées* like the raid of Robert Knolles on Auxerre and the Auvergne or the ravaging of Normandy and the Ile-de-France by James Pipe in 1358–9, and culminating between 1360–8 in confusing movements as far afield as Alsace, Provence and Languedoc by the Great Companies, hardened professional soldiers and adventurers wreaked havoc on many other regions.

It was now that English, Gascon, Breton and other captains with yet more exotic origins (German, Spanish, Italian, even Hungarian) established a stranglehold over many remote and inaccessible communities in central and southern France up to the Pyrenees and Alps: one such garrison used Lourdes as a base for several years, Tarbes likewise. Anse on the Rhône served as a repair for the band of Seguin de Badefol, whose death was attributed by Froissart to eating poisoned pears offered by Charles II of Navarre, anxious to terminate a contract with this notorious captain.[10] This was the period so colourfully recalled by the light of a November evening fireside by the Bascot of Mauléon, reminiscing to Froissart, 'At the sign of the Moon' at Orthez in 1388, and the one regretted by the famous *routier* Aymerigot Marchès (executed in 1391) after his loss of the castle of Aloise near St-Flour: 'Les villains d'Auvergne et de Limousin nous poureoient et amenoient en nostre chastel les bles et la farine, le pain tout cuit, l'avoine pour les chevaulx et la littiere, les bons vins, les buefs, les moutons, les brebis, tous gras et la poulaille et la vollaille'.[11]

The chronic fear and insecurity created by major invasions and localized warfare conducted by roving companies or permanent garrisons naturally prompted efforts by the indigenous population to protect itself. Town accounts are full of payments to scouts, spies and messengers sent to discover the proximity of enemy troops not only in fastnesses of the Massif Central but even in regions normally far distant from the main theatres of war like Provence. The authorities at Carpentras, for example, displayed an understandable paranoia over the whereabouts of the Companies and the no-less undisciplined Spanish troops who gathered around Henry of Trastamara during his exile in the Midi

---

[10] Jean Froissart, *Chroniques*, ed. S. Luce et al., 15 vols (Paris, 1869– continuing), vi. pp. xxxv n. 3, 74–6, 269–71 and *HL*, x, 1340–7 (Badefol); P. Tucoo-Chala, *Gaston Fébus et la vicomté de Béarn, 1343–1391* (Bordeaux, 1960), pp. 106, 305–6, 312 (Lourdes); M. Hébert, 'L'armée provençale en 1374', *Annales du Midi* 91 (1979), pp. 5–27 at p. 19 for Hungarians.

[11] [The peasants of Auvergne and Limousin feared[?] us and brought into our castle wheat and flour, baked bread, oats and litter for the horses, good wines, fat cattle and sheep, and poultry and fowls.] Jean Froissart, *Voyage en Béarn*, ed. A.H. Diverres (Manchester, 1953), pp. 87ff. (Mauléon); R. Delachenal, *Histoire de Charles V*, 5 vols (Paris, 1909–31), ii. 29 n. 2 (Marchès) citing Jean Froissart, *Oeuvres*, ed. Kervyn de Lettenhove, 28 vols (Brussels, 1867–77), xiv. 164.

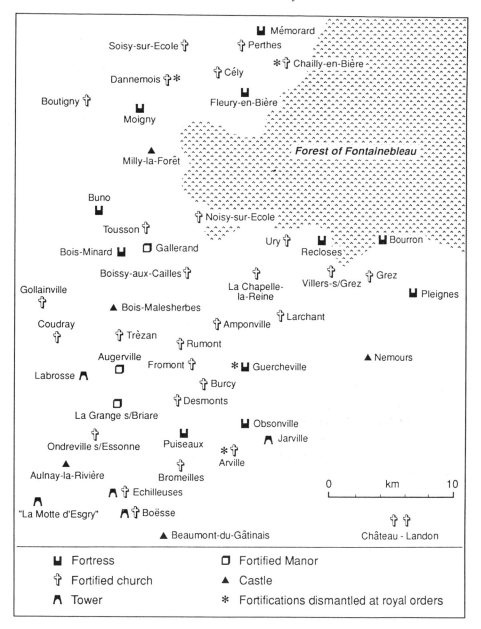

Fig. 3. Fortifications in the area south of Fontainebleau Forest in 1367
(after Contamine, 1972)

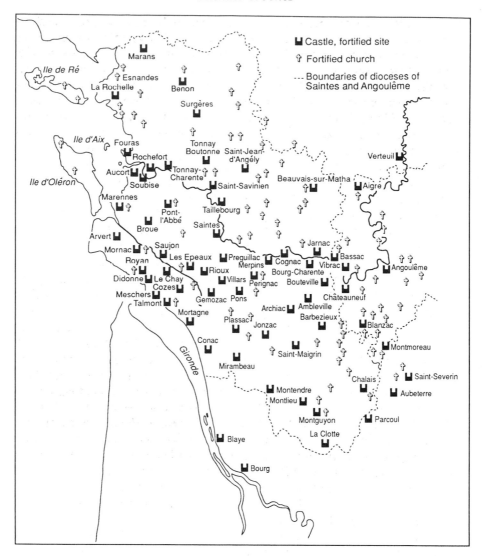

Fig. 4. Fortifications in Saintonge during the Hundred Years War
(after Favreau, 1986)

and menaced public order wherever they went.[12] The fortification of towns and castles and the hasty adaptation of civil buildings such as churches and monasteries to the needs of defence was another obvious response.

Figs 3 and 4 provide some indication of the intensity of efforts in this regard.

[12] R. André-Michel, ' "Anglais", Bretons et routiers à Carpentras sous Jean le Bon et Charles V', *Mélanges d'histoire offerts à M. Charles Bémont par ses amis et ses élèves* (Paris, 1913), pp. 341–52; *HL*, x. 1224, 1233–4 (Trastamara); K.A. Fowler, 'News from the Front:

In 1367, with the Companies still at large, Charles V instructed the *baillis* of Champagne, Burgundy, Auvergne, Bourbonnais and Nivernais to visit all the fortresses in their jurisdiction in the company of two knights in order to take appropriate measures for their defence or to destroy them if the former could not be easily effected. A return survives from the *bailli* of Melun which provides details on the density of fortified places bordering the forest of Fontainebleau, south-east of Paris. Within an area some 30 km by 40 km there were six major castles, four fortified manors, five towers, 12 forts and 28 fortified churches; a ratio of one strongpoint for each 20 or 25 km², though two forts and two churches were subsequently deemed untenable and were demolished.[13] Some of these defences naturally date from earlier periods, but many had been created as a direct response to the hostilities of recent decades.

Fig. 4 shows a similar dense configuration of fortified places on one of the most sensitive 'frontiers of war' in the fourteenth century: Saintonge.[14] Here the 'Hundred Years War' can be said to have begun in 1294, if not in 1259 when the treaty of Paris delivered the province into English hands, since its possession was hotly disputed both during Edward I's war with Philip IV and during the War of St-Sardos (1323–5). After Charles of Valois's invasion, the English regained Saintes in 1331 and the region saw some of the first military operations after the official outbreak of war in 1337. From that point onwards Saintonge normally remained divided into rival zones of allegiance. Even before the arrival of Lancaster in 1345, the province had witnessed many minor skirmishes with the capture or recovery of towns and castles from enemy hands: the daily coinage of warfare in France throughout this period. It was in Saintonge in the early 1350s that the leader of the Great Companies at the battle of Brignais (1362), the formidable Arnaud de Cervole, archpriest of Vélines in the diocese of Périgueux, who had recently forfeited his clerical status because of earlier acts of brigandage, gained his spurs and was rewarded by John II with a formal grant of the castellany of Châteauneuf-sur-Charente for services against the Anglo-Gascons. The iron hold which he exercised over his own men is demonstrated by his execution of 31 of them for 'homicides, rapines et viols' committed whilst they were holding Cognac in 1354–5.[15]

Later, by the treaty of Brétigny-Calais, Saintonge was officially handed over entirely to Edward III, much to the chagrin of many of its inhabitants. French campaigns to repossess it recommenced promptly in 1369, and 1372 saw them

letters and despatches of the fourteenth century', *Guerre et société en France, en Angleterre et en Bourgogne xive–xve siècle*, ed. P. Contamine, C. Giry-Deloison and M. Keen (Lille, 1991), pp. 63–92.

13 Contamine, *Guerre*, p. 10

14 Vale, *Angevin Legacy* and R. Favreau, *La commanderie du Breuil-du-Pas et la guerre de Cent Ans dans la Saintonge méridionale* (Jonzac, 1986) for all that follows on Saintonge.

15 Favreau, p. 41, Contamine, *Guerre*, p. 173, H. Denifle, *La désolation des églises, monastères et hôpitaux en France pendant la Guerre de Cent Ans*, 2 vols (Paris, 1897–9), i. 188–211 and A. Cherest, *L'Archiprêtre: episodes de la Guerre de Cent Ans au XIVe siècle* (Paris, 1879) for Cervole.

Plate II. The port defences of La Rochelle, after 1372.

Plate I. The castle of Montcontour (Vienne), finally retaken by the French in 1372.

Plate III. The fortified church of Esnedes (Charente-Maritime).

making major gains north of the Charente with the return to their allegiance of La Rochelle (plate II), Rochefort, Surgères and other strongholds. Cognac was regained in 1375 shortly before the truce of Bruges was agreed. When hostilities broke out again in 1377 the Charente continued to demarcate the frontier with English garrisons holding Taillebourg ('le plus bel chastel de Poictou . . . la clef de Poictou'), Bourg-Charente, La Faon and Verteuil. Though Bouteville fell briefly to the French in 1379, it soon returned to English hands and it required several campaigns by Louis, duke of Bourbon, and Louis de Sancerre, marshal of France, from 1384 to recover Taillebourg, St-Séverin and Verteuil, to demolish the castle at Jarnac and defences at Bourg-Charente considered too difficult to defend, and to relieve Rioux, though the otherwise isolated garrison at Bouteville still remained unconquered when the regime of general truces inaugurated in 1388 came into force and only fell finally to the French in 1392. Is it any wonder then that this map of Saintonge during the Hundred Years War shows more than 70 castles and fortified towns and almost 90 fortified churches, some like that of Esnandes in the *plat pays* north of La Rochelle not simply adapted from earlier work but designed *ab initio* for the physical defence it could offer as much as for any spiritual consolation it might provide (plate III). Or that Favreau comments bleakly and with only mild hyperbole that in Saintonge by the 1380s 'tout est reduit au désert'.[16]

The fear and suffering created by all this military activity is perhaps best caught in a letter to posterity written on the inside cover of a manuscript belonging to his house by the prior of Brailet (Yonne) in 1359. This was a year after the Jacquerie compounded the effects of foreign invasion by stirring up class hatred and civil war which had allowed Anglo-Navarrese and other lawless soldiery to ravage the Ile-de-France at will. First published in 1857,[17] it still retains its power to shock:

> In A.D. 1358 the English came to Chantecoq and took the castle on the eve of All Saints [31 Oct.]. At the same time they burned almost all the town and afterwards reduced the whole countryside to their control, ordering the towns, both great and small, to ransom all their possessions, viz., bodies, goods, and movables, or else they would burn the houses. This they did in many places. Confounded and completely terrorized in this fashion, very many of the people submitted to the English, paying them money by way of ransom and agreeing to provide them with cash, flour, oats, and many other necessary supplies [remember Aymerigot Marchès and the *rançons*!], if they would stop for a while the aforementioned persecution, because they had already killed many men in different places. Some they shut up in very dark dungeons, threatening them daily with death, and continually punishing them with whippings, wounds, hunger and want beyond belief. But others had nothing with which to pay ransom or they were unwilling to submit to the power of the English. To

16 Favreau, p. 50.
17 *Bibliothèque de l'école des chartes* xviii (1857), pp. 357–60, published here with minor amendments after *The Chronicle of Jean de Venette*, ed. and trans. R.A. Newhall and J.A. Birdsall (New York, 1953), pp. 253–4.

escape from their hands these made themselves huts in the woods and there ate their bread with fear, sorrow, and great anguish. But the English learned of this and they resolutely sought out these hiding places, searching numerous woods and putting many men to death there. Some they killed, others they captured, still others escaped. Among the latter I, Hugh de Montgeron, prior of Brailet in the parish of Domats in the deanery of Courtenay, diocese of Sens, contrived a hiding place in the Bois des Queues beyond the swamp of the lord of Villebon and there remained with many of my neighbours seeing and hearing every day about the vicious and wicked deeds of our enemies, namely, houses burned and many dead left lying in brutal fashion through the villages and hamlets. Seeing and hearing such things, I decided on the Sunday after St Luke's day [20 Oct.] to go to the city and remain there. But it happened that very night that these wicked English found their way to my hut so quietly that, in spite of the watchfulness of our sentinels, they almost captured me while I was asleep. But by God's grace and through the help of the Blessed Virgin Mary I was awakened by the noise they made and escaped naked, taking nothing with me because of my haste except a habit with a hood. Crossing into the middle of the swamp I stayed there shivering and shaking with the cold, which was very great at the time, while my hut was completely despoiled. Afterwards I went to Sens to the house of John Paysans, a priest and one of my relations, who received me kindly, showing me such charity from the goods that God had bestowed upon him that it is impossible for me adequately to describe it. And still [the English] never stopped coming to our aforementioned priory, sending me letters threatening destruction and intimating that they would set it on fire unless I came to them under safe conduct which they would send me. On this account I went and obtained from them a respite from the feast of St Peter's throne [22 Feb. 1359] until the feast of St John the Baptist [24 June 1359]. But little good this did because the man who was captain at the time was taken prisoner by the French and so all my trouble went for nothing. So I lived in the midst of troubles from the feast of All Saints until the feast of the Baptist. Again they took me prisoner but, not recognizing me, they left their booty behind because there was so little of it, for which God be praised. During this time they stripped the house of all movable goods, drank up four *queues* of wine, they carried off a *modius* of oats according to the measure in use at Courtenay, they took all my clothes, and at Easter [21 April 1359] and again on the Sunday after the feast of St Peter and St Paul [30 June 1359] they ate up the pigeons. And so by God's grace, I have escaped in the name of the Lord out of their hands up until now. But unless I wish to lose thirty arpents of the best grain, it is necessary to make again a settlement with these fellows lest worse happen and the last state of affairs be worse than the first.

I am writing this out behind our barn on Wednesday, the festival of St Martin 1359 [4 July 1359, though it was in fact a Thursday], because I do not dare write elsewhere. Do you who live in cities and castles ever see trouble equal to my trouble? Farewell.

Hugh

We need not dwell at length on the lot of the prior of Brailet and his kind: evidence of damage to ecclesiastical properties as a result of war in fourteenth-century France is overwhelming. Père Denifle's famous compendium, published between 1897–9 first traced the extent of the devastation; recent work simply refines and augments his findings.[18] Such information provides a valuable index to the regions where destruction was at its most severe as in the dioceses of Amiens, Tournai and St-Omer in the north-east, Cahors, Tulle, Rodez and Castres in the Midi, which Michèle Bordeaux estimated to have suffered even more than the group of central-western dioceses (Tours, Poitiers, Angers, Saintes, Limoges) and north-eastern ones (Reims, Laon, Cambrai, Noyon, Sens, Chalons, Troyes) from which evidence has already been cited for the devastation of war.[19] Whilst it is especially by exploiting accounts and other financial records of ecclesiastical corporations (which have survived more frequently than those from lay estates, though where these do they tell much the same story) that Boutruche and his successors have charted in such bold detail the fluctuating economic fortunes of landlords in the late fourteenth century.

This evidence has established for the countryside a pattern of decline in income and productivity, sometimes catastrophic in its incidence, more often cumulative, alternating with phases of reconstruction marking the periods when warfare ceased (truces were officially in force for two years out of three during the fourteenth-century phase of the war).[20] Thus, in northern France between c.1365 and c.1410, despite all that has been said so far about the impact of war, there was one such period of general remission. Fourquin heads a chapter in his *Campagnes de la région parisienne* 'tentative agrarian restoration, c.1365–1410'; Bois likewise speaks of 'the first reconstruction, c.1364–1410' in his account of neighbouring rural Eastern Normandy. Le Mené, dealing with Anjou, a region less directly afflicted by war than those two provinces (though not entirely immune from it as fig. 5 shows),[21] similarly discerns economic recovery, though its effects are deemed to be more patchy. Here there was no single great wave of destruction and desertion followed by a general movement of recolonization, but rather piecemeal efforts leading by the end of the century to 'l'impression . . . d'un pays en pleine convalescence'.[22] Rental values in the Angevin countryside, for example, had, perhaps fallen by 30–40% from the mid-century. Orchards and vineyards (as in Saintonge or the Bordelais) particularly suffered physical destruction and took a long time to re-establish, but arable land had rarely been entirely abandoned. Of that which had been between 1363–75, the period when

[18] Denifle, *La désolation, passim*; cf. Favreau, *La commanderie*.
[19] Michèle Bordeaux, *Aspects économiques de la vie de l'église aux XIVe et XVe siècles* (Paris, 1969).
[20] K.A. Fowler, 'Truces', *The Hundred Years War*, ed. K.A. Fowler (London, 1971), p. 184; R. Boutruche, 'The devastation of rural areas during the Hundred Years War and the agricultural recovery of France', *The Recovery of France in the Fifteenth Century*, ed. P.S. Lewis (London, 1972), pp. 23–59, an article originally published in 1947, first sketched the broad outlines of the story.
[21] *Atlas historique français (Monumenta Historiae Galliarum): Anjou*, ed. Robert Favreau (Paris, 1973), Pl. VIII no. 4.
[22] Le Mené, p. 221.

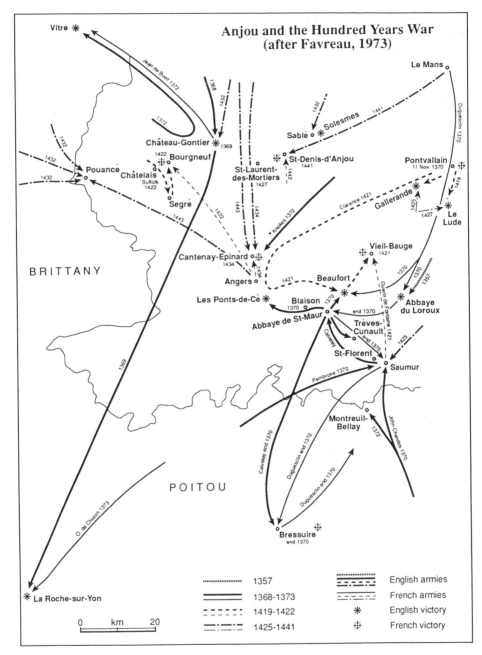

Fig. 5. Anjou and the Hundred Years War (after Favreau, 1973).

Anjou was most obviously affected by warfare, all but 10% was back in cultivation by 1400. As Bois demonstrated for Normandy, in Anjou too it seems it was easier to re-establish peasant holdings in late fourteenth-century conditions rather than larger seigneurial estates. These latter required considerable capital investment in mills, barns and other installations, so often the object of deliberate destruction, as well as administrative expertise and determination to restore them to their full revenue-earning potential.[23] With nuances, to take into account differing phases in the cycle of warfare and natural disaster which afflicted all of France during the period, the picture in the Angevin and Norman countryside seems to be repeated throughout much of the kingdom.

How did experience of war in towns compare? Perhaps even more than in the countryside the impact of war on towns is difficult to measure because of differences in size, variety of municipal institutions and forms of administration, economic and commercial interests, social complexion and many other factors distinguishing one urban community from another. Great cities already well-provided with sound defences when the war began like Bordeaux, even though in an exposed strategic position, were clearly less at risk than small *bourgades*. Unless there was some unfortunate accident such as treason or revolt, they were less likely to be besieged or suffer damage during a *chevauchée*, though unprotected suburbs were at risk like those of Narbonne and Carcassonne destroyed during the Black Prince's great raid of 1355. A full-scale siege of even a modest walled town was not undertaken lightly and required considerable logistical expertise: it would be an interesting exercise to establish the proportion of successful sieges during this phase of the war before combustible artillery helped to speed the process. But even the Companies, lacking the specialist technical services that regular authorities soon developed in response to the war, could inflict much damage directly on urban property besides laying waste the *plat pays*.

Failing to take Amiens in 1358, for example, Navarrese troops set fire to the suburbs and, according to Froissart, more than 3,000 houses were burnt in a conflagration the signs of which could still be seen fifty years later.[24] But systematic destruction of whole towns or even of *quartiers* was relatively rare as was massacring or expulsion of entire populations; even though it conformed with contemporary laws of war, the sacking of Limoges in 1370 by the Black Prince is exceptional.[25] In this respect at least the Anglo-French war in the fourteenth century appears less vicious in retrospect than the Albigensian Crusades when wholesale slaughter of civilian populations occurred. Nor, with the exception of the hapless inhabitants of Calais who found themselves in no-man's land between the English and French armies after their expulsion by Edward III, are

[23] Le Mené, pp. 211ff.
[24] Delachenal, ii. 17–21.
[25] Cf. M.H. Keen, *The Laws of War* (London and Toronto, 1965), *passim*. R. Barber, *Edward, Prince of Wales and Aquitaine* (London, 1978), pp. 225–6, critically surveys the evidence and concludes that Froissart exaggerates the casualties.

there any fourteenth-century incidents comparable to Louis XI's attempt to expunge Arras from the map in 1479 by ejecting its citizens, razing the town and renaming the site Franchise.[26] Nevertheless, some towns because they lay in the path of a *chevauchée* (like Caen in 1346) or because of their strategic or symbolic national or regional importance (Paris, Reims, Nantes and Rennes) naturally attracted the attention of enemy armies and were attacked or besieged on several occasions. A rich documentation allows us to take Reims (with a population in 1300 of about 20,000) as an extreme case of the way war affected urban life in this period.[27]

Like many French towns at the beginning of the war, its defences were in an unprepared state [fig. 6]: a new enceinte begun under Philip Augustus and pushed forward under Philip the Fair remained incomplete, often nothing more than earth banks and wooden palisading. As rumours of war began to spread in 1336 the échevins advised Philip VI of the need to inspect the defences which the *bailli* of Vermandois was ordered to repair in July 1337. But the town was still chiefly in the jurisdiction of the archbishop and division between ecclesiastical and lay authorities delayed action for several years though able-bodied men between the ages of 15 and 60 were formed into 'dizaines' (four of which formed a 'connétablie' about 100 strong) as an urban militia, the town walls and gates were temporarily reinforced, a system of watches was organized, especially at night, export of foodstuffs was prohibited, strangers in particular were carefully checked and the town was dispensed from sending recruits to the general *arrière-ban* so that it could better defend itself. Edward III's campaign in the Cambrésis (1339) added urgency to the citizens' efforts to complete their defences but it was the battle of Crécy that finally roused them to a frenzy of activity, with the clergy reluctantly accepting the necessity of contributing to the expenses of the fortifications.

As in many French towns which had not developed their own administrations during the thirteenth-century communal movement, Reims was a city where 'the ramparts gave birth to municipal institutions'.[28] Neighbouring Troyes and Chalons and more distant Tours, Angers, Nantes, Blois and Orléans were other important centres which evolved in the same way during the first decades of the war which saw the raising and completion of many major enceintes.[29] That of Avignon not only survives largely intact today but its construction between

---

[26] H. Sée, *Louis XI et les villes* (Paris, 1891), pp. 134–7; H. Stein, 'Les habitants d'Evreux et le repeuplement d'Arras en 1479', *Bibliothèque de l'école des chartes* lxxxiv (1923), pp. 284–97; *idem*, 'La participation du pays de Languedoc au repeuplement d'Arras sous Louis XI', *ibid.*, xcii (1931), pp. 62–9.

[27] Desportes, *Reims*, esp. pp. 526ff. for the following account.

[28] Cf. P. Contamine, 'Les fortifications urbaines en France à la fin du moyen âge: aspects financiers et économiques', *Revue historique* cclx (1978), pp. 23–47 [reprinted in his collected essays *La France au XIVe et XVe siècles. Hommes, mentalités, guerre et paix* (London, 1981), no. V at pp. 30–3].

[29] Cf. B. Chevalier, 'Pouvoir royal et pouvoir urbain à Tours pendant la guerre de Cent Ans', *Annales de Bretagne* 81 (1974), pp. 365–92.

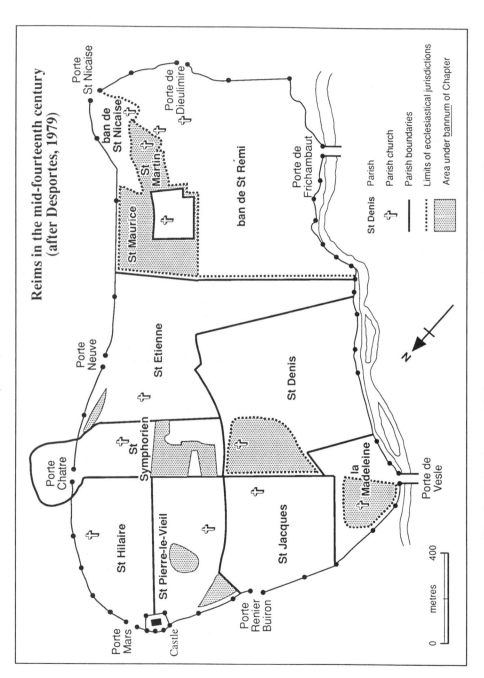

Fig. 6. Reims in the mid-fourteenth century (after Deportes, 1979).

1355–70 is well documented (plate IV).[30] At Reims, under Gaucher de Lor, appointed captain by Philip VI, a small committee was formed to supervise raising the necessary taxes and their expenditure. As Desportes comments, 'On peut voir en ce corps la première institution commune de la ville',[31] since it united for the first time representatives of the archbishop, the chapter and the abbey of St-Rémi as well as citizens.[32] More generally, a familiar pattern can be discerned; as Favreau has written, 'Un peu partout la guerre impose la défense, la défense exige le budget, la gestion du budget entraîne le développement des libertés muncipales.'[33]

Although the Black Death interrupted work on the defences at Reims, building continued at a more leisurely pace in the early 1350s before the battle of Poitiers had a galvanising effect similar to that of Crécy. Traditional artillery weapons were bought from Paris, St-Quentin and Rouen, an expert *artilleur* was hired from Verdun, metal and wooden grills were placed in the bed of the river Vesle to prevent horses crossing and agreements for mutual military aid were made with Chalons and the county of Rethel.[34] Despite further disputes between the towns-people and their archbishop over whether his castle of Porte-Mars should be incorporated into the enceinte (as it finally was in 1364), the summer of 1358 saw the effective enclosure of the town. But it was at a considerable material and human, as well as financial, cost (in the event an investment calculated at no less than 100,000 livres): houses, churches, hospitals and monasteries lying outside the enceinte were ruthlessly demolished and in the surrounding countryside woods were felled, villages cleared and *maisons-fortes* destroyed, their inhabitants being offered shelter within the city in an effort to create a *cordon sanitaire* around the city. It was not a moment too soon: on 4 December 1359 Edward III finally arrived before the newly-constructed defences to besiege the city. Nor was this the only occasion the defences of Reims were put to the test since the city later lay in the path of the successive *chevauchées* of Knolles (1370), Gaunt (1373) and Thomas of Woodstock (1380).[35]

The impact of war on Reims and its citizens was thus dramatic: alarms and excursions since 1337, institutional developments, especially in response to urban defence, the declining control of the archbishop, major alterations to the physical environment in and immediately around the town, social change too as

---

30 R. Michel, 'La construction des remparts d'Avignon au XIVe siècle', *Congrès archéologique de France, lxxvi session, Avignon 1909* (Paris, 1910), pp. 341–60; A.-M. Hayez, 'Travaux à l'enceinte d'Avignon sous les pontificats d'Urbain V et Grégoire XI', *Actes du 101e Congrès national des Sociétés savantes* (Paris, 1978), pp. 193–223.

31 [One can see in this body the first common institution of the town.]

32 Desportes, p. 542.

33 [Almost everywhere the war imposed defense, defense required a budget, the creation of the budget brought with it the development of municipal liberties.] Favreau, *Poitiers*, i. 188.

34 Desportes, p. 556 after P. Varin, *Archives administratives de la ville de Reims*, 10 vols (Paris, 1839–53), iii. 120–6.

35 Modern accounts have only marginally modified the classic narratives of these expeditions by Delachenal, iv. 301–42 (Knolles), 480–503 (Gaunt); v. 364–85 (Buckingham).

Plate IV. The town defences of Avignon, c. 1355–70.

the city provided a haven for refugees (in some years up to 50% of the population in some parishes were newcomers) whilst the role of the formerly dominant patriciate waned in worsening economic conditions. The Black Death, of course, contributed its share to the misery of these years: a quarter or third of the population was lost and it had similar consequences to those observed elsewhere – legal proceedings disrupted, rising wage rates, difficulties in filling tenancies, and so on. But because of a deteriorating military position, conditions became even worse in the Rémois between 1356–64. For part of this period the city was virtually cut off by routier bands and foreign invasion from its close trading partners, Laon, Soissons, Paris, Troyes, let alone its more distant markets. Scarcity drove up the price of basic cereals which doubled or tripled in cost; whilst the Anglo-French peace agreed in 1360 simply added to the inhabitants' tax burden. Reims owed 20,000 écus towards the first tranche of John II's ransom (600,000 écus) and was forced to raise loans to meet its obligations, including the maintenance of hostages in England, from Italians in Paris. These were still outstanding in 1365.

The extent to which Reims could take advantage of the rural economic recovery noted elsewhere from the 1360s was limited. Factors other than warfare need to be considered in explaining this. The town's textile industry, on which its economic fortune had been built, was by now in sad decline, in part because of the contraction of wider European markets and reduced demand but also because its products were no longer fashionable as replacement by products from the Low Countries, Germany and England in former Rémois markets shows. Yet we can see that the fiscal pressures generated by war (one of the factors to which Bois gives most attention in assessing changing social relations in rural Normandy in this period) also imposed an enormous burden on an impoverished urban population. Tax demands absorbed an increasing proportion of reduced urban wealth: the need to respond to royal requests for money, costs of maintaining the defences and equipping troops, problems caused by a continual flow of rural refugees into the city because of rural insecurity, all drained local resources. Despite its prestige as the city where the king was crowned, coronations were a mixed blessing since they cost the city dear (at least 7712 l. 18s 5d in 1364). Other fortuitous circumstances could similarly wreck careful budgeting. In 1382, for instance, the brother of Guy, marshal of Burgundy, Jean de Pontailler, *en route* for Flanders, was taken prisoner by some Rémois, and the city had to spend 35,000 francs it could ill-afford in legal costs and reparations to regain the good will of the duke of Burgundy.[36] To put this comparatively huge sum into perspective it may be noted that between 1364–80 about 60,000 francs had been raised from the citizens by means of *fouages* but often only after much protest. It was thus not until the late 1380s that Reims really began to show signs of a genuine revival of fortunes. In the event it was both a short and very partial period of remission: the second decade of the fifteenth century brought renewed crisis.

---

36 Desportes, pp. 589–90.

I had hoped to discuss some technical and specialised developments in warfare itself – the spread of gunpowder artillery and amphibious warfare along some of France's great river systems – as further illustrations of the changing impact of war in the fourteenth century.[37] But space precludes that and I must conclude. A succession of leading scholars, including last century Siméon Luce and Père Denifle, and in the early part of our own, Roland Delachenal, have all quoted the remarks of Petrarch returning to France after the treaty of Brétigny as testimony to the destructive effects of war in this period: 'I had difficulty in convincing myself that this was the country I had seen in former times . . . I scarcely recognized anything that I had once seen in this kingdom once so rich and now reduced to ashes, beyond city walls and fortresses there remained, it may be said, not a house which was left standing.'[38] Hyperbole, of course, nevertheless these are images which we do well to remind ourselves constituted the daily reality of war for many ordinary people in fourteenth-century France: images, moreover, that have been enhanced rather than diminished by the steady accumulation of detail culled from non-literary sources on which most serious scholars since the mid-nineteenth century have increasingly chosen to base their research on the effects of war on fourteenth-century France.

[37] For example, A. Merlin-Chazelas, *Documents relatifs au Clos des Galées de Rouen et aux armées de mer du roi de France de 1293 à 1418*, 2 vols (Paris, 1977–8) provides much material on ship and troop movements on the Seine from the late 1350s; for the amphibious siege of Rolleboise in 1363–4 see also Luce, *Du Guesclin*, pp. 417ff. and Delachenal, ii. 356–9.
[38] Cf. Delachenal, ii. 21.

Bibliography

I. Sources Cited by Short Title

SHORT TITLE	FULL CITATION
Allmand, *Society at War*	Allmand, Christopher T., ed. and tr. *Society at War.* Edinburgh: Oliver & Boyd, 1973 new edn, Woodbridge, 1998.
Anonimalle	*The Anonimalle Chronicle, 1333–1381*, ed. V. H. Galbraith. Manchester: Manchester University Press, 1927.
Ashley	Ashley, W. J., ed. and tr. *English History by Contemporary Writers: Edward III and His Wars, 1327–1360.* London: David Nutt, 1887.
Avesbury	Robert of Avesbury. *De gestis mirabilibus regis Edwardi Tertii*, ed. Edward Maunde Thompson. London: Rolls Series, 1889.
Barber, *Life and Campaigns*	Barber, Richard, ed. *The Life and Campaigns of the Black Prince.* London: The Folio Society, 1979.
Bridlington	*Gesta Edwardi Tertii auctore canonico Bridlingtonensi* in *Chronicles of the Reigns of Edward I and Edward II, vol. II*, ed. W. Stubbs. London: Rolls Series, 1883.
Carolus-Barré	Carolus-Barré, L. "Benoit XII et la mission charitable de Bertrand Carit dans les pays devastés du nord de la France. Cambrésis, Vermandois, Thiérarche. 1340." *Mélanges d'archéologie et d'histoire publiés par l'école française de Rome*, LXII (1950), 165–232.
Chron. Jean II et Charles V	*Chronique des règnes de Jean II et Charles V, tome II (1364–1380)*, ed. R. Delachenal. Paris: Société de l'histoire de France, 1916.
Cleopatra Brut	British Library, London. Cottonian MSS, Cleopatra D III. [An early redaction of the French *Brut d'Engleterre*.]
Foedera	*Foedera, conventiones, litterae etc.*, ed. Thomas Rymer, revised edition by A. Clarke, F. Holbrooke and J. Coley, 4 vols. in 7 parts. London: Record Commission, 1816–69.
Fordun	John of Fordun. *John of Fordun's Chronicle of the Scottish Nation* [Historians of Scotland, v. IV], ed. W. F. Skene, tr. F. J. H. Skene. Edinburgh: Edmonston and Douglas, 1872.
French Chronicle of London	*French Chronicle of London*, ed. G. J. Aungier, *Camden Series* XXVIII (1844).
Froissart, *Chronicles*	Sir John Froissart. *Chronicles of England, France, Spain &c.*, tr. Thomas Johnes. London: Bohn, 1852.

Froissart, *Oeuvres*   Jean Froissart. *Oeuvres*, ed. Baron Kervyn de Letten-hove. Brussels, 1867–77.

Grandes chroniques   *Grandes chroniques de France*, ed. Jules Viard. Paris: Société de l'histoire de France, 1920–53.

Historia Roffensis   William of Dene (?). *Historia Roffensis*. British Library, London. Cottonian MSS, Faustina B V. [An edition of the chronicle, which will include an English translation, is under preparation by Mark Buck for the Oxford Medieval Texts series.]

Jan de Klerk (Delpierre)   Jan de Klerk, *Edouard III, roi d'Angleterre, en Flandre*, tr. (into French by) Octave Delpierre. *Miscellanies of the Philobiblon Society*, X (1867). [For the original Dutch text, see *Van den derden Eduwaert*, ed. J. G. Heymans. Nijmegen: ALFA, 1983.]

Lanercost (Maxwell)   *The Lanercost Chronicle, 1272–1346*, tr. Sir Herbert Maxwell. Glasgow: Maclehose, 1913. [Latin: *Chronicle de Lanercost, MCCI–MCCCXLVI*. Ed. J. Stevenson. Edinburgh: The Bannatyne Club, 1839.]

Le Bel   Jean le Bel. *Chronique de Jean le Bel*, ed. Jules Viard and Eugène Déprez. Paris: Société de l'histoire de France, 1904.

Melsa   Thomas of Burton. *Chronica Monasterii de Melsa*, ed. E. A. Bond. London: Rolls Series, 1866–8.

MS CCC78   Corpus Christi College, Oxford, MS 78. [An independent continuation of the French *Brut* through the reign of Richard II.]

Murimuth   Adam Murimuth. *Continuatio Chronicarum*, ed. Edward Maunde Thompson. London: Rolls Series, 1889.

"Neville's Cross"   C. J. Rogers and M. C. Buck. "Three New Accounts of the Neville's Cross Campaign," *Northern History*, XXXIV (1988).

Original Letters   *Original Letters Illustrative of English History*, ed. Sir Henry Ellis. Third Series, vol. I. London: Bentley, 1846.

Pluscarden   *The Book of Pluscarden*, ed. and tr. Felix J. H. Skene. Edinburgh: William Paterson, 1880.

Quatre premiers Valois   *Chronique des quatre premiers Valois (1327–1393)*, ed. Siméon Luce. Paris: Société de l'histoire de France, 1862.

Rotuli Parliamentorum   *Rotuli Parliamentorum*, ed. J. Strachey et al., 6 vols. London: 1767–83.

Rotuli Scotiae   *Rotuli Scotiae etc., vol. I*, ed. David Macpherson. London: Record Commission, 1814.

St. Omer Chronicle   Bibliothèque Nationale, Paris, MS 693, fos. 248–279v. [C. J. Rogers is currently preparing an edition of this chronicle, which will include an English translation.]

Scalacronica (Maxwell)   Sir Thomas Gray. *Scalacronica*, ed. and tr. Sir Herbert Maxwell. Edinburgh: Maclehose, 1907.

Scalacronica (Stevenson)	Sir Thomas Gray. *Scalacronica*, ed. Joseph Stevenson. Edinburgh: Maitland Club, 1836.
Stones, *Anglo-Scottish Relations*	Stones, E. L. G. *Anglo-Scottish Relations 1174– 1328: Some Selected Documents*. London: Nelson, 1965.
"Tournai Bulletin"	Rogers, Clifford J. "An Unknown News Bulletin from the Siege of Tournai in 1340," *War in History*, 5 (1998), 359–367.
Venette	Jean de Venette. *The Chronicle of Jean de Venette*, tr. J. Birdsall, ed. R. A. Newhall. New York: Columbia University Press, 1953.
Villani	Giovanni Villani. *Cronica*, in *Cronisti del Trecento*, ed. Roberto Palmarocchi. Milan: Rizzoli, 1935.
Wrottesley, *Crecy and Calais*	Wrottesley, Maj. Gen. George. *Crecy and Calais from the Original Records in the Public Record Office [Reprinted from the William Salt Archaeological Society]*. London: Harrison and Sons, 1898.
Wyntoun	Andrew of Wyntoun. *Orygynale Cronykil of Scotland*, ed. David Laing. Edinburgh: Edmonston and Douglas [Historians of Scotland series, vols. II, III, IX], 1872–79.

II. Additional Primary Sources Available in English

The Anonimalle Chronicle 1307–1334, ed. and tr. Wendy R. Childs and John Taylor. Yorkshire Archaeological Society [Record Series vol. CXLVII], 1991.

Barbour, John. *The Bruce*, ed. and tr. A. A. M. Duncan. Edinburgh: Canongate Books, 1997.

The Brut; or, The Chronicles of England, ed. Friedrich W. D. Brie. London: Early English Text Society, 1906–8.

Chronicles of the Mayors and Sheriffs of London, A.D. 1188–1274, and The French Chronicle of London, A.D. 1259 to A.D. 1343, tr. Henry Thomas Riley. London: Trübner, 1863.

Knighton, Henry. *Knighton's Chronicle 1337–1396*, ed. and tr. G. H. Martin. Oxford: Clarendon, 1995.

Calendar of Documents Relating to Scotland, ed. Joseph Bain. Edinburgh: HMSO, 1887.

Calendars of Close Rolls.

Calendars of Patent Rolls.

Syllabus (In English) of . . . "Rymer's Foedera," vol. I, ed. Thomas Duffus Hardy. London: Longman's, 1869.

III. Suggestions for Further Reading

Note: The purpose of this section is to provide starting points for further study of the wars of Edward III, not to provide an exhaustive listing of all that has been written on the subject. It has also been limited to works in English. Those seeking more extensive bibliographies should refer in particular to Sumption's The Hundred Years War, *Ayton's* Knights and Warhorses, *and Allmand's* The Hundred Years War. *The footnotes to the articles in the Interpretations section, above, provide additional guidance.*

A. NARRATIVE HISTORIES AND BIOGRAPHIES OF THE PROTAGONISTS

Barber, Richard. *Edward, Prince of Wales and Aquitaine.* London: Allen Lane, 1978.

Barnes, Joshua. *The History of the Most Victorious Monarch Edward IIId etc.* Cambridge, 1688. [Remains in many ways the best, most detailed biography of Edward III.]

Burne, Alfred H. *The Crecy War.* London: Greenhill Books, 1990; reprint of 1955 Eyre and Spottiswoode edition. [Thought-provoking but not entirely reliable.]

Burne, Alfred H. *The Agincourt War.* London: Greenhill Books, 1991; reprint of 1956 Eyre and Spottiswoode edition.

Fowler, Kenneth. *The King's Lieutenant: Henry of Grosmont, First Duke of Lancaster, 1310–1361.* London: Elek, 1969.

Goodman, Anthony. *John of Gaunt.* Harlow, 1992.

Hewitt, H. J. *The Black Prince's Expedition of 1355–1357.* Manchester: Manchester University Press, 1958

Keen, Maurice H. *England in the Later Middle Ages.* London: Methuen, 1973.

Lucas, Henry Stephen. *The Low Countries and the Hundred Years War.* Ann Arbor: U. of Michigan Press, 1929. [Extremely detailed and well documented. Old, but unsurpassed.]

McKisack, May. *The Fourteenth Century, 1307–1399.* Oxford: Oxford U.P., 1959.

Miller, Edward. *War in the North.* Hull, 1960.

Nicholson, Ranald. *Edward III and the Scots. The formative years of a military career, 1327–1335.* Oxford: Oxford U.P., 1965. [An excellent study.]

Rogers, Clifford J. "The Scottish Invasion of 1346." *Northern History* XXXIV (1998).

Russell, P. *The English Intervention in Spain and Portugal in the Time of Edward III and Richard II.* Oxford, 1955.

Sumption, Jonathan. *The Hundred Years War, v. 1: Trial by Battle.* London: Faber and Faber, 1990.

B. OTHER

Allmand, Christopher. *The Hundred Years War.* Cambridge: Cambridge University Press, 1988.

Ayton, Andrew. "The English Army and the Normandy Campaign of 1346." *England and Normandy in the Middle Ages*, ed. D. Bates and A. Curry. London, 1987.

Ayton, Andrew. *Knights and Warhorses: Military Service and the English Aristocracy under Edward III*. Woodbridge: Boydell Press, 1994.

Ayton, Andrew. "War and the English Gentry under Edward III." *History Today* March 1992.

Barnie, John. *War in Medieval English Society: Social Values in the Hundred Years War 1337–99*. Ithaca: Cornell University Press, 1974.

Bradbury, Jim. *The Medieval Archer*. Woodbridge: Boydell Press, 1985.

Bradbury, Jim. *The Medieval Siege*. Woodbridge: Boydell Press, 1992.

Bridbury, A. R. "The Hundred Years War: Costs and Profits." In *Trade, Government and Economy in Pre-Industrial England*, ed. D. C. Coleman and A. H. John (1976).

Chaplais, P. "English Arguments Concerning the Feudal Status of Aquitaine in the Fourteenth Century," *B[ulletin of the] I[nstitute of] H[istorical] R[esearch]* 21 (1946–8).

Contamine, Philippe. *War in the Middle Ages*, tr. Michael Jones. Oxford: Basil Blackwood Ltd, 1987.

Cuttino, G. P. "Historical Revision: The Causes of the Hundred Years' War." *Speculum* 31 (1956).

Curry, Anne and Michael Hughes, eds. *Arms, Armies and Fortifications in the Hundred Years War*. Woodbridge: Boydell Press, 1994.

Fowler, Kenneth. *The Age of Plantagenet and Valois*. New York: Putnam, 1967.

Fowler, Kenneth (ed.). *The Hundred Years War*. London: Macmillan, 1971.

Fryde, E. B. "Parliament and the French War, 1336–40." In *Essays in Medieval History Presented to Bertie Wilkinson*, ed. T. A. Sandquist and M. R. Powicke. Toronto: University of Toronto Press, 1969

Fryde, Natalie M. "Edward III's Removal of his Ministers and Judges, 1340–1341." *BIHR* 48 (1975).

Gillingham, John. "Richard I and the Science of War in the Middle Ages." In Gillingham and Holt, eds., *War and Government in the Middle Ages*. Woodbridge: Boydell Press, 1984.

Haines, Roy M. "An English Archbishop and the Cerberus of War." In *The Church and War*, ed. W. J. Shiels. London: Ecclesiastical History Society/Basil Blackwell, 1983.

Haines, Roy Martin. *Archbishop John Stratford: Political Revolutionary and Champion of the Liberties of the English Church, ca. 1275/80 – 1348*. Toronto: Pontifical Institute, 1986.

Hardy, Robert. *Longbow: A Social and Military History*. Cambridge: Patrick Stephens, 1976.

Harriss, G. L. *King, Parliament, and Public Finance in Medieval England to 1369*. Oxford: Clarendon Press, 1975

Henneman, J. B. *Royal Taxation in Fourteenth Century France: The captivity and ransom of John II*. Philadelphia, 1976.

Henneman, J. B. *Royal Taxation in Fourteenth Century France. The development of war financing, 1322–1356.* Princeton, 1971.

Hewitt, H. J. *The Organization of War Under Edward III 1338–62.* Manchester: Manchester U. P., 1966.

Jenkins, H. *Papal Efforts for Peace under Benedict XII, 1334–42.* London, 1933.

Jones, Michael C. "Edward III's Captains in Brittany." In *England in the Fourteenth Century: Proceedings of the Harlaxton Symposium*, ed. W. M. Ormrod (1986).

Kaeuper, Richard W. *War, Justice and Public Order. England and France in the Later Middle Ages.* Oxford: Clarendon, 1988.

Keen, Maurice H. *Chivalry.* New Haven, Yale University Press, 1984.

Keen, Maurice H. *The Laws of War in the Late Middle Ages.* London, 1965.

Le Patourel, J. "The Treaty of Brétigny, 1360." *T[ransactions of the] R[oyal] H[istorical] S[ociety]*, 5th ser. 10 (1960).

Lewis, N. B. "The Organisation of Indentured Retinues in Fourteenth-Century England." *TRHS* (1944).

Lewis, N. B. "The Recruitment and Organization of a Contract Army, May to November 1337." *BIHR* 37 (1964).

Maddicott, J. "The Origins of the Hundred Years War." *History Today* 36 (1986).

McFarlane, K. B. "War, the Economy and Social Change. England and the Hundred Years War." *Past & Present* 22 (1962).

McHardy, Alison K. "The English Clergy and the Hundred Years War." In *The Church and War*, ed. W. J. Shiels. London: Ecclesiastical History Society/Basil Blackwell, 1983.

McKisack, M. "Edward III and the Historians." *History*, XLV no. 153 (1960).

Morgan, Philip. *War and Society in Medieval Cheshire, 1277–1403.* Manchester: Chetham Society, 1987.

Morris, J. E. "The Archers at Crecy." *EHR* 12 (1897).

Morris, J. E. "Mounted Infantry in Medieval Warfare." *TRHS* 3rd. ser, VIII (1914).

Noël, R. P. R. "Town Defence in the French Midi during the Hundred Years War." Ph.D. dissertation, University of Edinburgh, 1977.

Offler, H. S. "England and Germany at the beginning of the Hundred Years War." *EHR* LIV (1939).

Ormrod, W. M. "The Double Monarchy of Edward III." *Medieval History* 1 (1991).

Ormrod, W. M. "The Personal Religion of Edward III." *Speculum* 64 (1989).

Ormrod, W. M. *The Reign of Edward III. Crown and Political Society in England, 1327–1377.* New Haven: Yale U.P., 1990.

Postan, M. M. "The Costs of the Hundred Years War." *Past and Present* 27 (1964).

Prestwich, Michael. *Armies and Warfare in the Middle Ages. The English Experience.* New Haven: Yale University Press, 1996.

Prestwich, Michael. "English Armies in the Early Stages of the Hundred Years War: A scheme in 1341." *BIHR* 56 (1983)

Prestwich, Michael. *The Three Edwards: War and the State in England 1272–1377.* London: Weidenfeld and Nicholson, 1980.

Prince, A. E. "The Importance of the Campaign of 1327." *EHR* 50 (1935).

Prince, A. E. "The Indenture System under Edward III." In *Historical Essays in Honour of James Tait* (1937).

Prince, A. E. "The Payment of Army Wages in Edward III's reign." *Speculum* 19 (1944)

Prince, A. E. "The Strength of English Armies in the Reign of Edward III." *EHR* 46 (1931)

Rogers, Clifford J. "The Efficacy of the Medieval Longbow: A Reply to Kelly DeVries." *War in History* 5 (1998), pp. 233–42.

Rogers, Clifford J. "By Fire and Sword: *Bellum Hostile* and 'Civilians' in the Hundred Years War." In Mark Grimsley and Clifford J. Rogers, eds., *Civilians in the Path of War*, Nebraska, forthcoming.

Rogers, Clifford J. "The Military Revolutions of the Hundred Years War." *Journal of Military History* 57 (1993). Reprinted with revisions in C. J. Rogers (ed.) *The Military Revolution Debate*. Boulder: Westview, 1995.

Rogers, Clifford J. "The Offensive/Defensive in Medieval Strategy." In *From Crécy to Mohács: Warfare in the Late Middle Ages (1346–1526). Acta of the XXIInd Colloquium of the International Commission of Military History (Vienna, 1996)*. Vienna: Heeresgeschichtlichen Museum/Militärhistorisches Institut, 1997.

Sherbourne, J. W. "The Battle of La Rochelle and the War at Sea, 1372–5." *BIHR* 42 (1969).

Sherbourne, J. W. "The Cost of English Warfare with France in the Later Fourteenth Century." *BIHR* 1 (1977).

Sherborne, J. W. "John of Gaunt, Edward III's retinue and the French Campaign of 1369." In *Kings and Nobles in the Later Middle Ages*, ed. R. A. Griffiths and J. Sherborne. Gloucester: Sutton, 1986.

Stones, E. L. G. "The Anglo-Scottish Negotiations of 1327." *Scottish Historical Review* XXX (1951).

Stones, E. L. G. "The Treaty of Northampton, 1328." *History* NS XXXVIII (1953).

Tout, T. F. "Some Neglected Fights between Crecy and Poitiers." *EHR* (1905).

Tuck, J. A. "War and Society in the Medieval North." *Northern History* 21 (1985).

Vale, J. *Edward III and Chivalry*. Woodbridge: Boydell Press, 1982.

Vale, M. G. A. *The Origins of the Hundred Years War: the Angevin Legacy, 1250–1340*. Oxford: Oxford U.P., 1990 [2nd edn 1994].

Verbruggen, J. F. *The Art of Warfare in Western Europe During the Middle Ages. From the Eighth Century to 1340*. Tr. S. Willard and R. W. Southern, second English edition. Woodbridge: Boydell Press, 1997. [The best book on medieval warfare in general.]

Waugh, Scott L. *England in the Reign of Edward III*. Cambridge: Cambridge U. P., 1991.

Willard, J. F., et al. (eds). *The English Government at Work, 1327–1336*. Cambridge, Mass.: Medieval Academy of America, 1940–50.

Wright, N. "Ransoms of non-combatants during the Hundred Years War." *Journal of Medieval History* 17 (1991).

INDEX